WORLD SOCIETY:
THE WRITINGS OF
JOHN W. MEYER

World Society:
The Writings of
John W. Meyer

Editors
GEORG KRÜCKEN AND GILI S. DRORI

OXFORD
UNIVERSITY PRESS

OXFORD
UNIVERSITY PRESS

Great Clarendon Street, Oxford OX2 6DP

Oxford University Press is a department of the University of Oxford.
It furthers the University's objective of excellence in research, scholarship,
and education by publishing worldwide in

Oxford New York

Auckland Cape Town Dar es Salaam Hong Kong Karachi
Kuala Lumpur Madrid Melbourne Mexico City Nairobi
New Delhi Shanghai Taipei Toronto

With offices in

Argentina Austria Brazil Chile Czech Republic France Greece
Guatemala Hungary Italy Japan Poland Portugal Singapore
South Korea Switzerland Thailand Turkey Ukraine Vietnam

Oxford is a registered trade mark of Oxford University Press
in the UK and in certain other countries

Published in the United States
by Oxford University Press Inc., New York

© Oxford University Press 2009

British Library Cataloguing in Publication Data
Data available

Library of Congress Cataloging in Publication Data
Data available

Typeset by SPI Publisher Services, Pondicherry, India
Printed in Great Britain
on acid-free paper by
CPI Antony Rowe, Chippenham, Wiltshire

ISBN 978–0–19–923404–2

1 3 5 7 9 10 8 6 4 2

Contents

PART IV

List of Figures

Table

Foreword

It is institutional theory that introduced us, Georg and Gili: we met on a panel discussion of institutional theory, at the October 1996 meeting of the Society for Social Studies of Science (4S), held at Bielefeld University. Our conversation about institutional theory has not ended since. To develop our institutionalist thinking, we both draw inspiration from John W. Meyer and our work on this book is a tribute to this inspiration. We thank John for years of mentoring and cooperative work. We add thanks to John for the many conversations that led us to composing this work.

The work on this book – the selection of chapters and in particular the composition of Chapter 1 – benefitted greatly from conversations with, and editorial comments from, several dear colleagues. We thank Elaine Coburn, Anita Engels, Hokyu Hwang, Woody Powell, Chiqui Ramirez, Marc Schneiberg, and Marc Ventresca. Their wise reflections and sharp ideas were invaluable to the development of this project and to the writing of Chapter 1.

We thank Sabine Rechner-Ralle and Yujing Yue for their meticulous work to reconcile the various original texts into this uniform and coherent compilation.

We thank the editors at Oxford University Press for their support of this project. In particular, we note the encouragement provided by David Musson and Matthew Derbyshire throughout the process and we thank them their confidence in the importance of the project. We also thank Kate Walker, Joy Mellor, and others with Oxford University Press for their careful attention to the editing and production of this book. Last, we thank the three anonymous reviewers who provided us with helpful suggestions at the start of this project.

We thank the various publishers of John W. Meyer's work who graciously permitted the reprinting of the material in this compilation. Full citation of the original publications is noted in each chapter, but at the request of the copyright holders we note the following: Chapters 3 and 7 were originally published in the volume *Institutional Structure: Constituting State, Society, and the Individual* and the journal *International Sociology*, respectively, and are reprinted with permission from Sage. Chapters 4 and 8 were originally published in *American Journal of Sociology*. Chapters 5 and 14 originally appeared in the journal *Sociological Theory*. Chapter 6 was originally published as 'Institutional Conditions for Diffusion', in *Theory and Society*, vol. 22 (1993), pp. 487–511, and is reprinted with kind permission of Springer Science and Business Media. Chapter 9 was originally published as 'The World Institutionalization of Education' in Schriewer, Jürgen (ed.): *Discourse Formation in Comparative Education* (Comparative Studies Series, vol. 10), Frankfurt/M., Berlin, Bern, Bruxelles, New York, Oxford, Wien: Peter Lang 2000, pp. 111–132. Chapter 10 was originally published as 'The Structuring of a World Environmental Regime, 1870–1990' in *International Organization*, and is reprinted with the permission of Cambridge University Press. Chapter 11 was originally published as

x   *Foreword*

'World Society and the Authority and Empowerment of Science' in Drori, Meyer, Ramirez, and Schofer, *Science in the Modern World Polity*, © 2003 by the Board of Trustees of the Leland Stanford Jr. University, by permission of the publisher. Chapter 12 was originally published as 'Globalization and the Expansion and Standardization of Management' in Sahlin-Andersson and Engwall, eds., *The Expansion of Management Knowledge*, © 2002 by the Board of Trustees of the Leland Stanford Jr. University, by permission of the publisher. Chapter 13 is a revised version of a paper presented at the Conference on the Globalization of the Welfare State, Hanse Institute for Advanced Study, Delmenhorst, Germany, February 2004, and is published with the permission of Prof. Lutz Leisering, conference organizer, whose extensive comments greatly improved the paper. Chapter 15 was originally published in *Soziale Welt*, 49, 3: 213–32, 1998. Chapter 16 was originally published in *Institutional Approaches to the European Union*, edited by Svein S. Andersen, Arena: Oslo, 2001. Chapter 17 was originally published as 'The University in Europe and the World: Twentieth Century Expansion' by John W. Meyer and Evan Schofer, in *Towards a Multiversity? Universities between Global Trends and National Traditions*, (G. Krücken, A. Kosmützky, and M. Torka, eds.), pp. 43–60, Bielefeld, Germany: Transcript-Verlag, 2007. In adapting the various publications into this uniform editorial format, we made minor editorial changes to the chapters: we extracted a bibliography for Chapters 3, 11, and 12 from the combined bibliography of the volumes in which they were originally published; all other changes address spelling and formatting issues.

Last, but never least, we thank our families for bearing with us during the period of distraction and stress while we composed this work.

GK, GSD
January 2009
Speyer and Palo Alto

PART I
OVERVIEW

1

World Society: A Theory and a Research Program in Context

Gili S. Drori and Georg Krücken

In explaining the dynamics of world society, John W. Meyer often elaborates on what he calls "hypothetical worlds," namely, the alternative social orders that might have emerged from the dominance of European powers and the intellectual breakthroughs in religion, science, and politics of the Enlightenment era and the nineteenth century. The description of such alternative world orders offers a glimpse into the possible historical routes, each describing a counterfactual historical trajectory, not to say destiny, for the West and the world. This contemplation of "worlds that might have been" makes possible and directly useful reflections on the "world that is" and on the forces that came to shape it. Meyer's "reflections" on world history, as much as they draw from and comment on the study of specific sectors or institutions, provide a comprehensive explanation of the history of world society: describing patterns (such as structuration and globalization), detailing particular processes (such as the institutionalization of personhood and education), and pointing to causal mechanisms (such as international organizations and the professions). These historical accounts form the basis for provocative and counter-intuitive theoretical claims about how institutional forces of culture and legitimacy play key roles in sweeping social change and also its companion, local and global inertia of varied kinds. These chronicles of Western, now globalized, society combine into a sustained theoretical research program: a broad-ranging sociological theory of modernity in dialogue with, and generative for, a prolific body of empirical studies. Together, these studies by Meyer and his collaborators compose an integrated scholarship of world affairs, that is known as "world society theory," and that this book profiles in full form and detail for the first time.

Meyer is the central figure in this research tradition of world society theory, whose work marks the principal pieces of this body of argument, evidence, and theory. In this book, we "put the pieces" of this story together, to recognize and celebrate Meyer's contribution to sociology. The contribution extends beyond these studies of world society, and we note this with accounts of his breakthrough scholarship in institutional theory and his application of institutionalist methods and arguments to the wide variety of social institutions, issues, and processes. With Meyer offering his most recent articulation of these ideas and key theoretical matters in Chapter 2, this chapter introduces the broad ideas and frameworks for the accomplishment of world society theory by spotlighting the intellectual context of Meyer's writings and of world society theory. Following a brief description of the theory's stand (in the section "Theoretical Breakthroughs"), we draw the connections between Meyer's work and other bodies of scholarship (in the section "Connections"). Specifically, we relate Meyer's work and four bodies of scholarship with which his work converses and to which his work added his unique institutional perspective: organization studies and management, political science and international relations, social theory, and globalization. We conclude with an outline of the book, which comments on our selection of pieces from the long list of Meyer's publications (in the section "Organization of the Book").

THEORETICAL BREAKTHROUGHS

Meyer's work rests on several fundamental concepts that are captured in particular terms, which while often shared throughout the social sciences, are given distinct usages for the institutional project: embeddedness, rationalization, actorhood, legitimation, and scripts. These terms are common to Meyer's many works, and are combined with ideas about diffusion, globalization, the state, and education. Some phrases, like Meyer's "global imagined community," are a direct extension of the work of others (here, of Anderson 1991); other ideas, such as myth, ritual, and ceremony (Chapter 4), which are commonly used in several disciplines, are filled by Meyer with institutionalist meaning; yet other ideas, such as actorhood (Chapter 5), are original to world society theory. Most important, together they weave a tapestry that is a powerful alternative social theory to standard functionalisms, other critical accounts and "systems" theories, particularly the dominant rational choice and neoliberal views of actors, markets, and states. With these concepts, Meyer's work speaks broadly and compellingly about various matters: from law to stratification, from globalization to the person, Meyer describes modern society in a way that articulates trends, points at causal mechanisms, and outlines consequences that are distinctive in the modern social science corpus.

Meyer's approach is profoundly sociological, institutionalist, and phenomenological. The combination provides the basis for a distinctive voice and stance that adds value to the standard scholarship. For example, Meyer's approach to diffusion studies adds to the common description of the ecological features of the process by emphasizing theorization as an institutional component of diffusion. To similar effect, Meyer's reading of DiMaggio and Powell's canonical statement on institutional mechanisms of change (1983) sets out the process of "mimetic isomorphism" as conceptually distinct, in a meta-theoretical sense, from coercive and normative mechanisms (Chapter 2; Meyer 2008). In this sense, adding -hood to nation (nation-statehood), actor (actorhood), and person (personhood) articulates Meyer's approach to scripts and conveys his category-based and constructivist approach to issues that are frequently approached only from strategic or power/interests stands.

Meyer's constructivist and phenomenological insights are combined with quantitative methodologies. This combination is captured in the conceptually contradictory phrase "quantitative phenomenology," whose coining is attributed to Meyer's long-time colleague Francisco O. (Chiqui) Ramirez (Kamens 2007: 324). In its methodological approach, Meyer's work created a bridge between American empiricism and European-like sensibilities to a-rationality, the role of culture, and the power of social construction. On the one hand, Meyer was trained as a sociologist at the Columbia University in the early 1960s, working at Paul Lazarsfeld's Bureau for Applied Social Research which was one of the crucibles for the emerging empirical and quantitative tradition in American sociology; much like Lazarsfeld's, Meyer's experience built on his training in mathematics. Meyer later brought the power of these tools (both analytic and legitimacy) to studies of world society dynamics—a strong emphasis on quantitative data and statistical analysis and, most importantly, a concern with research design and methods that highlight variation and focus attention on longitudinal processes. Over four decades of empirical work, Meyer and his colleagues established a shared methodological imagination and jointly compiled a remarkable quantitative dataset extending from the early nineteenth century. These accomplishments have yielded a detailed description of the features of world society, key social entities (nation-states, international organizations, and firms) that are embedded in it, and key processes at work in both stabilizing and transforming it (for review of research strategies, see Schofer and McEneaney 2003). And with such rich comparative data, they also offered causal accounts, empirically detailing the antecedents and the implications of the described global institutional changes (for reviews, see Schneiberg and Clemens 2006; Drori 2008).

On the other hand, Meyer's statistical analyses – though data-rich and methodo-logically sophisticated – provide a platform for bold, provocative theoretical arguments. This is partially due to both empirical and conceptual reasons: empirically, there are limitations to small sample studies, as is the case in the study of cross-national processes; conceptually, there is a problem of reification of the same social entities that the study investigates, as the availability of these data is itself evidence of the institutionalization of the same trend that the studies formalize and quantify. With this combination of phenomenology and empiricism, Meyer turns what are otherwise inconsistent epistemological traditions into empirically productive schol-arship and bridges the conventional distinction between grand theory and empirical research programs. World society theory is indeed a theoretical research program (TRP) (Berger and Zelditch 2002), anchored in the breadth of its theoretical claims and the richness of the related researchable propositions (Jepperson 2002), and one of a few lines of modern sociology that delivers grandly on both the theoretical and empirical promise of a TRP.

The emphasis on researchable propositions, even in Meyer's nonempirical work, creates a tension in the corpus of research and is evident in the titles of Meyer's pieces. During the course of development, world society work evolved from being an approach, then a school, and now to being seen as a social theory. But Meyer, personally, is uneasy with the designation "theorist": Much like other American social science intellectuals, such as Erving Goffman (Collins 1986), Meyer's emphasis on research distinguishes him as an *American* theorist. By his own telling, his work results from a buildup of insights initially made to reinterpret the then-common sociological explanations of education and socialization. Indeed, world society work gradually matured intellectually through his efforts and the wider conversations that the early work provoked among colleagues, students, and several specialty fields across the social sciences. From his initial writings in the 1970s on particular institutions (Meyer 1977), organizations (Chapter 4), and cross-national processes (Meyer and Hannan 1979) through a series of comprehensive declarations of the theoretical stand (in particular, Meyer and Hannan 1979; Thomas et al. 1987; Meyer and Scott 1992; Scott and Meyer 1994; Meyer et al. 1997 [Chapter 8]) to more recent statements (Meyer et al. 2006), the work by Meyer and his colleagues consistently elaborates a distinctively institutionalist (and later neoinstitutionalist; Powell and DiMaggio 1991) sensibility and stance that is profoundly sociological as well.

The breadth of these conceptual claims and the span of the social institutions to which these concepts came to be applied led Meyer and his collaborators to continuously engage in a conversation with the then current social science theories. Such conversations, even if used for the purpose of highlighting the important distinctions among the worldviews, suggest strong intellectual connections between Meyer's scholarship and current social thought. The following section centers on such connections, elaborating on shared ideas, terminology, and subjects of study.

CONNECTIONS

The stature of Meyer's scholarship comes from the challenge that it poses to rational, or realist, approaches in the social sciences. Meyer's novel work of the 1970s challenged the dominant sociological theories of the day. On issues as central to sociological thinking as socialization, Meyer called for a reconsideration of the interplay between norms and social roles. Rather than seeing norms as being intern-alized by individuals (as is the image in Parson's and Merton's sociology), Meyer's phenomenological turn proposed viewing culture as outlining shared expectations codified into or constructed as models of how the world operates. And rather than people being socialized into their social roles through social institutions – primarily education but also medicine, science, and religion – Meyer shifted the discussion to the mythology carried by such institutions and to the ritualized nature of compliance with social expectations. In several seminal pieces from the 1970s (Chapter 4; Meyer 1977), Meyer breaks with American sociological thinking of the day and embraces the constructivist tone of phenomenology, primarily Berger and Luckmann's (1967) work (see Meyer 1992).

At the same time, Meyer's works then and now are thoroughly sociological, interpreting the main subject matters that concern many social scientists. Meyer's work analyzes a variety of social institutions that are the subject of study in all social science disciplines: from the state to the firm, from education to law, from the individual citizen to globalization, from social power to human rights. In the discussion of such substantive matters, there emerges a dialogue, even if contrarian at times, with a variety of social science schools of thought.

In this section, we discuss the intellectual connections between Meyer's scholarship and these various schools. We locate points of junction among them, on substantive and conceptual grounds, by identifying common concepts (such as diffusion or the social actor) or a shared interest in a particular social institution (such as education, science, and rights). The guiding questions of our review are (*a*) What are the points of connection between Meyer's work and other social science discussions? (*b*) How have Meyer and others influenced each other's work? This section samples some of the central connections between the world society theory and other intellectual endeavors or scholarly discussions, thus raising particular agendas as bridges across disciplinary or substantive subjects of study.

We organize the section by four fields of study: (*a*) organization studies and management, (*b*) political science and international relations, (*c*) social theory, and (*d*) globalization. Because the foundational concepts of world society theory, mentioned earlier, are used to interpret issues in all four scholarly fields, each discussion is organized around a specific concept or idea. In other words, we use the discussion of the connection between Meyer's work and each field of study as a lever for an elaboration of specific concepts or ideas that create obvious connections among them and to draw connections and distinctions among the theoretical approaches. Specifically, (*a*) we discuss the **open system** approach and ideas of **embeddedness** and **rationalization** to accentuate the connection between Meyer's work and the field of organization studies and management; (*b*) we use the discussion of **the state** and its related institutions to anchor the connection between Meyer's work and the field of political science and international relations; (*c*) we use the concepts of the **social system**, the **social actor**, and **governmentality** to draw connections with the field of social theory; and (*d*) we use the ideas about **diffusion** and **macroanalysis** to draw connections with the study of globalization. In line with recent calls to bridge across disciplinary divides (for example, Fearon and Wendt 2002; Tempel and Walgenbach 2007), we see the overall mission of this chapter as building bridges across scholarly discussions and as seeking conversations among academic disciplines.

Organization studies and management

Challenging the then common assumptions about the rationality of organizations, Meyer was central to the 1970s revolution in organizational studies. The dominant theories of the day regarded the organizations as rational, bounded, and autonomous entities: organizations, even when considered within the context of their environment, were regarded as "closed systems" and as deliberative decision makers. Then, with two influential pieces both of which were published in 1977 (Chapter 4; Meyer 1977), Meyer became pivotal in turning the field of organization studies on its head.

In his work on education (Meyer 1977), Meyer called for a focus on institutions rather than on specific social systems or organizations. Moreover, in this piece Meyer reorients the sociological understanding of education to carry a socialization function: more than teaching norms and more than changing the life of those educated in the system, education constructs social roles and identities, often through certification. In this way, education has a diffuse rather than direct impact on society because people learn the social myths (Jepperson 2002, particularly pages 231–3). This piece charted the path for institutionalist work on education (Kamens 1977; Meyer et al. 1978; Meyer et al. 1981), elaborating on, for example, the idea of the person. Still, education is not seen in this and in later work as a case study; rather, education is viewed as a key social institution. For that reason, this piece was also quickly followed by other institutionalist writings (Zucker 1977; Meyer and Scott 1983; DiMaggio and Powell 1983) that more generally laid the foundations for this tradition.

Even more influential was the article "Institutionalized Organizations: Formal Structure as Myth and Ceremony," written with Brian Rowan (Chapter 4, originally published in 1977). This piece is among the most cited papers in organizational institutionalism (Greenwood et al. 2008: 2). Meyer and Rowan's analysis is guided by the question why organizations develop ever-more elaborate formal-rational structures (such as organizational charts, formal communication systems, accounting and bookkeeping procedures, and detailed descriptions of positions and organizational units). This question obviously goes back to Max Weber (1968) and his early description of bureaucratic organizations. According to Meyer and Rowan, in the prevailing rationalist technological paradigm in organization studies of the mid 1970s, Weber's emphasis on the legitimacy of formal structures is left out. Instead, the rational approach regards formal rational structures as reflecting complex coordination tasks in organizations, as their function is to maximize efficiency. Meyer and Rowan challenge this basic assumption. According to them, the development of formal rational structures is driven not by the pursuit for efficiency but rather by the pursuit for legitimacy from the environment in which organizations are embedded. Formal structures, therefore, are first and foremost outward-oriented, with organizations influenced primarily by their institutional context. On this point, Meyer and Rowan again extend Weber's work. According to Meyer and Rowan, formal organizational structures hardly steer the organization's activities; rather, they are mainly display windows toward the environment, and are only loosely coupled to what they call the activity structure of an organization. Also, formal organizational structures do not reflect technological imperatives (Lawrence and Lorsch 1967; Thompson 1967/2003) or resource dependencies (Pfeffer 1972; Pfeffer and Salancik 1978); they reflect "the rules, norms and ideologies of the wider society" (Meyer and Rowan 1977: 84), the rationalized myths, and the taken-for-granted notions. In these ways, Meyer and Rowan's work is influential because of the relations it posed with sociological thought: engaging Weberian canon but challenging rational interpretations of Weber.

Meyer and Rowan's work is particularly influential because of the impact it had on the field of organizational studies. By emphasizing that formal structures adapt easily and often ritualistically to changing environmental conditions and that such adaptation leads to structural similarities between the organization and its environment, Meyer and Rowan's work charted a path to DiMaggio and Powell's (1983) renowned work on isomorphism. And in spite of Meyer's (2008) recent emphasis that DiMaggio and Powell's (1983) notion of mimetic isomorphism is conceptually distinct from coercive or normative mechanisms of isomorphism because it offers a constructivist image of the social actor, the strong conceptual link between these seminal neoinstitutional pieces is abundantly clear. Moreover, in his recent writing (2008), Meyer strengthens the connection between Meyer and Rowan (1977) and DiMaggio and Powell (1983) by yet again highlighting the cognitive dimensions and emphasizing the centrality of the enactment in producing isomorphism.

Both early works by Meyer (Chapter 4; Meyer 1977) were crucial in establishing a radical societal perspective on organizations that put (*a*) organizations in the context of their environment and (*b*) societal legitimacy at the center of social processes. These ideas became the trademarks for new institutionalism in organizational analysis (Powell and DiMaggio 1991; Scott 2004, 2008; Greenwood et al. 2008). And although early institutional work by Meyer and others focused on public sector institutions (e.g., Dobbin et al. 1988; Edelman 1990; Dobbin 1992, 1994), recently organization and management studies have increasingly used these early neoinstitutional concepts for the analysis of organizational behavior in the corporate sector. So while Powell (1991: 183) self-critically states that "much of the empirical research thus far has focused on nonprofit organizations and public agencies (schools, the mental health sector, health care, cultural institutions, etc.)," neoinstitutional concepts of legitimacy, institutional context, and isomorphism are used to describe processes in the for-profit sector too: the spread of the multidivisional form among large American corporations (Fligstein 1985), the establishment of investor relations departments in business firms (Rao and Sivakumar 1999), the adoption of quality management systems in German industry (Beck and Walgenbach 2005), and the symbolic management of strategic change among firms (Fiss and Zajac 2004). This development reflects the dramatic extension of organizational institutionalism: in some circles of management studies, institutional theory has become the most commonly used theory (Davis 2006: 114–115).

Meyer's foundational work in institutional thinking took place at a time of much theoretical innovation in organizational studies, particularly at Stanford University. Out of this intellectually vibrant environment came theories of organization as diverse as resource dependence, population ecology, and bounded rationality. Meyer's collaboration with Michael Hannan (Meyer and Hannan 1979) established common ground for the exploration of organizational fields (and also coined the methodology and early arguments for Meyer's subsequent and long focus on cross-national studies), and his work with W. Richard Scott (especially Meyer/Scott 1992, Scott/Meyer 1994) was particularly fruitful for the development of neoinstitutional theory and for the joint mentoring of several generations of scholars in this tradition.

Meyer's theoretical breakthroughs directly relate to the general field of organizational studies and management in three distinct realms: (*a*) embeddedness, with the "open system" approach, (*b*) expansion and structuration, with the formal organization approach, and (*c*) rationalization, with the constructivist approach. These relations create partially overlapping spheres: Meyer's work shared terminology or theoretical perspective with the three discussions, but the discussions only partially relate with each other. The relevance of Meyer's work to these three main issues in organizational studies and management reveals the extent of influence of Meyer's work: with shared ideas and concepts, Meyer's work relates to and connects various issues, theories, and specialties in the rapidly growing field of organizational studies.

First, in its emphasis on embeddedness as a foundational concept, Meyer's work is an obvious part of the "open system" approach, which regards organizations within the context of their relations with their environment. But whereas others describe the environment as primarily imposing technical requirements, transaction costs, or information-related imperatives (for example, contingency theory; Lawrence and Lorsch 1967), for Meyer the environment primarily consists of cultural models that are then enacted by embedded entities. The environment is, therefore, neither a Leviathan nor a market that imposes the logic of rational power. Rather, in Meyer's work as for other institutionalists (Scott 2008), the environment essentially involves normative preferences and the power of legitimacy. Again following Weber (1968), the form of the organization itself is seen as a strong cultural model in modern society because it codifies the logic of means-end rationality and sets social roles as the basis for interpersonal relations. As such, the institutional context of organizations creates indirect influences on the organization embedded in it: Meyer borrows Berger's (1968) idea of the "sacred canopy" to describe the diffuse and cultural influence of the institutional context. With that, organizations alter their form to reflect their relations with a rapidly changing institutional context. While for Weber the institutional context was primarily that of the large, centralized, hierarchical, and bureaucratic state, governance modes in the era following World War II are dramatically more diffuse. World society, which is built on the significant growth and legitimacy of international nongovernmental organizations, demonstrates the role of more cosmopolitan, egalitarian, and networked organizational actors (Chapters 7 and 8). By relying on Tocquevillian descriptions of authority, Meyer's work connects with research on the looseness of social networks: with network arcs creating a "sacred canopy" of shared understandings, rather than direct relations of power and exchange, authority of the cultural scripts is enhanced. For Meyer, embeddedness in a network embodies the increasingly associational rather than hierarchical nature of organizational fields, and further enhances the importance of cultural models. Such cultural models, shared among presumably equivalent actors, breed further structuration.

Second, Meyer's work is related to the formal organization approach through his study of expansion and structuration. Meyer's definition of the environment of organizations as cultural and diffuse (rather than economic, political, and direct) does not diminish his interest in the formal side of organizations. Moreover, the irrationality of rationality, which is evident in isomorphic and loose-coupling tendencies of organizations, does not contradict the impulse toward formalization. Structuration, he argues, comes not from imperatives but from scripts. Without diminishing the importance of organizations in modern society, Meyer negates the assumptions by Charles Perrow (1991) and others who define the "society of organizations," according to which organizations are the "independent variable" or the primary cause of societal development. For Meyer, organizations – like the individuals, *a-la* institutionalism – are the "dependent variable," or outcome, of the societal norms and expectations in which they are embedded. This embeddedness explains the expansion, in numbers and in scope, of organizations over time; it is also related to changes in organizational formats. For Perrow, society is peopled by organizations through which action occurs; for Meyer, society is formed by rationalization, which is expressed by and through formal organizations. Still, Meyer's focus on the formal is not a focus on structure alone: Meyer rejects the equating of formal structure with function (Chapter 4), and joins other institutionalists in seeing structure as an embodiment of meaning. In this sense, the structuration of organizational fields and the individual organizations therein is seen as conveying meanings of identity. Also, whereas organizations and meanings continuously change, Meyer's approach to social change is clear of modernization theory's normative tone. For example, the rapid expansion in numbers and scope of international organizations, particularly nongovernmental organizations, testifies to the institutionalization of a global society. Boli and Thomas (1997, 1999) sketch the nature of world society according to the thematic emphasis that organizational structuration marks. They show that the dominant global organizational field is economic, including trade and industry (see also Chabbott 1999), conveying the global cultural theme of progress (Chapters 3 and 8). Similarly, expressing the link between structure and meaning, the study of expansion and institutionalization trends is not specifically a matter of the life cycle of a field (in reference to population ecology literature; Hannan and Freeman 1977); rather, such structuration expresses the rise of a particular theme and thus reflects broader societal and organizational change. Several examples of this idea emerge in Meyer's work. For example, the nation-state, which is itself regarded as a formal organization (Chapter 7 and 8), tends to have a standardized set of ministries, and this format for ministerial duties reflects global policy trends, conveying the themes and policy emphases that are shared worldwide (Drori and Meyer 2007). In a similar vein, the rise of organizational work around governance conveys the alignment of management ideologies with the theme of participatory engagement or actorhood, which comes to be structured around procedures and the language of accountability and transparency (Drori 2006). This managerialist turn is particularly noticeable in education, where universities in very different countries, nowadays, have a fine-grained and differentiated structure with offices for a variety of tasks, which, like technology transfer, gender equality, and organizational development, previously were not regarded as part of the organization's responsibility (Krücken and Meier 2006; Ramirez 2006). Across these many examples – in the study of structuration of international organizations, firms, and public institutions – attention to the formal structure is complemented by attention to the meaning conveyed through formal structuration.

Third, in his work on rationalization, Meyer converses with the constructivist approach to organizational studies. As mentioned earlier, according to Meyer, the structuration of organizations and organizational fields, which is explained as increased formalization and structural elaboration, can hardly be equated with an increase of rational decision making. Rather, structuration is increasingly rationalized, or organized around means-ends logic in celebration of efficiency and credentialed expertise. In seeing organizational behavior not as driven by rational decision making, Meyer's work relates directly to the Carnegie School, and later articulation of the "garbage can model" of decision making (March and Olsen 1976). This work reveals how problems, solutions, and decision makers in organizations come to be independent from each other, thus directly challenging all kinds of rational decision-making models (March 1999). March's heralding work on decision making opened up intellectual space for Meyer's ensuing institutional commentary: Meyer builds on March's microlevel analyses, and adds the institutional concern with the wider context of organizational behavior.

Continuing with this emphasis on the irrationality of rationality, Meyer's collaboration with W. Richard Scott produced a stream of research on public sector organizations (Meyer and Scott 1992; Scott and Meyer 1994). Their use of the idea of rationalization again harks back to Weber: The neoinstitutionalist definition of rationalization as a cultural force (rather than the application of mechanistic routines) echoes Weber's emphasis on the nature, or "spirit," of the related routines. In Weber's words, "In the last resort the factors that produced capitalism are the rational permanent enterprise, rational accounting, rational technology, and rational law, but again not these alone. Necessary complementary factors were the rational spirit, the rationalization of the conduct of life in general and a rationalistic economic ethic" (Weber 1961: 260). This constructivist perspective resonates with what is called "Scandinavian institutionalism" (Czarniawska 2008: 772). Nils Brunsson (1989; also Brunsson and Olsen 1993) emphasizes rule making as a junction of rationalization where the traditional image of organizations whose rational, purposive actions are reversed and a world of standards emerges. Meyer's emphasis on diffuse cultural authority also resonates with Scandinavian ideas about "soft law," or voluntary schemes of compliance (Brunsson and Jacobsson 2000; Mörth 2006). And on the interpretative nature of the social construction of routines, Meyer's work on enactment and loose coupling relates to Weick's (1969, 1976) ideas of interlocked behavior and sense making. In general, Meyer's macrophenomenological approach to organizations emphasizes the socially constructed nature of these presumably rational entities and the related sense of agency (see Barley and Tolbert 1997). And although this conceptualization of the relationship between society and organizations is very much in line with Weber's original idea of rationalization, the consequences of such rationalization at the organizational level are seen differently. Instead of seeing organizations as the main symbol and driver of the "iron cage" – here relying on Parsons's commonly used yet imprecise translation of Weber's (1920) original term *stahlhartes Gehäuse* – the coupling between societal and organizational processes is much looser as, according to Meyer, organizations enact scripts of rational agency and engage in ritualistic compliance in order to gain legitimacy from a society that came to value rationalized ideals.

Meyer's work, placed at the junction of these three themes in organizational studies – embededdness, the formal organization, and rationalization – strongly emphasizes the role of the broader sociocultural environment as an explanatory variable for organization. This leaves room for various understandings of the carriers that are responsible for the diffusion of cultural models from the environment into the organization. In much of his work, Meyer points to the role of international organizations as diffusion agents (in particular, Chapter 8). But, as discussed in the section "Political science and international relations," international organizations are not necessarily explicit conduits of influence, surely not in a muscular way. Rather, they serve as the embodiment of global cultural values of an increasingly rationalized society. Their role is, therefore, as carriers of world culture, which is heavily scientized (Chapter 12; Drori and Meyer 2006) and professionalized (Chapter 11). In emphasizing the importance of knowledge in shaping practices and structures, Meyer joins with the sociologists of science who focus on the long-term trend of the scientization of society (Weingart 2003), and with sociologists of the professions who focus on the rationalizing and standardizing power of the professions (Power 1997; Sahlin-Andersson and Engwall 2002; Greenwood et al. 2006). In this way, Meyer's emphasis on the institutional context as primarily cultural and on the influence of such context as primarily diffuse, marks the phenomenological "pole" of institutional thinking in organizational studies. Meyer, who marked the emergence of this approach in the 1970s, stands this day in sharp contrast with the increasingly prevalent managerial and strategic institutionalist approach to organization (Meyer 2008; Chapter 2).

Political science and international relations

In keeping with the "open system" approach, Meyer came to treat the nation-state as an organization and to consider the nation-state as being shaped by its sociocultural environment. This approach puts Meyer's work in direct conversation with scholars from the disciplines of political science and international relations, who also consider states within the context of the international system. Still, because Meyer's work on organizations stems from criticizing rationality as the fundamental myth in organizational studies, his analyses of the state stand in contrast to the prevailing realism in political science and international relations. Here, Meyer criticizes the assumption that the state can be treated as a bounded and rational actor, which follows a distinct national trajectory and peruses singular distinct interests. His commentary on the political emerged from his sociological analysis of education and of formal organizations. As early as his 1970s analysis of education as an institution, he reflected on the role of policy as an institutionalized myth and developed the idea of the irrationality of rationality (Meyer 1977). This early commentary, which was initially directing its challenge at the literature on the state-sponsored institution of education, evolved into a comprehensive institutionalist statement about the nature of the modern nation-state.

Much like his approach to formal organizations, Meyer's analysis of the state can be divided along the main features of the institution of the modern nation-state: (*a*) its embeddedness in a wider – international and increasingly global – environment, (*b*) the results of this embeddedness in the structures and processes that constitute the state, and (*c*) the social institutions (such as education, development, and rights) that come to be intertwined with the modern state. On all these matters, Meyer's work participates in the current debates in political science and international relations, while departing from their often realist theoretical stand and offering a distinctly neoinstitutional interpretation of the state.

First, like the discursive shift in organizational studies toward an "open system" approach, the nation-state too is increasingly seen within the context of its relations with other international players. This approach obviously gave rise to discussions on globalization, which have come to define the international or global context as the taken-for-granted approach in the social sciences (what some call the globalization of globalization; also, Guillén 2001, and further discussion in the section "Globalization"). It also strengthened the tendencies toward comparative studies: state action and its patterns are analyzed in comparison with those in other states (even when the analysis takes little account of the influence by the international conditions or forces). Here, the theorization of the nation-state and the related universalization and rationalization of this "category" reified the embeddedness of the state in its international and global environment.

With the growing recognition, across disciplinary and theoretical lines, of the rise of the global, the debate shifted to the nature of the global or transnational system, which serves as the important context for nation-states. Recognizing the increasing heterogeneity of global governance (with the addition of private and public, international and transnational players) and the increased power of international instruments (of law and commercial interests), the central debate of the 1990s centered on the future of the nation-state. The recognition that international organizations, multinational firms, and transnational civil organizations now join states in formulating policies was expressed in an anxious discussion about the withering of the modern nation-state (for example, Evans 1997). The surprise was that neither a world-state nor a simple interstate system has emerged; nor has the world plunged into anarchy (for example, Rosenau 1997, 2003; Wendt 1999: 308). These discussions, which were rooted in dichotomous imagery (setting order and sovereignty versus anarchy and the porousness of boundaries; Milner 1991), now speak in terms of forms of global authority and the role nation-states play in it. For realists, the discussion on global authority is one of management, specifically the governance of a global system (for example, Rosenau 1995): the issue is how to coordinate global affairs when the players are increasingly transnational and the network is increasingly heterogeneous (for example, Ottaway 2001; Hall and Biersteker 2002; Pattberg 2005). Meyer replies to these discussions with a constructivist rebuttal: world society, in which nation-states are increasingly embedded, is organized in a highly Tocquevillian manner (Chapter 8: 180; Meyer et al. 2006: 25), with authority being both diffuse and normative in nature. Like Tocqueville's interpretation of social cohesion, world society is organized around cultural rules and associational networks rather than through centralized control. And whereas for some sociologists, embeddedness connotes the local roots of modern forms and thus explains cross-national variation (Evans 1995), for Meyer embeddedness connotes the relations of the nation-state with world society, conveys the influence of world society, and thus explains cross-national similarities. Second, the embeddedness of the nation-state in international and global networks results in profound changes to the practices, structures, and discourses of the state. Cross-nationally governments offer a similar range of social services (for example, mass education; Chapter 9), establish similar operational units (for example, ministries; Jang 2000; Kim, Jang, and Hwang 2002), and draft similar policies (most dramatically in national constitutions; Boli 1987). Such cross-national similarity, which appears in spite of the various configurations of local conditions and legacies, "makes sense only of common world forces at work" (Meyer et al. 1997: 152

[Chapter 8]). Discussions on the influence of global conditions and forces on the nation-state converged on the welfare state, focusing on the scope, trends, and future of the welfare state, which is now under the mounting challenge of globalization pressures (for example, Mishra 1999; Burgoon 2001; Montanari 2001; Brady et al. 2006; Detlef 2006). Specifically, they describe the resulting transformation of the welfare state (for example, Freeman et al. 1997; Gilbert 2002), assuming a mounting crisis due to a funding predicament and a rising tide of neoliberal ideals (for example, Huber and Stephens 2001; Castels 2004). Neoinstitutionalists, such as Lee and Strang (2006), join the debate by analyzing public sector downsizing in twenty-six OECD countries; yet Lee and Strang demonstrate this worldwide change in the state as a global diffusion process, and emphasize the role of institutional forces. From such a world society perspective, changes in the welfare state dynamics are understood against the backdrop of macrohistorical processes: worldwide changes to the state are driven by the diffusion of general societal norms, which, embodied in social policy, have become an integral part of the form and practice of modern nation-states (Chapter 7). Nation-states adhere to global norms of justice and progress and enact related scripts of social policy in order to be regarded as legitimate members of world society. In this sense, historical changes, here in the institution of the state, are a result of global constellations of actors and the culture that they carry. Meyer's work reinterprets this evidence of globalization effect on the nation-states by seeing such trends as isomorphic changes that produce weakly coupled state functions, thus highlighting the a-rational nature of state operation. Moreover, Meyer's work reinterprets the nature of global influence by regarding it as neither coercive nor direct, as presupposed by realists (Wallerstein 1973, 2000). On this point, the focus of academic discussion shifts to an analysis of the nature of global influence and to the associated mechanisms of influence, with the obvious nexus being not only the history of the state but also the implication in global governance (as reviewed in the section "Globalization"). On this point, Meyer's world society approach expanded the scope of study of even these global players: whereas political scientists focused their work on international organizations (for example, Diehl 1997), seeing the disciplinary commitment to interstate and formal exchanges, the neoinstitutional approach to the study of the global emphasizes the role of global civil society, international nongovernmental organizations, and the professional experts and consultants (for example, Boli and Thomas 1997, 1999).

Third, the expansion of state functions in accordance with global expectations reflects the changing content of the state (Meyer, 1999; Chapter 7). On this matter, Meyer and his colleagues document the cross-national and global institutionalization of various social rights and services, which are increasingly in the care of the state: from education to human rights to the environment, many issues move from the private domain to be taken-for-granted elements of the public sphere. Meyer's work notes the shift from particularistic principles toward universalistic rights. This is most clearly evident in the changing logic for the incorporation of women into the public sphere, where the social role of women was restated "from motherhood to citizenship" (Berkovitz 1999). In describing the influence of world society on such substantive changes to the state, Meyer's work departs from the growing body of work on the rise of international human rights in practice but more often in policy and legislation. For example, on the issue of ratification of international human rights treaties, realists describe the rampant ratification rate as a case of "cheap talk" (Hathaway 2003) or a tactical concession to international pressures (Sikkink 1993; Risse, Ropp, and Sikkink 1999). Others see this sweeping global rise as a result of action by organized social movements (Smith 1995; Keck and Sikkink 1998; Tsutsui 2004). According to Meyer's world society approach, however, these issues reflect more far-reaching changes to the social role of the state: the rise of universalistic rights, now anchored in a series of international laws and transnational action, constructed a global human rights regime and this regime, like world society in general, imprints nation-states through its rather diffuse authority. The nature of this global regime allows for extensive decoupling between legislation and practice (Hafner-Burton and Tsutsui 2005), revealing the extensive ceremonial and ritualized nature of state operations (also see Koenig 2008). Therefore, even "cheap talk" or "empty promises" which while describing noncompliance with the human rights "norm cascade" frame those as strategic moves, are interpreted by Meyer in the context of modeling and enactment processes. It is because enactment is ritualized that hypocrisy likewise becomes routine (Brunsson 1989; Krasner 1999).

Overall, Meyer's work offers a restatement of the role and nature of the modern nation-state in institutionalist terms. His statement engages him in current discussions in political science and international relations: Meyer, like many others, sees the state as being challenged from both market and global forces. Yet Meyer's restatement also marks his distinction from the prevailing perspectives by seeing the state as reified by the same institutions that presumably challenge it: "globalization certainly poses new problems for states, but it also strengthens the world-cultural principle that nation-states are the primary actors charged with identifying and managing those problems on behalf of their societies" (Meyer et al. 1997: 157 [Chapter 8]). The result is a dialectical process: not the weakening of the state that many political scientists were concerned about in the 1990s era of hyperglobalization, but rather further extension of the role of the state. This leads directly to a critical appraisal of Meyer's contribution to the burgeoning field of theoretical and empirical research on globalization.

Globalization

Meyer's comparative work predates any discussions on globalization per se: his collaborative work – initially focusing on cross-national development (Meyer and Hannan 1979) and subsequently maturing to a comprehensive statement of world society theory (Chapters 3 and 8) – sets the logic for comparative, historical, and later global studies even prior to the dramatic grip that the concept of globalization won in the social science imagination in the 1990s (Guillén 2001). With his constructivist tone, Meyer's work defines the world as the relevant "social horizon" (Beck 2000) or the "imagined community" (Anderson 1991), and describes more social issues as global (Hwang 2006). This concept departs from the vision of the world as a united system (Moore 1966; Wallerstein 1973, 2000) to a vision of mostly economic and political exchanges. Meyer's emphasis on world *society* led to a stream of research trying to define and describe the features of this society that go beyond the dimensions of transference and transformation (see Bartelson 2000) and emphasize transcendence, or the constitutive change of meanings.

In spite of the emphasis on the notion of world *society*, the label for Meyer's comparative work as late as 2003 was "world polity." The subsequent terminological shift – from highlighting the polity to emphasizing society – does not represent a shift of the basic tenets of the approach. Rather, it reflects the roots of world society theory in the intellectual context of American sociology: Meyer's hesitation to employ the term "society" comes as a reaction to the pre-1960 grand theories and from the post-1960 sociological rush to regard society as an aggregation of individuals (see section "Social theory"). Meyer's reaction develops into an emphasis on culture as the defining dimension of society, and thus world society is defined as a "broad cultural order with explicit origins in western society" (Meyer 1987: 41 [Chapter 3]). This understanding of society, on which we will elaborate in this section, draws directly on two of the founding fathers of sociology, namely, Emile Durkheim and Max Weber. From Durkheim, Meyer draws the emphasis on the shared moral understanding that underlies all social processes and structures and that cannot be reduced to individual or collective preferences; from Weber, Meyer draws the notion of occidental rationalization as specifying the basic cultural tenets of world society. On both, Meyer elaborates, for example, by spotlighting the universalistic norms of fairness and equality, voluntary and self-organized action, and cosmopolitanism as equally essential in specifying the cultural core of world society.

Though Meyer's image of world society is basically as a sweeping cultural complex, rather than a forceful ideology or doctrine that reflects the interests of powerful social agents (for example, Hannerz 1989), he deals extensively with the carriers of such global culture. According to his approach, formal organizations deserve closer attention here. As we pointed out in the section "Organization studies and management," organizations encapsulate societal myths of rationality and modernity. In particular, international organizations, governmental as well as nongovernmental, act as prime carriers of world society as they themselves can be seen as the embodiment of its cultural core. They constitute the organizational backbone of world society and promote global diffusion processes. Over time, not only could one witness the dramatic expansion of these carriers (Boli and Thomas 1997, 1999) but also the organizational backbone of world society became more heterogeneous. To the web of traditional international organizations, which is itself increasingly wider in scope and more networked (Diehl 1997), was added a rapidly intensifying network of global civil society organizations (Florini 2000; Hall and Biersteker 2002) and social movements (Tsutsui 2004). The main mechanism through which this heterogeneous configuration of global governance spread world cultural norms is what Strang and Meyer (Chapter 6) call "theorization." Theorization refers to general and abstract models that allow for concrete recipes for action by transcending local, idiosyncratic circumstances. Such models include causal and normative arguments on how different actors all over the world – from nation-states to individuals – should behave and organize their affairs to be recognized as legitimate, modern actors. And, theorization does not imply a strictly scientific understanding of the world, though scientific arguments are frequently employed.

Methodologically, Meyer's inclination toward empirical research results in a rich tradition of quantitative longitudinal analyses, in this case, analyses of globalization. Such empirical studies are conducted in order to track the impact of world society on collective and individual actors. Relying mostly on secondary data, the main tools for the analyses of these data are regression analyses, factor analyses, structural equation models, and event history analysis (for reviews, see Schofer and McEneaney 2003; Schneiberg and Clemens 2006; Drori 2008). And although most of these research methodologies are rather conventional in social research, event history analysis in particular is both a fairly novel approach, at that time, and is attuned to the time component inherent in social processes such as diffusion and globalization. With its origins lying in epidemiological research and thus with its suitability to measure the spread of an infectious disease, event history analysis became the most useful world society methodology for tracking the history of "contagious" global processes, such as the national ratification of international human rights treaties (Wotipka and Ramirez 2008) or the spread of environmental policies (Chapter 11).

With these characteristics, Meyer's approach plays a distinctive role in the burgeoning field of globalization studies. Based on both macrosociological and culturalist theoretical account and empirical research in the quantitative tradition, a broad theoretical and research agenda unfolds. Many of the chapters in this book give evidence of the fruitfulness and originality of this approach. Three issues in particular – diffusion, its carriers, and heterogeneity of outcomes – emerge from this research and offer not only a rich body of work to date but also possible directions for future research.

First, the notion of "diffusion," which was defined and elaborated on in a series of institutional studies (Strang and Macy 2001; Dobbin et al. 2007), is a central juncture for Meyer's engagement with the scholarship on globalization. The main emphasis of research by Meyer and his colleagues to date has been rebuttal of the realist descriptions of diffusion as either coercive imposition or strategic compliance. The intriguing puzzle to realist scholars is why states, some of which have the power to resist external pressures, would comply so faithfully with international norms, particularly those codified in international treaties (for example, Simmons 1998, 2000; Von Stein 2005; Simmons and Hopkins 2005; Avdeyeva 2007). It is commonly understood that diffusion is a process by which "external" influences come to determine "internal" forms: cross-national diffusion is evident in many social policies—from privatization (Levi-Faur 2003) and the rights of women (Ramirez, Soysal, and Shanahan 1997; Berkovitch 1999) to education (Chapter 9; Chapter 17; Schofer and Meyer 2005). Still, the debate rages on why (and how) global, or external, pressures come to mold processes and institutions that are internal to the nation-state. The debates revolve, therefore, not around the evidence for diffusion but rather around the issues of the sorts of influences and the varying degree of coercion involved in the process of diffusion. Meyer's work, which focuses on the impact of world culture on diffusion patterns over and above the coercive influence of economic and political dependencies, demonstrates the importance of shared models, or cultural modes (see also Lechner and Boli 2005). Here, there is an obvious connection with several common terms to describe the conduit of influence along which a practice or policy diffuses cross-nationally: terms such as "issue networks" (Sikkink 1993), "policy networks" (Dahan et al. 2006), and "international regimes" (Krasner 1983; Ruggie 1982, 1998) came to describe the social connections that transmit global models. This organization of global networks, as both heterogeneous and subject-oriented, leaves much room for cultural influence, as in Meyer's explanations, whereas micro- and macrorealists – from neoliberals (Keohane 2002) to world system theorists (Wallerstein 1973, 2000; Chase-Dunn 1998) and those focusing on the history of the state (most notably Charles Tilly and Theda Skocpol) – narrowly view culture as ideology and as subordinate to interests of power and influence.

Second, these divergent descriptions of global diffusion processes reflect the unique explanations of the means by which diffusion occurs. Commonly, the debates on this issue refer to the concept of "carriers" of globalization in an attempt to identify the social actors that encourage and guide globalization. Though it shares the "top down" model with many scholars of globalization who identify either economic forces (Wallerstein 1973, 2000) or rule-making organizations (Barnett and Finnemore 2004) as encouraging global diffusion, Meyer's understanding of the nature of such carriers is dramatically different. According to Meyer, the main carriers of globalization forces are not nation-states, global economic forces, or even international organizations per se. Rather, the force that powers global diffusion processes is world society, in a very broad sense. Therefore, while Wallerstein (1973, 2000) sees globalization processes as being driven by direct force and compliance, Meyer (Chapter 7) insists on the role of "soft" and diffuse mechanisms, in particular theorization and the elaboration of related role models. In this way, Meyer goes beyond the international relations scholars whose work centers on the teaching and normative role of international organizations (for example, Finnemore 1993; Barnett and Finnemore 2004; Barnett and Coleman 2005), by pointing out that the mechanisms of global influence are less tangible and direct, though not less effective. According to Meyer, the global source of influence is world society and its cultural core, demonstrating the importance of universalistic assumptions, of theorization, and thus of standardized models in creating the platform for global diffusion. To connote the diffuse nature of such influence, Meyer refers to it as the global social "ether" (Meyer 2004). And although many world society studies quantify embeddedness in world society in terms of interaction with international organizations, the idea is that such interaction is normative in nature, operating through diffuse and cultural forms of authority. With that, Meyer problematizes, if not undermines, the role of direct social contacts, physical interactions, and spatial proximity, which are so heavily emphasized in network analyses of globalization.

Analytically, global diffusion processes in the social world parallel diffusion processes in chemistry. According to world society research, cultural and structural patterns of the West diffuse through space like a gas, beginning with regions of high concentration of its molecules; eventually the gas molecules are equally distributed in space, if the process does not encounter obstacles. This "top down" model is accompanied by research methodologies measuring the diffusion of world societal standards as a process of binary coding (adopted/nonadopted). Equally clear seems to be the distinction between "sender" and "receiver" in global diffusion processes.

On the one hand, however, the existence of modernity as a cultural complex acting as a sender of world societal standards could be challenged on both theoretical and empirical grounds. In particular, the reception of S. N. Eisenstadt's (2003) historical and sociological work on multiple modernities could lead to a more differentiated concept of the underlying cultural bases of modernity. According to him and other scholars, different axes of modernity, which evolved in the context of different civilizations, have to be assumed and should be studied more thoroughly. Over the last years, civilizational comparisons at the interface of history and sociology have been one of the most fascinating contributions to the field of globalization, and a more intense dialogue between scholars assuming multiple modernities and those following the world society tradition as elaborated by Meyer could open new avenues in globalization research.

On the other hand, the culture and historicity of the different societal contexts being shaped by world society are not fully taken into account. In most world society analyses by Meyer and others, these contexts are conceptually underspecified. They mainly appear at the receiving end of globally diffusing cultural principles, neither as cultural contexts per se nor as actively shaping the cultural content of world society. In addition to closer investigations into the effect of world society on the culture and historicity of different societal contexts, further research is needed on the effects on world society's cultural content, resulting from the ever-increasing permeation of societal contexts. One could assume that world society as a virtual sender is also at the receiving end and hence subject to change.

Third, globalization with intense structuration and hyperrationalization creates complex situations rife with contradictions and hybrid forms through which emerge new patterns that cross-cut the alternative of adoption or nonadoption so familiar in diffusion research. And while Meyer's work is criticized for overly underscoring global convergence (Finnemore 1996), a stream of recent neoinstitutional scholarship shows that the interaction between transnational arrangements and national paths allows for diversity of outcomes (for example, Djelic and Quack 2007). The research recalls ideas about glocalization (Robertson 1994) and fragmegration (Rosenau 2003), and links with Appadurai's (1990) ideas about translocale cultures and Pieterse's (1995) ideas about coconstitution. Meyer's work regards hybridity as the evidence of loose coupling and a result of hyperrationalization (e.g., Meyer, Drori, and Hwang 2006). Indeed, cross-national heterogeneity also comes from the gap between policy charting and policy implementation, which is inherent in cross-national diffusion. Institutionalists readily accept that loose coupling is inherent in the process of diffusion in general and in particular in global diffusion of, or compliance with, policy. Drawing on these insights, researchers are challenged to describe heterogeneity of outcomes and loose coupling in specific terms. The research methodologies common to world society theory have not allowed for specific findings that explain different degrees of coupling or pointed to the cultural and historical specificity of the determining societal context. Research designs that combine case analyses (of national histories or organizational biographies) with an overview of the global field carry the promise of addressing this need to explain the global heterogeneity of outcomes.

Social theory

Meyer's work is squarely within the realm of neoinstitutional thinking in sociological theory. The bulk of neoinstitutional research is conceptualized as middle-range theory, which has had a strong and lasting impact on the interdisciplinary field of organizational research since the 1970s (Powell and DiMaggio 1991; Greenwood et al. 2008). Still, Meyer's work fills a macrosociological space in this field, which has been left open due to the reaction to the discreditation of "grand theories" after the demise of the structural functionalist approach of Talcott Parsons in American sociology. This reaction, unfortunately, conflated "*grand* theory" (focused on abstract explanations) with "*macro* analysis" (focused on systems and societies as a whole) and obscured the Durkheimian definition of sociology as the "science of institutions" and the related aspiration to develop a comprehensive account of society through the analysis of its institutions. Meyer's world society theory seems to be a special case within neoinstitutionalism since he and his colleagues developed a Durkheimian "grand theory" of society. And as much as Meyer's sense of social theory is grounded in researchable propositions and empirical analyses, thus fitting in with the American idea of a "theoretical research program" (Berger and Zelditch 2002; see discussion in the section "Organization studies and management"), the breadth of relevancy of his work defines it as a theory.

We highlight Meyer's contribution to sociological theory through discussions of two ideas: (*a*) actorhood and (*b*) rationalization. Both ideas draw from broad understandings of institutions, in which the sociology of knowledge as elaborated by Berger and Luckmann (1967) plays a pivotal role. Both ideas are also intertwined: notions of agentic actorhood are anchored in rationalization of the features of such entities, whereas rationalization is rooted in the sense of agency and control of social actors over their destiny.

According to the constructivist tone set by Berger and Luckmann, institutions embody the basic rules of society, which define who the actors are and what the actors are supposed to do. Formal rules, like laws that are set penalties for noncompliance, are less important than routines and habits, whose character is mainly implicit, informal, and taken for granted. Whereas this distinction between the formal and the informal is widely accepted in sociology, Meyer's work stands in opposition to the post-Parsonian era in American sociology, on two key points: (*a*) the dynamics of causation between levels of analysis and (*b*) the constituted nature of the social actor. First, in contrast to the "microsociological turn" in the post-Parsonian era in American sociology, according to which routines and habits as well as broader norms and values may be understood as locally constructed microphenomena, Meyer's perspective is clearly macrosociological. The macrostructures of society, which are conceptualized as a worldwide cultural frame with its historical roots in Western society, constitute individual and collective actors. For Meyer, macrostructures influence norms and behavior: It is not actors and their interests who constitute society ("bottom up"), but rather society, whose main cultural characteristics have become global over time, that constitutes actors in ongoing processes of rationalization ("top down").

Second, in strong contrast to the dominant realism in American sociology, in which bounded social actors are the taken-for-granted units of analysis, Meyer problematizes their constitution and the ongoing shaping of their behavior. This is an outcome of his emphasis on the cultural underpinnings of society. In this account, macrosociological structures are productive, creating new kinds of individual and collective actors. Here Meyer significantly expands the traditional focus on institutions, or "old" institutionalism: for him, institutions are intertwined with the constructions of the actor and thus they are far more than rules that limit or enhance individual and collective action. The construction of the modern actor, or the mythology of actorhood, is at the linchpin of Meyer's theoretical and empirical analyses, especially in recent years (Chapter 5).

Meyer points specifically to three kinds of actors: individuals, organizations, and nation-states. These actors increasingly prevail over alternative forms of societal actorhood, such as clans, families, or groups. What distinguishes modern actors is their unique sense of agency and strong sense of identity, which together form a sense of a rational and bounded agent (Frank and Meyer 2002; Jepperson and Meyer 2007). The development of this modern sense of actorhood, which is still going on, is explained as a historical process, in similar manner to macrosociological explanations by such authors as Durkheim, Weber, Simmel, and Elias. Societal rationalization, often through scientization (Drori and Meyer 2006), is the prerequisite for assuming individual actorhood and the loosening of the grip of traditional community structures (clans or families) into which one is born. Similar features of agency and identity are developing for organizations and nation-states, which too come to demonstrate rationalized expressions of identity and interest by them. The constitution of these various social actors is intertwined with extensive theorization of the actors' traits: for example, ideas about the life cycle are applied to firms, industrial sectors, and nations, as they would be applied to individuals. And, with such theorization comes profound standardization of what it means to become a modern, legitimate actor. Like most sociological theorists, Meyer contends that the actions of social actors are profoundly scripted, rather than rational calculations of means and ends. And while the social reward to scripted enactment is legitimacy, Meyer's approach is far from being strategic. Whereas other institutionalists (for example, Barnett and Finnemore 2004) consider enactment as a strategic move to gain legitimacy, Meyer contends that even strategic thinking, like other social action, is rationalized rather than rational. This ontology of the social actor contributes to "what Weber calls the 'rational restlessness' of the modern system" (Chapter 5: 109)

Rather than drawing solely on abstract reasoning, Meyer's ideas on the construction of actors in society are based on numerous quantitative and empirical research projects. This book is testimony to the strong empirical underpinnings of the world society theory, revealing how Meyer and his colleagues demonstrate that broader world society principles such as universalism, fairness, and the belief in progress are intimately linked to the construction of modern individuals, organizations, and nation-states in contemporary society (Chapter 5). This empirical research explains the dramatic expansion of education (Chapter 9; Chapter 17; Schofer and Meyer 2005) and the remarkable globalization of human rights (Chapter 13; Ramirez, Suarez, and Meyer 2006) as actorhood-driven and actorhood-producing trends. This empirical emphasis in Meyer's work often masks the link between his ideas and other developments in contemporary, mostly European, social theory. Nevertheless, while Meyer very rarely engaged European social theorists directly, his works expand on the issues of the social system, power, and agency. In the remainder of this section, we explicate Meyer's social theory by comparing his work with that of Michel Foucault, for the discussion of actorhood and with that of Niklas Luhmann, for the discussion of the contradictory trajectories (homogenization and differentiation) of the social system.

There are strong paradigmatic differences between Foucault's and Meyer's approaches: while Meyer stresses durable continuities in the long-term process of societal rationalization, Foucault recognizes historical discontinuities and individual contingencies whose specificities cannot be forced into a coherent "grand" narrative (Foucault 1972). Furthermore, there are obvious methodological differences between Meyer's rigorous quantitative approach and Foucault's equally rigorous focus on texts. Nevertheless, there are at least two clear junctions between their distinct theories (Krücken 2002: 248–253). First, both scholars see individual actors not as given entities, but rather as the result of ongoing construction processes. Meyer focuses his commentary on scripted actorhood, while Foucault argues that individual subjectivity is intimately linked to submission and obedience (Foucault 1990; Martin et al. 1993). Both demystify individuality by highlighting its standardization, even thus from actor-centered social theories, which – unlike traditional sociological thinking that in this instance can be traced back to Marx – take individual actors for granted and do not offer an explanation for their emergence in specific sociohistorical processes. In addition, in both approaches – with the notable exception of Foucault's early work on madness and civilization (1965) – there is no way out of rationalized society. Following both, one can hardly assume "lifeworlds" (Habermas 1985/1989), a "world of subjectivity" (Touraine 1995), or simply a "self" (Castells 1996) that can be set against broader rationalization processes. And, following both, rationalization processes are driven neither by political and economic forces (Habermas, Touraine) or technology (Castells). Rather, rationalization is driven by "soft" processes of influence: Meyer explains the impact of routines of organizations and Foucault emphasizes such media as textbooks and treatises. This emphasis on cultural forms of social impact, and in particular the role of science, is the second junction between Meyer and Foucault. Both scholars relate science and its taxonomies to identity formation: Foucault (1980) analyzes technologies for compiling, classifying, and statistically analyzing the ever-increasing amount of data as a source and the power to define social categories, while Meyer (Drori et al. 2003) stresses the recursive processes of the scientization of society and the socialization of science. For both, science is a lever for social order, including identity formation, structuration, and governmentality; for both, constituted order or control, come within the "iron cage" of one's own design (Foucault 1991; Drori et al. 2003). Finally, these junctions between Meyer and Foucault come to be reflected in some post-Foucauldian research: for example, the shaping of states and organizations by broader discourses is analyzed in a way that partly resembles neoinstitutional thinking (Rose and Miller 1992; McKinley and Starkey 1998). Still, an important difference between them comes from their distinct understandings of authority and power: according to Foucault, control is centralized and power is unevenly matched, whereas by Meyer's account, authority is diffuse and order emerges from theorized relations among formally equal and thus comparable social entities.

A second major contribution of Meyer's work to social theory lies in further developing Max Weber's insights into the rationalization of society (Weber 1958, 1968). In contrast to other interpretations of Weber's multifaceted work, Meyer sees Weber as the most explicit theorist of occidental rationalization, and he extends Weber's rationalization thesis into a globalization thesis by arguing that the main tenets of occidental rationalization – in particular, the belief in progress, justice, the spread of means/end-rationality, and, most importantly, the universality of such belief – become global. Still, Meyer's interpretation of rationalization as a homogenizing force leaves out the implicit images of conflict theory that underlie Weber's work. Weber (1949) argues that rationalization also leads to different "spheres of value" and results in societal struggles or conflicts (*Kampf*; see also Brubacker 1984; Oakes 2003). On this point of contention, between images of rationalization as setting a social trajectory of homogenization or differentiation, Meyer's work intersects with that of Niklas Luhmann.

Images of modern society as composed of different, at times conflicting, spheres are well established in European social theory. For example, Bourdieu (1984) argues that distinct societal fields (such as the economy, arts, and politics) may both overlap and be composed of diverse subfields, and that success in one field cannot easily be translated into other fields. Not unlike Bourdieu, Giddens (1986) distinguishes the distinct modularities in the structuration of institutions, where specific combinations of rules and resources constitute distinct political, economic, legal and other institutional domains. Luhmann's systems theory (1995, 1997) similarly defines society as functionally differentiated into autonomous systems.

Much like Weber and Meyer, Luhmann refers to a unique set of sociohistoric circumstances as the trigger of modernity (Hasse and Krücken 2008). Yet, as distinct from Meyer and Weber, Luhmann points to "functional differentiation" as the substitute of vertical stratification: the economy regulates the production and distribution of scarce products and services, science generates new knowledge, and the political system is unique in producing collectively binding decisions. For Luhmann, politics and science, for example, are distinct societal systems with characteristic rationalities that can be subordinated neither to the logic of other systems nor to a broader, all-encompassing kind of rationality as implied in Meyer's work. And whereas Meyer emphasizes the loose coupling among policy and practice or between subunits, Luhmann's idea of functional differentiation implies a high mutual dependency among subsystems. This has implications for outcomes: Luhmann's work, particularly on risk and the environment (1989, 1993) and in general on modernity (1998), shows how dependency is both a strength and a permanent source of vulnerability of modern society. From this perspective, societal integration or hom-ogenization on the basis of universal norms and cultural principles cannot be achieved; instead, modern society is shaped by very distinct yet fundamentally interrelated societal logics. For Meyer, while various trajectories are considered (Meyer et al. 1975), and variation is evident (Drori et al. 2003), the overall trend is one of isomorphism, particularly cross-nationally (see section "Globalization").

The differences between the two perspectives can be illustrated by referring to the environmental problems on which both authors have written (Luhmann 1989; Chapter 11). According to both Meyer and Luhmann, environmentalism cannot be traced to deteriorating conditions of the environment, but rather is attributed to macrosociological factors. From Meyer's perspective, the rationalization of the environment through scientific expertise and transnational environmental organiza-tions allows for the legitimacy of this emerging institution and for its institutional-ization and globalization. From Luhmann's perspective, while environmental problems transcend the binary logics of society's distinct functional systems, envir-onmental issues need to be translated into the binary logic of each functional system, in order to affect it. This implies two things. First, each social system will react to environmental problems only according to its own logic. Second, and following from the structural logic of modern society, no coherent answer can be given at a larger societal scale. According to Luhmann, the unity of society lies, paradoxically, in the diversity of its systems. Similar comparisons can be made on the study of the expansion of the welfare state (Luhmann 1995; Chapter 8; Drori and Meyer, forthcoming).

This comparison accentuates the profound differences between a homogenizing theory of rationalization (Meyer) and a theory of societal differentiation (Luhmann). Though these approaches can hardly be integrated at a meta-theoretical level, both Meyer's and Luhmann's works can be used as guidelines for reestablishing a socio-logical macroperspective. While Meyer's theory is particularly good at analyzing diffusion processes that transcend sectoral boundaries of society and shape all units of analysis, Luhmann's systems theory instead focuses on differences between societal systems that cannot be transcended. At the interface of these very different para-digms, there is scope for important new developments in theoretical and empirical research, taking into account contradictory societal pressures toward homogeniza-tion and differentiation.

Summary: Breadth of intellectual and empirical relevance

This review of world society theory places Meyer's theoretical and empirical contri-butions within the context of social science work in general. We relate world society theory with other intellectual endeavors in the social sciences, from other sociological approaches and social institutions to other social theories of world affairs, from colleagues to critics. Many of them share terminology with world society theory; others share a deeper conceptual understanding. Most clearly, "open system" ideas about the situated nature of social units, which came from the work of Meyer and his colleagues in the 1970s, have become commonsense notions in the social sciences;

here, obviously, the commonality between Meyer's institutionalism and other "open system" approaches is rather "shallow." Lately, several other concepts that are central to Meyer's world society theory have become commonly used by social scientists of different theoretical stands: in this list of shared concepts are "embeddedness," and "rationalization," and indeed "world society." Yet the common terminology does not translate to similarity of minds: the terminological "bridges" across the theoretical divides do not erase the substantial conceptual differences, some of which we allude to here.

This account of the commonalities and distinctions between Meyer's scholarship and other theories and issues in the social sciences reveals Meyer's relevance to current social theory and its wide appeal to scholars. For example, Meyer's work transcends the "Atlantic divide" in the social sciences. On various issues – from social theory and international affairs to organizations – European scholarship has an essential understanding of world society because there are many institutional insights available in European intellectual field. For example, European scholars from Luhmann to Bourdieu convey a constructivist image of the social actor, thus allowing a point of connection with institutionalist scholarship. At the same time, Meyer's work is American in its empirical emphasis and its ambivalence toward (grand) theory. Overall, therefore, this review of Meyer's work, placing it in the context of the social sciences, demonstrates Meyer's unique stand as a macro-phenomenological institutionalist. This intellectual perspective, with its richness of concepts and research tools, is engaging and reforging existing arguments about issues central to the social sciences. As the various chapters of this book attest, this theoretical approach has been applied by Meyer and his coauthors to the study of numerous issues.

ORGANIZATION OF THE BOOK

Following the commentary on the context and relevance of Meyer's work to social science research, this book proceeds with an overview of world society theory in Meyer's words. Chapter 2 offers a personal account of Meyer's intellectual journey, outlining the core tenets of world society theory. Meyer reviews the theory's intellectual history (its roots in Weberian thought and breakthrough ideas), outlines the theory's themes, summarizes the research agenda that opened the door to a highly prolific empirical tradition, and surveys the scope of research.

Part II reviews the concepts and processes that came to define world society theory and highlights four of them: rationalization (which strongly ties in with Meyer's later work on scientization), actorhood, diffusion, and globalization. These four concepts make up the scope of the theory's theoretical reach: by explicating the four key "building blocks" of world society theory, this part lays the foundation for Part III.

Part III demonstrates the breadth of world society theory by highlighting some of the numerous social institutions, varying from the nation-state and management to the European Union, that have been (re)interpreted from this theoretical stand. In spite of the variety in sectors and issues, the compilation reveals the far-reaching relevance of world society theory. These chapters speak of both the theoretical and the empirical: for example, the chapter on the environment tells of both the constitution of a global network of organizations and describes the global rise of environmentalism. Social scientists with different interests can find in this part a world society interpretation of their fields of interest, and they can also identify the "bridge" between their field and others.

The inclusion of these many chapters relating to social institutions creates two challenges. First, including ten chapters and thus the subject matters required us to make tough editorial choices: Meyer wrote extensively on many of these subjects, particularly about education, and we carefully chose the piece that accentuates his contribution or is most recent. Second, the inclusion of papers on ten different topics creates some redundancy in the presentation of the abstract arguments. Nevertheless, we chose not to edit Meyer's work but rather to maintain the rhythm and clarity of Meyer's pieces in their original form. We trust that the full-length version also allows for comprehensive institutional analysis of each institution, thus reinforcing the theme of the breadth of world society theory.

Part IV includes a bibliography of Meyer's work. This list is intended to serve as a source for readers, demonstrating the breadth and history of Meyer's contribution to sociological thinking and research.

REFERENCES

Anderson, Benedict. 1991. *Imagined Communities: Reflections on the Origin and Spread of Nationalism,* 2nd ed. London and New York: Verso.

Appadurai, Arjun. 1990. Disjunction and Difference in the Global Cultural Economy. *Theory, Culture and Society* 7 (2–3):295–310.

Avdeyeva, Olga. 2007. When Do States Comply with International Treaties? Policies on Violence against Women in Post-Communist Countries. *International Studies Quarterly* 51(4):877–900.

Barley, Stephen R. and Pamela S. Tolbert. 1997. Institutionalization and Structuration: Studying the Links between Action and Institution. *Organization Studies* 18 (1):93–117.

Barnett, Michael and Liv Coleman. 2005. Designing Police: Interpol and the Study of Change in International Organizations. *International Studies Quarterly* 49 (4):593–620.

—— and Martha Finnemore. 2004. *Rules for the World: International Organizations in Global Politics.* Ithaca, NY: Cornell University Press.

Bartelson, Jens. 2000. Three Concepts of Globalization. *International Sociology* 15 (2):180–96.

Beck, Nikolaus and Peter Walgenbach. 2005. Technical Efficiency or Adaptation to Institutionalized Expectations? The Adoption of ISO 9000 Standards in the German Mechanical Engineering Industry. *Organization Studies* 26 (6):841–66.

Berger, Peter. 1968. *The Sacred Canopy: Elements of a Sociological Theory of Religion.* New York: Doubleday.

—— and Thomas Luckmann. 1967. *The Social Construction of Reality.* New York: Doubleday.

Berger, Joseph, and Morris Zelditch Jr. (eds.) 2002. *New Directions in Contemporary Sociological Theory.* Lanham, MD: Rowman & Littlefield.

Berkovitch, Nitza. 1999. *From Motherhood to Citizenship: Women's Rights and International Organizations.* Baltimore, MD: Johns Hopkins University Press.

Boli, John. 1987. 'World-Polity Sources of Expanding State Authority and Organization, 1870–1970', in Thomas, G. M., J. W. Meyer, F. O. Ramirez, and J. Boli (eds.), *Institutional Structure: Constituting State, Society, and the Individual.* Newbury Park: Sage, pp. 71–91.

Boli, John and George M. Thomas. 1997. World Culture in the World Polity: A Century of International Non-governmental Organization. *American Sociological Review* 62 (2): 171–90.

—— —— (eds.) 1999. *Constructing World Culture: International Nongovernmental Organizations Since 1875.* Stanford: Stanford University Press.

Bourdieu, Pierre. 1984. *Distinction: A Social Critique of the Judgment of Taste.* Cambridge, MA: Harvard University Press.

Brady, David, Jason Beckfield, and Martin Seeleib-Kaiser. 2006. Economic Globalization and the Welfare State in Affluent Democracies, 1975–2001, *American Sociological Review* 70 (6):921–48.

Brubaker, Rogers. 1984. *The Limits of Rationality. An Essay on the Social and Moral Thought of Max Weber.* London: George Allen & Unwin.

Brunsson, Nils. 1989. *The Organization of Hypocrisy: Talk, Decisions and Actions in Organizations.* Chichester: John Wiley and Sons.

—— and Bengt Jacobsson. 2000. *A World of Standards.* Oxford University Press.

—— and Johan P. Olsen. 1993. *The Reforming Organization.* London: Routledge.

Burgoon, Brian. 2001. Globalization and Welfare Compensation: Disentangling the Ties that Bind. *International Organization* 55 (3):509–51.

Castells, Manuel. 1996. *The Rise of the Network Society. Vol. I. the Information Age: Economy, Society and Culture.* Oxford, UK: Blackwell Publishers.

Castels, Francis. 2004. *Future of the Welfare State: Crisis Myths and Crisis Realities.* New York: Oxford University Press.

Chabbott, Colette. 1999. Defining Development: 'The Making of the International Development Field, 1945–1990', in John Boli and George M. Thomas (eds.), *Constructing World Culture: International NGOs since 1875.* Stanford: Stanford University Press, pp. 222–48.

Chase-Dunn, Christopher K. 1998. *Global Formation: Structures of the World Economy.* Lanham, MD: Rowan and Littlefield.

Collins, Randall. 1986. The Rising of Intellectual Generations: Reflections on the Death of Erving Goffman. *Sociological Theory* 4 (1):106–13.

Czarniawska, Barbara. 2008. How to Misuse Institutions and Get Away With It: Some Reflections on Institutional Theory(ies), in Royston Greenwood, Christine Oliver, Kerstin Sahlin, et al. and Roy Suddaby (eds.), *The SAGE Handbook of Organizational Institutionalism.* London: Sage, pp. 769–82.

Dahan, Nicolas, Jonathan Doh, and Terrence Guay. 2006. The Role of Multinational Corporations in Transnational Institution Building: A Policy Network Perspective. *Human Relations* 59 (11):1571–600.

Davis, Gerald F. 2006. Mechanisms and the Theory of Organizations. *Journal of Management Inquiry* 15 (2):114–8.

Detlef, Jahn. 2006. Globalization as 'Galton's Problem': The Missing Link in the Analysis of Diffusion Patterns in Welfare State Development. *International Organization* 60 (2): 401–31.

Diehl, Paul F. (ed.) 1997. *The Politics of Global Governance: International Organizations in an Interdependent World.* Boulder, CO: Lynn Rienner.

DiMaggio, Paul and Walter W. Powell 1983. The Iron Cage Revisited: Institutional Iso-morphism and Collective Rationality in Organizational Fields. *American Sociological Review* 48 (2):147–60.

Djelic, Marie-Laure and Sigrid Quack. 2007. Overcoming Path Dependency: Path Gener-ation in Open Systems. *Theory and Society* 36 (2):161–86.

Dobbin, Frank. 1992. The Origins of Private Social Insurance: Public Policy and Fringe Benefits in America, 1920–1950. *American Journal of Sociology* 97:1416–50.

—— 1994. *Forging Industrial Policy: The United States, Britain, and France in the Railway Age.* New York: Cambridge University Press.

—— Lauren Edelman, John W. Meyer, W. Richard Scott, and Ann Swidler. 1988. The Expansion of Due Process in Organizations, in Lynne G. Zucker (ed.), *Institutional Patterns and Organizations: Culture and Environment.* Cambridge, MA: Ballinger, pp. 71–98.

—— Beth Simmons, and Geoffrey Garrett. 2007. The Global Diffusion of Public Policies: Social Construction, Coercion, Competition, or Learning? *Annual Review of Sociology* 33:449–72.

Drori, Gili S. 2006. Governed by Governance: The Institutionalization of Governance as a Prism for Organizational Change, in Gili S. Drori, John W. Meyer, and Hokyu Hwang (eds.), *Globalization and Organization: World Society and Organizational Change.* Oxford University Press, pp. 91–118.

—— 2008. Institutionalism and Globalization Studies, in Royston Greenwood, Christine Oliver, Kerstin Sahlin, and Roy Suddaby (eds.), *Handbook of Organizational Institutional-ism.* Thousand Oaks, CA: Sage, pp. 798–842.

—— and John W. Meyer. 2006. Scientization and Organization, in Gili S. Drori, John W. Meyer, and Hokyu Hwang (eds.), *Globalization and Organization: World Society and Organizational Change.* Oxford: Oxford University Press, pp. 50–68.

—— —— 2007. The Social State: A Comparative and Historical Study of the Change in the Social Concerns and Responsibilities of the State. Paper presented at American Sociological Association Annual Meeting.

—— —— Francisco O. Ramirez, and Evan Schofer. 2003. *Science in the Modern World Polity: Institutionalization and Globalization,* Stanford: Stanford University Press.

Edelman, Lauren B. 1990. Legal Environments and Organizational Governance: The Expan-sion of Due Process in the American Workplace. *American Journal of Sociology* 95 (6): 1401–40.

Eisenstadt, Shmuel Noah. 2003. *Comparative Civilizations and Multiple Modernities: A Col-lection of Essays.* Leiden: Brill.

Evans, Peter. 1995. *Embedded Autonomy: States and Industrial Transformation.* Princeton, NJ: Princeton University Press.

—— 1997. The Eclipse of the State? Reflections on Stateness in an Era of Globalization. *World Politics* 50 (1):62–87.

Fearon, James and Alexander Wendt. 2002. Rationalism v. Constructivism: A Skeptical View, in Walter Carlsnaes, Thomas Risse, and Beth Simmons (eds.), *Handbook of International Relations,* London: Sage Publications, pp. 52–72.

Finnemore, Martha. 1993. International Organization as Teachers of Norms: The United Nations Educational, Scientific, and Cultural Organization and Science Policy. *Inter-national Organization* 47:567–97.

—— 1996. Norms, Culture, and World Politics: Insights from Sociology's Institutionalism. *International Organization* 50:325–47.

Fiss, Peer C. and Edward J. Zajac. 2004. The Diffusion of Ideas over Contested Terrain: The (Non)adoption of a Shareholder Value Orientation among German Firms. *Administrative Science Quarterly* 49:501–34.

Fligstein, Neil. 1985. The Spread of the Multidivisional Form among Large Firms, 1919–1979. *American Sociological Review* 50 (3):377–91.

Florini, Ann M. (ed.) 2000. *The Third Force: The Rise of Transnational Civil Society.* Washington, DC: Carnegie Endowment for International Peace.

Foucault, Michel. 1965. *Madness and Civilization: A History of Insanity in the Age of Reason* (trans. Richard Howard). New York: Vintage Books.

—— 1972. *The Archaeology of Knowledge* (trans. A.M. Sheridan Smith). London: Tavostock.

—— 1975. *Discipline and Punish. The Birth of the Prison* (trans. A. Sheridan). New York: Vintage.

—— 1980. in Colin Gordon (ed.), *Power/Knowledge: Selected Interviews and Other Writings 1972–1977.* New York: Pantheon Books.

—— 1990. *The History of Sexuality* (Vol. 1; trans. Robert Hurley). London: Penguin.

Foucault, Michel. 1991. Governmentality, in Graham Burchell, Colin Gordon, and Peter Miller (eds.), *The Foucault Effect: Studies in Governmentaility.* Chicago: University of Chicago Press, pp. 87–103.

Frank, David and John W. Meyer. 2002. The Contemporary Identity Explosion: Individualizing Society in the Post-War Period. *Sociological Theory* 20 (1):86–105.

Freeman, Richard B., Robert H. Topel, and Birgitta Swedenborg, 1997. *The Welfare State in Transition.* Chicago: University of Chicago Press.

Giddens, Anthony. 1986. *The Constitution of Society: Outline of the Theory of Structuration.* Berkeley, CA: University of California Press.

Gilbert, Neil. 2002. *Transformation of the Welfare State: The Silent Surrender of Public Responsibility.* New York: Oxford University Press.

Greenwood, Royston, Christine Oliver, Kerstin Sahlin, and Roy Suddaby. 2008. Introduction, in Greenwood et al. (eds.), *Handbook of Organizational Institutionalism.* Thousand Oaks, CA: Sage, pp. 1–46.

—— Roy Suddaby, and Megan McDougal (eds.) 2006. *Professional Service Firms.* Elsevier.

Guillén, Mauro F. 2001. Is Globalization Civilizing, Destructive or Feeble? A Critique of Five Key Debates in the Social Science Literature. *Annual Review of Sociology* 27:235–60.

Habermas, Jürgen. 1985/1989. *A Theory of Communicative Action*, 2 Vols. Boston, MA: Beacon Press.

Hafner-Burton, Emilie M. and Kiyoteru Tsutsui. 2005. Human Rights Practices in a Globalizing World: The Paradox of Empty Promises. *American Journal of Sociology* 110 (5):1373–411.

—— —— and John W. Meyer. 2008. International Human Rights Law and the Politics of Legitimation: Repressive States and Human Rights Treaties. *International Sociology* 23 (1):115–41.

Hall, Rodney Bruce, and Thomas J. Biersteker (eds.) 2002. *The Emergence of Private Authority in Global Governance.* Cambridge: Cambridge University Press.

Hannan, Michael T. and John Freeman. 1977. The Population Ecology of Organizations. *American Journal of Sociology* 82 (5):929–64.

Hannerz, Ulf. 1989. Notes on Global Ecumene. *Public Culture* 1 (2):66–75.

Hasse, Raimund and Georg Krücken. 2008. Systems Theory, Societal Contexts, and Organizational Heterogeneity, in Royston Greenwood, Christine Oliver, Roy Suddaby, and Kerstin Sahlin (eds.), *The Handbook of Organizational Institutionalism.* Thousand Oaks, CA/London: Sage, pp. 539–59.

Hathaway, Oona. 2003. The Cost of Commitment. *Stanford Law Review* 55:1821–62.

Huber, Evelyn and John D. Stephens. 2001. *Development and Crisis in the Welfare State.* Chicago, IL: University of Chicago Press.

Hwang, Hokyu. 2006. Planning Development: Globalization and the Shifting Locus on Planning, in G. S. Drori, J. W. Meyer, and H. Hwang (eds.), *Globalization and Organization: World Society and Organizational Change.* Oxford: Oxford University Press, pp. 69–90.

Jang, Yong Suk. 2000. The Worldwide Formation of Ministries of Science and Technology, 1950–1990. *Sociological Perspectives* 43 (2):247–70.

Jepperson, Ronald L. 2002. The Development and Application of Sociological Neoinstitutionalism, in Joseph Berger and Morris Zelditch Jr. (eds.), *New Directions in Contemporary Sociological Theory.* Lanham, MD: Rowman & Littlefield, pp. 229–66.

—— and John W. Meyer 2007. 'Analytical Individualism and the Explanation of Macrosocial Change, in V. Nee and R. Swedberg (eds.), *On Capitalism.* Stanford, CA: Stanford University Press, pp. 273–304.

Kamens, David H. 1977. Legitimating Myths and Educational Organization: The Relationship between Organizational Ideology and Formal Structure. *American Sociological Review* 42:208–19.

—— 2007 Book Review – Reconstructing the University: Worldwide Shifts in Academia in the Twentieth Century, by David John Frank and Jay Gabler. *Comparative Education Review* 51 (4):323–525.

Keck, Margaret E. and Kathryn Sikkink. 1998. *Activists Beyond Borders: Advocacy Networks in International Politics.* Ithaca, NY: Cornell University Press.

Keohane, Robert. 2002. *Power and Independence in a Partially Globalized World.* New York: Routledge.

Kim, Young S., Yong Suk Jang, and Hokyu Hwang. 2002. Structural Expansion and the Cost of Global Isomorphism: A Cross-National Study of Ministries Structure, 1950–1990. *International Sociology* 17 (4):481–503.

Koenig, Matthias. 2008. Institutional Change in the World Polity: International Human Rights and the Construction of Collective Identities. *International Sociology* 23 (1):95–114.

Krasner, Stephen D. 1983. 'Structural Causes and Regime Consequences: Regimes as Intervening Variables', in S. D. Krasner (ed.), *International Regimes.* Ithaca, NY: Cornell University Press, pp. 1–22.

—— 1999. *Sovereignty: Organized Hypocrisy.* Princeton, NJ: Princeton University Press.

Krücken, Georg, 2002. Amerikanischer Neo-Institutionalismus – europäische Perspektiven. *Sociologia Internationalis* 40 (2):227–59.

—— and Frank Meier. 2006. Turning the University into an Organizational Actor, in G. S. Drori, J. W. Meyer, and H. Hwang (eds.), *Globalization and Organization: World Society and Organizational Change.* Oxford: Oxford University Press, pp. 241–57.

Lawrence, Paul R. and Jay W. Lorsch 1967. *Organization and Environment: Managing Differentiation and Integration.* Boston: Graduate School of Business Administration, Harvard University.

Lechner, Frank and John Boli. 2005. *World Culture: Origins and Consequences.* London: Blackwell.

Lee, Chang Kil and David Strang. 2006. The International Diffusion of Public-Sector Downsizing: Network Emulation and Theory-Driven Learning. *International Organization* 60:883–909.

Levi-Faur, David. 2003. The Politics of Liberalization: Privatization and Regulation-for-Competition in Europe's and Latin America's Telecoms and Electricity industries. *European Journal of Political Research* 42 (5):705–40.

Luhmann, Niklas. 1982. *The Differentiation of Society.* New York: Columbia University Press.
—— 1989. *Ecological Communication.* Chicago, IL: University of Chicago Press.
—— 1990. *Political Theory in the Welfare State.* Berlin/New York: de Gruyter.
—— 1993. *Risk: A Sociological Theory.* Berlin/New York, NY: de Gruyter.
—— 1995. *Social Systems.* Palo Alto, CA: Stanford University Press.
—— 1997. *Die Gesellschaft der Gesellschaft.* Frankfurt a.M.: Suhrkamp.
—— 1998. *Observations on Modernity.* Palo Alto, CA: Stanford University Press.
March, James G. 1999. Understanding How Decisions Happen in Organizations, *The Pursuit of Organizational Intelligence.* London: Blackwell Business, pp. 13–38.
—— and Johan P. Olsen. 1976. *Ambiguity and Choice in Organizations.* Bergen: Universitetsforlaget.
Martin, Luther H., Huck Gutman, and Patrick Hutton (eds.) 1993. *Technologien des Selbst.* Frankfurt a.M.: Fischer.
McKinlay, Alan, and Ken Starkey (eds.). 1998. *Foucault, Management and Organization Theory: From Panopticon to Technologies of Self.* London: Sage.
Meyer, John W. 1977. The Effects of Education as an Institution. *American Journal of Sociology,* 83:55–77.
—— 1987. World Polity and the Authority of the Nation-State, in G. Thomas, J. W. Meyer, F. O. Ramirez and J. Boli (eds.), *Institutional structure: Constituting State, Society, and the Individual.* Newbury Park: Sage, pp. 41–70.
—— 1992. From Constructivism to Neo-Institutionalism: Reflections on Berger and Luckman. *Perspectives* 15:11–12.
—— 1999. The Changing Cultural Content of the Nation-State: A World Society Perspective, in George Steinmetz (ed.), *State/Culture: State-Formation After the Cultural Turn.* Ithaca, NY: Cornell University Press, pp. 123–44.
—— 2004. Sociological Perspectives on Diffusion. Unpublished.
—— 2008. Reflections on Institutional Theories of Organizations, in R. Greenwood, C. Oliver, R. Suddaby, and K. Sahlin (eds.), *Handbook of Organizational Institutionalism.* Thousand Oaks, CA: Sage, pp. 790–811.
—— John Boli, and George M. Thomas 1987. Ontology and Rationalization in the Western Cultural Account, in G. M. Thomas, J. W. Meyer, F. O. Ramirez, and J. Boli, *Institutional Structure: Constituting State, Society, and the Individual.* Newbury Park, CA: Sage, pp. 12–40. Reproduced in Chapter 3.
—— John Boli-Bennett and Christopher Chase-Dunn. 1975. Convergence and Divergence in Development. *Annual Review of Sociology* 1:223–45.
—— John Boli, George Thomas, and Francisco O. Ramirez. 1997. World Society and the Nation-State. *American Journal of Sociology* 103:144–81. Reproduced in Chapter 8.
—— Gili S. Drori, and Hokyu Hwang. 2006. World Society and the Organizational Actor. in Drori, Gili S., John W. Meyer, and Hokyu Hwang (eds.), *Globalization and Organization: World Society and Organizational Change.* Oxford University Press, pp. 25–49.
—— and Michael T. Hannan (eds.) 1979. *National Development and the World System.* Chicago: University of Chicago Press.
—— and Brian Rowan. 1977. Institutionalized Organizations: Formal Structure as Myth and Ceremony. *American Journal of Sociology* 83:340–63.
—— and W. Richard Scott (eds.) 1992 (1983). *Organizational Environments: Ritual and Rationality.* Thousand Oaks, CA: Sage.
—— —— Sally Cole, and Jo-Ann K. Intili 1978. 'Instructional Dissensus and Institutional Consensus in Schools', in Marshall W. Meyer (ed.), *Environments and Organizations.* San Francisco: Jossey-Bass, pp. 290–305.

—— —— and Terrence E. Deal. 1981. Institutional and Technical Sources of Organizational Structure: Explaining the Structure of Educational Organizations, in Herman D. Stein (ed.), *Organization and the Human Services*. Philadelphia: Temple University Press, pp. 151–78.

Milner, Helen. 1991. The Assumption of Anarchy in International Relations Theory: A Critique. *Review of International Studies* 17:67–85.

Mishra, Ramesh. 1999. *Globalization and the Welfare State*. Northampton, MA: Edward Elger.

Montanari, Ingalill. 2001. Modernization, Globalization, and the Welfare State: A Comparative Analysis of Old and New Convergence in Social Insurance since 1930. *British Journal of Sociology* 52:469–94.

Moore, Wilbert E. 1966. Global Sociology: The World as a Singular System. *American Journal of Sociology* 71 (5):475–82.

Mörth, Ulrika. 2006. Soft Regulation and Global Democracy. in Djelic, Marie-Laure, and Kerstin Sahlin-Andersson (eds.), *Transnational Governance: Institutional Dynamics of Regulation*. Cambridge: Cambridge University Press, pp. 199–135.

Oakes, Guy. 2003. Max Weber on Value Rationality and Value Spheres: Critical Remarks. *Journal of Classical Sociology* 3 (1):27–45.

Ottaway, Marina. 2001. Corporatism Goes Global: International Organizations, Nongovernmental Organization Networks, and Transnational Business. *Global Governance* 7 (3):265–92.

Pattberg, Philipp. 2005. The Institutionalization of Private Governance: How Business and Nonprofit Organizations Agree on Transnational Rules. *Governance* 18 (4):589–610.

Perrow, Charles B. 1991. A Society of Organizations. *Theory & Society* 20 (6):725–62.

Pfeffer, Jeffrey. 1972. Merger as a Response to Organizational Interdependence. *Administrative Science Quarterly* 17:382–92.

—— and Gerald R. Salancik. 1978. *The External Control of Organizations*. New York: Harper & Row.

Pieterse, Jan Nederveen. 1995. 'Globalization as Hybridization, in Mike Featherstone, Scott Lash, and Roland Robertson (eds.), *Global Modernities*. Thousand Oaks, CA: Sage, pp. 45–68.

Powell, Walter W. 1991. 'Expanding the Scope of Institutional Analysis', in W. W. Powell and P. J. DiMaggio (eds.), *The New Institutionalism in Organizational Analysis*. Chicago: University of Chicago Press, pp. 183–203.

—— and Paul J. DiMaggio (eds.) 1991. *The New Institutionalism in Organizational Analysis*. Chicago: University of Chicago Press.

Power, Michael. 1997. *The Audit Society: Rituals of Verification*. Oxford: Oxford University Press.

Ramirez, Francisco O. 2006. The Rationalization of Universities, in Djelic, Marie-Laure and Kerstin Sahlin-Andersson (eds.), *Transnational Governance: Institutional Dynamics of Regulation*. Cambridge: Cambridge University Press, pp. 225–45.

—— Yasemin Soysal, and Suzanne Shanahan. 1997. The Changing Logic of Political Citizenship: Cross-National Acquisition of Women's Suffrage Rights, 1890 to 1990. *American Sociological Review* 62 (5):735–45.

—— David Suarez, and John W. Meyer. 2006. The Worldwide Rise of Human Rights Education, in Aaron Benavot and Cecilia Braslavsky (eds.), *School Knowledge in Comparative and Historical Perspective: Changing Curricula in Primary and Secondary Education*. Hong Kong: Springer, Comparative Education Research Centre, pp. 35–54.

Rao, Hayagreeva and Kumar Sivakumar. 1999. Institutional Sources of Boundary-Spanning Structures: The Establishment of Investor Relations Departments in the Fortune 500 Industrials. *Organization Science* 10 (1):27–42.

Risse, Thomas, Stephen C. Ropp, and Kathryn Sikkink. 1999. *The Power of Human Rights: International Norms and Domestic Change.* Cambridge: Cambridge University Press.

Robertson, Roland. 1994. Globalization and Glocalization *Journal of International Communication*, 1:33–52.

Rose, Nikolas and Peter Miller. 1992. Political Power Beyond the State: Problematics of Government. *British Journal of Sociology* 43 (2):173–205.

Rosenau, James N. 1995. Governance in the 21st Century. *Global Governance* 1:13–44.

—— 1997. *Along the Domestic-Foreign Frontier: Exploring Governance in a Turbulent World.* Cambridge: Cambridge University Press.

—— 2003. *Distant Proximities: Dynamics Beyond Globalization.* Princeton, NJ: Princeton University Press.

Ruggie, John. 1982. International Regimes, Transactions, and Change: Embedded Liberalism in the Postwar Economic Order. *International Organization* 36:379–415.

—— 1998. *Constructing the World Polity: Essays on International Institutionalization.* London: Routledge.

Sahlin-Andersson, Kerstin, and Lars Engwall (eds.) 2002. *The Expansion of Management Knowledge: Carriers, Flows and Sources.* Stanford, CA: Stanford Business Books.

Schneiberg, Marc and Elisabeth S. Clemens. 2006. The Typical Tools for the Job: Research Strategies in Institutional Analysis. *Sociological Theory* 24 (3):195–227.

Schofer, Evan and Elizabeth H. McEneaney. 2003. Methodological Strategies and Tools for the Study of Globalization, in Gili S. Drori, John W. Meyer, Francisco O. Ramirez, and Evan Schofer (eds.), *Science in the Modern World Polity: Institutionalization and Globalization.* Stanford, CA: Stanford University Press, pp. 43–74.

—— and John W. Meyer. 2005. The World-Wide Expansion of Higher Education in the Twentieth Century. *American Sociological Review* 70 (6):898–920.

Scott, W. Richard. 1983. Introduction: From Technology to Environment, in John W. Meyer and W. Richard Scott (eds.), *Organizational Environments: Ritual and Rationality.* Newbury Park, CA: Sage, pp. 13–17.

—— 2004. Reflections on a Half-Century of Organizational Sociology. *Annual Review of Sociology* 30:1–21.

—— 2008. Approaching Adulthood: The Maturing of Institutional Theory. *Theory and Society* 37 (5):427–42.

—— and John W. Meyer et al. 1994. *Institutional Environments and Organizations.* Thousand Oaks, CA: Sage.

Sikkink, Kathryn. 1993. Human Rights, Principle-Issue Networks, and Sovereignty in Latin America. *International Organization* 43 (3):411–41.

Simmons, Beth A. 1998. Compliance with International Agreements. *Annual Review of Political Science* 1:75–93.

—— 2000. International Law and State Behavior: Commitment and Compliance in International Monetary Affairs. *American Political Science Review* 94 (4):819–35.

—— and Daniel J. Hopkins. 2005. The Constraining Power of International Treaties: Theory and Methods. *American Political Science Review* 99:623–631.

Smith, Jackie. 1995. Transnational Political Processes and the Human Rights Movement, in L. Kriesberg, M. Dobkowski, and I. William (eds.), *Research in Social Movements.* Greenwood, CT: JAI Press, pp. 185–220.

Strang, David and Michael W. Macy. 2001. In Search of Excellence: Fads, Success Stories and Adaptive Emulation. *American Journal of Sociology* 107:147–182.

—— and John W. Meyer. 1993. Institutional Conditions of Diffusion. *Theory and Society* 22:487–511.

Tempel, Anne and Peter Walgenbach. 2007. Global Standardization of Organizational Forms and Management Practices? What New Institutionalism and the Business-Systems Approach Can Learn from Each Other. *Journal of Management Studies* 44 (1):1–24.

Thomas, George, John W. Meyer, Francisco O. Ramirez, and John Boli. 1987. *Institutional Structure: Constituting State, Society, and the Individual.* Newbury Park, CA: Sage.

Thompson, James W. 2003 (1967). *Organizations in Action.* Edison, NJ: Transaction Publishers.

Touraine, Alain 1995. *Critique of Modernity.* Oxford, UK: Blackwell Publishers.

Tsutsui, Kiyoteru. 2004. Global Civil Society and Ethnic Social Movement in the Contemporary World. *Sociological Forum* 19 (1):63–87.

Von Stein, Jana. 2005. Do Treaties Constrain or Screen? Selection Bias and Treaty Compliance. *American Political Science Review* 99:611–22.

Wallerstein, Immanuel. 1973. *The Capitalist World Economy: Essays.* Cambridge: Cambridge University Press.

—— 2000. Globalization or Age of Transition? A Long-Term View of the Trajectory of the World-System. *International Sociology*, 15 (2):249–65.

Weber, Max. 1920. *Gesammelte Aufsätze zur Religionssoziologie.* Vol. 1. Tübingen: Mohr Siebeck.

—— 1949. The Meaning of 'Ethical Neutrality' in Sociology and Economics, in Edward A. Shils and Henry A. Finch (eds.), *The Methodology of the Social Sciences.* New York: Free Press.

—— 1958: *The Protestant Ethic and the Spirit of Capitalism.* New York: Charles Scribner's Sons.

—— 1968: *Economy and Society: An Outline of Interpretive Sociology.* New York: Bedminster Press.

Weick, Karl. 1979 (1969). *The Social Psychology of Organizing,* 2nd edn. Boston: Addison-Wesley.

Weick, Karl E. 1976. Educational Organizations as Loosely Coupled Systems. *Administrative Science Quarterly,* 21:1–19.

Weingart, Peter, 2003. Growth, Differentiation, Expansion and Change of Identity – The Future of Science, in Bernward Joerges and Helga Nowotny (eds.), *Social Studies of Science and Technology: Looking Back Ahead.* Dordrecht: Kluwer Academic Publishers, pp. 183–200.

Wendt, Alexander. 1999. *Social Theory of International Politics.* Cambridge: Cambridge University Press.

Wotipka, Christine Min and Francisco O. Ramirez 2008. World Society and Human Rights: An Event History Analysis of the Convention on the Elimination of All Forms of Discrimination against Women, in Beth Simmons, Frank Dobbin, and Geoffrey Garrett (eds.), *The Global Diffusion of Markets and Democracy.* Cambridge: Cambridge University Press, pp. 303–43.

Zucker, Lynne G. 1977. The Role of Institutionalization in Cultural Persistence. *American Sociological Review,* 42:726–43.

2

Reflections: Institutional Theory and World Society

John W. Meyer

Sociological institutional (or neo-institutional) theory, as it has developed since the 1970s, has provided a useful perspective from which to understand the rise, nature, and impact of the modern world order or society. For many decades, social theories maintained postures that made it difficult to think of the world as a society, and theorists who did so (e.g., Heintz 1972; Luhmann 1975; Bull and Watson 1984; Robertson 1992) tended to be the exceptions. The world was seen as anarchical (by realists in political science) or as an economy without a regulating polity (by world systems students, following Wallerstein 1974) rather than as a society.

The core problem was that the social sciences are themselves creations of the post-Enlightenment nation-state system. Thus, they tend, mostly implicitly (as in Parsons' work), to conceive of societies as coterminous with nations and states. Societies were interdependent systems managed by an overriding sovereign organization. As the world did not have a sovereign state, and global interdependence was recognized only in a limited way, the world was, by definition, not a society.

Institutional theory, particularly in its more sociological versions, dramatically changed the scenario. Along with many other post-functionalist lines of thought, it emphasized a cultural conception of society as an "imagined community" (Anderson 1983), rather than a more realist model of actors involved in functional interdependencies. And it emphasized broad cultural themes and shifts in wider social environments as impacting actors of all sorts – organizations, but also individuals (Chapters 3, 4, 5, and 11). The application of this line of thought to the conceptualization of a world society and its impact was straightforward. Institutional theory made it easy to conceive of the world as a society (Chapter 7), and to analyze the impact of that society on all sorts of subunits, including national states (Chapter 8). Further, in a point I emphasize below, institutional theory described and called attention to great movements in the current world that were given neither description nor explanation in more conventional social theory. So institutional theory in addition

This chapter reflects many themes from my earlier work and collaborations. The first section parallels topics, vis-à-vis organization theory, in Meyer (2008). Work on the original paper was supported by a grant (to Francisco Ramirez and John Meyer) from the Spencer Foundation (20060003). Ronald Jepperson provided many detailed comments and suggestions.

to its explanatory value, has played a descriptive role. It calls attention to important features of the modern world order given little attention in earlier lines of thought.

World society, in this vision, is a good deal more than the set of actors (individuals, organizations, and national-states) envisioned in much more realist and functionalist social theory. And, it is more than the transactions of power and exchange among such actors. The modern world is filled with shared understandings of nature, humans, and society. It is also filled with understandings of a directly collective reality in a physical, moral, and social world (Jepperson and Swidler 1993–4). Obviously, many cultural elements in the world are not shared, but vary across several dimensions. And, many understandings are in no sense linked to conceptions of a common collective order, but rather envision only subunits. The surprising features of the contemporary world are: how much is shared, how much is universalized, and how strong collectivity is perceived, not that there is global unification.

Thus, world society is filled with associations with little agency for action, speaking to great collective goods and universal principles (as with the World Wildlife Fund and the environment, or Amnesty International, or a variety of treaty organizations). Then, there are the supra-national professions, like the scientific and legal and social scientific and medical and educational elites, that speak great supra-national truths to all the actors of the world. World society also has a broad range of social movements along all these axes, half-organizations and half-professional or ideological communities. And it is filled with nation-states shifting from their role as actors within a world society to postures of agency for collective truth and virtue in this society and transcending it: leading national states routinely parade themselves as instances of universal goods (the Americans illustrating enterprise and freedom; the Swedes sober community responsibility; the former Communists equality).

All this prominent social material makes up an envisioned world society that is of variable significance across social sectors and social regions. It is organized around collective and often transcendental goods – completely collective goods like the reified welfare of Mother Earth, and densely shared common interests like the health of the world exchange system. And, orientation toward it clearly penetrates, in many social sectors, far down into ordinary social life, as local people and organizations respond to global environmental problems (Chapter 10), or problems of violations of human rights (Chapter 13). Much social theory is inattentive to the dramatic expansions of such orientations, and focuses only on the internal dynamics of actors and their interdependencies. This has made it difficult for social scientists to explain great currents and movements of a more collective kind in the contemporary world (e.g., the environmental or human rights movements, or the worldwide accountability movements for organizational reforms). Interestingly, the same limitations apply to the social scientific analyses of historic Christendom – often seen more as parts than as a culturally constituted whole – and have made it difficult to understand many aspects of the long-term "rise of the West" (Meyer 1988; see Mann 1986, for a comprehensive analysis). A continuing conceptual problem in the more realist social sciences is a very thin conception of culture: at the world level, the term is more likely to refer to some musical tastes than to the academic field of economics, or to the highly developed doctrines of environmentalism (Chapter 10).

I begin (*a*) by reviewing the distinctive features of sociological institutional theory, and in particular, the more phenomenological versions that are useful in thinking about world society. Then I discuss (*b*) why this line of theorizing prospers in discussions of world society – that is, the features of world society that reflect processes theorized by the line of theory. In important ways, the kinds of variables emphasized in institutional theory play very prominent roles in the post-World War II world. So the theory describes and calls attention to, as well as offers explanations for, major historical developments. I then turn to a (*c*) substantive review of the core theoretical themes or propositions involved. These discuss the factors affecting the construction and expansion of modern "actorhood," creating powers and responsibilities for actors far beyond the plausible. The culture of the modern system greatly elaborates the imagined capacities and responsibilities of individuals, organizations, and national states, endowing them with extraordinarily agentic properties. This review leads to (*d*) an emphasis on Durkheimian aspects of contemporary world society – the extent to which this society contains (and is in good part an imagined community constructed by) a collective cultural cosmology, akin to a religious ideology, that penetrates very deeply into the identity and activity structures of the modern world. It also leads to (*e*) an emphasis on the social forces that rapidly expand this cosmology, providing instruction and therapy and consulting advice for actors from individuals to national states.

INSTITUTIONAL THEORIES

As the social sciences developed after the Enlightenment period, they routinely conceptualized human activity as deeply institutionalized – highly embedded in collective cultural patterns. People were creatures of habit, groups of customs, and societies of culture. Analyses consisted of models, often evolutionary, of variations in these habits and cultures, and of their changes over time.

At the same time, however, the Enlightenment generated many ideas that "man," now possessing formerly-divine powers, could use his developing knowledge of nature and society purposively, to accomplish his goals (Foucault 1994). Man, in this connection meant, variously, individual human persons in liberal contexts, and nation-states in statist ones (Toulmin 1990). And over time, it came to mean the bureaucracies derived from states, and the organizations constructed by individuals. In all these conceptions, persons, states, organizations, and bureaucracies were no longer seen as creatures of habit and culture; they were bounded and purposive and competent actors. In the twentieth century, indeed, the word habit disappeared from the social scientific vocabulary, and the word "actor" became central (Camic 1986). The choice of words is odd – in ordinary usage, "actor" implies a person playing a role written by someone else. But in social science, it means something like a goal oriented, bounded, integrated, technically effective entity.

With the rise of conceptions of modern society as built up around and by effective purposive actors, an intellectual division of labor developed. Primitive societies, the main focus of anthropology, were seen as embedded in culture. And to some extent, pre-modern societies in the west could be seen in the same way, as creatures of history. But, in the social sciences focusing on modernity – economics, sociology, psychology, political science, and so on – preferred analyses increasingly traced causal processes to the bottom-line choices and preferences of human actors (Meyer 1988). Institutions remained, of course, but now these institutions were seen as choices of human actors, or as values deeply internalized by these actors. And, while institutions might constrain actors, their choices were basic determinants of social outcomes. Modern humans and their groups, in short, created institutions and history, rather than being products of these elements.

With some simplification, one can call these emergent theoretical and normative emphases as realist (Chapters 3, 5, 6, and 8), and I employ this term for them here. They have a micro-social emphasis, especially as employed in the American context, in that they stress the centrality of the subunit actors rather than the wider system (e.g., individuals in societies, nation-state actors in the world). And they are realist in that they tend to see the actors involved as quite hard-wired entities, and the relations and interactions among these actors as quite tangible expressions of the material forces of power and exchange.

World War II gave great impetus to this general line of thought. Notions of humans and their society as embedded in collective culture were disparaged with the stigmatization of corporatism and statism, and liberal conceptions of the actorhood of people and groups greatly strengthened. Individuals could be liberated, and social psychologies proliferated. Groups could be rational organizations, and organization theory blossomed. Societies, with rational decision-making and planning (Hwang 2006), could all develop and progress, and associated theories in economics and political science elaborated. The more culturally based institutions of the past and the primitive world could be overcome with education and rationality. In general, institutions when recognized, got a bad reputation, as loci of inertia and irrationality: the unfortunate dependence of man on history, rather than history on man (Meyer 1988).

In this emergent social science of the post-War period, institutions were recognized, but as rather derivative structures. They were products of human action and decision, and could be produced and structured in rational ways by highly purposive (and often self-interested) actors. Society could be subjected to rational analysis, and the analyses used for policy purposes. So the dramatic twentieth century expansion of the social sciences intensified, in the composition of university faculties (Frank and Gabler 2006) and student enrollments (Drori and Moon 2006).

By the early 1970s, the extreme liberal optimism involved in these patterns faded. Development theories of society, institutionalized as policy, did not produce spectacular progress. Rationalistic organizational theory ran up against constant empirical findings of great gaps between the plans and policies of formal organization and the realities of practice in informal structure (e.g., Dalton 1959; Chapters 4, 11 and 15). And, studies of individual persons demonstrated great inconsistencies between their theoretical autonomous actorhood and their practical embeddedness in taken-for-granted culture and relationships.

Thus in every social science (except anthropology and history, where the old institutionalisms never died out), new institutionalisms developed (Jepperson 1991). Nation-states, formal organizations, and individuals – the "actors" of the new system – were conceived to be dependent on some sort of institutional structure. These new (or neo-) institutionalisms differed from the old ones in a very crucial way. In the new or neo-version, institutional structures worked by affecting and controlling and constraining "actors" – that is, people and groups with real or imagined properties as fairly bounded, autonomous, purposive, rational, and sovereign entities, capable of considerable technical skill and enormous self-control, and possessed of discrete resources. So in this new scheme, national states, rather than being embedded in history and culture, became actors operating under an institutional frame. So also, organizations were seen as actors rather than groups, and were similarly seen to operate under institutional constraints and opportunities. And, individual persons came similarly to be seen as highly agentic social actors (Chapters 5 and 14).

The New Institutionalisms

An expanded recognition of the importance of institutional contexts in affecting social activity has characterized social scientific thinking over the last three decades. But there are sharp differences among lines of theorizing in the extent and character of the driving institutional contexts recognized, and in the degree to which social actors are thought to be affected, penetrated, or constituted by the institutional forces. Many modern social scientific issues are between differing institutionalisms, rather than between institutional thinking and entirely distinct lines of thought. The issues are reviewed in many discussions: Jepperson (1991, 2002) is especially relevant here, but also see the broad reviews by Scott (2001), and Hasse and Kruecken (2005).

For simplicity, I lay out the distinctions among institutionalisms on a single dimension, though multiple components are involved. At one pole, there is realist institutionalism, with (*a*) very strong conceptions of the priority, boundedness, autonomy, and rationality of actors, and limited conceptions of the effects of any institutions, (*b*) notions of institutions as clear and operative rules rather than diffuse meaning systems, and (*c*) very narrow or limited conceptions of the important institutional environments which constrain and empower actors. At the other pole, there is phenomenological institutionalism, with (*a*) notions of actors as constructed by institutional models and meanings rather than as prior and fixed entities, (*b*) conceptions of institutions as cultural meanings rather than narrow organizational rules, and (*c*) very broad conceptions of institutions as general models constructing both actors and their activities.

At the realist extreme, we find ideas in economics that the whole modern system is made up of very strong actors and the single institutional rule of property rights (North and Thomas 1973). Parallel ideas in the political science field of international relations treat nation-states as actors in a completely anarchical context, except the single institutional principle of state sovereignty (Krasner 1999). Both lines of thought have tended to soften over time (e.g., North 1981; Mokyr 1992), with the empirical recognition of more and more elements of institutional contexts. In both cases, the emphasis on a social world of strong actors and anarchic contexts is so strong that there is a tendency to see the putatively single institutional rules crucial to modernity (that is, property rights, or national sovereignty) as having arisen almost by accident (e.g., at Westphalia in the case of sovereignty), since actors themselves are unlikely to cooperate in any trustworthy fashion.

Less extreme positions in political science (and economics) add elements to the institutional environment, and conceive the social actors as somewhat more penetrated or penetrable (see Katzenstein ed. 1996 for examples). Thus, political scientists imagine the environment contains "norms," and the actors involved may have created these norms (the more realist position) or become socialized to prior norms (slightly less realist). A norm might be, "don't use chemical weapons" or "treat your enemies' emissaries civilly." Parallel lines of thought in sociology emphasize the dependence of actors on social network relations.

Standard middle-of-the-road institutionalism in political science conceives international society as a regime made up of a variety of organizations and rules (e.g., Krasner 1983), and as having a good deal of cultural content perhaps generated and controlled by professional epistemic communities (Haas 1992).

This line of thought is central in modern sociology. The locus classicus is DiMaggio and Powell (1983), and broader summaries can be found in Powell and DiMaggio (1991) and Scott (2001 and elsewhere). The "regime" is here called the "organizational field," and the cultural content is again understood to be controlled and generated by professions. By and large, thinking in this important sociological tradition has a realist cast. So the institutional environment controls and empowers actors through coercive organizational powers and professional norms (Scott 2001 has a related typology).

But DiMaggio and Powell (1983) added an additional element in discussing the impact of institutional rules on actors: they called it "mimetic isomorphism," by which actors incorporate institutional rules by taking them for granted without much decision or reflection. At this point, actors are no longer actors in the realist sense, and we are in the domain of more phenomenological institutionalism.

This line of sociological thought, as it arose in the 1970s, is commonly traced to Meyer and Rowan (1977, included here as Chapter 4), which in turn has links back to earlier phenomenological thinking (esp. Berger and Luckmann, 1967). Here, the conception of institution is very broad – whole edited and translated models of the world and effective activity in it, culturally (Czarniawska and Sevón, eds. 1996); and whole arrangements of organizations and roles and relations, structurally. And the actors in this institutional system are conceived as constructed and constituted by it, deriving much of their purpose, technical rationality, boundedness, and sovereignty from the institutional environment. So, the line of thought is centrally sociological in character, in its analysis of the modern system, conceiving not only of social action as highly constructed, but social actors too: we will thus call the line of argument sociological institutionalism, or just institutionalism (see Chapter 3, and the overall review by Jepperson, 2002).

As illustrative imagery, here, if a realist looks at the silver screen of social life and perceives a John Wayne, he imagines that this reflects a real true John Wayne.

The sociological institutionalist supposes that what he sees is a very ordinary actor (perhaps even a wimp) playing the part of John Wayne – a part written by a screenwriter who isn't an actor at all, and who may not know how many legs a horse has.

Of course, in the wider world society to which we attend, the "scriptwriter" is a historical-cultural drama. For example, a 900-year history builds the great institutional complex we call the university, with the deepest cultural legitimations (notions about nature, rationality, the truth, and so on) and the most diverse specific instantiations (e.g., detailed analyses of a specific flower, or the culture of teenagers). And, the constructed actors are the individuals and groups taking identities as actors within this drama (e.g., the intellectual protagonists, as in Collins 1998). And the participants turn out, despite their exotic roles, to be ordinary people with clay feet. So we recognize, in the great gaps between the postures of the renowned intellectual "actors," and the realities of their daily life and practice, that a great deal of institutional construction has gone on.

As another example, a long, much-discussed history produces the complex of legitimations and meanings we call capitalism, or the modern economy (Jepperson and Meyer 2007). Elaborate and intense interpretive scripts are written, so that all sorts of odd actor roles and identities are formed – a complex system of definitions turns friendly advice into expensive therapy, a song into a worldwide commodity, and usury into a collective good. And enormous energy is put into the playing of stressful roles (laborer, entrepreneur, and so on) far removed from ordinary human life.

Institutional theory has been central in sociological thinking about world society. It offers descriptive and explanatory imagery about the organization of this society, about how and why models of national and individual actors are generated, and about how they play out in practice.

The Red Line: But, it must be emphasized that this theoretical perspective creates a certain discomfort in American sociology, and is often seen as in conflict with more realist perspectives. This is not really for theoretical or methodological reasons of a scientific character – the various institutional perspectives are not sharply inconsistent, and multivariate analyses can easily show the impact on particular outcomes of a wide variety of institutional forces. The problem is normative. The American economy, political system, and culture rest strikingly for their legitimation on principles of actorhood – particularly individual actorhood. The notion that actors are themselves constructions importantly violates a whole normative order that is deeply built into American social theory (e.g., Coleman 1986; see Jepperson and Meyer 2007 for an analysis). Thus, the phenomenological tradition, starting exactly at the point where DiMaggio and Powell noted a shift from coercive and normative institutional influences on actors to mimetic isomorphism, has been the target of considerable tension of an ultimately normative sort (e.g., Hirsch 1997). In fact, DiMaggio (1988) later made a kind of apology for his transgression – an apology paralleled also by Scott (2006). There is a sort of red line, in American social theory, exactly between more realist mechanisms and the idea of mimetic isomorphism, which denies the ultimate primacy of humans seen as small gods (or "actors"). Interestingly, the issue is much less central in European thought, where there are many parallels to sociological institutionalism in the work of Foucault (e.g., 1991) and his followers (e.g., Rose and Miller 1992; 2008), of Luhmann (e.g., 1975) and the later system theorists of all sorts of post-modern thinkers, and of Giddens (1984). The tensions about institutionalism in European thought reflect European tendencies toward functional models of collective purpose, often left-wing or critical ones. European intellectuals find it easy to understand that the individual is probably not a primordial purposive and rational or reasonable actor, but retain some belief that the king (or another sort of collective normative order) might be.

The tensions between institutional thinking and the modern normative emphasis on the priority and autonomy of actors have played out in many arenas of secondary relevance here. For instance, there is an odd reprise of the nineteenth century discussions of free will versus determinism. The issue now is the tension between the idea of structural or institutional effects and the modern doctrines, highly legitimated, of human agency (see Sewell 1992; and an enormous subsequent literature, mostly American, on this oddly formulated problem).

If sociological institutionalism runs against some normative currents in American social science, the question arises of why it has prospered so well in recent decades, generating a good deal of social research and receiving much attention. The answer, centrally, relates to the extremely rapid globalization characteristic of the last half century.

GLOBALIZATION, WORLD SOCIETY, AND INSTITUTIONAL THEORY

The period since World War II has seen a dramatic increase in the long-term world tendency toward the actualities and perceptions of global integration. The world of conflicting but autonomous national-states had run into disaster: it was seen as having created two crushing world wars, a massive global depression, gigantic deliberate destruction of human life including a Holocaust, and now a set of political conflicts between nuclear powers with the capacity to destroy life. It also confronted a most unruly set of social conditions, with much of the world escaping controlling empires and becoming independently acting national states. Further, rapid economic growth and change generated large scale interdependencies no longer under secure (e.g., imperial) control. In view of the disasters of the century, the dramatically increased perceived interdependence, and the obvious fact that the primordial nationalist state was more problem than solution, new visions were obviously needed.

The natural resolution to the recognition of such expanding interdependencies, in the history of the Western system, has been the creation and expansion of larger-scale controlling state organization. For a variety of reasons, this solution was not viable in that period. A weak UN was built, and eventually, a weak West European organization (Chapter 16). Some other regional associations and treaties were set up, too. But, nothing remotely resembling a true world state was conceivable, and the intellectual fantasies about a world federation characteristic of the previous hundred years or so essentially disappeared.

Given the threats and opportunities of rapidly expanding interdependence, and the absence of any state-building possibilities, other coordinating social and cultural structures evolved. The parallels with the construction of the United States in the nineteenth century, as analyzed by Tocqueville (1836 [1969]), are striking.

A host of intergovernmental and especially nongovernmental associations sprang up, devoted to the widest range of possible collective and transcendental goods (Boli and Thomas 1999). On the governmental level, these were often far from classic self-interest associations, and espoused broad goals related to general matters of global concern: regulating the sea-bed or Antarctica, or supporting science or human rights, as with the European Union (Chapter 16). Nation-states in this sense functioned as script-writers for a new world rather than actors in it. This is even more true of the exponentially-expanding nongovernmental system, through which the broadest range of collective goods has been promulgated: global scientific and medical and educational associations (Doctors Without Borders); organizations for the protection of human rights or endangered species (the World Wildlife Fund); advocates of global linguistic reform like Esperanto. These structures function primarily as script-writers, telling actors how to posture and behave in the good of the whole collectivity, rather than the interested actors of realist theory – I have sometimes called them "others," to contrast them with interested actor identities (see Chapters 5 and 7; Meyer 1999). The notion describes participants that function less as interested actors than as agents of collective goods and realities. They are thus less interested actors than significant or generalized others in the Meadian sense, addressing on general or universal principles what the imagined actors in the system should be like and what they should do.

The new global structures, and the societies within them, were at every point filled with rapidly expanding and globally-integrating professions. These have been expanding exponentially around the world, carrying supra-national models of activity commonly defined as in the interests of the most universal and most collective goods. They generally lack political or economic control authority, but are renowned as script-writers and consultants, instructing and advising the national, organizational, and individual actors of the modern system. They are not really actors, in the standard senses, but rather agents of wider principles – they tell actors how to be and what to do (Chapters 5 and 6). This is the meaning of the term "others." Social scientists are good examples. Economists provide universal prescriptions for progress and development, sociologists for human equality, and political scientists for proper governance. But similarly, medical professionals create worldwide standards, as do biologists and ecologists and engineers. And ultimately, actorhood management itself becomes a profession, and business schools with MBA programs spread all over the world (Sahlin-Andersson and Engwall, eds. 2002; Moon and Wotipka 2006).

The problems confronted by the collectively-oriented associations, professions, and actors of the post-War world, and the absence of any real possibility for authoritative resolution, have driven the properties of the world society they came to imagine. First, inevitably many of the resolutions they could produce in order to be successful had to take a broadly cultural form: no authoritative organization was possible. Second, the cultural rules and ideas developed had to be selected to promote a dream of a shared and collective and unified world, not one filled with threatening conflicts. Third, the world culture generated clearly had to locate ideologically its action principles, not in the absent central organizations, but in properly tamed or constructed versions of the legitimated participants in world society: national states, first of all, but also individuals and organizations. Thus, a broadly coherent set of constraints produced the evolution of the modern world culture, eliminating or subordinating many themes (e.g., the class conflicts emphasized by the Communists; or the excessively nationalist ideologies of the authoritarians; or the conflictful religious ideas arising out of previous world orders) that threatened possibilities for a new order.

Thus, we can consider how all these universalistic professionals, collective good organizations, and ordinary actors posturing as models and agents of the collective good, worked to construct order in a rapidly integrating, but stateless world. Two core questions were involved: (1) First, on what bases could they construct rules and realities of the new world society that appeared so obviously necessary? An imagined and desired world order would obviously require rule systems, but the absence of a proper global state made positive law difficult to formulate and legitimate. (2) Second, what were the bottom-line components of the new system? The absence of a world state made it necessary to find or create loci of ultimate responsibility for the new order. An obvious possibility in the Western cultural system involved the formulation of some very strong notions of rather sacralized actorhood, but who were the actors? Nationalism and the sovereign national state were very poor, partial, and delegitimated candidates, given the history.

The successful answers to these questions produced by the associations and professionals and posturing national agents giving birth to the new order have dominated the culture of world society throughout the post-War period. They reflect the same logics Tocqueville noted in interpreting an older American history. The answers take the form of formulations with something of a natural law character (in this case locating laws in science and rationality, rather than explicit religious ideas), given the absence of possible positive law bases (Chapters 12 and 15).

1. *Rationalization*: The bases of the rules that are to govern the new world society lie in the underlying laws of nature and rationality (Chapter 3). Thus, the sciences and especially social sciences experience their extraordinary expansion throughout the period (Chapter 12; Drori et al. 2003, 2006; Frank and Gabler 2006). They are thought to arise to deal with functional problems, and may play some role in this. But, they are involved even with the ongoing reconstruction and development of the cosmology for the new order (Frank and Meyer 2007; Drori and Meyer 2006). Global social integration and legal order are, thus, possible because humans act in a universe of common natural laws and social rationalities (Chapter 15). This makes possible, for instance, a scientized global environment movement (Chapter 10).

2. *Ontology*: The underlying entities of the global social world, entitled to its protection and empowered to manage it, are human individuals (Thomas et al. 1987; Berger et al. 1974; Chapters 3, 5, 13, and 14). They may operate through rational organizations, which derive from their choices. Or from national states, which similarly derive from their choices and are to respect their needs. Older notions not rooted directly in individual human rights and powers are delegitimated: nationalist models of corporate states, or bureaucratic or professional models of a Church (or university, or hospital, or business). The modern individual human, in principle, chooses a church, university, occupation, and even spouse (Chapters 13 and 14).

The overall outcome of global cultural re-rooting of all of society away from collectives like the state onto the human individual has been an expansive trans-formation in the social identity of this individual (Chapters 13 and 14). Many kinds of people (indigenous people, children, handicapped people, and so on) are now accorded global rights as human individuals. The rights have been enormously expanded over time. And their character has changed: from being entitled to autonomy and protection, individual humans are now, in principle, empowered. They are seen as having the rights and capacities to manage the entire world, economically, socially, religiously, and politically.

These dominating cultural achievements of the post-War period clearly generate globally standardized models of the organization of society (Chapters 3, 7, and 8). We can note two dramatic dimensions of these. Both of them are core devices for integrating the two dominating elements noted above – the rationalization and scientization of the natural and social environments, and the fundamental onto-logical standing of the individual.

3. *A Schooled World*: First, there is the universal, extraordinary, and extreme expansion of education (especially higher education) in population coverage, content coverage, and penetrative pedagogy. The expanded rationalized laws of nature and society are melded onto the minds and bodies of the empowered and entitled young to an astonishing degree (Chapters 9 and 17; Meyer et al. 1992; Schofer and Meyer 2005). And the whole enterprise has a strongly globalized and standardized flavor around the world (Chapter 9; Frank and Meyer 2007).

4. *An Organized World*: Second, there is the equally universal and extreme expansion of society as a collection of highly participatory formal organizations, with every sector of social life (including economy and state) coming to be organized in this fashion (Chapter 11; Drori et al. eds. 2006). The organizations involved are hyper-rationalized, and also highly incorporative of the participatory individual. All sorts of alternative structures – traditional bureaucracies, traditional professions, property- and land-owning forms, and families in all their corporate forms – decline relative to the organized society.

Institutional theory is well adapted to both the description and the explanation of all these changes. In contrast, realist models (stressing the power of dominant states and economic organizations) have the greatest difficulty explaining why there are universities in New Guinea, thousands of formal organizations in Uganda, scientific establishments in the Congo, efforts at accounting transparency in Honduras, and symbolically-recognized empowered individuals (with, e.g., gay and lesbian rights) everywhere.

Institutional theory can explain why the world generated so many models of proper actorhood during the period, why these models incorporated the elements they do (e.g., the modern individual), why the models have so much impact on putatively-autonomous national states everywhere, and why explosions of science and the rationalities, organizations and education, and human rights and powers, occur.

The continuing expansion of the world society on economic, political, social, and cultural dimensions through the whole post-War period has generated constant socio-cultural movements along the dimensions noted above. The professions and nongovernmental associations, of course, continually expand. Then, there is the rationalization of nature and society. The sciences expand, and new ones are created, and it becomes important to contemplate the question of ice on a moon of Jupiter. The social sciences expand even faster, and everything from childrearing to the diet of prehistoric man comes under their scrutiny. Similarly, there is a continuous expansion in the perceived rights and powers of individual persons: women, gay and lesbian rights, indigenous people's rights, the universal human entitlement to health and education and cultural choice, and powers of the young vis-à-vis their parents, their religious and military leaders, and even (tragically) their professors. And in consequence, education expands without a break (Chapter 9), so that now, about a fifth of a cohort of young people, worldwide, is enrolled in a university (Chapter 17; Schofer and Meyer 2005). In parallel, rational organizations expand everywhere too, and global policing tracks their transparency and rationality on worldwide scales of degrees of corruption.

Stabilization and equilibrium would stop these dramatic changes, and would probably also partly undercut the institutional theories that best analyze them. By the logic of these theories, under stable conditions, institutionalization works by locating cultural and social material in the proper motives and choices of constructed social actors. So, after a period of time, the modern institutional system constructs a drama of realist actorhood. This tendency is analyzed in the work of researchers who study the rise of equal employment requirements for organizations (e.g., Dobbin et al. 1993, 1998; Edelman et al. 1992, 1999). These reflect great social and legal movements, but after institutionalization, any ordinary organizational leader can, with the greatest assurance, explain why it is entirely rational for him to hire able women, minorities, and so on – and indeed, to have a program to do so more effectively. Order and realism are thus constructed and supported. Successful institutionalization has reconstructed actors so that they can give the properly motivated accounts of their proper activities. And when they do so, conventional realist social research can properly report these accounts as empirical findings and explanations.

A serious institutionalist would certainly find such accounts misleading, and would suppose the whole depicted realist world in fact rests on broadly institutionalized cultural models, but this idea would recede into the intellectual background of social thought, not the foreground of the business school. So it is well known that a factory in which everyone simply follows the rules will not work (rule-following is a classic oppositional union strategy) – participants have to believe in the enterprise to make it work. And it is well known that most social structures rely heavily on cultural credibility, not just organizational power: this understanding fuels the contemporary social psychological (and economic) emphasis on the importance of something called "trust" for the effective operation of modern social structures, and techniques are proposed to support such trust as a psychological property of individual persons. This is a deflection from the central idea that modern rationalized society depends very heavily on institutionalized models.

THE CORE ARGUMENTS OF INSTITUTIONAL THEORY

In giving an account of the rise, nature, and impact of the global society of the past half century or more, institutional theory employs a very few general ideas. These can be summarized simply, and they have proved to be quite convincing. Most of them, however, are strongly contested from realist perspectives, though as noted above there need not be any scientific conflict between lines of thought all of which can be true. These lines of thought often make different predictions, but that is a problem for substantive empirical research, not dogmatic resolutions. The real problem is rather a normative one, reflecting a need to stay on the right side of the red line: realist individualism is a reigning ideology of the modern system, and alternatives are seen as undercutting its legitimacy, or as improper and cynical depictions of actorhood in a cultural system resting on great respect for the competence and capacity of actors. So there is a good deal of tension about institutional propositions that, in fact, have obvious validity.

Argument 1: The rise of world models. Modern world society develops a great many models about what human actors – individuals, organizations, and national states – should be like. Far over and above the effects of political and economic powers and interests, these models are developed and elaborated by professions and associations organized around the collective good – and sometimes by established actors operating under collective good claims.

Clearly, there is no way to explain the great social changes of the post-War period that we have outlined above, starting with a realist picture emphasizing the great powerful states and corporations. These did not produce waves of human rights expansion (gay and lesbian rights; a worldwide right to education), nor did they generate global scientization and social scientization. Nor did they generate huge worldwide waves of educational expansion, or organizational rationalization. All these social changes are better seen as products of scriptwriters – "others" – than as products of interested actors. The same point can be made about the creation of supra-national associations like the UN and the European Union (Chapter 16) – much realist political theory has gone into explaining why these structures are not really possible.

But these observations generate much intellectual tension. Realists, who tend to recognize a social world made up only of interested actors, have great difficulty analyzing all these "others." And, because the issues are matters of normative tension, rhetoric becomes elaborate: there are defenses of a putative "old institutionalism" that properly recognized the role of power in rule-building (Hirsch and Lounsbury 1997; Stinchcombe 1997). One resolution is to imagine that the professionals, who generate much of the new and expanded cultural material, are doing so as self-interested projects, and manage to hoodwink all sorts of ordinary participants. But this is a weak account of the expanded professional authority of the modern system: it presents professionals as rational actors, but the rest of humanity as rubes.

A valiant attempt to see modern institutional rules as the product of hard-line social interests and functional requirements, with professionals serving mainly simply as mediators, is Stinchcombe's recent criticism of institutional theory (2001, see also 1997). He successfully finds examples that fit his realist arguments. For instance, rules in the construction business have to fit some very real constraints. But Stinchcombe does not attempt explanation of worldwide movements for gay and lesbian rights, or for education, scientization, and corruption control in the furthest peripheries of the world.

Note that a strong implication of Argument 1 is that the global models that arise in the modern system are models of the nation-state and other preferred actors as very nice and well-behaved, and thus as able, in principle, to get along well with each other. This follows from the Tocquevillian efforts of the professionals and the global associations to imagine and create a peaceful world order without a world state. The models (e.g., of the European Union – see Chapter 16) do not stress the old evolutionary virtues of actors that successfully destroy each other over the centuries.

Argument 2: The impact of global models on actors. Global models greatly impact the structures of the actors in world society – the national states, organizations, and individual identities involved (e.g., Chapters 7 and 8). This assertion, the original and surprising core idea of institutional theory, is now very widely accepted. It is empirically obvious that the great changes we have discussed have taken place on a worldwide basis, and enter into the structures and policies of essentially every society in the world. No place now escapes education, rational organization, science, social science, and the at least symbolic recognition of the rights and powers of the expanded human individual.

The assertion is obviously true and powerful, but realists have much difficulty with any conception of social actors as highly constructed and penetrated, so there is much tension about the point. The realist demands explanation of why "actors" in the world incorporate the global models – and demands explanation assuming the boundedness, priority, and rational self-interestedness of these actors. Therefore instrumental motives must be invoked. Typically, the realist idea is that national societies incorporate world models because "the World Bank makes them do it," or "powerful states make them do it." These arguments completely fail empirically much of the time – it is difficult to say the Americans make a third world country sign treaties the Americans themselves do not sign. And empirically, countries dependent on the World Bank adopt fashionable policies at rates no different than autonomous countries. But, the argument helps the realist maintain ideological realism.

One can see an expression of the tensions involved in the elaborate efforts of Mizruchi and Fein (1999) to understand the extraordinary popularity of the work of DiMaggio and Powell (1983). They adopt the posture of sociologists of science to investigate the question (a strategy that sometimes involves special pleading in the social sciences). They discover that the key popularity of the work is in the red-line-crossing idea of "mimetic isomorphism," or taking-for-granted copying of established models. They see this idea as a marginal part of the original work, and thus its popularity as an odd distortion in the history of the science. Thus, the popularity of the work reflects a kind of misdirection: the authors crossed the red line. Oddly enough, a related theme appears in the apology noted earlier by DiMaggio himself (1988; see also Scott 2006). Interestingly, Mizruchi himself later came to employ the notion of mimetic isomorphism (Mizruchi et al. 2006).

For a sociological institutionalist, there is no problem in explaining the adoption of external models by actors (Chapter 6 reviews the point). First, the expanded modern actor is built on external models in the first place, and readily adapts to their development. This is enhanced by the close supportive linkages between actors and the environments in which they are so deeply embedded. And it is enhanced by the routine incorporation by actors of the relevant professionals involved, who act as receptor sites for world models (Frank et al. 2000). Thus, Kogut and Macpherson (2008) show that countries with Chicago economists at their policy centers adopt preferred economic forms faster – presumably, such economists were able to pick up the neoliberal themes coming down from Professor Sachs at Harvard more quickly.

Second, the "others" of world society constantly elaborate the models so that adoption is facilitated, providing constantly intensifying guidance on how to do the correct things. It becomes increasingly clear just how to do education, or health, or organizational reform.

The origins of the models around which modern actors form in the wider world environment help explain why the dominant adopted models in the post-War period have emphasized actorhood that is deeply virtuous in terms of the global collective good. Good nation-states are cooperative participants in global society. Good organizations are rational, transparent, and law-abiding. Good individuals are expanded, schooled, and empowered participants in the world.

Argument 3: Models are decoupled from each other, from internal structure, and from activity. External models flow into the structures of actors in highly decoupled ways. Policies and structures tend to be poorly linked to each other, and often poorly linked to internal subunits and to practices. This is true on an individual case by case basis even when at the systemic level there is a good deal of overall coherence.

The decoupling idea has the most massive empirical support in studies of individual actors as in the famous gaps between norms and behavior. It is a central finding in the study of organizations, as with the dramatic inconsistencies between formal and informal organization (Dalton 1959), and the studied inconsistencies and disjunctions between policy and practice (Brunsson 1985, 1989, 2006). It is a routine observation in studies of nation-states, with their strikingly low case-level associations between formal policies and actual practices (e.g., Hafner-Burton and

Tsutsui 2005; Cole 2005). And it is well-theorized in institutionalist reasoning (Chapters 4 and 8). First, global models are elaborated as ideals to solve global problems of legitimation, not only to be useful in practice. Second, these models routinely reflect ideals beyond what is practicable in the most resourceful countries, let alone impoverished peripheries. Third, most actors do not have the capacity to conform to the best proprieties. Fourth, historic path dependencies and local interests may make conformity to standard models subject to some resistance. Finally, the adoption of exogenous models can create dialectic reactions. For instance, it is well understood that the long-term global emphasis on the importance and powers of individuals (e.g., democracy) creates some incentives to edit who the relevant individuals are, and thus has sometimes created impulses to genocide.

In fact, from an institutionalist point of view, decoupling is a necessary and stable feature of large-scale universalistic social organization (Brunsson 1989). And to maintain visions of universalistic rationality, modern actors devote enormous efforts at chronic reform activities (e.g., Brunsson and Olsen, eds. 1993). And when the reforms fail, they employ a very wide range of mechanisms to sustain hope for future reform (Brunsson 2006).

Realists have the greatest difficulty with the decoupling idea. They imagine that social structural rules arise because powerful political and economic actors want them in place, and want them implemented. If this doesn't happen, someone is cheating, or someone is asleep, and in any case great long-run stresses must be resolved. Permanent decoupling, as in the routine great inconsistencies between American criminal law and American criminal practice, is a problem for most realists. One can see the extreme tension, for instance, in an attack on a precursor of institutionalist thinking – the famously imagistic paper by Cohen, March and Olsen called "A Garbage Can Model of Organizational Choice" (1972) – by Bendor et al. (2001) thirty years after the original paper was published. The original paper had some creative imagery about decoupling at its core, and was widely cited for this: it also had some illustrative simulation models that were given little subsequent attention. Unable to effectively attack the core imagery, Bendor et al. devote extraordinary effort to destroy the simulation models, clearly attempting to undercut the whole subsequent institutionalist development (2001: 189): "We believe it is possible to revitalize the [theory] ... this operation would deprive the [theory] and the March-Olsen variant of the new institutionalism of a certain mystique. Without this bold move, however, there is little chance that these ideas will shed much enduring light on institutions." Crocodile tears lie thick on the page of the American Political Science Review.

Argument 4: Global models, independent of their adoption, impact internal structure and activity. Global institutional changes have pervasive effects, operating as waves running through the world (and through nominal actors in the world) rather than through point-by-point transmission through networks and organizational structures (Chapter 6).

The point here is an obvious one about the world. An enormous amount of planned change does not get effectively organizationally implemented, given the extreme decoupling of the modern system. But an enormous amount of change happens anyway, impacting both the actors that have adopted corrected policies and those that have not done so. The inflated character of the modern actor means that internal components and behaviors are under systemic control more than under agentic local control. The modern actor, constructed from the wider environment and maintained by linkages to that environment, has many internal components under environmental control. Becoming a properly modern rational actor, given inflated definitions, is possible only through a great deal of conformity, and by having many structural components (e.g., decisions) supported by the environment.

Thus Ramirez and his colleagues (e.g., Bradley and Ramirez 1996) study the impact of world norms on rapidly expanding female enrollments in higher education. They naturally observe pro-female policy changes in countries through the whole post-War period (perhaps greater in countries more closely tied to the world society). At the country level, such policy changes seem to have no direct effect at all, that is, countries with pro-female-education policies do not have more rapidly expanding female enrollment. Worldwide, female enrollments dramatically increase, but they increase in both adopters and non-adopters of virtuous policy. Exactly the same pattern appears in Abu Sharkh's (2002) cross-national study of child labor. Countries (especially well linked-in ones) ratify International Labor Organization principles against child labor, but doing so has no effect on practices. However, child labor declines sharply everywhere (especially in well-linked countries). Related findings characterize research on human rights (Cole 2005; Hathaway 2002; Hafner-Burton and Tsutsui 2005). And similar results characterize studies of worldwide changes in demographic transitions (Bongaarts and Watkins 1996).

The key idea here is that modern social actors are highly expanded and highly constructed: their components reflect exogenous principles and forces rather than right functional relations. So change in the wider environment can flow in and around actors in wave-like patterns, only very partially affected by tight network and organizational relationships.

This Durkheimian point about the embeddedness of social actors in diffuse collective cultural environments has powerful implications for the study of large-scale and long-run social change in the current world society. We turn to a discussion of this theme and the presentation of one final argument in the discussion of world society from the point of view of institutional theory.

WORLD SOCIETY, INSTITUTIONAL THEORY, AND LARGE-SCALE SOCIAL CHANGE

A striking feature of modern, highly developed social science has been its inability to predict, or even analyze after the fact, a great deal of worldwide social change. It is precisely in the areas to which the institutional theory of world society most directly attends that the failure is most extreme.

Thus the world has experienced a dramatic and exponential expansion of all sorts of inter- and nongovernmental organizational structure, without pause, through the whole post-War period (Boli and Thomas 1999; Drori et al. 2006). The expansion cuts across topic areas and regions of world society and involves organizations that penetrate far down into the world's societies so that local persons and groups are dramatically more likely to be linked in than in the past. But one can study the social scientific literature on organizations theory and get no real hint of this great change, and even long after the established fact get no real explanation.

Exactly the same sort of thing has gone on with the global expansion of the widest range of professions and professionals. Expansion goes on everywhere, and linking into world society. Lawyers and judges, supposedly prisoners of national boundaries, cite international precedents with abandon (Chapter 15). Educational change is worldwide (Chapters 9 and 17). Medical communication is worldwide, and so is managerialism (Chapter 11). The social work professionals talk about global social policies, and routinely communicate cross-nationally, in a way that was very implausible a few decades ago (Chapter 13). The widest range of academic professionals is linked in to worldwide communication and citation patterns (Chapter 12). Overall, the professionals are now a dominant category in the global occupational structure. But, the social sciences – having no real explanation – continue to reason as if we were in the older world of workers and farmers and capitalists and owners. The problem, essentially, is the limited social scientific awareness that modern participants are acting in relation to a world society. When a supra-national society is theorized, it is mainly seen as a production and exchange economy. But that conception cannot provide explanations of most of the crucial global expansions, which arise from a richly developed imagined world society (Anderson 1983).

The impact of all this machinery on the astonishing expansions and globalizations of science and social science is dramatic (Frank and Gabler 2006). And so is the impact on the extraordinary career of human rights, which expands its domain in the most dramatic ways to cover new groups, new rights, and details down to the local ground of social life (Chapters 5, 13, and 14; Soysal 1994; Ramirez et al. 1998; Berkovitch 1999; Frank and McEneaney 1999; Boyle 2002; Tsutsui and Wotipka 2004). The social scientific analyses of these changes, and of the processes by which they occur, are impoverished. Social scientific thought can comprehend, for instance, a Saudi Arabia that sharply restricts the public roles of women. It cannot readily comprehend a Saudi Arabia with extraordinarily expanded female educational enrollments all the way through the university level (Chapters 9 and 17; Bradley and Ramirez 1995).

Finally, the domestic consequences of all this – worldwide expansions in education and intra-societal formal organization, penetrating every society – have been extreme. But, it is most difficult to find serious social scientific attempts, even unsuccessful ones, to try to explain rapid educational expansion in Malawi, and intensive organization-building in the Republic of Georgia (both countries without the supposedly necessary economic infrastructures).

The Durkheimian vision embodied in Argument 4 above can help explain both, the problem and the solution here. Obviously, social scientific reasoning, especially in the American context, has stayed on the ideologically proper or realist side of the red line discussed above. Actors are taken very seriously as bounded, autonomous, prior, and purposive. So, explanations of how and why they might change are restricted to realist mechanisms – organizational and network processes that bring new information and incentives into fixed structures. Thus, a leading social scientist might explain the unpredicted women's movement with demographic arguments (Stinchcombe 1968) about expanded education, lowered birth rates, and efficient domestic machinery. Or, shifting to a demand side, the scientist might imagine changed work force needs requiring women. None of this makes all that much sense in explaining such a broad social change running through the whole population, and none of it explains a women's movement in Thailand.

Argument 4 works much better in accounting for the worldwide change in the educational status of women. Changed post-War global ideologies about human rights apply everywhere, can easily be developed to cover many different populations (certainly including women), and are available to the widest array of intra-societal groups everywhere. Women can pick up the new story, or school teachers, or lawyers and legislators, or young female students. And all these people can adopt the new story in their thinking, their activities, or in very partial versions of each. If we assume that each actor in modern world society – individuals, organizations, or national states – is a composite of decoupled components, each exposed to and indeed dependent on the exogenous cultural environment, explanations for the diffusion of all sorts of broad ideological constructions are easy to generate and test (Chapter 6). We can quickly understand the expansion of female educational enrollments in the most unlikely fields and countries (as per Bradley and Ramirez 1996; Ramirez and Wotipka 2001; Chapter 17).

The key idea is that as persons and groups and societies in the modern system become legitimated as "actors," they become very open systems (Chapters 5 and 14), highly exposed to and embedded in their environments on many dimensions and through many pathways. Dependencies on wider cultural and organizational environments are built in at every point. So even if an organizational manager forgets to adapt to a changed principle – say, a favorable attitude toward the employment of gay people – many internal participants will independently understand the new rule. And, because the organization will probably have expanded its actorhood by employing many schooled professionals paid and trained to be attuned to the wider environment, the flow of the appropriate cultural material into the organization will probably be quite rapid.

The same points can be made about the modern nation-states, as expanded and empowered but by the same token deeply embedded actors (Chapters 7 and 8; McNeely 1995). Their internal participants – increasing numbers of whom are highly professionalized and thus tied through schooling to the wider world order – rapidly bring in the culture of the wider system. And the same points can be made about the modern schooled individual, who quickly picks up the new social forms independent of internal preferences or of habituated activities.

Thus, the processes we have discussed above give an account of how the modern system turns people, groups, and societies into organized, empowered, and expanded actors. Plausible theories of an integrated but stateless system call for models of expanded actorhood. Classes of professional and associational model-producers arise quickly and expand, and the appropriate models of actorhood are produced. They diffuse throughout the world, as people and groups and societies find empowered actorhood an attractive prospect. Much decoupling and inconsistency results, but expanded actors are open systems, so the new cultural materials flow in anyway.

All these processes produce the strange world we now observe. It is a world with the most inflated claims about the rights and powers of human persons, the obligations and competencies of formal organizations in every sector of social life, and the extraordinary powers and responsibilities of national states. For all these structures, inflation produces expectations and standards far beyond any possible tightly coupled reality.

So no nation-state is really capable of being and doing what a nation-state now should be and do. All are failed states by the expanded modern criteria. Similarly, no organization can competently do all the things a modern organization should do according to expanded actorhood standards. And no individual is remotely competent to exercise all the powers and responsibilities a modern individual has: by now, all political, economic, social, and cultural outcomes are thought to be determined by, and in principle the responsibilities of, individual humans seen as actors. Individual identities are enormously expanded and proliferated (Chapters 5 and 14).

High aspirations and high self-esteem are everywhere, and have the highest legitimacy. Compared to them, reality looks almost like failure. By expanded current standards, all the actors in the world essentially require the most extensive therapies. This produces the contemporary astounding demand for therapists – the professionals and organizations and helpful actors that created the expanded demand in the first place.

Argument 5: Expanded modern actorhood creates expanded professionalism and consultancy. Worldwide, we can observe the most dramatic increases in the kinds of professional occupations that provide advice and therapy to actors on the widest range of dimensions. Every sector of social life generates expanded professional consultants. This is obviously true for individuals with huge and growing populations of consultants providing help: medical, psychological, educational, legal, economic, recreational, spiritual, and so on.

In the same way, organizations seem to need the help of ever-expanding arrays of consultancy. Some of this can be internalized, with the incorporation of the relevant professionals. But, much of it occurs in a globally-expanding market of consultants and consulting organizations. The consultants involved tend to cover most of the same domains dealt with by the therapists of the modern individual, suggesting the extent to which modern actorhood of every sort has many elements in common (Chapter 11; Sahlin-Andersson and Engwall, eds. 2002; Djelic and Sahlin-Andersson eds. 2006; Drori et al. eds. 2006).

National states turn out to need advice and instruction on the widest variety of issues, so a great and growing set of international organizations and professionals arises to provide the appropriate services (Chapter 8; Finnemore 1993; McNeely 1995).

Conflicts: The world social system we have described is built on visions of highly responsible participatory actors cooperating in an orderly global society. But in a number of ways, it can and does generate and intensify conflicts.

(1) By and large, the professionals and associations generating models for global society, and consultantship and therapies within this society, do so in ways that envision little conflict. These groups are rooted in the universalisms of science, social science, legal rights, education, rational organization, and so on. But of course many other participants in world society have their own visions of the global collective good, and produce more conflictful or less universalistic models of this good. So with expanding integration and expanding actorhood, all sorts of religious, national, and ethnic leadership arise and mobilize the expanding actors in directions that create conflicts. Economists do "jihad" for global progress, and sociologists for global equality, but other model-builders and advisors fill the same role with other forms of jihad.

(2) Models of expanding actorhood have built-in inconsistencies. First, there are the obvious inconsistencies between the expanded individual actor and the expanded organizational and nation-state actors. The individual is increasingly entitled to a self-chosen culture, and the organization to integrated cooperation.

Second, there are the legitimated inconsistencies between actors at each level. Individuals with expanded rights tread on each other's toes (in part generating the exceptional violence of American society, for example). Organizations are dramatically interpenetrated, with endless inconsistencies between, for example, professional and organizational obligations. Similarly, expanded national states have expanded possibilities for conflict with each other.

Third, there are the dramatic inconsistencies between actor powers and rights, on the one hand, and practical realities on the other. The world society celebrates the equality of individuals and nations, but is extraordinarily unequal in fact – and with expanded integration, these inequalities increasingly come to be seen as inequities. The world's models of national societies emphasize possibilities for progress and internal equality that are unrealizable, and increasingly seen as unjust. Everywhere, there are the legitimate perceptions of world society, national societies, organizational life, and individual life as involving failure. A world of high self-regard is a world with many possibilities for failure and the perception of failure and injustice. Thus, the modern system is filled with well-constructed legitimation crises, though not of the sort Habermas (1975) may have had in mind. The crises involved provide much fuel for mobilization, and for the expansion of markets for consulting and the mobilization of helpful professional and associational "others."

All these kinds of inconsistency provide fuel for social mobilization, and often conflict. And the mobilizations and conflicts involved often have high world-recognized legitimacy, permitting much mobilization, great ideological formulations, and massive collective action.

In a well-known treatise, Mancur Olson (1965) noted the extreme difficulty with which systems of self-interested rational actors and actions could generate collective action. He noted that this problem might not exist with other forms of action – for example, religious actors and their activities. As we obviously live in a world that has generated extraordinary levels of collective action, it may be fair to infer that our nominally-secular social modern world is a highly religious one.

MODERNITY AS A QUASI-RELIGIOUS SYSTEM

The social sciences have tended to take a micro-social and realist stance toward modern society. They have, in recent decades, brought "back in" actors: individuals as actors, nation-states as actors, and all sorts of organizations as actors. The imagery about collective life is aggregative – social forces work by affecting and constraining these (often individual) actors, who then scheme, employing power to achieve their interests (Coleman 1986; see Jepperson and Meyer 2007, for an analysis). Society is an aggregated product of their struggles. Much of the thinking involved works from economic metaphors, as if modern people are competing for something to eat in a scarce environment. And indeed, the field of economics has gained a great deal of centrality: within political science and sociology, and modified economic ways of thinking (e.g., "economic sociology") have also gained some prominence.

Central to all this thinking is a picture of the social world as made up of interested actors in some sort of organized or network relation to each other. The term "organizational field" is popular, as is the term "opportunity structure." The implication is indeed that the actors have strong interests and pursue them. The actors and their interests are prior, though in more sociological versions some network relationships and constraints on these may also be seen as exogenous, so the actors are very real actors, but are constrained (or sometimes empowered) by their embeddedness in organized social relations.

This scheme is applied very broadly. So, for example, the whole occupational structure is seen in light of economic metaphors – as a great labor market in which people produce products which they can then exchange for other products (adding up to a Gross National Product). This is very strange, because in modern societies, relatively few people engage in anything that might traditionally be defined as work or labor. And their jobs are often more organized around credentials than markets. And for most of them there is no very clear product and certainly no clear exchange of products in any traditionally economic sense of "products." In modern societies, for instance, the most common jobs are positions like schoolteacher, or manager. Indeed, most jobs lie entirely outside any sector with clear and tight links to a productive economy. They are in medicine, education, religion, recreation, the civil service, or the military, and both concepts and measures of "productivity" tend to be very opaque: very often operationalization consists simply of the tautological principle that if someone gets paid, they must have done something productive. From a traditional economic point of view, modern society is a ball game played without a ball, or with an elaborate set of sociocultural definitions substituting a ball. The roles and identities of the participants, similarly, cannot be seen as dominated by exogenous and prior actorhood if the interests and purposes of these participants are centrally socioculturally constructed.

So at the least, it is useful to set up models which start at the other end of things – with the socioculturally constructing "others" rather than the "actors" that are their products, and with the rationalized and scientized environment (or ball game) within which they interact. This was the spirit of the renowned "garbage can model" discussed above (Cohen et al. 1972), and is very much the spirit of the sociological institutionalism which followed it. More broadly, it is the spirit of almost any phenomenological sociology or cultural anthropology, identifying the cultural worlds that inhabitants are acting within. A key idea of sociological institutionalism is that modern cultural worlds identify these inhabitants as "actors."

If we do start with the cultural constructions, we immediately observe that they do not work by defining seamless webs of cultural authority as in the good old days of the oldest institutionalism. They work by defining "actors" at the front and center of the social stage. And they defined these actors as having interests, goals, and relationships. These relationships occur in a very highly rationalized context, involving the scientized analyses of nature and very detailed models of organized social structure: extraordinary levels of differentiation isolate special sectors of social life, so actors can have goals difficult to think of in an earlier world (stamp collecting, skiing, possessing a house with ten thousand square feet, achieving recognition for eating many hot dogs).

How is integration to be achieved in this constructed world? Clearly, money – rooted originally in economic imagery – plays a core role as a generalized medium of value (Jepperson and Meyer 2007; see Zelizer 1994, for instances of the fragmentation of this medium). Most of it is received for activities of little known significance for traditionally conceived economic activity (teaching, for instance, or doing economic or sociological research). And most of it is spent for things of little significance in traditional productive economy terms. But it does permit a rough sociocultural translation of activity and meaning around the world: one can fairly definitively relate violin playing in Mongolia to grave robbing in Rome through the medium. Neither of these activities has economic meaning in any traditional sense. But being able to relate them so tightly to each other maintains a reality in which standardized human social actors, behaving in a standardized and rationalized world, enter into a common conceptualized or imagined polity. The logic here is deeper than economistic reasoning: fundamental human "actors" have many utilities in common, and these can be well indexed by a standard criterion of value. Thus, more than a medium of economic exchange, money in the modern world society becomes an index of shared values. All these have a highly constructed ceremonial quality. This, presumably, is an essential element of an integrated but stateless world polity.

CONCLUSIONS

Institutional theory provides something of a systemic picture describing and explaining some important features of the modern world society. It is a picture at dramatic odds with realist emphases on a world economy and power structure, and accounts for many things that realist notions cannot explain well (or simply ignore).

The institutionalist vision stresses the world as, in good part, a culturally imagined community, with elements that parallel religious visions. Cultural leaders from the schooled professions, and public good associations incorporating their ideas, rise to play prominent roles. The analogues with religious leaders from other integrated but decentralized systems are direct (e.g., 19th century America; many periods in medieval Europe). And of course, participants who are interested actors in the world rise above their interests to enter the higher world of the collective good: nations like the United States or Sweden support grand disinterested visions of the world order, much like the kings (who were religious as well as secular leaders) of the medieval world.

Beyond this, more traditionally religious elites also mobilize to make increasingly global claims. They try to reconstruct explicitly spiritual commonalities and unifying principles for a world society. And they try to put forward claims for the global recognition of spaces and themes. These efforts have been successful at mobilizing subgroups within world society, and conflicts among them (as in Islamic efforts to extend their claims to the larger world), but have been surprisingly unsuccessful in generating explicitly religious world themes on a global collective level. The contrast with the normative successes of elites rooted in more secular traditions – the supporters of scientific and rationalistic norms, and legal principles of human rights – is notable. Even the new "traditions" of a global order, such as World Heritage Sites, tend to be supported with more rationalistic discourses.

All the main elites support religious-like visions of a world of modern virtuous actors, saved by schooling and organizational reform to be valid participants in a transformed global community. Models of policy and identity arise and adoption of these models will lead to universal progress and universal equality and justice. These models stress not the need for participants in the world to abase themselves before a dominating organizational structure, but the empowerment and entitlement of the participants themselves as sacralized and legitimated "actors."

Naturally, the actors themselves find such models attractive, and adoption is very common. Individual self-regard rises around the world, and former peasantries come to hold and express opinions, and to mobilize. Groups turn into organizations, with purposes and policies and programs; they take on strategies for effective action. And national states greatly expand their powers and responsibilities – they now assume primary responsibility for national progress and justice.

Whether or not particular entities take on their full roles as actors, with the rights and powers involved, the same cultural standards are likely to penetrate them anyway. Expanded actors in the modern system are highly decoupled open systems, subject to pervasive cultural flows.

In any event, the expanded and rather religious actorhood that spreads around the world vastly transcends the realistic capabilities of the participating actors. It creates a greatly expanded set of persons and groups at the top of the world stratification system who are not exactly actors in the ordinary social scientific sense. They are "others," schooled in university knowledge of natural and rational law, and in their understanding of the rights and obligations of actors. They have much in common with religious functionaries everywhere. They make their living telling actors what to do, analyzing the failures of actors, and creating expanded new models of what actors should be like.

The outcome, obviously, is a world of rapid integration, much conflict, and very high levels of collective action. The integration, conflict, and collective action occur around models that are sometimes explicitly religious but more often secular dramas of science, rationality, and legal rights. Whether or not they are explicitly religious, they clearly have an ultimately religious or transcendental character.

REFERENCES

Abu Sharkh, Miriam. 2002. History and Results of Labor Standard Initiatives. Unpublished doctoral dissertation, Free University of Berlin.

Anderson, Benedict. 1983. *Imagined Communities*. London: Verso.

Bendor, Jonathan, Terry M. Moe, and Kenneth W. Shotts. 2001. Recycling the Garbage Can: An Assessment of the Research Program. *American Political Science Review* 95 (1):169–90.

Berger, Peter L. and Thomas Luckmann. 1967. *The Social Construction of Reality*. New York: Doubleday.

——— , Brigitte Berger, and Hansfried Kellner. 1974. *The Homeless Mind: Modernization and Consciousness*. New York: Vintage Books.

Berkovitch, Nitza. 1999. *From Motherhood to Citizenship*. Baltimore: Johns Hopkins University Press.

Boli, John and George Thomas. 1999. *Constructing World Culture: International Non-Governmental Organizations Since 1875*. Stanford: Stanford University Press.

Bongaarts, John, and Susan C. Watkins. 1996. Social Interactions and Contemporary Fertility Transitions. *Population and Development Review* 22 (4):639–82.

Boyle, Elizabeth H. 2002. *Female Genital Cutting: Cultural Conflict in the Global Community*. Baltimore: Johns Hopkins University Press.

Bradley, Karen and Francisco Ramirez. 1996. World Polity and Gender Parity: Women's Share of Higher Education, 1965–1985. *Research in Sociology of Education and Socialization* 11:63–91.

Brunsson, Nils. 1985. *The Irrational Organization*. Chichester: Wiley.

——— 1989. *The Organization of Hypocrisy*. Chichester: Wiley.

——— and Johan P. Olsen. 1993. *The Reforming Organization*. London: Routledge.

——— 2006. *Mechanisms of Hope: Maintaining the Dream of the Rational Organization*. Copenhagen: Copenhagen Business School Press.

Bull, Hedley and Adam Watson. (eds.) 1984. *The Expansion of International Society*. Oxford: Oxford University Press.

Camic, Charles. 1986. The Matter of Habit. *American Journal of Sociology* 91:1039–87.

Cohen, Michael, James March, and Johan Olsen. 1972. A Garbage Can Model of Organizational Choice. *Administrative Science Quarterly* 17 (1):1–25.

Cole, Wade. 2005. Sovereignty Relinquished? Explaining Commitment to the International Human Rights Covenants, 1966–1999. *American Sociological Review* 70 (3):472–95.

Coleman, James S. 1986. Social Theory, Social Research, and a Theory of Action. *American Journal of Sociology* 91:1309–35.

Collins, Randall. 1998. *The Sociology of Philosophies*. Cambridge, MA: Belknap Press.

Czarniawska, Barbara and Guje Sevón. (eds.) 1996. *Translating Organizational Change*. Berlin: de Gruyter.

Dalton, Melville. 1959. *Men Who Manage*. New York: Wiley.

DiMaggio, Paul. 1988. Interest and Agency in Institutional Theory, in L. Zucker (ed.), *Institutional Patterns and Organizations.* Cambridge, MA: Ballinger, pp. 3–21.

——, and Walter W. Powell. 1983. The Iron Cage Revisited: Institutional Isomorphism and Collective Rationality in Organizational Fields. *American Sociological Review* 48 (2):147–60.

Djelic, Marie-Laure and Kerstin Sahlin-Andersson. (eds.) 2006. *Transnational Governance.* Cambridge: Cambridge University Press.

Dobbin, Frank and John R. Sutton. 1998. The Strength of a Weak State: The Employment Rights Revolution and the Rise of Human Resources Management Divisions. *American Journal of Sociology* 104:441–76.

—— —— John W. Meyer, and W. Richard Scott. 1993. Equal Opportunity Law and the Construction of Internal Labor Markets. *American Journal of Sociology* 99:396–427.

Drori, Gili S. and John W. Meyer. 2006. Scientization: Making a World Safe for Organizing, in M. Djelic and K. Sahlin-Andersson (eds.), Transnational *Governance: Institutional Dynamics of Regulation.* Cambridge: Cambridge University Press, pp. 31–52.

—— and Hyeyoung Moon. 2006. The Changing Nature of Tertiary Education: Cross-National Trends in Disciplinary Enrollment, 1965–1995, in David P. Baker and Alexander W. Wiseman (eds.), *The Impact of Comparative Education Research on Institutional Theory.* Oxford: JAI Press Elsevier Science, pp. 157–85.

—— —— , Francisco O. Ramirez, and Evan Schofer. 2003. *Science in the Modern World Polity.* Stanford: Stanford University Press.

—— —— and Hokyu Hwang. (eds.) 2006. *Globalization and Organization: World Society and Organizational Change.* Oxford: Oxford University Press.

Edelman, Lauren. 1992. Legal Ambiguity and Symbolic Structures: Organizational Mediation of Civil Rights Law. *American Journal of Sociology* 97:1531–76.

—— Christopher Uggen, and Howard S. Erlanger. 1999. The Endogeneity of Legal Regulation: Relevance Procedures as Rational Myth. *American Journal of Sociology* 105:406–54.

Frank, David John, and Elizabeth McEneaney. 1999. The Individualization of Society and the Liberization of State Policies on Same-Sex Sexual Relations, 1984–1995. *Social Forces* 77:911–44.

—— and Jay Gabler. 2006. *Reconstructing the University: Worldwide Changes in Academic Emphases over the 20th Century.* Stanford, CA: Stanford University Press.

—— and John W. Meyer. 2007. University Expansion and the Knowledge Society. *Theory and Society* 36:287–311.

—— Ann Hironaka, and Evan Schofer. 2000. The Nation-State and the Natural Environment Over the Twentieth Century. *American Sociological Review* 65 (1):96–116.

Finnemore, Martha. 1993. International Organizations as Teachers of Norms. *International Organization* 47 (4):565–97.

Foucault, Michel. 1991. Governmentality, in G. Burchell, C. Gordon, and P. Miller (eds.), *The Foucault Effect: Studies in Governmentality.* Chicago: University of Chicago Press, pp. 87–104.

—— 1994. *The Order of Things: An Archeology of the Human Sciences.* New York: Vintage Books.

Giddens, Anthony. 1984. *The Constitution of Society.* Berkeley: University of California Press.

Haas, Peter. 1992. Epistemic Communities and International Policy Coordination. *International Organization* 46:1–35.

Habermas, Jurgen. 1975. *Legitimation Crisis.* (trans. T. McCarthy.) Boston: Beacon Press.

Hafner-Burton, Emilie and Kiyoteru Tsutsui. 2005. Human Rights in a Globalizing World: The Paradox of Empty Promises. *American Journal of Sociology,* 110 (5):1373–411.

Hasse, Raimund, and Georg Kruecken. 2005. *Neo-Institutionalismus.* Rev. edn. Bielefeld: transcript Verlag.

Hathaway, Oona A. 2002. Do Human Rights Treaties Make a Difference? *Yale Law Journal* 111:1935–2042.

Heintz, Peter. 1972. *A Macrosociological Theory of Societal Systems; With Special Reference to the International System*. Bern: H. Huber.

Hirsch, Paul M. 1997. Sociology Without Social Structure: Neoinstitutional Theory Meets Brave New World. *American Journal of Sociology*, 102 (6):1702–23.

—— and Michael Lounsbury. 1997 Ending the Family Quarrel: Toward a Reconciliation of 'Old' and 'New' Institutionalism. *American Behavioral Scientist* 40: S.406–18.

Hwang, Hokyu. 2006. Planning Development: Globalization and the Shifting Locus of Planning, in G. Drori, J. Meyer, and H. Hwang (eds.), *Globalization and Organization*. Oxford: Oxford University Press, pp. 69–90.

Jepperson, Ronald. 1991. Institutions, Institutional Effects, and Institutionalism, in Walter W. Powell and Paul J. DiMaggio (eds.), *The New Institutionalism in Organizational Analysis*. Chicago: University of Chicago Press, pp. 143–63.

—— 2002. The Development and Application of Sociological Neo-Institutionalism, in J. Berger and M. Zelditch, Jr. (eds.), *New Directions in Contemporary Sociological Theory*. Lanham, MD: Rowman and Littlefield, pp. 229–66.

—— and John W. Meyer. 2007. Analytical Individualism and the Explanation of Macrosocial Change, in V. Nee and R. Swedberg (eds.), *On Capitalism*. Stanford: Stanford University Press, pp. 273–304.

—— and Ann Swidler. 1993–4. What Properties of Culture Should We Measure? *Poetics* 22 (4):359–71.

Katzenstein, Peter J. (ed.) 1996. *The Culture of National Security: Norms and Identity in World Politics*. New York: Columbia University Press.

Krasner, Stephen D. (ed.) 1983. *International Regimes*. Ithaca, NY: Cornell University Press.

—— 1999. *Sovereignty: Organized Hypocrisy*. Princeton: Princeton University Press.

Kogut, Bruce and J. Muir Macpherson. 2008. The Decision to Privatize: Economists and the Construction of Ideas and Policies, in B. Simmons, F. Dobbin, and G. Garrett (eds.), *The Global Diffusion of Markets and Democracy*. Cambridge: Cambridge University Press, pp. 104–40.

Luhmann, Niklas. 1975. Die Weltgesellschaft, in N. Luhmann (ed.), *Soziologische Aufklärung 2. Aufsätze zur Theorie sozialer Systeme*. Opladen: Westdeutscher Verlag, pp. 51–71.

Mann, Michael. 1986. *The Sources of Social Power*. Cambridge: Cambridge University Press.

McNeely, Connie L. 1995. *Constructing the Nation-State: International Organization and Prescriptive Action*. Westport: Greenwood Press.

Meyer, John W. 1988. Society Without Culture: A Nineteenth Century Legacy, in F. Ramirez (ed.), *Rethinking the Nineteenth Century*, New York: Greenwood, pp. 193–201.

—— 1999. The Changing Cultural Content of the Nation-State: A World Society Perspective, in G. Steinmetz (ed.), *State/Culture: State Formation after the Cultural Turn*. Ithaca: Cornell University Press, pp. 123–43.

—— 2008. Reflections on Institutional Theories of Organizations, in R. Greenwood, C. Oliver, K Sahlin, and R. Suddaby (eds.), *Handbook of Organizational Institutionalism*. Thousand Oaks, CA: Sage, pp. 790–811.

—— and Brian Rowan. 1977. Institutionalized Organizations: Formal Structure as Myth and Ceremony. *American Journal of Sociology* 83, 2:340–63. Reproduced in Chapter 4.

—— Francisco Ramirez, and Yasemin Soysal. 1992. World Expansion of Mass Education, 1870–1970. *Sociology of Education* 65 (2):128–49.

Mizruchi, Mark S. and Lisa C. Fein. 1999. The Social Construction of Organizational Knowledge: A Study of the Uses of Coercive, Mimetic, and Normative Isomorphism. *Administrative Science Quarterly* 44 (4):653–83.

—— Linda B. Stearns, and Christopher Marquis. 2006. The Conditional Nature of Embeddedness. *American Sociological Review* 71 (2):310–33.

Mokyr, Joel. 1992. *The Lever of Riches*. Oxford: Oxford University Press.

Moon, Hyeyoung and Christine Min Wotipka. 2006. The World-Wide Diffusion of Business Education, 1881–1999, in G. Drori, J. Meyer, and H. Hwang (eds.), *Globalization and Organization*. Oxford: Oxford University Press, pp. 121–36.

North, Douglass C. 1981. *Structure and Change in Economic History*. New York: Norton.

—— and Robert Paul Thomas. 1973. *The Rise of the Western World*. Cambridge: Cambridge University Press.

Olson, Mancur. 1965. *The Logic of Collective Action*. Cambridge, MA: Harvard University Press.

Powell, Walter W., and Paul M. DiMaggio (eds.) 1991. *The New Institutionalism in Organizational Analysis*. Chicago: University of Chicago Press.

Ramirez, Francisco O. and Christine Min Wotipka. 2001. Slowly but Surely? The Global Expansion of Women's Participation in Science and Engineering Fields of Study, 1972–92. *Sociology of Education* 74 (3):231–51.

—— Yasemin Soysal, and Suzanne Shanahan. 1998. The Changing Logic of Political Citizenship: Cross-National Acquisition of Women's Suffrage. *American Sociological Review* 62:735–45.

Robertson, Roland. 1992. *Globalization: Social Theory and Global Culture*. London: Sage.

Rose, Nikolas and Peter Miller. 1992. Political Power Beyond the State: Problematics of Government. *British Journal of Sociology* 43 (2):173–205.

—— —— 2008. *Governing the Present: Administering Economic, Social and Personal Life*. Cambridge: Polity Press.

Sahlin-Andersson, Kerstin and Lars Engwall (eds.) 2002. *The Expansion of Management Knowledge*. Stanford: Stanford University Press.

Schofer, Evan, and John W. Meyer. 2005. The World-Wide Expansion of Higher Education in the Twentieth Century. *American Sociological Review* 70 (6):898–920.

Scott, W. Richard. 2001. *Institutions and Organizations*, 2nd edn. Thousand Oaks: Sage.

—— 2006. Approaching Adulthood: The Maturing of Institutional Theory. *Theory and Society*, Forthcoming.

Sewell, William H., Jr. 1992. A Theory of Structure: Duality, Agency, and Transformation. *American Journal of Sociology* 98 (1):1–29.

Soysal, Yasemin. 1994. *Limits of Citizenship*. Chicago: University of Chicago Press.

Stinchcombe, Arthur L. 1968. *Constructing Social Theories*. New York: Harcourt, Brace.

—— 1997. On the Virtues of the Old Institutionalism. *Annual Review of Sociology* 1997:1–18.

—— 2001. *When Formality Works*. Chicago: University of Chicago Press.

Thomas, George, John W. Meyer, Francisco Ramirez, and John Boli. 1987. *Institutional Structure: Constituting State, Society, and the Individual*. Beverly Hills: Sage.

Tocqueville, Alexis de. 1836 (1969). *Democracy in America*. J. P. Maier (ed.) (trans. G. Lawrence). Garden City: Anchor Books.

Toulmin, Stephen. 1990. *Cosmopolis: The Hidden Agenda of Modernity*. New York: Free Press.

Tsutsui, Kiyoteru and Christine Min Wotipka. 2004. Global Civil Society and the International Human Rights Movement. *Social Forces* 83 (2):587–620.

Wallerstein, Immanuel. 1974. *The Modern World-System*, Vol. 1. New York: Academic Press.

Zelizer, Viviana. 1994. *The Social Meaning of Money*. New York: Basic Books.

PART II
CONCEPTS AND PROCESSES

3

Rationalization

Ontology and Rationalization in the Western Cultural Account

In this book, we develop the view that social action in modern societies is highly structured by institutionalized rules. These rules take the form of cultural theories, ideologies, and prescriptions about how society works or should work to attain collective purposes, especially the comprehensive and evolving goals of justice and progress. The collective goods themselves are linked to other institutional elements that define the moral order and the natural world. Following the terminology of the sociology of knowledge, we conceptualize Western society as essentially a cultural project organizing human activity to forge the proper links between the moral and natural worlds.

A central concern of our analysis is the way in which the institutional structure of society creates and legitimates the social entities that are seen as "actors." That is, institutionalized cultural rules define the meaning and identity of the individual and the patterns of appropriate economic, political, and cultural activity engaged in by those individuals. They similarly constitute the purposes and legitimacy of organizations, professions, interest groups, and states, while delineating lines of activity appropriate to these entities. All of this material has general cultural meaning in modern systems and tends to be universal across them, so that all aspects of individual identity, choice, and action (a vote, a consumer purchase, a job decision) are depicted in the institutional system as related to the collective purposes of progress and justice.

It is revealing that the terms institution and institutionalization have vague and variable meaning in modern sociological discussions. They refer to the broad patterning of social structure and activity around general rules, but with much uncertainty about the nature of such rules: Are they statistical summaries of practice or are they empirical analyses of the interactions among a given and prior set of units such as individuals, organizations, or some sort of cultural forms? We see institutions as cultural rules giving collective meaning and value to particular entities and activities, integrating them into the larger schemes. We see both patterns of activity

Originally published as:

John W. Meyer, John Boli, and George M. Thomas. 1987. Ontology and Rationalization in the Western Cultural Account, in George M. Thomas, John W. Meyer, Francisco O. Ramirez, and John Boli (eds.), Institutional Structure: Constituting State, Society, and the Individual. London: Sage, pp. 2–37.

and the units involved in them (individuals and other social entities) as constructed by such wider rules. Institutionalization, in this usage, is the process by which a given set of units and a pattern of activities come to be normatively and cognitively held in place, and practically taken for granted as lawful (whether as a matter of formal law, custom, or knowledge).

Most social theory takes actors (from individuals to states) and their actions as real, a priori, elements of modern social processes and institutional forms. We see the "existence" and characteristics of actors as socially constructed and highly problematic, and action as the enactment of broad institutional scripts rather than a matter of internally generated and autonomous choice, motivation, and purpose.

It is important to note that in taking an institutionalist view, we do not postulate a society without people in it. It is rather that we find it problematic – as requiring explanation and analysis – that people invoke and rely on cultural accounts in defining themselves as individuals (persons, human beings, or world citizens) with rights, dignity, and value. It is problematic when they invoke and rely on cultural accounts to define their actions as matters of individual choice and decision, filled with individual motives and perceptions and involving such legitimated resources as individual property. The social psychology involved is that of Goffman (1974) and Swanson (1971), and its linkage to institutional structures is that of Mills (1940). But we add the important point that the ontological status of the individual is a social construction, which can be a social resource that actors can draw on to support their actions or can also be a liability, as in Berger et al.'s (1973) conception of the homeless mind.

In this introductory chapter, we consider the problems of actor-centered social theories, discussing first models that are based on individuals and then those based on collective actors such as interest groups, organizations, and states. Such models, we argue, ultimately fall back on soft conceptions of culture as the backdrop of action. Culture is allowed too little content and too much reified inevitability. In the next section, we develop a model of modern cultural systems as institutionalized accounts that map out the entities and processes of modern society and integrate them together within general frameworks.

In the third section of this chapter, we use this institutionalist model to argue that the rationalization of activity and its incorporation in legitimated models of collective life are interdependent with the construction of the entities given status as purposeful actors. This line of thought is pursued by describing the religious and cultural aspects of Western history that led to the prevalent institutional models of actors, organizational forms, and rationalized action. We conclude with a brief overview of the book, noting how the specific studies fit within the general institutional analysis proposed here.

ACTORS, ACTION, AND THEIR REIﬁCATION

Most explanatory models produced by social theorists in recent decades take much of the organizational and ideological individualism of modern society for granted. Two foundation stones underlie these models: Society consists essentially of individual actors and social activity ordinarily involves the purposive behavior of individuals. There is an intellectual naturalness about these models that derives from modern society itself – many ideological currents of the social system reinforce far more than any alternative conceptions. Thus, the economy is modeled as the dynamic of individual investment, consumption, and labor market "decisions." The polity is modeled as being built up through individual electoral choices and organizational commitments; and religion and culture are modeled as resulting from individual beliefs, values, and knowledge.

In such models, social structure is relevant as a way of analyzing the processes by which individual choice and consequent action influence the choices and actions of others. Economists tend to allow social structure into their models only insofar as it involves exchange processes that can be expressed in terms of costs and benefits. Psychologists allow for more complex effects, bringing in individual attachments, interaction, and communication. Sociologists are somewhat more reckless. Their analyses of exchange, attachment, and interaction typically uncover highly structured arrangements of individuals – in groups, organizations, networks, and the like – that have strong independent effects on such matters as job choices, electoral preferences, and cultural tastes and values.

For some purposes, such models can be highly fruitful, but they tend to understate the institutional underpinnings of the individual effects that are found; furthermore, with respect to the study of structural change and variation, they are severely limiting. Their naturalness in analyzing contemporary social processes and outcomes is accompanied by strained awkwardness when they attempt to account for the emergence and stability of such recurring social forms as the complex and stable job market, the democratic election, or the highly structured system of education and educational allocation. That such phenomena could be sustained solely or even primarily by the choices and actions of individuals is immediately problematic. One obvious problem is that these forms are so widespread. Is it reasonable to believe that the values and technical knowledge of masses of highly disparate individuals really are so uniform?

This problem leads individualistic social models to conceptualize culture as a general value system for society and socialization as a mechanism for instilling culture into individuals, as exemplified in the work of Parsons (1951). Socialization is the glue that keeps society together, instilling a cultural set of universalistic, rational norms and values into the character of all (or at least most) individuals. Culture is both a set of values that leads to individual preferences and a system of technical knowledge that informs individuals about which means to choose in order to achieve specified ends.

This heavy reliance on individual socialization and internalized cultural values has met sharp criticism from a number of viewpoints (consider, for example, the critique by Wrong 1961). For one thing, attempts to establish the existence and strength of cultural values and the ability of diffuse socialization to implant those values appear to be largely unsuccessful. Second, the presupposition that cultural values are largely universal and consensual is contradicted by glaring inconsistencies within the cultural system itself and the obvious centrality of conflicts and competing interests in modern society. Third, and most important for our purpose, the claim that such powerful institutions as the market economy, the bureaucratic state, or the citizen-based polity derive from abstract values internalized by individuals through social-ization simply leaves out too much. With this claim, the central features of modern society are "explained" by a residual approach that lumps a number of powerful social forces under the vague concept of culture but does not analyze them further.

One reaction to these problems was a return to a more intensified sociological individualism – the painstaking construction of more elaborate reductionist models of individuals. In Homans's (1964) phrase, theorists had "to bring men back in." Throughout the social sciences – not only in economics and psychology, of course, but also in political science and sociology – there have been attempts to develop an account of society based on rigid models of individual action. For example, under the general rubric of network analysis, many attempts have been made to squeeze more explanatory value out of theories focused on patterns of human interaction (see the papers in Marsden and Lin 1982; Burt and Minor 1983).

These attempts still run into the roadblock erected by the focus on individual dispositions generated by socialization and interaction patterns structured around individuals. In explaining elections and electoral behavior, for example, one can go only so far with an individualistic approach. At some point, one must come to terms with the massive institutional features of the social system itself. People are likely to vote only if there are elections. Education is pursued (and is more likely to affect electoral choices) if there is a universal educational system linked to the system of status allocation. Occupational careers are constituted (and are more likely to determine party affiliation) if there are organized occupations linked to the stratifica-tion system. Religious commitments are made (and are more likely to affect political participation) if religious practices are organized, legitimated, and culturally linked to the political sphere. In all these areas, an institutionalist approach suggests the importance of wider cultural issues and the culturally constructed character of micro-sociological effects.

The main route taken by research in recent years to get around this roadblock has been to abandon the fascination with the individual and turn instead to other "actors" in the social system such as interest groups, organizations, and associations. Social processes and social changes thus result, at least in part, from the actions and interactions among large-scale actors. The modern polity, for example, is seen as a network of interorganizational relations (Warren 1967; Scott 1983). At center stage, we find the state, which is also conceived as a coherent organizational actor engaged in purposive behavior on both the domestic and the international scene (Evans, Rueschemeyer, and Skocpol 1985). These lines of analysis retain the realism of sociological individualism, where the actors are engaged in purposive behavior through the more or less rational selection of means, but the analysis is much more complex and can involve several levels at once.

Taking collectivities seriously as actors resolves some of the difficulties of indi-vidualistic models. Much of what was earlier relegated to the grab bag of culture and propagated in the social system by socialization is now located explicitly in the structure and policies of organized actors. These organizations may channel interests in ways far removed from their starting points, as when the concerns of the handicapped come to be organizationally structured in terms of civil rights laws. Individuals and their free-floating networks of interaction become dependent variables, while causal analysis concentrates on the formally structured rules generated by organized groups. Much of the substantive stuff of society is described in this way: Welfare systems, job markets, and cultural structures become products of organizations or sets of organizations engaged in action and interaction (see Wilensky 1976; Baron and Bielby 1980; Baron 1984; DiMaggio and Stenberg 1985; Wuthnow 1980*a*, 1985). Accordingly, the political participation of individuals receives less attention than the organized systems of participation, which determine electoral choices through class or interest group processes that are more situational than socializing. The educational attainments of individuals receive less attention than the education system itself, which induces individual educational participation through a combination of incentives and coercion.

Accompanying this shift to collectivities as reified actors is a widespread concern for the broader environment in which these actors operate. Just as individualistic models ultimately invoke a surrounding web of interaction and relationships, so also do organizational models embed the actors in a wider system – a world economy (Wallerstein 1974), a system of militarily competitive states (Tilly 1975; Skocpol 1979), or a road map of international cultural diffusion (Inkeles and Sirowy 1983). But the neorealism of the thinking involved imposes a reluctance to see the wider system as having autonomous cultural content that might construct and legitimate as well as channel the collective actors. Content is postulated to lie in the purposes, properties, resources, and sovereignty of the organizational actors, while the encompassing environment is largely culturally vacuous – a set of raw resources, opportunities, or constraints. There is a preference for ecological or resource dependency models that limit the outside environment to little more than the patterns of interactions and competition among states, corporations, social movements, and the like.

These interactions usually are depicted as exchange relations within a competitive order. A given organization or interest group faces an environment providing resources and imposing costs. It acts by engaging in economic, political, military, or communication exchange, often very one-sided, in competition with other organizations. If the wider environment is given any content, that content is tamed as a commodity called legitimacy, which actors can exchange with each other (see McCarthy and Zald 1977; Pfeffer and Salancik 1978; Tilly 1975). The content, purposes, technical structure, and integration attributed to a given actor are thus viewed as properties of the actor, quite independent of the wider setting. The open-system assumptions of some such models (see Scott 1981, on the literature on organizations) imply that the organized actors are involved in complex interaction with the environment at many different boundaries, but the boundaries remain – the actor as an entity is clearly distinct from the environment in which action occurs.

The shift to collective actors as the muscle of the social system alleviates some of the problems of individualistic models, but it tends to exacerbate others. Even if many levels of collectivities are postulated (from the individual to the nation-state) and rational-choice assumptions are loosened to allow for political and symbolic depictions of action, reducing social life to the interaction of organized collectivities meets with considerable difficulties.

There is, first, the crucial problem of explaining the existence of the collectivities themselves – where they come from, how they grow, and why they persist. The usual tendency in this theoretical line is to treat them as aggregations of the interests and capacities of lower-level units (perhaps under certain vaguely described ecological or resource conditions). For example: The nation-state is the product of the accumu- lated interests and conflicts of classes, military factions, or other social groups. Successful collectivities are those that function most efficiently in the competitive environment, and the latter's influence on the outcome is restricted to the general pressures imposed by resource limitations and niche opportunities (Tilly 1975; Skocpol 1979).

This line of thought greatly understates the extent to which organizational structures are not only influenced but also internally constituted by the wider environment. The wider setting contains prescriptions regarding the types of organ- izational actors that are socially possible and how they can be conceivably structured. Collectivities are thus as much the embodiment of the prescriptions of the available cultural forms as they are the aggregation of lower-level units and interests (Chapter 4, DiMaggio and Powell 1983; Zucker 1983). In other words, the boundary between the environment and the actor is not only highly fluid but also highly problematic. In the chapters that follow, we pursue this argument with respect to such large-scale structures as the modern state, the educational and welfare systems, the social movements, and the rules of modern individualism itself.

A second problem in the reification of collective actors and the focus on their distinctive properties and behavior is that the extraordinary uniformity of their fundamental character is ignored: state bureaucracies, policies, and budgets as well as elections and citizenship; occupational and interest groups and the claims that they make within the polity; the formal organization of schools as well as enrollments, teacher certification, and learning technologies. If such institutions were simply the products of competing interests and political negotiation, there should be much less uniformity in these dimensions across national societies. The source of that uni- formity lies in an institutional environment common to organizations in national societies throughout the world system. Common definitions and theories of social organization generate structural similarities in highly disparate societies.

Third, the realist view of collective actors assumes that organizational structure is tightly linked to internal components and activities. There is massive empirical evidence that such is not the case. Research on organizations repeatedly finds very loose coupling at every level – between formal and informal structure, among different structural elements, between structure and action, and between policy and actuality (e.g., Weick 1976; March and Olsen 1976). Studies of the behavior of the state find that the implementation of policy is a highly problematic process (Pressman and Wildavsky 1973; Bardach 1977; Berman and McLaughlin 1975–1978). The assumption that collectivities are produced by internal forces is thus empirically countered by the weak relationship between the policy structures of these collectivities and the putative forces that were supposed to control them. This parallels similar findings at the individual level: Action often works obliquely to stated goals and norms; the knowledge and technical competence attributed to individuals by political and economic theory are conspicuous by their absence; the theoretically postulated minimal requirements of consistency in personality and action at a given time or over the life cycle are not met (e.g., Mischel 1971; Brim and Kagan 1983).

The common response to this sort of criticism is the charge that the discontinuities between structure and action, or principles and behavior, are themselves largely deliberate. States express commitment to broad-based economic development as a smoke screen to deal with "problems of legitimacy" with respect to their impoverished citizens. School systems are employed to maintain false consciousness on the part of the masses so they will not understand the true nature of the social system. Individuals hide their true intentions and values in order to bluff their way to social power and position.

Such responses provide some reasonable answers but beg the larger question: Where do these legitimacy problems come from? More forcefully, what powerful exogenous factors make possible and necessary the sweeping but unrealistic claims of modern institutions? What forces empower the educational system or the open election to serve as legitimating structures and thus support the disparate and inconsistent activities going on within them? What is gained, and from what source, when individuals or organizations dress their motives and questionable competence in acceptable guises? When questions like these do get attention, the notion of culture is again brought in through the back door as an unanalyzed residual force of such plasticity that it can be stretched to fill the holes in the argument.

CULTURE AS INSTITUTIONAL RULES

Theories that reify social actors, whether individual or collective, thus sweep the big problems under the rug of "culture" without dealing with the debris lying under this idea. Their rather primitive usage limits the concept of culture to a cluster of consensual general values (e.g., religious morality) and a body of consensual knowledge or technique (e.g., scientific rules). Culture becomes important only inasmuch as it surfaces in the conscious structure or policy of actors – in individuals' values and information or in collective values and technologies (if collectivities are reified as actors). Culture thus enters in only as an influence on the condition of the actors involved.

We employ a broader conception in which culture is more than vague ideas about the moral or natural environment of society. Culture includes the institutional models of society itself. The cultural structure of these models defines and integrates the framework of society, as well as the actors that have legitimate status and the patterns of activity leading to collective goods. Lines of thought treating culture as only rules of value and technique at the moral and natural boundaries of society ignore the fact that the central cultural myths of modern society are those giving meaning and value to society and its components. Beyond a sociology of religion or of science, a proper analysis must focus on institutions – the cultural rules of society itself.

Culture has both an ontological aspect, assigning reality to actors and action, to means and ends; and it has a significatory aspect, endowing actor and action, means and ends, with meaning and legitimacy. In a narrower view, for instance, American culture contains "values" that influence individuals to be assertive and achievement oriented in all sorts of exchange relations. In the broader view, American culture comprises a set of well-established theories giving reality and meaning, "value," to individual action organized in patterns of exchange as the surest path to progress and justice. At the same time, these rules deny (usually implicitly) the reality and meaning of alternative means, ends, actors, and actions; in America, for instance, undercutting the possibilities for immersing individuality in community. The individual may be conscious of these theories only in limited cognitive and normative ways that situationally range in inclusiveness (Douglas 1966). Yet, these theories are the heart of the social system – such rule structures as political and legal definitions concerning property, contracts, association, and the like; economic definitions of the meaning of labor, production, and consumption; and more purely social definitions of such constructs as childhood and the self.

In the narrow view, culture is a set of ideas and values, sharply distinguished from material interests and action. Is the law of property economic (i.e., materialist) or political and religious (i.e., idealist)? Are the rules legitimating the formation of such associations as business corporations materialist or idealist? What about the Reformation doctrines Weber called the *Protestant Ethic*? This idealism/materialism distinction makes sense only if the underlying social theory gives actors (especially individuals) and their motives prior social reality. From a narrow actor-centered posture, all such matters concern ideas that are more or less reducible to material factors.

At the institutional level, this polemical distinction breaks down. Western economic and political forces operate at a high level of generality as rule structures that create, among other things, a peculiar emphasis on the legitimacy of the individual and individual purposes. This emphasis is cultural, not natural. In our view, Western culture is a system of rules that make the production and consumption of something like the electric toothbrush a matter of universal value (like groceries or gasoline, it contributes to GNP) and propagate convincing reasons (of health, child hygiene, aesthetics, or social relations) for individuals to choose to produce and consume such a device, thus enhancing the meaning and significance of the individual at the same time. Culture involves far more than *general values* and knowledge that influence tastes and decisions; it defines the *ontological value* of actor and action.

Both social actors and the patterns of action they engage in are institutionally anchored. The particular types of actors perceived by self and others and the specific forms their activity takes reflect institutionalized rules of great generality and scope. It is in this sense that social reality – including both social units and socially patterned action – is "socially constructed" (Berger and Luckmann 1966). Institutionalized rules, located in the legal, social scientific, customary, linguistic, epistemological, and other "cultural" foundations of society, render the relation between actors and action more socially tautological than causal. Actors enact as much as they act: What they do is inherent in the social definition of the actor itself. Consequently, rules constituting actors legitimate types of action, and legitimated action constitutes and shapes the social actors. For example, changes in Western notions of labor result in changes in the rules and organization governing work. On the other hand, political and economic rules of wage labor as a self-interested class devolve from rules about the collective value of work; the working class changes as legitimate rules of labor value change. As another example, expansion of the types of commodities people may properly consume increases the complexity of the individual, adding new motives and sometimes rights; conversely, adding new aspects to the personality expands the possible commodities one can legitimately consume. For instance, the elaboration of theories of self-esteem leads to personal projects and rights to self-actualization and fulfillment, resulting in both organizational programs and commodities that promise these outcomes. Conversely, commodities from the automobile, television, and personalized personal computers to a shampoo that meets the "ever-changing needs" of one's hair or a tennis racket that is made of material and strung so as to correct one's particular weaknesses all greatly expand the legitimate domain of the self and highly articulate subtle nuances of fulfilled selfhood. At other organizational levels, the same reciprocal, tautological processes occur. The definition and standing of the modern organization are constitutively linked to what is legitimate and necessary. In this way, environmental concerns, a broadened conception of worker rights, or more organized conceptions of the economy and its function must be incorporated in the structure and action of the organization. For instance, the new right to pure air produces organizational expansion to manage this right.

Hence the common notion that the actor performs the action is only a half-truth – at the institutional level, action also creates the actor. Not only does the institutionalization of certain forms of organization, such as the corporation, generate rationalized goals and goal-oriented action, but also the institutionalization of rationalized goals and action creates highly general models from which organizations draw their identity and structure. The same can be said of individuals, states, and other social units.

This is not to say, however, that society is a matter of continuous negotiation, communication, and exchange of meaning. Symbolic interactionism and sociopsychological variants of phenomenology employ an institutional view of social behavior, but they depict the meanings and rules constructing actors and action as operating at the same level of analysis as the actors affected by them. The local interplay between interaction and its meaning, whereby actors (usually people, in these formulations) continually discover and construct who they are through looking-glass feedback processes, allows for no level of reality external to the phenomenological situation itself. This tradition of research ignores the extraordinary power of exogenous institutionalized definitions of reality. The individual may work out identity details (e.g., an aggressive style to counterbalance a putative socialization defect in assertiveness) and nuances of meaning in the way described by this tradition, but little negotiation at all is required for the individual to know that individuals exist, that they are organized into groups, that rational action is required in the workplace, or that a proper pilot does not snort cocaine in the cockpit.

A fully institutional analysis, then, calls attention to the extent to which, both in the modern world polity and throughout much of Western history, the cognitive and moral frames of activity at all levels are anchored in the broadest institutional (societal and world) levels. Actors and action are illuminated by universalistic lights. The interaction of people buying and selling in a supermarket occurs under the aegis of highly general historical rules legitimating and constructing the economy and its participants: There are rules of property, the collective good in exchange, the principles of autonomous consumption and impersonal exchange, and so on and on. These rules cannot easily be observed and may be completely transparent in the ordinary course of events, but something as concrete and material as the supermarket is an impossible flight of fancy in their absence.

RATIONALIZATION AND THE CONSTRUCTION OF ENTITIES

A key task of institutional analysis is to describe the content and coherence of the Western, now worldwide, institutional order and to develop a theory of its origin and evolutionary dynamics. The diverse analyses reported here each focus on a particular aspect of this task and thereby take tentative steps toward our long-range goal. In doing so, our work is informed greatly by the Weberian tradition and in particular by the concept of rationalization. There is a large literature produced by Weberian scholars on the conceptual and historical nuances of types of rationality (e.g., Roth and Schluchter 1979; Kalberg 1980; Schluchter 1981). We do not explore these nuances and typologies. Rather, we use a working definition of rationalization, moving from abstract concept to particular empirical referents or variables that reflect rationalization processes. To summarize concisely, we use the generic term rationalization to refer to purposive or instrumental rationalization: the structuring of everyday life within standardized impersonal rules that constitute social organization as a means to collective purpose. Denotatively, through rationalization, authority is structured as a formal legal order increasingly bureaucratized; exchange is governed by rules of rational calculation and bookkeeping, rules constituting a market, and includes such related processes as monetarization, commercialization, and bureaucratic planning; cultural accounts increasingly reduce society to the smallest rational units – the individual, but also beyond to genes and quarks.

The instrumental and purposive nature of Western rationalization results in the constitution of society as a means to collective ends. In this sense, Western, and now worldwide society, is a rational project of creating progress and justice – in the traditional West, the millennium. We refer to this character of the world polity as a project, following the lead of the sociology of knowledge. One can also refer to this project as the state, distinguishing the broad referent of state as project from its identification with the bureaucratized state (Thomas and Meyer 1984); for historical reasons, this usage is more common in French or German than in English.

An institutional analysis rests on two central themes. First, the rationalization of social activity stands in a reciprocal relation to the social construction of the actors given ontological status in society. Second, the institutional rules undergoing rationalization and social ontology operate at a very general (now often worldwide) level, not simply at the level of local negotiation.

The emergence of social entities in the process of rationalization

Rationalization involves restructuring action within collective means and ends. In the most general sense, the means are technical development and the expansion of exchange; the ends are the twin pillars of Western thought, progress and justice (most often defined in terms of equality). Rationalization through the elaboration of means–ends chains requires the specification of entities at the end of the causal chain: Equality, for instance, is not attainable without a precise unitary definition of the entities that are to be equal. Rationalization around the goal of equality compels a sharpened conception of the individual and the delineation of the dimensions in which equality is to be sought, yielding notions of human rights and individual personality. The further rationalization is pushed, the more the individual must be enhanced and expanded. In the same way, doctrines and measures of progress and profit require and create bounded entities: individuals, firms, and states.

Thus Weber's argument that the strong ontological status of the individual is one source of Western rationalization tells only part of the story. In our terms, including the more institutional version of Weber's theory (Collins 1980), the individual is an institutional myth evolving out of the rationalized theories of economic, political, and cultural action.

This myth leads people to posture as individuals, in a loosely coupled way, and they can be fairly convincing about it. The contrast with systems in which people are immersed in corporate identities (e.g., age, gender, familial, communal, or corporate occupational statuses) has often seemed striking to researchers. Modern "individuals" give expression to the institutionalized description of the individual as having authorized political rights, efficacy, and competence; they consider themselves effective choosers of their occupations, investments, and consumption goods; and they willingly give vent to an extraordinary range of cultural judgments, offhandedly responding to questionnaires with their views of the polity, the economy, even the exact properties, including being, of God. Given the possibilities and inducements of the modern system, they also perform a wide range of economic, political, and cultural actions – and *ex post facto* can explain in great detail how their activity was carefully selected as efficient for their particular purposes. This enactment of the institutionalized theory of rational behavior is rarely troubled by the internal inconsistencies and self-contradictions that are so typical of human action. It is precisely that this status of rational actor is a culturally supported posture that explains much specific inconsistency.

Of course, not only the individual but also many other social units are generated by the institutionalized rationalizing project. Rationalization around the goal of progress helps generate several kinds of units. Progress cannot be attained without specifying the boundaries within which it has to occur; hence, the nation-state is reified as the unit within which GNP or life expectancy or book production is measured. The more elaborate the concept of progress, the more reified the nation-state (yielding, among other things, more boundary maintenance activity around the rules defining the national unit). Similarly, rational analysis of the means by which progress is to be achieved leads to a reification of the productive entities that enter into the expansion of technique and exchange – labor, occupational roles, professions, and corporations are all thereby enhanced. The strengthening and elaboration of the cultural rules and definitions of progress support the empowering of the individual and collective actor involved. For instance, groups mobilizing around labor and capital appear in societies that have little to be conceived of practically in either way.

The generality of institutional rules

The institutions constructing and giving meaning to modern social entities and their rationalized action have a much wider and more universal character than any particular setting they constitute. This is true in two closely related senses. First, these institutions embody universalized claims linked to rules of nature and moral purpose. Economic, educational, or political action is legitimated in terms of quite general claims about progress, justice, and the natural order. Thus, particular conflicts or claims are couched within general cultural elements that are in principle applicable everywhere across classes and societies. For example, general principles of human rights or economic growth are held to be applicable to any modern or modernizing order. The differences that do arise within local settings are limited and remain within the context of the broader cultural frame. For example, teachers adopt different styles, organizations different management techniques, and state regimes different ideological stances – all within the constitutive order of what it means to be a teacher, a business organization, and a nation-state.

Second, specific institutional claims and definitions tend, in practice, to be very similar almost everywhere. Differences across particular settings result from the organization of that setting around varying emphases or interpretations of more general institutional rules. For example, socialist notions of justice, progress, and technique are remarkably similar to their capitalist counterparts; albeit specified somewhat more around equality than liberty and organized more corporately by the bureaucratic state. Moreover, beyond the given differences, quite similar goals and means are specified and pursued, even down to the details of particular industries, or welfare and educational progress.

The degree of uniformity of institutional structures points to a strategy for analysis: One must see these institutions in all of the diversity not only as built up out of human experience in particular local settings, but also *as devolving from a dominant universalistic historical culture*. The diverse version of these general themes is interpretable by the differential penetration and historical syntheses of distinct (sometimes contradictory) elements of this culture.

The institutions of the West devolve from Western religion and the church at least as much as they are built up by the strategies of sub-units (Anderson 1974; Strayer 1970). The frame derives directly from the Christian church and the invisible conceptual "Kingdom of God" that the earthly church organization was supposed to represent in an imperfect way. Consider this church at an early point (perhaps 1500) in the modern era.

The church was, first, transnational in character. It was a unified symbolic structure encompassing a wide variety of cultures and people – "nations" in the older sense. As such, it provided a common frame of reference for the West – not entirely uniform, to be sure, but in both a literal and a symbolic sense, there was a common language that dominated the cultural arena. Second, the church was universalist, in that it had the duty to bring "the way, the truth, and the life" to all of humanity, recognizing no boundaries to its mission. Its constant proselytizing was remarkably successful, and to an extraordinary degree, it succeeded by the "power of the Word," particularly before the modern era. But for our purposes, the key fact is that the spread of Christianity meant the spread of universalist ideology as such – it became not only common but also natural to develop theories and ideologies of sweeping, all-encompassing scope.

Third, the church as a symbol system provided the fundamental ontological structure of the West. The church consisted, in essence, of a set of institutional definitions – of transcendental reality (God, Christ, and Spirit), of humanity (God's creation/children) and human nature (sinful yet creative), and of earthly existence and its ultimate purpose (the glory of God). These definitions constituted the ultimate source of authority: That which *is* was an issue that could be addressed only within the context of the church's symbolic structure. The church also provided guidelines for action: It was no distant theological bastion but penetrated every limb of the social body.

This, then, was the overarching cathedral within which the modern cultural system developed: a common, highly legitimated, boundaryless polity where ultimate authority was located at the peak of the vaulted dome (God) and devolved on human entities (popes and priests, kings and nobles) as subordinate beings, with much to say about social ontology, actors, and the relationships among action, nature, and the ultimate.

The content of the overarching framework has changed with the transition of the West from feudal agrarianism to state-directed technical/economic progressivism, but the location of authority and definitions of reality have remained at the highest level, transcending all of the social entities (including the nation-state) that it encompasses. A number of detailed studies show how this structure led to the particular features of the modern institutional framework. For example, Bendix (1978) describes the development of institutional conceptions of the sovereignty of the state from Roman law and the doctrines of the church as a legal and ideological process characterizing Europe as a whole. We should not be misled by the view that modern authority structures are "secular" rather than "religious." Authority structures define the sacred and relate it to the profane. Whether the sacred involves transcendent deities (Jehovah, God, and Allah) or transcendental concepts (equality, freedom, rights, and livelihood) at its ultimate root is irrelevant, for the sacred in a sociological sense is always religious. Thus, the "secular" content of the world polity's ontological structure is no less religious than that of the Christian church (see Ellul 1973; Wuthnow 1980*b*).

Hence, in modern social systems, it is fruitful to see social structure not as the assembly of patterns of local interaction but as ideological edifices of institutionalized elements that derive their authority from more universal rules and conceptions. The disjuncture between social structure and observable patterns of activity and inter- action, which is the bread and butter of much sociological research, makes sense in this light. The formal structures of society, ranging from the definition and proper- ties of the individual to the form and content of such organizations as schools, firms, social movements, and states, arise from, or are adjusted to fit, very general rules that often have worldwide meaning and power.

CULTURAL ACCOUNTS

In this usage, institutions can be described as cultural accounts under whose author- ity action occurs and social units claim their standing. The term account here takes on a double meaning. Institutions are descriptions of reality, explanations of what is and what is not, what can be and what cannot. They are accounts of how the social world works, and they make it possible to find order in a world that is disorderly. At the same time, in the Western rationalizing process, institutions are structured accounting systems that show how social units and their actions accumulate value (in monetary, scientific, moral, historical, and other forms) and generate progress and justice on an ongoing basis. The meaning of the individual, or the corporation, or the state in the cultural account of the West is to a large extent contained in prescriptions for rational action producing increasing amounts of value that are taken as the ultimate goals of the human project. The enormous amount of financial and bureaucratic record-keeping (accounting) that goes on in modern society is one result.

The Western cultural account is distinctive and has generated a transformation of society of extraordinary thoroughness and depth. What general features of this account are most central?

First, the cosmos outside of human society is distinctively simplified and abstracted (Bellah 1964). Moral authority is integrated in a single high god whose authority is unitary and universalistic. The properties of the single god are elaborated over time, becoming increasingly universal, abstract, and separated from human activity. The god is pervasive and inactive (i.e., in a sense, dead). Other spiritual entities, with their potential for direct intervention in society and nature, are excluded (Weber's "disenchantment of the world"). The natural world is similarly unitary and universalistic, in the sense that nature is objective, lawful, and structured according to discoverable invariant principles. Nature too is removed from human society, something separate and exploitable. The cosmos is radically dualistic. Moral authority and the laws of nature are not linked directly to each other, either through webs of spiritual intervention in nature or the subjection of the spiritual world to natural processes. Contrast the situation described by Geertz (1980) in his description of the Balinese theater-state: There, much political activity is linked to a complex and active cosmos; much natural activity is linked to a complex and lively physical world; and the two are integrated more outside human agency than through it.

Second, the links between moral authority and nature are provided by society. Human beings and human society have value and responsibility as moral projects in nature. People and society can achieve progress through activity in the natural world, and they can fail to progress. Hence much purposive rational organization is possible, necessary, and highly legitimate as evidenced by the movement from early monasticism to the universal church and from the nascent medieval state to the modern welfare state and corporation (Coleman 1982). Individuals too can be organized as rational, purposive actors. All of this progress-oriented activity occurs in a universalistic cultural frame and the degree of success achieved can be evaluated by means of general value measures (which are increasingly expressed in monetary terms as with the GNP).

Third, individual human beings have distinctive moral standing. The human soul or personality is tied directly to ultimate moral authority. The links between the individual and the moral and natural cosmos may be mediated by social structure, but any such structure must contain cultural accounts explaining how individual action generates moral value. Thus, in Western terms, human society can and should be assessed in terms of justice – a concept that, when reduced to the notion of equality, is difficult to define or operationalize in systems that do not reify the individual. Thus, justice, like progress, is linked to both moral authority and nature. Justice is a culturally available perspective with respect to both individual participation in society (work, voting, and consuming popular culture) and the distribution of the benefits of nature (income, standard of living, and possession of things).

These cultural properties have long been discussed as distinctive features of the West, although there has often been a tendency to adopt a teleological view of them, describing Western history as some kind of necessary unfolding of these features. The teleology should be seen as a property of the Western system and not the perspective of the analyst: Western institutional models are functional ones and for research purposes must be analyzed rather than adopted. Much can be gained by analyzing the role these features have played in the evolution of modern social organization – the rise of the state system, the institutions of private and public property, the shift from absolutism to parliamentarianism, or the changing nature of long-distance exchange. All embody cultural purpose.

By the same token, the social organization generated by the early Western cultural account has amplified and altered the original themes. For example, both the intensive development of the state as a rational project and the expansion of exchange and rationalized production have greatly amplified and secularized the cultural account: An amazing array of activities and commodities, up to and including sociological research and meetings, now enter into the cultural account of progress (GNP) almost everywhere in the world. Notions of justice likewise now cover a range of human rights that is very broad, from the traditional civil and political domains to very comprehensive claims regarding material consumption, cultural participation, and protection from discrimination (Marshall 1948; Bendix 1964).

The consequences of the Western cultural account for social organization constitute a central concern of this book. Our general themes can be summed up as follows. First, rationalization in the context of the radical dualism of the West leads to the formation of an extraordinary array of legitimated actors reified as purposive and rational individuals, associations, classes, organizations, ethnic groups, or nation-states. The chronic tendency of social theory to depict action as the choices and decisions of purposive rational actors has strong cultural roots in the conception of human beings as agents of sovereign moral authority or as morally sovereign themselves. We have to step outside this taken-for-granted view in order to analyze Western cultural functionalism, or we are all too likely to let our theories be dominated by it. Second, collective actors command greater legitimacy and authority if they are founded on a theory of individual membership and activity such as the nation-state or the rationalized firm. Other types of actors that reflect more communal structures and submerge the individual within the collective, command less authority. Third, organizational entities that are tied into the theories of justice and progress gain special standing above all others – the individual and the nation-state are the most real of all (the only certainties are death and taxes), with the balance between the two varying from one society to another.

Fourth, because they derive from universalistic cultural ideology, dominant organizational forms, including the structure and boundaries of collective action, are relatively standardized across societies. There is only a loose relationship between organizational forms and practical needs and goals operating in local situations. In this sense, Western organizational structures are to be seen as ritual enactments of broad-based cultural prescriptions rather than the rational responses to concrete problems that the cultural theories purport them to be. In any complex society, there is bound to be considerable disjunction between ritual forms and practical affairs, but the universalization and high degree of abstraction of the cosmos – both ultimate moral authority and nature – make this disjunction seem more inconsistent in the modern West than elsewhere and hence more of a pressure for further elaboration and change.

AN OVERVIEW OF THE BOOK

The chapters that follow carry out the themes of our institutionalist perspective and apply them to an explanation of many of the dominant social organizational forms of the modern system. They conceptualize social structure as involving large-scale collective organization; they view this organization, along with its activities, as constructed by historical processes operating at very general levels. Moreover, this organization reflects the general rules of a distinctive Western cultural system in which the construction and legitimation of actors takes a central place and in which such actors (from the individual to the state) take on distinctive forms.

The various chapters examine diverse topics and in part were written for diverse audiences. Consequently, different appellations for concepts such as the accounting structure and the world cultural system are used in order to emphasize aspects that are particularly relevant to the specific analysis. The following, while highlighting different nuances, all refer to the same concept: world polity, culture, system, political-economy, institutional order or environment, and transnational order. Similarly, accounting structure, institutional order or environment, ontological order, ideology, and culture reflect different subject matter, audience, and emphasis rather than different concepts. For some purposes, it might be useful to distinguish more technically among these appellations; but it does not seem necessary for the purposes of the present work. For similar reasons, there is some repetition of the general institutionalist argument across chapters, but in each case, these are tailored to address the specific issues involved in the particular topic being examined.

We begin, in Part II, with the nation-state, which lies at the heart of the rational project and whose origins and nature are the subject of much current sociological discussion. Chapter 2 takes an explicitly institutionalist view: The authority of the state and the extension of the state system derive from a wider world polity, which both provides a necessary legitimacy and defines appropriate and necessary arenas of jurisdiction and form for the state. The modern expansion of state jurisdiction, the extension of the state system to unlikely areas of the Third World, and the formal and purposive homogeneity of modern states, are all traced to this institutional cultural starting point. Chapter 3 carries out empirical analyses documenting the surprising isomorphism of constitutional authority around the world, its rapid expansion in the modern system, and the associated rise in the organizational power of the state. Important aspects of these analyses discredit any view that these processes arise within the internal social structural patterns of particular societies; they suggest, rather, that they derive from the wider world polity.

An implication of this interpretation is pursued in Chapter 4: If the state is indeed an exogenous, but highly supported and legitimated, institution as it arises in the world periphery, it should be found to be disconnected from society in a variety of ways – in regime instability that is greater when the state is stronger, and in expanding state strength that occurs more rapidly under conditions of turbulence. Both of these expectations – which run against more functionalist analysis of the state as a local actor – find support in comparative empirical analyses.

The theses of Part II are synthesized in Chapter 5, which summarizes a variety of lines of theory and research on the modern expansion of the state and its authority and power. A review of this research suggests the utility and power of explanations focused more directly on the institutions of a world polity and culture to deal with evidence other theoretical lines find more intractable.

Part III describes and explains the manner in which the state project reconstitutes society as a rationalized nation, focusing on citizenship and national institutions as core features of the modern state and state system. Contemporary states, in practice, universally penetrate society, reconceptualizing people as citizens, expanding their rights and obligations, incorporating them into national structures, and defining state authority as legitimated in terms of citizen rights and welfare. Chapter 6 traces this evolution in constitutional doctrine over the last century, with empirical data showing both extraordinary isomorphism among states and great expansion in the formal meaning of citizenship on a worldwide basis.

Within this context, Chapters 7 and 8 analyze the rise and expansion of a central institution's building modern citizenship and personhood – the educational system. One of the surprises to classic functional theories of the modern system has been the rapid expansion of both mass and elite education, ordinarily under state auspices, in the furthest peripheries of the world. These chapters suggest that the dominance of this institution is part of the reconstruction of society around the authority of the nation-state via the political expansion of individual membership through citizenship. The dialectic of individual and state captured in the institution of citizenship arises from the broader nature of the Western cultural system and is driven by contemporary world ideological forces. In Chapter 9, the same perspective is taken on another dominant modern institution – the national welfare system – that is similarly seen as reconstituting society as a rationalized nation. Welfare institutions built on modern individual rights are enactments, often ritualized and loosely coupled with concrete welfare, of the state as defined and legitimated within the world institutional environment. This chapter also takes tentative steps in extending this interpretation to include the expansion of modern land reform programs throughout the periphery.

At the base of the institutionalization of citizenship are the institutional rules giving authority and reality to the individual person, which are greatly expanded and secularized in the modern period. The individual is both the source of modern state authority and the primary object of its legitimate purposes. Part IV considers the contemporary expansion of individualism in a number of areas. Chapter 10 reviews the construction of the ideology of childhood and its linkage with state powers and obligations, showing great expansion in constitutional emphasis on childhood in the last century, and also showing the widespread and homogeneous character of this expansion – thus calling attention, again, to the cultural and institutional character of the changes in the world political system.

In Chapter 11, a parallel analysis is applied to the social construction of the individual life course in general, entailing social–psychological implications. The creation and regularization of rules of the life course, and the creation of much social organization around the steps of this life course, are all built on Western myths of the subjective individual and its rights and powers: The modern flowering of legitimate subjectivity and its relative disconnection from the social structure can be usefully seen as consequences of this evolution. Chapter 12 discusses the implication of this individualism for traditional male political solidarity and the political constitution of sexual violence – rape. As the polity is reconstructed around the abstract individual, the polity is less dominated by male solidarity, resulting in significant changes in public definitions of rape and victimization.

The modern rationalization of public life, a central theme of this book, is built on the expansion of the ontological status of the individual – legitimate motives, interests, perceptions, and reality – and the sovereignty of the nation-state as the guarantor of that status. All this provides a fertile field for social movements and collective action reconstructing and organizing identity oriented toward the state. Most lines of theory conceive of this in terms of the stresses of rationalization and the reactions of individuals and groups. The argument pursued here has modern collective action as more enacting than reacting to modern world culture. Chapter 13 summarizes the recent comparative literature on social movements. It assesses the adequacy of research mobilization and crisis integrationist theories and suggests a more institutional, world system approach. In Chapter 14, an institutionalist model is developed, with a focus on how collective action has the goal of reconstituting society; because of this work on the broad institutional order, many of these movements are religious in nature. This perspective is used to interpret nineteenth century American religious revivalism. Revivalism was an integral aspect of the expansion of the American polity parallel, and in causal relation, to rationalization through the market: revivalism framed the project of progress in terms of a radical individualistic religion and the creation of a new moral–political order.

Finally, Chapter 15 reviews and integrates the empirical and theoretical stance developed here. It summarizes research findings and outlines a research agenda for the institutional analysis of the origins, formation, and dynamics of the world cultural accounting system.

SUMMARY: INSTITUTIONS AND INSTITUTIONALIZATION

Much of our work in this book consists of unpacking the code words sociologists use to sweep troublesome explanatory issues under the rug of culture. It is commonplace to describe social situations and structure as conditioned by legitimacy, or as involving issues of authority, or as determined by the distribution of knowledge. All too often these terms are disembodied and almost devoid of substance. Legitimacy is not an abstract principle but an established and elaborated accounting theory that links situations and structures to collective purposes. Authority is not a metaphysical concept but an explanation of substantive sovereignty and coordination. Thus the authority of any given actor is not some abstract principle standing alone, but a functional account of how things properly are to work, and the legitimacy of this authority is a cognitive and normative cultural account of how the actor promotes general collective ends. Knowledge is not an abstract feature of consciousness but quintessentially validated content.

By *institution*, we mean a set of cultural rules that give generalized meaning to social activity and regulate it in a patterned way. Institutionalization, then, involves processes that make such sets of rules seem natural and taken for granted while eliminating alternative interpretations and regulations. In the Western tradition, rules become institutionalized as they are linked more closely to universal moral authority and lawful order in nature. They are institutionalized as they become more complete and integrated accounts of social activity in a given domain and as they provide explanations of more aspects of that activity. They are institutionalized as they become more invisible and eliminate more alternatives. Hence, they are institutionalized as they become less challengeable and less subject to manipulation by the people involved.

Institutionalization, then, involves the building of relationships that organize action, on one hand, and locate action in expanding cultural theories and ideologies, on the other. The theories at issue, ordinarily functional in nature, are both normative and descriptive, but it is a mistake to see these two dimensions as sharply distinct. Institutionalization implies the construction of both means and ends, of both actor and activity, and the linking of these elements to general goods and truths. As it is only institutionalized conceptions of reality that allow us to distinguish the good and the true, our understanding of the social world is best advanced by considering both normative and descriptive theories as fundamentally problematic.

REFERENCES

Anderson, Perry. 1974. *Lineages of the Absolutist State*. New York: Schocken.

Bardach, Eugene. 1977. *The Implementation Game: What Happens After a Bill Becomes a Law*. Cambridge, MA: MIT Press.

Baron, James N. 1984. Organizational Perspectives on Stratification. *Annual Review of Sociology* 10: 37–69.

—— and William T. Bielby. 1980. Bringing the Firms Back In: Stratification, Segmentation, and the Organization of Work. *American Sociological Review* 45:175–88.

Bellah, Robert N. 1964. Religious Evolution. *American Sociological Review* 29:358–74.

Bendix, Reinhard. 1964. *Nation-Building and Citizenship*. New York: John Wiley.

—— 1978. *Kings or People: Power and the Mandate to Rule*. Berkeley: University of California Press.

Berger, Peter and Thomas Luckmann. 1966. *The Social Construction of Reality*. New York: Doubleday.

——, Brigitte Berger, and Hansfried Kellner. 1973. *The Homeless Mind*. New York: Random House.

Berman, Paul and Milbrey McLaughlin. 1975–1978. *Federal Programs Supporting Educational Change*, Vols. 1–8. Santa Monica, CA: Rand.

Brim, Orville G. and Jerome Kagan. (eds.) 1983. *Constance and Change in Human Development*. Cambridge, MA: Harvard University Press.

Burt, Ronald and Michael J. Minor. (eds.) 1983. *Applied Network Analysis*. Newbury Park, CA: Sage.

Coleman, James. 1982. *The Asymmetric Society*. Syracuse, NY: Syracuse University Press.

Collins, Randall. 1980. Weber's Last Theory of Capitalism: A Systematization. *American Sociological Review* 45 (December):925–42.

DiMaggio, Paul and Walter W. Powell. 1983. The Iron Cage Revisited: Institutional Isomorphism and Collective Rationality in Organizational Fields. *American Sociological Review* 48 (April): 147–60.

—— and Kirsten Stenberg. 1985. Conformity and Diversity in the American Residential Stage in Judith Balfe and Margaret Wyszonirski (eds.), *Sociology and the Arts*. New York: Praeger.

Douglas, Mary. 1966. *Purity and Danger*. Harmondsworth: Penguin.

Ellul, Jacques. 1973. *The New Demons*. New York: Seabury.

Evans, Peter, Dietrich Rueschemeyer, and Theda Skocpol. (eds.) 1985. *Bringing the State Back in*. Cambridge: Cambridge University Press.

Geertz, Clifford. 1980. *Negara: The Theatre State in Nineteenth-Century Bali*. Princeton, NJ: Princeton University Press.

Goffman, Erving. 1974. *Frame Analysis*. New York: Harper Colophon.

Homans, George. 1964. Bringing Man Back In. *American Sociological Review* 29:809–18.

Inkeles, Alex and Larry Sirowy. 1983. Convergent and Divergent Trends in National Educational Systems. *Social Forces* 62 (December):303–34.

Kalberg, Steven. 1980. Max Weber's Types of Rationality: Cornerstones for the Analysis of Rationalization Processes in History. *American Journal of Sociology* 85:1180–201.

March, James G. and Johan P. Olsen. 1976. *Ambiguity and Choice in Organizations*. Bergen: Universitetsforlaget.

Marsden, Peter V. and Nan Lin (eds.) 1982. *Social Structure and Network Analysis*. Newbury Park, CA: Sage.

Marshall, T. H. 1948. *Citizenship and Social Class*. New York: Doubleday.

McCarthy, John D. and Mayer Zald. 1977. Resource Mobilization and Social Movements: A Partial Theory. *American Journal of Sociology* 82 (May):1212–43.

Meyer, John W. and Brian Rowan. 1977. Institutional Organizations: Formal Structure as Myth and Ceremony. *American Journal of Sociology* 83 (September):340–63. Reproduced in Chapter 4.

Mills, C. Wright. 1940. Situated Actions and Vocabularies of Motive. *American Sociological Review* 5:904–13.

Mischel, Walter. 1971. *Introduction to Personality*. New York: Holt, Rinehart & Winston.

Parsons, Talcott. 1951. *The Social System*. New York: Free Press.

Pfeffer, Jerry and Gerald Salancik. 1978. *External Control of Organizations*. New York: Harper & Row.

Pressman, Jeffrey L. and Aaron Wildavsky. 1973. *Implementation*. Berkeley: University of California Press.

Roth, Guenther and Wolfgang Schluchter. 1979. *Max Weber's Vision of History: Ethics and Methods*. Berkeley: University of California Press.

Schluchter, Wolfgang. 1981. *The Rise of Western Rationalism: Max Weber's Development History*. Berkeley: University of California Press.

Scott, W. Richard. 1981. *Organizations: Rational, Natural and Open Systems*. Englewood Cliffs, NJ: Prentice-Hall.

—— 1983. The Organization of Environments: Network, Cultural, and Historical Elements, in J. W. Meyer and W. R. Scott (eds.), *Organizational Environments: Ritual and Rationality*. Newbury Park, CA: Sage, pp. 155–75.

Skocpol, Theda. 1979. *States and Social Revolutions*. Cambridge: Cambridge University Press.

Strayer, Joseph. 1970. *On the Medieval Origins of the Modern State*. Princeton, NJ: Princeton University Press.

Swanson, Guy. 1971. An Organizational Analysis of Collectivities. *American Sociological Review* 36:607–23.

Thomas, George M. and John W. Meyer. 1984. The Expansion of State. *Annual Review of Sociology* 10:461–82.

Tilly, Charles. 1975. *The Formation of National States in Western Europe*. Princeton, NJ: Princeton University Press.

Wallerstein, Immanuel. 1974. *The Modern World-System I: Capitalist Agriculture and the Origins of the European World-Economy in the 16th Century*. New York: Academic Press.

Warren, Roland. 1967. The Interorganizational Field as a Focus for Investigation. *Administrative Science Quarterly* 12:396–419.

Weick, Karl E. 1976. Educational Organizations as Loosely Coupled Systems. *Administrative Science Quarterly* 21:1–19.

Wilensky, H. 1976. *The New Corporatism, Centralization and the Wellfare State*. Newbury Park, CA: Sage.

Wrong, Dennis. 1961. The Oversocialized Conception of Man in Modern Sociology. *American Sociological Review* 26:183–93.

Wuthnow, Robert. 1980a. The World Economy and the Internationalization of Science in Seventeenth-Century Europe, in Albert Bergesen (ed.), *Studies of the Modern World-System*. New York: Academic Press, Ch. 3.

—— 1980b. World Order and Religious Movements, in Albert Bergesen (ed.), *Studies of the Modern World-System*. New York: Academic Press, Ch. 4.

—— 1985. State Structures and Ideological Outcomes. *American Sociological Review* 50: 799–821.

Zucker, Lynne G. 1983. Organizations as Institutions, in Samuel Bacharach (ed.), *Research in the Sociology of Organizations*. Vol. 2. Greenwich, CT: JAI Press.

4

Myth and Ritual

Institutionalized Organizations: Formal Structure as Myth and Ceremony

Many formal organizational structures arise as reflections of rationalized institutional rules. The elaboration of such rules in modern states and societies accounts in part for the expansion and increased complexity of formal organizational structures. Institutional rules function as myths which organizations incorporate, gaining legitimacy, resources, stability, and enhanced survival prospects. Organizations whose structures become isomorphic with the myths of the institutional environment – in contrast with those primarily structured by the demands of technical production and exchange – decrease internal coordination and control in order to maintain legitimacy. Structures are decoupled from each other and from ongoing activities. In place of coordination, inspection, and evaluation, a logic of confidence and good faith is employed.

Formal organizations are generally understood to be systems of coordinated and controlled activities that arise when work is embedded in complex networks of technical relations and boundary-spanning exchanges. But in modern societies, formal organizational structures arise in highly institutionalized contexts. Professions, policies, and programs are created along with the products and services that they are understood to produce rationally. This permits many new organizations to spring up and forces existing ones to incorporate new practices and procedures. That is, organizations are driven to incorporate the practices and procedures defined by prevailing rationalized concepts of organizational work and institutionalized in society. Organizations that do so increase their legitimacy and their survival prospects, independent of the immediate efficacy of the acquired practices and procedures.

Originally published as:

John W. Meyer and Brian Rowan. 1977. Institutionalized Organizations. Formal Structure as Myth and Ceremony. American Journal of Sociology 83:340–56.

Work on this chapter was conducted at the Stanford Center for Research and Development in Teaching (SCRDT) and was supported by the National Institute of Education (contract no. NE-C-00–3–0062). The views expressed here do not, of course, reflect NIE positions. Many colleagues in the SCRDT, the Stanford Organizations Training Program, the American Sociological Association's work group on Organizations and Environments, and the NIE gave help and encouragement. In particular, H. Acland, A. Bergesen, J. Boli-Bennett, T. Deal, J. Freeman, P. Hirsch, J. G. March, W. R. Scott, and W. Starbuck made helpful suggestions.

Institutionalized products, services, techniques, policies, and programs function as powerful myths, and many organizations adopt them ceremonially. But conformity to institutionalized rules often conflicts sharply with efficiency criteria and, conversely, to coordinate and control activity in order to promote efficiency undermines an organization's ceremonial conformity and sacrifices its support and legitimacy. To maintain ceremonial conformity, organizations that reflect institutional rules tend to buffer their formal structures from the uncertainties of technical activities by becoming loosely coupled, building gaps between their formal structures and actual work activities.

This chapter argues that the formal structures of many organizations in post-industrial society (Bell 1973) dramatically reflect the myths of their institutional environments instead of the demands of their work activities. The first part describes prevailing theories of the origins of formal structures and the main problem the theories confront. The second part discusses an alternative source of formal structures: myths embedded in the institutional environment. The third part develops the argument that organizations reflecting institutionalized environments maintain gaps between their formal structures and their ongoing work activities. The final part summarizes the argument by discussing some research implications.

Throughout the paper, institutionalized rules are distinguished sharply from prevailing social behaviors. Institutionalized rules are classifications built into society as reciprocated typifications or interpretations (Berger and Luckmann 1967: 54). Such rules may be simply taken for granted or may be supported by public opinion or the force of law (Starbuck 1976). Institutions inevitably involve normative obligations but often enter into social life primarily as facts which must be taken into account by actors. Institutionalization involves the processes by which social processes, obligations, or actualities come to take on a rule-like status in social thought and action. So, for example, the social status of doctor is a highly institutionalized rule (both normative and cognitive) for managing illness as well as a social role made up of particular behaviors, relations, and expectations. R&D is an institutionalized category of organizational activity which has meaning and value in many sectors of society as well as a collection of actual R&D activities. In a smaller way, a 'No Smoking' sign is an institution with legal status and implications as well as an attempt to regulate smoking behavior. It is fundamental to the argument of this chapter that institutional rules may have effects on organizational structures and their implementation in actual technical work which are very different from the effects generated by the networks of social behavior and relationships which compose and surround a given organization.

PREVAILING THEORIES OF FORMAL STRUCTURE

A sharp distinction should be made between the formal structure of an organization and its actual day-to-day work activities. Formal structure is a blueprint for activities which includes, first of all, the table of organization: a listing of offices, departments, positions, and programs. These elements are linked by explicit goals and policies that make up a rational theory of how, and to what end, activities are to be fitted together. The essence of a modern bureaucratic organization lies in the rationalized and impersonal character of these structural elements and of the goals that link them.

One of the central problems in organization theory is to describe the conditions that give rise to rationalized formal structure. In conventional theories, rational formal structure is assumed to be the most effective way to coordinate and control the complex relational networks involved in modern technical or work activities (see Scott 1975 for a review). This assumption derives from Weber's (1930, 1946, 1947) discussions of the historical emergence of bureaucracies as consequences of economic markets and centralized states. Economic markets place a premium on rationality and coordination. As markets expand, the relational networks in a given domain become more complex and differentiated, and organizations in that domain must manage more internal and boundary-spanning interdependencies. Such factors as size (Blau 1970) and technology (Woodward 1965) increase the complexity of internal relations, and the division of labor among organizations increases boundary-spanning problems (Aiken and Hage 1968; Freeman 1973; Thompson 1967). Because the need for coordination increases under these conditions, and because formally coordinated work has competitive advantages, organizations with rationalized formal structures tend to develop.

The formation of centralized states and the penetration of societies by political centers also contribute to the rise and spread of formal organization. When the relational networks involved in economic exchange and political management become extremely complex, bureaucratic structures are thought to be the most effective and rational means to standardize and control subunits. Bureaucratic control is especially useful for expanding political centers, and standardization is often demanded by both centers and peripheral units (Bendix 1964, 1968). Political centers organize layers of offices that manage to extend conformity and to displace traditional activities throughout societies.

The problem. *Prevailing theories assume that the coordination and control of activity are the critical dimensions on which formal organizations have succeeded in the modern world.* This assumption is based on the view that organizations function according to their formal blueprints: coordination is routine, rules and procedures are followed, and actual activities conform to the prescriptions of formal structure. But much of the empirical research on organizations casts doubt on this assumption. An earlier generation of researchers concluded that there was a great gap between the formal and the informal organization (e.g., Dalton 1959; Downs 1967; Homans 1950). A related observation is that formal organizations are often loosely coupled (March and Olsen 1976; Weick 1976): structural elements are only loosely linked to each other and to activities, rules are often violated, decisions are often un-implemented, or if implemented have uncertain consequences, technologies are of problematic efficiency, and evaluation and inspection systems are subverted or rendered so vague as to provide little coordination.

Formal organizations are endemic in modern societies. There is a need for an explanation of their rise that is partially free from the assumption that, in practice, formal structures actually coordinate and control work. Such an explanation should account for the elaboration of purposes, positions, policies, and procedural rules that characterizes formal organizations, but must do so without supposing that these structural features are implemented in routine work activity.

INSTITUTIONAL SOURCES OF FORMAL STRUCTURE

By focusing on the management of complex relational networks and the exercise of coordination and control, prevailing theories have neglected an alternative Weberian source of formal structure: the legitimacy of rationalized formal structures. In prevailing theories, legitimacy is a given: assertions about bureaucratization rest on the assumption of norms of rationality (Thompson 1967). When norms do play causal roles in theories of bureaucratization, it is because they are thought to be built into modern societies and personalities as very general values, which are thought to facilitate formal organization. But norms of rationality are not simply general values. They exist in much more specific and powerful ways in the rules, understandings, and meanings attached to institutionalized social structures. The causal importance of such institutions in the process of bureaucratization has been neglected.

Formal structures are not only creatures of their relational networks in the social organization. In modern societies, the elements of rationalized formal structure are deeply ingrained in, and reflect, widespread understandings of social reality. Many of the positions, policies, programs, and procedures of modern organizations are enforced by public opinion, by the views of important constituents, by knowledge legitimated through the educational system, by social prestige, by the laws, and by the definitions of negligence and prudence used by the courts. Such elements of formal structure are manifestations of powerful institutional rules which function as highly rationalized myths that are binding on particular organizations.

In modern societies, the myths generating formal organizational structure have two key properties. First, they are rationalized and impersonal prescriptions that identify various social purposes as technical ones and specify in a rule-like way the appropriate means to pursue these technical purposes rationally (Ellul 1964). Second, they are highly institutionalized and thus in some measure beyond the discretion of any individual participant or organization. They must, therefore, be taken for granted as legitimate, apart from evaluations of their impact on work outcomes.

Many elements of formal structure are highly institutionalized and function as myths. Examples include professions, programs, and technologies:

> Large numbers of rationalized professions emerge (Wilensky 1965; Bell 1973). These are occupations controlled, not only by direct inspection of work outcomes but also by social rules of licensing, certifying, and schooling. The occupations are rationalized, being understood to control impersonal techniques rather than moral mysteries. Further, they are highly institutionalized: the delegation of activities to the

appropriate occupations is socially expected and often legally obligatory over and above any calculations of its efficiency.

Many formalized organizational programs are also institutionalized in society. Ideologies define the functions appropriate to a business – such as sales, production, advertising, or accounting; to a university – such as instruction and research in history, engineering, and literature; and to a hospital – such as surgery, internal medicine, and obstetrics. Such classifications of organizational functions, and the specifications for conducting each function, are prefabricated formulae available for use by any given organization.

Similarly, technologies are institutionalized and become myths binding on organizations. Technical procedures of production, accounting, personnel selection, or data processing become taken-for-granted means to accomplish organizational ends. Quite apart from their possible efficiency, such institutionalized techniques establish an organization as appropriate, rational, and modern. Their use displays responsibility and avoids claims of negligence.

The impact of such rationalized institutional elements on organizations and organizing situations is enormous. These rules define new organizing situations, redefine existing ones, and specify the means for coping rationally with each. They enable, and often require, participants to organize along prescribed lines. And they spread very rapidly in modern society as part of the rise of post-industrial society (Bell 1973). New and extant domains of activity are codified in institutionalized programs, professions, or techniques, and organizations incorporate the packaged codes. For example:

> The discipline of psychology creates a rationalized theory of personnel selection and certifies personnel professionals. Personnel departments and functionaries appear in all sorts of extant organizations, and new specialized personnel agencies also appear.
>
> As programs of research and development are created and professionals with expertise in these fields are trained and defined, organizations come under increasing pressure to incorporate R & D units.
>
> As the prerational profession of prostitution is rationalized along medical lines, bureaucratized organizations – sex-therapy clinics, massage parlors, and the like – spring up more easily.
>
> As the issues of safety and environmental pollution arise, and as relevant professions and programs become institutionalized in laws, union ideologies, and public opinion, organizations incorporate these programs and professions.

The growth of rationalized institutional structures in society makes formal organizations more common and more elaborate. Such institutions are myths which make formal organizations both easier to create and more necessary. After all, the building blocks for organizations come to be littered around the societal landscape; it takes only a little entrepreneurial energy to assemble them into a structure. And because these building blocks are considered proper, adequate, rational, and necessary, organizations must incorporate them to avoid illegitimacy. Thus, the myths built into rationalized institutional elements create the necessity, the opportunity, and the impulse to organize rationally, over and above pressures in this direction created by the need to manage proximate relational networks:

Proposition 1. *As rationalized institutional rides arise in given domains of work activity, formal organizations form and expand by incorporating these rules as structural elements.*

Two distinct ideas are implied here: (1*a*) As institutionalized myths define new domains of rationalized activity, formal organizations emerge in these domains. (1*b*) As rationalizing institutional myths arise in existing domains of activity, extant organizations expand their formal structures so as to become isomorphic with these new myths.

To understand the larger historical process, it is useful to note that:

Proposition 2. *The more modernized the society, the more extended the rationalized institutional structure in given domains and the greater the number of domains containing rationalized institutions.*

Modern institutions, then, are thoroughly rationalized, and these rationalized elements act as myths giving rise to more formal organization. When Propositions 1 and 2 are combined, two more specific ideas follow: (2*a*) Formal organizations are more likely to emerge in more modernized societies, even with the complexity of immediate relational networks held constant. (2*b*) Formal organizations in a given domain of activity are likely to have more elaborated structures in more modernized societies, even with the complexity of immediate relational networks held constant.

Combining the ideas above with prevailing organization theory, it becomes clear that modern societies are filled with rationalized bureaucracies for two reasons. First, as the prevailing theories have asserted, relational networks become increasingly complex as societies modernize. Second, modern societies are filled with institutional rules which function as myths depicting various formal structures as rational means to the attainment of desirable ends. Figure 4.1 summarizes these two lines of theory. Both lines suggest that the post-industrial society – the society dominated by rational organization even more than by the forces of production – arises both out of the complexity of the modern social organizational network and, more directly, as an ideological matter. Once institutionalized, rationality becomes a myth with explosive organizing potential, as both Ellul (1964) and Bell (1973) – though with rather different reactions – observe.

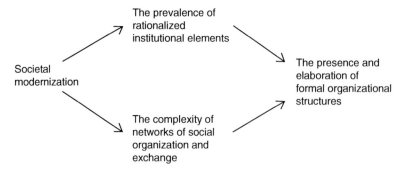

Figure 4.1. The origins and elaboration of formal organizational structures

The relation of organizations to their institutional environments

The observation is not new that organizations are structured by phenomena in their environments and tend to become isomorphic with them. One explanation of such isomorphism is that formal organizations become matched with their environments by technical and exchange interdependencies. This line of reasoning can be seen in the works of Aiken and Hage (1968), Hawley (1968), and Thompson (1967). This explanation asserts that structural elements diffuse because environments create boundary-spanning exigencies for organizations, and that organizations which incorporate structural elements isomorphic with the environment are able to manage such interdependencies.

A second explanation for the parallelism between organizations and their environments – and the one emphasized here – is that organizations structurally reflect socially constructed reality (Berger and Luckmann 1967). This view is suggested in the work of Parsons (1956) and Udy (1970), who see organizations as greatly conditioned by their general institutional environments and therefore as institutions themselves in part. Emery and Trist (1965) also see organizations as responding directly to environmental structures and distinguish such effects sharply from those that occur through boundary-spanning exchanges. According to the institutional conception as developed here, organizations tend to disappear as distinct and bounded units. Quite beyond the environmental interrelations suggested in open-systems theories, institutional theories in their extreme forms define organizations as dramatic enactments of the rationalized myths pervading modern societies, rather than as units involved in exchange – no matter how complex – with their environments.

The two explanations of environmental isomorphism are not entirely inconsistent. Organizations both deal with their environments at their boundaries and imitate environmental elements in their structures. However, the two lines of explanation have very different implications for internal organizational processes, as will be argued below.

The origins of rational institutional myths

Bureaucratization is caused in part by the proliferation of rationalized myths in society, and this in turn involves the evolution of the whole modern institutional system. Although the latter topic is beyond the scope of this chapter, three specific processes that generate rationalized myths of organizational structure can be noted.

The elaboration of complex relational network – As the relational networks in societies become dense and interconnected, increasing numbers of rationalized myths arise. Some of them are highly generalized: for example, the principles of universalism (Parsons 1971), contracts (Spencer 1897), restitution (Durkheim 1933), and expertise (Weber 1947) are generalized to diverse occupations, organizational programs, and organizational practices. Other myths describe specific structural elements. These myths may originate from narrow contexts and be applied in different ones. For example, in modern societies the relational contexts of business organizations in a single industry are roughly similar from place to place. Under these conditions, a particularly effective practice, occupational specialty, or principle of coordination can be codified into myth-like form. The laws, the educational and credentialing systems, and public opinion then make it necessary or advantageous for organizations to incorporate the new structures.

The degree of collective organization of the environment – The myths generated by particular organizational practices and diffused through relational networks have legitimacy based on the supposition that they are rationally effective. But many myths also have official legitimacy based on legal mandates. Societies that, through nation building and state formation, have developed rational–legal orders are especially prone to give collective (legal) authority to institutions which legitimate particular organizational structures. The rise of centralized states and integrated nations means that organized agents of society assume jurisdiction over large numbers of activity domains (Swanson 1971). Legislative and judicial authorities create and interpret legal mandates; administrative agencies – such as state and federal governments, port authorities, and school districts – establish rules of practice; and licenses and credentials become necessary in order to practice occupations. The stronger the rational–legal order, the greater the extent to which rationalized rules and procedures and personnel become institutional requirements. New formal organizations emerge and extant organizations acquire new structural elements.

Leadership efforts of local organizations – The rise of the state and the expansion of collective jurisdiction are often thought to result in domesticated organizations (Carlson 1962) subject to high levels of goal displacement (Clark 1956; Selznick 1949; Zald and Denton 1963). This view is misleading: organizations do often adapt themselves to their institutional contexts, but they often play active roles in shaping those contexts (Dowling and Pfeffer 1975; Parsons 1956; Perrow 1970; Thompson 1967). Many organizations actively seek charters from collective authorities and manage to institutionalize their goals and structures in the rules of such authorities.

Efforts to mold institutional environments proceed along two dimensions. First, powerful organizations force their immediate relational networks to adapt to their structures and relations. For instance, automobile producers help create demands for particular kinds of roads, transportation systems, and fuels that make automobiles virtual necessities; competitive forms of transportation have to adapt to the existing relational context. But second, powerful organizations attempt to build their goals and procedures directly into society as institutional rules. Automobile producers, for instance, attempt to create the standards in public opinion defining desirable cars, to influence legal standards defining satisfactory cars, to affect judicial rules defining cars adequate enough to avoid manufacturer liability, and to force agents of the collectivity to purchase only their cars. Rivals must then compete both in social networks or markets and in contexts of institutional rules which are defined by extant organizations. In this fashion, given organizational forms perpetuate themselves by becoming institutionalized rules. For example:

School administrators who create new curricula or training programs attempt to validate them as legitimate innovations in educational theory and governmental requirements. If they are successful, the new procedures can be perpetuated as authoritatively required or at least satisfactory.

New departments within business enterprises, such as personnel, advertising, or research and development departments, attempt to professionalize by creating rules of practice and personnel certification that are enforced by the schools, prestige systems, and the laws.

Organizations under attack in competitive environments – small farms, passenger railways, or Rolls Royce – attempt to establish themselves as central to the cultural traditions of their societies in order to receive official protection.

The impact of institutional environments on organizations

Isomorphism with environmental institutions has some crucial consequences for organizations: (*a*) they incorporate elements which are legitimated externally, rather than in terms of efficiency; (*b*) they employ external or ceremonial assessment criteria to define the value of structural elements; and (*c*) dependence on externally fixed institutions reduces turbulence and maintains stability. As a result, it is argued here, institutional isomorphism promotes the success and survival of organizations. Incorporating externally legitimated formal structures increases the commitment of internal participants and external constituents. And the use of external assessment criteria – that is, moving toward the status in society of a subunit rather than an independent system – can enable an organization to remain successful by social definition, buffering it from failure.

Changing formal structures – By designing a formal structure that adheres to the prescriptions of myths in the institutional environment, an organization demonstrates that it is acting on collectively valued purposes in a proper and adequate manner (Dowling and Pfeffer 1975; Meyer and Rowan 1975). The incorporation of institutionalized elements provides an account (Scott and Lyman 1968) of its activities that protects the organization from having its conduct questioned. The organization becomes, in a word, legitimate, and it uses its legitimacy to strengthen its support and secure its survival.

From an institutional perspective, then, a most important aspect of isomorphism with environmental institutions is the evolution of organizational language. The labels of the organization chart as well as the vocabulary used to delineate organizational goals, procedures, and policies are analogous to the vocabularies of motive used to account for the activities of individuals (Blum and McHugh 1971; Mills 1940). Just as jealousy, anger, altruism, and love are myths that interpret and explain the actions of individuals, the myths of doctors, of accountants, or of the assembly line explain organizational activities. Thus, some can say that the engineers will solve a specific problem or that the secretaries will perform certain tasks, without knowing who these engineers or secretaries will be or exactly what they will do. Both the speaker and the listeners understand such statements to describe how certain responsibilities will be carried out.

Vocabularies of structure which are isomorphic with institutional rules provide prudent, rational, and legitimate accounts. Organizations described in legitimated vocabularies are assumed to be oriented to collectively defined, and often collectively mandated, ends. The myths of personnel services, for example, not only account for the rationality of employment practices but also indicate that personnel services are valuable to an organization. Employees, applicants, managers, trustees, and governmental agencies are predisposed to trust the hiring practices of organizations that follow legitimated procedures – such as equal opportunity programs or personality testing – and they are more willing to participate in or to fund such organizations. On the other hand, organizations that omit environmentally legitimated elements of structure or create unique structures lack acceptable legitimated accounts of their activities. Such organizations are more vulnerable to claims that they are negligent, irrational, or unnecessary. Claims of this kind, whether made by internal participants, external constituents, or the government, can cause organizations to incur real costs. For example:

> With the rise of modern medical institutions, large organizations that do not arrange medical-care facilities for their workers come to be seen as negligent – by the workers, by management factions, by insurers, by courts which legally define negligence, and often by laws. The costs of illegitimacy in insurance premiums and legal liabilities are very real.
>
> Similarly, environmental safety institutions make it important for organizations to create formal safety rules, safety departments, and safety programs. No Smoking rules and signs, regardless of their enforcement, are necessary to avoid charges of negligence and to avoid the extreme of illegitimation: the closing of buildings by the state.
>
> The rise of professionalized economics makes it useful for organizations to incorporate groups of economists and econometric analyses. Though no one may read, understand, or believe them, econometric analyses help legitimate the organization's plans in the eyes of investors, customers (as with Defense Department contractors), and internal participants. Such analyses can also provide rational accountings after failures occur: managers whose plans have failed can demonstrate to investors, stockholders, and superiors that procedures were prudent and that decisions were made by rational means.

Thus, rationalized institutions create myths of formal structure which shape organizations. Failure to incorporate the proper elements of structure is negligent and irrational; the continued flow of support is threatened and internal dissidents are strengthened. At the same time, these myths present organizations with great opportunities for expansion. Affixing the right labels to activities can change them into valuable services and mobilize the commitments of internal participants and external constituents.

Adopting external assessment criteria – In institutionally elaborated environments, organizations also become sensitive to, and employ, external criteria of worth. Such criteria include, for instance, such ceremonial awards as the Nobel Prize, endorsements by important people, the standard prices of professionals and consultants, or the prestige of programs or personnel in external social circles. For example, the conventions of modern accounting attempt to assign value to particular components of organizations on the basis of their contribution – through the organization's production function – to the goods and services the organization produces. But for many units – service departments, administrative sectors, and others – it is utterly unclear what is being produced that has clear or definable value in terms of its contribution to the organizational product. In these situations, accountants employ shadow prices: they assume that given organizational units are necessary and calculate their value from their prices in the world outside the organization. Thus, modern accounting creates ceremonial production functions and maps them onto economic production functions. Organizations assign externally defined worth to advertising departments, safety departments, managers, econometricians, and occasionally even sociologists, whether or not these units contribute measurably to the production of outputs. Monetary prices, in post-industrial society, reflect hosts of ceremonial influences, as do economic measures of efficiency, profitability, or net worth (Hirsch 1975).

Ceremonial criteria of worth and ceremonially derived production functions are useful to organizations: they legitimate organizations with internal participants, stockholders, the public, and the state, as with the Internal Revenue Service (IRS) or the U.S. Securities and Exchange Commission (SEC). They demonstrate socially the fitness of an organization. The incorporation of structures with high ceremonial value, such as those reflecting the latest expert thinking or those with the most prestige, makes the credit position of an organization more favorable. Loans, donations, or investments are more easily obtained. Finally, units within the organization use ceremonial assessments as accounts of their productive service to the organization. Their internal power rises with their performance on ceremonial measures (Salancik and Pfeffer 1974).

Stabilization – The rise of an elaborate institutional environment stabilizes both external and internal organizational relationships. Centralized states, trade associations, unions, professional associations, and coalitions among organizations standardize and stabilize (see the review by Starbuck 1976).

Market conditions, the characteristics of inputs and outputs, and technological procedures are brought under the jurisdiction of institutional meanings and controls. Stabilization also results as a given organization becomes part of the wider collective system. Support is guaranteed by agreements instead of depending entirely on performance. For example, apart from whether schools educate students or hospitals cure patients, people and governmental agencies remain committed to these organizations, funding and using them almost automatically year after year.

Institutionally controlled environments buffer organizations from turbulence (Emery and Trist 1965; Terreberry 1968). Adaptations occur less rapidly as increased numbers of agreements are enacted. Collectively granted monopolies guarantee clienteles for organizations like schools, hospitals, or professional associations. The taken-for-granted (and legally regulated) quality of institutional rules makes dramatic instabilities in products, techniques, or policies, unlikely. And legitimacy as accepted sub-units of society protects organizations from immediate sanctions for variations in technical performance:

Thus, American school districts (like other governmental units) have near monopolies and are very stable. They must conform to wider rules about proper classifications
and credentials of teachers and students, and of topics of study. But they are protected
by rules which make education as defined by these classifications compulsory.
Alternative or private schools are possible, but must conform so closely to the required
structures and classifications as to be able to generate little advantage.

Some business organizations obtain very high levels of institutional stabilization.
A large defense contractor may be paid for following agreed-on procedures, even if the
product is ineffective. In the extreme, such organizations may be so successful as to
survive bankruptcy intact – as Lockheed and Penn Central have done – by becoming
partially components of the state. More commonly, such firms are guaranteed survival
by state-regulated rates which secure profits regardless of costs, as with American public
utility firms.

Large automobile firms are a little less stabilized. They exist in an environment that
contains enough structures to make automobiles, as conventionally defined, virtual
necessities. But still, customers and governments can inspect each automobile and can
evaluate and even legally discredit it. Legal action cannot as easily discredit a high
school graduate.

Organizational success and survival – Organizational success, thus depends on
factors other than efficient coordination and control of productive activities.
Independent of their productive efficiency, organizations which exist in highly elaborated institutional environments and succeed in becoming isomorphic with these
environments gain the legitimacy and resources needed to survive. In part, this
depends on environmental processes and on the capacity of given organizational
leadership to mold these processes (Hirsch 1975). In part, it depends on the ability of
given organizations to conform to, and become legitimated by, environmental institutions. In institutionally elaborated environments, sagacious conformity is required:
leadership (in a university, a hospital, or a business) requires an understanding of
changing fashions and governmental programs. But this kind of conformity – and the
almost guaranteed survival which may accompany it – is possible only in an environment with a highly institutionalized structure. In such a context, an organization
can be locked into isomorphism, ceremonially reflecting the institutional environment in its structure, functionaries, and procedures. Thus, in addition to the conventionally denned sources of organizational success and survival, the following
general assertion can be proposed:

*Proposition 3. Organizations that incorporate societally legitimated rationalized elem-
ents in their formal structures maximize their legitimacy and increase their resources and
survival capabilities.*

This proposition asserts that the long-run survival prospects of organizations increase
as state structures elaborate and as organizations respond to institutionalized rules. In
the United States, for instance, schools, hospitals, and welfare organizations show
considerable ability to survive, precisely because they are matched with – and almost
absorbed by – their institutional environments. In the same way, organizations fail
when they deviate from the prescriptions of institutionalizing myths: quite apart

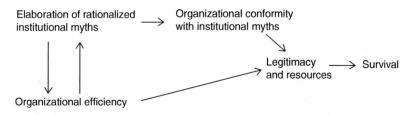

Figure 4.2. Organizational survival

from technical efficiency, organizations which innovate in important structural ways bear considerable costs in legitimacy.

Figure 4.2 summarizes the general argument of this section, alongside the established view that organizations succeed through efficiency.

INSTITUTIONALIZED STRUCTURES AND ORGANIZATIONAL ACTIVITIES

Rationalized formal structures arise in two contexts. First, the demands of local relational networks encourage the development of structures that coordinate and control activities. Such structures contribute to the efficiency of organizations and give them competitive advantages over less efficient competitors. Second, the interconnectedness of societal relations, the collective organization of society, and the leadership of organizational elites create a highly institutionalized context. In this context, rationalized structures present an acceptable account of organizational activities, and organizations gain legitimacy, stability, and resources.

All organizations, to one degree or another, are embedded in both relational and institutionalized contexts and are therefore concerned both with coordinating and controlling their activities and with prudently accounting for them. Organizations in highly institutionalized environments face internal and boundary-spanning contingencies. Schools, for example, must transport students to and from school under some circumstances and must assign teachers, students, and topics to classrooms. On the other hand, organizations producing in markets that place great emphasis on efficiency build in units whose relation to production is obscure and whose efficiency is determined, not by a true production function, but by ceremonial definition.

Nevertheless, the survival of some organizations depends more on managing the demands of internal and boundary-spanning relations, while the survival of others depends more on the ceremonial demands of highly institutionalized environments. The following discussion shows that whether an organization's survival depends primarily on relational or on institutional demands determines the tightness of alignments between structures and activities.

Types of organizations

Institutionalized myths differ in the completeness with which they describe cause and effect relationships and in the clarity with which they describe standards that should be used to evaluate outputs (Thompson 1967). Some organizations use routine, clearly defined technologies to produce outputs. When output can be easily evaluated a market often develops, and consumers gain considerable rights of inspection and control. In this context, efficiency often determines success. Organizations must face exigencies of close coordination with their relational networks, and they cope with these exigencies by organizing around the immediate technical problems.

But the rise of collectively organized society and the increasing interconnectedness of social relations have eroded many market contexts. Increasingly, such organizations as schools, R & D units, and governmental bureaucracies use variable, ambiguous technologies to produce outputs that are difficult to appraise, and other organizations with clearly defined technologies find themselves unable to adapt to environmental turbulence. The uncertainties of unpredictable technical contingencies or of adapting to environmental change cannot be resolved on the basis of efficiency. Internal participants and external constituents alike call for institutionalized rules that promote trust and confidence in outputs and buffer organizations from failure (Emery and Trist 1965).

Thus, one can conceive of a continuum along which organizations can be ordered. At one end are production organizations under strong output controls (Ouchi and McGuire 1975) whose success depends on the management of relational networks. At the other end are institutionalized organizations whose success depends on the confidence and stability achieved by isomorphism with institutional rules. For two reasons it is important not to assume that an organization's location on this continuum is based on the inherent technical properties of its output and therefore permanent. First, the technical properties of outputs are socially defined and do not exist in some concrete sense that allows them to be empirically discovered. Second, environments and organizations often redefine the nature of products, services, and technologies. Redefinition sometimes clarifies techniques or evaluative standards. But often organizations and environments redefine the nature of techniques and output so that ambiguity is introduced and rights of inspection and control are lowered. For example, American schools have evolved from producing rather specific training that was evaluated according to strict criteria of efficiency to producing ambiguously defined services that are evaluated according to criteria of certification (Callahan 1962; Tyack 1974; Meyer and Rowan 1975).

Structural inconsistencies in institutionalized organizations

Two very general problems face an organization if its success depends primarily on isomorphism with institutionalized rules. First, technical activities and demands for efficiency create conflicts and inconsistencies in an institutionalized organization's efforts to conform to the ceremonial rules of production. Second, because these ceremonial rules are transmitted by myths that may arise from different parts of the environment, the rules may conflict with one another. These inconsistencies make a concern for efficiency and tight coordination and control problematic.

Formal structures that celebrate institutionalized myths differ from structures that act efficiently. Ceremonial activity is significant in relation to categorical rules, not in its concrete effects (Merton 1940; March and Simon 1958). A sick worker must be treated by a doctor using accepted medical procedures; whether the worker is treated effectively is less important. A bus company must service required routes whether or not there are many passengers. A university must maintain appropriate departments independently of the departments' enrollments. That is, activity has ritual significance: it maintains appearances and validates an organization.

Categorical rules conflict with the logic of efficiency. Organizations often face the dilemma that activities celebrating institutionalized rules, although they count as virtuous ceremonial expenditures, are pure costs from the point of view of efficiency. For example, hiring a Nobel Prize winner brings great ceremonial benefits to a university. The celebrated name can lead to research grants, brighter students, or reputational gains. But from the point of view of immediate outcomes, the expenditure lowers the instructional return per dollar expended and lowers the university's ability to solve immediate logistical problems. Also, expensive technologies, which bring prestige to hospitals and business firms, may be simply excessive costs from the point of view of immediate production. Similarly, highly professionalized consultants who bring external blessings on an organization are often difficult to justify in terms of improved productivity, yet may be very important in maintaining internal and external legitimacy.

Other conflicts between categorical rules and efficiency arise because institutional rules are couched at high levels of generalization (Durkheim 1933) whereas technical activities vary with specific, unstandardized, and possibly unique conditions. Because standardized ceremonial categories must confront technical variations and anomalies, the generalized rules of the institutional environment are often inappropriate to specific situations. A governmentally mandated curriculum may be inappropriate for the students at hand, a conventional medical treatment may make little sense given the characteristics of a patient, and federal safety inspectors may intolerably delay boundary-spanning exchanges.

Yet another source of conflict between categorical rules and efficiency is the inconsistency among institutionalized elements. Institutional environments are often pluralistic (Udy 1970), and societies promulgate sharply inconsistent myths. As a result, organizations in search of external support and stability incorporate all sorts of incompatible structural elements. Professions are incorporated although they make overlapping jurisdictional claims. Programs are adopted which contend with each other for authority over a given domain. For instance, if one inquires who decides what curricula will be taught in schools, any number of parties from the various governments down to individual teachers may say that they decide.

In institutionalized organizations, then, concern with the efficiency of day-to-day activities creates enormous uncertainties. Specific contexts highlight the inadequacies of the prescriptions of generalized myths, and inconsistent structural elements conflict over jurisdictional rights. Thus, the organization must struggle to link the requirements of ceremonial elements to technical activities and to link inconsistent ceremonial elements to each other.

Resolving inconsistencies

There are four partial solutions to these inconsistencies. First, an organization can resist ceremonial requirements. But an organization that neglects ceremonial requirements and portrays itself as efficient may be unsuccessful in documenting its efficiency. Also, rejecting ceremonial requirements neglects an important source of resources and stability. Second, an organization can maintain rigid conformity to institutionalized prescriptions by cutting off external relations. Although such isolation upholds ceremonial requirements, internal participants and external constituents may soon become disillusioned with their inability to manage boundary-spanning exchanges. Institutionalized organizations must not only conform to myths but must also maintain the appearance that the myths actually work. Third, an organization can cynically acknowledge that its structure is inconsistent with work requirements. But this strategy denies the validity of institutionalized myths and sabotages the legitimacy of the organization. Fourth, an organization can promise reform. People may picture the present as unworkable but the future as filled with promising reforms of both structure and activity. But by defining the organization's valid structure as lying in the future, this strategy makes the organization's current structure illegitimate.

Instead of relying on a partial solution, however, an organization can resolve conflicts between ceremonial rules and efficiency by employing two interrelated devices: decoupling and the logic of confidence.

Decoupling – Ideally, organizations built around efficiency attempt to maintain close alignments between structures and activities. Conformity is enforced through inspection, output quality is continually monitored, the efficiency of various units is evaluated, and the various goals are unified and coordinated. But a policy of close alignment in institutionalized organizations merely makes public a record of inefficiency and inconsistency.

Institutionalized organizations protect their formal structures from evaluation on the basis of technical performance: inspection, evaluation, and control of activities are minimized and coordination, interdependence, and mutual adjustments among structural units are handled informally.

Proposition 4. *Because attempts to control and coordinate activities in institutionalized organizations lead to conflicts and loss of legitimacy, elements of structure are decoupled from activities and from each other.*

Some well-known properties of organizations illustrate the decoupling process:

> Activities are performed beyond the purview of managers. In particular, organizations actively encourage professionalism, and activities are delegated to professionals.

Goals are made ambiguous or vacuous, and categorical ends are substituted for technical ends. Hospitals treat, not cure, patients. Schools produce students, not learning. In fact, data on technical performance are eliminated or rendered invisible. Hospitals try to ignore information on cure rates, public services avoid data about effectiveness, and schools deemphasize measures of achievement.

Integration is avoided, program implementation is neglected, and inspection and evaluation are ceremonialized.

Human relations are made very important. The organization cannot formally coordinate activities because its formal rules, if applied, would generate inconsistencies. Therefore individuals are left to work out technical interdependencies informally. The ability to coordinate things in violation of the rules – that is, to get along with other people – is highly valued.

The advantages of decoupling are clear. The assumption that formal structures are really working is buffered from the inconsistencies and anomalies involved in technical activities. Also, because integration is avoided, disputes and conflicts are minimized, and an organization can mobilize support from a broader range of external constituents.

Thus, decoupling enables organizations to maintain standardized, legitimating, formal structures while their activities vary in response to practical considerations. The organizations in an industry tend to be similar in formal structure, reflecting their common institutional origins, but may show much diversity in actual practice.

The logic of confidence and good faith – Despite the lack of coordination and control, decoupled organizations are not anarchies. Day-to-day activities proceed in an orderly fashion. What legitimates institutionalized organizations, enabling them to appear useful in spite of the lack of technical validation, is the confidence and good faith of their internal participants and their external constituents.

Considerations of face characterize ceremonial management (Goffman 1967). Confidence in structural elements is maintained through three practices-avoidance, discretion, and overlooking (Goffman 1967: 1218). Avoidance and discretion are encouraged by decoupling autonomous subunits; overlooking anomalies is also quite common. Both internal participants and external constituents cooperate in these practices. Assuring that individual participants maintain face sustains confidence in the organization, and ultimately reinforces confidence in the myths that rationalize the organization's existence.

Delegation, professionalization, goal ambiguity, the elimination of output data, and maintenance of face are all mechanisms for absorbing uncertainty while preserving the formal structure of the organization (March and Simon 1958). They contribute to a general aura of confidence within and outside the organization. Although the literature on informal organization often treats these practices as mechanisms for the achievement of deviant and subgroup purposes (Downs 1967), such treatment ignores a critical feature of organization life: effectively absorbing uncertainty and maintaining confidence requires people to assume that everyone is acting in good faith. The assumption that things are as they seem, that employees and managers are performing their roles properly, allows an organization to perform its daily routines with a decoupled structure.

Decoupling and maintenance of face, in other words, are mechanisms that maintain the assumption that people are acting in good faith. Professionalization is not merely a way of avoiding inspection – it binds both supervisors and subordinates to act in good faith. So, in a smaller way, does strategic leniency (Blau 1956). And so do the public displays of morale and satisfaction which are characteristic of many organizations. Organizations employ a host of mechanisms to dramatize the ritual commitments which their participants make to basic structural elements. These mechanisms are especially common in organizations which strongly reflect their institutionalized environments.

Proposition 5. *The more an organization's structure is derived from institutionalized myths, the more it maintains elaborate displays of confidence, satisfaction, and good faith, internally and externally.*

The commitments built up by displays of morale and satisfaction are not simply vacuous affirmations of institutionalized myths. Participants not only commit themselves to supporting an organization's ceremonial facade but also to making things work out backstage. The committed participants engage in informal coordination that, although often formally inappropriate, keeps technical activities running smoothly and avoids public embarrassments. In this sense, the confidence and good faith generated by ceremonial action is in no way fraudulent. It may even be the most reasonable way to get participants to make their best efforts in situations that are made problematic by institutionalized myths that are at odds with immediate technical demands.

Ceremonial inspection and evaluation – All organizations, even those maintaining high levels of confidence and good faith, are in environments that have institutionalized the rationalized rituals of inspection and evaluation. And inspection and evaluation can uncover events and deviations that undermine legitimacy. So institutionalized organizations minimize and ceremonialize inspection and evaluation.

In institutionalized organizations, in fact, evaluation accompanies and produces illegitimacy. The interest in evaluation research by the American federal government, for instance, is partly intended to undercut the state, local, and private authorities which have managed social services in the United States. The federal authorities, of course, have usually not evaluated those programs which are completely under federal jurisdiction; they have only evaluated those over which federal controls are incomplete. Similarly, state governments have often insisted on evaluating the special funding they create in welfare and education but ordinarily do not evaluate the programs which they fund in a routine way.

Evaluation and inspection are public assertions of societal control which violate the assumption that everyone is acting with competence and in good faith. Violating this assumption lowers morale and confidence. Thus, evaluation and inspection undermine the ceremonial aspects of organizations.

Proposition 6. *Institutionalized organizations seek to minimize inspection and evaluation by both internal managers and external constituents.*

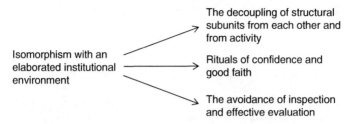

Figure 4.3. The effects of institutional isomorphism on organizations

Decoupling and the avoidance of inspection and evaluation are not merely devices used by the organization. External constituents, too, avoid inspecting and controlling institutionalized organizations (Meyer and Rowan 1975). Accrediting agencies, boards of trustees, government agencies, and individuals accept ceremonially at face value the credentials, ambiguous goals, and categorical evaluations that are characteristic of ceremonial organizations. In elaborate institutional environments, these external constituents are themselves likely to be corporately organized agents of society. Maintaining categorical relationships with their organizational subunits is more stable and more certain than is relying on inspection and control.

Figure 4.3 summarizes the main arguments of this section of our discussion.

SUMMARY AND RESEARCH IMPLICATIONS

Organizational structures are created and made more elaborate with the rise of institutionalized myths, and, in highly institutionalized contexts, organizational action must support these myths. But an organization must also attend to practical activity. The two requirements are at odds. A stable solution is to maintain the organization in a loosely coupled state.

No position is taken here on the overall social effectiveness of isomorphic and loosely coupled organizations. To some extent, such structures buffer activity from efficiency criteria and produce ineffectiveness. On the other hand, by binding participants to act in good faith, and to adhere to the larger rationalities of the wider structure, they may maximize long-run effectiveness. It should not be assumed that the creation of microscopic rationalities in the daily activity of workers affects[1] social ends more efficiently than commitment to larger institutional claims and purposes.

Research implications

The argument presented here generates several major theses that have clear research implications.

1. Environments and environmental domains which have institutionalized a greater number of rational myths generate more formal organization. This thesis

---

[1] GK, GSD: In the original text, this word appears as "effects."

leads to the research hypothesis that formal organizations rise and become more complex as a result of the rise of the elaborated state and other institutions for collective action. This hypothesis should hold true even when economic and technical development are held constant. Studies could trace the diffusion to formal organizations of specific institutions: professions, clearly labeled programs, and the like. For instance, the effects of the rise of theories and professions of personnel selection on the creation of personnel departments in organizations could be studied. Other studies could follow the diffusion of sales departments or research and development departments. Organizations should be found to adapt to such environmental changes even if no evidence of their effectiveness exists.

Experimentally, one could study the impact on the decisions of organizational managers, in planning or altering organizational structures, of hypothetical variations in environmental institutionalization. Do managers plan differently if they are informed about the existence of established occupations or programmatic institutions in their environments? Do they plan differently if they are designing organizations lot more or less institutionally elaborated environments?

2. Organizations which incorporate institutionalized myths are more legitimate, successful, and likely to survive. Here, research should compare similar organizations in different contexts. For instance, the presence of personnel departments or research and development units should predict success in environments in which they are widely institutionalized. Organizations which have not institutionalized structural elements in their environments should be more likely to fail, as such unauthorized complexity must be justified by claims of efficiency and effectiveness.

More generally, organizations whose claims to support are based on evaluations should be less likely to survive than those which are more highly institutionalized. An implication of this argument is that organizations existing in a highly institutionalized environment are generally more likely to survive.

Experimentally, one could study the size of the loans banks would be willing to provide organizations which vary only in (*a*) the degree of environmental institutionalization and (*b*) the degree to which the organization structurally incorporates environmental institutions. Are banks willing to lend more money to firms whose plans are accompanied by econometric projections? And is this tendency greater in societies in which such projections are more widely institutionalized?

3. Organizational control efforts, especially in highly institutionalized contexts, are devoted to ritual conformity, both internally and externally. That is, such organizations decouple structure from activity and structures from each other. The idea here is that the more highly institutionalized the environment, the more time and energy organizational elites devote to managing their organization's public image and status and the less they devote to coordination and to managing particular boundary-spanning relationships. Further, the argument is that in such contexts managers devote more time to articulating internal structures and relationships at an abstract or ritual level, in contrast to managing particular relationships among activities and interdependencies.

Experimentally, the time and energy allocations proposed by managers presented with differently described environments could be studied. Do managers, presented with the description of an elaborately institutionalized environment, propose to spend more energy maintaining ritual isomorphism and less on monitoring internal conformity? Do they tend to become inattentive to evaluation? Do they elaborate doctrines of professionalism and good faith?

The arguments here, in other words, suggest both comparative and experimental studies examining the effects on organizational structure and coordination of variations in the institutional structure of the wider environment. Variations in organizational structure among societies, and within any society across time, are central to this conception of the problem.

REFERENCES

Aiken, Michael and Jerald Hage. 1968. Organizational Interdependence and Intraorganizational Structure. *American Sociological Review,* 33 (December):912–30.

Bell, Daniel. 1973. *The Coming of Post-industrial Society.* New York: Basic.

Bendix, Reinhard. 1964. *Nation-Building and Citizenship.* New York: Wiley.

—— 1968. Bureaucracy, in David L. Sills, *International Encyclopedia of the Social Sciences.* New York: Macmillan, pp. 206–19.

Berger, Peter L. and Thomas Luckmann. 1967. *The Social Construction of Reality.* New York: Doubleday.

Blau, Peter M. 1956. *Bureaucracy in Modern Society.* New York: Random House.

—— 1970. A Formal Theory of Differentiation in Organizations. *American Sociological Review* 35 (April):201–18.

Blum, Alan F. and Peter McHugh. 1971. The Social Ascription of Motives. *American Sociological Review,* 36 (December):98–109.

Callahan, Raymond E. 1962. *Education and the Cult of Efficiency.* Chicago: University of Chicago Press.

Carlson, Richard O. 1962. *Executive Succession and Organizational Change.* Chicago: Midwest Administration Center, University of Chicago.

Clark, Burton R. 1956. *Adult Education in Transition.* Berkeley: University of California Press.

Dalton, Melville. 1959. *Men Who Manage.* New York: Wiley.

Dowling, John and Jeffrey Pfeffer. 1975. Organizational Legitimacy, *Pacific Sociological Review,* 18 (January):122–36.

Downs, Anthony. 1967. *Inside Bureaucracy.* Boston: Little, Brown.

Durkheim, Emile. 1933. *The Division of Labor in Society.* New York: Macmillan.

Ellul, Jacques. 1964. *The Technological Society.* New York: Knopf.

Emery, Fred L. and Eric L. Trist. 1965. The Causal Texture of Organizational Environments, *Human Relations* 18 (February):21–32.

Freeman, John Henry. 1973. Environment, Technology and Administrative Intensity of Manufacturing Organizations. *American Sociological Review* 38 (December):750–63.

Goffman, Erving. 1967. *Interaction Ritual.* Garden City, NY: Anchor.

Hawley, Amos H. 1968. Human Ecology, in David L. Sills (ed.), *International Encyclopedia of the Social Sciences.* New York: Macmillan, pp. 328–37.

Hirsch, Paul M. 1975. Organizational Effectiveness and the Institutional Environment. *Administrative Science Quarterly* 20 (September):327–44.

Homans, George C. 1950. *The Human Group.* New York: Harcourt, Brace.

March, James G. and Johan P. Olsen. 1976. *Ambiguity end Choice in Organizations.* Bergen: Universitetsforlaget.

—— and Herbert A. Simon. 1958. *Organizations.* New York: Wiley.

Merton, Robert K. 1940. Bureaucratic Structure and Personality. *Social Forces* 18 (May): 560–8.

Meyer, John W. and Brian Rowan. 1975. Notes on the Structure of Educational Organizations. Paper presented at annual meeting of the American Sociological Association, San Francisco.

Mills, C. Wright. 1940. Situated Actions and Vocabularies of Motive. *American Sociological Review,* 5 (February):904–13.

Ouchi, William and Mary Ann Maguire. 1975. Organizational Control: Two Functions. *Administrative Science Quarterly* 20 (December):559–69.

Parsons, Talcott. 1956. Suggestions for a Sociological Approach to the Theory of Organizations I. *Administrative Science Quarterly* 1 (June): 63–85.

—— 1971. *The System of Modern Societies.* Englewood Cliffs, NJ: Prentice-Hall.

Perrow, Charles. 1970. *Organizational Analysis: A Sociological View.* Belmont, CA: Wadsworth.

Salancik, Gerald R. and Jeffrey Pfeffer. 1974. The Bases and Use of Power in Organizational Decision Making. *Administrative Science Quarterly* 19 (December):453–73.

Scott, W. Richard. 1975. Organizational Structure, in Alex Inkeles (ed.), *Annual Review* of *Sociology. Vol. 1.* Palo Alto, CA: Annual Reviews, pp. 1–20.

Scott, Marvin B. and Stanford M. Lyman. 1968. Accounts. *American Sociological Review* 33 (February):46–62.

Selznick, Philip. 1949. *TVA and the Grass Roots.* Berkeley: University of California Press.

Spencer, Herbert. 1897. *Principles of Sociology.* New York: Appleton.

Starbuck, William H. 1976. Organizations and their Environments, in Marvin D. Dunnette (ed.), *Handbook of Industrial and Organizational Psychology.* New York: Rand McNally, pp. 1069–23.

Swanson, Guy E. 1971. An Organizational Analysis of Collectivities. *American Sociological Review* 36 (August):607–24.

Terreberry, Shirley. 1968. The Evolution of Organizational Environments. *Administrative Science Quarterly* 12 (March):590–613.

Thompson, James D. 1967. *Organizations in Action.* New York: McGraw-Hill.

Tyack, David B. 1974. *The One Best System.* Cambridge, MA: Harvard University Press.

Udy, Stanley H., Jr. 1970. *Work in Traditional and Modern Society.* Englewood Cliffs, NJ: Prentice-Hall.

Weber, Max. 1930. *The Protestant's Ethic and the Spirit of Capitalism.* New York: Scribner's.

—— 1946. *Essays in Sociology.* New York: Oxford University Press.

—— 1947. *The Theory of Social and Economic Organization.* New York: Oxford University Press.

Weick, Karl E. 1976. Educational Organizations as Loosely Coupled Systems. *Administrative Science Quarterly* 21 (March):1–19.

Wilensky, Harold L. 1965. The Professionalization of Everyone? *American Journal* of *Sociology* 70 (September):137–58.

Woodward, Joan. 1965. *Industrial Organization, Theory and Practice.* Oxford: Oxford University Press.

Zald, Mayer N. and Patricia Denton. 1963. From Evangelism to General Service: The Transformation of the YMCA. *Administrative Science Quarterly* 8 (September): 214–34.

5

Actorhood

The "Actors" of Modern Society: The Cultural Construction of Social Agency

Much social theory takes for granted the core conceit of modern culture, that modern actors—individuals, organizations, nation states—are autochthonous and natural entities, no longer really embedded in culture. Accordingly, while there is much abstract metatheory about "actors" and their "agency," there is arguably little theory about the topic. This article offers direct arguments about how the modern (European, now global) cultural system constructs the modern actor as an authorized agent for various interests via an ongoing relocation into society of agency originally located in transcendental authority or in natural forces environing the social system. We see this authorized agentic capability as an essential feature of what modern theory and culture call an "actor," and one that, when analyzed, helps greatly in explaining a number of otherwise anomalous or little analyzed features of modern individuals, organizations, and states. These features include their isomorphism and standardization, their internal decoupling, their extraordinarily complex structuration, and their capacity for prolific collective action.

INTRODUCTION

Modern culture depicts society as made up of "actors" – individuals and nation-states, together with the organizations derived from them. Much social science takes this depiction at face value, and takes for granted that analysis must start with these actors and their perspectives and actions. We refer, for instance, to elaborate

Originally published as:

John W. Meyer and Ronald L. Jepperson. 2000. The 'Actors' of Modern Society: The Cultural Construction of Social Agency. Sociological Theory 18:100–120.

An original version of this chapter was prepared for a conference on institutional analysis at the University of Arizona, March 1996. We appreciate the support of the Institute for International Studies at Stanford University in its preparation and the comments of Al Bergesen, John Boli, Thomas Fararo, David Frank, Edgar Kiser, Walter W. Powell, Francisco Ramirez, Evan Schofer, participants in the Arizona conference, and anonymous reviewers. We also draw upon previous discussions with Shmuel Eisenstadt, Ann Swidler, and Morris Zelditch, Jr.

interest-based theories so committed to assuming actorhood that they leave its actual properties unanalyzed. Modern actors are seen as autochthonous and natural entities, no longer really embedded in culture (Meyer 1988). Out of the unspecified core of actorhood emanate the utilities and preferences said to produce the entire social world. In the background of such analyses, one sometimes finds mention of prior cultural rules – for example, a system of property rights in part culturally derived – but these rules are typically presented as preconditions, operating mainly at some earlier point in history. The modern social system at present is imagined to operate via fully realized and unfettered actors pursuing their goals (if under institutional "incentives" and "constraints," understood as background conditions).

This realist (as opposed to phenomenological) imagery[1] is so dominant and legitimated that it is taken as a kind of faith by scholars in most North American circles, and recently in many European ones as well. Standard culturalist imagery departs only somewhat from this vision. It often features a dramatic emphasis on human voluntarist interpretation and action (Alexander 1986; Sewell 1992), but it also provides little specification of what the modern agent is like. Such scholars add attention to "meanings," but often seem to assume, we think erroneously, that they arise out of the raw (untutored, unscripted) social experience of actors. In so doing, these scholars often underplay the highly constructed, scripted, and legitimated character of modern actorhood – despite their emphasis on culture.

Accordingly, there is more abstract metatheory about "actors" and their "agency," than substantive arguments about the topic. This characterization is arguably valid even if one takes into account European discussions, which have perhaps been more attentive to the constructed features of actorhood, and less prone to reify actors. In social theory generally, modern actorhood is routinely treated as a given condition or attainment – or even a universal telos of human or social nature. Assumptions about actorhood are now so taken for granted that social scientists use the term "actor" with little reflexivity to denote people or organized groups, as if such entities are by definition actors.

In this chapter, in contrast, we take seriously the idea that the modern "actor" is a historical and ongoing cultural construction, and that the particulars of this construction should help to account for a number of specific features of actorhood, including anomalous and unnoticed ones. We offer direct social theory taking up this topic. In doing so, we depend upon two main analytical departures.

First, we see the actorhood of individuals, organizations, and national states as an elaborate system of social *agency* that has a long and continuing religious and

---

[1] As indicated, by "realism" we invoke a contrast with more "phenomenological" or "constructivist" imagery. The underlying analytical dimension demarcates the degree to which units or relations under analysis are thought to be relatively generic (i.e., not very historically or contextually specific in "realist" imagery) versus highly constructed (i.e., quite historically or contextually generated); see Thomas, Meyer, Ramirez, and Boli (1987: ch. 1); Jepperson (1991). "Realism" also often entails actor-centric arguments that see activity as controlled by tightly connected incentives and resources. These may arise from the purposes of actors themselves (who may be conceived to be hard-wired [natural] systems [e.g., rational actors]), or from purposes built into wider networks or systems of control.

postreligious evolution.[2] Our main theme on this issue concerns the ongoing relocation into society of agency originally located in transcendental authority (gods) or in natural forces environing the social system. Over time these exogenous forces (e.g., godly powers) have been relocated as authority immanent within society itself, enlarging social agency, relocating authority from god to church, from church to state, from church and state to individual souls and later citizens. Recognizing the spiritual immanence of Western societies (as Durkheim did) will help us see the development of modern actorhood more as a cultural devolution – from god to society, on to individuals and organizations – than a natural evolution from less to more social complexity, or an aggregate product of interest-based struggles over naturally given goals.

Second, we call attention to the ways in which this cultural system constructs the modern actor as an *authorized agent* for various interests (including those of the self). This agentic construction, we will argue, accounts for much of the uniqueness of modern actorhood. Notably, participants in modern society enact in their identities substantial agency for broad collective purposes. Under the terms of a wider rationalized and universalistic culture, they are constructed as having the capacity and responsibility to act as an "other" to themselves, to each other, and indeed for the wider cultural frame itself (as with Mead's "generalized other"). We see this authorized agentic capability as an essential feature of what modern theory calls an "actor."

In the following section, we sketch the continuously evolving cultural rules that construct, maintain, and elaborate actors. The subsequent section analyzes the types of agency that the modern actor takes up. The following section locates the origins of this system of agency in the modern, especially liberal, polity. The following section then derives a number of propositions about common structural and dynamic features of modern individuals, states, and organizations – the similarities of the three types of actors itself both motivation and subject for our analysis. In this last section, we also present propositions about a number of structural features of modern society as a distinctive action system.

In undertaking this analysis, we apply and elaborate one line of contemporary sociological theory, the so-called sociological institutionalism (Thomas, Meyer, Ramirez, and Boli 1987). We purposefully employ the theoretical and empirical resources of this research program rather than attempting to synthesize or address other contemporary theoretical efforts.[3]

---

[2] By "agency" we refer to legitimated representation of some legitimated principal, which may be an individual, an actual or potential organization, a nation-state, or abstract principles (like those of law or science, or more prosaically, high culture or even etiquette). Note that the concept "agency" directly draws attention to the devolution of external authority, and to the external legitimation and chartering of activity. We draw the concept from the standard principal/agent in contrast, though we broaden the typical usage.

[3] We should note that we see our discussion as solidaristic with some European efforts. Foucault's work (and related work) on technologies of the self is obviously directly relevant (Foucault 1979, 1990; Miller and Rose 1994; Miller and O'Leary, 1987), with the idea that specific features of actorhood are generated by specific institutional structures. In this article, we pay less attention to specific meso-institutional structures (such as prisons, asylums, clinics) and more to the basic institutional matrix of the modern Western polity. Most theorists have used agency more as a means of isolating cultural rule

THE CULTURAL RULES OF MODERN ACTORHOOD

We first address the question: What are the cultural rules that constitute agentic actorhood in the first place and that subsequently structure it? We attempt to isolate and explicate rules of actorhood located within the modern Western cultural framework. (We do not attempt to offer an explanation of their origins or development, or a commentary upon such explanations.[4])

It is routinely noted (but as often forgotten) that the Western cultural framework reflects the development, expansion, and secularization of the principally religious models of Western Christendom, a sustained cultural evolution extending into the human rights movements of the contemporary period (Weber 1927; Parsons 1966; McNeill 1963; Eisenstadt 1986, 1987; Mann 1986; Hall 1986; Thomas et al. 1987; Meyer 1989). These models involve a sharp delineation of, and "axial tension" (Eisenstadt 1986) between, society and its natural and spiritual environments. This differentiation is historically associated with the distinctive ongoing "rationalization"[5] of cultural representations of nature, the spiritual domain, and society.

In the Western picture, humans have the capacity and responsibility to modify society and to intervene in lawful nature, in order to reduce discrepancies between mundane realities and transcendentally chartered goals (Eisenstadt 1986). Further, the resolution for this "axial tension" is to be this-worldly, attained through the joint transformation of society and the individual. Society is instrumentalized as a modifiable vehicle for salvation (later, progress and justice) (Bellah 1964; Thomas and Meyer 1984), but in the Western tradition it is the cultural project that is sacred, not some specific control structure in itself. The contrast with China in this respect, from an early historical period, is striking (Weber 1927; Needham 1954; Eisenstadt 1986, 1987).

The spiritual environment in the Western ontology is increasingly simplified and abstract over time, consolidated in a high god who is rendered eternal, lawful, and relatively non-invasive in both nature and society – and thus not what modernists would consider much of an actor. The natural environment in this ontology is represented as unified and lawful, and over time is purged of animist or spiritual forces; it is deadened, and again not filled with what modernists would call actors. The modern cultural dramatics of human actorhood – what Weber called the "rational restlessness" of the modern system – are in good part a precipitate or devolution of these distinctive cultural properties.

---

systems, rather than studying the basic parameters of agentic actorhood as a topic itself (e.g., Bourdieu [1977] has used agency as a theoretical entry in this way). We recognize that Luhmann (1982) developed an elaborate system theory of types of action in different institutional systems. We hesitate to position our work vis-a-vis his, except to say that Luhmann did not, to our knowledge, focus directly on the specific agentic features of modern actorhood.

   [4] For a complementary explanatory sketch, see Meyer (1989).

   [5] By "rationalization" we refer (conventionally) to the cultural accounting of society and its environments, in terms of articulated, unified, integrated, universalized, and causally and logically structured schemes (Weber 1927; Parsons 1966; Kalberg 1994).

The rationalization of representations of nature

In Western culture, nature is tamed and demystified through the extraordinary development, expansion, and authority of science. Nature is represented by elaborate, lawfully defined entities set in imagined lawful relation to each other; the laws involved are held to be universally binding rather than culture-specific. More and more domains are incorporated over time into this cognitive system: psyches, elements of human society, the ecosystem, the forces of the history of the universe and its current physical operation, the evolution of life, species, and human language. Animist and spiritual forces are marginalized or purged, relative to other cultural ontologies (e.g., ancestor spirits disappear from nature). This process is a continuing one, and to this day one finds new rationalizations of previously opaque entities and relations: for instance, particularistic conceptions of life, the earth, and the human race are undercut by discoveries of life in rocks from Mars and far inside the earth, of new planets and stars, of more details of primate evolution, and so on. Or human behavior previously seen as arbitrary is analyzed in terms of psychological, medical, or environmental bases. To be sure, pseudo- and nonscientific spiritualism and naturalism remain as core elements of the cultural ontology (as we discuss below), but they are under constant encroachment and displacement by putatively scientific accounts, which then routinely receive public authoritativeness and standing.

This cultural development has been globalized to an astonishing degree, so that the "scientific outlook" has public authority in most parts of the world, with scientists attaining substantial public (even philosophic) standing in world culture. In most versions of high modernity, the scientific outlook in fact comes to define both rationality and the progressive society, with obviously enormous effects.

Responsible individual and social actors are to take scientific knowledge into account in their activities; in fact, doing so becomes, in an ever-broadening array of world regions, a desideratum of rational behavior (Inkeles and Smith 1974). Individual persons, including business and political leaders, may privately have little scientific knowledge or faith. Routinely they have idiosyncratic, syncretic, mixtures of beliefs, privately consulting all sorts of carriers of spiritual or mystical authority, medical functionaries far removed from scientific grounding, and so on. Scientists themselves declare religious beliefs, but these private belief systems are no longer adequate bases for the posture of proper rational modern actorhood. A competent defense in a trial court or a legislative hearing, or before the court of public opinion, must claim that one's actions were guided by the best scientific and professional advice: the claim that one acted under advice from a palm reader has little standing.[6]

---

[6] We are focusing upon *scientism* – to science as a powerful post-Enlightenment ideology – rather than the actual scientific practices problematized by the "science studies" literature (e.g., Latour 1987; Barnes, Bloor, and Henry 1996). Concern for these meso- and microlevel features of science in principle, complement our macroscopic ones. In fact, the ways in which the disorder and interest of actual scientific activity are cloaked in modern society – so stressed by the "science studies" literature – is a natural product of the extreme legitimacy and prestige of science in the modern polity. This status generates the loose coupling of image and doctrine to actual practice, in ways analyzed in the institutionalist literature about organizations (e.g., Meyer and Scott 1983).

The rationalization of the picture of nature creates some of the elements of modern actorhood. This rationalization creates a constantly expanding set of recognized entities with their functional interrelations and often associated legitimated "interests." New elements and functions are recognized, such as wetlands, species diversity, the functions of the rain forest, the declining whale population, scarce or dangerous metals, and so on. Some of these entities can be seen as having interests that require protection or recognition: one can now argue for the *rights* of whales, or of species in general, or even of geological forms (as in the Gaia movement). Shifting from functional analyses of nature to ideas about rights moves beyond simple scientific rationalization, and obviously adds moral elements. But the underlying rationalized scientific analysis is almost always a crucial component of these rights claims: It is much easier to argue for the rights of whales if one also does an analysis of whales' sentient qualities or their crucial roles in an ecology.

New properties and interests are also discovered in aspects of human society that are represented as being rooted in nature. For instance, new natural properties of the individual, and thus potential rights, are conceived (e.g., self-esteem). New laws and functions defining society are articulated (economic and social development, the costs of dependency), producing definitions of new rights and interests. And new elements of social organization acquire analytic standing, producing organizations that may claim legitimate interests and rights (for women, ethnic groups, the physically limited, fetuses, and also such functionally defined groups as occupations and professions).

Thus the rationalization of nature and the rationalization of society are highly interpenetrated. Proper human activity and social organization must take into account the imagined lawful entities and relations in the natural environment (including the natural laws thought to govern human individuals and social organization, as proclaimed by the psychological and social sciences). But the enriched analysis of nature, in this broad sense, also provides agendas for expanded rational human activity: new analyses create a constant flow of new social problems and possibilities (see Schofer 1999).

Implicit in much realist theoretical imagery is the idea that the processes of rationalization of nature and society more or less inevitably produce the phenomenon of actorhood. For instance, differentiated individuals in a complex society are thought naturally to acquire individual consciousness and actorhood (Simmel, and many others). Differentiated structures in a complex environment are thought naturally to produce formal organizational actors through pressures for efficiency or stability (e.g., North and Thomas 1973). World or regional complexity, differentiation, and conflict are thought to produce naturally the nation-state as a rational actor (Wallerstein 1974; Tilly 1992).

Putting aside the particulars of such analyses, the underlying assumption seems fundamentally mistaken. The rationalization of nature does produce an expanded set of recognized entities and relations. In the social domain, these may be entities accorded with natural functions that have the character of social rights, but they are not yet actors. Whales may be accorded rights of a sort, and validated human actors may represent these rights (as we discuss below), but whales are not actors. Nor are the ethnic cultures displayed in museums, or fetuses, or interest groups not yet formally organized (e.g., labor or women in premodern societies). For an entity with recognized interests to be seen as a legitimate actor requires another step: the cultural construction of the capacity and authority to act for itself. We argue that in the modern system, this capacity comes from the wider cultural system, and can best be seen as the cultural devolution of originally spiritual agency.

The rationalization of representations of the spiritual world, and the rise of the agentic actor

As with the natural world, the spiritual one has been highly rationalized in the Western ontology. There has been a remarkably continuous unification, generalization, and taming of the spiritual domain and spiritual authority (a process discussed by both Durkheim and Weber; also by Bellah 1964; Collins 1982: chap. 2; Eisenstadt 1986; Thomas et al. 1987). Spiritual forces have been progressively consolidated into a single high god, in a relatively linear religious evolution. In a strikingly stepwise way, god "takes leave of time and space" (Durkheim), and his anthropomorphic qualities decline. God does not so much die (contrary to Nietzsche), but is deadened in the sense of greatly reduced agency. This evolution continues in the contemporary period, with the reconstruction of god as basic principles (as evidenced, for instance, in much modern religious thought of the high culture sort, or in "the force" of *Star Wars*).

Further, in the modern Western ontology, there is an ongoing diminishment of the domain under direct transcendental-spiritual control. This domain becomes more truly transcendental over time, with the pullout of god from society. It is also highly rationalized, as in the ongoing and aggressive search for more common and universal principles of justice and morality (as in modern attempts to create and elaborate global conceptions of "human rights" and to implement them in legal systems [Chapter 15]).

With the increasing transcendence and inertness of god, agency and authority are relocated immanently in society's structures and rationales. Some agency is built into modern pictures of the agentic authority and responsibility of the state and other organizations; much devolves to the modern individual, who is empowered with more and more godlike authority and vision.

Social and individual actors thereby attain greater reality and standing, and more functions and responsibilities – they are now agents of higher principles, and hence highly legitimated in ways unique to modern Western culture. Elaborate schemas of socioeconomic development become the responsibilities and purposes of nation-states. These states are truly projects in ways far more elaborated than for other polities (Thomas and Meyer 1984). The status of the individual as responsible creature and carrier of purpose and the moral law is greatly enhanced (McNeill 1963; Hall 1986; Dumont 1986; Thomas et al. 1987). Individuals attain sacral standing across more and more dimensions: age, sex, race, ethnicity, sexuality, and physical limitations. Accordingly, they enact both more self and more public standing than do people outside the modern system (Inkeles and Smith 1974; Jepperson

1992). Structured social organizations arise to pursue, with great legitimacy, validated individual and collective purposes and responsibilities. Whole societies are
reconstructed around a network of historically distinctive rationalized purposive
associations (Coleman 1973). Individuals and societies together are seen as the
authorized centers and sources of all social action (hence the dominance of actor
and action theories in social science). "Man" as actor – individuals, organizations,
states – carries almost the entire responsibility for the now-sacralized human project,
with gods, other spiritual forces, ancestors, or an animated nature drained of agency.

We should note that all this cultural development has been globalized to a very
substantial (in fact, astonishing) degree in the period following World War II. First,
both the cultural system and the associated roster of agentic actors have expanded on
a nearly worldwide basis: The nation-state form, with individuals as citizens, and
organizations as components, is found worldwide. Second, while there are attempts
in Asia and the Islamic world to limit the spread of models originating in the West,
a surprising feature of the modern system is how completely the Western models
dominate world discourse about the rights of individuals, the responsibilities and
sovereignty of the state, and the nature of preferred organizational forms. One can as
yet find little impact of other huge civilizational forces (China, Islam) on the standardized rule structures found in those institutions, organizations, and associations
operating on a world scale (see, e.g., Chapter 8). Third, and most recently, the
various formal "others" of this system – collectives representing sciences, professions,
and rationalized world associations – explicitly deploy the expanded standards and
putative truths as collective culture for the world, with substantial influence (Boli and
Thomas 1999). In effect, Christendom had some modest attainments as a missionary
movement, but has achieved vastly greater hegemony in its transformation into
science, law, and rationalized education.

The resulting identity of "The Actor"

We have discussed what seem to be the essential cultural ingredients of modern
actorhood. First, stemming from the rationalization of the realm of nature, and of
aspects of humans and human society seen as part of nature, one finds the natural
human entity with valid and lawful functions and interests. This is the human
individual or group that can be represented as behaving in terms of natural
(scientifically expressible) laws. Second, devolving from rationalized spiritual authority, one finds the legitimated agent and carrier of authority, responsibility, and
capacity to act in history. The integration of these two elements in a single, imagined
natural and spiritual entity is what modernists mean by the term "actor."

FEATURES OF THE AGENTIC ACTOR

The constructed capacity for responsible agency is the core of modern actorhood. In
this section, we try to isolate the different sorts of agency that constitute modern

actors. We distinguish agency for a self, for other actors, for entities that are not actors, and for principle (i.e., for cultural authority).

Agency for the self

The modern actor is a mobilized agent for its self (or for other "principals," as we will discuss below). Modern culture creates an agentic individual managing goals thought to reside in a personality or life course (the "principal" for individuals); a sovereign state managing goals of a national society; and an organizational structure managing its legitimated interests.

The two cultural sources of this structure discussed above both introduce a great deal of standardization and scripting. A first aspect is widely recognized: modern cultural formulations defining individual, organizational, or state entities and interests are highly standardized, and evolve and expand in similar ways over time. For example, discourses of self-esteem, originally reflective of alternative lifestyles, over time transform into standard technology of the self, thereby elaborating it. The modern organization similarly has elaborated over time, with the expansion of accounting, personnel, information, planning, safety, and environmental elements. The modern state is an agent for an expanding array of domains of national society, from economic or scientific development to education to individual health – with each domain itself conceived more expansively over time.

Most social theory has recognized one way or another that core social entities have been more elaborately constructed over time. The agentic aspect and its underlying spiritual devolution are less well recognized. Modern individuals, organizations, and nation-states, in becoming legitimated agents for their underlying interests, incorporate the highly standardizing responsibility to enact imagined moral and natural principles. The proper modern agentic individual, for instance, manages a life, carrying a responsibility not only to reflect self-interest but also the wider rationalized rules conferring agency. Helplessness, ignorance, and passivity may be very natural human properties, but they are not the properties of the proper, effective agent. Modern agentic actors involve themselves in all sorts of efforts elaborating their agentic capabilities, efforts that often have only the most distant relation to their raw interests. Organizations, for example, develop improved information systems toward no immediate goal (Feldman and March 1981; Brunsson 1989), or management training programs stressing individual self-development and organizational culture (Scott and Meyer 1994). Nation-states clearly devote resources to the development of agentic capabilities that are little related to their actual political agendas: for example, science policy (Finnemore 1996a), or the elaboration and celebration of internal cultural features (e.g., Hobsbawm 1983; Anderson 1991).

Agency for other actors

Assisted by elaborate structures of otherhood, individuals and collectives take up available cultural technology for developing actorhood (Brunsson 1989). Thus mobilized in standardized and stylized ways, supported by a host of external cultural definitions and social structures, modern actors can easily shift from agency for the self to agency for other actors – from actorhood to otherhood – whether these other actors be states, organizations, or individuals.

In fact, a striking feature of the modern system is the extreme readiness with which its actor participants can act as agents for other actors. They can do this, with rapidity and facility, as employees and consultants, as friends and advisors, as voters and citizens. They can do it in exchange for resources, or as a free good to the world around them. And they do it much more often and more easily than do participants in less rationalized cultural systems. Ready opining, on the widest range of issues, is a notable feature of modern individuals and is distinctive to them (Lerner 1959; Inkeles and Smith 1974). Organizations display their successes on every occasion (rather than conceal them from their competitors, as in older and more typically rational behavioral forms); national states are eager to serve as models for the world around them with cascades of assistance programs, publicity, and displays before international organizations (Chapter 8).

Since individuals and organizations and nation-states incorporate an enormous amount of standardizing rationalized material, it becomes very easy for them to put their standardized agency at the service of other actors. Individuals in an instant can advise others of their true interests, or can participate in complete good faith as advisors and consultants to organizations that they might have known nothing about previously. And, of course, they can nearly instantaneously become, as voters, agents of the greater national collectivity. Modern organizations and states have similar and more powerful agentic capabilities, and can advise and collaborate in all sorts of collective activity: they also serve as agents of their own individual members or citizens.

Agency for nonactor entities

Modern actors also mobilize as agents for the imagined interests of nonactor entities recognized in the cultural system. For instance, individuals, organizations, and nation-states now mobilize their agency on behalf of the ecosystem, whales, trees, birds, plants, or species in general: that is, on behalf of nonactors. They similarly mobilize agency for imagined potential actors, such as fetuses, the unorganized poor, the unrecognized and unorganized groups of women or laboring classes, dying languages and cultures, and so on. The capacity to do so arises from the modern actor's imagined competence in applying natural and moral law, competence that can be put to the service of the widest variety of legitimated entities, whether the entities are themselves actors or not.

Agency for principle (i.e., for cultural authority)

As we have discussed, the modern actor is in good part an agent operating under very general rules, and can serve as agent or consulting others for a wide variety of legitimated principals having recognized functions or interests: selves, other actor individuals or organizations, entities without actorhood. But one third-party principal is, in practice, always involved: in becoming an authorized agent (of the self, or of any other), the proper modern actor assumes responsibility to act as agent of the imagined natural and moral law. Otherwise the actor risks either incompetence or corruption.

At the extreme, agentic actors represent not any recognized entity or interest, but instead become purely agents of principle. This priestly stance is the most highly developed and respected role running through the modern system and carrying much authority in it. Thus moral and legal theorists pursue and develop abstract models independent of any practical interest, and are highly admired. Honored scientists attend to matters of presumed truth remote from any consequence: the moons of Jupiter (the matter that put Galileo in trouble once again receives attention); the origins of the universe, or of humankind, or language; attempted communication with putative intelligent life elsewhere. The authoritative voice of the sciences and professions stems from the posture of pure otherhood; that is, from their claim to speak for wider truths and standards, beyond any local situation or interests (Meyer 1994a).

Prevailing social theory has little to offer in explanation of the extraordinary prestige attached to agency for principle, and (as we discuss below) very poorly accounts for the social authority of the professions and professionals involved. The prestige and authority of this form of agency become explicable if we explicitly recognize the dependence of modern actorhood on a rationalized culture of natural and moral law. The carriers of this law can be seen as crucial authorities in the maintenance of actorhood. If fostering the actorhood of states, organizations, and individuals is a crucial desideratum in the modern system, the consultants who help actors do so are prized authorities (Brunsson 1989; Meyer 1994a).

THE LINKAGE OF AGENTIC ACTORHOOD TO MODERN, ESPECIALLY LIBERAL, SYSTEM

The agency system we are analyzing is very much a historical construction in the general sense already discussed: it arises from the religious and legal history of the West. It is also a construction in a more specific sense: its elaboration is tied to the liberal model of sociopolitical organization that has dominated the post-World War II epoch, with its emphasis on individual rather than diffuse corporate or state authority, on democratic forms and the market economy, and so on. The dominance of the United States during the period, and the collapse of Europe (and, relatedly, corporatism) at the beginning of the period, are obviously consequential historical factors.

The cultural model of the liberal system is Protestant and Anglo-American in origin, but has been carried worldwide in the latter half of the twentieth century. Versions can be found throughout the global system and its organizations (e.g., the United Nations system, the World Bank, and so on). The liberal model legitimates an actor (a self or an interest) as an abstract, rather contentless, entity in social space. It also constructs a standardized agent who manages, elaborates, and standardizes that self, employing the latest cultural recipes: elaborate psychological theories for individuals (e.g., self-development [Frank, Meyer, and Miyahara 1995]), organizational theories for firms (participatory management, budgeting systems), development theories for nation-states (neoclassical economics [Biersteker 1992], science management [Finnemore 1996a], and welfare policies [Strang and Chang 1993]). The liberal model is distinctive in foregrounding "action," creating extensive psychological, biological, and organizational theory about this action, and focusing upon proper agency arrangements and enactment.

Cultural devolutions other than this liberal form occurred within the broader Western tradition, producing different distributions of social agency. Some featured subunit actorhood much less. The varying devolutions reflect secularized versions of the different religious formations within Western Christendom (McNeill 1963; Jepperson and Meyer 1991). In these religious polities, and in the secularized formations that eventually built upon them, spiritual charisma could be distributed across three main locations: (*a*) in a central institutional complex (a monarchy, a high Church, a state); (*b*) in the community as an organic body (that is, in a sacralized matrix of relations [e.g., a system of corporate orders]); or (*c*) in spiritualized subunits (namely, individuals empowered as souls carrying responsibility for responsible action, whether individually or associationally).

Variations in the social construction of agentic actorhood follow. If a center arrogates spiritual authority and agency, organizations and individuals (and civil society) will tend to have less autonomous agentic standing. If instead relations are more sacralized, then both the center (for instance, a state) and subunits will tend to have less charismatic standing. In the more liberal forms that became dominant in the world polity after World War II, much more charisma was located in subunits (individuals and associations in civil society), producing the system of agentic actorhood under analysis here. In each case, godly authority and powers devolve into social organization, but find different institutionalization.

Consider for instance the more corporate Western traditions such as the Germanic and Scandinavian ones. Locating more authority and charisma in a social community as an organic body (i.e., in a relational system), they gave more substantive content to their constituent (more corporate) social entities: For instance, some organizations or corporate structures may be seen as having long-standing natural rights; theories of personality (and gender) feature more biological grounding (Jepperson 1992; Frank, Meyer, and Miyahara 1995). While this (extrasocial) content of the self (or interests) is expanded, the idea of agentic actorhood is less developed and less central.

Even in the current period, after much standardizing pressure, the more corporatist national variants of the modern system (Germany, Scandinavia, and Westernized Japan) more overtly specify the tasks and functions that specific entities are naturally supposed to want and do. Such corporatist arrangements tend to trap entities in explicitly articulated role and hierarchic structures, and less in scripted agency – placing more emphasis on direct training, control, and discipline (Hofstede 1980; Laurent 1983; Meyer 1983; Jepperson and Meyer 1991). Insuring a proper agency is a source of much uncertainty and anxiety, hence organizational theories are notoriously more power-oriented in Central Europe than in the Anglo-American tradition (Crozier 1964; Hofstede 1980; Laurent 1983). In contrast, the liberal system organizes more directly around the agency: it is in a literal sense more an action system than a control structure (thus the notoriously loose, ill-defined, overlapping, and sprawling organizing structures of the liberal system [Meyer and Scott 1983]). Organizational theories vary accordingly, with their historically distinctive emphasis on informal, tacit, associational coordination, rather than control.

The individual in both these models is "embedded" in social organization, but in the more dominant liberal variant of the modern system, the individual is entrapped in a standardized agency more than in explicit social control schemes. Correspondingly, the modern (especially liberal) individual displays more standardized "public virtues" (Dahrendorf 1967) relative to nonmodernists, and relative to elaborated private qualities. This is the flattened selfhood but exaggerated actorhood – in our language, the agency profile – so noted for American individuality (classically by Tocqueville; and analyzed by Dahrendorf 1967; Varenne 1977; Thomas et al. 1987; Jepperson 1992).

IMPLICATIONS FOR UNDERSTANDING FEATURES OF MODERN ACTORHOOD AND SOCIAL STRUCTURE

More direct explanations of a number of features of contemporary social structure become possible if one begins with an analysis of an expanding system of social agency, with a system of constructed "actors" as its carrier. Unacknowledged agency dynamics permeate and shape modern social structure. "Actors" are agents for larger realities and larger imagined truths: they are in substantial part monads of a larger cultural project. Accordingly, they celebrate ideals of mobilized agency, and enter into the sweeping collective action that is distinctive to modern society. In this section, we call attention first to features of modern actorhood that come into clearer relief once one attends to its agentic character. Then we bring to attention a number of features of collective authority and action that otherwise go unnoticed or are only arduously accounted for in conventional lines of argument.

The structure of the modern actor

1. The tension between principal and agent within the actor – between legitimated self and agency for this self – generates consequential inconsistencies and contradictions (as in any principal-agent relationship), and occasions ongoing cultural evolution.

Many of the deepest contradictions of "interest" faced by modern actors are those between the interests of the underlying self and those of highly standardized and enacted agency. The underlying self has goals to pursue or interests to protect; the agent is charged to manage this interestedness effectively, but in tune with general

principles and truths. This structure creates contradictions and tensions. For instance, the interests of the university as a raw actor[7] involve the production of
education and research at low cost; in contrast, the goals of the university as agent
are to have effective management control, the maximum number of expensive
professors, and the complete array of prestigious programs. In parallel fashion,
interests of the nation include socioeconomic development and the enhancement
of individual welfare; in contrast, goals of the state as agent involve expensive
structures and controls (e.g., the creation and expansion of decorative economic
plans and policies, the maintenance of expensive universities) far removed from these
objectives.

This same tension is dramatic for individuals, and is celebrated in classical
psychological dualisms (I versus Me, long-run versus short-run interests) and in
associated analytical conundra (weakness of the will, self-deception, altruism, attitudes versus behavior). Individuals follow their Id (or Inner Child, or whatever) and
sacrifice agentic effectiveness, or they build up their agency in canonical ways, but
then lose touch with their self. To escape highly standardized agency, actors search
for new authenticities or for particularistic cultures in which to express their selves;
more contradictions and cultural evolutions follow (e.g., therapists and consultants
struggle to reconcile the demands of "the new organization" with the desiderata of
personal growth).

Much cultural production arises around both the principal and agent elements of
actorhood. In connection with the "principal," there are ideologies of self-development
and expression for individuals, participatory and representational structures in organizational life, and rituals of authenticity in collective life (for example, democracy itself,
or evolving ideologies of diversity). Cultural models of legitimate selfhood or interests
continually evolve, reconceptualizing what natural motives and purposes are supposed
to be: for example, editing (and taming) the imagined true nature of the nation and its
heritages; socializing the true purposes of the organization; developing conceptions of
the natural individual that are harmonious with responsible agency.

Models of agency become ever more encompassing as well: political and organizational theories of information, control, and coordination (and sometimes
suppression of raw actorhood) become more elaborate; psychological models of
self-management become more elaborate as well (and occupy a large share of
American popular culture). Much professional work then goes into the improvement
of the principal–agent linkage. As new stresses are discovered in individuals and
organizations, there is further theorization and modification of the associated prin-
cipal/agent technologies. All this production expands the structural complexity of the
modern actor and also expands its reliance on consultation with a wide range of
others. Models of the individual, the organization, and the state are all much more
ramified, as is the structure of otherhood supporting the enactment of these more
complex models.

---

[7] By "raw actor" we intend to connote an entity pursuing rather unselfconsciously its built-in
purposes – built in either through socialization or prior to socialization (e.g., by biology). These
purposes can be nonlegitimated (e.g., some sexual ones), or legitimated self-interests (e.g., a person
wanting a nice car).

2. The highly standardized and scripted nature of agency produces highly isomorphic actors.

Modern actors enact highly standardizing models for agency and scripts for activity, producing two notable sorts of isomorphism. First, modern agentic actors are highly isomorphic within actor types: people enact highly standardized individualism (Inkeles and Smith 1974; Inkeles 1983; Thomas et al. 1987; Jepperson 1992); organizations are highly (and increasingly) structurally similar (Meyer and Rowan 1977; DiMaggio and Powell 1983; Hannan and Freeman 1989); so are nation-states (see the reviews by Finnemore 1996b; and Chapter 8). This phenomenon is most difficult to explain if these entities are seen as raw actors, as they vary so extremely in resources (100-to-1 in the case of states), and also in backgrounds and conditions.

For instance, the model of the effective modern individual is remarkably isomorphic everywhere, and people in fact come to talk and behave in similar ways when they enact these models (Inkeles and Smith 1974; Inkeles 1983). This is also true, and increasingly so, of organizations, so that management texts and consulting firms now flow rapidly into and across sectors and countries, and organizations have in fact become more isomorphic in their structures, procedures, and accounts (Meyer 1994a). Standardized models and recipes are widespread for nation-states too (e.g., UNESCO or World Bank models), and these entities have also become more isomorphic (McNeely 1995).

Second, the isomorphism of the different actor elements of the modern system is also remarkable: individuals, organizations, and states reveal strikingly similar agentic structures and dynamics – the motivation for this paper. Despite the obvious substantive differences among individuals, groups, and states, the cultural reduction of all to the agent–actor identity produces great commonalities, commonalities that have been taken for granted in most theorizing. Agentic actors at any level are to form clear boundaries and purposes, effectively integrated sovereignty, coherent control systems, and rational technologies.

3. The standardization of agency also helps to account for the decoupling of structural elements of the modern actor.

Institutional lines of argument such as ours have striking advantages in the explanation of the decoupling of structural elements of modern individuals and organizational actors. If these entities are in fact mobilized agents assembled within an expanding rationalistic culture, they are often laboring to enact high policies of the most elaborate and standardized forms. However, they are trying to do so with limited and highly variable resources under great local and variable constraints. Imagine, for instance, a Third World country trying to maintain a broadly legitimated stance toward women's rights in a traditional peasant economy (Berkovitch 1999). In such a situation, decoupling can understandably be extreme.

For individuals, attitudes and opining will be disconnected from actual behavior (a renowned instance of decoupling that has seemed so problematic for conventional theories of personhood, yet seems such a fundamental and consequential characteristic). For organizations, decision-making discourse will be disconnected from decision-making, and both from action (Brunsson 1989). Nation-state constitutional claims and policies are notoriously decoupled from local practices (Boli 1987). In all these cases, the efforts of a highly agentic actor, immersed in general principles of agency, are only loosely coupled to the structures of acting. Many specific decouplings and inconsistencies follow from this underlying structural feature.

One specific decoupling in modern individuals, insufficiently problematized, is revealed in the capacity of individuals to transition quickly from mundane experience into agency for high culture. Marx noted long ago that the Protestant revolutions transformed people into their own priests, and Tocqueville noted how the Americans he met could, at a moment's notice, posture as if they were advisors to the president. Such comportments seem endemic to the modern system, as when professors move from banal private experience to dispensing high cultural principles in their lectures, or when friends deploy the psychological wisdom of the ages to one another (independent of their own competencies). The agentic empowerment from the broader culture here seems obvious, especially in the liberal polities: the modern individual carries a little piece of ex-godly agency, and has a little role in society's mission to act in history. The properly agentic actor is always partly an agent of the broader historical telos of the modern system, and its postures reveal this telos.

4. The ongoing rationalization and expansion of social agency in modern culture greatly heightens the overall structuration of modern actors.

A most remarkable feature of modern actors, neglected or marginalized by most theorizing, is how complexly structured they are, and how much this structuration has increased over time, and continues to increase (Meyer 1994a). Nation-states, holding constant overall resources and basic functions, are much more elaborate than they were even a few decades ago: they have programs, ministries, and policies covering a much wider range of activities (see Finnemore [1996b] and Chapter 8 for general reviews; Barrett and Frank [1999] for population control policy; Berkovitch [1999] for policies on the status of women; Frank, Hironaka, Meyer, Schofer, and Tuma, [1999] for the environment). Organizations too have tended toward structural elaboration, holding constant reasonable measures of size and technical complexity (Meyer 1994a; for specific examples, see Edelman [1990]; Dobbin, Sutton, Meyer, and Scott [1993]; Sutton, Dobbin, Meyer, and Scott [1994]). Older academics can easily remember a time when a university entailed the most modest personnel, accounting, legal, safety, environmental, medical, and counseling offices. The expansion in these structures is apparent in most world regions, and covers every sort of organized social sector. Similarly, the inclination of modern individuals everywhere to form plans and policies of an articulated kind seems clear, and their self-proclaimed dimensions and capacities, fueled by the agentic emphases of modern education, are now legion (Inkeles and Smith 1974; Inkeles 1983; Jepperson 1992; Meyer, Ramirez, and Soysal 1992).

To be sure, expanded structuration partly follows from increased complexity and scale in local activities and resources, as is conventionally theorized. But holding these factors constant, structuration also follows directly from the great cultural rationalization of domains that the agentic society, and hence its responsible actors, must take into account; that is, from the elaboration of the principals and principles of proper agency. The less capable student may now be diagnosed as dyslexic, and if so, s/he should do something about it, in proper agentic fashion. Correspondingly, the agentic university and nation-state should provide otherhood for such students, and incorporate proper policies. Both individual and collective goods are thereby enhanced in this process. The changes represented would proceed much more haltingly (if at all) without the high legitimation involved.

The society of agentic actors

A society of these standardized, decoupled, complexly structured agentic actors is necessarily a distinctive one, quite different from a society of raw actors imagined by some realist social theorists.

1. **A society of agentic actors generates an elaborate social structure of othering activity, given that the modern actor (*a*) shifts routinely from agency for the self into otherhood for the widest variety of other actors, and (*b*) is remarkably receptive to othering.**

(*a*) In an instant, modern actors transform into others; they brim with rule-laden and intendedly thoughtful counsel for each other. This posturing is taken as natural both by them and their principals, with the obvious hypocrisies largely neglected and unproblematic. Modern individuals also stand ready to offer their services as agents for organized actors, as members (of organizations, of polities), and as consultants. A defining characteristic of the virtuous agentic actor is the capability to enter in good faith the structure of an organized actor, and to assume with little question its purposes. And of course, modern individuals comport themselves as advisory others to whole nation-states, in their identities as citizens: they are filled with putative disinterested and relevant opinion. Relatedly, modern organizations and states assume agency responsibilities for the individuals within them, making advice available on the widest variety of topics (from mental health to childrearing).

A "desire for prestige" seems patently inadequate to account for all this enactment of otherhood, given that it is so obviously an institutional construction. Nor is straightforward self-interest sufficient, as much othering is at odds with the more obvious actor interests. For instance, modern actors will take time from their own pursuits to advise and instruct others in general truths, or even to reveal the grounds for their successes to their competitors. This is an inexplicable phenomenon absent attention to the generalized agency of the system.

(*b*) Note too that modern actors show extreme proclivity to avail themselves of the services of these advisory others. As the natural and spiritual environments are rationalized, anarchic uncertainties are tamed and transformed into rationalized uncertainties, with a myriad of others available to help proper agents deal with them. The exorbitant claims to effective and encompassing agency built into modern actors make them eager markets for this othering.

Three forms of otherhood have rapidly expanded. First, organized actors employ professionalized others, such as therapists or accountants or external consulting firms. Second, they show preference for employing those credentialed in the imagined principles of proper agency, via educational programs that are generally far removed from actual practical demands or competencies (Berg 1970; Collins 1979). Third, relatedly, actors themselves seek direct instruction in general principles of agency as much or more than training in actual practice.

Consultants without direct action responsibility are found everywhere the modern system reaches. Nation-states employ them and respond to their teachings in every modern policy domain, from family law to education, medicine, and economics. Organizations structure themselves to depend upon a host of professionalized consultants in every sector, and further, internalize the relevant professionals. And modern individuals are well known for their rampant use of such informal and formal consultancy, helping to manage the mobilization of a proper self and its deployment over a (itself standardized) life course (Meyer 1987).

This ritualized and routinized otherhood might be thought to follow unproblematically from the interests of raw actorhood, on the assumption that the information carried by others is instrumentally useful in accomplishing actor goals. However, this representation is not very credible, for well-known empirical reasons (see, e.g., March 1988). That is, few studies can demonstrate the marginal utility of an economics consultant or a more professionally trained manager or a more highly educated employee, or of a training program in the abstract principles of selfmanagement (Berg 1970). Modern actors nevertheless employ otherhood in the absence of demonstrated utility, or even in cases of highly suspect utility.

This practice becomes comprehensible if one sees the modern actor as mainly a legitimated agent for actorhood. Such an entity would obviously devote resources to the elaboration and demonstration of mobilized agency. Doing so may not help actual action – it may even interfere[8] – but openness to otherhood certainly helps with the construction of legitimated and accountable decisions, and for facilitating talk about rational action (Brunsson 1989).

2. The continuing scientization of nature and rationalization of the moral universe creates constant new discoveries of collective problems occasioning agentic pursuit and fueling the sweeping collective action of the modern system.

There is a continuing search for integrating scientific and legal/moral principles, to respond to inconsistencies, and to enable more effective agency. Differences in economic development, for instance, receive explication in terms of general economic laws, and are then subject to attempted agentic control.

This rationalization becomes an ongoing process, and fosters the extraordinary collective action that is a continuing characteristic, and sometimes even social problem, of the modern system. Thus, the nation-states of this system have been generators of waves and waves of religious and social movements. Human "actors" turn out to be able to mobilize on a large scale around a wide variety of issues, from the welfare of songbirds (Frank et al. 1999) to the worldwide movement for the protection of gay and lesbian rights (Frank and McEneaney 1999), to the abstract pursuit of world economic development (Chabbott 1999). The interstate system

---

[8] See Brunsson (1989) for organizations; March (1988) for individuals (and organizations); Shenhav and Kamens (1991) for states.

itself has been able to mobilize extraordinary levels of war and public commitment to war (notably, as with recent wars, mobilized more around abstract ideological visions than around clear raw-actor interests). Organizations have been able to pursue expansive collective visions: conventional actor theories can sometimes explain "private" behavior of this sort in terms of simple interests, but they have great difficulties explaining the worldwide rise of the various nonprofit structures of the contemporary world.[9]

In fact, theories that see the modern system as made up of unremarkable raw actors have the greatest difficulty in explaining modern collective action in general. They tend instead to erect a supposed failure of collective action – in rather extraordinary denial of empirical evidence – as a descriptive nostrum and analytic problem. The actually massive collective action of the modern system becomes explicable if one situates the now standard "logic of collective action" (Olson 1965; Coleman 1990) within a broader logic of collective agency.[10] Specific agents share in the general social agency of the system. In negotiating the definitions and rules of this broader system, agents negotiate the bases of their own existence and authority. Nominally altruistic collective action can then readily be seen as the expression of self-interest on the part of agents, but it is an interest often at odds with the self-interest of the selves they are to manage.

3. Much authority for collective action, and even social status, is tied to putatively disinterested agency for cultural standards, reflecting the peculiar structural idealism of the modern system.

The great enhancement of the centrality of "disinterested" professionalized others is a notable development of modern society, one difficult to account for in terms of interests or functional requirements. (Indeed demonstrations of functionality are conspicuous by their absence.) The definers and carriers of social agency – especially those more removed from direct responsibility for mundane self-interested actorhood – are granted substantial authority and prominence. The most canonical authority is that of the professional who serves no actor but rather the high truths of the rationalized natural and moral universe: pure otherhood, with no tainting by any particular (i.e., partly profane) actor. In fact, the admixture of pure agency with more mundane interests by professionals is a source of minor pollution-reactions. The therapist, accountant, or lawyer who must bring agency to the service of trivial individual problems is readily seen as tawdry; the scientist who must sacrifice larger concerns with high truth for the practical good of the corporation is readily seen as

---

[9] The recent Rio conference on the environment, for instance, found many thousands of nonprofit organizations (including hundreds of international ones) eager to participate (Frank et al. 1999; see also Boli and Thomas 1999).

[10] Olson (1965) indicated that his "logic of collective action," which specifies self-limiting features of collective action, might not obtain well in religious settings, among others. We are providing a rationale for this scope limitation, in part by specifying and generalizing the "religious" restriction. As we have argued, we see the cultural model of the Western system as religious in character – with substantial implications for expectations about collective action.

partly fallen; the social or physical scientist who entertains policy demands is readily seen as a lesser figure.

Naturally, this system produces expansion of professionals beyond the requirements of function,[11] and it produces the centrality of professionals in the modern system of authority – surely a core feature of modern society. Power comes from many sources in the modern system, but authority seems to flow more from the relative purity of otherhood.

This relative proximity to high culture, and the putatively disinterested carrying of it, helps to account for peculiar idealist features of the modern stratification system, ones not adequately addressed in the literature (Meyer 1994b). The lowest status in this system is accorded to those categorized as simply self-interested actors, that is, those coded as merely working. A little higher are those certified agent-actors with more agency, in more rationalized and universalized structures, that is, those who manage work, or (receiving more status) provide services (if often invisible ones). High status is accorded to those who do not really work at all (in any conventional sense), or even manage work, but rather serve the great exogenous cultural principles: the professionals and scientists who are often agents of no real principal (Treiman 1977). These are people who get the Nobel prizes, or more prosaically, the highest prestige ratings in surveys.[12] Reflective of this cultural structure, educational credentials everywhere become the master ingredient of status (with credentialism expanding in tandem with the increasing structuration of agentic actors). Further, the single biggest predictor of the relative prestige of an occupation is the educational credentialing that it represents.

Given this stratification system, the explosive expansion in numbers of professionals and scientists, along with professional and scientific authority (and discourse), becomes comprehensible. The inflated cultural system depicting humans and their groups as agent-actors creates a social world in which the most valued roles are those with little raw actorhood.

---

[11] The literature on professions is well-developed in its discussion of careerist interests and structures (e.g. Starr 1982; Friedson 1986), and in the exposure of the extraordinary arbitrariness and subjectivity involved in professional work (Latour 1987). It is almost helpless in discussing the extraordinary authority of these bodies (for partial exceptions see Parsons [1954] and Abbott [1988]). Usually, there is an inclination to analyze the professions reductively and exclusively as successful conspiracies. This vision reflects fealty to the dominant analytic realism, but it seems highly limited in substance.

[12] The sociological literature on stratification, much of it doggedly attached to nineteenth-century ideology, earnestly debates whether modern social status derives from the realities of public and collective ("political") actor-resources or private and organizational/individual ("economic") ones. This entire academic discourse has proceeded in scholastic disconnection from the evidence. It is odd – and indicative of social science's rigid resistance to phenomenological challenges – that those researching stratification (an identity constructed via the principle of individual equality) and those researching economic organization (an identity constructed via the principle of collective progress) have no convincing analysis of their own surprisingly elevated social status (let alone of their existence, an even bigger problem). Although these researchers are essentially functionless, and serve no clear actor, they insist on theories of status that feature function and actorhood: a conspicuous example of nonreflexive social science.

SUMMARY AND CONCLUSIONS

We have tried to contribute to a more substantive account of the modern actor, by trying to recover a proper anthropological and historical distance from the modern system. The literatures that might actually situate such actors in history and culture – and thereby actually theorize them – have been strangely peripheralized (sometimes self-peripheralized) in current discourse. Cultural and symbolic anthropologies are peripheralized precisely because they are seen as dealing with highly embedded social participants, wearing masks reflecting the authority of the gods – rather than being proper (and properly analyzable) actors. The religious history of the West is peripheralized as dealing with cultural matters irrelevant to the continuing operation of a world of now properly realized actors. Much political doctrine is similarly peripheralized as representing legal and institutional detail, or "ideas," irrelevant to social theory.

We think social theory should be concerned about these elisions. Modern social participants wear masks, too, now carrying the devolved authority of a high god. The modern mask is actorhood itself, and in wearing it modern participants acquire their agentic authority for themselves, each other, and the moral (and natural) universe (Berger, Berger, and Kellner 1973). They become agents for themselves, true, but under the condition that they are also agents for and under constructed rationalized and universalistic standards. These ideas help explain the distinctive features of the modern actor, we have suggested: its historical and anthropological peculiarity, standardization and professionalization, high structuration, isomorphism within and across types of actors, and extraordinary decoupling. Every one of these features is problematic in conventional realist theorizing – and in the more humanist cultural and interpretive work that has arisen in partial reaction.

The notion of culturally devolved agency also helps explain distinctive features of the modern system of actors. Generations of realist theories, starting from a narrow conception of the actor, have struggled to explain how collective action is possible. They have better conceptions of the blockages to collective action (and of the dynamics of raw actor interests) than of the contextual cultural forces that enable and facilitate it. The one-sided analytic preoccupation has been odd, given the demonstrated capacities and practices of the modernists in building imagined communities on expansive national and world scales – operating as others to each other, and as agents for all sorts of nonactor interests, including the core high principles on which they all depend. Analysis of this matter is greatly furthered if one starts with the matrix of Western culture, and the idea that actorhood in the first place involves agentic authority devolved from a very distant and very high god. Legitimate actorhood has expanded continuously in this cultural system, and as part of its construction so has the capacity for expanded collective action. The dominant realist imagery has also erected a very peculiar "problem of social order" by seeing modern society as featuring a structure/agency tension between great raw social structural actors (principally the state) and raw subunit actors (especially individuals). This theorized tension is decentered (and downsized) if one sees actor agency as itself a central structure of the system: much of modern structuration exists in the formation, standardization, enactment, and celebration of agentic actorhood. It is further reconceptualized if one recognizes that central structures in the modern stratification system – its most distinctive feature a panoply of authoritative sciences and professions – build around relatively pure agency for high and universalistic collective principles.

Contemporary theorists constantly enjoin us to theorize modern society by "bringing actors back in." This injunction has coincided with little actual analysis of actorhood. To develop such analysis, we have argued, one must necessarily see modern individuals, organizations, and states as taking up standardized technologies of agentic authority, devolved from an elaborate Christian and then post-Christian culture.

REFERENCES

Abbott, Andrew. 1988. *The System of Professions*. Chicago: University of Chicago Press.

Alexander, Jeffrey. 1986. *Twenty Lectures on Sociological Theory*. New York: Columbia University Press.

Anderson, Benedict. 1991. *Imagined Communities*. London: Verso.

Barnes, Barry, David Bloor, and John Henry. 1996. *Scientific Knowledge*. London: Athlone.

Barrett, Deborah and David Frank. 1999. Population Control for National Development: From World Discourse to National Policies, in John Boli and George M. Thomas (eds.), *Constructing World Culture: International Nongovernmental Organizations Since 1875*. Stanford, CA: Stanford University Press, pp. 198–221.

Bellah, Robert. 1964. Religious Evolution. *American Sociological Review* 29:358–74.

Berg, Ivar. 1970. *Education and Jobs*. New York: Praeger.

Berger, Peter, L., Brigitte Berger, and Hansfried Kellner. 1973. *The Homeless Mind*. New York: Vintage.

Berkovitch, Nitza. 1999. The International Women's Movement: Transformations of Citizenship, in John Boli and George M. Thomas (eds.), *Constructing World Culture: International Nongovernmental Organizations Since 1875*. Stanford, CA: Stanford University Press, pp. 100–126.

Biersteker, Thomas. 1992. The Triumph of Neoclassical Economics in the Developing World, in James Rosenau and Ernst-Otto Czempiel (eds.), *Governance without Government: Order and Change in World Politics*. Cambridge: Cambridge University Press, pp. 102–31.

Boli, John. 1987. World Polity Sources of Expanding State Authority and Organization, 1870–1970, in George Thomas, John W. Meyer, Francisco Ramirez, and John Boli (eds.), *Institutional Structure: Constituting State. Society, and the Individual*. Newbury Park, CA: Sage, pp. 71–91.

—— and George Thomas (eds.) 1999. *Constructing World Culture: International Nongovernmental Organizations Since 1875*. Stanford, CA: Stanford University Press.

Bourdieu, Pierre. 1977. *Outline of a Theory of Practice*. New York: Cambridge.

Boyle, Elizabeth Heger, and John Meyer. 1998. Modern Law as a Secularized and Global Religious Model: Implications for the Sociology of Law. *Soziale Welt* 49:213–32. Reproduced in Chapter 15.

Brunsson, Nils. 1989. *The Organization of Hypocrisy: Talk, Decisions, and Action in Organizations*. New York: Wiley.

Chabbott, Colette. 1999. Defining Development: The Making of the International Development Field, 1945–1990, in John Boli and George M. Thomas (eds.), *Constructing World Culture: International Nongovernmental Organizations Since 1875*. Stanford, CA: Stanford University Press, pp. 222–48.

Coleman, James S. 1973. *Power and the Structure of Society*. New York: Norton.

—— 1990. *Foundations of Social Theory*. Cambridge, MA: Harvard University Press.

Collins, Randall. 1979. *The Credential Society*. New York: Academic Press.

—— 1982. *Sociological Insight*. New York: Oxford University Press.

Crozier, Michel. 1964. *The Bureaucratic Phenomenon*. Chicago: University of Chicago Press.

Dahrendorf, Ralf. 1967. *Society and Democracy in Germany*. New York: W.W. Norton.

DiMaggio, Paul and Walter W. Powell. 1983. The Iron Cage Revisited: Institutional Isomorphism and Collective Rationality in Organizational Fields. *American Sociological Review* 48:147–60.

Dobbin, Frank, John Sutton, John Meyer, and W. Richard Scott. 1993. Equal Opportunity Law and the Construction of Internal Labor Markets. *American Journal of Sociology* 99:396–427.

Dumont, Louis. 1986. *Essays on Individualism*. Chicago: University of Chicago Press.

Edelman, Lauren. 1990. Legal Environments and Organizational Governance. *American Journal of Sociology* 95:1401–40.

Eisenstadt, Shmuel. 1986. *The Origins and Diversity of Axial Age Civilizations*. Albany: State University of New York Press.

—— 1987. *European Civilization in a Comparative Perspective*. Oslo: Norwegian University Press.

Feldman, Martha and James G. March. 1981. Information in Organizations as Signal and Symbol. *Administrative Science Quarterly* 26:171–86.

Finnemore, Martha. 1996a. *National Interests in International Society*. Ithaca, NY: Cornell University Press.

—— 1996b. Norms, Culture, and World Politics: Insights from Sociology's Institutionalism. *International Organization* 50:325–47.

Foucault, Michel. 1979. *Discipline and Punish*. New York: Vintage.

—— 1990. *The History of Sexuality*. New York: Vintage.

Frank, David and Elizabeth McEneaney. 1999. The Individualization of Society and the Liberalization of State Policies on Same-Sex Sexual Relations, 1985–1995. *Social Forces* 77:911–44.

—— John Meyer, and David Miyahara. 1995. The Individualist Polity and the Centrality of Professionalized Psychology. *American Sociological Review* 60:360–77.

—— Ann Hironaka, John Meyer, Evan Schofer, and Nancy Tuma. 1999. The Rationalization and Organization of Nature in the World Culture, in John Boli and George M. Thomas (eds.), *Constructing World Culture: International Nongovernmental Organizations Since 1875*. Stanford, CA: Stanford University Press, pp. 81–99.

Friedson, Elliot. 1986. *Professional Powers*. Chicago: University of Chicago Press.

Hall, John. 1986. *Powers and Liberties*. New York: Penguin.

Hannan, Michael and John Freeman. 1989. *Organizational Ecology*. Cambridge, MA: Harvard University Press.

Hobsbawm, E. J. (ed.) 1983. *The Invention of Tradition*. Cambridge: Cambridge University Press.

Hofstede, Geert. 1980. *Culture's Consequences*. Beverly Hills, CA: Sage.

Inkeles, Alex. 1983. *Exploring Individual Modernity.* New York: Columbia University Press.
—— and David H. Smith. 1974. *Becoming Modern.* Cambridge, MA: Harvard University Press.
Jepperson, Ronald L. 1991. Institutions, Institutional Effects, and Institutionalism, in Walter W. Powell and Paul J. DiMaggio (eds.), *The New Institutionalism in Organizational Analysis.* Chicago: University of Chicago Press, pp. 143–63.
—— 1992. National Scripts: The Varying Construction of Individualism and Opinion Across the Modern Nation-States. PhD dissertation. Boston: Yale University, Department of Sociology.
—— and John W. Meyer. 1991. The Public Order and the Construction of Formal Organizations, in Walter W. Powell and Paul J. DiMaggio (eds.), *The New Institutionalism in Organizational Analysis.* Chicago: University of Chicago Press, pp. 204–31.
Kalberg, Stephen. 1994. *Max Weber's Comparative-Historical Sociology.* Cambridge: Cambridge University Press.
Latour, Bruno. 1987. *Science in Action.* Cambridge, MA: Harvard University Press.
Laurent, Andre. 1983. The Cultural Diversity of Western Conceptions of Management. *International Studies of Management and Organization* 13:75–96.
Lerner, Daniel. 1959. *The Passing of Traditional Society.* Glencoe, IL: Free Press.
Luhmann, Niklas. 1982. *The Differentiation of Society.* New York: Columbia.
Mann, Michael. 1986. *The Sources of Social Power.* Cambridge: Cambridge University Press.
March, James. 1988. *Decisions and Organizations.* Oxford: Blackwell.
McNeely, Connie. 1995. *Constructing the Nation-State.* Westport, CT: Greenwood.
McNeill, William. 1963. *The Rise of the West.* Chicago: University of Chicago Press.
Meyer, John W. 1983. Conclusion: Institutionalization and the Rationality of Formal Organizational Structure, in John W. Meyer and W. Richard Scott (eds.), *Organizational Environments.* Beverly Hills, CA: Sage, pp. 261–82.
—— 1987. Self and Life Course: Institutionalization and its Effects, in George Thomas et al. (eds.), *Institutional Structure.* Newbury Park, CA: Sage, pp. 242–60.
—— 1988. Society without Culture: A Nineteenth-Century Legacy, in Francisco Ramirez (ed.), *Rethinking the Nineteenth Century.* New York: Greenwood Press, pp. 193–201.
—— 1989. Conceptions of Christendom: Notes on the Distinctiveness of the West, in Melvin Kohn (ed.), *Cross-National Research in Sociology.* Newbury Park, CA: Sage, pp. 395–413.
—— 1994a. Rationalized Environments, in W. Richard Scott, John W. Meyer et al., *Institutional Environments and Organizations.* Newbury Park, CA: Sage, pp. 28–54.
—— 1994b. The Evolution of Modern Stratification Systems, in David B. Grusky (ed.), *Social Stratification in Sociological Perspective.* Boulder, CO: Westview Press, pp. 730–37.
—— and Brian Rowan. 1977. Institutionalized Organization: Formal Structure as Myth and Ceremony. *American Journal of Sociology* 83:340–63. Reproduced in Chapter 4.
—— and W. Richard Scott. 1983. *Organizational Environments.* Beverly Hills, CA: Sage.
—— Francisco Ramirez, and Yasemin Soysal. 1992. World Expansion of Mass Education, 1870–1970. *Sociology of Education* 65:128–49.
—— John Boli, George M. Thomas, and Francisco O. Ramirez. 1997. World Society and the Nation-State. *American Journal of Sociology* 103:144–82. Reproduced in Chapter 8.
Miller, Peter and Timothy O'Leary. 1987. Accounting and the Construction of the Governable Person. *Accounting, Organizations and Society* 12:235–65.
—— and Nikolas Rose. 1994. On Therapeutic Authority: Psychoanalytical Expertise under Advanced Liberalism. *History of the Human Sciences* 7:29–65.

Needham, Joseph. 1954. *Science and Civilization in China*. Cambridge: Cambridge University Press.

North, Robert, and Robert Thomas. 1973. *The Rise of the Western World*. New York: Cambridge University Press.

Olson, Mancur. 1965. *The Logic of Collective Action*. New York: Schocken Books.

Parsons, Talcott. 1954. The Professions and the Social Structure. *Essays in Sociological Theory*. Glencoe, IL: The Free Press, pp. 34–49.

—— 1966. *Societies: Evolutionary and Comparative Perspectives*. Englewood Cliffs, NJ: Prentice-Hall.

Schofer, Evan. 1999. Science Associations in the International Sphere, 1875–1990: The Rationalization of Science and the Scientization of Society, in John Boli and George M. Thomas (eds.), *Constructing World Culture: International Nongovernmental Organizations Since 1875*. Stanford, CA: Stanford University Press, pp. 249–66.

Scott, W. Richard, John W. Meyer et al. 1994. *Institutional Environments and Organizations*. Thousand Oaks, CA: Sage.

Sewell, William H., Jr. 1992. A Theory of Structure: Duality, Agency, and Transformation. *American Journal of Sociology* 98:1–29.

Shenhav, Yehuda, and David H. Kamens. 1991. The 'Costs' of Institutional Isomorphism: Science in Non-Western Countries. *Studies of Science* 21:527–45.

Starr, Paul. 1982. *The Social Transformation of American Medicine*. New York: Basic Books.

Strang, David and Patricia Chang. 1993. The International Labor Organization and the Welfare State: Institutional Effects on National Welfare Spending, 1960–80. *American Sociological Review* 47:235–62.

Sutton, John, Frank Dobbin, John Meyer, and W. Richard Scott. 1994. Legalization of the Workplace. *American Journal of Sociology* 99:944–71.

Thomas, George and John W. Meyer. 1984. The Expansion of the Stile. *Annual Review of Sociology* 10:461–82.

—— —— Francisco Ramirez, and John Boli. 1987. *Institutional Structure: Constituting State, Society, and the Individual*. Beverly Hills, CA: Sage.

Tilly, Charles. 1992. *Coercion, Capital, and European States*. Cambridge, MA: Basil Blackwell.

Treiman, Donald. 1977. *Occupational Prestige in Comparative Perspective*. New York: Academic Press.

Varenne, Herve. 1977. *Americans Together*. New York: Teachers' College Press.

Wallerstein, Immanuel. 1974. *The Modern World System*. New York: Academic Press.

Weber, Max. 1927. *General Economic History*. New York: Greenberg.

6

Diffusion

Institutional Conditions for Diffusion

Much social scientific inquiry seeks to specify the conditions and mechanisms underpinning the flow of social practices among actors within some larger system. Sociology, rural sociology, anthropology, geography, economics, and communication studies all have rich traditions of diffusion research.[1] Virtually everything seems to diffuse: rumors, prescription practices, boiled drinking water, totems, hybrid corn, job classification systems, organizational structures, church attendance, and national sovereignty. Whether viewed as a hindrance to structural-functional analysis (Naroll 1965), the deposited trace of social structure (Burt 1987), or a fundamental source of social control and change (Skog 1986), diffusion seems critical to social analysis.

Most sociological analysis treats diffusion as a primarily, or even exclusively, relational phenomenon. When diffusing practices and adopter identities are rich in social and cultural meaning, however, connectedness seems an insufficient explanatory principle. Our aim is to suggest how institutional conditions operating in wider social systems affect the rate and form of diffusion. We argue that diffusion is importantly shaped and accelerated by culturally analyzed similarities among actors, and by theorized accounts of actors and practices. These institutional conditions are argued to be especially rife in "modern" social systems, and help to account for the intimate connections between socioscientific interest in diffusion and its empirical prevalence.

PREVAILING THEORY AND ITS WEAKNESSES

Diffusion connotes the socially mediated spread of some practice within a population. In Rogers's widely cited definition, diffusion occurs when "an innovation is

Originally published as:

David Strand and John W. Meyer. 1993. Institutional Conditions for Diffusion. Theory and Society 22: 487–511.

This chapter was presented at the "Workshop on New Institutional Theory" Ithaca, NY, November 1991. The authors have made equal contributions to this chapter. We thank Frank Dobbin, Ronald Jepperson, Douglas McAdam, Francisco Ramirez, Arthur Stinchcombe, Sid Tarrow, Marc Ventresca, Harrison White, and the Editors and reviewers of *Theory and Society,* for their helpful comments. Research support was provided by the National Science Foundation (SES 9213152, SES 9213258).

[1] For a general review, see Rogers 1983.

communicated through certain channels over time among the members of a social system."[2] This quite general formulation includes communication and influence processes operating both on and within populations of adopters.[3] It excludes atomistic decision-making processes where actor choices are uninformed by the activities or choices of others.

The aspect of diffusion that most intrigues sociologists is the opportunity it offers for a network analysis. Considerable attention has been paid to mapping lines of effective communication and influence within populations, particularly via direct contacts between prior and potential adopters.[4] Such point-to-point diffusion processes resonate with the "sociological realism" dominating contemporary sociological analysis. In such accounts, social entities (often seen as purposive, rational "actors") and their network relations are understood as jointly providing a sufficient basis for the explanation of social behavior.

Relational models suggest that rates of diffusion should vary with levels of interaction between prior and potential adopters. When the adopted practice is socially meaningless (for example, in the spread of measles), physical proximity may be all that is required for transmission to occur. When adoption is socially meaningful, it is common to think of actors as making different choices cognitively available to each other, developing shared understandings, and exploring the consequences of innovation through each other's experience.

Exchange dependence is generally thought to increase further the flows of elements. Narrowly, common conventions or protocols are needed or advantageous at the boundaries where exchange occurs. Handshaking arrangements aid in interpersonal (and electronic) exchange, and common accounting systems in interorganizational exchange. Businesses benefit when they buy the kinds of keyboards secretaries are familiar with, and typewriting schools benefit when they train secretaries to use the kinds of keyboards businesses own (David 1985). More broadly, similarities in internal structure may arise from transactions. The flow from secondary to tertiary education promotes common definitions of students, subjects, and grading, and the values arising from the exchange may homogenize internal structures too.

Theories of diffusion emphasize the rationalities involved. This occurs in part through attention to the characteristics of practices that spread widely. A core idea is that practices are adopted to the extent that they appear more effective or efficient than the alternatives. Further ideas elaborate on conditions that facilitate rational choice: consistency with prior attributes or policies, the simplicity of the novel practice, opportunities for experimentation, and so on (Fliegel and Kivlin 1966).[5]

---

[2] Rogers 1983: 14. We use the terms "practice" and "innovation" interchangeably to refer to the diffusion item, which may take a variety of forms (a structural element, a policy, an attitude, and so on).

[3] Reviews of mathematical models include Bartholomew 1982; Mahajan and Peterson 1985.

[4] An alternative approach treats actors as immediately sensitive to the number of prior adopters, rather than indirectly affected via a point-to-point transmission mechanism. See Granovetter and Soong 1983.

[5] Also see Rogers 1983.

In addition, diffusion itself is often described as a rational process. Learning from the experiences of others appears a sensible and even optimal strategy where means–ends relationships are not well understood or defy calculation (Banerjee 1982). Where the actions of others objectively change costs and benefits (as when the fact that others routinely drive on the right side of the road increases the benefits of doing so), diffusion is again rational (Arthur 1989). And in a more phenomenological vein, the process underlying diffusion can be seen as an inherently sense-making one, where actors jointly construct an understanding of the appropriateness and worth of some practice.

Sociological realism, with its focus on actors and relationships, has generated much useful diffusion research. Coleman, Katz, and Menzel's work on the prescription of an antibiotic is a classic in this tradition (Coleman, Katz, and Menzel 1966). Coleman and his colleagues demonstrated the relational basis of diffusion by noting that temporal patterns of adoption differed for socially integrated and socially isolated doctors. An S-shaped curve of adoptions among socially integrated doctors suggested a contagion process, where physicians learned about and adopted the drug through interaction with prior adopters. By contrast, socially isolated physicians adopted the drug at a constant rate, suggesting dependence on sources of information outside the adopting population.

Much continuing work seeks to specify further the relational basis of diffusion. A number of analyses treat diffusion as a spatial process, where the probability of transmission is some function of geographical distance.[6] Others have used diffusion processes to examine social structure, generally conceived as a network of social relations.[7] Relational analyses have become increasingly sophisticated: for example, Burt's reanalysis of the Coleman et al. data argues that structurally equivalent actors – individuals whose relations to all others are similar – influence each other more than do directly connected actors.

Despite the vigor of these lines of research, problems remain. Empirically, many systems witness rapid and unstructured diffusion unpredicted by the above considerations. For example, the modern world system has been observed to exhibit remarkable homogeneity in organizational structures and ideologies. Ikenberry notes a few of the policies that have diffused internationally – nineteenth-century free-trade policy, social Darwinism, Keynesian economic planning, liberal multilateralism, and privatization (Ikenberry 1989). Institutions for mass education and social security have spread rapidly among states, and even national sovereignty diffused among colonial dependencies.[8] Yet levels of international interaction and interdependence are not self-evidently high, relative to national or local settings.

Similar patterns are obtained in the American polity. Flows of educational practices among American states are rapid, despite a weak federal role and little obvious interdependence. Most prominently, despite the diversity, size, and lack of centralization

---

[6] Examples include Hagerstrand 1967; Spilerman 1970; Knoke 1982; Land, Deane, and Blau 1991.

[7] See Friedkin 1986; Carley 1990.

[8] For welfare, see Collier and Messick 1975. For education, see the papers in Meyer and Hannan 1979. For national independence, see Strang 1990 and 1991a.

of American society, commentators have for two centuries noted the homogeneity in the characters of American individuals and organization. De Toqueville, as we note further, had useful ideas to add to sociological realism.

The theoretical problem is that relational models underspecify the variety of effects that may be induced by interaction and interdependence. Granted, interaction can increase solidarity and similarity; it can also increase conflict and boundary formation. And while exchange can create some small boundary isomorphisms (e.g., trading roles and languages), it can also generate cultural divisions of labor of great stability (Barth 1969; Cohen 1969). Where asocial processes, such as the spread of infectious disease are concerned, relational models are more than adequate. But where diffusion involves the social construction of identity, whether and when intensified relations promote homogeneity rather than differentiation seems unclear.

We need, at minimum, to formulate the wider conditions under which expanded social relationships lead to rapid diffusion. In doing so, we call attention to a class of quite distinct factors that act to increase and redirect the flow of social material.

CULTURAL LINKAGES

We begin with the observation that linkages may be cultural as well as relational. That is, the cultural understanding that social entities belong to a common social category constructs a tie between them. Such ties, while easily represented in graph theoretic terms, invoke a different substantive imagery from that of direct relations such as friendship and exchange.[9] We argue that where actors are seen as falling into the same category, diffusion should be rapid.

Such effects may operate via perceptions built into the actors involved. The individual or organization's cognitive map identifies reference groups that bound social comparison processes. Rational mimicking requires prior and potential adopters be understood as fundamentally similar, at least with respect to the practice at issue. Perceptions of similarity may enhance rates of diffusion for additional reasons, as actors find themselves enmeshed in competitive emulation.

Categories are also defined and institutionalized at levels above that of the actor's perceptions, producing structural conditions that accelerate diffusion. This is the thrust of DiMaggio and Powell's discussion of institutional isomorphism (DiMaggio and Powell 1983). DiMaggio and Powell forcefully point to the homogenizing effects of coercive pressures from the state or dominant organizations within the field, imitation among organizations unable to calculate individually optimal strategies, and linkages to standardized and recalcitrant professions.

For example, rapid diffusion within the world system seems linked to the homogeneous cultural construction of contemporary nation-states. States subscribe to remarkably similar purposes – economic growth, social equality, the political and

---

[9] Culturally recognized similarities may induce high levels of interaction, and thus might be motivated as proxies for high levels of direct relations. We instead argue for the direct impact of culturally defined similarity on diffusion.

human rights of the individual (Thomas, Meyer, Ramirez, and Boli 1987). States are also understood as possessing identical legal standing as sovereign, despite extreme disparities in military and economic capacity. And while these cultural definitions can be and are violated, they provide fertile ground for the rapid diffusion of public policies and institutional structures. Consider how much diffusion would be slowed if nation-states were wholly primordial, or if they occupied formally differentiated positions within a hierarchical global political structure.

In the same way, institutionalized conceptions of formal organization produce rapid diffusion. Standardized categories make it plausible for organizational analysts to provide recipes for successful management and motivate public authorities to dictate or provide incentives for approved forms. As these models gain a taken-for-granted or rulelike status, it becomes advantageous for organizations to comply in at least symbolic ways (Chapter 4).

Socio-scientific researchers are of course part of the cultural system in question, and they share common understandings about the nature of the actors they study. Assumptions of similarity are thus built into almost all diffusion research. Where researchers study diffusion – that is, where they assume actors are not only connected but also ultimately similar – flows between actors are, by our argument, more likely to occur.

The construction of cultural categories expands interaction among their members. Organizations systematically monitor their competitors or fellows, or are influenced by independent monitoring efforts. American states communicate through participation in the Council of State Governments; the United Nations and its specialized agencies play similar roles within the international system. Such forums serve as more than opportunities for communication, however; they are designed specifically to promote the homogenization of their members around models of progressive policy. For example, Strang and Chang argue that the International Labour Organization has successfully promoted the expansion and modernization of social security programs, especially among the welfare laggards of the industrialized world (Strang and Chang 1993).[10]

Despite these forms of sponsored interaction, cultural linkages generally outstrip direct relations. The pervasiveness of similarity in modern systems means that diffusion is often less structured by interaction and interdependence than expected. Practices diffuse along the lines of social relations, but also to other actors broadly considered similar. American educational researchers, for instance, are often quite depressed about the likelihood that progressive reforms will diffuse from central nodes, but at the same time they are overwhelmed by the overall faddishness of the systems they study (Meyer and Scott 1983).

THEORIZATION

Diffusion within cultural categories is accelerated and redirected by their *theorization*. By theorization we mean the self-conscious development and specification of

---

[10] For a parallel argument about science policies, see Finnemore 1990.

abstract categories and the formulation of patterned relationships such as chains of cause and effect. Without general models, cultural categories are less likely to arise and gain force. And without such models, the real diversity of social life is likely to seem as meaningful as are parallelisms. Both points are central to the work of Mead, who stressed both the constitutive importance of the generalized other and the social control significance of the wider community's model of the internal structure of the "self" (Mead 1934).

Thus, the theorization of childrearing practices around elaboration models of the social and intellectual development of the individual enhances the diffusion of these practices. The theorization of organizational control and communication processes expands the diffusion of associated reforms (novel budgeting and accounting practices, leadership training, and matrix organizational forms). The theorization of environmental issues, or of educational structures, or of welfare policies speeds policy diffusion across national states. Marxist theorizations of world history hasten the diffusion of socialist revolution (to unanticipated sites, a common outcome where theories are really compelling).

Theoretical formulations range from simple concepts and typologies to highly abstract, complex, and rich models. We make two general arguments. First, diffusion becomes more rapid and more universal as cultural categories are informed by theories at higher levels of complexity and abstraction. For example, the elaborate theorization of the individual, or the formal organization, or the national society should produce rapid diffusion (in contrast to relatively slow diffusion among "natural," untheorized entities such as the family or religious communities).

Second, theorization renders diffusion less structured by social relations and differences across adopters. General models facilitate meaningful communication and influence between weakly related actors, and between theorists and adopters. Diffusion may still require direct contact,[11] but in more modest amounts. Standard organizational forms spread widely, and into contexts where the technical need for formalization seems absent (Chapter 4).

Theorizing is a strategy for making sense of the world. As such, it is employed in individual-specific ways by the potential adopters themselves. Further, interaction between potential adopters may construct shared theories of the world, the nature of the interacting pair, and the mutual relevance of different practices.

These forms of "bottom up" theorizing should impact diffusion, but in rather local ways. Individual-specific theories affect the individual's adoption patterns, but not those of other adopters. Shared understandings generated by an interacting pair may homogenize the actors involved, but not larger populations. Ideas about adopter-level theorizing thus provide a mechanism motivating arguments about the individual rationality of adoption or the effects of network relations.

Rather than stressing ubiquitous theorizing by potential adopters, we emphasize globally available models imported into local situations or used to inform the

---

[11] For a discussion of the diffusion of social movements wedding ideas about cultural constructions with an analysis of interaction patterns, see McAdam and Rucht 1992.

construction of new social arrangements.[12] More global theorizations are able to induce much broader diffusion processes, as their effects do not vary across sites or adopters. And they tend to be more distinctive (and thus observable) than individual theorizing, providing the basis for explanatory accounts that can complement or counter relational arguments and notions of individual utility maximization.

This focus leads to an emphasis on culturally legitimated theorists: scientists (including popular analysts disesteemed within the academic community), intellectuals, policy analysts, and professionals. The relevant groupings vary across national societies: in the United States academic researchers and professionals seem most central, while in most European societies more broadly construed and less institutionally defined intellectual communities may occupy a dominant position. These groups produce especially complex and highly integrated models. They are also free of pressing needs to apply their theories to concrete problems, which increases not only foolishness but also abstraction.

We do not suggest that the mere appearance of a general model within an intellectual community induces diffusion. In fact, it seems clear that diffusion is halting where practices are identified solely with the specialized theorist. For example, Cole contrasts the rapid diffusion of quality circles in Japan and Sweden with slow adoption in the United States (Cole 1985).[13] He argues that quality circles were embraced in Japan by centrally placed corporations as a strategy for expanding productivity, and by organized labor in Sweden as a means of instilling workfloor democracy. But in the United States, the main supporters of quality circles were politically and organizationally isolated foundations, management consultants, and academic analysts.

This kind of finding is probably quite general. But we would argue that the effects of theoretical models cannot be divorced from consideration of how compelling these models are to relevant audiences. Thus the small-group logic informing quality circles may have more strongly resonated with Japanese understandings of how human beings interact and work together than with the psychologically bounded, rationalized understandings of the individual that dominate American academic and commonsense theorizing. One might expect theoretically articulated models of human motivation stressing individual properties would provide a more persuasive basis for innovations in the United States (helping to produce widespread counseling for the victims of job "burnout," psychological profiling, and aptitude testing).

The diffusion-generating power of theoretical models thus varies with the extent to which they are institutionalized – built into standard and authoritative, rather than highly specialized and marginal, interpretations and schemas. One reason for

---

[12] There are many unexplored complexities in the relationship between individual theorizing and legitimated collective theorization. For example, it is often noted that theories again appeal by running counter to common sense, or emanating from exotic locales. On the other hand, theories resonating with standard thinking are more accessible and reproducible. We do not make much effort here to speak about the relationship between different forms of theorizing, or the broader issue of what characteristics make for especially compelling theories.

[13] We thank Paul DiMaggio for suggesting this example and the general issue of purely professional social movements.

emphasizing the sciences and professions is that these communities are relatively central, prestigious, influential, and so not only construct models but are able to promote them vigorously.[14] But diffusion obviously requires support from other kinds of actors as well: state authorities, large corporate actors, grassroots activists. In some way, models must make the transition from theoretical formulation to social movement to institutional imperative.

As a model is institutionalized, it is codified in organizational routines, while the theorist or his/her disciples become self-interested reformers or nascent professionals or agents of the state. Analyses may then treat diffusion not as grounded in theorization but as driven by organizational routines and promoted by self-interested actors. We would instead emphasize the continuing role of a compelling logic in permitting such movements to gain support, and in defusing self-interested opposition.

Below we discuss ways in which theorization enters into diffusion processes: in accounts of adopters, in accounts of practices, and in diffusion mechanisms. We note expected consequences of theorization for observable features of diffusion patterns.

THE THEORIZATION OF ADOPTERS

Theorizing identifies and interprets regularities in ways that define populations within which diffusion is imaginable and sensible. This occurs when theoretical accounts identify forms of similarity within culturally recognized categories: for example, when psychological discoveries of the need for children to engage in creative play supports movement toward unstructured kindergarten curricula. It also occurs when theoretical accounts define and popularize new categories of actors: for example, when psychologists define dyslexia and by implication dyslexics, promoting the diffusion of new reading technologies.

All theorizations propose homogeneities within the populations or categories they analyze, because all models simplify the real diversity of social life. This is of course true for typological efforts, which explicitly aim at identifying categories and making salient what characteristics they share. But it is also true for explanatory models, which theorize parallelisms in structure and behavior across classes of actors or systems. It is even true of elaborate conceptual models intended to sensitize observers to sources of variation. Armed with Weber's depiction of bureaucracy, for example, observers have identified many "superficially" distinctive organizations as having much in common.

But only the most empty typological exercise simply clarifies bases on which social units can be grouped. Theories actively motivate certain groupings as meaningful and consequential. Theories are often precisely about the way similar systems respond in consistent ways to environmental inputs, and to modifications in

---

[14] The sciences and professions are also globally connected and legitimated, making their impact particularly broad. The extra-national character of the sciences in particular is longstanding: see Wuthnow 1980; Riddle 1989.

structure and operations. Theories thus predict that similar practices can be adopted by all members of a theoretically defined population, with similar effects. They advise masses of individuals to adopt standard therapies; organizations to adopt stylized management schemes; and practically all nation-states to adopt standard schemes to promote economic growth.

The point is made nicely in William Ouchi's *Theory Z*, a discussion of the features of Japanese management styles that might be more widely adopted by American corporations. Ouchi writes,

To a specialist in the Japanese society and culture, the differences between Japan and the United States are so great that a borrowing of social organization between them seems impossible. To a student of business organization, however, the underlying similarity in tasks between Japanese and American business suggests that some form of the essential characteristics of Japanese companies must be transferable. The objective became to separate the culturally specific principles from those universally applicable to economic organizations (Ouchi 1981).

Note that here a research tradition treating organizations as arrangements for accomplishing complex tasks explains why diffusion is sensible within the population "economic organizations," rather than within but not between the two populations "Japanese organizations" and "American organizations."

Actors theorized as equivalent may differ substantially along a variety of untheorized dimensions. In such cases, social rules and practices are likely to flow in ways often decried as unrealistic or maladaptive. In American society, even individuals of extremely marginal status often acquire the standard stances and aspirations of citizenship. And organizations such as schools adopt standard forms despite wide variation in resources and constituencies (Meyer and Rowan 1978). A striking feature of many social systems penetrated by theorization is ritualized isomorphism.

THE THEORIZATION OF DIFFUSING PRACTICES

Just as the theorization of adopters defines populations within which diffusion can occur, the theorization of innovative practices expands their diffusion potential. Theoretical accounts of practices simplify and abstract their properties, and specify and explain the outcomes they produce. Such accounts make it easier to perceive and communicate about the practice. And while sometimes theoretical investigation documents the flaws and unwanted side effects of an innovation, more often theorization documents the many virtues involved, in terms of standardized notions of efficiency or justice or progress.

For example, much educational research is devoted to identifying administrative, curricular, and pedagogic reforms, demonstrating their effectiveness, and specifying them in generalizable and transferable ways. Much operations research is devoted to the specification of optimal decision-making procedures for complex problems.

Much medical research is devoted to locating and advocating therapeutic techniques and developing these in ways that facilitate their diffusion.[15]

The theorization of the adopting population and that of the diffusing practice could have separate, additive effects. But in fact, the two are often theorized jointly. This has the powerful effect of matching the adopter to the practice, and the practice to the adopter.

Such a theory of a social form (such as an "organization") emphasizes certain features as central and relevant, while treating others as variable, or unnecessary, or derivative. Practices related to theoretically emphasized and articulated activities become privileged candidates for diffusion. And a theory of a practice typically specifies conditions necessary for its effective operation.

To illustrate, consider the interplay of organizations and theories about organizations. A tradition of research[16] and professional practice (in accounting and managerial science) conceptualizes organizations as information processing systems. Many proposals for organizational structure and practice are inspired by this theorization. Strategic planning schemes, information gathering and processing technologies, budgeting and goal-setting routines, and organizational structures designed to combat bounded rationality flow rapidly.

On the other hand, theories conceptualizing organizations as groups engaged in cooperative interdependent action privilege alternative kinds of flows. Small armies of human relations and resources consultants, industrial psychologists, and personnel specialists suggest organizational reforms. Job enlargement, job rotation, suggestion boxes, and management training diffuse.

THEORIZATION AS A DIFFUSION MECHANISM

Finally, theorization enters not only through the social construction of the adopter and the practice, but as a diffusion mechanism. Most concretely, theorists may become central conduits of diffusion. For example, members of the Harvard economics department were active in bringing Keynesian fiscal policy to Washington, and American economists helped spread Keynesian policies through much of the post-war world.[17]

These efforts lead diffusion to flow along the lines of relations linking theorists, rather than along the lines of relations linking adopters. Hirschman thus notes that West Germany and Japan did not adopt Keynesian policies in the post-war era, even

[15] The taken-for-granted nature of these efforts may make them appear trivial examples of theorization. But consider the work required to construct the professional communities involved (for medicine, the social mobilization attending the Flexner Report), the mistakes that these communities may promulgate (the virtues of oat bran, recent news that we should stop drinking milk), the difficulty of overcoming common practices and entrenched interests (movements against smoking and drinking), and the possibility of alternative theoretical logics (holistic models of health).

[16] Distinguished contributions to this perspective include Simon 1957; March and Simon 1958.

[17] See the papers in Hall 1989. For an analysis emphasizing the capacities of adopters rather than cross-national diffusion, see Weir and Skocpol 1985.

though American occupation made for very high levels of interaction with and dependence on the United States (Hirschman 1989). He explains that military officers and corporate managers dominated American delegations to Germany and Japan, while economists played more central roles in delegations to countries where the American presence was less massive.

Generally, knowledge of the relational structure, orientation, and influence of relevant theorists seems useful in mapping diffusion. We should emphasize, however, that the main consequence of theorizing an activity is not simply to add a new set of relational structures channeling diffusion. Theorists have little impact when their analysis is unpersuasive. And compelling theoretical arguments may diffuse very rapidly themselves, attenuating point-to-point diffusion. The very aim and character of theories means that they are less tied to concrete actors than are the practices they describe. Where potential adopters internally reproduce and act on the basis of the theoretical model, we might describe theorization itself as the diffusion mechanism.

CONSEQUENCES OF THEORIZATION FOR DIFFUSION

We have argued throughout that cultural linkages, and particularly those informed by compelling models of behavior, should accelerate the pace of diffusion within the populations they describe. Theorization should affect the content and form of diffusion as well.

If theorization shapes diffusion, what flows is not a copy of some practice existing elsewhere. When theorists are the carriers of the practice or theorization itself is the diffusion mechanism, it is the theoretical model that is likely to flow. Such models are neither complete nor unbiased depictions of existing practices. Instead, actual practices are interpreted as partial, flawed, or corrupt implementations of theorized ones.

For example, the peculiar organization of American education (the absence of unified national authority, considerable local autonomy, and the parent–teacher association [PTA]) is less copied around the world than are abstract models of a liberal, expanded, and unified curriculum. Individuals take on abstracted models of the theorized individual (in forming standard opinions and ideas about political efficacy) as much as concrete properties individually observed (Jepperson 1992). New nation-states adopt organizational forms built up and legitimated as models in the United Nations and its specialized agencies (McNeely 1989). They embellish existing models rather than mimic extant forms, so that over time more and more individual rights and state powers are written into national constitutions (Boli 1987).

Theorized diffusion is also likely to be relatively unconstrained by relational structures. Theorization provides a substitute for close, inductive examination of the experiences of others. It facilitates communication between strangers by providing a language that does not presume directly shared experience. It provides rationales for adoption that run counter to simple interaction-based processes such as direct mimicry and superstitious learning (where adopted practices are temporally rather than causally linked to desired outcomes; March 1988).

At an arelational extreme, theorization helps innovation masquerade as diffusion. It is a common theoretical gambit to claim that the elements proposed for diffusion are actually found somewhere. Contemporary organizational innovators in the United States may strategically present their ideas as standard practice in Japan, while in previous decades the United States was the supposed source of many organizational innovations. Proposals for social reform often claim to be built on the Swedish model, while theorists have seen the future work in the Soviet Union, Cuba, China, and even Nicaragua. In all these cases, we often have not so much faithful copying as theoretically mediated diffusion or disguised innovation.

Finally, we note the complex relationship between theorization and rationality. Theorization specifies why the potential adopter should attend to the behavior of one population and not some other, what effects the practice will have, and why the practice is particularly applicable or needed given the adopter. All this permits the actor to see through the confusing evidence of others' mixed successes and detect the "true" factors at work. In short, theorization may be regarded as turning diffusion into rational choice.

However, theorization as described here will produce patterns of behavior quite different from those generally flowing from rational decision-making at the individual (adopter) level. As we have emphasized throughout, global theorization defocuses individual variability, assuming equivalences that are perceptibly inaccurate given the local information. Behavior using such models as scripts will produce much more homogeneous action than would decisions generated from personal information. And global theorization diminishes the perceived relevance of local examples of success, exorcising "superstition" but diminishing the rationality of diffusion from a naive perspective. The unpersuaded observer will see in theorized diffusion only ritualized isomorphism.

MODERNITY AND DIFFUSION

By the above logic, diffusion should be most rapid where theorization is central to the construction of both units and specific elements, where partial theorizations articulate with each other, and where a network of congruent theories forms a hegemonic cultural frame. The outstanding instance of this in the contemporary world is modernity itself. A core substantive point in our argument is thus that the more social entities are constructed and legitimated as modern entities (and particularly as modern "actors"), the more social materials flow among them.

A specification of the conventional meanings of "modernity" makes the logic of this situation clearer. Modernity connotes the organization of society and the nation-state around universalized notions of progress and justice, as built up of rationalized organizations and associations, and as composed of autonomous, rational, and purposive individual citizens. And it implies the integrated functioning of these elements so that collective goods are enhanced by individual and organizational progress and contribute to such progress.

Analyses from a modern point of view can call attention to dissimilarities across local contexts, and hence to differing strategies appropriate to each. But in a more basic sense such analyses are a powerful force for homogenization. Modern theories advocate a more universalistic moral order, a more scientific and standardized analysis of nature and means-ends relationships, and a more ahistorical view of human nature and human society. The construction of actors around these notions makes them more similar, in easily perceived and communicated ways.

From this point of view, the rapidity of flows among contemporary social actors becomes comprehensible. After all, they have the same legitimate purposes, so they are susceptible to die for the same social demands. They depend on the same technologies legitimated on the same grounds, so flows of improved techniques can be rapid and little-constrained by traditional loyalties. And they have the same relatively scientific conceptions of basic resources, remarkably similar definitions of human nature, collective authority, and social control, permitting "innovations" in these areas to flow rapidly (Boli-Bennet and Meyer 1978).

We would thus argue that the more societies are organized as nation-states (and not as "primordial" religious or ethnic groups) the more social structures diffuse among them. Within nation-states, the more collective action occurs within rationalized formal organizations, the more they become isomorphic with each other and with the rules of both nation-states and world society. And at the individual level, the rise of expanded and unified notions of citizenship, capacity, and moral worth (in short, the world-cultural construction of "actorhood") leads individuals rapidly to adopt attitudes and practices from each other, and from national and world centers (Jepperson 1992).

The density of globally organized analysis has expanded rapidly, particularly since World War II. In the late nineteenth century, Japan sent delegations to the major Western societies to observe modern institutions: parliaments, police forces, the army, the navy, and so on (Westney 1989). They chose from among the menu of extant systems, selecting models such as the British navy, and the French police and military (the latter fortunately exchanged for the Prussian model, some years later).

In the late twentieth century, theorists do the traveling. When state socialism collapsed in Eastern Europe and the Soviet Union, Western academics rushed to the rescue, bearing analyses of optimal economic and political arrangements (Sachs 1989; Peck and Richardson 1992). In the contemporary world, communities of researchers and theorists actively help to construct new policy domains, issues, and interests (see especially the recent work on the role of epistemic communities in national policymaking; Haas 1989).[18]

Rules and practices linked to prevailing theories of the modern are most likely to diffuse. Thus a mechanism to enhance the productivity of the physically challenged will flow more readily than will one justified by paternalistic notions of charity. A scientifically rationalized medical therapy will flow more than one backed only by testimonials. Forms of political participation grounded in the rights of the

---

[18] Also see the 1992 issue of *International Organization* devoted to epistemic communities, edited by Haas.

individual will diffuse more rapidly than ones grounded in the rights of social collectivities.[19]

The sciences and the professions are central to the modernizing project. They are devices for turning local and parochial practices into universally applicable principles that can "rationally" be adopted by all sorts of superordinate authorities, implemented by subordinate ones, and copied by modern entities everywhere. As social rules and practices come under scientific and professional analysis, they become potential candidates for rapid diffusion in the modern system.

For instance, it is clear that modern arrangements of mass education have flowed very rapidly around the modern world system. These flows have been more rapid in the post-World War II period, in which both the political and economic benefits have been scientifically defined and elaborated (Meyer, Ramirez, and Soysal 1992). Education is prestigious, is thought functional for all sorts of goods, and is seen as both individually and collectively beneficial. Every country, now, has highly legitimate reasons to pursue educational expansion.

DIFFUSION AND THE SUBSTANCE OF MODERNITY

We have motivated the relationship between modernity and diffusion in formal terms, as arising out of the effects that any dominant, integrated conception of the social order might have on flows of social material. But the impact of modernity on diffusion seems to go beyond the simple effect of standardization. It has to do with the substance of the sociological vision embodied in the modern.

Modern perspectives locate much value and responsibility in social "actors," both individual human beings and purposive rationalized organizations. The sovereignty and the competence of these actors are celebrated. Social structures that rest upon the self-interested choices of autonomous actors are formally demonstrated to generate optimal outcomes.

The cultural construction of empowered actors carrying ultimate values seems especially favorable for diffusion. Such actors are assumed to have the capacity to innovate and reform; they also have the moral duty to do so. And as highly valued entities, actors can sensibly look to one another as models for their action. In the more liberal, more egalitarian, and more reductionist versions of modernity, actors

---

[19] As noted by a reviewer, attempts at modernization generally carry some traditional baggage. Nationalism, the prime political expression of modernity, is constructed in part by the selective regeneration (or invention) of various traditions. See Anderson 1983; Hobsbawm and Ranger 1983. National projects involve the recording of traditional stories, the revival of old forms of dress and dance. Once sanctified as expressions of national identity, such forms may be retained even where they appear economically or politically costly. These kinds of practices are often valued precisely because they are distinctive, and may diffuse in only formal ways (i.e., proclamations of national costumes may diffuse, but not the clothes themselves). And where modernizing projects are overcome by aggressively xenophobic appeals to the ethnically or religiously distinctive, we might expect generalized resistance to diffusion. On the other hand, it is easy to understate how stylized the cultures involved often are. This is most true for contemporary organizations, which may hire outside experts to sensitize organizational participants to the putatively unique culture of the organization.

are powerfully drawn to copy each other and identify with collective standards. This, in fact, was de Tocqueville's argument about the homogeneity of individuals and groups within the American polity.

MODERNIZATION AND DIFFUSION RESEARCH

Diffusion research is built fundamentally around assumptions of modernity. Diffusion analyses nearly always investigate the spread of "innovations": boiled drinking water, improved seed corn, new prescription drugs. Both the anthropological and sociological traditions of diffusion research are grounded in the study of marginally modern peoples exposed to modern practices. But in the contemporary world, marked by the obliteration of nonmodern communities, both practice and adopters are likely to be modern.

The modernity of both practices and adopters is so pervasive in contemporary diffusion research that its consequences are generally ignored. But the cultural match between practice and adopter may substantially alter patterns of diffusion, an effect noted in an earlier generation of studies in rural sociology. For example, Marsh and Cole-man found that network centrality predicts early adoption within progress-oriented communities, but not within communities opposed to innovation (Marsh and Coleman 1956). Becker showed that items with "high adoption potential" (defined in terms of attractiveness and communicability to professionals) were adopted early by centrally placed authors, while items with "low adoption potential" were adopted early by social isolates (Becker 1970).

In both cases, the researchers connected their findings to the social meaning of the diffusing items and the adopters. Where adoption is highly prestigious, because the practice is obviously modern and the community values modernity highly, relationally central actors initiate adoption. Where the practice is less obviously modern or the community devalues modernity, it will be the "marginal men," those relatively unconstrained by community norms, that adopt early. Clearly the predictions of simple relational models will go astray if they are not made conditional on the larger cultural context.[20]

ANALYTIC STRATEGIES

Several research strategies seem useful in empirically examining the ideas discussed above.

Better specify relational models: Some of the arguments above predict the absence of diffusion effects across conditions generally thought to promote adoption.

[20] Relational models can account for these kinds of results by arguing that centrally placed actors in modern communities typically have extensive relations to the outside world, while in nonmodern communities it is the marginal men who have outward-looking relations. See Menzel 1960. Marsh and Coleman (and we) would prefer to frame an explanation in terms of the location of actors within communities of discourse.

For example, theorization implies insensitivity to patterns of interaction and inter-dependence. Recent advances in the capacity directly to model relational structures and individual level effects in diffusion research make it possible to test for the role of network linkages.[21] We may then wish to ascribe some portion of the residual variation to the impact of the sorts of cultural processes discussed in this chapter. For instance, notions of a larger "world polity" gain plausibility when it can be shown that the cross-national expansion and content of mass education seems unrelated to exogenous factors such as level of economic development, and unmediated by rela-tions such as those connecting metropoles and former colonies (Meyer, Kamens and Benvaot 1992).[22]

This research design is fairly weak, since residual variation is employed as evidence for an argument of central interest. It is always possible that structures of interaction or interdependence are poorly specified. Positive evidence would be more persuasive.

Specify theorized linkages: A second strategy, which is methodologically a variant of the first, provides such evidence. Theorized similarities can be measured and treated as a particular kind of channel of diffusion, methodologically playing the same role as interaction or interdependence in the models above. Or the location and relational structure of theorists may be used to predict patterns of diffusion. It would then be possible to examine the impact of social definitions on diffusion in a more positive vein.

Examine variation among populations: A third strategy takes a somewhat differ-ent tack. One can compare the diffusion of some practice across different popula-tions, where the population as an aggregate is measured in terms of interaction, interdependence, and socially constructed similarity. Further, we can qualitatively capture the degree to which the social construction of the population is theoretically informed, and the degree to which relevant theories are institutionalized. In general, it becomes possible to examine the degree to which the rate of diffusion, or other aggregate characteristics of the diffusion process, are functions of both relational and cultural characteristics of the population.

Examine variation among diffusing practices: A fourth strategy compares the diffusion of different kinds of practices across the same population, contrasting more or less "modern" practices, or more or less theoretically privileged practices. One could also study practices before and after they are theorized or become understood as "modern." For example, Tolbert and Zucker found that the adoption of civil service procedures became disconnected from city characteristics once the reform movement had been authoritatively and discursively institutionalized (Tolbert and Zucker 1983).

Examine the content of diffusion: An alternative approach is to examine the content of adopted practices, rather than the timing of adoption. Content analyses of diffusing policies may be particularly useful in examining evidence for theoretically mediated diffusion. Similarity in content to known theoretical models provides

---

[21] One approach to modeling complex relational structures directly is to estimate diffusion processes within an event history framework. See Marsden and Podolny 1990; Strang 1991b; Strang and Tuma (forthcoming).

[22] Also see Meyer, Ramirez, and Soysal 1992.

direct evidence of such connections.[23] In addition, if actors are drawing on a theorized model rather than on each other, variability in adopted content should be low and covariances should be time stationary (i.e., average differences between adopted practices should not increase with the interval between their adoption times). The latter holds because "transmission errors" do not cumulate over time when actors respond to an external model. Comparisons could be drawn across populations or practices, in line with the strategies outlined above.

CONCLUSION

We have argued that flows of social elements in a wider system are enhanced by the cultural codification of adopter identities, by the rise of theorized models of adopters and practices that motivate diffusion, and thus by the rise of universalized and integrated models of the "modern." We see such cultural factors as adding to relational understandings of diffusion, as pointing to distinctively patterned outcomes, and as suggesting alternative designs for diffusion analyses.

These arguments give importance to legal, and especially professional and scientific, cultural materials. These forms of theorization, and their rise to dominance in the modern world, greatly speed the diffusion of rules and practices. They define or construct social entities as comparable, and theorize the universal and beneficial relevance of new and otherwise alien social materials. By reconstituting adopters and by redefining social elements, modern theorization greatly expands the motives and rationales for society-wide and worldwide standardization. As these forms of theorizing penetrate more and more aspects of society (from agricultural extension services to educational innovations to the rights of wives and children), standardizing flows increase.

Following Tocqueville, we call attention to the anomalous character of modernity. Its careful analysis of the bounded individual, the rationalized organization, and the purposive society create powerful standardizing forces. The diffusion processes involved directly oppose the internal rationalization sought by the modernizing project and presupposed in its analysis. The modern actors whose uniqueness and autonomy are most celebrated are precisely those most subject to the homogenizing effects of diffusion.

REFERENCES

Anderson, Benedict. 1983. *Imagined Communities*. London: Verso.
Arthur, W. Brian. 1989. On Competing Technologies and Lock-in by Historical Events: The Dynamics of Allocation Under Increasing Returns. *Economic Journal* 99: 116–31.

[23] Content analyses of diffusing practices also permit an insight into network transmission patterns. In exploring diffusion patterns among the states, Walker notes that the California Fair Trade law was "followed either verbatim or with minor variations by twenty states; in fact, ten states copied two serious typographical errors in the original California law." See Walker (1969: 881).

Banerjee, Abhijit V. 1982. A Simple Model of Herd Behavior, *Quarterly Journal of Economics* 107: 797–817.

Barth, Frederik (ed.) 1969. *Ethnic Groups and Boundaries: The Social Organization of Culture Difference*. Boston: Little, Brown.

Bartholomew, David J. 1982. *Stochastic Models for Social Processes*. New York: Wiley.

Becker, M. H. 1970. Sociometric Location and Innovativeness: Reformulation and Extension of the Diffusion Model. *American Sociological Review* 35: 267–82.

Boli, John. 1987. World Polity Sources of Expanding State Authority and Organization, 1870–1970 and Human Rights or State Expansion? Cross-national Definitions of Constitutional Rights, 1870–1970, in G. M. Thomas, J. W. Meyer, F. O. Ramirez, and J. Boli (eds.), *Institutional Structure*. Newbury Park: Sage, pp. 71–91 and 133–49.

Boli-Bennett, John and John W. Meyer. 1978. The Ideology of Childhood and the State. *American Sociological Review* 43: 797–812.

Burt, Ronald S. 1987. Social Contagion and Innovation: Cohesion Versus Structural Equivalence. *American Journal of Sociology* 92: 1287–335.

Carley, Kathleen. 1990. Structural Constraints on Communication: The Diffusion of the Homomorphic Signal Analysis Technique Through Scientific Fields. *Journal of Mathematical Sociology* 15: 207–46.

Cohen, Abner. 1969. *Custom and Politics in Urban Africa: A Study of Hausa Migrants in Yoruba Towns*. Berkeley: University of California Press.

Cole, Robert W. 1985. The Macropolitics of Organizational Change: A Comparative Analysis of the Spread of Small-group Activities. *Administrative Science Quarterly* 30: 560–85.

Coleman, James S., Elihu Katz, and Herbert Menzel. 1966. *Medical Innovation*. New York: Bobbs-Merrill.

Collier, David and Richard Messick. 1975. Prerequisites Versus Diffusion: Testing Alternative Explanations of Social Security Adoption. *American Political Science Review* 69: 1299–315.

David, Paul A. 1985. Clio and the Economics of QWERTY. *American Economic Review* 75: 332–7.

DiMaggio, Paul J. and Walter W. Powell. 1983. The Iron Cage Revisited: Institutional Isomorphism and Collective Rationality in Organizational Fields. *American Sociological Review* 48: 147–60.

Finnemore, Martha. 1990. International Organizations as Teachers of Norms: UNESCO and Science Policy. Unpublished doctoral dissertation, Stanford University.

Fliegel, Frederick C. and Joseph E. Kivlin. 1966. Attributes of Innovations as Factors in Diffusion. *American Journal of Sociology* 72: 235–48.

Friedkin, Noah E. 1986. A Formal Theory of Social Power. *Journal of Mathematical Sociology* 12: 103–26.

Granovetter, Mark and Roland Soong. 1983. Threshold Models of Diffusion and Collective Behavior. *Journal of Mathematical Sociolog* 9: 165–79.

Haas, Peter M. 1989. Do Regimes Matter? Epistemic Communities and Mediterranean Pollution Control. *International Organization* 43: 377–404.

Hagerstrand, Torben. 1967. *Innovation Diffusion as a Spatial Process*. Chicago: University of Chicago Press.

Hall, Peter A. (ed.) 1989. *The Political Power of Economic Ideas: Keynesianism Across Nations*. Princeton: Princeton University Press.

Hirschman, Albert O. 1989. How the Keynesian Revolution was Exported from the United States, and Other Comments, in P. A. Hall (ed.), *The Political Power of Economic Ideas: Keynesianism Across Nations*, pp. 347–60.

Hobsbawm, Eric and Terence Ranger. 1983. *The Invention of Tradition*. Cambridge: Cambridge University Press.

Ikenberry, John. 1989. Explaining the Diffusion of State Norms: Coercion, Competition, and Learning in the International System. Paper presented at the annual meetings of the International Studies Association, London.

Jepperson, Ronald L. 1992. National Scripts: The Varying Construction of Individualism and Opinion across the Modern Nation-States. Unpublished doctoral dissertation, Yale University.

Knoke, David. 1982. The Spread of Municipal Reform: Temporal, Spatial, and Social Dynamics. *American Journal of Sociology* 87: 1314–39.

Land, Kenneth C., Glenn Deane, and Judith R. Blau. 1991. Religious Pluralism and Church Membership: A Spatial Diffusion Model. *American Sociological Review* 56: 237–49.

Mahajan, Vijay and Robert A. Peterson. 1985. *Models for Innovation Diffusion*. Beverly Hills: Sage.

March, James G. 1988. *Decisions and Organizations*. Oxford: Basil Blackwell.

—— and Herbert A. Simon. 1958. *Organizations*. New York: Wiley.

Marsden, Peter V. and Joel Podolny. 1990. Dynamics Analysis of Network Diffusion Processes, in H. Flap and J. Weesie (eds.), *Social Networks Through Time*. Rijksuniversiteit Utrecht: Utrecht NL, pp. 197–214.

Marsh, Paul C. and A. Lee Coleman. 1956. Group Influences and Agricultural Innovations: Some Tentative Findings and Hypotheses. *American Sociological Review* 61: 588–94.

McAdam, Douglas and Dietrich Rucht. 1992. Cross National Diffusion of Social Movement Ideas and Tactics. Presented at the annual meetings of the American Sociological Association, Pittsburgh.

McNeely, Connie. 1989. Cultural Isomorphism among Nation-States: The Role of International Organizations. Unpublished doctoral dissertation, Stanford University.

Mead, George Herbert. 1934. *Mind, Self, and Society*. Chicago: University of Chicago Press.

Menzel, Herbert. 1960. Innovation, Integration, and Marginality: A Survey of Physicians. *American Sociological Review* 25: 704–13.

Meyer, John W. and Michael T. Hannan (eds.) 1979. *National Development and the World System*. Chicago: University of Chicago Press.

—— and Brian Rowan. 1977. Institutionalized Organizations: Formal Structure as Myth and Ceremony. *American Journal of Sociology* 83: 440–63. Reproduced in Chapter 4.

—— —— 1978. The Structure of Educational Organizations, in M. Meyer et al. (eds.), *Environments and Organizations*. San Francisco: Jossey-Bass, pp. 78–109.

—— and W. Richard Scott. 1983. *Organizational Environments: Ritual and Rationality*. Newbury Park: Sage.

—— David Kamens, and Aaron Benavot. 1992. *School Knowledge for the Masses: World Models and National Cunicular Categories in the Twentieth Century*. Philadelphia: Falmer.

—— Francisco O. Ramirez, and Yasemin Soysal. 1992. World Expansion of Mass Education, 1870–1980. *Sociology of Education* 63: 128–49.

Naroll, Raoul. 1965. Galton's Problem: The Logic of Cross-cultural Analysis. *Social Research* 32: 429–51.

Ouchi, William. 1981. *Theory Z*. New York: Addison-Wesley.

Peck, Merton J. and Thomas J. Richardson (eds.) 1992. *What is to be Done? Proposals for the Soviet Transition to the Market*. New Haven: Yale University Press.

Riddle, Phyllis. 1989. University and State: Political Competition and the Rise of Universities, 1200–1985. Unpublished doctoral dissertation, Stanford University.

Rogers, Everett M. 1983. *Diffusion of Innovations*. Detroit: The Free Press.

Sachs, Jeffrey. 1989. My Plan for Poland. *International Economy* 3: 24–9.

Simon, Herbert A. 1957. *Administrative Behavior*. New York: Macmillan.

Skog, Ole-Jorgen. 1986. The Long Waves of Alcohol Consumption: A Social Network Perspective on Cultural Change. *Social Networks* 8: 1–32.

Spilerman, Seymour. 1970. The Causes of Racial Disturbances: A Comparison of Alternative Explanations. *American Sociological Review* 35: 627–49.

Strang, David. 1990. From Dependency to Sovereignty: An Event History Analysis of Decolonization. *American Sociological Review* 55: 846–60.

—— 1991a. Global Patterns of Decolonization, 1500–1987. *International Studies Quarterly* 35: 429–54.

—— 1991b. Adding Social Structure to Diffusion Models: An Event History Framework. *Sociological Methods and Research* 19: 324–53.

—— and Patricia M. Y. Chang. 1993. The International Labor Organisation and the Welfare State: Institutional Effects on National Welfare Spending, 1960–80. *International Organization* 47: 235–62.

—— and Nancy B. Tuma. Spatial and Temporal Heterogeneity in Diffusion. *American Journal of Sociology* (forthcoming).

Thomas, George M., John W. Meyer, Francisco O. Ramirez, and John Boli. 1987. *Institutional Structure: Constituting State, Society, and the Individual*. Newbury Park: Sage.

Tolbert, Pamela S. and Lynne G. Zucker. 1983. Institutional Sources of Change in the Formal Structure of Organizations: The Diffusion of Civil Service Reform. *Administrative Science Quarterly* 28: 22–39.

Walker, Jack. 1969. The Diffusion of Innovation Among the American States. *American Political Science Review* 63: 881.

Weir, Margaret and Theda Skocpol. 1985. State Structures and the Possibilities for 'Keynesian' Responses to the Great Depression in Sweden, Britain, and the United States', in P. B. Evans, D. Rueschemeyer, and T. Skocpol (eds.), *Bringing the State Back In*. Cambridge, MA: Cambridge University Press.

Westney, D. Eleanor. 1987. *Imitation and Innovation: The Transfer of Western Organizational Patterns to Meiji Japan*. Cambridge, MA: Harvard University Press.

Wuthnow, Robert. 1980). The World-Economy and the Institutionalization of Science in Seventeenth-Century Europe, in A. Bergesen (ed.), *Studies of the Modern World-System*. New York: Academic, pp. 22–55.

7

Globalization

Globalization: Sources and Effects on National States and Societies

The world polity and cultural system are relatively stateless, but they legitimate strong nation-state identities as the dominant actors. This produces very strong tendencies for the adoption of common models of modernity, despite extraordinary differences in resources and local culture. Local distinctiveness is also legitimated, so long as it is not inconsistent with homogeneity on the main dimensions of stratification and identity.

Globalization has a number of dimensions. First, it means the increased political and military interdependence of a set of sovereign nation-states and the expanded and strengthened set of organizations involved: here, states are the main actors conceptualized. Second, it means the increased economic interdependencies of a set of national or subnational economies and the relevant multilateral and international public and private organizations: here, states and firms are the main originating actors. Third, it means an expanded flow of individual persons among societies through socioeconomic migration, travel and political expulsion: states and individuals are the main actors discussed.

Fourth, globalization means the expanded interdependence of expressive culture through intensified global communication. Themes from music to ethnic revival spread like fads through the world society, and organizational structures arise to spread them. All types of actors from individuals to organizations to national states are involved.

Fifth, globalization means the expanded flow of instrumental culture around the world. Put simply, common models of social order become authoritative in many different social settings. This article focuses on this dimension of globalization: on why it arises, how it is organized and what consequences it has.

Originally published as:

John W. Meyer 2000. Globalization: Sources, and Effects on National States and Societies. *International Society* 15: 235–250.

This chapter is based on a paper that was prepared for the conference on 'Globalizations: Dimensions, Trajectories, Prospects,' Stockholm 1998. It is compiled from collaborative work done over the last decade. I am indebted to a number of colleagues for their help. For a summary, see Chapter 8.

THE PHENOMENON

There is, by now, little dispute about the facts of the matter. In many areas of social life, common models organized in world discourse arise and penetrate social life worldwide. At the nation-state level, the theme is highly developed (see the review by Meyer et al. Chapter 8).

1. The world society creates, increasingly, common models of national state identity and purpose (McNeely 1995). These scripted forms, as they change over time, show up in national constitutions (Boli 1987), depiction of national purpose, (Fiala and Gordon-Lanford 1987; McNeely 1995) and data systems (Ventresca 1995). Essentially, all national states now define their fundamental purposes as having to do with socioeconomic development or welfare and individual justice, rights, and equality.

2. Common models of socioeconomic development are also scripted, and national policies change with changes in world scripts. Thus, science is seen as central to development, and associated policies and investments expand and spread rapidly (Finnemore 1996; Schofer 1999). The same holds for population control in a mid-century reversal from pro-natalist to anti-natalist doctrines (Barrett and Frank 1999); actual demographic patterns follow similar paths (Bongaarts and Watkins 1996). Economic policies change in worldwide waves (Hall 1989), including recent waves that stress markets and privatization. A huge wave of policy and practice change is created by the recent world environment movement (Chapter 10; Frank et al. 1999). Broad shifts, such as a great expansion in numbers of national parks, are worldwide, so are narrow ones in the spread of environmental impact assessment policies.

3. Common models of human rights are also scripted and produce waves of national policy and practice changes in areas such as the status of ethnoracial minorities or women (McNeely 1995; Bradley and Ramirez 1996; Berkovitch 1999). Movements such as current efforts to extend rights to gays and lesbians are worldwide in character and produce waves of local social organization and national policy (Frank and McEneaney 1999). More broadly, a general world wave emphasizing both, human rights and democratization, has had much impact.

4. Education, linking both ideologies of human rights and of social progress, has been highly scripted with enormous impact on educational expansion around the world (Riddle 1993; Meyer, Ramirez et al. 1992a).

    Educational curricula show the same scripted and standardized qualities, both, at the mass and at the elite levels (Meyer, Kamens et al. 1992).

If we shift from the national to the organizational level, it is more difficult to find comparative and longitudinal research. Most work in this field is intranational. But, clearly, much cultural globalization is going on, as organizations in many different societies come under the influence of standard models of organizing, and consulting firms and professionals helping them to do this spread very rapidly. In areas like accounting, sweeping reforms take a worldwide character (Olson et al. 1998). This is also true of information systems, management styles, organizational training programs, and modern models of proper formal organizational structure. Schools, hospitals, businesses, and government agencies come to see themselves – and to be analyzed by others – as organizations and actors of a generally universalized sort and thus as subject to standardizing rationalization (Brunsson and Sahlin-Andersson 1997).

At the individual level, many analyses also suggest rather sweeping forms of modernization – the reconstruction of the individual as a standardized unit with standard rights and capacities (Inkeles and Smith 1974; see the review by Jepperson 1992). This is aided by the very rapid expansion of systems of universal mass education (Meyer, Ramirez et al. 1992), which is known to play a dominant role in constructing the standard "modern" individual. At the global level, of course, highly elaborated standard models of the rights and standing of the human and citizen individuals are developed. These build into something like law – in both, liberal models of the human as an authoritative participant in society (freedoms of speech, association, religion, culture, and the like) and more corporatist versions of the human as a bundle of welfare rights.

The overall phenomenon is clear: global models of the instrumental structure and actorhood of nation-states, organizations, and individuals have much impact in the contemporary system. The intellectual questions are now not about the phenomenon itself but about its explanation. These questions are addressed in this chapter. First, why do these global structures arise? Second, how are they organized at the global level? Third, through what mechanisms do they impact national societies?

FORCES FOR THE GLOBALIZATION OF MODELS OF ACTORHOOD

The globalization of instrumental models of actorhood follows from the structure of world society, as it has become more integrated over time. Two core properties of this society are central: the fact that the modern world is stateless and that it is made up of strong, culturally constituted actors.

First, as is commonly recognized, the world society is a stateless polity. It has no central, controlling political organizations in it – no state organization with legitimate sovereignty over or responsibility for the whole. There are some important organizations such as the UN system and the World Bank/IMF. But these are not sovereign – they derive such authority, as they have, from delegation by the subunit nation-state actors that make them up. There are also some rather dominating subunit actors, such as very powerful nation-states and some very strong economic actors, but these too have no direct or authoritative sovereignty over the system as a whole.

Two important consequences follow from the statelessness of the world polity. First, almost all the interests that push for sociopolitical regulation in the world work toward building a broad world polity of shared rules and models, rather than trying to assemble a stronger world state bureaucracy. These interests may reflect the goals of nation-states, business firms, concerned human individuals, and all sorts of specialized groups. For instance, as concerns arise about the world environment, they are channeled principally toward the construction of rather binding cultural (mainly scientific) rules and models, not toward the formal imposition of bureaucratic authority by (non-existent) world state organizations. As concerns arise about the stability and growth of the (increasingly recognized) world economy, these are channeled into the creation of appropriate common economic models for states. As concerns arise about human rights and welfare, they are channeled similarly. In all these areas, there is no point in imagining a controlling world state. It is more reasonable to try to construct common cultural principles that can produce the desired actions in subunits of the world society.

Thus, from every side, candidate models for appropriate action by national states, organizations, and even individuals are produced at a very rapid rate. The exponential growth in this cultural material is indicated by the extraordinary expansion in international governmental and nongovernmental associations in the current period (Boli and Thomas 1997). It is also indicated by the explosion in scientific activity covering the widest variety of domains in the current system (Schofer 1999).

Second, there is no central controlling structure to regulate or stop the expansion in world political culture that is produced. Faced with a knowledge system and groups that give attention to a problem with the ozone layer, an older (e.g., Chinese) imperial system could resort to simple suppression of the intellectuals and groups involved, thus eliminating the problem. The statelessness of the current system means that nobody is in a position to stop an environmental, human rights, or expansive economic development model.

Thus a great deal of cultural material – much of it imposing extraordinary costs on the actors involved – is produced in the contemporary system, with few mechanisms for control. Indeed, the intellectuals and associations involved gain much prestige and importance by developing costs for actors. For instance, the social scientists who discover new forms of unjust inequality (among countries, genders, classes, ethnic groups, races, or persons of varying disabilities) gain world attention and preferment – prizes go to such people. They do not bear the costs of correction: the subunit nation-state and organizational actors in the system do.

Third,[1] world society is itself stateless and lacks much of a collective actor. But it contains much cultural and associational material that defines itself as made up principally of very strong and highly legitimated actors. These arise from a rationalized (scientific) analysis of nature as universal and lawful and thus suited to rational and purposive action.

They arise even more from a secularized analysis of a universal and lawful moral or spiritual authority: the high god no longer acts in history, but sacralized human actors do, carrying legitimated agency for their own actions under valid and universal collective principles (Chapter 5). There are the modern nation-states. There are human and citizen persons, who now carry the banner of legitimated individuality

---

[1] GK, GSD: In the original text, this word was mistakenly worded 'Second'; it has been corrected here.

and actorhood. And there are many types of formalized organizational actors, ultimately constituted by individuals and/or by states.

Modern culture and the strongest modern social theories define social life as the product of these actors in all sectors of social life: the economy, the political system, and other institutional domains. Each actor is empowered, and the empowerment is highly legitimated, so that, in principle, they all respect the actorhood of the others.

Tremendous premiums in the modern system go with actorhood, so that social life tends to be reorganized around its claims. Essentially, every society now forms itself around the model of autonomous nation-state actorhood. Within and among societies, individuals mobilize around principles of actorhood (e.g., human rights). And all sorts of social structures reform themselves as formal organizations and thus as legitimated actors.

The claims of actorhood are rewarding, exorbitant, and utterly unrealistic. Under elaborate, standardized, and very general rules, actors are thought to have clear purposes, means–ends technologies, and analyzed resources. They are to have unified decision sovereignty, effective control over their internal activities, and clearly defined boundaries. They are to have complete and accurate analyses of their environments. They are, in short, to be little gods. And all of this occurs under universalized legitimating rules and in a rationalized and standardized environment. So proper actors have a great deal in common and are exposed to a common wider environment.

In this situation, real social actors, because of the exorbitant claims built into their identities, face very great uncertainty about every property of their actorhood, from sovereignty and purpose to needed technologies to effective control systems to analyses of their environments. Real social entities of a more traditional kind, unconstrained by the claims of actorhood might face the same uncertainties but would have no obligation to deal with them. The pretenses of actorhood require and facilitate mobilization.

Faced with now-rationalized uncertainties and the legitimated requirements of actorhood to deal with these uncertainties, modern actors stabilize themselves by creating and using rules of various kinds. This is a driving force for globalization. The point is that the first "interest" or problem of the modern actor is not to accomplish prior goals of some sort but to be an actor. This requires discovering goals, technologies, resources, sovereignty, control, and boundaries. It is much easier to accomplish this if wider stabilizing rules can be created and utilized.

So modern actors create and consult collective rules. Nation-states employ common definitions of nation-state goals: principally, socioeconomic development and justice or equality. They consult and respect wider cultural analyses about how to accomplish these goals and use common analyses (e.g., accountings) of their resources. They mobilize standardized ways of organizing sovereignty and control. And, while none of these things work very well, they are at least legitimate demonstrations of actorhood, which is, after all, the core purpose. Actors, in short, establish their existence by adopting common forms and supporting the creation of such common forms (even when these forms might be quite costly to them).

Organizations, as is well known, follow similar patterns, structuring themselves, with the aid of elaborate consulting machineries, around common and established models: they devote many resources to the construction of such models. Individuals too, in the modern system, consult a myriad of external rule systems (lawyers, therapists, accountants, and the like) in propping up their individuality. One achieves strong status as a rational actor by becoming much like everyone else.

In other words, the drive to create common globalized models of instrumental culture is produced by a system that defines actorhood as a core principle. It feeds on itself: each step forward in globalization produces more and more definitions of the requirements and responsibilities of effective actorhood (e.g., modern environmental principles), which motivates actors even further to support the construction of more demanding theories of their responsibilities.

GLOBAL CONFLICT

The extreme dependence of modern actors on wider legitimating models that sustain their actorhood generates much global instrumental culture. The cultural models in question vary, but they rest on common rationalistic (e.g., scientific) assumptions and there is more integration than is commonly supposed. But absent a unifying state, there is a good deal of conflict too. The issues take great importance, as sub-unit actors depend on the wider models for legitimation. So differences that might otherwise seem small can loom very large, and modern global conflict is often about variations among fairly similar models of modernity. The Second World War, for instance, can be seen to have been about variations between more corporatist and statist models of individual and society. The Cold War can be seen to have been about modest variations in models of the social control of the economy. At present, similar fractionating lines appear between older western models and emerging, more fundamentalist Islamic ones. It is important to note that these conflicts are only secondarily about the "interests" of the rational actors of the system; they are principally about the properties of proper actorhood and thus have a constitutive or religious character.

OTHERHOOD: THE NATURE OF THE GLOBALIZED CULTURAL SYSTEM

We have discussed the modern system's drive or demand for a globalized instrumental culture and turn now to analyze the supply of this material. A core factor arises from the nature of modern actorhood. This actorhood involves two components (Meyer and Jepperson, forthcoming). First, mainly derived from the modern scientific analysis of nature, there is the recognized existence of physical and social entities with natural interests and functions: actors are entities with rights. These are not only individuals, societies, and functional groups within society (like "labor"), but also many entities outside society – like whales or other species, or the ecosystem as a whole, or social entities not yet proper actors (fetuses, unformed indigenous social groups and so on).

Actorhood proper arises from an additional principle mainly derived from western and now worldwide moral law. Actors are entities with rights or interests *and* with the assigned right and capacity to represent these interests. Actors, thus, are assigned agency – derived mainly from the moral universe: it is in this sense that they are small gods. Agency is, in effect, moral action and occurs with a great deal of universalized standardization. There are proper ways to set goals, choose technologies, organize effective sovereignty and self-control, and to relate rationally to the environment. And the good agent, because legitimated agency is derived from a common moral frame, has a great deal in common with other agents: the rational state, rational organization, and rational individual have a great deal in common (and often consult the same therapeutic authorities).

Modern actors thus have great capacities to transfer their agency to others; in short, they function as Others. Modern individuals do this to others, sometimes for pay and sometimes for free. They also do it to the organizations they serve and to national states. Modern individuals are renowned for their ability to opine to each other and the wider world (including surveying social scientists). Similarly, states and other organizations serve the purpose of advising Others and each other and individuals. Collective action of this sort is endemic in the modern system, contrary to realist theories.

All this activity occurs under the moral law: consultants and agents are to reflect the wider truths of the law in acting as Others to actors. In extreme cases, as with the sciences and professions, elite participants serve as agents almost purely of the wider extrasocial truths: agents for the Mind of God as reflected in nature (the sciences) and/or the moral universe (as in the legal professions and their kin).

Agency of this sort is very highly valued in the modern system, and the most virtuous and admired participants are those who serve most purely as agents of general truths. Indeed, in the modem stratification system, occupations are valued in terms of their nearness to pure Otherhood and their distance from self-interested actorhood. Unadmired roles are those that involve real work and the exercise of real narrow power. Consultant Others are more admired. Most admired, worldwide, are the Others who act as agents of the high truths of science and law: these are the ones who get the high prizes (Meyer 1994).

Thus, modern world society is filled with eager participants in the formation of universalized global culture. These are the direct creators of the general principles of social progress and social equality, the analysts of technologies for actors to accomplish their ends, the therapists who create general principles of sovereignty and self-control, and all the scientific analysts of the wider natural environment.

ORGANIZATIONAL FORMS OF GLOBALIZED AND RATIONALIZED OTHERHOOD

Nation-state, organizational, and individual actors are seeking models of their actorhood. And these structures, equipped with and valuing universal agency, readily supply othering on a global scale.

Most directly, the modern system is seen as an explosion of scientific and professional activity and the organization of this activity on a global scale. Scientific and professional organizations, of both governmental and non-governmental sorts, have expanded exponentially (Schofer 1999). So have investments in these activities, and so have the numbers of personnel trained in them. The activities and ideologies involved make global, universalistic claims and are used in just these ways. They provide grounding for globalized environmental and technological othering, globalized instruction on human rights and personhood, and global instruction on the proper organization of society (e.g., the market economy, the democratic political system, and proper intrafamilial social relationships).

Between the pure Otherhood that is involved in the scientific and professional contemplation of universal law and the practical world of actors, a thick layer of applied professionalism arises. This is the most significant area of scientific expansion at the global level (Schofer 1999). And it generates huge, global consulting industries that instruct national states, organizations, and individuals on procedures for properly agentic actor-hood. This is one of the most rapidly expanding industries in the world, and its services are widely utilized by claimant actors. It is an industry that almost entirely rests on universalized scientific and professional assumptions, so its output can, in principle, be used everywhere and by all actors.

It should be noted that a certain role distance between the purer Otherhood of the elite sciences and professions and the more applied Otherhood of the agentic consultants is maintained. Pure theory is too unclear and inconsistent to be used effectively by those who maintain the faith in practically agentic actorhood. So, application fashions and fads arise and provide simplifications, for instance, in the contemporary "standards" and "quality assurance" programs supplied to modern organizations or in the recipes for the production of economic development by national states or in the therapies promoted for individuals. But the claims of the particular advocates rest almost entirely on the assumptions of true, universalized laws.

Then, on a more concrete level, it can be seen that agentic othering is produced by a welter of international governmental and non-governmental associations. These have expanded exponentially in the current period (see the reviews by Boli and Thomas 1997, 1999). They are built by agentic state and non-state actors, who (often eagerly) participate in their formation. They contain codified recipes and models for proper actor structuring and activity in all the areas of recognized instrumental social life: very few of them are concerned with arational or expressive domains of social life. They share models of medicine, science, education, economic organization, human rights, environmental protection, technical development, rational political and social organization, and so on. The models put forward rest on rationalized scientific and professional analyses, and this justifies their putative universality, though the purely theoretical scientists and professionals often have little direct involvement. The spirit is applied and practical and often highly professionalized, but behind it is the mobilization of the true faith in a wider rationality.

Participation in these globalized associational networks is known to be a strong predictor of proper mobilized actorhood: this is true not only of national states (Chapter 8) but also of formal organizations and, undoubtedly, of individuals too. At the individual level, the promotion of globalized actorhood is most dramatic through national educational systems which expand isomorphically around the world and which tie individuals into globalized models of modernity: education tends to be the main predictor at the individual level (Inkeles and Smith 1974, and many others).

Next, these associations shade over into wider social movements, varying in degree of formal organization. All sorts of agentic human actors support as universalizing Others: discursive models of human rights, social organization in all its areas, and the wider natural environment. Elaborate languages, universalized and often resting on very general scientific or professional ideologies, support the rapid expansion of human rights into unforeseen areas (e.g., gay and lesbian rights – see Frank and McEneaney 1999) or the generalization of environmental principles to quite elaborate levels.

Finally, the actors themselves, in their eagerness to demonstrate universality, put their own models – often heavily edited by transmitting scientists, professionals and consultants – forward for general emulation. And, eager for stabilization, other actors try to copy the most admired ones. National states searching for models of proper individual welfare have beaten pathways to Sweden, which has been most happy to be copied. others, searching for the true route to economic development, have often tried to copy the USA (which clearly finds self-enhancement by advancing itself as a model; but the recent tendency to try to copy Japanese models has abated). At the organizational level, admired firms put themselves forward as models, and whole sets of consulting firms and business school academics make a business out of aiding in the diffusion.

All this increasingly rapid "diffusion" of models of actorhood rests on underlying assumptions that rational human actorhood is and should be a universal matter (Chapter 6), and that successful models must represent some sort of scientific truth.

Rationalistic and realist theories treat the sorts of collective action discussed above as rare and difficult (Olson 1965; Coleman 1986). In fact, it is routine in global society and makes for globalization. The theoretical issue is simple: if rational actorhood is a prior and natural state, as realist theories assume, then collective mobilization is likely to be difficult (unless built into the genetics or prior socialization of the actors). If, as we assume, rational actorhood is an elaborate sociocultural construction and at great odds with actual human life and possibilities, then collective action is a very natural outcome.

MECHANISMS OF TRANSMISSION

The core mechanism by which the wider global instrumental culture is transmitted to subunits, as outlined above, is through the structuring of actor identities. Once national societies enter the world as nation-state actors, they acquire proper identity and purpose and seek out approved forms rather eagerly. Once social groups have been reorganized as formal organizations, they come to be open to wider models of rationalization. Once persons become modern individuals, they eagerly acquire the forms of modern individualism.

Thus, standardized purposes, technologies, resource definitions, sovereignty and control forms, and analyses of the wider environment are quickly adopted. Nation-states, organizations and individuals, at least in their formal identity claims, tend to be very nice. Of course, this is all enhanced by the active Otherhood provided by the global system and floods of (also very nice) consultants, international associations, and scientific and professional bodies. This is, in realist analyses, seen as imposed and potentially oppressive: the surprise of the modern world, obvious in our analyses, is how eagerly the forms of modernity (e.g., universal education) are sought out, and how little they are resisted. The core mechanism here is the identity mechanism which opens up essentially the whole social structure of the world to rather rapid penetration.

Beyond this, the models of modern actorhood are simultaneously supplied to national states, organizations (e.g., interest groups), and individuals. These various actor-levels affect each other a great deal, so that states which neglect to incorporate an approved model from the global system come under much pressure from world-legitimated internal actors to do so. Similarly, modernizing states press their internal actors (e.g., firms) to conform to proper models of actorhood.

SOME CONSEQUENCES FOR ACTORS

A first and obvious consequence of the globalized system of instrumental culture for actor subunits is unexpected isomorphism. Societies vary by factors of 100 to 1 in resources and enormously in their own traditions. But, they adopt surprisingly similar forms of modernity (in the state, the educational system and the economy). Bradley and Ramirez (1996), for instance, consider the world expansion in female participation in higher education. If this took place in developed countries only, realist theories could make sense of it: if it were slowed in Islamic ones, standard cultural theories would fit. In practice, it has been worldwide, and types of countries vary little in the matter.

A second consequence is the high internal structuration of modern actors: their extreme tendency to organize, plan, make policy, and posture around the goods of modern actorhood. Even Third World national states and rather functionally simple organizations and quite marginal individuals adopt rationalized structures of plan. A modern university, for instance, will have a much more elaborate structure than a university of the same size and diversity in an earlier period. So will a modern state, firm, or individual person (who can now spell out [e.g., to an interviewer, or occasionally in the mass media] all sorts of matters a more traditional person would have left implicit). Structuration follows from the great inconsistency between high models of complete, rational actorhood and the practical capabilities and resources of actual putative actors. Core national states, for instance, can often simply carry out forms of modernity without too much centralized structuration. Semi-peripheral strugglers have to mobilize structure and peripheral ones have to plan. The countries in the furthest periphery, with little capacity to do anything, then write the new forms into their identities, and their national constitutions are often some of the most progressive documents in the world (Boli 1987).

A third consequence of globalization is local decoupling. Actors adopt high forms but are unable to carry them out in practice (e.g., human rights). They adopt inconsistent structures from different global sources (e.g., educational and labor market policies). They adopt symbolic frames without substantive meaning and so on. The exalted character of global frames of actorhood virtue naturally means that hypocrisy – the respect vice pays to virtue – is enlarged in the modern system.

Analysts of decoupling often take it to mean that nothing really changes with the adoption of modern forms of actorhood, but this is unrealistic. In a Durkheimian way, local relationships between modern institutions and between these institutions and practices (e.g., between attitudes and actions) are very weak, but over time both systems are penetrated by wider models. For instance, Bradley and Ramirez (1996) show that the spread of world standards that encourage female participation in universities affects both national policy adoptions and actual enrollments, but these two variables are themselves little related. The point is that wider global changes penetrate all levels relatively independently, so that there are high correlations over time collectively and low correlations across units cross-sectionally.

In practice, the extensive decoupling characteristic of the modern system provides fertile soil for the discovery of social problems and social inconsistencies and the construction of much reform. Reform is, in fact, endemic and stimulates both local and global expansive change in modernity. New problems are discovered in the environment, socioeconomic development, and human conditions (e.g., inequalities and injustices); these provide the fuel for further expansive reform. Global models expand faster than any possible correction, so the system is in a kind of permanent crisis that calls for more rapid expansion and reform.

THE CONSTRUCTION OF THE LOCAL: GLOCALIZATION

The mobilization of social entities, in the modern system, around legitimated global models of actorhood is built on the principle that the local actors, in fact, have their own distinctive identities on which their nominal choices are rooted. Standardized actorhood arises around the principle of actor unique identity. Thus, with globalization, actors systematically generate and expand their own self-conscious, unique bases. But, they do this within global models of effective instrumental action. This Tocquevillian phenomenon is called "glocalization" by Robertson (1992). Nations celebrate their unique heritages while moving into standardized models. Organizations, as they become standard rational structures, dramatize their supposedly unique organizational cultures. Individuals parade their individual subjectivities.

The cultures produced and celebrated face the problem that true agentic actorhood has a standardized-model character in instrumental ways. This means that uniqueness – the dramatization of the local – inevitably takes an expressive character. Nation-states do not usually direct their uniqueness toward the arational and unique character of their divisions of labor, their forms of state structure, their educational or medical systems, and the like. Too much uniqueness on such matters violates the principles of rational actorhood.

Uniqueness and identity are thus most legitimately focused on matters of expressive culture: variations in language, dress, food, traditions, landscapes, familial styles, and so on. These are precisely the things that do not matter in the modern system, which is to say they have no direct rational relation to instrumental actorhood. Nation-states and organized ethnic groups within them do not claim to have their own styles of wife- or child-beating, of economic production, and so on. Such claims would violate global principles and pressures, and actual traditions along these lines are suppressed in reconstructions or revitalizations of history and tradition.

CONCLUSION

The globalization of instrumental culture is a striking empirical feature of the modern system, as models of proper actorhood for national states, individuals, and organizations spread around the world. The empirical phenomenon is difficult to contest – we have concentrated on its explanation.

Globalization of instrumental culture is a product of a stateless world that is filled with "social actors" who are legitimated in rationalistic and universalistic terms. Actorhood is a high and constructed form, far beyond the capacities of real social units. These units thus work to create stabilizing rules at the collective level, providing legitimacy to their structures and activities. They do this even when costs are high. The rules involved, of course, are rationalistic and universalistic and apply everywhere.

The supply of globalized models also expands with socially constructed actorhood. The legitimated agency of social actors readily transforms itself into agency for others or for the natural and moral universe beyond society: modern world society is, in a sense, dominated by its clergy. Thus, globalized models are produced by the sciences and professions (the highest status groups in the modern national and world stratification system) by rapidly expanding international associations that rest on scientized and universalized pretenses, by social movements on a global scale and by actors themselves who present their forms as universal models.

The adoption of actor identities by national states, organizations, and individuals produces units that are eager and ready to adopt legitimating global models. This is, of course, facilitated by the available otherhood in a world of helpful consultants. It is also facilitated by the multilayered character of actorhood in the modern system, as individuals and organizations press national states (and conversely) to assume their world-legitimated responsibilities.

Consequences include massive unexpected isomorphisms among social units, the high structuration of these units, and a great deal of internal decoupling within them. They also include the empowered production of much subjectivity and uniqueness within each constructed actor: scripted expressive culture that is edited to be consistent with the more instrumental models of global culture.

REFERENCES

Barrett, Deborah and David John Frank. 1999. Population Control for National Development: From World Discourse to National Policies, in J. Boli and G. Thomas (eds.), *Constructing World Culture*. Stanford, CA: Stanford University Press, pp. 198–221.

Berkovitch, Nitza. 1999. The Emergence and Transformation of the International Women's Movement, in J. Boli and G. Thomas (eds.), *Constructing World Culture*. Stanford, CA: Stanford University Press, pp. 100–26.

Boli, John. 1987. World Polity Sources of Expanding State Authority and Organization, 1870–1970, in G. Thomas et al. (eds.), *Institutional Structure*. Beverly Hills, CA: Sage, pp. 71–91.

—— and George Thomas. 1997. World Culture in the World Polity: A Century of International Non-Governmental Organization. *American Sociological Review* 62:171–90.

—— and —— (eds.) 1999. *Constructing World Culture: International Nongovernmental Organizations Since 1875*. Stanford, CA: Stanford University Press.

Bongaarts, John and Susan Watkins. 1996. Social Interactions and Contemporary Fertility Transitions. *Population and Development Review* 22 (4):639–82.

Bradley, Karen and Francisco Ramirez. 1996. World Polity Promotion of Gender Parity: Women's Share of Higher Education, 1965–85. *Research in Sociology of Education and Socialization* 11:63–91.

Brunsson, Nils and Kerstin Sahlin-Andersson. 1997. Constructing Organizations, Working Paper. Stockholm: Stockholm Center for Organizational Research.

Coleman, James. 1986. *Individual Interests and Collective Action*. New York: Cambridge University Press.

Fiala, Robert and Audri Gordon-Lanford. 1987. Educational Ideology and the World Educational Revolution, 1950–1970. *Comparative Education Review* 31 (3):315–32.

Finnemore, Martha. 1996. *National Interests in International Society*. Ithaca, NY: Cornell University Press.

Frank, David John and Elizabeth H. McEneaney. 1999. The Individualization of Society and the Liberalization of State Policies on Same-Sex Sexual Relations, 1984–1995. *Social Forces* 77 (March):911–44.

—— Ann Hironaka, John W. Meyer, Evan Schofer, and Nancy Brandon Tuma. 1999. The Rationalization and Organization of Nature in World Culture, in J. Boli and G. Thomas (eds.), *Constructing World Culture*. Stanford, CA: Stanford University Press, pp. 81–99.

Hall, Peter (ed.) 1989. *The Political Power of Economic Ideas*. Princeton, NJ: Princeton University Press.

Inkeles, Alex and David Smith. 1974. *Becoming Modern*. Cambridge, MA: Harvard University Press.

Jepperson, Ronald. 1992. National Scripts: The Varying Construction of Individualism and Opinion across the Modern Nation-States. PhD dissertation, Yale University.

McNeely, Connie. 1995. *Constructing the Nation-State: International Organization and Prescriptive Action*. Westport, CT: Greenwood.

Meyer, John W. 1994. The Evolution of Modern Stratification Systems, in D. Grusky (ed.), *Social Stratification*. Boulder, CO: Westview Press, pp. 28–54.

—— and Ronald Jepperson. 2000. The "Actors" of Modern Society: The Cultural Construction of Social Agency. *Sociological Theory*. Reproduced in Chapter 5.

—— Francisco Ramirez, and Yasemin Soysal. 1992. World Expansion of Mass Education, 1870–1980, *Sociology of Education* 65 (2):128–49.

—— David Kamens, and Aaron Benavot. 1992. *School Knowledge for the Masses: World Models and National Primary Curricular Categories*. London: Falmer Press.

—— John Boli, George Thomas, and Francisco Ramirez. 1997. World Society and the Nation-State, *American Journal of Sociology* 103 (1):144–81. Reproduced in Chapter 8.

—— David John Frank, Ann Hironaka, Evan Schofer, and Nancy Brandon Tuma. 1997. The Structuring of a World Environmental Regime, 1870–1990. *International Organization* 51 (4):623–51. Reproduced in Chapter 10.

Olson, Mancur. 1965. *The Logic of Collective Action*. Cambridge, MA: Harvard University Press.

Olson, Olov, James Guthrie, and Christopher Humphrey (eds.) 1998. *Global Warning: Debating International Developments in New Public Financial Management*. Oslo: Cappelen Akademisk Forlag.

Riddle, Phyllis. 1993. Political Authority and University Formation in Europe, *Sociological Perspectives* 36 (1):45–62.

Robertson, Roland. 1992. *Globalization: Social Theory and Global Culture*. London: Sage.

Schofer, Evan. 1999. Science Associations in the International Sphere, 1875–1990, in J. Boli and G. Thomas (eds.), *Constructing World Culture*. Stanford, CA: Stanford University Press, pp. 249–66.

Strang, David and John Meyer 1993. Institutional Conditions for Diffusion, *Theory and Society* 22:487–511. Reproduced in Chapter 6.

Ventresca, Marc. 1995. Counting People when People Count. PhD dissertation, Stanford University.

PART III
APPLICATIONS

8

The Nation-State

World Society and the Nation-State

The authors analyze the nation-state as a worldwide institution constructed by
worldwide cultural and associational processes, developing four main topics: (1)
properties of nation-states that result from their exogenously driven construction, including isomorphism, decoupling, and expansive structuration; (2)
processes by which rationalistic world culture affects national states; (3) characteristics of world society that enhance the impact of world culture on national
states and societies, including conditions favoring the diffusion of world models,
expansion of world-level associations, and rationalized scientific and professional
authority; (4) dynamic features of world culture and society that generate
expansion, conflict, and change, especially the statelessness of world society,
legitimation of multiple levels of rationalized actors, and internal inconsistencies
and contradictions.

This chapter reviews arguments and evidence concerning the following proposition:
*Many features of the contemporary nation-state derive from worldwide models con-
structed and propagated through global cultural and associational processes.* These
models and the purposes they reflect (e.g., equality, socioeconomic progress,
human development) are highly rationalized, articulated, and often surprisingly
consensual. Worldwide models define and legitimate agendas for local action,
shaping the structures and policies of nation-states and other national and local
actors in virtually all of the domains of rationalized social life – business, politics,
education, medicine, science, even the family and religion. The institutionalization
of world models helps explain many puzzling features of contemporary national
societies such as structural isomorphism in the face of enormous differences in

Originally published as:

John W. Meyer, John Boli, George M. Thomas, and Francisco O. Ramirez. 1997. *World Society and the
Nation-State.* American Journal of Sociology 103:144–81.

Work on this chapter was facilitated by funds provided by the Sovereignty Project of the Institute
for International Studies, Stanford University. Helpful comments were provided by many colleagues, including Neil Fligstein, Steve Krasner, Ron Jepperson, Walter Powell, participants in
Stanford's Comparative Workshop, and seminar participants at Cornell, Columbia, Northwestern,
and Princeton Universities. We also thank several *AJS* referees. Some ideas here are developed from
earlier work by Thomas et al. (1987) and Meyer (1994). Direct correspondence to John W. Meyer,
Department of Sociology, Stanford University, Building 12, Room 160, Stanford, California
94305–2047.

resources and traditions, ritualized and rather loosely coupled organizational efforts, and elaborate structuration to serve purposes that are largely of exogenous origins. World models have long been in operation as shapers of states and societies, but they have become especially important in the postwar era as the cultural and organizational developments of world society have intensified at an unprecedented rate.

The operation of world society through peculiarly cultural and associational processes depends heavily on its statelessness. The almost feudal character of parcelized legal-rational sovereignty in the world (Meyer 1980) has the seemingly paradoxical result of diminishing the causal importance of the organized hierarchies of power and interests celebrated in most "realist" social scientific theories. The statelessness of world society also explains, in good measure, the lack of attention of the social sciences to the coherence and impact of world society's cultural and associational properties. Despite Tocqueville's ([1836] 1966) well-known analysis of the importance of cultural and associational life in the nearly stateless American society of the 1830s, the social sciences are more than a little reluctant to acknowledge patterns of influence and conformity that cannot be explained solely as matters of power relations or functional rationality. This reluctance is most acute with respect to global development. Our effort here represents, we hope, a partial corrective for it.

We are trying to account for a world whose societies, organized as nation-states, are structurally similar in many unexpected dimensions and change in unexpectedly similar ways. A hypothetical example may be useful to illustrate our arguments, and we shall carry the example throughout the chapter. If an unknown society were "discovered" on a previously unknown island, it is clear that many changes would occur. A government would soon form, looking something like a modern state with many of the usual ministries and agencies. Official recognition by other states and admission to the UN would ensue. The society would be analyzed as an economy with standard types of data, organizations, and policies for domestic and international transactions. Its people would be formally reorganized as citizens with many familiar rights, while certain categories of citizens – children, the elderly, the poor – would be granted special protection. Standard forms of discrimination, especially ethnic and gender based, would be discovered and decried. The population would be counted and classified in ways specified by world census models. Modern educational, medical, scientific, and family law institutions would be developed. All this would happen more rapidly, and with greater penetration to the level of daily life, in the present day than at any earlier time because world models applicable to the island society are more highly codified and publicized than ever before. Moreover, world-society organizations devoted to educating and advising the islanders about the models' importance and utility are more numerous and active than ever.

What would be unlikely to happen is also clear. Theological disputes about whether the newly discovered *Indios* had souls or were part of the general human moral order would be rare. There would be little by way of an imperial rush to colonize the island. Few would argue that the natives needed only modest citizenship or human rights or that they would best be educated by but a few years of vocational training.

Thus, without knowing anything about the history, culture, practices, or traditions of this previously unknown society, we could forecast many changes that, upon "discovery," would descend on the island under the general rubric of "development." Our forecast would be imprecise because of the complexity of the interplay among various world models and local traditions, but the likely range of outcomes would be quite limited. We can identify the range of possibilities by using the institutionalist theoretical perspective underlying the analysis in this chapter to interpret what has already happened to practically all of the societies of the world after their discovery and incorporation into world society.

Our institutionalist perspective makes predictions somewhat at variance with those of three more established theoretical approaches to world society and the nation-state (for reviews, see Powell and DiMaggio 1991; Jepperson, Wendt, and Katzenstein 1996; and Finnemore 1996b). In multivariate analyses of properties of nation-states, researchers would inevitably consider hypotheses from all four perspectives. But none of the prevailing theories would effectively predict many of the profound social and organizational changes that would occur on our hypothetical island, not least because they do not adequately consider the cultural processes involved.

Microrealist analyses, dominant in the field of international relations under the banner of neorealism, assume that the nation-state is a natural, purposive, and rational actor in an essentially anarchic world (Waltz 1979; Gilpin 1981). State action reflects inherent needs and interests; culture is largely irrelevant, though it may be invoked to explain particular, often historically rooted patterns of policy or behavior. In any case, culture is only local or national, not global. Much contemporary theory about globalization has this microrealist character, stressing a conception of world society as involving nothing more than dense networks of transactions and interdependence (Jacobson 1979) among autonomous nation-state actors. Variants like neoliberalism (Keohane 1986) and regime theory (Krasner 1983) pay attention to institutional frameworks created by states that, once in place, act as constraints on state action, but they rely on microeconomic realist arguments to explain the emergence of institutions and their durability. Power and interests come first, leaving little room for culture.

Partly in reaction to microrealism, macrorealist arguments such as world-system theory (Wallerstein 1974; Chase-Dunn 1989) and state-competition theory (Skocpol 1979; Tilly 1992) see the nation-state as the creature of worldwide systems of economic or political power, exchange, and competition. The nation-state is less a bounded actor, more the occupant of a role defined by world economic and political/military competition. Culture, most often seen as self-serving hegemonic ideology or repressive false consciousness, is of only marginal interest; money and force, power and interests are the engines of global change. World-system theory develops this line of thought most consistently: The dynamism of the world economy and state system depend greatly on the absence of centralized world authority (a world state or empire), and global culture is essentially a by-product of hegemony with no causal significance in its own right (Chase-Dunn 1989).

The third perspective, also developed partly in response to microrealism, adopts a microphenomenological approach that conceptualizes the nation-state as the product of national cultural and interpretive systems. The state is embedded in institutions whose cultural character matters, but these institutions reflect world processes only indirectly or not at all. Simple arguments (e.g., Almond and Verba 1963) are content to give a nod to local political culture as background material, while more complex versions (March 1988; March and Olsen 1989) see cultural interpretation and purposive action as simultaneously shaping one another. Application of this perspective to global cultural processes could be fruitful, but most discussions extending this line of thought to the world level (e.g., Mattelart 1983; Sklair 1991) treat culture superficially as flows of relatively arbitrary and expressive Western tastes in media products, fashion, art, or fast foods (Ritzer 1996). They fail to appreciate sufficiently the substantive significance of culture and its organizational presence in world society.

Our own perspective, macrophenomenological in orientation, builds on contemporary sociological institutionalism (Thomas et al. 1987; Powell and DiMaggio 1991). We see the nation-state as culturally constructed and embedded rather than as the unanalyzed rational actor depicted by realists (Meyer 1997). We find that the culture involved is substantially organized on a worldwide basis, not simply built up from local circumstances and history (Meyer 1980; Thomas et al. 1987). We see such transnational forces at work throughout Western history, but we argue that particular features and processes characteristic of world society since World War II have greatly enhanced the impact of world-institutional development on nation-states.

Below, we further develop this theoretical background. Then we turn to our causal argument which is organized in four sections: (*a*) distinctive properties of the nation-state as constructed in world culture; (*b*) processes operating at the world-society level that produce and shape nation-states; (*c*) features of world society that enhance the impact of world culture on national states and societies; and (*d*) dynamics of world society, especially global cultural processes that promote inconsistency and conflict in the production and modification of world-societal structures and characteristics.

THEORETICAL BACKGROUND

For realist perspectives, the world is either anarchic (actors pursue interests without interference from an overarching authority structure) or networked (actors intentionally construct interdependent systems of economic and political competition from the ground up). Microphenomenological analysts take culture and interpretation more seriously but restrict them to action processes operating at local or national levels.

Our opening proposition suggests, in contrast, that the world level of social reality is culturally transcendent and causally important in several different senses. First, the contemporary constructed "actors," including nation-states, routinely organize and legitimate themselves in terms of universalistic (world) models like citizenship, socioeconomic development, and rationalized justice. Second, such models are

quite pervasive at the world level, with a considerable amount of consensus on the
nature and value of such matters as citizen and human rights, the natural world and
its scientific investigation, socioeconomic development, and education. Third, the
models rest on claims to universal world applicability; for example, economic models
of development and fiscal policy and medical models of the human body and health
care delivery are presumed to be applicable everywhere, not just in some locales
or regions.

The authority of these general models, legally nonbinding though it may be, goes
far in explaining why our hypothetical discovered island society would rapidly adopt
"modern" structures and purposes upon incorporation into world society. Alternative
models, including whatever traditional structures were in place, have little legitimacy.
The correct modern forms are highly developed and articulated with elaborate
rationalized justifications. Particularistic or local models find it difficult to compete
with these legitimations.

Culture

Realist analyses view culture functionally as expressive material that integrates
collectivities or supports the domination of powerful actors. Microphenomenological
analysts give greater heed to culture's meaning-generating properties and cognitive
import (Berger and Luckmann 1967) but limit their scope to local situational
knowledge and reality construction. These approaches miss the essential elements
of the cultural dimension of world society – the cognitive and ontological models
of reality that specify the nature, purposes, technology, sovereignty, control, and
resources of nation-states and other actors (Meyer 1997). These models, organized in
scientific, professional, and legal analyses of the proper functioning of states, societies, and individuals, are more cognitive and instrumental than expressive. The
analyses involved are highly rationalized and universalistic, describing integrated,
functioning, rational actors. They thus constitute functional theories serving as
ideologies of actor-centric rationalization (Thomas et al. 1987).

To avoid misunderstanding on this point, we emphasize that the functionalism of
world culture is inscribed in commonsense descriptions and social-scientific theories
of "the way things work," but such theories may not mesh well with practical
experience. For example, conventional legitimations for mass schooling insist that
formal education is necessary and beneficial for economic growth, technical innovation, citizen loyalty, and democratic institutions, among other things. Such functional justifications of schooling are rarely questioned, even though careful studies of,
for example, education's effects on economic growth suggest that this functional
relationship is at best weak and highly conditional (Rubinson and Browne 1994).

Diffuse functional models of this sort about actors, action, and presumed causal
relations are centrally constitutive of world culture. As they are implemented in the
furthest corners of the globe, they operate as framing assumptions producing
consequences that in no reasonable way can be seen as "functional" for the societies
that implement them. For instance, the implementation of standard scripts for
educational development in countries of all sorts, without regard to their particular

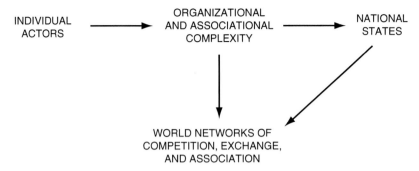

Figure 8.1. The world as aggregated action

circumstances, produces results that often seem quite bizarre, especially when viewed through the rationalized lenses of the functional theories that justify these scripts. Children who will become agricultural laborers study fractions; villagers in remote regions learn about chemical reactions; members of marginalized groups who will never see a ballot box study their national constitutions (Meyer, Nagel, and Snyder 1993). Deeming such practices rationally functional requires a breathtaking leap of faith.

In our island society, the implementation of world models embodying "functional" or "modernity" theories of development would be rampant. For example, any economist comes equipped with powerful models with which to interpret the island economy. These can be applied, with considerable authority, without even visiting the place. A few standardized data tables would be sufficient to empower policy proposals. Similarly, any sociologist comes equipped with the capability to propose measures, analyses, diagnoses, and policy prescriptions for the correction of gender inequalities on the island. On a broad range of economic and social indicators, the island would be categorized and compared with other nation-states in the same way that every newly independent geopolitical entity has been processed in the past several decades. These data collection and comparison processes would greatly enhance the cultural standing and membership of the island society in the nation-state community (McNeely 1995), helping it to transform quickly into a "real" national entity.

Explanatory models

Most analyses see nation-states as collective actors – as products of their own histories and internal forces. Figure 8.1 depicts such conventional models. We emphasize instead models of the sort depicted in Figure 8.2.

Figure 8.2 presents the view that nation-states are more or less exogenously constructed entities – the many individuals, both inside and outside the state, who engage in state formation and policy formulation are enactors of scripts rather more than they are self-directed actors. The social psychology at work here is that of Goffman (1969, 1974) or Snow (Snow and Benford 1992), emphasizing

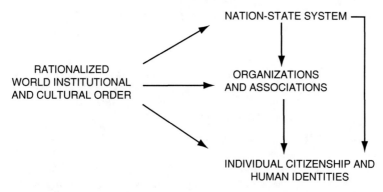

Figure 8.2. The world as enactment of culture

dramaturgical and symbolic processes in place of the hard-boiled calculation of interests assumed by rationalistic actor-centric approaches (see Thomas and Meyer 1984; or cf. Skocpol 1985, pp. 3–20, with pp. 20–28).

We have deliberately oversimplified Figure 8.2 because the proposition we are examining focuses on the enactment dimension of world-societal development. Of course, states, organizations, and individuals also contribute to the content and structure of world culture, and much world-cultural change and elaboration occur within transnational organizations and associations independent of lower-level units. A more complete figure would depict recursive processes among the constituent parts of world society, but here we concentrate on enactment processes. We take up some issues of world-cultural change in the chapter's last section, on the dynamics of world culture.

The exogenous cultural construction of the nation-state model makes it easy and "natural" for standard sociopolitical forms to arise in our island society. Models and measures of such national goals as economic progress and social justice are readily available and morally compelling. Also available are model social problems, defined as the failure to realize these goals, which make it easy to identify and decry such failures as inefficient production methods or violations of rights. Alongside these are prescriptions about standardized social actors and policies that are to be engaged in the effort to resolve these newly recognized problems. All this is widely known and ready for implementation.

PROPERTIES OF THE CULTURALLY CONSTITUTED NATION-STATE

As we develop our argument, we want to keep in the forefront a number of empirical observations about contemporary nation-states. First, nation-states exhibit a great deal of isomorphism in their structures and policies. Second, they make valiant efforts to live up to the model of rational actorhood. Third, and partly as a result of the second observation, they are marked by considerable, and sometimes extraordinary, decoupling between purposes and structure, intentions and results. Fourth, they undergo expansive structuration in largely standardized ways. The generality of these observations makes sense only if nation-states are understood as, in part, constructions of a common wider culture rather than as self-directed actors responding rationally to internal and external contingencies.

Isomorphism and isomorphic change

Given other perspectives' emphases on the heterogeneity of economic and political resources (realist theories) or on local cultural origins (microphenomenological theories), most lines of thought anticipate striking diversity in political units around the world and in these units' trajectories of change. Our argument accounts for the similarities researchers often are surprised to find. It explains why our island society, despite all the possible configurations of local economic forces, power relationships, and forms of traditional culture it might contain, would promptly take on standardized forms and soon appear to be similar to a hundred other nation-states around the world.

Take the example of women in higher education. Microrealist or functional actor-centric models, following Harbison and Myers (1964), suggest that female enrollments in universities would increase in developed economies much more than elsewhere. Macrorealist arguments imply that female enrollments would expand in the core much more than the periphery (Ward 1984; Clark 1992), while microphenomenological arguments point to rising female enrollments in Western but not Islamic countries. However, female enrollments have expanded rapidly everywhere and in about the same time period (Ramirez 1987; Bradley and Ramirez 1996) – a period in which world societal discourse has emphasized female equality (Berkovitch 1997). This finding makes sense only if common world forces are at work.

Isomorphic developments leading to the same conclusion are reported in studies of many other nation-state features: constitutional forms emphasizing both state power and individual rights (Boli 1987), mass schooling systems organized around a fairly standard curriculum (Meyer, Kamens, and Benavot 1992; Meyer, Ramirez, and Soysal 1992), rationalized economic and demographic record keeping and data systems (McNeely 1995; Ventresca 1995), antinatalist population control policies intended to enhance national development (Barrett and Frank 1997), formally equalized female status and rights (Ramirez and Weiss 1979; Charles 1992; Berkovitch 1997; Ramirez, Soysal, and Shanahan, in press), expanded human rights in general (Ramirez and Meyer 1992), expansive environmental policies (Frank et al. 1997), development-oriented economic policy (Hall 1989; Finntinore 1996*a*), universalistic welfare systems (Collier and Messick 1975; Thomas and Lauderdale 1987; Abbott and Deviney 1992; Strang and Chang 1993), standard definitions of disease and health care (Thornton 1992), and even some basic demographic variables (Watkins 1987). Theories reasoning from the obviously large differences among national economies and cultural traditions have great difficulty accounting for these observed isomorphisms, but they are sensible outcomes if nation-states are enactments of the world cultural order.

Rational actorhood

As we discuss further below, in world culture, the nation-state is defined as a fundamental and strongly legitimated unit of action. Because world culture is highly rationalized and universalistic, nation-states form as rationalized actors. Out of all the possible forms political entities might take, one – the model of the rational and responsible actor – is utterly dominant. This is how nation-states routinely present themselves, both internally (e.g., in their constitutions) and externally (e.g., in seeking admission to the UN and other intergovernmental bodies). They claim all the features of the rational state actor: territorial boundaries and a demarcated population; sovereign authority, self-determination, and responsibility; standardized purposes like collective development, social justice, and the protection of individual rights; authoritative, law-based control systems; clear possession of resources such as natural and mineral wealth and a labor force; and policy technologies for the rational means–ends accomplishment of goals.

Consider this last item – goals. Nation-states are remarkably uniform in defining their goals as the enhancement of collective progress (roughly, gross domestic product [GDP] per capita) and individual rights and development (roughly, citizen enhancement and equality). This occurs in constitutions which typically emphasize goals of both national and equitable individual development (Boli 1987), in general statements on national education, which frequently follow suit (Fiala and Gordon-Lanford 1987), in depictions of the nation and the individual citizen in educational curricula (Wong 1991), and in vast amounts of formal economic policy (McNeely 1995). Goals outside the standard form (the nation in service to God, a dynasty, an ethnic or religious group, or imperial expansion), while still common enough, are usually suspect unless strongly linked to these basic goals of collective and individual progress.

Nations have traditions of piling up the skulls of their neighbors in war, but these are no longer announced as goals. War is no longer an acceptable "continuation of politics by other means"; war departments have been relabeled departments of defense (Eyre and Suchman 1996). Nation-states present themselves as not simply rational actors but rather nice ones at that.

Thus, our island society would likely adopt a purposive nation-state structure, almost immediately, with the appropriate goals of economic development, equality, and enhancement of individual opportunity. A purposive nation-state actor would be constructed to take formal responsibility for such matters, even under the most unlikely social and economic circumstances (Meyer 1980; Jackson and Rosberg 1982).

Decoupling

Both realist and microphenomenological arguments suggest, for different reasons, that nation-states should be tightly coupled structures – due to functional require-ments, the control structures imposed by external powers, or their own domestic cultures and interpretive schemes. This is notoriously not the case. For example, commitments to egalitarian citizenship, which are ubiquitous in constitutions and public discourse, are frequently contradicted by policies that make formal distinctions between genders and among ethnic groups. At the same time, both the claims and the policies are frequently inconsistent with practice.

Decoupling is endemic because nation-states are modeled on an external culture that cannot simply be imported wholesale as a fully functioning system (Chapter 4; Riggs 1964). World culture contains a good many variants of the dominant models which leads to the eclectic adoption of conflicting principles. Diffusion processes work at several levels and through a variety of linkages, yielding incoherence. Some external elements are easier to copy than others, and many external elements are inconsistent with local practices, requirements, and cost structures. Even more problematic, world cultural models are highly idealized and internally inconsistent, making them in principle impossible to actualize (Chapter 6).

Having few rationalized resources, our imagined island society would find it much easier to adopt the latest structural forms than to make them work effectively. It is easier to create a cabinet ministry with appropriate policies for education or for the protection of women than to build schools and organize social services implementing these policies. It is easier to plan for economic development than to generate capital or technical and labor skills that can make development happen.

Hence, the logic of copying externally denned identities promotes profound decoupling. Any rationalized "actor," whether an individual, organization, or nation-state, reveals much decoupling between formal models and observable practices (for organizations, see Chapter 4 and Weick 1976; for individuals, see Cancian 1975; Jepperson 1992; Brim and Kagan 1980; and Goffman 1974). Resource-rich "actors" facing exogenous pressures to assume a given posture may be able to do so convincingly: Core countries often have the resources and organizational capacity to adopt, for example, a curricular innovation in education (Meyer, Kamens, and Benavot 1992) even if, like the United States, they lack a central educational authority structure. Weaker actors faced with the same imperative may emphasize formal structuration instead. Peripheral nation-states do a good deal of symbolic educational reform via national policies and control systems (Ramirez and Rubinson 1979), but they have more difficulty bringing change into the classroom.

If formal structuration and centralization are difficult, state managers may retreat simply to planning for future progress. National planning is especially common in the world's peripheries (Meyer, Boli-Bennett, and Chase-Dunn 1978). If even planning cannot be accomplished, policymakers and bureaucrats may settle for incorporating the required principle in general statements of values and identity. Peripheral countries' constitutions are especially likely to specify comprehensive principles of rationalized progress, including detailed assertions of state responsibility for both individual welfare and national economic growth (Boli 1987; Boli-Bennett and Meyer 1978), that their states cannot live up to.

We can predict that our island society would likely adopt a rather advanced constitution and engage in formal social and economic planning. Repeated rounds of planning and policy-making would occur as it became clear that the idealized rational models were far from effective implementation. Cynicism would emerge, but its main concrete result would be still more planning and reform.

The decoupling of general values from practical action is, of course, quite different from the relationship predicted by realist and microphenomenological lines of argument (Parsons 1951). Realist theories see actor policy and structure as deliberate means of controlling action, not as conformity to exogenous models. Microphenomenological perspectives see policy and structure as constructed in hermeneutic consistency with action. Thus, the prevalence of decoupling has led to much befuddlement (Cancian 1975; for an extended discussion, see Jepperson 1992): How can values and action be so habitually inconsistent? Such inconsistency is an obvious actor characteristic from an institutional point of view, particularly for actors like nation-states that have broad and diffuse goals (Meyer and Rowan 1977; March 1988; Brunsson 1989).

One should not be too cynical about decoupling, however. True, for any set of constructed actors, the correlations between policy and practice may be very low (e.g., the correlation between constitutional state authority and government revenue as a proportion of GNP is slightly negative (Boli 1987)). But systemically this relationship is strong. The same time periods and civilizations that foster expanded images of state authority also generate highly elaborated state organizations.

Expansive structuration

By structuration we mean the formation and spread of explicit, rationalized, and differentiated organizational forms. Here we argue that the dependence of the modern nation-state on exogenous models, coupled with the fact that these models are organized as cultural principles and visions not strongly anchored in local circumstances, generates expansive structuration at the nation-state and organizational levels.

The structuration of the nation-state greatly exceeds any functional requirements of society, especially in peripheral countries. Impoverished countries routinely establish universities producing overqualified personnel, national planning agencies writing unrealistic five-year plans, national airlines that require heavy subsidization, and freeways leading nowhere – forms of "development" that are functionally quite irrational. This observation poses a problem for both realist and microphenomenological theories.

One common intellectual response to this decoupled structuration is neglect of its generality. Typically, political and organizational theorists try to explain the apparent irrationalities of specific structural changes as products of local constellations of power and interests – the delusions of a self-aggrandizing leader, perhaps, or the interests of dominant elites. But the process operates everywhere and in many different sectors of social life. Holding constant the functional pressures of size, resources, and complexity, in recent decades nation-states and other organizations have clearly expanded inordinately across many different social domains. This is precisely the period during which world society has been consolidated (Meyer et al. 1975; Strang 1990), making world models universally known and legitimated.

Nation-states and organizations may have distinct and complex histories, but they all have expanded structurally in similar ways in the same historical period (Jepperson and Meyer 1991; Dobbin 1994; Guillen 1994; Soysal 1994).

Present-day universities and firms, for instance, have a multitude of offices that an organization of the same size and goals would not have had just a few decades ago: accounting, legal, personnel, safety, environment, and counseling offices, among others. After the fact, all of these seem functionally necessary and the power coalitions that produced them can certainly be identified, but this sort of explanation simply does not account for the worldwide simultaneity of the process. So also with nation-states, which undergo structuration to manage the expanding, externally denned requirements of rational actorhood. Common evolving world-societal models, not a hundred different national trajectories, have led states to establish ministries and other agencies purporting to manage social and economic planning, education (Ramirez and Ventresca 1992), population control (Barrett and Frank 1997), the environment (Frank et al. 1997), science policy (Finnemore 1996a), health, gender equality (Berkovitch 1997), the welfare of the old and the young (Boli-Bennett and Meyer 1978), and much more. This worldwide process affects both core and peripheral countries, though with variable impact depending on local resources and organizational capacities.

The enormous expansion of nation-state structures, bureaucracies, agendas, revenues, and regulatory capacities since World War II indicates that something is very wrong with analyses asserting that globalization diminishes the "sovereignty" of the nation-state (Duchacek et al. 1988; Nordenstreng and Schiller 1979). Globalization certainly poses new problems for states, but it also strengthens the world-cultural principle that nation-states are the primary actors charged with identifying and managing those problems on behalf of their societies. Expansion of the authority and responsibilities of states creates unwieldy and fragmented structures, perhaps, but not weakness. The modern state may have less autonomy than earlier but it clearly has more to do than earlier as well, and most states are capable of doing more now than they ever have done before.

PROCESSES OF WORLD SOCIETY'S IMPACT ON NATION-STATES

So far, we have argued that the observable isomorphism among nation-states supports our proposition that these entities derive from models embedded in an overarching world culture. What processes in world society construct and shape these "actors" to produce such isomorphism? The usual approach to answering this question would seek to identify mechanisms whereby actors rationally pursuing their interests make similar choices and decisions. This approach implicitly assumes that actor definitions and interests are largely fixed and independent of culture. We find it more useful and revealing to focus on processes that produce or reconstruct the actors themselves. We identify three processes by which world-societal elements 'authorize and fashion' national states: the construction of identity and purpose, systemic maintenance of actor identity, and legitimation of the actorhood of such subnational units as individuals and organized interests.

Construction of nation-state identity and purpose

World society contains much cultural material authoritatively defining the nation-state *is* the preferred form of sovereign, responsible actor. The external recognition and construction of sovereign statehood have been crucial dimensions of the Western system for centuries (Krasner 1995–96), with new claimants especially dependent on obtaining formal recognition from dominant powers. With the anticolonial and self-determination movements of the twentieth century, all sorts of collectivities have learned to organize their claims around a nation-state identity, and the consolidation of the UN system has provided a central forum for identity recognition that diminishes the importance of major states. Entry into the system occurs, essentially, via application forms (to the UN and other world bodies) on which the applicant must demonstrate appropriately formulated assertions about sovereignty and control over population and territory, along with appropriate aims and purposes (Meyer 1980; Jackson and Rosberg 1982; McNeely 1995).

More than 130 new nation-state entities have formed since 1945. They consistently proclaim, both internally and externally, their conformity to worldwide models of national identity and state structure. So, too, would our island society. But older states, too have learned to adapt to changes in these models. Thus, through both selection and adaptation, the system has expanded to something close to universality of the nation-state form. Realist theories, grounding their analyses in each country's particular resources and history, would predict a much wider variety of forms, including the retention of older statuses such as formal dependency or indirect incorporation of small or weak entities (Strang 1990).

World-cultural models of sovereign identity take concrete form in particular state structures, programs, and policies. As described above, worldwide models of the rationalized nation-state actor define appropriate constitutions, goals, data systems, organization charts, ministry structures (Kim and Jang 1996), and policies. Models also specify standard forms for the cultural depiction of national identity. Methods of constructing national culture through traditions (Hobsbawm and Ranger 1983), museums (Anderson 1991), tourism (MacCannell 1976), and national intellectual culture (Gellner 1983) are highly stylized. Nation-states are theorized or imagined communities drawing on models that are lodged at the world level (Anderson 1991).

Often, copying world models or conventions amounts to simple mimesis (DiMaggio and Powell 1983) that has more to do with knowing how to fill in forms than with managing substantive problems. For instance, to compile comparable educational enrollment data in the 1950s, UNESCO statisticians chose to report enrollments for a six-year primary level and three-year junior and senior secondary levels. In ensuing decades, many countries structured their mass schooling systems around this six-year/three-year/three-year model, generally without investigating whether it would best meet any of the presumed purposes of schooling.

Strang (1990) shows the extraordinary impact of the legitimized identity system on the survival and stability of states. Throughout modern history, dependent territories have moved to sovereign statehood at a steadily increasing rate that accelerated rapidly in the postwar period. Once sovereign, countries almost never revert to dependence. Even the breakup of the Soviet Union produced not dependent territories but formally sovereign nation-states, unprepared as some of the former republics were for this status. Thus, it is highly unlikely that our island society would be incorporated as a dependent territory of an extant nation-state; this would be too great a violation of the legitimized right to self-determination. Moreover, establishing the island society's sovereign status in the international system would stabilize its new state, though it would not preclude, and might even increase instability in the state's government (Thomas and Meyer 1980).

Orientation to the identity and purposes of the nation-state model increases the rate at which countries adopt other prescribed institutions of modernity. Having committed themselves to the identity of the rationalizing state, appropriate policies follow – policies for national development, individual citizenship and rights, environmental management, and foreign relations. These policies are depicted as if they were autonomous decisions because nation-states are denned as sovereign, responsible, and essentially autonomous actors. Taking into account the larger culture in which states are embedded, however, the policies look more like enactments of conventionalized scripts; even if a state proclaims its opposition to the dominant world identity models, it will nevertheless pursue many purposes within this model. It will develop bureaucratic authority and attempt to build many modern institutions, ranging from a central bank to an educational system. It will thereby find itself modifying its traditions in the direction of world-cultural forms.

Systemic maintenance of nation-state actor identity

If a specific nation-state is unable to put proper policies in place (because of costs, incompetence, or resistance), world-society structures will provide help. This process operates more through authoritative external support for the legitimate purposes of states than through authoritarian imposition by dominant powers or interests. For example, world organizations and professionalized ideologies actively encourage countries to adopt population control policies that are justified not as good for the world as a whole but as necessary for national development (Barrett and Frank 1997). National science policies are also promulgated as crucial to national development; before this link was theorized, UNESCO efforts to encourage countries to promote science failed to diffuse (Finnemore 1996a). As this example illustrates, international organizations often posture as objective disinterested others who help nation-states pursue their exogenously derived goals.

Resistance to world models is difficult because nation-states are formally committed, as a matter of identity, to such self-evident goals as socioeconomic development, citizen rights, individual self-development, and civil international relations. If a particular regime rhetorically resists world models, local actors can rely on legitimacy myths (democracy, freedom, equality) and the ready support of activist external groups to oppose the regime. Nation-state "choices" are thus less likely to conflict with world-cultural prescriptions than realist or microphenomenological theories anticipate because both nation-state choices and world pressures derive from the same overarching institutions.

Legitimation of subnational actors and practices

World-cultural principles license the nation-state not only as a managing central authority but also as an identity-supplying nation. Individual citizenship and the sovereignty of the people are basic tenets of nationhood. So too are the legitimacy and presumed functional necessity of much domestic organizational structure, ranging from financial market structures to organizations promoting individual and collective rights (of labor, ethnic groups, women, and so on). World-society ideology thus directly licenses a variety of organized interests and functions. Moreover, in pursuing their externally legitimated identities and purposes by creating agencies and programs, nation-states also promote the domestic actors involved. Programs and their associated accounting systems increase the number and density of types of actors, as groups come forward to claim newly reified identities and the resources allocated to them (Douglas 1986; Hacking 1986).

A good example is the rise of world discourse legitimating the human rights of gays and lesbians, which has produced both national policy changes and the mobilization of actors claiming these rights (Frank and McEneaney 1994). As nation-states adopt policies embodying the appropriate principles, they institutionalize the identity and political presence of these groups. Of course, all these "internally" generated changes are infused with world-cultural conceptions of the properly behaving nation-state.

Hence, if a nation-state neglects to adopt world-approved policies, domestic elements will try to carry out or enforce conformity. General world pressures favoring environmentalism, for example, have led many states to establish environmental protection agencies, which foster the growth of environmental engineering firms, activist groups, and planning agencies. Where the state has not adopted the appropriate policies, such local units and actors as cities, schools, scout troops, and religious groups are likely to practice environmentalism and call for national action. Thus, world culture influences nation-states not only at their centers, or only in symbolic ways, but also through direct connections between local actors and world culture. Such connections produce many axes of mobilization for the implementation of world-cultural principles and help account for similarities in mobilization agendas and strategies in highly disparate countries (McAdam and Rucht 1993).

Explicit rejection of world-cultural principles sometimes occurs, particularly by nationalist or religious movements whose purported opposition to modernity is seen as a threat to geopolitical stability. While the threat is real enough, the analysis is mistaken because it greatly underestimates the extent to which such movements conform to rationalized models of societal order and purpose. These movements mobilize around principles inscribed in world-cultural scripts, derive their organizing capacity from the legitimacy of these scripts, and edit their supposedly primordial claims to maximize this legitimacy. By and large, they seek an idealized modern community undergoing broad-based social development where citizens (of the right sort) can fully exercise their abstract rights. While they violate some central elements of world-cultural ideology, they nonetheless rely heavily on other elements. For example, religious "fundamentalists" may reject the extreme naturalism of modernity by making individuals accountable to an unchallengeable god, but they nevertheless exhort their people to embrace such key world-cultural elements as nation building, mass schooling, rationalized health care, and professionalization (on the striking case of postrevolutionary Iran, see Rajaee 1993; and Tehranian 1993). They are also apt to reformulate their religious doctrine in accordance with typical modern conceptions of rational-moral discipline (Juergensmeyer 1993; Thomas 1996). In general, nationalist and religious movements intensify isomorphism more than they resist it (Anderson 1991).

Realist models envision chains of organizational control from major powers downward through national powers and into local arenas. Therefore, they miss the direct effects of world-cultural models on the creation and sustenance of domestic actors. Microphenomenological and conventional "cultural" models stress the tradition-based resistance of local life-worlds to the exogenous pressures of modernization. They miss the extent to which, in the contemporary world, the local is itself cosmopolitan (Hannerz 1987).

ELEMENTS OF COLLECTIVE WORLD SOCIETY

The stateless character of world society has blinded many scholars to the enormous accumulation in recent decades of world social organization and cultural material. The culture involved clearly champions the principle that nation-states, organizations, and individuals are responsible, authorized actors. World-level entities, however, are not conceptualized in the same way. World society is mainly made up of what may, loosely following Mead (1934), be called "rationalized others" (Meyer 1994): social elements such as the sciences and professions (for which the term "actor" hardly seems appropriate) that give advice to nation-state and other actors about their true and responsible natures, purposes, technologies, and so on. Rationalized others are now everywhere, in massive arrays of international associations (Boli and Thomas 1997b) and epistemic communities (Haas 1992), generating veritable rivers of universalistic scientific and professional discourse. In this section, we concentrate on the social structural frame that organizes, carries, and diffuses world cultural models, leaving the content of the models aside. The content is widely discussed in the literature under the heading of "modernization": well-known, highly abstract, and stylized theories of the "functional requirements" of the modern society, organization, and individual, and the linkages among them. In these theories, the legitimated goals of properly constructed actors center on collective socio-economic development and comprehensive individual self-development. Society and individuals are bound together by rationalized systems of (imperfectly) egalitarian justice and participatory representation in the economy, polity, culture, and social interaction. These are global conceptions, not local, expressed as general principles to be applied everywhere (e.g., the World Congress of Comparative Education's [1996] sweeping affirmation of education's importance for justice and peace in all countries). Many other international professional associations, and nongovernmental organizations more generally, express similar goals (Chabbott 1997).

In world culture, almost every aspect of social life is discussed, rationalized, and organized, including rules of economic production and consumption, political structure, and education; science, technique, and medicine; family life, sexuality, and interpersonal relations; and religious doctrines and organization. In each arena, the range of legitimately defensible forms is fairly narrow. All the sectors are discussed as if they were functionally integrated and interdependent, and they are expected to conform to general principles of progress and justice. The culture of world society serves as a "sacred canopy" for the contemporary world (Berger 1967), a universalized and secularized project developed from older and somewhat parochial religious models. This section shows how this material is structured and rendered authoritative in world society.

Organizational frame

The development and impact of global sociocultural structuration greatly intensified with the creation of a central world organizational frame at the end of World War II. In place of the League of Nations, which was a limited international security organization, the UN system and related bodies (the International Monetary Fund, World Bank, General Agreement on Tariffs and Trade [GATT]) established expanded agendas of concern for international society, including economic development, individual rights, and medical, scientific, and educational development (Donnelly 1986; Jones 1992). This framework of global organization and legitimation greatly facilitated the creation and assembly of expansive components of an active and influential world society, as we discuss below. A wide range of social domains became eligible for ideological discussion and global organization. The forces working to mobilize and standardize our island society thus gain strength through their linkage to and support by the UN system and the great panoply of nongovernmental organizations clustered around it.

Diffusion among nation-states

The organization of a Tocquevillian world, made up of formally equal nation-states having similar rationalized identities and purposes, has intensified diffusion processes among nation-states (Chapter 6). In the West, since at least the seventeenth century, nation-states have claimed legitimacy in terms of largely common models; this commonality led them to copy each other more freely than is usual in systems of interdependent societies. The institutionalization of common world models similarly stimulates copying among all nation-states, in sharp contrast to traditional segmental societies in which entities jealously guard their secrets of success and regard copying as cultural treason.

Realist models expect this sort of copying only as a result of direct interdependence, especially domination, or in response to functional requirements imposed by competitive systems. Therefore, they overlook the broad cultural thrust involved. Microphenomenological models, emphasizing local traditions and interpretive schema, overlook the extent to which the modern actor is a worldwide cultural construction whose identity and interpretations derive directly from exogenous meanings, which makes the local arena less determinative of actor structuration.

The contemporary world is rife with modeling. Obviously, much of this reflects the main dimensions of world stratification – the poor and weak and peripheral copy the rich and strong and central. The Japanese, on entering the system in the nineteenth century, self-consciously copied successful Western forms (Westney 1987). Aspiring to core status in the same period, the Germans and Americans paid careful attention to each other's educational successes (Goldschmidt 1992). In the twentieth century, there has been a pronounced tendency to copy such American forms as the corporation (Takata 1995) and the liberal educational system. More recently, attention has shifted to Japanese work organization (Cole 1989) and education (Rohlen 1983). The emerging elites of our island society would undoubtedly turn first to American, Japanese, or European models for much of their social restructuring.

The world stratification system, however, is multidimensional; different countries parade distinctive virtues. For planning welfare programs, Sweden is the paragon of virtue. For promoting social equality, such "radical" countries as Maoist China and Cuba have been major models. On the other hand, even economically successful countries, if deemed opprobrious due to their failure to conform to important world principles, are unlikely models for imitation. South Africa is the best example.

Associations, organizations, and social movements

As with any such polity, the decentralized world made up of actors claiming ultimate similarity in design and purpose is filled with associations. Both governmental and nongovernmental voluntary organizations have expanded greatly, particularly since 1945 (Feld 1972; Boli and Thomas 1997a). Hundreds of intergovernmental entities cover a broad range of rationalized activity, including science, education, the economy and economic development, human rights, and medicine. Thousands of nongovernmental organizations have even broader concerns, organizing almost every imaginable aspect of social life at the world level. They are concentrated, however, in science, medicine, technical fields, and economic activity – the main arenas of rationalized modernity and, thus, arenas where rationalized nation-states are seen as the principal responsible actors. Less often, they focus on more expressive solidarities such as religion, ethnicity, one worldism, or regionalism (Boli and Thomas 1997a). World organizations are, thus, primarily instruments of shared modernity.

Many of the international nongovernmental organizations have a "social movement" character. Active champions of central elements of world culture, they promote models of human rights (Smith 1995); consumer rights (Mei 1995); environmental regulation (Frank et al. 1997); social and economic development (Chabbott 1997); and human equality and justice (Berkovitch 1997). They often cast themselves as oppositional grassroot movements, decrying gaps or failures in the implementation of world-cultural principles in particular locales and demanding corrective action by states and other actors. Agents of social problems, they generate further structuration of rationalized systems.

Clearly, our island society would quickly come under the scrutiny of all these international organizations. Its state and people would be expected to join international bodies, and they would find it advantageous to do so, gaining access to leading-edge technologies and ideas and enhancing their legitimacy as participants in the great human endeavor. The organizations themselves would also directly "aid" our island society in "developing." They would provide models for data, organization, and policy; training programs to help the island's elites learn the correct high forms of principle, policy, and structuration; consultants to provide hands-on assistance; and evaluation schemes to analyze the results. International organizations would collect data to assess the island's population, health care, education, economic structure (labor force, production, investment), and political status, all in fully rationalized terms redefining the society as a clear candidate for modernity.

Thus, the whole panoply of external organizations would set in motion efforts to increase social value and development on the island. Eventually, the locals would know how to push the process relatively autonomously, establishing such movements as a green party, women's organizations, and consumer rights' bodies to protect the new identities being constructed in the reorganizing society.

Sciences and professions

Scientists and professionals have become central and prestigious participants in world society. Their authority derives not from their strength as actors – indeed, their legitimated postures are defined as disinterested rationalized others rather than actors – but from their authority to assimilate and develop the rationalized and universalistic knowledge that makes action and actorhood possible. This authority is exceptionally well organized in a plethora of international organizations, most of them nongovernmental. These organizations are usually devoted to specific bodies of knowledge and their dissemination, but their ultimate aims include the broad development of societies (Drori 1997; Schofer 1997).

Especially in the more rationalized and public arenas of social life, the sciences and professions are leading forces; the occupations involved are the most prestigious in stratification systems almost everywhere (Treiman 1977). Sustainable socioeconomic development calls for the knowledge of economists who can advise on production functions, natural scientists and engineers to create and manage technologies and a variety of scientists to analyze environmental problems and costs. Individual development, rights, and equalities call for the expertise of social scientists, lawyers, psychologists, and medical professionals. These legitimated experts appeal to and further develop transnational accounts and models, yielding a self-reinforcing cycle in which rationalization further institutionalizes professional authority.

Scientific and professional authority is rooted in universal, rationalized ultimate principles of moral and natural law (on the rise of universities along these lines, see Riddle 1993). Their rationalized knowledge structures constitute the religion of the modern world, replacing in good measure the older "religions" that have been spiritualized and reconstructed as more ordinary organizational actors, and they underlie the other mechanisms of world influence noted above. The models of national development or human rights carried by international associations have their roots in scientific and legal knowledge such as theories and measures of national economic development or of individual social and economic equality. Similarly, diffusion among nation-states is heavily mediated by scientists and professionals who define virtuous instances, formulate models, and actively support their adoption. The current wave of Japanization in American economic and educational organization is defined and carried not directly by Japanese elites or American managers but by professors of business and education (Smith and O'Day 1990).

Organizations and consultants would flock around our island society, operating almost entirely in terms of scientific and professional (legal, medical, educational) models and methods. Very little would be presented to the island society as a matter of arbitrary cultural imposition; advice would be justified in terms of rational scientific authority. Scientists and professionals carry ultimate, rational, unified, universal truth, by and large shunning the image of self-interested power brokers. Science as authority is much more influential than scientists as an interest group (Meyer and Jepperson 1996).

Summary

The rapidly intensifying structuration of a world society made up of rationalized cultural elements and associational organizations rather than a centralized bureaucratic state is insufficiently appreciated in social research (Thomas et al. 1987; Robertson 1992). To show the coherence of what has happened, Boli and Thomas (1997a) present correlations among longitudinal variables describing many dimensions of world-level development. The period covered is the last 80–100 years; variables are world totals, by year, for economic production, energy consumption, foundings of governmental and nongovernmental organizations, educational enrollments, urban population, trade, treaties in force, and so on. The point is not to sort out causal relations among these variables but to show the consistency of the trends involved. Almost all correlations are extremely high (.90 or above). The current period of intensive international organization (more treaties, nongovernmental organizations, intergovernmental bodies, trade, and international scientific and professional discourse) is also a period of intensive national organization and development and individual rationalization and modernization. World society is rationalizing in an extraordinarily comprehensive way.

SOURCES OF DYNAMISM AND CHANGE
IN WORLD CULTURE

Few lines of sociological theory entirely discount the existence or impact of world culture. Microrealists may imagine that the world is made up solely of interest-driven national and local actors, but macrorealist perspectives often invoke an influential collective cultural sphere. Usually, though, macrorealists describe the cultural sphere as a matter of hegemony, that is, a function of the resources amassed by dominant actors (capitalists in world-system theory or states in state-competition theory). Expansion and change in stratified structures of interaction thus produce expansion and change in cultural rules, with advantages always accruing to the dominant. Such arguments seem quite reasonable in some respects, and one explanation for the current world-cultural preference for market systems and political democracy is surely a half century of dominance by the United States. Our island society would obviously evolve quite differently in a world with a hegemonic China.

Microphenomenological arguments can add some useful ideas here. Power and interests aside, the cultural styles or tastes of dominant actors might readily replicate themselves in global cultural models. Some dimensions of world culture may therefore be relatively gratuitous reflections of American culture as opposed to deeper underlying structures. For example, the more exotic aspects of American individualism, such as its peculiar interest in self-esteem and the inner child, may fade from world culture when the United States has lost its hegemonic position.

It is thus plausible to argue that dominant actors directly shape world culture. It is not plausible to argue, however, that institutionalization and change occur solely through the purposive action of constructed actors. This argument takes the cultural ideology of the modern world at face value, insisting on the exclusive power of humans as actors to give dynamism to the secular world. Much more is at work, however: Contemporary world culture is not passive and inert but highly dynamic in its own right. World-cultural forces for expansion and change are incorporated in people and organizations as constructed and legitimated actors filling roles as agents of great collective goods, universal laws, and broad meaning systems, even though the actors themselves interpret their action as self-interested rationality. Cultural forces defining the nature of the rationalized universe and the agency of human actors operating under rationalized natural laws play a major causal role in social dynamics, interacting with systems of economic and political stratification and exchange to produce a highly expansionist culture (Meyer and Jepperson 1996).

These cultural dynamics appeared early on, in the distinctive culture of Western Christendom (McNeill 1963; Hall 1986; Mann 1986) that provides much of the foundation for modern world culture. In this cultural complex, a demystified, lawful, universalistic nature forms the common frame within which social life is embedded (Weber 1946), and unitary moral laws and spiritual purposes are clearly differentiated from nature (Eisenstadt 1986, 1987). Spiritual obligations and rights originally devolving from an active and interventionist god are now located in humans and their communities, making individuals the ultimate carriers of responsible purposive action. As legitimated actors having agency for themselves and others, individuals orient their action above all toward the pursuit of rationalized progress.

Contemporary world culture thus posits a system of action, in contrast to more ceremonial or status-oriented cultures (including the premodern West, at various periods) that locate actorhood in transcendent entities and depict humans as subject to fate or the gods. Action is initiated and carried out by "actors" who dominate the cultural stage in virtually all current cultural theories (including most social-scientific work). Individuals, organizations, and states are highly legitimated entities whose interests are defined in universalistic terms, and they are both expected and entitled to act as agents of their interests (Meyer and Jepperson 1996). Faithful and energetic enactment of this cultural framework yields collective authority: Proper actors reciprocally legitimate each other.

Intense dynamism inheres in social and cultural arrangements that make human actors the core carriers of universal purposes (Eisenstadt 1987). The distinctive structure of actorhood that characterizes world society pushes the limits in this regard, for several reasons. First, no universal actor (world state) has central control or the repressive capacity to limit lower-level action. Second, the universalistically legitimated actors of world society are defined as having similar goals, so competition for resources is enhanced. Third, legitimated actorhood operates at several levels (national, organizational or group, and individual) that partially compete with one another. Fourth, internal contradictions and inconsistencies in world-cultural models make certain forms of struggle inevitable in world society. Taken together, these factors generate widespread conflict, mobilization, and change.

The statelessness of world society

A powerfully organized and authoritative worldwide actor would obviously lower the dynamism of world society. Wallerstein (1974) makes this point regarding the world economy, but it applies culturally as well. Agents of a world actor responsible for general human welfare would find the invention of new cultural goods and problems costly and disorderly. They would discourage rights-based claims by subunits and the self-righteousness of heteronomous intellectuals challenging central authority on moral grounds (Eisenstadt 1987). Perhaps the best historical example is the well-known pattern of Chinese imperial repression directed at innovative intellectuals (Collins 1986), scientists (Wuthnow 1980), and merchants (Hall 1986). The continuously expanding rationalization of natural and moral law, so characteristic of the sciences and professions, would seem wasteful and destabilizing, not value enhancing.

In present world society, intellectuals who discover new truths (about gender inequality, say, or science's contribution to economic growth, or the probability of asteroid collisions) gain much honor and preferment. They also create many costs by impelling collective action and structuration to deal with their discoveries. These costs are borne not by the cultural innovators themselves, who are pitched as rationalized others, but by responsible actors, especially states.

A centralized world actor might approach our island society like a medieval king, taking steps to protect his peasants from the joys and temptations of urban life by limiting their exposure to the high forms of cultural modernity. Such steps would be interpreted as paternalistic or repressive violations of basic human and social rights – a discriminatory denigration of the islanders as incapable of rational actorhood. Widespread internal and external opposition movements would ensue.

The structure of multiple actors in a common frame

Instead of a central actor, the culture of world society allocates responsible and authoritative actorhood to nation-states. They derive their rights and agency from the relatively unified culture of natural and moral law institutionalized by the sciences and professions. Many features of state action and interaction involve the application of general principles and the further elaboration or modification of these principles.

Given actors' common identity and ultimate similarity, competition is not only the prevailing theory of interaction but a source of collective moral meaning. The successes and failures of particular actors engender extensive theorization, learning, and diffusion (Chapter 6). Global depression produced and popularized Keynesian economic models (Hall 1989); more recently, the dislocations and challenges theorized as due to globalization have popularized neoclassical economic models (Biersteker 1992). Similarly, relative ineffectiveness in reducing poverty and inequality promotes welfare-system expansion or reform (Strang and Chang 1993), while scientized measurement of hitherto unsuspected forms of pollution pushes the expansion of environmental ministries (Frank et al. 1997).

In this cultural context, practical problems reflect neither fate nor the gods but crises of action and technical systems, provoking further cultural theorization. The actors involved – for example, the economic clergy charged with advising states on means of dealing with economic downturn – may suffer a modest loss of face, but the proposed solutions do not include burning a few economists at the stake. Instead, more resources go to economics graduate programs and state regulatory agencies.

Study of our island society would reveal an array of social problems. Its traditions, interpreted as prerational culture, might well be stored in museums (as they are elsewhere), but they would also be reinterpreted as problems. World culture is a factory of social problems that are both products of theorization and occasions for further cultural growth. In addition, these problems foster diverse forms of moral entrepreneurship that collide with one another. Diverse responses to problems are guaranteed because of the legitimacy endowed on multiple actors and their interests; collisions are frequent because of the universalism of the definitions and rules of world culture. The greater the number of entities, whether individuals, organizations, or nation-states that pursue similar interests requiring similar resources, the more the entities will come into conflict with each other and develop theories of one another as sources of social ills.

Local variations in a universalistic society become anomalies or deviations unless they are justified in terms of general cultural principles. Due to their dependence on the wider culture, local actors thus discover that their interests lie in defending local arrangements not as locally legitimate but as instances of more universal rules. This process fills world society with dynamic ideological conflicts over matters that on the face of it seem inconsequential, including a considerable number of wars fueled partly by clashes over modest variations on shared cultural or religious models.

Thus, if our island society elite wishes to maintain distinctive local patterns of, say, gender differentiation, it would be well advised to invoke universalistic cultural principles of some sort and join with others in generalizing the issue to the world level. African intellectuals have shown the way here, activating principles of self-determination and cultural autonomy to resist the application of Western feminist scholarship to their societies (Mohatny 1984).

The forces motivating local actors (including states) to incorporate, employ, and legitimate world theorists and theories thereby strengthening the authoritative worldwide network of sciences, professions, and consultants. They also reinforce and modify, in continuing contest, the elements of world culture that undergird them. Global discourse intensifies and becomes ever more complex as the world-societal arena of interaction is ever more routinely activated.

Multiple levels of legitimated actorhood

World society would be a good deal less dynamic if only one type of actor were legitimated, but actors at several levels enjoy appreciable legitimacy. Individuals and states mutually legitimate each other via principles of citizenship while individuals and international organizations do the same via principles of human rights. Between individuals and nation-states lie any number of interest and functional groups that have standing as legitimated actors due to their connections with individuals and states. These include religious, ethnic, occupational, industrial, class, racial, and gender-based groups and organizations, all of which both depend on and conflict with actors at other levels. For example, individual actors are entitled to demand equality while collective actors are entitled to promote functionally justified differentiation. Individual actors claim primordial ethnic and familial rights while collective actors impose homogenization. Such dualisms, once peculiarly Western (Eisenstadt 1987), are now common world-cultural features.

In virtually every contested arena, both sides can rely on the wider cultural canopy for a good deal of legitimation, especially if they imaginatively adapt the general frame to fit local circumstances. A major result of contestation is thus even more expanded cultural modeling and structuration. In our island society, economic, psychological, and biological analysts would discover a variety of purportedly functional inequalities and individual handicaps while educational and sociological analysts would specify methods of correcting or managing these problems. International organizations would send experts to help mobilize grassroots movements to demand solutions to the problems. The solutions would require structuration and, in the long run, cultural or theoretical elaboration.

Cultural contradictions

Most social theories, scholarly or not, treat change as the product of actors rightly pursuing their interests. The cultures (if any) in which these actors are embedded are assumed to be closed, internally consistent, and rather static. This is the dominant interpretation of the work of Parsons (1951), and its obvious inadequacy, given the openness, inconsistencies, and flux of the culture of modernity, readily leads critics to discount the importance of culture in the production of change.

What critics of cultural analysis overlook is the dynamism that is generated by the rampant inconsistencies and conflicts within world culture itself. Beyond conflicts of interests among individuals or among states, beyond the dualistic inconsistencies between individuals and organizations or groups and national collectivities, there are also contradictions inherent in widely valued cultural goods: equality versus liberty, progress versus justice, standardization versus diversity, efficiency versus individuality. Contestation thus often centers on such contradictory pairs as too much state regulation (inhibiting growth) or too little (permitting excessive inequality), too much individual expressiveness (producing profanity) or too little (infringing liberty), too much nationalism (yielding genocide) or too little (producing anomie).

These contradictory elements are integrated in different ways in different variants of world-cultural models – at the world level, within each national society, even locally (Friedland and Alford 1991). Adherents of competing models suspiciously regard others as violators of quasi-sacred definitions and boundaries; thus, they are primed to perceive potential and at least partially legitimated dangers, sins, and impurities (Douglas 1966). Economists are primed to perceive legitimate efforts to reduce inequality as threatening the equally legitimate economic growth; sociologists are primed to perceive rationalizing technique as a leviathan threatening the face-to-face community; ecologists interpret economic and technical development as a threat to the natural base of the entire system. All of these priesthoods preach in terms of ultimate values and with considerable authority, reflecting and reproducing a remarkably dynamic culture.

In summary, analysis of the expanding and changing culture of world society must take into account dynamic properties of world culture as such, not just interaction and power relations among actors. The cultural construction of rational actorhood endows individuals and groups (to a lesser extent, organizations as well) with exalted spiritual properties that justify and motivate mobilization, innovation, and protest. Further, the decentralized and multilevel character of modern actorhood ensures that interests will conflict and meaning structures will develop contradictions, especially in the absence of a stabilizing central world actor.

Ironically, world-cultural structuration produces more mobilization and competition among the various types of similarly constructed actors than would occur in a genuinely segmental world. Increasing consensus on the meaning and value of individuals, organizations, and nation-states yields more numerous and intense struggles to achieve independence, autonomy, progress, justice, and equality. Greater good becomes possible and likely but so too does greater evil, as good and evil become more derivative of world culture and therefore of greater scale than in earlier times.

CONCLUSION

A considerable body of evidence supports our proposition that world-society models shape nation-state identities, structures, and behavior via worldwide cultural and associational processes. Carried by rationalized others whose scientific and professional authority often exceeds their power and resources, world culture celebrates, expands, and standardizes strong but culturally somewhat tamed national actors. The result is nation-states that are more isomorphic than most theories would predict and change more uniformly than is commonly recognized. As creatures of exogenous world culture, states are ritualized actors marked by extensive internal decoupling and a good deal more structuration than would occur if they were responsive only to local cultural, functional, or power processes.

As the Western world expanded in earlier centuries to dominate and incorporate societies in the larger world, the penetration of a universalized culture proceeded hesitantly. Westerners could imagine that the locals did not have souls, were members of a different species, and could reasonably be enslaved or exploited. Inhabiting a different moral and natural universe, non-Western societies were occasionally celebrated for their noble savagery but more often cast as inferior groups unsuited for true civilization. Westerners promoted religious conversion by somewhat parochial and inconsistent means, but broader incorporation was ruled out on all sorts of grounds. Education and literacy were sometimes prohibited, rarely encouraged, and never generally provided, for the natives were ineducable or prone to rebellion. Rationalized social, political, and economic developments (e.g., the state, democracy, urban factory production, and modern family law) were inappropriate, even unthinkable. Furthermore, the locals often strongly resisted incorporation by the West. Even Japan maintained strong boundaries against many aspects of modernity until the end of World War II, and Chinese policy continues a long pattern of resistance to external "aid."

The world, however, is greatly changed. Our island society would obviously become a candidate for full membership in the world community of nations and individuals. Human rights, state-protected citizen rights, and democratic forms would become natural entitlements. An economy would emerge, denned and measured in rationalized terms and oriented to growth under state regulation. A formal national polity would be essential, including a constitution, citizenship laws, educational structures, and open forms of participation and communication. The whole apparatus of rationalized modernity would be mobilized as necessary and applicable; internal and external resistance would be stigmatized as reactionary unless it was couched in universalistic terms. Allowing the islanders to remain imprisoned in their society, under the authority of their old gods and chiefs and entrapped in primitive economic technologies, would be unfair and discriminatory, even though the passing of their traditional society would also occasion nostalgia and regret.

Prevailing social theories account poorly for these changes. Given a dynamic sociocultural system, realist models can account for a world of economic and political absorption, inequality, and domination. They do not explain well a world of formally equal, autonomous, and expansive nation-state actors. Microcultural or phenomenological lines of argument can account for diversity and resistance to homogenization, not a world in which national states, subject to only modest coercion or control, adopt standard identities and structural forms.

We argue for the utility of recognizing that rationalized modernity is a universalistic and inordinately successful form of the earlier Western religious and postreligious system. As a number of commentators have noted, in our time, the religious elites of Western Christendom have given up on the belief that there is no salvation outside the church (Illich 1970; Shils 1971). That postulate has been replaced by the belief among almost all elites that salvation lies in rationalized structures grounded in scientific and technical knowledge – states, schools, firms, voluntary associations, and the like. The new religious elites are the professionals, researchers, scientists, and intellectuals who write secularized and unconditionally universalistic versions of the salvation story, along with the managers, legislators, and policymakers who believe the story fervently and pursue it relentlessly. This belief is worldwide and structures the organization of social life almost everywhere.

The colossal disaster of World War II may have been a key factor in the rise of global models of nationally organized progress and justice, and the Cold War may well have intensified the forces pushing human development to the global level. If the present configuration of lowered systemic (if not local) tensions persists, perhaps both the consensuality of the models and their impact on nation-states will decline. On the other hand, the models' rationalized definitions of progress and justice (across an ever broadening front) are rooted in universalistic scientific and professional definitions that have reached a level of deep global institutionalization. These definitions produce a great deal of conflict with regard to their content and application, but their authority is likely to prove quite durable.

Many observers anticipate a variety of failures of world society, citing instances of gross violations of world-cultural principles (e.g., in Bosnia), stagnant development (e.g., in Africa), and evasion of proper responsibility (in many places). In our view, the growing list of perceived "social problems" in the world indicates not the weakness of world-cultural institutions but their strength. Events like political torture, waste dumping, or corruption, which not so long ago were either overlooked entirely or considered routine, local, specific aberrations or tragedies, are now of world-societal significance. They violate strong expectations regarding global integration and propriety and can easily evoke world-societal reactions seeking to put things right. A world with so many widely discussed social problems is a world of Durkheimian and Simmelian integration, however much it may also seem driven by disintegrative tendencies.

REFERENCES

Abbott, Andrew and Stanley DeViney. 1992. The Welfare State as Transnational Event: Evidence from Sequences of Policy Adoption. *Social Science History* 16 (2):245–74.

Almond, Gabriel and Sidney Verba. 1963. *The Civic Culture.* Princeton, NJ: Princeton University Press.

Anderson, Benedict. 1991. *Imagined Communities,* 2nd edn. London: Verso.

Barrett, Deborah and David Frank. 1997. Population Control for National Development: From World Discourse to National Policies, in John Boli and George M. Thomas (eds.), *World Polity Formation since 1875: World Culture and International Non-Governmental Organizations,* in press. Stanford, CA: Stanford University Press.

Berger, Peter. 1967. *The Sacred Canopy.* Garden City, NY: Doubleday.

—— and Thomas Luckmann. 1967. *The Social Construction of Reality.* New York: Doubleday.

Berkovitch, Nitza. 1997. The International Women's Movement: Transformations of Citizenship, in John Boli and George M. Thomas (eds.), *World Polity Formation since 1875: World Culture and International Non-Governmental Organizations,* in press. Stanford, CA: Stanford University Press.

Biersteker, Thomas. 1992. The Triumph of Neoclassical Economics in the Developing World, in James Rosenau and Ernst Otto Czempiel (eds.), *Governance without Government: Order and Change in World Politics.* Cambridge: Cambridge University Press, p. 10231.

Boli, John. 1987. World Polity Sources of Expanding State Authority and Organizations, 1870–1970, in George M. Thomas, John W. Meyer, Francisco O. Ramirez, and John Boli (eds.), *Institutional Structure.* Beverly Hills, CA: Sage, pp. 71–91.

—— and George M. Thomas. 1997a. World Culture in the World Polity: A Century of International Non-Governmental Organization. *American Sociological Review* 62:171–190.

—— (eds.) 1997b. *World Polity Formation since 1875: World Culture and International Non-Governmental Organizations,* in press. Stanford, CA: Stanford University Press.

Boli-Bennett, John and John W. Meyer. 1978. The Ideology of Childhood and the State. *American Sociological Review* 43 (6):797–812.

Bradley, Karen and Francisco O. Ramirez. 1996. World Polity Promotion of Gender Parity: Women's Share of Higher Education, 196S–8S. *Research in Sociology of Education and Socialization* 11:63–91.

Brim, Orville, Jr., and Jerome Kagen (eds.) 1980. *Continuity and Change in Human Development.* Cambridge, MA: Harvard University Press.

Brunsson, Nils. 1989. *The Organization of Hypocrisy: Talk, Decisions and Action in Organizations.* New York: Wiley.

Cancian, Francesca. 1975. *What Are Norms?* Oxford: Oxford University Press.

Chabbott, Colette. 1997. Denning Development: The Making of the International Development Field, 1945–1990, in John Boli and George M. Thomas (eds.), *World Polity Formation since 1875: World Culture and International Non-Governmental Organizations,* in press. Stanford, CA: Stanford University Press.

Charles, Maria. 1992. Cross-National Variation in Occupational Sex Segregation. *American Sociological Review* 57 (4):483–502.

Chase-Dunn, Christopher. 1989. *Global Formation: Structures of the World Economy.* Cambridge: Basil Blackwell.

Clark, Roger. 1992. Multinational Corporate Investment and Women's Participation in Higher Education in Noncore Nations. *Sociology of Education* 65 (1):37–47.

Cole, Robert. 1989. *Strategies for Learning: Small-Group Activities in American, Japanese and Swedish Industry.* Berkeley and Los Angeles: University of California Press.

Collier, David and Richard Messick. 1975. Prerequisites versus Diffusion: Testing Alternative Explanations of Social Security Adoption. *American Political Science Review* 69:1299–315.

Collins, Randall. 1986. Heresy, Religious and Secular, in Randall Collins (ed.), *Weberian Sociological Theory.* Cambridge: Cambridge University Press, pp. 213–46.

DiMaggio, Paul J. and Walter W. Powell. 1983. The Iron Cage Revisited. *American Sociological Review* 48 (2):147–60.

Dobbin, Frank. 1994. *Forging Industrial Policy: The United States, Britain, and France in the Railway Age*. New York: Cambridge University Press.

Donnelly, Jack. 1986. International Human Rights: A Regime Analysis. *International Organization* 40:599–642.

Douglas, Mary. 1966. *Purity and Danger*. London: Penguin.

—— 1986. *How Institutions Think*. Syracuse, NY: Syracuse University Press.

Drori, Gili. 1997. Science Education for Economic Development: Policy Discourse, Empirical Evidence, and Re-evaluation. Paper presented at the annual meetings of the American Sociological Association, Toronto.

Duchacek, Ivo D., Daniel Latouche, and Garth Stevenson (eds.) 1988. *Perforated Sovereignties and International Relations: Trans-Sovereign Contacts of Subnational Governments*. New York: Greenwood.

Eisenstadt, Shmuel. 1986. *The Origins and Diversity of Axial Age Civilizations*. Albany: State University of New York Press.

—— 1987. *European Civilization in a Comparative Perspective*. Oslo: Norwegian University Press.

Eyre, Dana and Mark Suchman. 1996. Status, Norms, and the Proliferation of Conventional Weapons, in Peter Kat-zenstein (ed.), *Culture and Security*, New York: Columbia University Press, pp. 79–113.

Feld, Werner. 1972. *Non-Governmental Forces and World Politics*. New York: Praeger.

Fiala, Robert and Audri Gordon-Lanford. 1987. Educational Ideology and the World Educational Revolution, 1950–1970. *Comparative Education Review* 31 (3):31532.

Finnemore, Martha. 1996a *National Interests in International Society*. Ithaca, NY: Cornell University Press.

—— 1996b. Norms, Culture, and World Politics: Insights from Sociology's Institutionalism. *International Organization* 50:325–47.

Frank, David and Elizabeth McEneaney. 1994. The Legalization of Sex: Cross-National Variation in Lesbian and Gay Rights. Paper presented at the annual meetings of the American Sociological Association, Los Angeles.

—— Ann Hironaka, John W. Meyer, Evan Schofer, and Nancy Tuma. 1997. The Rationalization and Organization of Nature in World Culture, in John Boli and George M. Thomas (eds.), *World Polity Formation since 1875: World Culture and International Non-Governmental Organizations*, in press. Stanford, CA: Stanford University Press.

Friedland, Roger, and Robert Alford. 1991. Bringing Society Back In: Symbols, Practices, and Institutional Contradictions, in Walter W. Powell and Paul J. DiMaggio (eds.), *The New Institutionalism in Organizational Analysis*. Chicago: University of Chicago Press, pp. 232–63.

Gellner, Ernest. 1983. *Nations and Nationalism*. Oxford: Oxford University Press.

Gilpin, Robert. 1981. *War and Change in World Politics*. Cambridge: Cambridge University Press.

Goffman, Erving. 1969. *The Presentation of Self in Everyday Life*. New York: Doubleday Anchor.

—— 1974. *Frame Analysis*. New York: Harper & Row.

Goldschmidt, Dietrich. 1992. Historical Interaction between Higher Education in Germany and in the USA. *German and American Universities*. Kassel: Wissenschaftliches Zentrum fiir Berufs- und Hochschulforschung der Gesamthochschule, pp. 11–33.

Guillen, Mauro. 1994. *Models of Management: Work, Authority, and Organization in a Comparative Perspective*. Chicago: University of Chicago Press.

Haas, Peter. 1992. Epistemic Communities and International Policy Coordination. *International Organization* 46:1–35.

Hacking, Ian. 1986. Making Up People, in Thomas C. Heller, Morton Sosna, and David Wellbery (eds.), *Reconstructing Individualism: Autonomy, Individuality, and the Self in Western Thought*. Stanford, CA: Stanford University Press, pp. 222–36.

Hall, John. 1986. *Powers and Liberties*. New York: Penguin.

Hall, Peter (ed.) 1989. *The Political Power of Economic Ideas*. Princeton, NJ: Princeton University Press.

Hannerz, Ulf. 1987. The World in Creolisation. *Africa* 57 (4):546–59.

Harbison, Frederick, and Charles Myers. 1964. *Education, Manpower, and Economic Growth*. New York: McGraw-Hill.

Hobsbawm, Eric, and T. Ranger. 1983. *The Invention of Tradition*. Cambridge: Cambridge University Press.

Illich, Ivan. 1970. *Deschooling Society*. New York: Harper & Row.

Jackson, Robert and Carl Rosberg. 1982. Why Africa's Weak States Persist: The Empirical and the Juridical in Statehood. *World Politics* 35 (1):1–24.

Jacobson, Harold K. 1984. *Networks of Interdependence: International Organizations and the Global Political System,* 2nd edn. New York: Knopf.

Jepperson, Ronald. 1992. National Scripts: The Varying Construction of Individualism and Opinion across the Modern Nation-States. PhD dissertation. Yale University, Department of Sociology.

—— and John W. Meyer. 1991. The Public Order and the Construction of Formal Organizations, in Walter W. Powell and Paul J. DiMaggio (eds.), *The New Institutionalism in Organizational Analysis*. Chicago: University of Chicago Press, pp. 204–31.

—— Alexander Wendt, and Peter Katzenstein. 1996. Norms, Identity, and Culture in National Security, in Peter Katzenstein (ed.), *Culture and Security*. New York: Columbia University Press, pp. 33–78.

Jones, Philip W. 1992. *World Bank Financing of Education: Lending, Learning, and Development*. London: Routledge.

Juergensmeyer, Mark. 1993. *The New Cold War: Religious Nationalism Confronts the Secular State*. Berkeley and Los Angeles: University of California Press.

Keohane, Robert O. (ed.) 1986. *Neorealism and Its Critics*. New York: Columbia University Press.

Kim, Young and Yong Suk Jang. 1996. Structural Expansion and the Cost of Global Isomorphism: A Cross-National Study of Modern Ministerial Structure, 1950–1990. Paper presented at the annual meetings of the American Sociological Association, New York.

Krasner, Stephen (ed.) 1983. *International Regimes*. Ithaca, NY: Cornell University Press.

—— 1995–96. Compromising Westphalia. *International Security* 20 (3):115–51.

MacCannell, Dean. 1976. *The Tourist: A New Theory of the Leisure Class*. New York: Schocken Books.

Mann, Michael. 1986. *The Sources of Social Power*. Cambridge: Cambridge University Press.

March, James. 1988. *Decisions and Organizations*. Oxford: Blackwell.

—— and Johan P. Olsen. 1989. *Rediscovering Institutions*. New York: Free Press.

Mattelart, Armand. 1983. *Transnationals and the Third World: The Struggle for Culture*. South Hadley, MA: Bergin & Garvey.

McAdam, Doug, and Dieter Rucht. 1993. The Cross-National Diffusion of Movement Ideas. *Annals of the American Academy of Political and Social Science* 528:56–74.

McNeely, Connie. 1995. *Constructing the Nation-State: International Organization and Prescriptive Action.* Westport, CN: Greenwood.

McNeill, William. 1963. *The Rise of the West: A History of the Human Community.* Chicago: University of Chicago Press.

Mead, George Herbert. 1934. *Mind, Self, and Society.* Chicago: University of Chicago Press.

Mei, Yujun. 1995. The Consumer Rights Sector in the World Polity: Its Rise and Diffusion. Master's thesis. Arizona State University, Department of Sociology.

Meyer, John W. 1980. The World Polity and the Authority of the Nation-State in Albert J. Bergesen (ed.), *Studies of the Modern World-System.* New York: Academic Press, pp. 109–37.

—— 1994. Rationalized Environments in W. Richard Scott and John W. Meyer (eds.), *Institutional Environments and Organizations.* Newbury Park, CA: Sage, pp. 28–54.

—— 1997. The Changing Cultural Content of the Nation-State: A World Society Perspective, in George Steinmetz (ed.), *New Approaches to the State in the Social Sciences.* Ithaca, NY: Cornell University Press, in press.

—— and Ronald Jepperson. 1996. The Actor and the Other: Cultural Rationalization and the Ongoing Evolution of Modem Agency. Paper presented at the Institutional Analysis Conference, Tucson, Arizona, April.

—— John Boli-Bennett, and Christopher Chase-Dunn. 1975. Convergence and Divergence in Development. *Annual Review of Sociology* 1:223–46.

—— and Brian Rowan. 1977. Institutionalized Organizations: Formal Structure as Myth and Ceremony. *American Journal of Sociology* 83 (2):340–63. Reproduced in Chapter 4.

—— David Kamens, and Aaron Benavot, with Yun-Kyung Cha and Suk-Ying Wong. 1992. *School Knowledge for the Masses: World Models and National Primary Curricular Categories in the Twentieth Century.* London: Falmer Press.

—— Francisco O. Ramirez, and Yasemin Soysal. 1992. World Expansion of Mass Education, 1870–1980. *Sociology of Education* 65 (2):128–49.

—— Joanne Nagel, and Conrad W. Snyder. 1993. The Expansion of Mass Education in Botswana: Local and World Society Perspectives. *Comparative Education Review* 37 (4):454–75.

Mohanty, Chandra. 1984. Under Western Eyes: Feminist Scholarship and Colonial Discourses. *Boundary Z* 12 (3):333–57.

Nordenstreng, Kaarle and Herbert I. Schiller (eds.) 1979. *National Sovereignty and International Communication.* Norwood, NJ: Ablex.

Parsons, Talcott. 1951. *The Social System.* Glencoe, HI: Free Press.

Powell, Walter W. and Paul J. DiMaggio (eds.) 1991. *The New Institutionalism in Organizational Analysis.* Chicago: University of Chicago Press.

Rajaee, Farhang. 1993. Islam and Modernity: The Reconstruction of an Alternative Shi'ite Islamic Worldview in Iran in Martin E. Marty and R. Scott Appleby (ed.), *Fundamentalisms and Society.* Chicago: University of Chicago Press, pp. 103–25.

Ramirez, Francisco O. 1987. Global Changes, World Myths, and the Demise of Cultural Gender, in Terry Boswell and Albert J. Bergesen (ed.), *America's Changing Role in the World-System,* New York: Praeger, pp. 257–73.

—— and John W. Meyer. 1992. The Institutionalization of Citizenship Principles and the National Incorporation of Women and Children, 1870–1990. Manuscript. Stanford University, Department of Sociology.

—— and Richard Rubinson. 1979. Creating Members: The Political Incorporation and Expansion of Public Education in John W. Meyer and Michael T. Han-nan (eds.), *National Development and the World System.* Chicago: University of Chicago Press, pp. 72–82.

Ramirez, Francisco O. and Marc Ventresca. 1992. Building the Institutions of Mass Schooling, in Bruce Fuller and Richard Rubinson (eds.), *The Political Construction of Education.* New York: Praeger, pp. 47–59.

—— and Jane Weiss. 1979. The Political Incorporation of Women, in John W. Meyer and Michael T. Hannan (eds.), *National Development and the World System,* Chicago: University of Chicago Press, pp. 238–49.

—— Yasemin Soysal, and Suzanne Shanahan. In press. The Changing Logic of Political Citizenship: Cross-National Acquisition of Women's Suffrage, 1890–1990. *American Sociological Review.*

Riddle, Phyllis. 1993. Political Authority and University Formation in Europe, 1200–1800. *Sociological Perspectives* 36 (1):45–62.

Riggs, Fred. 1964. *Administration in Developing Countries: The Theory of Prismatic Society.* Boston: Houghton Mifflin.

Ritzer, George. 1996. Cultures and Consumers: The McDonaldization Thesis: Is Expansion Inevitable? *International Sociology* 11 (3):291–308.

Robertson, Roland. 1992. *Globalization: Social Theory and Global Culture.* London: Sage.

Rohlen, Thomas. 1983. *Japan's High Schools.* Berkeley and Los Angeles: University of California Press.

Rubinson, Richard and Irene Browne. 1994. Education and the Economy, in Neil J. Smelser and Richard Swedberg (eds.), *The Handbook of Economic Sociology.* Princeton, NJ: Princeton University Press, pp. 581–99.

Schofer, Evan. 1997. Science Association in the International Sphere, 1875–1990: The Rationalization of Science and the Scientization of Society, in John Boli and George M. Thomas (eds.), *World Polity Formation since 1875: World Culture and International Non-Governmental Organizations.* Stanford, CA: Stanford University Press, in press.

Shils, Edward. 1971. No Salvation outside Higher Education. *Minerva* 6 (July):313–21.

Sklair, Leslie. 1991. *Sociology of the Global System.* Baltimore: Johns Hopkins University Press.

Skocpol, Theda. 1979. *States and Social Revolutions.* New York: Cambridge University Press.

—— 1985. Bringing the State Back In, in Peter B. Evans, Dietrich Rueschemeyer, and Theda Skocpol (eds.), *Bringing the State Back In.* Cambridge: Cambridge University Press, pp. 3–37.

Smith, Jackie. 1995. Transnational Political Processes and the Human Rights Movement. *Research on Social Movements, Conflict and Change* 18:185–220.

Smith, Michael and Jennifer O'Day. 1990. Systemic School Reform, in Susan Fuhrman and Betty Malen (eds.), *The Politics of Curriculum and Testing.* Bristol, PA: Falmer Press, pp. 233–67.

Snow, David A. and Robert D. Benford. 1992. Master Frames and Cycles of Protest, in Aldon Morris and Carol Mueller (eds.), *Frontiers in Social Movement Theory.* New Haven, CN: Yale University Press, pp. 135–55.

Soysal, Yasemin. 1994. *Limits of Citizenship: Migrants and Post-national Membership in Europe.* Chicago: University of Chicago Press.

Strang, David. 1990. From Dependency to Sovereignty: An Event History Analysis of Decolonization, 1870–1987. *American Sociological Review* 55:846–60.

—— and Patricia Chang. 1993. The International Labor Organization and the Welfare State: Institutional Effects on National Welfare Spending, 1960–1980. *International Organization* 47:235–62.

—— and John W. Meyer. 1993. Institutional Conditions for Diffusion. *Theory and Society* 22:487–511. Reproduced in Chapter 6.

Takata, Azumi Ann. 1995. From Merchant House to Corporation: The Development of the Modern Corporate Form and the Transformation of Business Organization in Japan, 1853–1912. PhD dissertation. Stanford University, Department of Sociology.

Tehranian, Majid. 1993. Islamic Fundamentalism in Iran and the Discourse of Development, in Martin E. Marty and R. Scott Appleby (eds.), *Fundamentalisms and Society*. Chicago: University of Chicago Press, pp. 341–73.

Thomas, George M. 1996. Social Movements in Rationalized Institutional Contexts: Religions and World Culture. Paper presented at the Institutional Analysis Conference, Tucson, Arizona, April.

—— and Pat Lauderdale. 1987. World Polity Sources of National Welfare and Land Reform, in George M. Thomas, John W. Meyer, Francisco O. Ramirez, and John Boli (eds.), *Institutional Structure*. Beverly Hills, CA: Sage, pp. 92–110.

—— and John W. Meyer. 1980. Regime Changes and State Power in an Intensifying World System, in Albert J. Bergesen (ed.), *Studies of the Modern World-System*. New York: Academic Press, pp. 139–58.

—— —— 1984. The Expansion of the State. *Annual Review of Sociology* 10:461–82.

Thomas, George M., Francisco O. Ramirez, and John Boli. 1987. *Institutional Structure: Constituting State, Society, and the Individual*. Beverly Hills, CA: Sage.

Thornton, Patricia. 1992. Psychiatric Diagnosis as Sign and Symbol: Nomenclature as an Organizing and Legitimating Strategy, in Gale Miller and James A. Holstein (eds.), *Perspectives on Social Problems, vol. 4*. Greenwich, CN: JAI Press, pp. 155–76.

Tilly, Charles. 1992. *Coercion, Capital, and European States, A.D., 1990–1992*. Cambridge: Basil Blackwell.

Tocqueville, Alexis de. (1836) 1966. *Democracy in America*. New York: Doubleday.

Treiman, Donald. 1977. *Occupational Prestige in Comparative Perspective*. New York: Academic Press.

Ventresca, Marc. 1995. Counting People when People Count: Global Establishment of the Modern Population Census, 1820–1980. PhD dissertation. Stanford University, Department of Sociology.

Wallerstein, Immanuel. 1974. *The Modern World System, vol. 1*. New York: Academic Press.

—— 1995. *After Liberalism*. New York: New Press.

Ward, Kathryn. 1984. *Women in the World System*. New York: Praeger.

Waltz, Kenneth M. 1979. *Theory of International Politics*. Reading, MA: Addison-Wesley.

Watkins, Susan. 1987. The Fertility Transition: Europe and the Third World Compared. *Sociological Forum* 2 (4):645–73.

Weber, Max. 1946. Science as a Vocation, in H. H. Gerth and C. Wright Mills (eds.), *From Max Weber*. New York: Oxford University Press, pp. 129–56.

Weick, Karl. 1976. Educational Organizations as Loosely Coupled Systems. *Administrative Science Quarterly* 21 (1):1–19.

Westney, Eleanor. 1987. *Imitation and Innovation: The Transfer of Western Organizational Patterns to Meiji Japan*. Cambridge, MA: Harvard University Press.

Wong, Suk-Ying. 1991. The Evolution of Social Science Instruction, 1900–86. *Sociology of Education* 64 (1):33–47.

World Congress of Comparative Education. 1996. Call for Papers: Educating All for Peace and Justice. World Congress of Comparative Education, Sydney.

Wuthnow, Robert. 1980. The World Economy and the Institutionalization of Science in Seventeenth-Century Europe, in Albert J. Bergesen (ed.), *Studies of the Modern World-System*. New York: Academic Press, pp. 25–55.

9

Education

The World Institutionalization of Education

INTRODUCTION

Mass education, throughout its modern history, has been justified by functional theories and ideologies. These ideas stress its contribution to the development of national society, seen as an integrated and bounded social system. For over a century, elite education has also been reorganized and justified around such conceptions. Both mass and elite education are supposed to be closely tied to the distinctive needs and direction of a particular society. A good deal of social theory argues that close linkages indeed occur empirically and drive educational creation and change. When close linkages fail to materialize, the favored response and strategy are to undertake educational research, planning, and reform designed to better align schooling with societal needs.

This tradition is not without critics. Mostly from the left, these critics proceed from the premise that mass and elite education function to maintain societies dominated by economic and/or political elite interests. Education functions not for the good of society as a whole, but rather to reproduce structures of domination that benefit elites. Both lines of thought, however normatively different, emphasize the tight linkages between societal or elite needs and interests and the mass and higher educational arrangements that arise and develop in these societies. The underlying premise seems to be that different societies or elites have different personnel requirements and get the educational systems that train or socialize the next generation to meet these needs. This is the received wisdom both in educational theories of social order (the right) and in educational theories of class or elite reproduction (the left).

This received wisdom continues to influence the field of comparative education and mislead much of its research enterprise. Both the functionality and uniqueness of

Originally published as:

John W. Meyer and Francisco O. Ramirez. 2000. The World Institutionalization of Education, in Jürgen Schriewer (ed.), Discourse Formation in Comparative Education. *Frankfurt: Peter Lang Publishers,* pp. 111–32.

The authors share equal responsibility for this chapter which has evolved from our earlier work on the subject: Francisco O. Ramirez and John W. Meyer 1992; John W. Meyer, John Boli, George Thomas, and Francisco O. Ramirez 1997 (see Chapter 8).

educational systems are greatly overestimated in country-specific studies. Many important cross-national educational similarities are both overlooked within the case study tradition and undertheorized in the conventional disputes between social order and reproduction theories. A compelling insight from comparative educational research needs to be re-asserted: national educational systems originate and become institutionalized in national societies that aspire to development and progress along quite standard lines. Standardized education arises then as an agreed upon core feature of development and progress as well as a crucial instrument intended to attain these transnationally legitimated goals. To explain national educational developments one must go beyond "national traditions" and situate nation-states within a broader nation-state system. Only then does the world institutionalization of education emerge as a major dynamic to be analyzed.

Conventional functional theories, both of the left and the right, have two characteristics that limit their capacity to interpret the global standardization of education (Chapter 8). First, since modern education tends to be formally organized and controlled at national levels, functional theories suppose that distinctive national needs and interests tend to determine the character of education. Nations are seen as distinct social systems, and education is tightly integrated with the national socio-cultural system. Since nations vary enormously in economy (by factors of one hundred to one) and polity and culture, education should vary too. Standardization, if it occurred, would be a slowly arising consequence of tight economic and political integration. In fact, educational standardization seems to occur at faster, not slower, rates than other forms of world integration. Thus, with respect to world society, functional theories focus on the level of the national actor and have a microsociological character.

Second, functional theories tend to be realist. They suppose that education is tied into rather hard-wired national social systems made up of clearly defined interests and requirements. The society that creates and manages education is thought to be an inherently cohesive functioning system of power and interest, of technical requirements, and so on. Again, societies around the world differ greatly in such matters, and educational standardization is an unlikely outcome if this picture is correct. But suppose that the society that constructs and reconstructs education is a phenomenological rather than a natural entity – a cultural vision (and a rather standardized one at that). Then it becomes easy to understand the world institutionalization of education.

Functionalism, both on the left and the right, tends to be microsociological and realist. The institutional theory we put forward below alters both these dimensions, seeing education as part of a universalistic and global model (i.e., macrosociologically) and seeing it as indeed a model – and organized in relation to society itself as a cultural model of development and justice (i.e., cultural or phenomenological rather than realist in character). Here we may note two lines of sociological argument about world society that alter one but not both of the functionalist assumptions.

First, one important sociological reaction to nation-level functionalism has been macrosociological in character, while retaining the realism of functional theories. Society and education are seen as organized in a global political economy and driven by the powers, interest, and needs built into this global system. This line of thought is highly developed in sociological "world systems" theories (Wallerstein 1974) and has frequently been applied to the explanation of world education (Dale 2002). For the most part, this world systems argument emphasizes the driving forces of inequality in the world economy and tends to suppose that institutions like education would develop very differently in core and peripheral parts of world society – extreme versions of the argument would have dominant power in the world suppressing educational development in the periphery. Such ideas make it hard, of course, to explain world educational standardization, since they propose that global forces enforce differentiated education on different parts of the world. But in a provocative paper, Yehudi Cohen discussed how the increasing integration of the world by a dominating neoimperial system might be creating homogeneity in at least elite education as a kind of management strategy (Cohen 1970).

A second social scientific reaction to functionalism retains its national or subnational level of analysis, but moves from realism to a more culturalist or phenomenological perspective on the relation of education and society. Here, the core conception is that educational systems tend to reflect the distinctive cultural values and perspectives characteristic of national societies, not necessarily tight functional requisites or even power and interest systems. Much historical work on education has this character, emphasizing unique national trajectories linked to variations in religion, political culture, and the like. Even when educational outcomes are very much linked to power and interest competitions,[1] the linkages are less functional than matters of cultural and status-group competition. These lines of argument, thus, are far removed from the explanation of educational globalization, and tend to emphasize the uniqueness of national educational systems.

Standardization, on the other hand, is an expected outcome in the sociological neoinstitutionalist perspective we advance here (see Thomas et al. 1987). From this point of view – both macrosociological and culturalist in character – modern education tends almost inherently to be a world enterprise, universal and universalistic in aspiration and in some measure in outcome. We see the nation-state that organizes education as embedded in a world society – in other words, a nation-state system. This system produces and incorporates national entities that, of course, differ enormously in resources, power, and culture. But these national entities tend to be symbolically transformed into nation-states with formally similar rights (and responsibilities, as well as other qualities) in the world.

THE NEOINSTITUTIONALIST CONCEPTION

Nation-states indeed vary, from great powers with large populations and much national wealth to less than visible and often struggling ones. But all of these entities present themselves to the nation-state system – and are entitled and indeed obligated

---

[1] As in the works of Randall Collins 1979; Ivor Goodson 1983.

to present themselves – as national societies with standard modern goals and standard strategies to attain these goals (Chapter 8; Thomas et al. 1987). All aspire to national economic development measured in very standard ways, that is, the gross national product per capita. Practically all constitutionally view their people as humans with formal rights and as entitled to developments as citizen-persons (see Donelly 1986; Ramirez and Meyer 1998). And practically all, following world standardized ideas on the question, emphasize education as a crucial instrument in attaining the desired national and individual development (see Fiala and Gordon-Lanford 1987; Chabbot and Ramirez 2000).

Education, in short, is a core and causal part of the cultural model of the modern society or nation-state. Education is adopted as part of this model and this adoption symbolizes commitment to becoming a respectable member or "imagined community" legitimated by world society (Anderson 1983). The "imagined community" and the centrality of education in its construction is a cultural principle exogenous to any specific nation-state and its historical legacy. Education is thus not much adapted to the endlessly varying idiosyncrasies of social reality but is homogenized around both common development goals or projects and common technological ideas about how to achieve these goals. Loose linkages between educational policies and prescriptions and actual local resources and structures are in many ways expected and perhaps even inevitable outcomes of world pressures toward nation-state standardization and educational homogeneity.

Education is standardized because it is part of a general model of the modern nation-state. But modern education is itself also spelled out as a model, with much professional, intellectual, and scientific support. There are clearly defined conceptions of educational structure, e.g., principles of universal enrollment, of educational curricular content, e.g., social studies instruction, of educational organization, e.g., the idea of the professionalized teacher, and so on. The elaboration of education as a relatively specific model in itself greatly increases global standardization.

The intensity of world pressures toward nation-state standardization has obviously increased over time (Hüfner et al. 1987). Several factors explain this phenomenon. First, the world is generally more integrated in terms of communication as well as exchange. Second, normative models of the nation-state, its proper goals, and the nature and rights of the citizenry have intensified, greatly affecting education. Third, technical social scientific ideas – the human capital revolution in education, for example – have symbolically tied education ever more closely to basic individual and collective desiderata. Fourth, professional models of the education system have intensified over time, with worldwide professional and organizational integration. Finally, doctrines about the nation-state, citizen, and human rights and education as both an individual and collective good have been institutionalized in concrete world organizations such as the World Bank, UNESCO and other parts of the UN system, the OECD, other world and regional organizations, and a multitude of proliferating international governmental and nongovernmental organizations (Jones 1992 and 1990).

MECHANISMS

The institutional theory pursued here suggests that the core mechanisms of the rapid diffusion of such modern institutions as education lie in (a) the common and rationalized identities of nation-states, (b) the common rooting of these identities in doctrines of individual citizenship, and (c) their rationalistic cultural immersion in common technical ideas such as those promoting education (Chapter 6; Ramirez 1997). These commonalities organize the world society so that flows of standardized educational ideas are rapid. Diffusion is further enhanced by the worldwide integration of the educational sciences and professions and by the organizations that carry this material providing detailed models of the proper national educational system.

But one may think of mechanisms in a more conventional sense. Much sociological research describes the ways in which organizations, professionals, and social movements promulgate flows of standardized cultural material. Some elements of world society facilitate this process. First, an integrated world stratification system provides dominant models to be copied. In a world culture defining education as central to progress, educational policies in dominant countries are among the first things to get copied. Japanese industrial success in the 1970s and 1980s directs worldwide attention toward Japanese schools and to their educational standards. There was much faith in a causal connection between their educational and economic performance. Much of the American policy fascination with the need for national curricular frameworks illustrates this phenomenon (Smith and O'Day 1990). In earlier periods, American models were copied on the same basis; note, for example, European efforts to emulate comprehensive secondary schooling. And still earlier, before World War I, German models were fashionable.[2] It is unclear which concrete national cases will acquire heroic status in the twenty-first century. But while the world as a stratification system certainly continues to generate diffusion from cores to peripheries, world organizational and cultural changes have in recent decades constructed more direct and organized mechanisms for diffusion (Meyer, Ramirez, and Soysal 1992). That is, in addition to direct borrowing or imitation, there is a rise in national enactments of educational blueprints or scripts of a more general or abstract character such as pedagogies and curricula that purport to foster active learning or the acquisition of higher order thinking skills.

Thus, a second point needs to be emphasized: an explicit world order now helpfully provides models for countries to copy. Clear definitions of the widespread problems to which education is the solution and the types of education that are putatively the best solutions are generated through an elaborate network of international governmental and nongovernmental organizations including UNESCO and the World Bank (McNeely 1995; Chabbot 1996). For instance, the education of women, both as a sound individual and national investment and as a matter of

---

[2] For a general discussion of the diffusion of educational ideas, policies, and practices, see Schriewer et al. 1998.

human rights, has been championed throughout this international network, influencing national educational policies and practices (Berkovitch 1998).

Third, and probably most important, education as a rationalized institution is ever more scientized, and educational practitioners are increasingly professionalized. Elaborate, standard scientific and professional analyses of the virtues and properties of education permeate world communication. The sciences and professions involved rest on the universal authority of their disciplines (e.g., economics or psychology) and their methods (e.g., cost accounting or experimental studies of learning), not principally on idiosyncratic national authority. They are automatic carriers of virtues that enjoy worldwide legitimacy, such as the enhanced academic achievement of learners due to better prepared teachers or the greater organizational efficiency of schools and universities due to more rational resource allocation. The professionalization and scientization of education greatly speeds up worldwide communication and standardization, just as the latter clearly facilitates the former. These processes reciprocally influence and strengthen each other.

THESES

Thus, the arguments of this essay may be straightforwardly stated:

1. The rise of rationalized models of the nation-state and of mass and elite education in the nineteenth and twentieth centuries produced institutions that are more homogenous across countries than would be predicted by the actual variability of national societies and cultures.

2. World models exercise increasing force over time on national educational systems, producing diffusion and standardization at an increasing rate.

3. Educational models increasingly diffuse from international organizations and from the educational sciences and professions; educational models decreasingly diffuse directly from core nations to peripheral ones.

4. The impact of particular endogenous national political, social, and economic characteristics on national educational systems declines over time.

5. Factors affecting national educational change have mainly and increasingly to do with the extent and character of national links to world society. The more a nation-state is immersed in world society and linked to its organizational carriers, the more its educational system will correspond to world models and will change in directions attuned to changes in world emphases.

Mass schooling has been most directly and thoroughly influenced by world models of progress and justice. Some institutions of higher education originated prior to the crystallization of these models and the concomitant project of constructing the modern nation-state. These institutions may continue to reflect the organizational forms and styles of the eras in which they were born (Stinchcombe 1965). However, higher education has not been immune to the worldwide standardization and rationalization processes; higher education has also been attuned to worldwide educational emphases. The student movements of the 1960s, for instance, affected a wide range of universities across the world, in part, because student politics in that era was frequently framed around world issues of progress and justice and the rights of students as citizen-persons.

DIMENSIONS OF WORLD STANDARDIZATION

In the following sections, we briefly review the progress of the world's "school board" of organizations and professions in generating a common world educational system in several areas: the structure, organization, and content of national educational systems, their direct international links, and the internationalization of their content.

Basic educational structure

There is already much evidence that basic educational patterns diffuse across the world, and with increasing rapidity, though more research is obviously needed. Mass schooling itself spreads via diffusion with rates of adoption increasing over time and highly dependent on links to the world society rather than on internal societal characteristics (Meyer, Ramirez, and Soysal 1992). The same thing seems to be true with respect to the basic principles of compulsory schooling (Ramirez and Ventresca 1992). What was a hotly contested issue in the older European culture of state or church struggles over control of education has become taken for granted in the contemporary world. Schooling the masses is a core theme on national agendas, and any erosion in primary educational enrollments is everywhere treated as evidence of severe national crisis (Fuller and Heyneman 1989).

The call for educational expansion has also affected higher education. The modern university system has certainly spread everywhere, with more universities being founded after World War II than in the history of the world prior to 1945 (Riddle 1996). Moreover, higher educational enrollments have increased in most parts of the world, despite the many obvious obstacles to, and costs of, such growth (Ramirez and Riddle 1991).

Further, worldwide variability in the patterning of the educational career sequence seems to be giving way to standardized sequences closely conforming to the tacitly preferred UNESCO model of 6–3–3 years (Benavot and Riddle 1988). Standard models of educational sequencing also seem to have tended to replace older and more tracked "models." Aaron Benavot discusses the long-term decline in specialized vocational education: the UNESCO year-books suggest a parallel decline for specialized teacher training arrangements (Benavot 1983). These developments have been triggered by the rise of comprehensive models of secondary education (Kamens, Meyer, and Benavot 1996). While universities continue to be regarded as elite institutions, there is a consistent worldwide decline in any programs that officially and formally restrict access on the basis of stratificational criteria. Thus, women's participation in higher education has increased worldwide (Bradley and Ramirez 1996). This pattern holds even when one examines traditionally masculine fields of study such as science and engineering, where women's relative share is also on the ascent in the last three decades (Ramirez and Min Wotipka 1998).

With respect to both mass and higher education, forms of differentiation based on ascribed status characteristics such as ethnicity, class, and gender are increasingly stigmatized in the larger world. International conventions calling for equal educational opportunity and prohibiting discrimination are passed in international organizations and affirmed in international conferences. Professional and scientific educational discourse clearly supports egalitarian educational principles. For example, despite the fact that adult roles for men and women continue to vary and vary across national societies, the worldwide tendency has been to create uniform mass educational curricula and increasingly similar enrollment patterns for the two genders (Ramirez and Cha 1990).

Content and instruction

Educational systems utilize increasingly world standardized curricula. Our recent review of the world's primary educational curricula in the twentieth century provides evidence for much increased standardization and diffusion (Meyer et al. 1992). Remarkably similar sets of subjects are covered worldwide, with much homogeneity in the amount of curricular time allocated to particular subjects. For instance, Suk-Ying Wong, working with these data, shows a striking tendency for the world's mass educational systems to shift toward the American "social studies" model and away from the traditional subjects of geography and history (Wong 1991). In a related study, Mary Rauner examines the content of civics education curricula and finds a cross-national pattern of change from a solely national focus to one in which world issues and international organizations are also emphasized (Rauner 1998). In both of these studies change was slower in the old European centers, suggesting that the process of diffusion involved more than simply poorer countries copying the curricula that prevailed among the richer ones. What appears to be the case is that countries with strong linkages to international communication relative to their own histories are most likely to promote the more "global" civic education emphases. The relative balance of international over historical trajectories is greatest among newly developed and less developed countries. Old European centers may be best linked to world educational communication, but have even stronger lateral capacities to maintain some domestic distinctiveness.

A cross-national focus on science and mathematics curricula has also emerged. David Kamens and Aaron Benavot demonstrate that what are now highly legitimate school subjects were once more controversial ones (Kamens and Benavot 1996). This seems to be especially the case with respect to content and instruction in science. A more recent content analysis of science textbooks, from the early twentieth century to the present era, shows a trend in the direction of greater pedagogical emphasis on the child as an active learner and away from an earlier stress on science as a set of canonical facts to be transmitted to pupils (McEneaney 1998). This study further shows that a greater curricular and textbook emphasis on child-centric active learning is more likely to be found in countries where large numbers of professional schools of

Education generate a more liberal pedagogical authority. A broader review of curricular trends and patterns also emphasizes global institutionalization dynamics (McEneaney and Meyer 2000).

In policy circles the focus on curricula and instruction is subordinated to the overriding interest in the cross-national achievement "horse race." There is much faith in strong linkages between curricula and instruction, on the one hand, and academic achievement and economic performance, on the other. This immediate "bottom line" perspective unfortunately deflects attention away from important issues of historical origins and cross-national commonalities in curricular matters. Recent efforts to examine pedagogical flows and curricular emphases in cross-national perspective are likely to be of value in their own right, however loosely related these may turn out to be to achievement and economic outcomes (Schmidt et al. 1996).

Fewer cross-national materials pertain to curricula and instruction in higher education. One research effort has focused on what counts as history in university catalogues or courses and degrees. Data are available for universities in a large number of countries over different time periods. A content analysis of the materials suggests that the focus of university history has changed from an emphasis on Western civilization to emphases on both international or global and more dispersed national histories (Frank et al. 1998). This study also documents the worldwide rise of civil society actors as opposed to military and political elites in what counts as history. Obviously much more work in comparative higher education is needed.[3]

Educational organization

Present evidence for the diffusion of standard models of educational funding and governance and the resultant world homogeneity is weak (see Inkeles and Sirowy 1983; Noah and Eckstein 1992). It can be argued that one should expect less standardization insofar as educational organization has been historically linked to the political control of education by a set of state bureaucracies with somewhat distinct organizational traditions (see Meyer and Scott 1983; Jeperson and Meyer 1991). But clearly, long-term trends toward more nation-level control over education continue; the proportion of countries with national ministries of education has increased over time and this institution becomes a virtually universal reality (Ramirez and Ventresca 1992). As standardized education spreads around the world, especially in less developed countries, it is carried out with national central organizational controls. Though such ministries first rose in Western Europe, their globalization, especially after World War II, cannot be attributed to American hegemony since the United States did not establish a ministry until very late. Current calls for decentralization and experiments with decentralization need to be placed in historical perspective and are not likely to result in a permanent and thorough de-nationalization of education.

---

[3] For some work on the topic, see Schriewer et al. 1998.

The core organizational area which clearly touches most on educational technology is the local school and classroom. Here the evidence for homogenizing tendencies is strong. The principle of the classroom rather than alternative forms of organizing instruction is worldwide, and attempts to alter it have failed. Nearly everywhere one finds the nominally professionalized and somewhat autonomous teacher. Attempts to de-skill teaching are replaced by standardized models of professionalized teacher training requiring higher and higher levels of certification. Educational instruction everywhere is professionalized in surprisingly standardized ways. Evidence of efforts to professionalize is found even under very difficult local conditions (Meyer 1998; Ramirez 1998).

The rise of an internationalized educational sector

The dimensions discussed above concern national educational change toward homogeneity. We turn here to consider the expansion of the international or global educational system and the increased density of national links to it.

One issue is the rise of strong international organizational models influencing national educational systems. There has clearly been a long-term rise in worldwide tendencies to identify centers of educational virtue. These tendencies emerge in part, because higher degrees of global integration and communication facilitate the identification of educational policies and practices elsewhere. More importantly, the rise of the universalistic world society makes it less likely that these policies and practices will be dismissed as "alien curiosities." Rather, the plausibility of adoption is increasingly imagined everywhere. Thus, core national educational systems receive enormous, worldwide attention and are commonly cited as models. However, there is not much by way of systematic research that traces this trend with empirical data.

Educational models and agendas are also increasingly defined by international organizations. This is characteristic of both the World Bank and UNESCO, though the models preferred by these organizations tend to differ over time (see Hüfner et al. 1987; Chabbot 1996). The research question is the degree to which such standardized international models find organizational nodes that gain sustained attention in national policy systems. The literature suggests, at times optimistically and at times critically, that there has been an intensification of ties between international and national educational organizations, professionals, and reform movements. An assessment of the degree of importance of the international models is much needed.

A second issue is a substantive one: what dimensions of educational are identified in world policy discourse in different periods? There seem to be variations over time in world emphases on maximizing educational participation and extending rights to previously excluded groups in maximizing student achievement levels. The former encompasses a range of discussions valuing diversity regarding race, gender, ethnicity, class and a variety of handicaps. The resulting discourse is one of rights, fairness, and justice. Achievement discourse emphasizes standards, effort, performance, excellence, and values productivity. An earlier and perhaps renewed interest in civic education is informed by a world emphasis on participation, rights, and the national value of good citizenship. The current emphasis on science and science achievement in national reform agendas is shaped by forces or images of economic globalization, international competition, and the national value of enhanced productivity. The stable relationship throughout this century between changes in world emphases and changes in national agendas is clearly a research question worth pursuing. It seems evident that educational agendas worldwide are increasingly similar with respect to both the educational framing of important problems and the educational solutions to them.

Beyond isomorphism?

There is finally the question of whether educational systems become not only parallel or similar but also in a sense the same. Educational sameness occurs in two fronts. First, educational systems seem increasingly to organizationally recognize each others' credentials and standards. It appears that degrees and certificates acquire more common meaning around the world; this principle of equivalence is no doubt an ideal strongly favored by educational professionals and scientists worldwide. However partial and tentative, developments in this direction are found not only in the European Community but also more generally.

Second, there is substantive sameness in the educational definition of the world. The latter is decreasingly defined as a space populated by peoples living in the same legal, social, and physical forms. Common humanity is a theme that permeates the intended curricula in the social sciences and in the humanities. Both in lower levels of schooling (Rauner 1998) and in higher education (Frank et al. 1998), there is some evidence of a more inclusive vision of history, of viewing other countries and their problems and efforts to solve them as relevant, and of imagining transnational peoples as engaged in a common project to promote peace and progress. All of this is quite fragile and has its critics. But this emphasis on global commonality also has its counterpart in the natural sciences. Here one can observe the growing emphasis on a common world ecology and the rise of an integrated science emphasis in world educational models and in national educational curricula.

Both of these developments in the social and in the natural sciences are facilitated by the rise of an international educational sector and an increase in national links to the sector and to the models articulated by global educational professionals and scientists. Not surprisingly the latter often hail from the more developed countries. The rapid diffusion of curricular ideas in less developed countries is sometimes critiqued as a continuing form of domination. Alternatively lapses in implementation are sometimes cited as evidence of bad faith or worse. Both criticisms miss the mark, because they continue to think of nation-states as unique natural entities that should either buy or reject the models based on a bounded calculation of national interest. We, on the contrary, argue that rapid diffusion in less developed countries reflects the degree to which their identities as nation-states are contingent on their adherence to international models and educational emphases. The same nominally autonomous nation-state identities, however, make it nearly impossible for external agencies to thoroughly monitor and manage the implementation of educational models. The resultant loose coupling is endemic; educational standardization is a manual cut and paste process in which what exactly gets cut and how precisely it gets pasted varies. Given these cross-national and temporal variations, the multiple observable trends toward educational isomorphism are striking and call our attention to the world institutionalization of education.

A note on "glocalization"

We have stressed on a variety of forces generating global educational standardization. It is important to note that this standardization occurs in a frame that emphasizes the sovereignty of the modern individual and the modern nation-state. Like Alexis de Tocqueville's American individuals (de Tocqueville 1966), all these entities are homogenized in status but on the peculiar ground that each has its own unique sovereign identity. This amounts to a celebration, within a universalistic frame, of the local and particular value in each individual and setting. Thus, we have what Roland Robertson calls "glocalization" – the universal celebration and legitimation of the putative uniqueness of each individual, community, and nation (Robertson 1992).

Much of this celebration takes on the form of expressive culture. It is after all highly illegitimate to stress the instrumental superiority and dominance of some individuals, classes, ethnicities, communities, or nations. Furthermore, it is clearly improper to treat instrumental economic or political success as reflective of inherent superiority. The proper form is to treat the special features of each legitimated individual or collective unit as a matter of personality, national character, cultural style, or its equivalent. Nations and individuals may, and indeed often must, claim some unique value in their styles or backgrounds. These claims apply to a wide range of domains, from issues of food and clothing styles to artistic and literary representations to constructions of national history and indigenous culture.

Educational systems worldwide reflect and re-direct this celebration in ways that generate or legitimate cultural diversity without claim to stratificational distinction. There is the curricular emphasis on relevance to the particular individual student and the corresponding organizational expansion of course and program choices for each individual. There is much celebration of local cultural material, with artistic, literary, and historical instruction decreasingly emphasizing standard canons and increasingly legitimating diversity. All cultures and their products are assigned equal value and their study is in part left to the tastes of individuals, communities, and to some extent, nations.

So, within the standard and universalized educational forms, much legitimated diversity can appear. This shows up in every subject area. History is no longer a sacred canonized text, but can cover diverse times, places, and peoples. Literature, art, and music become more eclectic. Social studies directly emphasize legitimated diversity within and across nation-states. Science, too, becomes a meta-frame, within which almost anything can be analyzed, depending on the interests and tastes of individual students, teachers, and curriculum developers. Standardized educational models thus celebrate and increasingly equalize diversity. In one sense the weakening of canons in an expanding system of knowledge production involves a loss of meaning and authority. But it is also true that there is a great deal of homogenization in the structure and character of the frame within which this diverse schooled material acquires meaning. The educational models may celebrate multiple intelligence, the achievements of indigenous peoples, and even diverse paths to national development, but everywhere the individual and collective effort to cultivate intelligence and achievement has a strong educational flavor and is strongly linked to world models of progress and justice.

CONCLUSION

The logic of rationalized modern mass and elite education has always meant that a high degree of international homogenization was involved. Within the framework of a world society the process of becoming a nation-state and of competing with other nation-states led to the adoption of remarkably similar projects and commitments to remarkably similar technologies, such as education. This process has produced pressures toward institutional isomorphism throughout the nineteenth and twentieth centuries.

The recent period following World War II was characterized by the rise of much relevant international organizational structure and the triumph of the authority of more common and worldwide scientific and professional groups and ideologies. These developments have greatly intensified pressures for international diffusion and standardization of educational models.

Diffusion and the resultant isomorphism clearly characterize basic educational structures. Types of programs, and educational sequences and differentiation, seem strikingly homogenous and change in similar ways around the world. This appears to be also true of formal curricular content in both mass and elite education. It may be less true of educational organizational structure. The latter shows strong worldwide isomorphism at the bottom, with respect to school and classroom technology for example. However, there appears to be more variability at the top, with respect to levels of political control and management. The international educational sector has also become more institutionalized; international educational organizations are playing a sharper role in defining and transmitting educational models for individual and national development. Moreover there has been an intensification of national linkages to the world educational apparatus. Finally, there has been a great deal of internationalization of educational content at both mass and elite educational levels and a rise in the educational definition of the world as common humanity and common habitat.

Though often grounded in empirical research this paper offers a good deal of speculative argument. The kind of comparative educational research that directly addresses these arguments has emerged, but its development remains rather limited. There are, of course, substantial research difficulties in collecting and analyzing cross-national longitudinal educational data. But there are other obstacles, that may be both more difficult to justify and harder to eradicate. First, educational researchers have tended to create standards of data quality that produce microscopic studies and fine data with little evidentiary value on large scale comparative issues. These studies justify inferences about individuals or about specific societies; in this tradition, comparative education mostly either compares individuals across societies or provides a book cover for mostly unrelated case studies. These studies do not allow us to examine cross-national trends or to test hypotheses that seek to explain cross-national variation.

More importantly and perhaps paradoxically, the standard world ideologies relating education to each social system in which it is found pervade the research community too. Thus, there is a great reluctance to view education as a central world myth and its spread around the world more as an organizing and even mobilizing myth rather than as a functional arrangement. This stifles the development of comparative research designs and analyses that examine particular national educational arrangements as resulting from worldwide flows and global institutionalization.

REFERENCES

Anderson, Benedict. 1983. *Imagined Communities: Reflections on the Origin and Spread of Nationalism.* London: Verso Press.

Benavot, Aaron. 1983. The Rise and Decline of Vocational Education. *Sociology of Education* 56 (2):63–76.

—— and Phyllis Riddle. 1988. National Estimates of the Expansion of Mass Education, 1870–1840. *Sociology of Education* 61 (3):191–210.

Berkovitch, Nitza. 1998. The Emergence and Transformation of the International Women's Movement, in John Boli and George Thomas (eds.), *World Polity Since 1875: World Culture and International Non-Governmental Organizations.* Stanford, CA: Stanford University Press.

Bradley, Karen and Francisco O. Ramirez. 1996. World Polity and Gender Parity: Women's Share of Higher Education, 1965–1985. *Research in Sociology of Education and Socialization* 11:63–92.

Chabbot, Colette. 1996. Constructing Educational Development: International Development Organizations and the World Conference of All. PhD dissertation. Standord University.

—— and Francisco O. Ramirez. 2000. Development and Education, in Maureen Hallinan (ed.), *Handbook of Sociology of Education.* New York: Plenum, pp. 163–87.

Clark, Roger. 1992. Multinational Corporate Investment and Women's Participation in Higher Education in Non-Core Nations. *Sociology of Education* 65 (1):37–47.

Cohen, Yehudi. 1970. School Systems and Civilizational States, in Joseph Fischer (ed.), *Social Sicience and the Comparative Study of Educational Systems.* New York: In Text Press.

Collins, Randall. 1979. *The Credential Society: An Historical Sociology of Education and Stratification.* New York: Academic Press.

Dale, Roger. 2000. Globalization: A New World for Comparative Education?, in Jürgen Schriewer (ed.), *Discourse Formation in Comparative Education.* Frankfurt am Main: Peter Lang, pp. 87–109.

de Tocqueville, Alexis. 1966. *Democracy in America.* New York: Doubleday.

Donelly, Jack. 1986. International Human Rights: A Regime Analysis. *International Organization* 40:599–642.

Fiala, Robert and Audrey Gordon-Lanford. 1987. Educational Ideology and the World Educational Revolution, 1950–1970. *Comparative Education Review* 31 (3):315–33.

Frank, David, Suk-Ying Wong, John W. Meyer, Francisco O. Ramirez, and Sue Duncan. 1998. What Counts as History: A Cross-National and Longitudinal Study of History Curricula. Unpublished paper.

Fuller, Bruce and Stephen Heyneman. 1989. Third World School Quality: Current Collapse and Future Potential. *Educational Researcher* 18 (2):12–19.

Goodson, Ivor. 1983. *School Subjects and Curriculum Change.* London: Croom Helm.

Hüfner, Klaus, Jens Naumann, and John W. Meyer. 1987. Comparative Education Policy Research: A World Society Perspective, in Meinolf Dierkes, Hans N. Weiler, and Ariane Berthoin Antal (eds.), *Comparative Policy Research: Learning From Experience.* Aldershot: Gower.

Inkeles, Alex and Larry Sirowy. 1983. Convergent and Divergent Trends in National Educational Systems. *Social Forces* 62 (2):303–33.

Jeperson, Ronald L. and John W. Meyer. 1991. The Public Order and the Construction of Formal Organizations, in Walter Powell and Paul DiMaggio (eds.), *The New Institutionalism in Organizational Analysis.* Chicago, IL: University of Chicago Press.

Jones, Philip. 1990. Unesco and the Politics of Global Literacy. *Comparative Education Review* 34 (1):41–60.

—— 1992. *World Bank Financing of Education: Lending, Learning, and Development.* New York: Routledge.

Kamens, David H. and Aaron Benavot. 1996. Elite Knowledge for the Masses: The Origins and Spread of Mathematics and Science Education in National Curricula. *American Journal of Education* 99 (2):137–80.

—— and John W. Meyer. Theories and Research on the Content of the Curriculum, in Maureen Hallinan (ed.), *Handbook of Sociology of Education.* New York: Plenum, pp. 189–211.

—— —— and Aaron Benavot. 1996. Worldwide Patterns in Academic Secondary Education Curricula. *Comparative Education Review* 40 (2):116–38.

McEneaney, Elizabeth H. 1998. The Transformation of Primary School Science and Mathematics: A Cross-National Analysis, 1900–1995. PhD disssertation. Stanford University.

McNeely, Connie. 1995. *Constructing the Nation State: International Organization and Prescriptive Action.* Westport, CT: Greenwood Press.

Meyer, John W. 1998. Training and Certifying Unqualified Teachers in Namibia, in Wes Snyder, Jr. and Friedhelm Voigts (eds.), *Inside Reform Policy and Programming Considerations in Namibia's Basic Education Reform.* Windhoek, Namibia: Gamsberg Macmillan.

—— and W. Richard Scott. 1983. *Organizational Environments: Ritual and Rationality.* London: Sage.

—— David H. Kamens, Aaron Benavot, Yun-Kyung Cha, and Suk-Ying Wong. 1992. *School Knowledge for the Masses: World Models and National Curricular Categories in the 20th Century.* London: Falmer Press.

—— Francisco O. Ramirez, and Yasemin Soysal. 1992. World Expansion of Mass Education, 1870–1970. *Sociology of Education* 65 (2):128–49.

—— John Boli, George Thomas, and Francisco O. Ramirez. 1997. World Society and the Nation-State. *American Journal of Sociology* 103 (1):144–81. Reproduced in Chapter 8.

Noah, Harold J. and Max A. Eckstein. 1992. Comparing National Systems of Secondary School Leaving Examinations, in Robert F. Amove, Philip G. Altbach, and Gail P. Kelly (eds.), *Emergent Issues in Education: Comparative Perspectives.* Albany, NY: State University of New York Press.

Ramirez, Francisco O. 1997. The Nation-State, Citizenship, and Educational Change: Institutionalization and Globalization, in William Cummings and Noel F. McGinn (eds.), *International Handbook of Education and Development: Preparing Schools, Students and Nations for the Twenty-First century.* New York: Garland Publishing.

—— 1998. Comparing Assessment and Gender Equity: Constructing the Progressive Learner in Northern Namibia, in Wes Snyder, Jr. and Friedhelm Voigts (eds.), *Inside Reform Policy and Programming Considerations in Namibia's Basic Education Reform.* Windhoek, Namibia: Gamsberg Macmillan.

—— and Yun-Kyung Cha. 1990. Citizenship and Gender: Western Educational Developments in Comparative Perspective. *Research in Sociology of Education and Socialization* 9:153–74.

—— and John W. Meyer. 1992. Educational Globalization: The Effect of World Models on National Educational Systems. Unpublished Research proposal.

—— —— 1998. Dynamics of Citizenship Development and the Incorporation of Woman: A Research Agenda, in Connie McNeely (ed.), *Public Rights, Public Rules: Constituting Citizens in the World Polity and National Policy.* New York: Garland, pp. 59–80.

—— and Phyllis Riddle. 1991. The Expansion of Higher Education, in Philip G. Altbach (ed.), *International Higher Education: An Encyclopedia.* New York: Garland.

—— and Marc Ventresca. 1992. Building the Institution of Mass Schooling: Isomorphism in the Modern World, in Bruce Fuller and Richard Rubinson (eds.), *The Political Construction of Education.* New York: Praeger.

—— and Christine Min Wotipka. 1998. Women's Access to Science and Engineering Fields of Study: Trends and Analysis. Paper presented at the Annual Meetings of the American Education Research Association.

Rauner, Mary. 1998. The Worldwide Globalization of Civics Education Topics, 1955–1995. PhD disssertation. Stanford University.

Riddle, Phyllis. 1996. The University and Political Authority: Historical Trends and Contemporary Possibilities. *Research in Sociology of Education and Socialization* 11:43–62.

Robertson, Roland. 1992. *Globalization: Social Theory and Global Culture.* London: Sage.

Schmidt, William et al. 1996. *Characterizing Pedagogical Flow: An Investigation of Mathematics and Science Teaching in Six Countries.* Dordrecht: Kluwer Academic Publishers.

Schriewer, Jürgen et al. 1998. Konstruktionen von Internationalität. Referenzhorizonte pädagogischen Wissens im Wandel gesellschaftlicher Systeme, in Hartmut Kaelble and Jürgen Schriewer (eds.), *Gesellschaften im Vergleich.* Frankfurt am Main: Peter Lang, pp. 151–258.

Smith, Michael and Jennifer O'Day. 1990. Systemic School Reform, in Susan Fuhrman and Betty Malen (eds.), *The Politics of Curriculum and Testing.* Bristol, PA: Falmer Press.

Stinchcombe, Arthur. 1965. Social Structure and Organizations, in James G. March (ed.), *Handbook of Organizations.* Chicago, IL: Rand McNally.

Strang, David and John W. Meyer. 1993. Institutional Conditions for Diffusion. *Theory and Society* 22 (4):487–511. Reproduced in Chapter 6.

Thomas, George, John W. Meyer, Francisco O. Ramirez, and John Boli. 1987. *Institutional Structure: Constituting State, Society, and the Individual.* Beverly Hills, CA: Sage.

Wallerstein, Immanuel. 1974. *The Modern World System: Capitalist Agriculture and the Origins of the European World-Economy in the Sixteenth Century.* New York: Academic Press.

Wong, Suk-Ying. 1991. The Evolution of Social Science Instruction, 1900–1986: A Cross-National Study. *Sociology of Education* 64 (1):33–47.

10

Environment

The Structuring of a World Environmental Regime, 1870–1990

In recent decades, a great expansion has occurred in world environmental organization, both governmental and nongovernmental, along with an explosion of worldwide discourse and communication about environmental problems. All of this constitutes a world environmental regime. Using the term *regime* a little more broadly than usual, we define world environmental regime as a partially integrated collection of world-level organizations, understandings, and assumptions that specify the relationship of human society to nature. The rise of an environmental regime has accompanied greatly expanded organization and activity in many sectors of global society (see Robertson 1992; Smith et al. 1994; Boli and Thomas 1998). Explaining the growth of the environmental regime, however, poses some problems. The interests and powers of the dominant actors in world society – nation-states and economic interests – came late to the environmental scene. Thus, these forces cannot easily be used to explain the rise of world mobilization around the environment, in contrast with other sectors of global society (for example, the international economic and national security regimes).

We see the world environmental regime as produced through another process, starting from the rise of much international nongovernmental association and discourse and leading to interstate treaties and later to intergovernmental organization. Behind this long process, we argue, lie two larger forces that help drive its development: the long-term expansion of rationalized and authoritative scientific interpretation, which structures perceptions of common environmental problems, and the rise of world associational arenas – principally the United Nations (UN) system – with agendas open to broad concerns such as the environment.

Originally published as:

John W. Meyer, Frank, David John, Hironaka, Ann, Schofer, Evan, and Tuma, Nancy Brandon. 1997. The Structuring of a World Environmental Regime, 1870–1990. *International Organization* 51:623–51

An earlier version of this chapter was presented at the 1994 Annual Meeting of the American Sociological Association. The research was supported by a grant from the National Science Foundation to Nancy Brandon Tuma and John W. Meyer. Work on the article was aided by suggestions from Henrich Greve, Francisco O. Ramirez, David Strang, and project colleagues in Stanford's Comparative Workshop.

We lay out a brief description of the environmental regime and consider several explanations, including our own, for its expansion. We then describe in more detail the processes by which the world environmental regime expanded, and provide quantitative event history analyses that show the impact of the main forces involved. Finally, we consider the characteristics of different patterns of regime development in world society – for instance, why the environment regime developed differently from the international security regime commonly taken as canonical.

EVIDENCE OF INCREASING DOMAIN STRUCTURE

World society is filled with communication, association, and organizational structure concerned with the relation of society to the natural environment. This has greatly increased over time. There is much world-level scientific (and broader cultural) discussion of environmental issues such as the greenhouse effect and the overproduction of carbon dioxide, the ozone layer and methane generation from the expanded production and consumption of cattle, declining biological diversity and species extinction, deforestation, and the effects of a wide variety of dangerous chemicals (including DDT, heavy metals, and plutonium). In addition, many international nongovernmental associations focus on the environment; for example, the International Union for the Conservation of Nature, which had representatives from 118 countries in 1990 and takes policy positions on a wide range of issues.

Much activity of an official sort also occurs. Many intergovernmental treaties are concerned with the environment, such as the 1973 Convention on International Trade in Endangered Species, which had been ratified by 107 countries in 1990. Many formal intergovernmental organizations deal with the environment; for example, the International Whaling Commission has been joined by 40 countries (an increasing number of which do not hunt whales but choose to have input on whaling decisions). Following the 1972 Conference on the Human Environment held in Stockholm (attended by 114 governmental representatives and a great many representatives of nongovernmental organizations) the UN Environment Programme (UNEP) was formed. UNEP is a special body within the UN Secretariat established by resolution of the UN General Assembly and has taken some jurisdiction over the environmental domain.

Quantitative data describing the extraordinary expansion of international nongovernmental and governmental organizations (and treaties) concerned with the environment are presented in Figures 10.1 and 10.2. (The data, sources, and coding rules for these figures are discussed later; an overview is presented here to make clear the dramatic changes involved.) Figure 10.1 shows the cumulative numbers of organizations and treaties in existence at any given time; Figure 10.2 shows the rates of formation of these new entities and how they vary over time. Both figures show patterns of extreme growth.[1]

---

[1] When we plot the logarithm of variables on the vertical axis against year, the relationships are roughly linear, suggesting exponential growth of environmental activity.

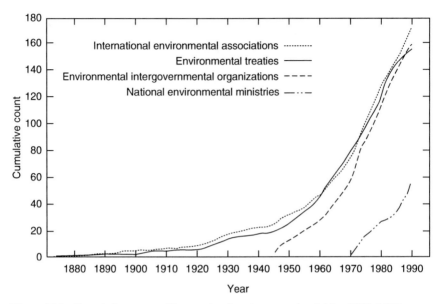

Figure 10.1. Cumulative counts of international environmental activities, 1870–1990

Examining data on how the environmental regime has developed since 1870, we describe and analyze its developmental process. The core intellectual problem is how so much organized collective action has arisen in a world society that so clearly lacks a strong central actor (or state), that organizationally resembles an anarchy, and in which the dominant state organizations, until recently, formed few and weak environmental agendas.[2] (To illustrate this point, Figures 10.1 and 10.2 also show the recent expansion in national ministries concerned with the environment.) Our core answer is that this same world is a strong, though stateless, polity increasingly integrated around a common rationalistic and scientized culture.

The world environmental regime is filled with both, discourse and organization, and these obviously affect each other. By discourse, we mean worldwide discussion and communication, universalistic, rationalized, and authoritative in character, occurring in international public arenas among policy professionals, scientists, and representatives of nation-states, in intergovernmental organizations, and in international nongovernmental associations. Our analyses focus on explaining the organizational side of the world environmental regime, and discourse enters as an explanatory factor. A parallel analysis would focus on explaining the discursive side of the system. We offer commentary on this, but lacking the necessary data, we do not analyze it.

The foci of this chapter are the explanation of (a) the overall rise of environmental organization, indicated by international environmental nongovernmental associations,

[2] The anarchy image is taken very seriously in the field of international relations, compare Gilpin (1981).

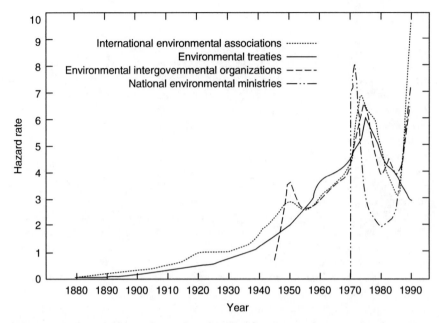

Figure 10.2. Smoothed hazard rates for initiation of international environmental activities, 1870–1990

international environmental treaties, intergovernmental environmental organizations, and national environmental ministries; and (b) the change over time in the character of this organizational system. Our main arguments are that the overall rise of environmental organization occurs with the expansion of a worldwide scientific culture and the creation of a broad world organizational structure, and that the character of the environmental regime shifts over time from informal international discourse and association to more official intergovernmental activity and organization.

ALTERNATIVE EXPLANATIONS

If we imagine that collective action must be built on individuals as natural actors, or on nation-states as natural actors, it becomes difficult to explain the extraordinary profusion of world-level collective action in such arenas as the environment.[3] By common agreement and observation, no strong world collective actor exists. Without such an actor, collective action in a generalized domain such as the environment should be extremely difficult and tenuous.

[3] For individuals as natural actors, see Olson 1965; and Coleman 1986. For nation-states as natural actors, see Waltz 1979; and Gilpin 1981.

Existing analyses of the world-level environmental structure tend to emphasize precisely this fragility. Whether focused on the emergence of a single international environmental treaty or intergovernmental organization or on the general conditions under which such structures appear, theories of international relations underscore the conflicts inherent in nation-state negotiations and delineate the exceptional circumstances under which such conflicts may be resolved (Young 1989; Benedick 1991; Levy 1993; Sprinz and Vaahtoranta 1994). In empirical reality, however, great and highly collective environmental goods have been rather quickly created, and much mobilization has ensued. All this has occurred in a world society without a sovereign collective actor.

Realist accounts root the explanation of the rise of world collective action on the environment in the powers and interests of dominant state actors. There is some discussion of the idea that the world environmental regime appeared at the behest of powerful Western nation-states, for example, to control resource flows or to tip the scales of environmental security (see Homer-Dixon 1994; Gould et al. 1995). Although such factors may motivate particular treaties or organizations, there is scant support for a theory of Western hegemony on a wider scale. Western nation-states have proved to be at least as reluctant as others to participate in international environmental structures – whether reluctance is measured by speed to ratify, discipline to comply, or willingness to lead. The roots of modern environmentalism clearly lie in Western societies and cultures as we elaborate later, but they do not principally lie in dramatic state action and purpose. In this matter, the environment sector provides an important contrast with others (for example, the national security sector).

As a second possible line of explanation, the environment movement itself, as with all such movements, provides its own story of its rise: a highly functional one. The claim is that the urgency of the problems created by environmental degradation makes collective mobilization functionally necessary (see Walsh 1981; and McCoy and McCully 1993). This is unconvincing. First, massive environmental degradation has been occurring for a long time without much corresponding mobilization; for example, world croplands doubled between 1700 and 1850 and nearly doubled again by 1920, with devastating losses to biodiversity (see Turner et al. 1990; and Groombridge 1992). This problem did not "cause" much world-level action until the 1990s. Likewise, fishery collapses (for example, during the Hanseatic League), the degradation of international rivers and seas (for example, in nineteenth-century Europe), and air pollution throughout the industrial period generated few visible responses. Even now, poorly understood but potentially disastrous problems, such as those posed by industrial gas "cocktails," barely appear on the global agenda (Yearley 1996). The point is that no matter how dire or widespread, environmental problems do not automatically generate organized solutions, nationally or internationally. Second, like all functional explanations, this one, hinging on degradation, can explain why environmental action is needed but not why it happens in the absence of a collective actor. We need an explanation for the presence of environmental mobilization after World War II that also explains the absence of much activity before.[4]

---

[4] On an organization-by-organization or treaty-by-treaty basis, other explanations of international environmental structure are available; for example, some have emphasized the promise of CFC substitutes in facilitating the ozone treaty. Such explanations, however useful, do not attempt to address the rise of the whole world environmental structure, as we do here.

Our argument starts from the sociological assumption that modern individuals, organizations, and nation-states by their construction have been deeply embedded in a wider world society, polity, and rationalistic culture (see Thomas et al. 1987; Robertson 1992; Meyer 1994, 1997; McNeely 1995; and Finnemore 1996a). This wider system defines, legitimates, and supports the identities of these entities; constructs appropriate purposes and technologies for them; and helps enforce their sovereignty, responsibility, and control capabilities (see DiMaggio and Powell 1983; and Powell and DiMaggio 1991). In our view, the world environmental regime derives fundamentally from changes in this wider polity rather than from changes in the interests and capabilities of individuals and states as prior natural actors. Of course, in a world in which nation-states have primacy as actors, world changes mainly occur through changes in the social construction and modification of the goals and interests of these scripted "actors."

The sociological conception of a world polity is closely related to two conceptions employed more often by political scientists: the idea that much international behavior is structured by more or less organized regimes, and the more recent idea that important components of these regimes are rooted in discursive or epistemic communities and a world civil society.[5] In comparison, the sociological conception of a world polity calls attention to the underlying cultural and organizational base that facilitates and helps to empower specific organizational (regime) structures and the associated epistemic communities; we use the term *regime* in this broader sense (Thomas et al. 1987). Using *regime* in this way helps avoid two limitations sometimes built into narrower uses of the term: the assumption that regimes are almost by definition organizational products of state action, and the assumption that regimes can be defined in terms of their effectiveness in controlling practical state policy and action (a matter we separately address in our concluding discussion). Neither assumption helps describe or understand the rise of an elaborated world environmental regime. A broader conception of regimes is useful for our analysis, which traces the formation of – and the sociocultural roots of – an international system and epistemic community, with uncertain and diffuse effects on specific state policies and actions over a long period of time.

EXPLAINING THE RISE OF THE ENVIRONMENTAL REGIME

The preceding discussion suggests two conditions that make the environmental regime distinctive. The first condition is the long-term degradation of the environment – a continuous feature of modern history that continually provides issues that could, at any time, become arenas for collective action. The second condition is the

[5] Compare chapters in Krasner 1983; and Haggard and Simmons 1987. See Young 1986; Adler and Haas 1989; Nadelman 1990; Falk 1992; Haas 1992; and Wapner 1996. This overall line of thought is developed in Rosenau and Czempiel 1992.

absence of strong collective actors (either at the world or the national state level) with environmental issues central to their agendas. At the end of this chapter, we suggest how variations in these conditions might be expected to produce variations in the development of different sectors of world society (such as international security, international economic organization, human rights, education, or the status of women). Our arguments – and the environmental example – may be of special use to a field of international organization that has tended to focus on social domains that are central to nation-state agendas throughout the modern period. Ronald Jepperson, Alexander Wendt, and Peter Katzenstein, for instance, argue that academic research in international relations has tended to form its agenda by looking principally at those social domains that are foci of interstate purpose and contest and by remaining inattentive to others (Jepperson et al. 1996). Considering the environmental case may provide a useful corrective.

Under these conditions, we argue that two dramatic changes in world society serve as variables that explain the rise of the contemporary environmental regime. The first change is cultural in character and involves the expansion of rationalized scientific analyses of nature that define and codify environmental degradation in terms that enable widespread collective mobilization and action. The other change is organizational and involves the rise of an international associational framework, principally the UN system that provides arenas that encourage mobilization around broad interests, transcending nation-state agendas. Together, these two forces provide an expanded world-level frame within which interaction and discourse about environmental issues could expand rapidly. The current literature on the rise of social movements and collective action increasingly emphasizes the importance of such frames (see Goffman 1974; Snow et al. 1986; Garrison 1995). In our view, the rise of the world environmental regime and many of its properties follow from changes in the wider frame involved. We discuss our two explanatory variables in turn.

The scientific rationalization of nature

Early efforts to mobilize environmental concerns around sentimental attachment to nature – or around nature as a set of resources to be allocated – provided weak frames for the mobilization of international activity (see Pepper 1984, and Frank 1997). Western-style sentimentalization presumed values that were parochial. Even now, animal-rights principles are not widely accepted in the larger world society. Thus, an early attempt at selective conservation failed to garner much support: The 1900 Convention for the Protection of Savage Species in Africa aimed to protect the magnificent fauna of Africa, including giraffes, elands, and hippos. To do so, the treaty sought the reduction of other, "noxious" species, such as lions, baboons, and pythons. The distinction between magnificent and noxious species earned the treaty disapprobation from international conservation associations, such as the Fauna and Flora Preservation Society, and contributed to the treaty's failure to win ratification (Hayden 1942).

The same limited success resulted from an early attempt to see whales as a resource to be partitioned: A few whaling countries were involved in this effort, but the resource frame pitted national interests against one another and inhibited the matter from being generalized as a worldwide concern. Thus the 1937 Agreement for the Regulation of Whaling, "desiring to secure the prosperity of the whaling industry and, for that purpose, to maintain the stock of whales," received only eight ratifications or accessions, and some major whaling countries, such as Japan, refused to be involved (Hayden 1942).[6]

By contrast, the scientific view of nature, which has spread with increased scientific knowledge and public awareness, asserts the existence of a global and interdependent ecosystem that encompasses human beings and sustains the very possibility of life (see Nanda 1983; Haas 1989; Stern et al. ;1992 Taylor and Buttel 1992; and Dunlap 1994).[7] Some components of this ecosystem are local and regional; others are intercontinental and global; rarely are they coterminous with national boundaries. The universalized conception of interdependence inherent in such a view of nature provides a much stronger frame for international discourse and activity around the environment than did sentimental or resource views.

The ecosystemic view has grown more prevalent with the massive expansion of both national and international scientific activity in the twentieth century.[8] As an example, the International Council of Scientific Unions (ICSU) was founded in 1919 with five scientific organizations involving people from a limited set of countries. Expansion of the organization, both in the number of sciences involved (it is now twenty) and the number of countries represented (currently almost all, in one or another specific field), has been rapid. From its origins, the ICSU has acted as a platform for advocates for the environment in international forums, though environmental organizations are not included in it (see Hayden 1942; McCormick 1989).

In a world in which most countries are organized around rationalistic models of state and society, a scientific conception of nature can frame environmental issues in a way that involves the legitimate and almost universal interests and perspectives of people, organizations, and nation-states (see Thomas et al. 1987; Schott 1993; Drori 1997). Thus, when scientists first suggested in 1973 that chlorofluorocarbons (CFCs) break down in the stratosphere and release ozone-destroying catalysts, they raised the possibility of global environmental damage (see Benedick 1991; and Parson 1993). Developing countries, responsible only for a tiny portion of the CFCs released, nevertheless took part in the international negotiations that ensued because they too faced risks to human health and declines in agricultural and fishery production.

Viewed scientifically as an ecosystem, nature lacks clear national boundaries. Thus, our first guiding hypothesis is

> The worldwide expansion of scientific discourse and association over this century facilitated the rise of world environmental organization.

---

[6] The eight parties were the United States, Great Britain, Norway, Germany, Ireland, New Zealand, Mexico, and Canada.

[7] Models of moral integration have arisen with models of the scientific integration of humans and nature; see, for example, Bergesen 1995.

[8] See, for example, Finnemore 1993, 1996b; and Schofer 1998.

The formal organization of the world polity

A great barrier to constructing a world environmental regime early in this century lay in the fact that no organizational frame existed within which environmental issues could enter the world's agenda. There was neither a central authoritative world actor (a situation that remains) nor any organizational structure within which environmental issues might legitimately fall (Nanda 1983). Thus, early environmentalist discourse could occur at informal world conferences (for example, the International Congresses for the Protection of Nature) but only on an ad hoc basis. Later, and very rapidly after World War II, many intergovernmental organizations arose, and these increasingly provided platforms for environmental mobilization.[9]

In the earlier period, the international organizational frame did little to facilitate environmental organizing. Specifically, the creation of the League of Nations in 1919 helped little. The League was defined principally as an international security system and actively resisted adoption of agenda items that might seem to constitute interference in the affairs of sovereign countries. Thus efforts to encourage the League to act on environmental issues failed in every instance except in the case of whale protection.[10] In 1935, for example, under pressure from the Conseil International de la Chasse and the British government, the League authorized a subcommittee to draft a treaty to reduce oil dumping on the high seas. After some exploratory efforts, however, including two international conferences, the issue was dropped from the League's agenda (see Hayden 1942; and Mitchell 1993).

The UN system, weak as it is in terms of sovereign authority, changed this. A broad agenda was established by the mostly liberal powers that won World War II. It included concern for national and international development, for national and international human rights, and for a world society collectively concerned with a worldwide view of nature. Thus the Food and Agricultural Organization and the World Health Organization provided a legitimate structure within which to consider worldwide environmental issues (see Caldwell 1990; and McCormick 1989). So too did the UN Educational, Scientific, and Cultural Organization, where scientized concerns about the world as an overall natural environment became organizationally central (Finnemore 1993, 1996b).

In this period, mobilizing worldwide concerns around the environment made practical organizational sense. Individuals could reasonably assemble to create legitimated interests and associations. Nation-states could forward their concerns and propose rules and treaties to each other with perfect propriety, and scientific bodies could find arenas and agendas in terms of which to formulate their general concerns and models. Thus, our second guiding hypothesis is

> The rise of a world organizational regime with an agenda broad enough to include environmental issues facilitated the expansion of organization around these issues.

[9] Over seventeen hundred intergovernmental organizations existed by 1994; see Union of International Associations 1994.

[10] For a discussion of the League's environmental activities, see Hayden (1942: 148) who notes that "the whale question alone was treated by the League" since there was never "any unit of the League's structure specifically charged with handling items of this nature."

A note on the changing form of world environmental organization

A further hypothesis in our analysis qualifies the two main hypotheses. We envision an evolutionary sequence in the forms of world environmental organization. We see the expansion of the forms of organization we study as driven by expanded scientific rationalization and by generally expanded and open international association, as we argued earlier. We also argue – though we are unable to examine this argument very rigorously due to methodological limitations – that expanded informal international environmental association leads to more formal intergovernmental transactions (such as treaties), which in turn lead to the expansion of more permanent intergovernmental organization.

First, since the world polity had a stateless and Tocquevillian character, especially in the environment domain, worldwide social mobilization around world environmental issues almost inevitably began with decentralized and nongovernmental associational activity, as is characteristic of such systems. Only as a result of later extensive associational activity was there much development and expansion of more official state and state-like activity in the international arena. Thus nongovernmental discourse and associational activity preceded and helped to produce the formation of more formal and official organizational structure. The extraordinary success of the environmental movement in gaining the attention of world society has ultimately produced central official world organizations concerned with the environment, most prominently, UNEP.

Because the variables in our analysis are too highly correlated, we are unable to directly examine quantitative evidence supporting the hypothesized evolutionary sequence of the rise of environmental organizational structures, over and above our two main hypotheses. We support the idea of an evolutionary sequence with descriptive information showing that the sequence, in time, follows the pattern we propose.

One indirect implication of the argument, however, can be examined empirically. The institutionalization of environmental concern in a central world organization (UNEP, in 1972) seems to have modestly affected the character of the whole world environmental enterprise. Extant nongovernmental organizations gained structural strength, resources, and centrality, but the rate of formation of new international associations in the domain (holding constant the effects of our two main explanatory variables) may have slowed. The growth rate in new intergovernmental treaties also slowed as treaties became less common instruments of world activity, in deference to the administrative and regulatory expansion of the official organizations involved. We will examine evidence on the more derivative proposition that

> The formation of official world environmental organizations structures and organizes the whole environmental system, slowing rates at which new nongovernmental and multilateral activity increase.

We argue that this effect is produced by expanded and centralized intergovernmental organization. One could argue that the effect is simply produced by the overall exhaustion of topics in the environmental domain. This argument, however, is unrealistic. While seeming to slow rates of new activity, the formation of official world environmental organizations clearly expands the meaning and enhances the legitimacy of existing associations and treaties. Once UNEP was formed, for example, many existing world environmental associations expanded rapidly in terms of membership, budget, and staff size (Frank et al. 1998). Likewise, some treaties experienced resurgent attention; for example, in the years surrounding the 1972 Stockholm conference at which UNEP received its charter, seven countries (including Belgium, France, and Spain) acceded to the 1958 Convention on Fishing and Conservation of the Living Resources of the High Seas. With heightened official attention to the environment, nation-states were eager to prove their credibility. The point is that official world organization has consolidated the environmental realm, slowing the proliferation of new associations and multilateral activity and simultaneously authorizing and strengthening that which already exists.

In what follows, we bring evidence to bear on these ideas, first with descriptive data and then with event history analyses of the hazard rate, over time, of several types of events. In particular, we discuss the dramatic expansion in international nongovernmental association, the rise in international treaties, and the expansion of official governmental organizations concerned with the environment. We show, with event history analyses, the effect on each of these variables of our hypothesized explanatory variables: the expansion of scientific discourse and organization and the rise of a general and open international associational system.

FROM INFORMAL TO MORE OFFICIAL STRUCTURES

The rise of discourse and association

Figure 10.1 graphs the cumulative number of international nongovernmental associations concerned with the environment from the late nineteenth century, along with several other measures of world environmental activity discussed later. Figure 10.2 gives the same information using a smoothed plot of the hazard rate at which international nongovernmental associations concerned with the environment have been founded.[11] (Few of these organizations have disappeared.[12]) Here, we define an international association as an organized body that has not been established by intergovernmental agreement, has members from at least three countries, and has environmental matters

---

[11] A hazard rate is defined as the limit of the probability of the occurrence of an event per unit of time; see Tuma and Hannan 1984. Here, the event being considered is the founding of another international non-governmental association. Later, we consider other events. We use the approach to smooth hazard rates developed by Wu 1989; the basic notion is analogous to forming a running or moving average.

[12] The data are from *Yearbook of International Organizations 1995* and include all organizations from sections A–D, including inactive organizations but excluding internationally oriented organizations grounded in a particular country; see Union of International Associations 1995. Naturally, some associations are not recorded in the data, though the compilers have, over many decades, made efforts at completeness. For other uses of similar data from the same sources, see Boli and Thomas 1997. Editions of the yearbook begin in 1906 but contain information on the founding dates of associations formed long before then.

prominent on its agenda (Union of International Associations 1995). An association was categorized as concerned with the environment if its stated aims mentioned environmentally related goals or concerns. We intentionally employed a broad conception of the environment, including mention of natural resources, energy, and mining, but we excluded associations concerned principally with agriculture or with science. Examples of organizations (with founding dates) included are the Fauna and Flora Preservation Society (1903), the International Fur Trade Federation (1949), and the International Organization for Human Ecology (1980).

Three key points are revealed by the graphs in Figures 10.1 and 10.2. First, the number of nongovernmental environmental associations has increased extraordinarily, especially since World War II, after which, we argue, the official international agenda made it easier and more legitimate to raise environmental matters in world discourse. Similar increases in rates of association formation occur in many other sectors of "modern" activity, including health, science, and business and trade (Boli and Thomas, in press).[13]

Second, the expansion of international associational activity in the environmental domain occurs a little earlier than the rise of treaties and considerably earlier than the rise of the intergovernmental organizations and ministries plotted in Figures 10.1 and 10.2. We argue that this temporal order reflects a substantively meaningful sequence in which the development of world social discourse and activity (of which international associations are one element) creates the grounding for more official multilateral and international structuration.

The rise in the rate of formation of international environmental associations seems to continue, but the growth occurs at a slower pace in the most recent decades. We argue that this reflects changes resulting from the relatively recent rise of official governmental and intergovernmental activity in the environmental domain; we test this idea controlling for other causal factors that drive expansion. We suspect that more centralized and official institutionalization tend to produce growth in existing international associations rather than proliferation of new ones (Frank et al. 1998). As an example, the recent attention to acid rain has been accompanied by few new international associations devoted to its cause; however, many older organizations, including Greenpeace, Friends of the Earth, and the International Union for the Conservation of Nature, have added acid rain to their agendas (Levy 1993).

In the post-UNEP period, the central environmental associations expanded not only their agendas but also their memberships and resources (Frank et al. 1998). International Greenpeace, for example, was founded in 1971, one year before UNEP. Since then, Greenpeace has gained more than six million members worldwide and has an estimated income of more than $100 million, making it one of the largest international environmental associations in the world (Wapner 1996).

We argued earlier and show later that the scientific legitimization of environmental discourse in world society increases the hazard rate of formation of new

---

[13] For the environment as well as other sectors, periods of war temporarily slow rates of formation of associations. Taking this minor factor into account does not modify the discussion or results reported later.

associations. A qualitative inspection of the types of such organizations founded over time supports the point. Through the first third of the century, such organizations tended to be formed around sentimentalized concerns with specific aspects of nature, as exemplified by the International Friends of Nature (1895) and the International Bureau of Antivivisection Societies (1925). Other organizations were formed around a conception of nature as a set of resources to be organized and allocated – for example, the International Union of Forestry Research Organizations (1891) and the Commonwealth Forestry Association (1921). In recent decades, environmental associations have tended to form based on much more general and more scientized conceptions of nature as an ecosystem – for example, the Asian Environmental Society (1972) and the International Society for Ecological Modelling (1978).[14]

In the background (we argue as an important causal force) is the enormous rise in world structuration and discourse in the scientific domain. Structuration refers to the creation and elaboration, within and among social actors, of organizational structures with increased capabilities, rights, duties, and obligations (Giddens 1979). Actors become more elaborately organized in a domain and enter into more differentiated and more elaborate formal and informal relations with one another. The creation and expansion of the world science system established a frame in which all sorts of environmental issues could be seen as universally significant and in which many kinds of policy activities could be seen as rational. To describe the expansion of "scientization" in world society we show, in Figure 10.3, cumulative data on indicators

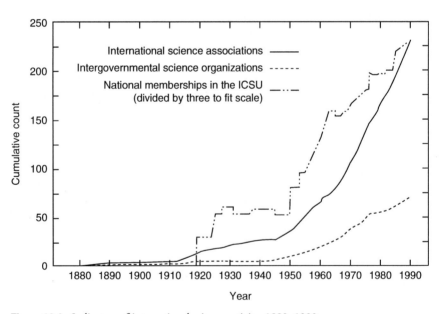

Figure 10.3. Indicators of international science activity, 1880–1990

[14] For a more complete analysis of the distinctions here, see Frank 1994, 1995.

of the emerging scientific organizational system of world society. Each indicator shows dramatic changes, especially after World War II. Clearly, the expansion of this system produced many organizations and professions that could speak authoritatively and with putative objectivity on a wide range of environmental issues.

Treaties

Official involvement in world environmental issues by nation-states, the central (and powerful) actors legitimated in world society, arose slowly. Nation-states often took some jurisdiction over internal environmental matters (for example, by forming national parks or managing natural resources). For the most part, however, the environment did not become a major focus of intergovernmental relations until scientific associations and developments created an appropriate arena in world political culture. World political culture is the broad set of institutionalized conceptions and assumptions, often taken for granted, that define, permeate, and support the modern nation-state system (see Thomas et al. 1987; and Meyer 1994; see also Jepperson et al. 1996). Thus, a long-term rise occurred in the number of intergovernmental treaties concerned with the environment, as shown in Figures 10.1 and 10.2, but this rise is somewhat slower and later than the growth of international association in this arena.[15] Early treaties tended to be specific, signed by limited numbers of developed countries, and concerned with the management of specific international dependencies, as was the case with the 1911 Fur Seal Convention. A few treaties, very much restricted to core Western countries given to a distinctive sentimentalization of nature, took a more romantic view, as exhibited by the 1933 Convention Relative to the Preservation of Fauna and Flora in their Natural State. None of the early treaties took a broadly ecosystemic view; this view arose later with the scientific rationalization of the field.

More recent treaties, following scientific rationalization and the rise of worldwide environmental association, have a very different character.[16] They emphasize regional and global interdependencies, and they are rooted in a broad and universalistic scientific conception of nature as an ecosystem with which human society must come into balance. Recent treaties include the 1979 Convention on Long-Range Transboundary Air Pollution and the 1985 Convention for the Protection of the Ozone Layer.

The total number of international environmental treaties has continued to rise in recent decades, but growth in the rate of treaty formation has slowed, reflecting the emergence of more official intergovernmental organization. New issues are increasingly likely to be handled by the expansion of extant official organizations rather than by the signing of new, specialized treaties. This process is clear, for example, in various recent proposals to extend the domain of the International Whaling Commission to include porpoises, dolphins, and other cetaceans, rather than to negotiate new, special-purpose agreements.

[15] We define an environmental treaty as one that is primarily focused on some aspect of the relationship between human society and nature and that involves three or more nation-state parties. For a description of the coding rules and a list of the treaties involved, see Frank (1994).

[16] For a detailed analysis of the content of environmental treaties, see Frank (1997) from which the present analysis is derived.

Intergovernmental organizations

The twentieth century buildup of world-level discourse and association concerned with the environment, and the creation of a world organizational frame broad enough to include an environmental agenda, culminated in an extraordinary profusion of official intergovernmental organizations in this domain, as Figures 10.1 and 10.2 show.[17] Early organizations of this sort tended to be specialized in focus and membership (for example, the International North Pacific Fisheries Commission, founded in 1952). Later, organizations were broader on both dimensions. Especially prominent in this sense was the creation of a genuine umbrella organization in the domain, UNEP, in 1972. Its central office is in Nairobi, and more than ten thousand nongovernmental associations have found it useful to maintain a liaison there, through the Environmental Liaison Center (Trzyna and Childers 1992). UNEP now has several subcomponents that deal with specialized environmental matters, such as the ozone layer and regional seas.[18]

The creation of a more centralized official world environmental structure slows the rate of formation of new official intergovernmental organization. This process is analogous to the notion of "competition" found in population ecology approaches.[19] The more elaborated and dominating the extant official structure, the more likely that new functions and activities will be absorbed by it in preference to the creation of new organizations.[20] World concerns about ozone, for example, led not to the creation of a new official organization but to the elaboration of the structure of UNEP (see Benedick 1991; and Parson 1993). As another example, the 1972 Convention for the Protection of the World Cultural and Natural Heritage directly produced the World Heritage Foundation. The 1973 Convention for the Prevention of Pollution from Ships led to the addition of executive functions to the International Maritime Organization (Mitchell 1993).

Of course, overall international activity has increased in the most recent period, though not through new organizations; for example, both the European Union and the Council of Europe have pressed for vigorous environmental activities among their nation-state members. They have done so, however, through the elaboration of existing organizational structures rather than through the creation of new independent ones.

A note on nation-level structuring

It is sociologically easiest to think of the creation of rationalized and organized world society as a bottom-up process in which activities are rationalized in local and then

---

[17] Data are from *Yearbook of International Organizations 1995* (intergovernmental organizations, sec. A-F; inactive organizations, sec. H). We define an intergovernmental environmental organization as one established by official agreement (often in the form of a treaty) between three or more countries, which has some aspect of the natural environment as its primary concern.

[18] For descriptions, see Caldwell 1990; and Trzyna and Childers 1992.

[19] For example, Hannan and Freeman 1989.

[20] For national-level discussions of parallel processes, see Hamilton and Biggart 1988; Fligstein 1990; and Dobbin 1994.

national settings and only gradually evolve to the world level through international interdependencies and perhaps cultural processes. This picture probably describes many aspects of world society (for example, features of economic regulation).

The bottom-up view, however, describes the environmental domain poorly. Widespread and mobilized world concern about the environment is heavily dependent on universalistic and scientific ideologies and principles. These have tended to arise and achieve codification in world discourse before, not after, they became local and national issues in most nation-states. In fact, the rise of the world environmental domain clearly precedes and causes the formation of generalized national structures that formalize and manage the issues involved.

To illustrate this point, consider again the cumulative number of and the hazard rate of formation of national ministries concerned with the environment (shown in Figures 10.1 and 10.2, respectively).[21] Strikingly, national ministries arose only in the period since the creation of the world-level UNEP in 1972.

One might view this matter cynically, with the idea that formalized national ministries arise only when enough international conferences and organizations exist for ministers to attend, and that such ministries are only ritual showpieces.[22] It is probably more reasonable to see the distinctive situation here as reflecting the highly abstract, rationalized, and scientized nature of the modern conception of the natural environment – a conception that arises in a transnational cultural system and achieves an organizational base there before entering most national states.[23]

STATISTICAL ANALYSES OF INTERNATIONAL STRUCTURATION

We turn now to a statistical analysis of the rise of the various measures of international environmental structuration discussed earlier. The aim is to show that measures of our two main explanatory variables – the rise of international scientific discourse and organization and the expansion of the international associational arena – affect the rise of nongovernmental and governmental organization and international treaties concerned with the environment. Because the variables under analysis are so highly correlated, we are unable to show that the different forms of environmental organization affect each other in a causal sequence, but we can

[21] Data are from *Europa World Yearbook 1970–96*. All ministries with the words "environment," "conservation," and "ecology" in their titles are included. The first national environmental ministry appeared in 1971. There were 52 ministries by 1989 (the final year of our analysis) and 57 more by 1996. National environmental agencies, which are often but not always directly connected with national environmental ministries, proliferated during the same period, rising from 25 in 1972 to 140 in the current period; see Wapner (1996).

[22] For example, one recent study found 180 international environmental bodies with some claim on the active involvement of the Swedish government; see Levy et al. (1993).

[23] Treaty ratification demonstrates the same pattern: the nation-states that ratify the most treaties are consistently the ones that participate most actively in the world environmental, scientific, and political sectors, even when environmental degradation and economic infrastructure are controlled; see Frank (1997).

examine one implication of this idea: the rise of official intergovernmental organization in the domain, other things being equal, slows down the hazard rates of expansion of numbers of treaties and nongovernmental and intergovernmental organizations (that is, these rates continue to grow over time, but more slowly).

We analyze the dependent variables using event history (or hazard rate) analysis, a method for analyzing the processes generating change over time in categorical dependent variables, usually as a function of the current or earlier values of certain hypothesized explanatory variables (Tuma and Hannan 1984).[24] We examine the effect of several indices reflecting the underlying forces discussed earlier on the hazard rates of formation or founding of international environmental nongovernmental associations, environmental treaties, and intergovernmental organizations.[25] The following analyses are exploratory in character and cannot produce definitive confirmation of our hypotheses. First, the variables we discuss are, for the most part, interrelated with one another, and they all covary markedly with time as we have shown. Hence, it is difficult to show convincingly and consistently the independent effects of scientific expansion and of the rise of an open system of international association. It also means that we cannot examine whether nongovernmental association, treaties, and intergovernmental organization form a causal sequence, though we can study whether expanded intergovernmental organization slows growth rates in the other two variables (with the other variables controlled). Second, it is difficult to find independent indicators that can be measured over a long time period and that clearly capture the separate effects we propose. It is also hard to show that the indicators of the different explanatory variables form distinct clusters. We must rely on the face validity of the indicators we use, rather than on strong statistical support for their clustering. Third, because of a lack of data covering a long time period and for statistical reasons, we are limited in the range of control variables we can employ to control the hypothesized effects of other factors. Our basic aim is to show three main effects on world environmental organization corresponding to our three guiding hypotheses: a positive effect of the increased rationalization of scientific discourse and organization, a positive effect of the increased formal structuration of a world agenda hospitable to environmental issues, and a negative effect of the more recent consolidation of this agenda (for example, through the formation of UNEP). A further goal is to show that measures of environmental degradation do not eliminate these effects; we show that measures of environmental degradation do not add much by way of explanatory power. Our analyses are highly suggestive of the processes involved but by no means conclusive from the viewpoint of formal statistical tests.

---

[24] Whereas time-series analysis is the standard method of analyzing change over time in an outcome measured with a continuous or metric scale (for example, variables measured in dollars), event history analysis is a method for analyzing change over time in an outcome measured as a categorical variable. Here, we analyze longitudinal data on several categorical outcomes: founding of a new international environmental association, formation of a new environmental treaty, and creation of a new intergovernmental organization.

[25] The data set is available from the authors.

Discourse

To capture the scientific rationalization of world discourse about nature, we use three world-level indicators that vary over time: the cumulative number of scientific unions in the International Council of Scientific Unions (ICSU), the logarithm of the cumulative number of science-oriented international nongovernmental associations, and the cumulative number of nation-states (of those in existence throughout the time period) with at least one national park.[26] We suppose that this last indicator captures not only the scientific rationalization of nature but also something of the earlier sentimentalization of it.[27] We are trying, with these indicators, to capture the causal impact of general scientific rationalization of nature on environmental structuration. Note that no directly environmental organizations are in the ICSU, and no environmental organizations are included in our count of science-oriented nongovernmental associations.

Structuration

To measure the structuration of the world polity in terms hospitable to an environmental agenda, we employ four indicators: the cumulative number of independent nation-states in existence; the cumulative number of intergovernmental organizations (not counting those in the environment sector itself); the cumulative number of multilateral treaties (other than environmental treaties); and a trichotomy scored zero for the period before the League of Nations, 1 for the League period, and 2 for the period since the UN has been in existence.[28]

---

[26] The cumulative worldwide total of domestic environmental non-governmental associations would also be a plausible, though indirect, measure of the scientific rationalization of nature in world discourse; see Princen and Finger (1994); and Wapner (1996). It is difficult, however, to get reliable data on these associations over time. Domestic environmental non-governmental associations certainly facilitate the rise of the world environmental structure, as the National Resources Defense Council did in advocating international ozone regulations; see Benedick (1991). In general, however, the effects of these associations are similar to those of other indicators of the scientific rationalization of nature in world discourse. Thus, the World Meteorological Organization (an international science association) served as an important advocate of international ozone regulation, as did the National Resources Defense Council. The sources of the data are as follows: ICSU (International Research Council 1922–1952; International Council of Scientific Unions 1954–90); international science associations (Union of International Associations 1994); national parks (International Union for the Conservation of Nature 1990).

[27] For analyses supporting this view, see Schofer (1996).

[28] The sources of the data are as follows: for nation-states, see Europa Yearbook (1990); for intergovernmental organizations, see Union of International Associations (1994); for multilateral treaties, see Mostecky (1965); and Bowman and Harris (1984, 1993). In the case of multilateral treaties, no single source covers the whole period. Therefore, we used two sources that employ different criteria for counting treaties; see Lechner (1991). To render the two compatible, we calculated the average multiplier for a ten-year period of overlap that made counts based on the less comprehensive source equal counts based on the more comprehensive source. We used this multiplier to adjust the counts for the remaining years covered by the less comprehensive source.

Consolidation

To measure the central consolidation of the official intergovernmental environment domain, which we argue has negative effects (with the other forces controlled) on the creation of separate new structures, we employ three indicators: the cumulative number of intergovernmental environmental organizations, the cumulative number of nation-states with an environmental ministry (from a fixed set composed of the nation-states that were independent in 1971, the date of the first environmental ministry), and the staff size of UNEP (which is zero before the founding of the organization).[29]

Size and degradation

As a control variable, we employ the logarithm of the total world population (in billions). The purpose is to capture the effect of the overall size of world society, along with the commonly argued effects of environmental degradation produced by population growth. In preliminary analyses not reported here, we also included direct measures of this degradation.[30]

Indicators of each of the three main independent variables (discourse, structuration, and consolidation) were separately factor analyzed using SPSS, and factor scores were computed based on these analyses.[31] Event history analyses were conducted using the RATE program (Tuma 1992). The model employed assumes that the hazard rate of an event (for example, founding of an environmental organization) depends not on any inherent characteristics of time but rather on the time-varying explanatory variables included in the analysis.

Results

Table 10.1 reports the results of the main analyses. In each analysis, our measure of the hospitable structuration of the world polity shows a positive effect, as

[29] The sources of the data are as follows: for intergovernmental environmental organizations, see Union of International Associations 1995; for environmental ministries, see Statesman's Year-Book (1960–89); for UNEP staff, see United Nations Environment Programme (1992).

[30] In other analyses, we have also considered direct measures of environmental degradation; see Frank (1997). Factor indicators used were the logarithm of anthropogenic carbon dioxide emissions; see Keeling et al. (1989); and United Nations Environment Programme (1991); and the logarithm of CFC emissions; see Council on Environmental Quality (1991). The resulting factor shows almost no effect when included in analyses such as those discussed later. Of course, emissions are not the same as perceived effects – the latter are much closer to the discursive and associational variables that we emphasize.

[31] SPSS (1988). In each of the three cases, indicators were loaded on a single common factor and had very high weights. Given high multicollinearity among all ten indicators used to construct the three measures, it was not possible to differentiate clearly among the three concepts by factor analysis of all ten indicators simultaneously. Our grouping of indicators into three different constructs and factors rests on substantive and theoretical grounds rather than on statistical evidence. The factors for the international environmental associations and treaty analyses were constructed with data beginning in 1870, corresponding to the starting time for their analyses. Likewise, the factors for the intergovernmental organizations analysis were constructed from 1919.

hypothesized. An expanded world structure open to environmental issues produces more intergovernmental and international nongovernmental organizations and more multilateral environmental treaties.

In each analysis, our measure of the central consolidation of an official international governmental sector around the environment also has the expected negative effects. With other factors controlled, consolidation operates to slow the growth rate in the creation of new governmental and nongovernmental organizations and of new intergovernmental treaties. We do not argue that this indicates a weakening of the structures involved. Although centralization may lower the creation of new nongovernmental environmental associations, it clearly increases the size and strength of the older ones.

Our measure of the scientific rationalization of nature in world social discourse shows the hypothesized positive (and significant) effects on the creation of international nongovernmental associations and of international environmental treaties. In the analysis of the formation of intergovernmental organizations, the effect is positive but is significant only at the .17 level in a one-tailed test. Our measure of discursive rationalization seems to be rather distant from the process by which intergovernmental organizations are created.[32]

Overall, the analyses in Table 10.1 support our guiding hypotheses. In the face of high multicollinearity among our explanatory variables, however, we took one further step to check the robustness of these findings. We disaggregated the factors back into single indicators. For each of the three dependent variables, we then estimated the resulting thirty-six event-history models (three indicators of rationalization × four indicators of structuration × three indicators of consolidation, each including the logarithm of world population); we hoped that the directions and significance levels of effects would be consistent with the results reported in Table 10.1.

For international environmental associations, the effect of the indicator for the rationalization of nature in world discourse was positive in twenty-nine of thirty-six equations and significant in eighteen of these (.05 level, one-tailed test). The effect of the indicator for the structuration of the world polity was positive in thirty-two of thirty-six equations and significant in fifteen of these. The indicator for the consolidation of an official intergovernmental environmental domain had a negative effect in twenty-seven of thirty-six equations and was significant in twenty-four of these.

For international environmental treaties, the effect of the indicator for the rationalization of nature in world discourse was positive in all thirty-six equations and significant in sixteen of these (.05 level, one-tailed test). The effect of the indicator for the structuration of the world polity was positive in thirty-two of thirty-six equations and significant in six of these. The effect of the indicator for the consolidation of an

---

[32] In our preliminary exploratory analyses, the rationalization of nature in world discourse factor consistently showed positive effects on the rate of formation of intergovernmental environmental organizations. These effects varied in statistical significance, depending on the exact time periods used for the construction of the factor and on the time periods used for the analysis (here, the analysis begins in 1919, with the formation of the League of Nations). In a few cases, however, the effects were highly significant.

Table 10.1. Maximum likelihood estimates of the hazard rate at which international environmental associations, treaties, and intergovernmental organizations are formed in the world[a]

Indicators	Independent variables	Associations, 1870–1989	Treaties, 1870–1989	Intergovernmental organizations, 1919–90
Cumulative number of unions in the ICSU	Rationalization of	1.44*	2.13**	0.72
	nature in world discourse	(.82)[b]	(.88)	(.77)
Cumulative number of science international nongovernmental associations, logged	Structuration of world	2.61**	1.96*	2.99**
Cumulative number of nation-states with national parks (constant cases)	polity	(.86)	(.85)	(.76)
Cumulative number of international treaties (nonenvironmental)				
World organization (0 = pre-League; 1 = League; 2 = UN)				
Cumulative number of intergovernmental organizations (nonenvironmental)	Consolidation of official	-0.59**	-0.41*	-0.61*
Cumulative number of independent nation-states	intergovernmental	(.19)	(.19)	(.30)
Cumulative number of intergovernmental environmental organizations				
Cumulative number of nation-states with environmental ministries (constant cases)	environmental domain			
Staff of UNEP				
World population in billions, logged	Population	-5.90*	-5.96*	-6.90*
		(3.28)	(3.36)	(4.09)
Constant		4.25	4.19	9.78*
		(2.63)	(2.69)	(5.14)
Chi-squared improvement over baseline		196.31**	201.97**	158.44**

Note. $N = 153$ associations, 156 treaties, 157 intergovernmental organizations.

[a] Each column reports analysis of a separate dependent variable. As a guide to interpretation, we report statistical significance levels, even though we are studying the whole population of cases.

[b] Standard errors are shown in parentheses.

**$p < .01$ (one-tailed test).

*$p < .05$.

official intergovernmental environmental domain was negative in thirty of thirty-six equations and significant in eighteen of these.

For intergovernmental organizations, the indicator for the rationalization of nature in world discourse showed a positive effect in twenty-one of the thirty-six equations but was significant in only three cases (.05 level, one-tailed test). As in the main analyses reported in Table 10.1, our measure of discourse seems to be too remote from the processes producing official international organization. The indicator for the structuration of the world polity had a positive effect in only eighteen of the thirty-six cases and was significant in only seven. Of the four indicators on which the factor is based, two (the number of independent states in existence and the cumulative number of intergovernmental organizations) tended to show negative effects, though the overall effect of the factor was positive and significant. These two indicators appear to capture some of the negative effect accompanying the consolidation of the official environment. The indicator of the consolidation of the official intergovernmental environmental domain had the expected negative effect in twenty-nine of the thirty-six analyses and was significant in eighteen of these.

In these disaggregated analyses, the effects are fairly stable and usually have the expected signs; the significance levels are encouraging. Overall, the results are consistent with the findings in Table 10.1. The results are less convincing in the analyses of intergovernmental organizations than in the other two cases; however, we take the results of these disaggregated analyses as offering some support for our three guiding hypotheses.

Limitations

We have noted some limitations that make our statistical analyses exploratory in character, rather than more definitive. First, the explanatory variables describing scientific rationalization and the world associational system vary together over time. This turns out not to be a major problem, as we have been able to show stable differential effects of these variables. Second, although the indicators of each explanatory variable statistically covary, they cannot be clearly differentiated in a statistical sense into separate clusters, and much of the justification for treating them separately is conceptual. The findings that they have distinct effects, two of which are positive and one of which is negative, lend support to the differentiation of the concepts involved. Third, we are limited in the control variables that we can use to examine other possible effects, but we note that our control variables have weak effects and do not alter our main conclusions.

DISCUSSION

We have traced the rise of a large-scale sector of world society concerned with the environment. The rise of scientific discourse and association has been central. It universalized and legitimated earlier and narrower conceptions of the environment as the locus of either sentiment or particular resources (Frank 1997). The creation of an open, world organizational frame in the UN system greatly facilitated mobilization. In contrast, highly organized and interested action by nation-states – the bread and butter of international organization in much theory and practice – seems to be a later and less important feature of the system. Most nation-states had no central organized structures (such as ministries) dealing with the environment until late in the process. This reflects, in a sense, a top-down history, in which the rise of universalistic discourse and organization rather belatedly construct nation-states' aims and responsibilities more than the bottom-up political processes of power and interest that are mentioned more often.

There is no reason to generalize this situation across sectors or domains of actual or potential world sociocultural organization. Speculatively, we suggest two properties of a sector that affect trajectories of its organization in world society. First, to what extent do strong universalistic and rationalized cultural frames make a particular sector of common and general interest beyond local or national levels? Second, to what extent do the constituted nation-state models give the state monopoly or dominant responsibilities, interests, and international aims in that arena? Thus sectors that fit with the liberal, individualistic organization of world society will develop more quickly at the world level.

In the absence of either factor, we might anticipate little world-level mobilization or structuration in the domain. The lack of much world-level mobilization around ethnic and religious claims, especially given the intensity of local mobilization on these issues, illustrates a domain where our perspective predicts little world-level activity (see Boli and Thomas 1998). Religious and ethnic claims tend to apply to only a fraction of the world polity rather than the entirety, and they emphasize alternatives to the state system rather than rationalized action in it. These matters tend to be low on the agendas of legitimated states, and it is difficult to universalize these ideas in modern world culture.

When the opposite holds, as in the contemporary world economic or "development" sectors, we expect rapid sector development with a complex mix of intergovernmental and nongovernmental world activity (Chabbott 1998). States clearly see national and world development as central to their mission. Beyond this, however, a wider and now scientized culture of human progress and development fuels an enormous amount of nongovernmental activity at the world level.

When states take monopoly and sovereign responsibility for a domain, and when weakly rationalized or universalized common interests are available, a sector dominated by intergovernmental relations and organizations may result. This seems roughly to describe the international security sector. In view of practical human concerns, it is striking that during most of this century, the international nongovernmental arena concerned with peace, arms control, and international security has been weakly developed. It was probably relatively more central in international life at the turn of this century than now. Unfortunately, this sector seems to dominate academic discussion of organized world society, leading to misleading generalizations that overemphasize the role of national interests, state action, and intergovernmental organization (Jepperson et al. 1996).

Finally, in sectors such as the environment, human rights, the status of women, education, or the status of children, world concerns, rationalized and universalized in terms of general legal and scientific principles may transcend the limited international interests of states in these areas and foster worldwide movements, associations, and mobilizations.[33]

Whatever the trajectories involved, sectors change their status over time. Deborah Barrett and David John Frank show that a rationalized world movement concerned with population control operated throughout this century, against the considerable resistance of both states and intergovernmental bodies (Barrett and Frank 1998). In the 1950s, as states took on increasing functions for managing economic development, and as economic development came to be scientifically analyzed as requiring population control, an official governmental and interstate sector blossomed.

A note on effectiveness

The preceding discussion bears directly on the question of whether the international environmental sector is "effective" in managing environmental problems. It clearly has *affected* a wide range of policies and practices, from the recent extraordinary rise in numbers of national parks to widespread protection for air, water, and forests and the routine employment of environmental impact assessments.[34] How well it actually *solves* environmental problems is unclear (see Haas et al. 1993).

The environmental sector is clearly ineffective in comparison to the rapidly expanding claims on it. This follows from the nature and trajectory of the sector as we have described it. A sector arising out of highly legitimated but essentially unlimited discourse and association, rather than fixed and limited state interests or a fixed and limited world order, is a factory that creates and defines problems at a rate faster than that at which feasible solutions can be organized. The Tocquevillian features of modern world society can be expected to produce continued collective problem definition and mobilization around the environment, producing (as in the U.S. case) much more collective action than narrow theories can explain.

As we have shown, however, the rise of an official intergovernmental system, together with highly codified national interests and structures, may have slowed the rate of nongovernmental mobilization in the area. Although the system may not solve problems, it may tame them, and it may even slow the rate of formation of new problems.

CONCLUSION

We have examined the rise of a world environmental regime in a discursively volatile but organizationally stateless world society. In such a system, it makes sense that this

---

[33] For human rights, see Smith, Pagnucco, and Romeril (1994); Smith (1995); and Boli and Thomas (1998). For the status of women, see Berkovitch (1994). For education, see Hüfner et al. (1987).
[34] On national parks, see IUCN (1990).

regime arises in discourse and association, and that its growth depends heavily on the rise of a worldwide scientific culture. The regime turns out to have also depended heavily on the creation of a world organizational structure (principally, the UN system) with a frame and agenda broad enough to include environmental matters.

An associational system began to develop late in the nineteenth century. Facilitated by the broader world structure, the structure and discourse involved in this associational system clearly led to an expanded wave of intergovernmental treaties and then to an official world intergovernmental environmental system. Only at that point did nation-states begin to formalize environmental issues as central to their internal agenda-setting structures.

Given the dependence of the modern world on rationalized scientific culture, it has been difficult for states and their intergovernmental bodies to obtain the kind of monopoly authority over environment issues that would be required to slow down the development of the broader movements involved. Some "progress" has been made in creating formal structures that at least co-opt expansive forces of discourse and association, but it is plausible to expect continuing rapid creation and discovery of environmental issues, continuing conceptions of failure to deal with them effectively, and continuing world-level social mobilization around them.

REFERENCES

Adler, E. and Peter Haas. 1992. Conclusion: Epistemic Communities, World Order, and the Creation of a Reflective Research Program. *International Organization* 46:367–90.

Barrett, Deborah and David John Frank. 1998. Population-Control for National Development: From World Discourse to National Policies, in J. Boli and G. M. Thomas (eds.), *World Polity Formation Since 1875*. Stanford, CA: Stanford University Press.

Benedick, Richard E. 1991. *Ozone Diplomacy.* Cambridge, MA: Harvard University Press.

Bergesen, Albert. 1995. Eco-Alienation. *Humboldt Journal of Social Relations* 21:111–26.

Berkovitch, Nitza. 1994. From Motherhood to Citizenship: The World-wide Incorporation of Women into the Public Sphere in the Twentieth Century. PhD dissertation. Department of Sociology, Stanford University.

Boli, John and George M. Thomas. 1997. World Culture in the World Polity. *American Sociological Review* 62:171–90.

—— —— (eds.) 1998. *World Polity Formation Since 1875*. Stanford, CA: Stanford University Press.

Bowman, M. and David John Harris. 1984. *Multilateral Treaties: Index and Current Status.* London: Butterworths.

—— —— 1993. *Multilateral Treaties: Index and Current Status: Cumulative Supplement.* London: University of Nottingham Treaty Centre.

Caldwell, Lynton Keith. 1990. *International Environmental Policy,* 2nd edn. Durham, NC: Duke University Press.

Chabbott, Colette. 1998. Defining Development: The Making of the International Development Field, 1945–1990, in John Boli and George M. Thomas (eds.), *World Polity Formation Since 1875*. Stanford, CA: Stanford University Press.

Coleman, James S. 1986. *Individual Interests and Collective Action.* New York: Cambridge University Press.

Council on Environmental Quality. 1991. *Environmental Quality: 22nd Annual Report.* Washington, DC: U.S. Government Printing Office.

DiMaggio, Paul and Walter Powell. 1983. The Iron Cage Revisited. *American Sociological Review* 48:147–60.

Dobbin, Frank. 1994. *Forging Industrial Policy: The United States, Britain, and France in the Railway Age.* New York: Cambridge University Press.

Drori, Gili. 1997. The National Science Agenda as a Ritual of Modem Nation-Statehood. PhD dissertation. Department of Sociology, Stanford University.

Dunlap, Riley. 1994. International Attitudes Towards Environment and Development, in H. O. Bergesen and G. Parmann (eds.), *Green Globe Yearbook 1994.* Oxford: Oxford University Press, pp. 115–26.

Europa Yearbook. 1970–96. *The Europa World Yearbook.* London: Europa Publications.

Falk, Richard. 1992. *Explorations at the Edge of Tone: Prospects for World Order.* Philadelphia, PA: Temple University Press.

Finnemore, Martha. 1993. International Organizations as Teachers of Norms. *International Organization* 47:565–97.

—— 1996a. Sociology's Institutionalism. *International Organization* 50 (2):325–47.

—— 1996b. *Defining National Interests in International Society.* Ithaca, NY: Cornell University Press.

Fligstein, Neil. 1990. *The Transformation of Corporate Control.* Cambridge, MA: Harvard University Press.

Frank, David John. 1994. Global Environmentalism: International Treaties in World Society. PhD dissertation. Department of Sociology, Stanford University.

—— 1997. Science, Nature, and the Globalization of the Environment, 1870–1990. *Social Forces* 76 (2):409–37.

—— Ann Hironaka, John W. Meyer, Evan Schofer and Nancy Brandon Tuma. 1998. The Rationalization and Organization of Nature in World Culture, in John Boli and George M. Thomas (eds.), *World Polity Formation Since 1975: A Century of Non-Governmental Organization.* Stanford, CA: Stanford University Press.

Garrison, William A. 1995. Hiroshima, the Holocaust, and the Politics of Exclusion. *American Sociological Review* 60:1–20.

Giddens, Anthony. 1979. *Central Problems in Social Theory: Action, Structure, and Contradiction in Social Analysis.* Berkeley: University of California Press.

Gilpin, Robert 1981. *War and Change in World Politics.* Cambridge: Cambridge University Press.

Goffman, Erving. 1974. *Frame Analysis.* Cambridge, MA: Harvard University Press.

Gould, Kenneth, Adam Weinberg, and Allan Schnaiberg. 1995. Natural Resource Use in a Transnational Treadmill. *Humboldt Journal of Social Relations* 21:61–93.

Groombridge, Brian (ed.) 1992. *Global Biodiversity: Status of the Earth's Living Resources.* London: Chapman and Hall.

Haas, Peter M. 1989. Do Regimes Matter? Epistemic Communities and Mediterranean Pollution Control. *International Organization* 43:377–403.

—— 1992. Introduction: Epistemic Communities and International Policy Coordination. *International Organization* 46:1–35.

—— Robert O. Keohane and Marc A. Levy (eds.) 1993. *Institutions for the Earth.* Cambridge, MA: MIT Press.

Haggard, Stephan and B. A. Simmons. 1987. Theories of International Regimes. *International Organization* 41:491–517.

Hamilton, Gary and Nicole Biggart. 1988. Market, Culture, and Authority: A Comparative Analysis of Management and Organization in the Far East. *American Journal of Sociology* 94:S52–S94.

Hannan, Michael T. and John Freeman. 1989. *Organizational Ecology*. Cambridge, MA: Harvard University Press.

Hayden, Sherman Strong. 1942. *The International Protection of Wild Life*. New York: Columbia University Press.

Homer-Dixon, Thomas F. 1994. Environmental Scarcities and Violent Conflict: Evidence from Cases. *International Security* 19:5–40.

Hüfner, Klaus, John W. Meyer and Jens Naumann. 1987. Comparative Education Policy Research: A World Society Perspective, in M. Dierkes, H. Weiler, and A. Antal (eds.), *Comparative Policy Research*. Aldershot, UK: Gower, pp. 188–243.

International Council of Scientific Unions (ICSU). 1954–90. *Year Book*. Paris: ICSU Secretariat.

International Research Council. 1922–52. *Reports of Proceedings of the General Assembly*. London: International Research Council.

International Union for the Conservation of Nature (IUCN). 1990. *1990 United Nations List of National Parks and Protected Anas*. Gland, Switzerland: IUCN.

Jepperson, Ronald, Alexander Wendt and Peter Katzenstein. 1996. Norms, Identity, and Culture in National Security. in Peter Katzenstein (eds.), *The Culture of National Security*. New York: Columbia University Press.

Keeling, C. D., R. B. Bacastow, A. F. Carter, S. C. Piper, T. P. Whorf, M. Heimann, W. G. Mook, and H. Roeloffzen. 1989. A Three-Dimensional Model of Atmospheric CO2 Transport Based on Observed Winds. *Geophysical Monograph* 55:165–236.

Krasner, Stephen. (ed.) 1983. *International Regimes*. Ithaca, NY: Cornell University Press.

Lechner, F. J. 1991. Religion, Law, and Global Order, in R. Robertson and W. R. Garrett (eds.), *Religion and Global Order*. New York: Paragon House.

Levy, Marc A. 1993. European Acid Rain, in P. M. Haas, R. O. Keohane, and M. A. Levy (eds.), *Institutions for the Earth*. Cambridge, MA: MIT Press, pp. 75–132.

—— Robert O. Keohane and Peter M. Haas. 1993. Improving the Effectiveness of International Environmental Institutions, in P. M. Haas, R. O. Keohane, and M. A. Levy (eds.), *Institutions for the Earth*. Cambridge, MA: MIT Press, pp. 397–426.

McCormick, John. 1989. *Reclaiming Paradise*. Bloomington: Indiana University Press.

McCoy, M. and Patrick McCully. 1993. *The Road from Rio: An NGO Action Guide to Environment and Development*. Utrecht: International Books.

McNeely, Connie. 1995. *Constructing the Nation-State: International Organization and Prescriptive Action*. Westport, CT: Greenwood.

Meyer, John W. 1994. Rationalized Environments, in W. R. Scott and J. W. Meyer (eds.), *Institutional Environments and Organizations*. Thousand Oaks, CA: Sage, pp. 28–54.

—— 1997. The Changing Cultural Content of the Nation-State. in G. Steinmetz (ed.), *New Approaches to the State in the Social Sciences*. Ithaca, NY: Cornell University Press.

Mitchell, Ronald. 1993. International Oil Pollution of the Oceans, in P. M. Haas, R. O. Keohane, and M. A. Levy (eds.), *Institutions for the Earth*. Cambridge, MA: MIT Press, pp. 183–247.

Mostecky, Vaclav (ed.) 1965. *Index to Multilateral Treaties*. Cambridge, MA: Harvard Law School Library.

Nadelman, Ethan. 1990. Global Prohibition Regimes: The Evolution of Norms in International Society. *International Organization* 44:479–526.

Nanda, Ved P. 1983. Global Climate Change and International Law and Institutions. in V. P. Nanda (ed.), *World Climate Change: The Role of International Law and Institutions.* Boulder, CO: Westview Press, pp. 227–39.

Olson, Mancur. 1965. *The Logic of Collective Action.* Cambridge, MA: Harvard University Press.

Parson, Edward A. 1993. Protecting the Ozone Layer. in P. M. Haas, R. O. Keohane, and M. A. Levy (eds.), *Institutions for the Earth.* Cambridge, MA: MIT Press, pp. 27–73.

Pepper, David. 1984. *The Roots of Modern Environmentalism.* London: Croon Helm.

Powell, Walter, and Paul DiMaggio (eds.) 1991. *The New Institutionalism in Organizational Analysis.* Chicago: University of Chicago Press.

Princen, Thomas, and Matthias Finger. 1994. *Environmental NGOs in World Politics: Linking the Local and the Global.* New York: Routledge.

Robertson, Roland. 1992. *Globalization.* London: Sage.

Rosenau, James, and E. O. Czempiel (eds.) 1992. *Governance Without Government: Order and Change in World Politics.* Cambridge: Cambridge University Press.

Schofer, Evan. 1998. Science Association in the International Sphere, 1875–1990: The Rationalization of Science and Scientization of Society, in John Boli and George M. Thomas (eds.), *World Polity Formation Since 1875.* Stanford, CA: Stanford University Press.

—— 1996. National Parks in the World: The Rise and Diffusion of an Environmental Model, 1850–1990. Working Paper. Department of Sociology, Stanford University.

Schott, Thomas. 1993. World Science. *Science, Technology, and Human Values* 18:196–208.

Smith, Jackie. 1995. Transnational Political Processes and the Human Rights Movement. *Research on Social Movements, Conflict, and Change* 18:185–220.

—— Ron Pagnucco, and Winnie Romeril. 1994. Transnational Social Movement Organizations in the Global Political Arena. *Voluntas* 5:121–54.

Snow, David A., E. Burke Rochford, Jr., Steven K. Worden, and Robert D. Benford. 1986. Frame Alignment Processes, Micromobilization, and Movement Participation. *American Sociological Review* 51:464–81.

Sprinz, Detlef and Tapani Vaahtoranta. 1994. The Interest-Based Explanation of International Environmental Policy. *International Organization* 48:77–105.

SPSS. 1988. *SPSS-X User's Guide.* Chicago: SPSS.

Statesman's Year-Book. 1960–89. *Statesman's Year-Book.* New York: St Martin's Press.

Stern, Paul G., Oran R. Young, and Daniel Druckman. (eds.) 1992. *Global Environmental Change.* Washington, DC: National Academy.

Taylor, Peter J. and Frederick H. Buttel. 1992. How Do We Know We Have Environmental Problems? Science and the Globalization of Environmental Discourse. *Geoforum* 23:405–16.

Thomas, George M., John W. Meyer, Francisco O. Ramirez, and John Boli. 1987. *Institutional Structure.* Newbury Park, CA: Sage.

Trzyna, Thaddeus C. and Roberta Childers. 1992. *World Directory of Environmental Organizations,* 4th edn. Sacramento: California Institute of Public Affairs.

Tuma, Nancy Brandon. 1992. *Invoking RATE.* Palo Alto, CA: DMA Corporation.

—— and Michael T. Hannan. 1984. *Social Dynamics: Models and Methods.* Orlando, FL: Academic Press.

Turner, B. L., W. C. Clark, R. W. Kates, J. F. Richards, J. T. Mathews, and W. B. Meyer (eds.) 1990. *The Earth as Transformed by Human Action.* Cambridge: Cambridge University Press.

Union of International Associations. 1994, 1995. *Yearbook of International Organizations.* Munich: K. G. Saur.

United Nations Environment Programme (UNEP). 1991. *Environmental Data Report,* 3rd edn. Oxford: Basil Blackwell.

—— 1992. *Annual Report.* Nairobi, Kenya: UNEP.

Walsh, Edward J. 1981. Resource Mobilization and Citizen Protest in Communities Around Three Mile Island. *Social Problems* 29:1–21.

Waltz, Kenneth. 1979. *Theory of World Politics.* Reading, MA: Addison-Wesley.

Wapner, Paul Kevin. 1996. *Environmental Activism and World Civic Politics.* Albany: State University of New York Press.

Wu, Lawrence L. 1989. Issues in Smoothing Empirical Hazards, in C. C. Clogg (ed.), *Sociological Methodology 1989.* Washington, DC: American Sociological Association, pp. 127–59.

Yearley, Steven. 1996. *Sociology, Environmentalism, Globalization.* London: Sage.

Young, Oran R. 1986. International Regimes: Toward a New Theory of Institutions. *World Politics* 39:104–22.

—— 1989. The Politics of International Regime Formation: Managing Natural Resources and the Environment *International Organization* 43:349–75.

11

Management

Globalization and the Expansion and Standardization of Management

INTRODUCTION

The chapters in this book have common roots of a striking phenomenon observed in recent decades in the world of organizations. Cultural models of expanded organizational management spread rapidly around the world (and perhaps especially around Europe), with ideas, rules, and practices flowing more freely than in the past. The contrast with the situation a few decades ago is notable: Guillen (1994) can write about past management ideologies and cultures as fairly distinctive to the political and social structures of the national societies he treats as his cases, though with some processes of diffusion and influence. Now, and in these chapters, however, the center of gravity shifts to ideas about management as flowing generally around the world. National characteristics are now seen as operating to restrict or facilitate the flow (see, e.g., Røvik in chapter 6 or Tiratsoo in chapter 8 of the Sahlin-Andersson and Engwall volume), rather than as constitutive determinants of the principles of management (but see Byrkjeflot in Chapter 10 of the Sahlin-Andersson and Engwall volume).

This shift describes the observable realities of the management theories carried by the worldwide – and perhaps especially European – spread of consulting firms (Ruef in chapter 4 of the Sahlin-Andersson and Engwall volume), social movements (Røvik in chapter 6), or training systems and principles (Luo in chapter 9 of the Sahlin-Andersson and Engwall volume). It also describes the social science models put forward to explain the changes. These tend to shift from "particle theories" of diffusion, which emphasize the histories and motives of the polities and firms to which ideas do or do not flow, to "wave theories," which emphasize the immersion of particular entities in a general context or medium that supports diffusion (Czarniawska and Sévon 1996).

Originally published as:

John W. Meyer 2002. Globalization and the Expansion and Standardization of Management, in Kerstin Sahlin-Andersson and Lars Engwall (eds.), *The Expansion of Management Knowledge*. Stanford, CA: Stanford University Press, pp. 33–44 .

What has changed in the broader context that makes a worldwide diffusion of management ideologies seem routine and central rather than surprising and peripheral? Behind their diversity, the chapters in the Sahlin-Andersson and Engwall (2002) book have a common picture, not just of the phenomenon they are dealing with but of a basic explanatory variable: globalization (and its close relative, Europeanization). The rapid diffusion or management ideology is facilitated by the rise of a conception of society as transcending national boundaries.

Globalization, of course, has many meanings or dimensions. The aim of this chapter is to spell out some of the different aspects of globalization that are involved, and some of the different pathways through which these differing dimensions work to make a world that is safer for a worldwide McKinsey (Armbrüster and Kipping in Chapter 5; Ruef in Chapter 4, both in the Sahlin-Andersson and Engwall volume).

TWO MEANINGS OF THE SPREAD OF MANAGEMENT IDEAS

The expanded diffusion of management ideas around the world has two related aspects, and it is useful to distinguish between these aspects. Each, in turn, is complex.

First, there is the intensified diffusion of standardized models of organization. Ideas about organization flow more rapidly across countries in the world, so principles of proper organizational supervision, accounting, structure, training, and so on, apply everywhere. And ideas about organization flow more rapidly across social sectors or arenas, so the principles of proper business organization extend quickly from one industry to another, and outside the business system to public agencies, hospitals, schools, prisons, and so on (Olson et al. 1998). Clearly, this situation helps us understand the causal forces behind the diffusion: the ideas spread faster because organizations in different countries and different business and public sectors are seen as ultimately more similar than they were in the past (Chapter 6).

Second, and closely related, there is a general intensification of focus on management as a common core element to all forms of structuring (Brunsson and Sahlin-Andersson 2000). The contrast is with older concerns with formal structuring as authoritative bureaucracy, ownership, or specific professionalism (e.g., schools, hospitals, or shoe manufacturers). This shift, indeed, is partly captured in the modern preference for the general term *organization,* rather than *bureaucracy* or *association,* and rather than substantive specification of the work involved. Thus, the head of a hospital or school is increasingly defined as a manager rather than a doctor or educator: the leaders of a utility company are seen as managers rather than electrical engineers, and so on.

The key to conceptions of *organization* as the crucial entity and *management* as core to organization lies in the extraordinary agentic actorhood attributed to organized entities in the modern system (Chapter 5). They are no longer passive, trustworthy servants of the king or the public or their owners: they are rational bounded decision-making actors, with purposes and technologies and free resources of their own, with the sovereign authority to decide and act, and the capacity to control their internal structures to conform to their decisions.

Hence, public agencies are to become privatized or decentralized or autonomous managed organizations to more efficiently meet their responsibilities (Olson et al. 1998). Shoemaking organizations are to be managed to such an extent that they may decide not to make and sell shoes any longer. Even schools, which may be privatized and which may contract out teaching services, are in any case to become organizations that make decisions about how to serve their publics and enter into contractual relations with these publics.

The explanatory problem, therefore, is to explain how globalization produces a world of agentic, empowered, and managed organizations that function as rational and dramatic actors.

DIMENSIONS OF GLOBALIZATION

Enlarged markets: experiences and myths

A conventional and widespread notion is that on every side, from suppliers to regulators to consumers, organizations face with globalization (and especially the new Europe) markets that are much larger than before. The idea is that these expanded markets pose many new uncertainties and require much more effective decision-making, control, and activity than were needed in the old village societies. The phrasing of the idea may emphasize the threatening character of the expanded markets (a common theme in pessimistic European interpretations) or stress the positive opportunities involved (as always, the American story), but the arguments are essentially the same.

In either case, it is essential to note, the idea of expanded *markets* is involved. This idea carries the implication that the new globalized world, although very complex (one meaning of the term uncertainty), is nonetheless very highly ordered, so the uncertainties can in principle be resolved by improved efficacious actorhood. Were globalization to simply imply disorder and anarchy (another meaning of uncertainty), expanded organization and management would not be likely consequences – prayer and defensive passivity would be wiser. Reliance on god and the state would be wiser than attempts at rational planning and action.

Expanded markets may be experienced by organizations, or with varying degrees of intensity, they may be anticipated. People may see European or global competition coming down the line. Or associated organizations may be experiencing it. Or advisors and business associations may predict it. In all these cases, the globalization involved brings in new uncertainty, but uncertainty of a highly rationalized sort, which responsible organizations need to mobilize to deal with.

At the extreme, globalization functions as a myth – a generally new and expanded picture of a standardized world with high expectations. In this sense, it can confront any organization even in the absence of any effective direct competition. Hence, modern public school organizations, even with effective monopolies, begin to envision a world of expanded educational competition (or economic competition to which their training must respond). Hospitals confront larger standards, perhaps carried by their real or imagined clientele – the old local people are now national and European and global citizens, carrying (in themselves or by attribution) high expectations for treatment. The old locals are now members of world society, and are understood to require treatment in light of the best practices obtaining anywhere. In the expanded global world, markets and market standards are part of a myth of enhanced rationalization.

Thus, the inputs, technologies, and outputs of modern organizations come to be seen against the background of a much larger, more complex, and more rationalized world than in the past. This requires more effective organizational structures, empowered to make the needed complex decisions and to take a broader range of actions across a much wider front of uncertainty.

But other elements of organization require similar mobilizations. Not only technologies but also sovereign decision-making capabilities and coordination, and control systems need to be upgraded in the globalized world.

The sovereign organization in a weakened state and national community

Globalization, and especially Europeanization, has dramatically undercut the old sovereignties and protections provided to organizations by the national state and the national community. This development provides changed experiences for organizations but even greater changes in anticipations and in myths.

In the past, many organizations could effectively function as subunits of the national state and community rather than as autonomous entities. This is most obviously true of public agencies, which could often claim to simply be bureaucratic components of the national state, controlled and protected by its laws and regulations. The answers to questions about, say, the efficacy of a school could simply be that this school is in complete compliance with, and a dedicated professionalized servant of, the national state. In the same way, a hospital might be seen as the proper embodiment of the rules of the national professional medical community (Brunsson and Sahlin-Andersson 2000). In neither case does the organization posture as an autonomous decision maker or actor. The decisions are to be made in a ministry or professional community, not in the organization, which is more a faithful trustee than an organized actor. Mobilization as a bounded actor for such an organization would unreasonably sacrifice the protection of its monopoly position and would be in violation of its sworn responsibility. Secure under the umbrella of the nation and state, the proper posture is professionalism in Weber's sense – the loyal and competent servant, not the decision maker.

The same mentality describes much traditional private business organization too. The organization is not a mobilized decision maker or actor, but a servant or trustee of owners or occupational communities, or a local community. Demobilization is a more appropriately humble posture than is mobilized empowerment under such conditions.

One can see the traditional embeddedness of an organization in national or local control systems in several ways. For instance, it can be seen as constraining possible choices, which are ruled out by national law or policy, professional authority, and so on. From this point of view, modern globalization represents a great expansion in organizational freedom and empowerment, as for the first time all sorts of new decisions can be made and new actions taken. However, the new freedom can be seen to have destroyed a mass of old protections that provided a secure and certain – however depressingly constrained – environment. In any case, the old monopolies are weakened, whether they are seen as protective or constraining.

In the new globalized system, sovereignty devolves on organizations, which are now to confront directly the problems of decision and action. They can no longer hide behind the state or local or national communities (e.g., professional ones), but must become more rational and rationalized actors on a grand scale. The constructed space created in this expanded vision, of course, is one in which many new social movements supporting expanded managerial capacity spread rapidly.

Globalization and the expanded person

Organizations organize people. And globalization changes the practices, rules, and myths defining what people are, what they are entitled to, and what they can do. On all these dimensions, the changes amount to expansion of the personhood that organizations can and must deal with.

It is easiest to see this as creating new constraining uncertainties. If the old rules of local and national communities are applied, fairly passive persons could be managed bureaucratically or with even more traditional mechanisms of the sort used to manage peasants. Now, with great expansions in principles of individual citizenship, and the translation of this onto a global scale with principles of human rights, major new problems for organizing are created everywhere. Old technologies violate safety or medical or environment principles, which are now rationalized worldwide. Old control systems violate (worldwide) human rights, as do old exercises of organizational sovereignty. Old adaptations to market uncertainty violate modern employment principles. Old principles of employment or promotion violate the human rights of individuals or groups or both (e.g., gendered employment). And the new principles sweep around the world, so that an organization doing customary labor control in Southeast Asia can generate a consumer strike on human rights grounds in San Francisco.

However, the new globalized persons provide new possibilities for organizing, too. They have extraordinary capacities and can be educated or trained to become part of a new expanded management system, having learned to create their own jobs, manage their own time, engage in their own proper human relations, and so on (see Luo in chapter 9 of the Sahlin-Andersson and Engwall volume). So all sorts of new organizational forms become possible, far beyond traditional bureaucracy, professional community, or family firm structures. The global citizen can be a part of a new enhanced and empowered organization, which may be achieved by decentralization, weekend therapy sessions, or complex new computer systems. And with the rise of organization comes the rise of management possibilities – and then the social movements that spread expanded management ideologies everywhere.

The rationalized global environment

It is common to see globalization as involving forces that break down the basis and autonomy of the state and liberate demonic forces of irrationality and localism in new tribalisms. And certainly, events occur (e.g., in Rwanda, Columbia, or Indonesia) that make such a view seem plausible. The view, however, is of no help to our present purposes. The "risk society" would not be likely to generate expanded organization and expanded management if the new risks were essentially arbitrary and anomic (Beck 1992). Rather, it would generate a sense of powerlessness and meaninglessness that promote lower, not higher, levels of organizational mobilization.

But the view of globalization as a breakdown is fundamentally an error. As I have stressed, contemporary globalization involves the construction of new domains of rationality, not only the collapse of some old ones. The new economic world is imagined as a market with expanded rationality. The new polity and society expand worldwide, with common models of societal organization and development reflecting a great deal of social scientization and rationalization (Chapter 8). The new persons are empowered and rational, with expanded human rights and capabilities (Frank et al. 1995). And all this occurs in a physical and technical and human environment increasingly scientized – in principles of engineering but also in ecological, biological, and medical analyses.

All this rationalization occurs on a worldwide basis, penetrating most societies, sectors, and organizational settings. It provides fertile ground for the mobilization of organization and management, and for the rapid diffusion of new models and fashions for both. Perhaps the term *risk society* carries the wrong image, and we should employ the phrase *opportunity society* in parallel (Beck 1992).

To deal with all the expansions in the domains of rationality, an organization must rapidly expand, and managerial capability must especially expand (Meyer 1994). And as the new rationalities are worldwide in character, the models of how to properly manage may be found everywhere and spread everywhere. Thus, whole new doctrines spring up – here a new accounting system (Wallerstedt in chapter 11 of the Sahlin-Andersson and Engwall volume), there an informative one (Walgenbach and Beck in chapter 7 of the Sahlin-Andersson and Engwall volume), over to the side a new system for training employees (Luo in chapter 9 of the Sahlin-Andersson and Engwall volume), and new mechanisms for making decisions. And everywhere, new forms of standardization, measurement, and data (Tiratsoo in chapter 8 of the Sahlin-Andersson and Engwall volume).

CARRIERS OF MODELS FOR EXPANDED ORGANIZATION AND MANAGEMENT

In many ways, as discussed above, globalization creates a new space or vacuum – the possibility and necessity for rapidly expanded organization and management capability or responsibility. This space – a greatly expanded, unfilled domain of rationalized uncertainty – has been filled with rapidly evolving promoters of managerial ideology. These are discussed extensively in the chapters of this book and may simply be noted here.

First, we may note the expansion in numbers, and importance of the academic clergy – the intellectuals creating new management ideas and models. Institutionally this involves the rapid expansion and worldwide spread of business schools, which provide not only training but also intellectual centrality for the movement (Luo in chapter 9 of the Sahlin-Andersson and Engwall volume). It also involves the production and spread around the world of academic publications supporting the new fashions. Second, these business schools increasingly provide a training base from which managers are recruited. The shift from technical training (e.g., in engineering, education, medicine, or other occupations) to generalized management training is a core indicator of the whole expansion in conceptions of organization and management that we are concerned with here. One indicator of the diffusion of management ideology is the spread of the MBA, or business training in general (Luo in chapter 9 of the Sahlin-Andersson and Engwall volume). This is not only an indicator but also a cause of further diffusion, as each executive who obtains his/her position because of "management" education rather than training in substantive matters is likely to be a permanent node facilitating further diffusion. Dependent on faith in the existence of generalized management capabilities, he or she is especially susceptible to further expansions or developments of such doctrines. So presumably the expanded employment of people trained as generalized managers in overarching business schools directly increases the subsequent diffusion of new ideologies of expanded management.

Third, a whole set of specialists arises, translating more academic models into practical form and penetrating local organizational practice. Here, we have the explosion of the consulting industry that is noted in many chapters of this book (e.g., Ruef in chapter 4, Wallerstedt in chapter 11, Ernst and Kieser in chapter 3, all in the Sahlin-Andersson and Engwall volume).

Fourth, but less discussed in the chapters here, is the dramatic rise in organizational linkages to all sorts of associations. These associations may be general business groups or specialized to specific industries and activities. They may also be professional associations to which particular managers (e.g., personnel or safety managers) belong. In any case, such associations of organizations become major carriers of general management information. For instance, they clearly provide the basis for the rapid expansion of standardized personnel practices in response to American affirmative action pressures (Edelman et al. 1992; Dobbin and Sutton 1998): the same process operates on a worldwide basis, too.

Finally, we may note that the rise of generalized conceptions of management as an activity – and of this management as going on in a rather standardized and globalized world – creates a strong tendency for organizations everywhere to look at an array of other organizations as potential models. If, on the one hand, an organization sees itself as an entity unique to a particular country, community, business setting, and so on, it is unlikely to look for (or be exposed to) management models drawn from

258 *World Society: The Writings of John W. Meyer*

around the world. If, on the other hand, it is seen as a modern organized actor, models are everywhere and the possibilities for diffusion are endless. The entire communication system around such an organization changes: its own elites look elsewhere, as do its ordinary participants. But so do customers and suppliers giving advice, and even members of the general public. If everyone within and without an organization examines it from the point of view of universal rationalities rather than local community, there is a great deal of exposure to expanded ideologies of organization and management. In practice, attention goes to the successful – Apple or IBM are models when things go well, and massive publicity in academic, professional, and mass media promulgates their organizational forms. And it is organization and management, more than technical accomplishments that now circulate most widely (Røvik in chapter 6 of the Sahlin-Andersson and Engwall volume). These, indeed, are the kinds of changes generated by modern globalization.

DIMENSIONS OF GLOBAL ORGANIZATIONAL RATIONALIZATION: SOME SPECULATIONS

Worldwide changes in recent decades strike at some dimensions of management and organization more than others, providing some focal points for further changes.

In many kinds of organized activities, global rationalization has been going on for a long time. This may especially describe technologies dealing with the physical world, as such matters have been rationalized for centuries. Thus engineering technologies and production management may have been diffusing rapidly for a long time. It is probably not reasonable to see special globalization going on in these areas in recent decades (Schofer 1999).

In contrast, in the pre-World War II world there was a considerable tendency to see people and organizations as local – tied to distinctive patterns of national citizen-membership and state structure. Thus it was reasonable, until recently, to imagine that managerial patterns for different national societies might be very different, and the possibilities for diffusion very limited (Hofstede 1980). With the rise of scientized modern psychologies, and of human rights systems extended worldwide, and with the decline in the special sacred meaning of national citizenship, we may suppose that there have been rapid expansions in those aspects of organization and management concerned with persons and many diffusing and contending ideologies in the area.

In exactly the same way, recent globalization has hit hard in standardizing the meaning of social value and values – briefly, money in some of its various meanings (especially finance, credit, and investment, which have rapidly globalized). We may assume that there has been a great expansion in standardized organizational control and management in areas related to monetary value – accounting, finance, measurement, and the like (Fligstein 1990). Social movements to improve the management on these dimensions can flourish.

The point here is simply that the diffusion of cultural material on organizations and management is enhanced by the rise of standard models in these matters but also by rapid change in the areas, as this generates the space in which consultants and theorists and new training systems blossom.

CONCLUSION

Globalization has a variety of meanings and dimensions. Many of these operate to create more standardized pictures of organization across the boundaries of nations or social sectors. And they operate to create stronger pictures of organizations as empowered and managed actors.

One causal pathway, here, is through the expansion of all sorts of markets and myths, and ideologies of markets. New uncertainties confront organizations (even in supposedly monopoly situations such as state educational systems). The market idea implies that these expanded environments have a rationalized character of a kind that demands and legitimates expanded organization and management, rather than the sort of threatening chaos that might undercut the expanded organization. Even if the new world is threatening, it can and must be dealt with. So much structuration results.

A second causal pathway lies through the weakened control and legitimacy of the national community and nation-state. Organizations are no longer so protected (or constrained) by their position as subunits in national professional and bureaucratic structures. They are more exposed – and again, exposed to a highly rationalized environment of markets and standards. More organizations and managements are called for and legitimated.

Third, globalization has produced a kind of natural law expansion in models of the persons that make up organizations – their rights, capacities, and ability to be organized. The new organizational forms must and can incorporate these people in dynamic participation, but in doing so must become more mobilized and managed. Whole domains are created or expanded having to do with personnel, decision-making participation, safety, the environment, and all sorts of rights connected with employment and promotion.

Finally, globalization has expanded the overall scientization of the world, with great schemes defining the physical environment, the nature of social development, and indeed the capacities of human persons. Scientization generates the kind of rationalized uncertainties that are recipes for organizing.

In the space created by all these rapid social changes, many new movements and institutions are created to diffuse new and expanded models of organization and management. New training institutions built around management provide the employment base, and expanded post-employment training is organized. All sorts of academics generate new models expanding management capacity, and all sorts of consultants arise to diffuse them. And in a world in which disembodied organization is seen as subject to the same standards of high managerial capacity, models and exemplars are discussed in all sorts of media. All these processes greatly intensify diffusion, and break down the boundaries (of nation, or social sector) that might restrict it.

REFERENCES

Beck, Ulrich. 1992. *Risk Society.* London: Sage.

Brunsson, Nils and Kerstin Sahlin-Andersson. 2000. Constructing Organizations: The Case of the Public Sector Reform. *Organization Studies* 21 (4):721–46.

Czarniawska, Barbara, and Guje Sevón (eds.) 1996. *Translating Organizational Symbolism.* New York: de Gruyter.

Dobbin, Frank and John Sutton. 1998. The Strength of a Weak State: The Rights Revolution and the Rise of Human Resources Management Divisions. *American Journal of Sociology* 104 (2):441–76.

Edelmann, Lauren, Steven Abraham, and Howard Erlanger. 1992. Professional Construction of the Legal Environment: The Inflated Treat of Wrongful Discharge Doctrine. *Law and Society Review* 26:47–83.

Fligstein, Neil. 1990. *Transformation of Corporate Control.* Cambridge, MA: Harvard University Press.

Frank, David, John Meyer, and David Miyahara. 1995. The Individualist Polity and the Centrality of Professionalized Psychology. *American Sociological Review* 60 (3):360–77.

Guillén, Mauro F. 1994. *Models of Management: Work, Authority, and Organization in a Comparative Perspective.* Chicago: University of Chicago Press.

Hofstede, Geert. 1980. *Culture's Consequences.* Beverly Hills: Sage.

Meyer, John W. (1994). 'Rationalized Environments, in W. R. Scott and J. W. Meyer (eds.), *Institutional Environments and Organizations: Structural Complexity and Individualism.* London: Sage, pp. 28–54 and 228–54.

—— and Ronald L. Jepperson. 2000. The 'Actors' of Modern Society: The Cultural Construction of Social Agency. *Sociological Theory* 18:100–20. Reproduced in Chapter 5.

—— John Boli, George Thomas, and Francisco Ramirez. 1997. World Society and the Nation State. *American Journal of Sociology* 103 (1) (July):144–81. Reproduced in Chapter 8.

Olson, Olov, James Guthrie, and Christopher Humphrey (eds.) (1998). *Global Warning: Debating International Developments in the New Public Financial Management.* Oslo: Cappelen Akademisk Forlag.

Schofer, Evan. (1999). Science Associations in the International Sphere 1875–1990, in J. Boli and G. Thomas (eds.), *Constructing World Culture.* Stanford, CA: Stanford University Press, pp. 249–66.

Strang, David, and John W. Meyer. (1993). International Conditions for Diffusion, in W. R. Scott, and J. W. Meyer (eds.), *Institutional Environments and Organizations: Structural Complexity and Individualism.* London: Sage, pp. 100–12. Reproduced in Chapter 6.

12

Science

World Society and the Authority and Empowerment of Science

OVERVIEW

In this chapter, we put forward explanations of the expanded and institutionalized authority of science in modern societies. As we suggest in Chapter 1, the contemporary worldwide expansion of scientific activity can be seen as reflecting this expanded collective authority, as a cultural matter, rather than producing authority through accretions of functional success and organizational power. And the core element of the expansion of science is indeed its broad authority, rather than its instrumental functions, powers, and interests. In this sense, science operates as the secular equivalent of a "sacred canopy" for the modern order, generating a modern, rational interpretation of world order, and offering this logic as a secular interpretive grid for natural and social life.

Science arises and expands in close conjunction with the modern cultural invention and expansion of the model of the rational and purposive social "actor," whether individual, organization, or nation-state. For this highly agentic and competent actor, science serves functions far beyond those of an instrumental tool: it plays a broad role analogous to religious ones, providing constitutive and legitimate (i.e., ontological and cosmological) supports for the hubris involved in claims to actorhood.

An explanation for the contemporary explosion of scientific authority and activity, then, may be the recent rapid expansion in the rights and responsibilities of a variety of social actors from individuals to national states. And this expansion, in turn, is clearly a product of the rapid globalization of the current period, with the rise of a world public society, or polity. Worldwide, individuals, accepted as human beings, are accorded rights and capacities that were previously unrecognized or restricted to the citizens of a few core countries. National states, with greatly expanded rights and

Originally published as:

Gili S. Drori, John W. Meyer, Francisco O. Ramirez and Evan Schofer. 2003. World Society and the Authority and Empowerment of Science, in Science in the Modern World Polity: Institutionalization and Globalization. Stanford, CA: Stanford University Press, pp. 23–42.

duties and attributed capacities, cover a globe in which previously only a few had much standing. And rational organizations, with elaborate responsibilities and capacities, are found everywhere, in every domain. The idea that all sorts of entities function as actors, with exaggerated rights and capacities, pops up everywhere in the modern world society. This idea implies that a wide range of actors enjoy an enormous capacity for a human agency that is conceived as a rational, purposeful, and ultimately predictable articulation of valid interests. Supporting this idea and its triumphant dissemination as a cultural frame, a world scientific culture expands and intensifies. The current structure/agency debates on the social sciences underestimate both the degree to which an agency itself is a worldwide standardized social construction, and the extent to which scientific authority supports and legitimates the agentic actor.

Taking this view to the authority of science in the modern system helps explain many features of science: its rapid spread around a world that in instrumental or functional terms is very diverse, its spread across many different social domains despite limited effectiveness, the worldwide standardization of its forms and contents, and its tendency to focus on a variety of questions far removed from any instrumental significance.

Thus explaining the modern global explosion of scientific activity, discourse, and organization, we need to understand the ways that the contemporary world polity has expanded the conceptions of human social actorhood, as carried by persons, states, and organizations. Globalization has built up expanded sets of truths that are to apply everywhere, with science as the obvious cultural vehicle. And it has expanded and standardized the meaning, responsibilities, and rights of all sorts of social actors. Science comes into play to prop up the necessary model of the agentic actor, who with the proper approach and socialization can understand everything (Meyer 1986). So science props up the necessary model of the universalized and lawful environment in response to which a scientifically understandable agentic actorhood is obviously correct and desirable.

EXPANSION AND AUTHORITY

All the sectors of the rationalized society – the economy, political system, family and socialization, medicine, and others – rest on a cultural base that is substantially scientific in character. These sectors also change rapidly with scientific developments; for example, the introduction of modern ecological, economic, or human rights arrangements relies heavily on scientific advances and draws extensively from the scientific discourse. Or consider the raising of children: a variety of medical, biological, psychological, and social sciences define how it should best be done. These sciences generate clear cultural rules, and also generate categories of scientifically trained persons who can instruct (e.g., in court) on correct or negligent forms of childrearing. The sciences have clear authority, but this authority is cultural in character. That is, the scientists do not raise the children. Rather, they instruct "real" social actors how it should be done. Individual actors are to do it. States are to provide legislation and resources. Organizations of various sorts (childcare, medical, or educational) are to manage parts of it. All are to play their parts in a cultural drama laid out by the sciences.

The modern scientized society can be contrasted with more "traditional" societies, in which some religious or traditional authority over a limited range of social life is vested in a few elite interpreters, but in which much authority is embedded in mundane society. The priests may make some rules, for instance, about childrearing, but more are carried along by generations of grandmothers. The authority is now more concentrated. It moves to science, which penetrates far down into society and spreads across all the different modern sectors and national societies. Direct reference to scientific authority routinely appears in legislative and courtroom hearings, in business decisions, or for that matter in conflicts between spouses. Religious leaders, too, now gain stature to the degree that they appear to be scientific: even the grandmothers may try to do so.

The scientization of society, or the penetration of science into everyday life, is extreme (chapter 3 in Drori et al. 2003). Science, thus, is no longer confined to exotic academic locales; it also resides in the states and other organizations, and in the routine thoughts and practices of ordinary individuals (including children; see, chapter 6 in Drori et al. 2003). Also, beyond physical nature, science addresses social and psychological worlds, and something close to the divine (as in theories of the big bang, or of extraterrestrial intelligence). The domain expansion makes science a label of expertise and specialization available for a wide variety of cultural materials, so we can have "food science" or "sports science." The scientization of society extends to expressive issues as well: in order to resolve matters of observance of the Sabbath, rabbinical discussions focus on the technical details of the operations of elevators and the physics of gravitational forces; and in order to define death, authority goes to doctors and biologists and psychologists. Finally, social concerns are defined in scientific and technical terms from the naming of periods by their scientific advances (the Green Revolution or the Space Age) to the use of scientific methods in everyday discourse (the display of synoptic maps in weather reports or statistical error margins in polling reports).

CURRENT EXPLANATIONS OF SCIENTIFIC EXPANSION

Explanations for the modern expansion in scientific authority are less well developed than one might expect. One tradition sees expanded scientific authority as reflecting the expansion of science itself – the greatly increased numbers of scientific personnel, activities, research products and investments in modern national societies (Ben-David 1990; Cozzens 1997). In this tradition, scientific expansion can simply be described, with explanations taken to be almost self-evident. Science expands and is frequently referred to because it "works" and provides functional advantages. The implied causal arguments here are that scientific expansion arises from the pressures, or needs, of powers and interests governing modern society. Science, in other words, is functionally necessary, either for the social system as a whole or for the dominating political and economic interests within it. Seeing science as an instrumental or functional necessity is clearly part of the modern culture itself. But science often spreads more as a faith than as a system of well-established and clearly known functional relationships (Wuthnow 1987a). It has been unexpectedly difficult to document the functional necessity of, or contribution of, science in the modern system (see Kuhn 1977; Shenhav and Kamens 1991; chapters 4 and 10 in Drori et al. 2003). It is easy to show the important social consequences or benefits of particular scientific or technical developments, but much more difficult to show strong and consistent positive effects of overall scientization. Our own research reveals that some dimensions of scientization enhance economic growth, while others show negative effects (see chapter 10 in Drori et al. 2003).

Moreover, this faith in the utility of science, in general, obscures the obvious lack of functionality of many particular scientific ventures. Much scientific activity has always seemed to have few instrumental benefits for the modern system, or for particular elites in it, as with the current and expensive exploration of various distant and receding galaxies, or the reproductive behavior of various organisms. Economists, mostly as a matter of theoretical commitment rather than strong evidence, subscribe to doctrines of the economic benefits of science, but have not even convincingly demonstrated the marginal utility of an economist: for most social research, it would be most difficult to specify directly the functional consequences.

A second, and more critical, explanatory theme in this field is that the expansion of science is produced by the interests of scientists, themselves, and the scientific organizational system (Merton 1973; Ben-David 1990). This line of reasoning can suppose that functionally successful science can build up strong organizational and professional support, or it can imagine that the whole process is a kind of successful political strategy (Abbot 1988). Scientists clearly do perpetuate their own necessity to justify their professional standing, to encourage further sponsorship of their activities, and to support their social status (see, e.g., Finnemore 1996). But unless scientists are seen as having extraordinary manipulative power and competence, and unless everyone else is seen as foolishly taken in, this explanation assumes what it sets out to explain. Why would scientific elites have such extraordinary authority or legitimated empowerment to pursue their interests, given that they directly master neither the economic structures (capital) nor the political ones (the state) understood to be controlling in modern society? It seems clear that any form of power in the modern system depends on scientized conceptions of reality; understanding why this is so makes it clear that the scientists are much more than simply servants of power (see chapters 12 and 13 in Drori et al. 2003).

A third explanatory theme sees expansion as built into the nature of scientific activity itself. A less critical version, here, sees science as reflecting a natural human curiosity, and as developing by creating endless new arenas for this quality: science, thus, endogenously feeds itself, providing agendas and incentives for autonomous expansion (e.g., Cole 1973). A more critical version – the "sociology of scientific work" – emphasizes the social embeddedness of this process, and the arational and arbitrary ways in which both social and scientific interests feed into a path-dependent expansion (see, e.g., Callon et al. 1986). But this essentialist perspective on the

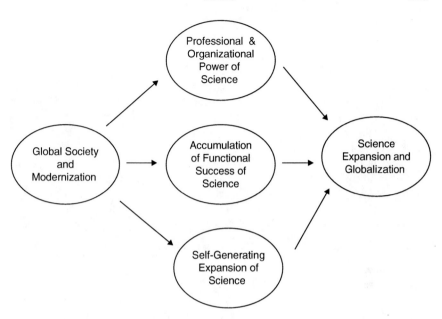

Figure 12.1. Factors affecting the global expansion of science

motives for scientific expansion offers no explanation for the recent phenomenal rates of global proliferation, and the recent intense global structuration of the whole arena of science (chapters 3 and 4 in Drori et al. 2003).

Figure 12.1 shows the three dominant explanations of the global expansion of science in recent decades. A first theme emphasizes scientific functional success, aggregating across a microcontext to a macrosocial effect, as a driving force. A second theme, directly macrosociological, emphasizes the professional power, organization, and interests of the scientists themselves. A third theme emphasizes the natural or cultural spirit of exploration, and the self-reinforcing effects of scientific development over time. In a broad sense, all three themes see science as a very natural (for good or ill) product of the long-term process of social modernization, becoming global as the modernization process itself becomes worldwide.

THE PROBLEM

The core explanatory issue has been poorly formulated in two ways. First, the real problem is to explain the legitimation, authority, resources, and attention given to science in the wider system, not the particular organizations and activities involved. Why does the extraordinary modern legitimated empowerment of science arise and expand? Why do all sorts of social forces – and both populations and elites pour attention, prestige, and resources into scientific activity? Scientific authority is to be found not in scientists and their particular activities themselves, but rather in wider societies that create, confer, expand, and concretely uphold this authority. It is built up by nations, states, and organizations that support scientific activity, and that rest policies and activities on scientific knowledge. It is built by people – especially elites – who en masse in the modern world send their young to study the sciences in universities, who help expand these universities and incorporate in them much scientific work in the name of various common goods, and who create the rules conferring social and economic advantage on the properly trained and credentialed persons so produced.

A central feature of every modern stratification system is that the greatest social prestige, and often status and income, are given to the schooled professionals. This is in sharp contrast to dominant theories, which stress the importance of state power and control over economic capital, as the engines of stratification. In fact, the elite professionals, who dominate the prestige system, commonly do so through claims to scientific knowledge (Treiman 1977; Abbott 1988; Meyer 1994a, b). We need to explain why this is so. It is unlikely to be the manipulative product of the professionals themselves, since the behavior of others and of whole societies is involved in this conferral of status and authority.

As a second aspect of the explanatory problem, the broad social authority involved goes principally to science in general, as a broad cultural abstraction. It does not go mainly to specific (and possibly functional) activities and analyses. All sorts of scientists, from engineers to social scientists to astronomers, carry the prestige of science. All sorts of scientific roles, from educators to lab technicians to MBAs, are elaborated in the universities. All sorts of scientific training, from sociology to biology to abstract physics, are institutionalized and sought after. Instrumental theories try to explain variations in social investment among fields and there are indeed such variations to explain; but in explaining the trees, the forest of a huge overall social and educational investment in science, in general, is underemphasized. For a parallel, one must imagine an economy in which profitable firms are greatly rewarded, and less profitable ones almost as much and firms with no intention or hope of making a profit only a bit less. Obviously, such a situation reflects a society attaching great meaning and value to the general category "firm." In the same way, a wide range of activities linked to the category "science" get great support, legitimacy, and often resources (as in the allocation of university positions), in the modern system.

Thus, science is to be seen as a broad and general authoritative cultural canopy covering an enormous domain of valued activity in the modern system. The problem is, thus, to explain the character of the institution as an authoritative one in modern society, not the specific activities, roles, and organizations involved. One cannot explain the modern general authority of science by looking mainly at the often-careerist and often-chaotic activities of the scientists and their organizations. The general and expanded authority of science is a property of the modern society, not mainly the scientists. A neo-institutionalist perspective emphasizes that such a focus on scientists themselves and their interests is itself scripted and shaped by global myths, located in a polity that is substantially a cultural construction, and that is worldwide in both claims and realities.

SCIENCE AND THE MODERN ACTOR

The global and cultural dimensions of modern science establish it as a core feature of modernity and as one axis of the modern, initially western and now global, polity. It is the stand of science as a global cultural institution, and its cultural qualities that are central to understanding its social role and the impact of its globalization. And it is in its capacity as a global cultural institution that science alters all other modern institutions. We need to understand the forces that so strongly support this transcending cultural institution.

Science, seen as an authoritative and general cultural system, has close links with the construction of the modern agentic social actor. Science is thus not only socially employed for practical purposes (the instrumentalist view), but is elaborated as a vital cultural frame (the institutionalist perspective), supporting the constitution or legitimacy of social entities as social actors. Actorhood is the principle that social life is built up of actors – human individuals, organizations and national states with valid interests that others are to respect, and with the capacity (i.e., agency) to validly represent those interests in activity (Chapter 5). Rational and responsible human actorhood that everyone else is to respect only makes sense if (a) the world is a rather lawful and orderly (i.e., scientizable) place, and if (b) the human social actors can understand it (i.e., be scientists). But if the world indeed has these properties, working with and having science are practically an obligation, and a highly valued one. In the contemporary world, the cultural authority is such that a great scientist, Einstein, can be defined as "Man of the Century" by *Time Magazine*.

It is generally understood that the rise of modern science and the rise of the rationally organized actorhood of individuals and states (and derived formally as organized actors) go together (e.g., Ezrahi 1990). Out of a medieval matrix in which the order (and thus real actorhood and action) occurred only in a spiritual plane, and in which the natural world was seen as chaotic and "fallen," arose both concepts of strong human actors, empowered by their access to the wider spiritual and natural laws, and an orderly and scientized conception of the nature which these actors could comprehend and in which they could properly act. The Renaissance, Reformation, and Enlightenment progressively built modern individuals and states. They also, in the subsequent revolutions, linked these together in the modern nation-state, which during the nineteenth and twentieth centuries led to organizational revolutions creating all sorts of organized actor structures in both state and society. Each step of the process also expands the scientization of the environment within which the empowered actors take form: actorhood expands science, and science expands actorhood (Toulmin 1990).

The modern society is culturally constituted as made up of these social actors, with changing content and meaning over time. Foundationally, actors include human individuals. This conception has greatly intensified on a worldwide scale over time, and individual actorhood is increasingly seen as a matter of global human, rather than national citizen rights (Soysal 1994). States (increasingly over time, nation-states) are also foundationally seen as legitimate actors both domestically and on a world scale: this is a core meaning of the principle of sovereignty (Krasner 1999). Many other recognized organized actors are built by individual actors in association (as with the modern corporation), or by devolution from state actors (as with public bureaucracies). In contemporary societies, mixtures of both are common, as in public good, or non-governmental organizations in civil society (contrast Coleman 1974; Perrow 1991; and Meyer 1994b for general perspectives).

The modern liberal society sees itself as produced and maintained by such actors, with a polity, economy, and culture almost entirely driven by their choices, rather than by nature, tradition, history, or spiritual powers. In this sense, actors are seen as bounded, or as disembedded from wider spiritual, natural, and social forces: they carry an autonomous capability to act on their own purposes. Thus, the defining elements of actors include boundaries and purposes, coherent means-ends technologies using analyzable resources to achieve the purposes, unified sovereign authority, and effective control systems over behavior. Such actors can understand and manage these aspects of their identity, and do so with a comprehension of the lawful and orderly physical and social nature within which they are to act. This conception of the actor as a sort of all-competent "good guy" is of course very unrealistic, particularly on the agency side, and much religious and cultural – and in the modern period, scientific – support is needed to sustain it. The myths of actorhood require that individuals and organizations and states are understood to maintain elaborate information systems, extraordinary searches of the environment, extremely complex decisions, and highly effective control and implementation systems. Science, nominally taming the environment while nominally empowering the actor, is a great support (see Brunsson 1989; Brunsson and Sahlin-Andersson 2000).

Each of the specific properties of the modern actor is interdependent with a rationalized or scientized picture of the environment (prominently the natural environment, but increasingly also the social and psychological ones). Purposive human action makes little sense if the environment is utterly disordered, chaotic, corrupted, and unpredictable. In such disordered situations, means-ends technologies, and the rationalized use of resources toward goals, are similarly disabled, and the sovereignty of the agentic actor and effective control over the machinery of action lose meaning and legitimacy. Thus in order to sustain actorhood, some science is vital. For example, if societies and individuals are to be responsible on matters of health, a coherent knowledge system must be assumed. Or as another example, a rationalized and universal educational system requires much scientized educational theory, and those who wish to put forward such a system generally support the sciences involved.

The scientific rationalization of the environment is, thus, crucial to the constitution of human agentic actorhood. If people can know the laws of disease, they acquire the capability and responsibility to control their behavior, as rational or rationalized actors, in light of these laws by such means as hygiene and immunization. If the technical and resource environment of economic production is scientized, states and organizations similarly gain legitimate authority and responsibility to take action, such as planning the production cycles and manipulating currency exchange rates. Thus, the scientific rationalization of the environment of action creates the orderly uncertainties (making matters lawful and releasing them from the grip of arbitrary or chaotic forces) and calls for the consolidation of empowered actorhood.

In this sense, historically strong conceptions of the human (and state, and organizational) actor arise in interdependence with the rise of the scientization of nature, including the nature of human actors themselves. And there is a continuing cultural interdependence between strong models of actorhood (e.g., liberal individualist ones) and the scientization of nature (Frank et al. 1999; see Schofer 1999a, b for discussions on the general relationship). Scientized domains (e.g., greater control over energy resources, yet also human sexuality) expand the authority, responsibility, and capacity of the human actors involved. And, such a call for the display of actorhood (authority, responsibility, and capacity) is translated into social mobilization around claims of uniqueness. Thus, the scientization of human sexuality helps consolidate the claims for the rights of gay and lesbian people (Frank and McEneaney 1999). Similarly, the scientization of the human life course formalizes the status and conditions of childhood, and sets the foundation for children's rights in labor laws, custody battles, and international educational aid (chapter 12 in Drori et al. 2003).

Causal relations between scientization and the expansion of social actorhood run both ways, and operate at both actor and cultural levels. At the cultural level, expanded scientific rationalization creates expanded models of proper human actorhood. For instance, the eighteenth century development of modern scientific analyses of the economy created an enormously expanded model of the competencies and responsibilities of the proper human actor, who became empowered and responsible to make the widest variety of rational choices about consumption, productive investment, exchange, and technical improvement. The same processes operate also at the actor level: the new and scientifically legitimated market society created incentives for actorhood competencies that were previously much less important, or even stigmatized. In a similar process, the human capital and human rights revolutions after World War II, with their scientific groundings, dramatize the triumph of actorhood.

In the other causal direction, expanded religious and secular conceptions of the role of human actors in society and state made an encyclopedic expansion of human scientific knowledge culturally proper and necessary. They also generated motives along these same lines for the emerging individual and state actors. For example, the expansion of genetic knowledge can help gay and lesbian activists refer to actual or potential genetic characteristics to establish their claims for recognition. Similarly, consumer or labor interests can refer to knowledge and analyses on their market positions as such market relations are elaborated on by economists. Overall, then, scientization supports the claims of actors, while the notion of actorhood encourages further investigation of knowledge on potential characteristics.

SCIENCE AS INSTRUMENT AND ONTOLOGY
FOR ACTORHOOD

Two kinds of ties link scientization and actorhood: instrumental and ontological interdependence. In conventional thinking, only the first is relevant. But, to understand the authority and cultural significance of science in the modern system, the second is more important.

On the instrumental side, much modern theory imagines that actors are rather complete, given, and naturally evolving entities. These entities/actors may lack needed information, or may demand information that expands their capabilities. Science and scientization meet such needs and provide knowledge required for actor functioning. Knowledge may improve the specification of goals (e.g., education, medicine, or economic survival), the analysis of resources and of means-ends relations (e.g., for efficient production), the overall analysis of the social and physical environment (e.g., mapping and taxonomies), and the ability to integrate and organize sovereignty and self-control (e.g., economic, organizational, and psychological capacities). As rationalized and rational individuals and collective actors behave and compete, demands for improved knowledge are crucial. Obviously, much modern scientific activity can be analyzed as responses to such social demands.

But it is a mistake to take competent agentic human actorhood as a given. Instead, it is necessary to recognize that cultural claims for this actorhood have been enormously inflated in the modern system. Political, economic, and social institutions rest on assumptions of actor capacity and competence beyond any plausibility. Similar expectations arise about organizations – and nation-states, which are now seen as a responsibility for all sorts of human progress and equity. Faced with this situation, there are great pressures for scientization, less as instrumentally valuable for given actors than for the validation of actorhood itself. This highly institutional or ontological (or expressive) function of science becomes overwhelmingly important in the modern actor-centric system.

Thus throughout the whole modern period, and perhaps especially in recent decades, even the search for nominally-instrumental scientific knowledge and competence clearly takes on more than instrumental meaning. Over and above the utility of great rockets going to the moon or delivering warheads, dramatic and symbolic elements that transcend ordinary social interests are present (which might benefit more from a mundane new fertilizer). The universal knowledge and capability of human actorhood are demonstrated, or highlighted, by such memorable quotes as " . . . one giant step for mankind." This and other demonstrations are ordinarily seen as emotional or expressive, but in our view might better be seen as reflecting the ontological role of science in the modern system.

Beyond this, much modern scientific activity cannot be seen as substantially instrumental at all. The current literature imagines that science has something of a life – at least, an inertial force – of its own, in an organized "natural curiosity," or a suboptimizing drive of the scientific establishment itself (e.g., Cole 1973). One can better analyze the global expansion of science by seeing it, in relation to human actorhood, as having an ontological role. During the modern era and more intensely during the twentieth century, science provides elaborated, rationalized, and more complete conceptions of the nature of things, including the nature of the human and organizational actors themselves. Science, thus, establishes a cosmos in which responsible and authoritative human actorhood is enhanced: (*a*) an eternal frame within which human actors exist, and (*b*) a demonstration of the all-knowing agentic competence of these actors.

This ontological dimension becomes more important if one sees the pretenses of human actorhood as deeply problematic. As much modern organizational theory emphasizes, human (and organizational) actorhood is constructed, fragile, filled with uncertainty, and very incomplete. The first problem of any legitimated modern actor is to create and sustain actorhood itself – not to act rationally and effectively. Brunsson (1989), for instance, makes it a central theme that modern organizations, in order to maintain their actorhood, often make decisions and act in ways that seem highly a-rational (e.g., in making decisions, they avoid wide-scoped searches and concentrate on only one alternative; see also March 1988, and Kahneman et al. 1982).

The link between science and human actorhood helps explain some of the distinctive features of science as it developed in, and integrated into, the modern educational system (McEneaney 1998; chapter 6 in Drori et al. 2003). Curricula and textbooks emphasize greatly and increasingly over time, general all-purpose value of thinking scientifically, and for the broadest range of individual human participants. They do not emphasize narrowly instrumental, technical, or disciplinary structures: the idea is to build in the child a strong human actor who is a sort of "participatory scientist," rather than a passive student who knows a lot of science and accepts it as a higher authority. Science is more a part of the umbrella of understanding for proper actors, than an instrument that they control (and that controls them); the form emphasizes participation.

An important role of scientization, in the modern system, is to sustain cosmologies – or abstract and general pictures of the wider universe – within which human social actors exist and maintain their universal status, or legitimacy, as agentic entities. Two aspects of this seem important.

First, there is a continuing concern with the location of the human actor in the wider lawful and rationalized universe. This involves, far beyond instrumental considerations, a concern with the fundamental nature of human social, psycho-logical, and physical life, and of the context of existence. Such are the fascinations with the linguistic, evolutionary and sociocultural pre-histories, including pre-histories of the earth, the solar system, and indeed the universe. It becomes important to know about the Big Bang, the existence of life on Mars, or the potential location of other intelligent life forms in the universe. It also becomes important to trace the evolution of the human species and its cultures. Decisions about such questions seem to have meaning, less for rational and instrumental action, but more for an understanding and stabilization of existence. It strengthens the ontological status of the rational human actor to establish the known and lawful character of all of nature, stretching out from the actor to infinity on every horizon.

Second, derived from religious origins and spiritual concerns, legitimated claims for the modern human actor involve the agency far beyond instrumental or realistic considerations. The human actor is, thus, assumed to hold the capacity for informed and rational knowledge, understanding, and action (Chapter 5). The "full" human actor, human or organization, is to have an extraordinary level of consciousness and the capacity for a conscious rational action on a universal level. Science clearly reflects this concern. It shows up in commitments to universal theorization, to an extraordinary emphasis on logical and mathematical formalization, and to an investigation of all sorts of questions as relevant to the achievement of true and universal theory (Toulmin 1990). It is, thus, important in constructing agentic human actorhood to establish, not only that the universe is a lawful and rational place, but that humans can and do figure it out: gratuitous displays of knowledge, information, and analysis help to do this (see chapter 6 in Drori et al. 2003, on the importance of "science as fun" in the modern school curriculum).

Both these ontological foci of scientific activity help explain why so much of modern scientific expansion occurs in culturally-focused, rather than instrumental, settings. Science is to be found in industry and in industrial research settings, to be sure, along with a variety of instrumentally-oriented special institutions. But its main place is in the rapidly expanding university systems of the world (Riddle 1989), and in the curricula of universal mass education (Benavot et al. 1991; Kamens and Benavot 1992). These locales support a broad and ontological, rather than narrow and instrumental, conception of science.

GLOBALIZATION, ACTORHOOD, AND THE DEMAND FOR SCIENCE

The contemporary period, especially since World War II, has involved a very great expansion in human social actorhood. Individuals have more recognized human rights (McNeely 1995, 1998). Nation-states (present in far greater numbers) take on greatly broadened rights and powers (Chapter 8). And, the formal organizations derived from these fundamental actors have greatly expanded their functions – to the rational management of personnel, legal matters, environmental concerns, safety matters, and research and innovation (Brunsson and Sahlin-Andersson 2000). Further, nation-state actorhood, organizational expansion, and the celebration of individual human status have become worldwide, extending to the whole territory and population of the world.

Behind this dramatic expansion in rationalized actorhood lie the forces that come under the common title "globalization." Many specific components of the general concept are involved. (*a*) The disasters of World War II brought individual human rights to global prominence (Rauner 1998; Lauren 1998). (*b*) The corresponding breakdown of colonial empires created a large number of independent and sovereign nation-states. Both the Cold War and the nuclear age called attention to the importance of the responsibility of these states for the condition of the whole world. (*c*) Economic integration, as reality and as myth, made the conditions of both states and human individuals matters of global relevance and significance. In all these ways, the situation called for responsible articulate actorhood, rather than raw Darwinian competition among mute powers. (*d*) The entire scenario was played out in the almost complete absence of anything such as an integrating and controlling world state (Wallerstein 1974 makes this a defining condition for the whole system). If any order were to be found and maintained, the actors would have to do it.

In this situation, many immediate purposes of many different parties expanded the demands and claims for the actorhood of states and individuals and all sorts of organizations in between. Groups internal to society had legitimate claims for equity and progress – the state was the obvious agent to respond to these. Similarly, in a world of high interdependence, states had every incentive to maintain their internal controls by assuming expanded powers. In the wider world, claimant social groups and states had every reason to insist on the expanded responsibilities of other states in the system to meet their obligations; few alternatives existed in the absence of the old (colonial) system or a new world state replacing it.

All these forces assembled in an exploding set of professions (Haas 1992 calls them "epistemic communities") and international organizations (Boli and Thomas 1999) during the period. These structures were not themselves agentic actors, with real line authority and with direct responsibilities for action. They can be discussed best as presumably disinterested "others" who tell actors what to do (Chapter 8; Meyer 1994b). Their existence generates expanded actorhood rights and responsibilities in the putatively real actors of the system. And the language they speak is principally the language of science, as every expert or consultant knows.

The expansion in responsible actorhood has clearly been reflected in the expansion of rationalized and scientized knowledge systems: as new domains are tamed by scientization, new arenas of rightful and responsible actorhood are created (e.g., in scientifically analyzed "economies"). All this has gone worldwide (see Schofer 1999a, b; chapters 4 and 5 in Drori et al. 2003).

There are, therefore, instrumental demands for scientific knowledge in all sorts of domains coming under the legitimate responsibilities of various actors: for everything from medical and psychological knowledge to population and reproductive control to information systems, environmental understanding, and production technologies. As more and more domains of human life are rationalized in terms of the rights, responsibilities, and powers of human actors, instrumental pressures for scientization process are increasing. Such pressures result in an explosion of scientization, with more intense penetration of particular domains and extension of it across domains. As rationalized, or scientized, society (and its related feature of collective actorhood) expands, science becomes socialized in a well-known sense, applied to the widest variety of issues, and scientific organizations proliferate at both national and world levels.

By itself, this instrumentalized use of science leads in some analyses, to a taming and debasement of true science. In other analyses, it leads to the penetration of society by a scientific leviathan, and a subjection of society to instrumental reasoning. Either way, these lines of thought leave out the cosmological or ontological side of the science/society relationship, and thus mistakenly describe what is happening. Pure theory does not disappear into application: it is reinforced by the demands of the empowered modern human actor for ontological status as an entity in the universe and as a rational "knower" of the universe. Thus every step in the expansion of human actorhood produces both an expansion of instrumental science (the technical gadgetry of applications) and an expansion in cosmological, universal, and logical/mathematical theorization. The same human actors who now take an interest in scientifically managing the details of diet, administration, and poverty, now also avidly support massive expenditures for the study of miles of Antarctic ice, of theories about the origins of both humankind and the universe, and so on. The instrumental scientific rationalization of the human actor and his/her environment is accompanied by the ontological quest for understanding of when the sun will burn out.

Key indicators of the "ontological" rather than instrumental status of modern expanded science, as noted above, can be found in the fact that so much scientific expansion occurs in educational systems, with their diffuse foci. For instance, it occurs in the educational and public attention given to scientific discoveries of extraordinarily little instrumental significance: the discovery that a species of crow can make and use tools may be relevant to ontological questions about the human condition, but is not likely to lead to increases in the gross national product.

GLOBALIZATION OF SCIENCE

We discussed above ways in which globalization in the contemporary period expands the responsibilities and rights of agentic human actorhood (at several organizational levels), generating enormous demand for science of all sorts to provide accounts of both actor and the tamed environment permitting rational action. But of course, globalization also works to supply scientific expansion meeting – but also creating and enlarging – the demand. Thus Haas' (1992) epistemic communities of experts both respond to and create international agendas for expanded actor responsibility (e.g., for air and water pollution, or for global warming, or to control child labor). And the greatly expanded set of international organizations formed in the current period, often relying on scientific presumptions, works the same way (Boli and Thomas 1999), simultaneously generating supply of and actor demand for scientization. Through both broad routes, an explosion in globalized scientific discourse and activity is produced (chapters 3 and 4 in Drori et al. 2003).

Science, throughout its history, has a universalizing character. In the contemporary period, it has achieved effective global status. The abstract commitment to science, in general, transcends variations in time and space that might generate variations in rational or functional investment patterns. Science – and science in general – expands rapidly not only in developed core economies and societies, but in the Third World too. Scientific activity expands, in fact, in every sort of country worldwide (see chapter 9 in Drori et al. 2003). Scientific practices, policies, organizational forms, and ideas proliferate worldwide.

First, there is the globalization of the scientific system. Scientific data, laws, and organizations are developed to apply everywhere in the world (and beyond). Biological and socioscientific knowledge, as well as physio-scientific knowledge, applies everywhere: it is understood to be useful everywhere, and to extend its ontology everywhere. The furthest tribe remaining has a society and economy that can be analyzed socioscientifically, and it exists in a biological ecosystem that can be analyzed scientifically. And the knowledge involved should in principle be applied everywhere, with appropriate policies. Thus, even very peripheral people and societies can and must develop properly within the "laws" of science. The dominance of this perspective helps explain the very rapid world-level expansion, in recent decades, of all sorts of international (both governmental and non-governmental) scientific organizations, with widespread participation from all sorts of countries (Boli and Thomas 1999; chapter 3 in Drori et al. 2003).

Second, there is an essentially universal extension of the scientific system itself into national-level societies. Almost every peripheral country now builds universities, which handle the great and expanding bulk of post-secondary schooling, in contrast to particular institutes that might be relevant to local functional needs (Riddle 1989). National states, operating under world-level encouragement, create governmental scientific establishments, and organize (at least formally or constitutionally) as if the principles of a universal knowledge system are locally empowered and authoritative (Finnemore 1996). Domestic non-governmental scientific organizations also expand greatly in the current period (Schofer 1999a). And, in every type of country – from richest and most economically complex to the poorest and most economically simple – scientific instruction is increasingly emphasized in mass education (Benavot et al. 1991; Kamens and Benavot 1992; chapter 6 in Drori et al. 2003). The researchers who study the question find essentially no economic correlates: the process is worldwide, and occurs in every type of country with the most minor variants (see chapter 9 in Drori et al. 2003, or Lee 1990, on the development of "Islamic science" in Malaysia).

Given the extreme international differences in available resources, it is not surprising that world scientific activity and production are dominated by the core countries. What is surprising is how much such scientific activity goes on in the furthest peripheries of the world, and how rapidly this expands.

CONCLUSION

Our overall argument on the way in which the modern globalized system has supported the expansion of scientific activity is illustrated in Figure 12.2.

As we have argued, science expands in the modern system as a secularized version of a "sacred canopy" providing a cultural base for expanded and now globalized human actorhood. Far beyond instrumental considerations, the perverse influences of the scientists themselves or of the products of natural curiosities, science provides a cultural umbrella sustaining the ontological status of the rationalized human actor. It defines a lawful and universal nature (including human social nature) in which the rationalized human actor can make sense, and it provides a system of knowledge that establishes the capacity of this actor for complete comprehension of, and access to, this nature.

This suggests that the science that spreads around the world is quite homogeneous in content or focus – since it relates to general abstract principles and cosmologies rather than to particular functional problems. The available studies of worldwide scientific expansion reinforce this conclusion. Despite enormous economic and cultural variation around the world, general abstract models of actorhood and scientized environment are remarkably similar. Science curricula and textbooks in mass education are remarkably homogeneous, and change over time isomorphically (McEneaney 1998; chapter 6 in Drori et al. 2003). Standard models of science in the universities are worldwide. University enrollments expand in every type of country; this expansion involves growth in male and female enrollments, even in the sciences (chapter 8 in Drori et al. 2003). Similar general guidelines for science policy are institutionalized across national variations (Finnemore 1996), and the same domains of scientific research are to be found everywhere (chapter 9 in Drori et al. 2003).

Some cross-national variations appear: these seem to be related to the extent to which national societies support scientific activity beyond the narrower "hard science" base that might link most tightly to immediate functional drives for national development (chapter 10 in Drori et al. 2003). Western liberal countries seem

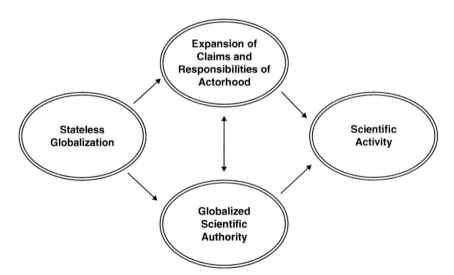

Figure 12.2. The global expansion of science: An institutional perspective

to support scientific activities in ways far beyond "hard science," with large socioscientific and medical research systems. Typical developing countries show a more limited range, particularly involving less social science research. Both Communist countries and some newly industrializing Asian countries dramatically emphasize "hard science" research (and presumably instruction) in fields such as mathematics, physics, chemistry, and engineering (chapter 9 in Drori et al. 2003).

Overall, however, a broadly defined scientific system expands and proliferates worldwide. It expands as a global system, and also as a highly penetrative one into every type of country. With science carrying both instrumental and cosmological/ ontological meanings, such global penetration is also highly consequential for nation-states worldwide. Science globalization alters their structure by establishing scientific institutions locally. Most importantly, it changes their nature by allowing its rationale to become the axis of their social life: from defining the relationship between social and natural, to rationalizing social explanations and claims, and ultimately empowering all forms of actorhood.

REFERENCES

Abbot, Andrew. 1988. *The System of Professions*. Chicago: University of Chicago Press.

Benavot, Aaron, Yun-Kyung Cha, David Kamens, John W. Meyer, and Suk-Ying Wong. 1991. Knowledge for the Masses: World Models and National Curricula, 1920–1986. *American Sociological Review* 56:85–100.

Ben-David, Joseph. 1990. *Scientific Growth*. Berkeley: University of California Press.

Boli, John and George M. Thomas. 1999. *Constructing World Culture: International Nongovernmental Organizations since 1875*. Stanford, CA: Stanford University Press.

Brunsson, Nils. 1989. *The Organization of Hypocrisy*. Chichester: Wiley.

—— and Kerstin Sahlin-Andersson. 2000. Constructing Organizations. *Organization Studies* 21:721–46.

Callon, Michel, John Law, and Arie Rip. 1986. *Mapping the Dynamics of Science and Technology: Sociology of Science in the Real World*. Houndmills: Macmillan.

Cole, Jonathan R., and Stephen Cole. 1973. *Social Stratification in Science*. Chicago: University of Chicago Press.

Coleman, James. 1974. *Power and the Structure of Society*. New York: Norton.

Cozzens, Susan. 1997. The Discovery of Growth, in J. Krige, and D. Pestre (eds.), *Science in the Twentieth Century*. Amsterdam: Harwood Academic Publishers, pp. 127–42.

Ezrahi, Yaron. 1990. *The Descent of Icarus: Science and the Transformation of Contemporary Democracy*. Cambridge, MA: Harvard University Press.

Finnemore, Martha. 1996. *National Interests in International Society*. Ithaca: Cornell University Press.

Frank, David J. and Elizabeth McEneaney. 1999. The Individualization of Society and the Liberalization of State Policies on Same-Sex Sexual Relations, 1984–1995. *Social Forces* 77:911–44.

—— Ann Hironaka, John W. Meyer, Evan Schofer, and Nancy Tuma. 1999. The Rationalization and Organization of Nature in the World Culture, in J. Boli and G. Thomas (eds.), *Constructing World Culture*. Stanford, CA: Stanford University Press, pp. 81–99.

Haas, Peter. 1992. Introduction: Epistemic Communities and International Policy Coordination. *International Organization* 46:1–35.

Kahneman, Daniel, P. Slovic, and Amos Tversky. 1982. *Judgment Under Uncertainty.* Cambridge: Cambridge University Press.

Kamens, David, and Aaron Benavot. 1992. A Comparative and Historical Analysis of Mathematics and Science Curricula 1800–1986, in J. Meyer, David Kamens, and Aaron Benavod (ed.), *School Knowledge for the Masses: World Models and National Primary Curricular Categories in the Twentieth Century.* London: Falmer Press, pp. 101–23.

Krasner, Stephen D. 1999. *Sovereignty: Organized Hypocrisy.* Princeton: Princeton University Press.

Kuhn, Thomas S. 1977. *The Essential Tension.* Chicago: University of Chicago Press.

Lauren, Paul. 1998. *The Evolution of International Human Rights.* Philadelphia: University of Pennsylvania Press.

Lee, Molly. 1990. Structural Determinants and Economic Consequences of Science Education: A Cross-National Study, 1950–1986. PhD dissertation, Stanford University.

March, James. 1988. *Decisions and Organizations.* Oxford: Blackwell.

McEneaney, Elizabeth H. 1998. The Transformation of Primary School Science and Mathematics: A Cross-National Analysis, 1900–1995. PhD dissertation, Stanford University.

McNeely, Connie. 1995. *Constructing the Nation-State: International Organizations and Prescriptive Action.* Westport: Greenwood Press.

—— 1998. *Public Rights, Public Rules: Constituting Citizens in the World Polity and National Policy.* New York: Garland Publishing.

Merton, Robert K. 1973. *The Sociology of Science: Theoretical and Empirical Investigations.* Chicago: University of Chicago Press.

Meyer, John W. 1986. Myths of Socialization and Personality, in T. Heller, M. Sosna, and D. Wellbery (eds.), *Reconstructing Individualism.* Stanford: Stanford University Press, pp. 212–25.

—— 1994a. The Evolution of Stratification Systems, in David Grusky (ed.), *Social Stratification.* Boulder, CO: Westview Press, pp. 730–7.

—— 1994b. Rationalized Environments, in W. R. Scott and J. W. Meyer (eds.), *Institutional Environments and Organizations.* Thousand Oaks, CA: Sage, pp. 28–54.

—— and Ronald Jepperson. 2000. The 'Actors' of Modern Society: The Cultural Construction of Social Agency. *Sociological Theory* 18:100–120. Reproduced in Chapter 5.

—— John Boli, George Thomas, and Francisco O. Ramirez. 1997. World Society and the Nation-State. *American Journal of Sociology* 103:144–81. Reproduced in Chapter 8.

Perrow, Charles. 1991. A Society of Organizations. *Theory and Society* 20:725–62.

Rauner, Mary. 1998. *The Worldwide Globalization of Civics Education Topics, 1955–1995.* PhD dissertation, Stanford University.

Riddle, Phyllis. 1989. *University and State: Political Competition and the Rise of Universities, 1200–1985.* PhD dissertation, Stanford University.

Schofer, Evan. 1999a. The Rationalization of Science and the Scientization of Society: International Science Organizations, 1870–1995, in J. Boli, and G. Thomas (eds.), *World Polity in Formation.* Stanford: Stanford University Press, pp. 249–66.

—— 1999b. The Expansion of Science as Social Authority and Institutional Structure in the World System, 1700–1990. PhD dissertation, Stanford University.

Shenhav, Yehouda and David Kamens. 1991. The 'Costs' of Institutional Isomorphism in Non-Western Countries. *Social Studies of Science* 21:427–545.

Soysal, Yasemin. 1994. *The Limits of Citizenship.* Chicago: University of Chicago Press.

Toulmin, Stephen E. 1990. *Cosmopolis.* New York: Free Press.

Treiman, Donald. 1977. *Occupational Prestige in Comparative Perspective*. New York: Academic Press

Wallerstein, Immanuel. 1974. *The Modern World System*, Vol. 1. New York: Academic Press.

Wuthnow, Robert. 1987a. The Institutionalization of Science, in R. Wuthnow (ed.), *Meaning and Moral Order*. Berkeley: University of California Press, pp. 265–98.

13

Human Rights

World Society, the Welfare State, and the Life Course: An Institutionalist Perspective

Globalization is obviously a main theme in contemporary life and in current social scientific thinking. Attention to it occurs everywhere, but may be especially distinct in Europe, where the impact of supranational forces is intensified by the similar and parallel rise of the European Union and other regional institutions.

The various phenomena involved in globalization are widely understood to have strong impacts on individual lives and on the traditional – often national – social institutions thought to structure lives. In this paper, we develop the more specific idea that globalization is closely related to the "life course" as a modern institution and that education and social welfare systems are major factors in this process. By "life course," we mean much more than the distributions of patterns and sequences that describe individual roles and experiences in a society. We mean the institutionalized sociocultural organization of legitimate roles and expectations and perspectives. Thus in contemporary developed societies, an individual can expect and is expected to receive an education that develops both a self and a broad set of social rights for future roles. These roles are organized by institutions that support a whole set of individual perspectives (e.g., job satisfaction, security, and the like) and rights, and that lead naturally through a set of phases toward a socially protected retirement. What is especially distinctive about the modern life course, which we argue here comes under global scrutiny and (at least symbolic) protection, is its pronounced legitimation and organization of the subjective perspective of the individual. Life is supposed to make sense from the point of view of individual people, even more than such social groups as nations.

We approach the matter from the perspective of sociological institutionalism (Thomas et al. 1987). This means that we emphasize two themes that may be

This chapter is a revised version of a paper presented at the conference led by Lutz Leisering on the "Globalization of the Welfare State" at the Hanse-Wissenschaftskolleg (Hanse Institute for Advanced Study), Delmenhorst, Germany, February 6–8, 2004.

Work on the chapter was facilitated with support from the National Science Foundation and the Bechtel Center of the Institute for International Studies, Stanford University. The chapter reflects ongoing research with Francisco Ramirez and other colleagues in the Comparative Sociology Workshop at Stanford. The present version benefited from extensive and generous and detailed comments by and conversations with Lutz Leisering, whose efforts were supported by his fellowship at the Hanse Institute for Advanced Study.

different from the emphases in many discussions of the issues. First, we see global-ization as an institutional matter, not simply the rise of supranational economic and political forces. We see a whole array of world institutions – organizations and discourses – arising to articulately develop and expand models bearing on individual lives and perspectives. Second, we see the individual life course as itself a changing institutional or cultural construction, not simply a series of demographic events reflecting wider socioeconomic forces (as, for example, in Mills and Blossfeld 2003). The proper life course is, in other words, the direct focus of much regulatory and ideological attention, not a derivative consequence.

We begin by reviewing meanings and dimensions of globalization, and then consider ways in which these dimensions effect the social structuring of the life course. We review ways in which some classic life-course institutions are weakened and ways in which others are changed and strengthened. Expanding global society increasingly legitimates the structuring of the life course as built around the project of the individual's life and perspective, and decreasingly derives life-course rules from the needs, projects, and perspectives of corporate groups and national societies. In a sense, with modern globalization we are seeing the increased world-level develop-ment of institutionalized individualism (Meyer 1986).

MEANINGS AND DIMENSIONS OF GLOBALIZATION

The globalization of national societies

Most meanings of the term globalization reflect the idea that the national societies of the modern world come under sustained world influences. This may take the simple forms of expanded trade, but broader influences involving the direct diffusion of institutional arrangements, such as life-course patterns, are increasingly emphasized. The larger point is that, beyond simple economic interaction, the global models of what ought to be a proper nation-state tend to diffuse. Conceptions of society and state, in other words, do not simply reflect local economic and cultural arrangements and resources, but incorporate worldwide forms.

Economic Exchange. Most discussions of globalization emphasize relatively raw economic forces. And those that do so tend to see globalization as having some negative impacts on the institutions – particularly welfare state institutions – supporting the individual life course. There is the expansion of trade, particularly obvious in Europe. There are greatly increased flows of investment and technologies. In one way or another, labor is made subject to international markets. As a consequence, at least on some dimensions, there may be a competitive "race to the bottom," with the under-cutting of employment, incomes, and welfare protections – concern about such issues arises in all sorts of countries (Alber and Standing 2000).

Another consequence is particularly to be found in Europe, with its modern history of welfare state institutions. Here, "globalization" is also a discourse (some-times referred to as "neoliberal"), which stipulates the need for nation-states to deregulate their welfare states and the life course of their citizens in response to economic globalization. This involved the sense that Europeanization and globalization generate anomie, uncertainty, and deregulation. Whether or not there is deprivation, there are all sorts of normative inconsistencies of the kind that greatly activate legal and social scientific policy intellectuals. An American social scientist visiting Europe now can only with great difficulty avoid long excited normative or policy discussions on questions that seem arcane: What exactly are the rights of a Portuguese worker injured in France on the way to work for a Dutch construction firm in Berlin? Such legitimation crises are, with globalization, present everywhere.

Economic Institutions. Interpretations of globalization broaden if the term is understood to include, not simply raw economic variables, but the world economy as an institutional system involving extensive legal and cultural legitimation. The justifications of expanded trade and investment must ultimately resort to globalized conceptions of the rights of individuals (and globalized conceptions of societies) around the world. Global markets of a capitalist sort are substantially legitimated only if the participants can be seen as having equal status in principle. Thus in the world context as in earlier national and regional ones, the institutions (not necessarily the instrumental realities) of modernity and, in particular, its capitalist forms legitimate a great deal of individualism. This amounts to the "institutionalized individualism" of Parsons and Platt (1973) – with much social protection and regulation of the individual life course. This is done with much theoretical emphasis on the individual as competent and empowered choice- and decision-maker, since the capacity for choice is crucial to the legitimation of markets. In other words, whatever damage worldwide trading patterns may do to individual choice capacities, world economic institutional principles are designed to expand these capacities and to legitimate this expansion. Sometimes, as with the institutions of human capital, like education, effects seem fairly dramatic.

The Social Institutions of Modernity. But modern meanings of globalization go far beyond economic arrangements, whether these are seen as practical matters of trade or as institutional matters of legitimation. It has become clear that every social institution of modernity comes under global influences and spreads globally, particularly in the expansive post-1945 world. The sociological institutionalists have made this a main theme, with accounts of a world polity or society (see the reviews and citations in Chapter 8; Thomas et al. 1987; Finnemore 1996; Hasse and Kruecken 1999; Jepperson 2002). From a different background, the systems theory of society converges with institutionalism in this respect (see Luhmann 1997; Stichweh 2000). Centrally, all sorts of models of social progress and of individual development have spread pervasively around the world. The spread is not principally in response to the spread of socioeconomic development as the narrower economic theories suppose – it is a matter of direct constitutive influence. So it has long been known that the protective institutions of the welfare state spread (as political programs, often with the weakest implementation, given resource constraints) widely around the world (Strang and Chang 1993). And so, dramatically, do the more liberal institutions of expansive education, individual political and social participation, and the like (Meyer et al. 1992).

Liberal Dominance. The models of society that spread most dramatically, in the last half-century, have obviously been those celebrating the logics of expansive modernity. Such logics, carried by a variety of contending forces, all have at their core quite aggressive notions of the membership of the individual person in the larger society. Liberals, corporatists, and statists, from far right to far left, all see society (as well as, sometimes, other structures) as rooted in individual persons, and individual persons as deriving benefits from society. All construct citizenship, claiming to represent and attempting to control individuals. In this sense, all carry out versions of modern development and modernity that expand the recognition of, and control over, the individual life course (Jepperson 2002). Institutions managing every state of the life course expand from birth and infancy to old age and death. Stages and transitions come under inspection and control or regulation – more tangibly, not only in advanced welfare states but also in more market-oriented societies. The perspective of the individual, in one form or another, is increasingly celebrated.

But among the contesting forms of modernity, and hence of the institutionally constructed life course, one form has obviously had a good deal of precedence in the last half-century. One rightist alternative, fascism, was destroyed and stigmatized in World War II, and a left version, communism, in the Cold War. In noncommunist countries after 1945, statist structures were weakened in some measure quite deliberately (Djelic 1998). And the doctrinally liberal (but by no means what is now called "neo-liberal" with its raw economistic meanings) and individualist United States was quite hegemonic. The United States had much precedence with regard to military power and the ideals of freedom and democracy. So as the European welfare states developed, in good part on older European models, they tended to evolve in liberal formats, emphasizing human rights and individual development perspectives rather than older corporatist models.

Conclusion. The spread of the life-course institutions is by no means an accidental process produced by high rates of contact, communication, or exchange (Strang and Meyer 1993). It is highly intentional, purposive, and even driven, both from the sending side and the receiving side. As for the recipients of modernity, societies around the world, as they enter the nation-state system, aggressively pursue the institutions of modern rationalization and differentiation. And the institutions of the life course are central to their conceptions of the proper national society, as they indicate and produce both national development and the welfare of the people conceived as individuals and citizens.

The sending side of the diffusion of modernity is also strikingly aggressive. The world is now filled with all sorts of international organizations and professional associations who have, as main functions, the diffusion of the appropriate modern institutions (Berkovitch 1999; Boli and Thomas 1999, with regard to social policy Deacon et al. 1997; and many of the works of Kaufmann, e.g., 1986).

The rise of a global society

The overwhelming modern awareness that interdependencies of all sorts transcend the boundaries of national societies generates forms of globalization that go far beyond the enhanced diffusion of standard models of national society and state. They go beyond even the diffusion of models edited to fit more smoothly into a global interstate society (less warlike, less ethnocentric, more friendly participants in regional neighborhoods and world organizations, and so on). Increasingly, "society" and "polity" themselves come to be conceived, discussed, and organized at a global level.[1] This has great impact on both the global focus on the individual life course and on the way this life course is conceived and defined.

Statelessness. A commonly noted central feature of the rising world political system is its dramatic statelessness. Even its European regional counterpart, the European Union, though filled with organizational structures, lacks the properties of unity, sovereignty, and citizenship that are central to the modern national state. The direct impact on life-course institutions is clear. The world has no capability, and Europe has a very weak capacity, to build up the traditional styles of welfare protections associated with highly corporate nation-states. It is difficult to imagine state-like protections against unemployment organized at a global level or a traditionally structured world pension system. A certain amount of world welfare support exists, but until very recently advocated almost entirely on the ancient base of charity – notably "humanitarian aid" – not the modern one of welfare entitlement. Lacking a state, a world welfare state of a sort highly structured around statist or corporatist traditions is not plausible. As we observe below, many traditional notions of welfare survive and indeed expand globally, but they do so justified by foci on expanded individualist models and are appreciably altered in the process.

Welfare and the Nation-State. Further, the capacity of existing welfare states to operate is, as is often noted, undercut. We noted above that it may be undercut by raw economic forces of competition. Here, we need to add the point that the communal integration and sovereignty, on which the corporatist welfare state's legitimacy is based, is undercut. This is true in several senses. First, it is more and more difficult, and lacks legitimacy, to exclude foreigners from the rights of membership in the national family (Soysal 1994). Second, it is difficult to sustain the unique definitions of national culture and virtue required to support the closed national system. People have more and more human rights, defined exogenously. They can resist the restrictive classificatory efforts of the welfare state and can demand new rights and resources. The national bureaucracies and professional establishments (e.g., medicine) can no longer so successfully impose their definitions and procedures. Closed and exclusionary definitions of proper education, health, welfare, age-related rights, and so on lose power and legitimacy.

Universalism. Stateless global society, as it expands, rests on and reinforces universalistic definitions. Science gains authority (Drori et al. 2003). So do social scientific principles of rationalization (Sahlin-Andersson and Engwall 2002; Drori et al. 2006), which recently come to the fore in the institutional design of social security systems as propagated by international policy consultants and international

---

[1] Sociological systems theory assumes that today there is only one society, the world society (Luhmann 1973).

organizations. And at the center lies not the national state or corporate society, but rather the expanded human individual (Ramirez and Meyer 2002). This theorized person has an enormously expanded set of rights. The rights are held as a natural human being, not the citizen of any specific enterprise. The rights are claims, not simply against some state authorities, but in principle against the whole world. And in fact claims based on human rights are now routinely addressed to the world in general, through international courts and organizations, nongovernmental organizations, and the global media.

Thus, given the global statelessness and the weakening of the sovereignty of national states, globalization intensifies models rooted in an expansive individualism. The individual involved is less an entitled beneficiary of a national (or other) community and more depicted as a proactive project and perspective of his own. This has powerful effects on the expansion of social regulation of the life course and on the character of that life course. Life-course institutions of liberalism are intensified, and those reflecting more corporate welfare arrangements are weakened or rearranged in more individualistic formats.

IMPLICATIONS OF GLOBALIZATION FOR THE INSTITUTIONALIZED LIFE COURSE

We reviewed, above, a variety of dimensions of modern globalization, with an eye to assessing their impact on life-course institutions and arrangements around the world. This review, essentially, supports a set of core ideas about how these institutions are changing.

General effects

First, almost all the changes associated with globalization move the individual person toward the center of the social stage and weaken the corporate or communal groups (e.g., familial) in which the individual might previously have been seen as embedded. Much associational life, including a reconstructed and individualized family life, remains and intensifies, but obviously the dependencies associated with corporate family and community are undercut at every turn. We live in societies of vastly expanded organizational structures, but these organizations are rationalized and are structured in terms of individual persons rather than corporate groups.

Second, while social controls increasingly reach down to reflect and affect and incorporate individual persons, the forces of globalization tend to reinforce the legitimacy of the individual's perspective as a project. The global individual is a choosing entity – an actor – with purposes and interests of his own. Many social situations are properly evaluated as they reflect interests and purposes of the individual: for example, the interests of the family have less legitimate opportunity to block a divorce (or an abortion), and the interests of the autonomous divorcing individual have much more standing, worldwide, than in the past.

Third, while all sorts of institutions around the individual make gains, those associated with the liberal model of the active, autonomous, choosing individual gain special strength, while those associated with the individual as protected welfare beneficiary of strong corporate or collective processes lose relative strength. This involves two shifts: First, some structures, such as education, gain much prominence. Second, many life-course structures, such as health institutions, change character to reflect changed models of the individual and the life course. Changes of this sort are endemic in the modern system: welfare arrangements focus on individuals in new ways, but so do educational systems, career mobility patterns, retirement arrangements, and so on.

Thus the forces of globalization create a period with an enormous explosion of human ideas and standards – structured at the world level – organized broadly around human rights ideas (Ramirez and Meyer 2002). Goals that might once have been phrased in terms of the collective goods of societies are now organized around the life courses of individuals, and individuals seen as projects of their own. Thus traditional welfare arrangements are reconstructed around conceptions of an active choosing individual, and the "state" of the welfare state loses much of its dramatic corporate character. The modern welfare state becomes a service organization trying to carry out global norms.

In the following sections, we look at implications and concomitants of globalization in specific institutional areas.

Schooling

Educational Expansion. Heidenheimer (1981; Flora and Heidenheimer 1981) developed a classic distinction between countries modernizing with an emphasis on educational expansion – with the individual seen as the central actor in progress – and those emphasizing welfare arrangements in which the collective society is the central actor and the individual a beneficiary. While liberal globalization, as is well known, has put barriers in the way of traditional welfare systems, it has helped produce an explosion in educational enrollments. This explosion characterizes every educational level from kindergarten through postdoctoral study. It characterizes the whole world, every type of specific country that can be identified, and the whole past half-century. A number of studies, using worldwide data from UNESCO show the dramatic increases in primary and secondary schooling, such that over ninety per cent of the world's children spend appreciable time in schools (for analyses, see Meyer et al. 1977, 1992). A current project analyzes the explosion of enrollments, over the last half-century, in higher education (Schofer and Meyer 2005). It turns out that these enrollments, in every type of country, expand by factors of ten and twenty over the period. So a typical Third-World country has higher educational enrollments than those of Germany, England, or France thirty years ago. Something like twenty percent of an age-cohort, worldwide, experiences higher education – a figure unthinkable a few decades ago. Thus, in a global society built around individuals, education becomes – for individuals and countries alike – an expansive format for improvement.

Nonformal Education. Aside from the formal educational system, there is a world-wide explosion in foci on training. Lifelong learning is a main theme, and training is to be found in all sorts of settings from firms to government offices to the personal-development marketplace (Jakobi 2006; Luo 2006).

Educational Foci. Over and above the general expansion of education, we may note features of the educational system that reflect global liberalism, or the expansion of life-course institutions focused on the perspective and development of individuals. A major loser, worldwide, is vocational training in the narrow sense (Benavot 1983). Education, even in firms, is now increasingly organized around logics of personal choice and personal development (Monahan, Meyer, and Scott 1994; Luo 2006).

This is strikingly true of the development of the formal educational system, worldwide. The great fear that this system would develop simply as an instrument of the political or economic Leviathan has turned out to be quite misplaced. Educational systems expand general, not technical, training. They increasingly organize curricula around individual choice and participation, and extend such forms to earlier and earlier phases of the mass educational cycle. They emphasize active participatory learning of a student-centered sort and decreasingly focus on developing knowledge of canonical sorts. In science, for example, instructional changes worldwide deemphasize highly disciplinary forms, deductive forms, and the elaboration of formal or technical knowledge: they now emphasize student involvement, participation, interest, and choice (McEneaney 2003). The whole effort is to appeal to the student's interest and understanding, not to the subordination of the student to the canonical requirements of science as a priesthood.

Similarly, as is well-known, modern instruction in the humanities (arts, literature, music, and language) decreasingly emphasizes any sort of canonical cultural knowledge and increasingly emphasizes individual choice, participation, and the equality of cultures. As Frank and Gabler (2006) might suggest, lower proportions of educated people know who Rembrandt is, and more have painted a painting.

Along the same lines, Frank and Gabler note that the great expansions in modern university systems have been in social science, not technical, areas. And of course, those social sciences grounded in liberal individualism have been the biggest gainers.

Education as a Global Human Right. For many years, education has been seen as a right of citizens and a responsibility for the virtuous state to provide. External forces, such as international nongovernmental organizations, might push states to assume their responsibilities. And they could criticize negligent states as defective, especially if these states had made (as has been common) abstract commitments to universal education.

In recent decades, globalization has produced the "Education for All" movement, defining universal education as the right of all and the responsibility of all to support. All states are to provide it, and all other states and people have to drive them to do so. Massive social efforts around the world are made to fulfill the dream involved.

In very recent years, an even newer movement has arisen to set out the goal of "Universal Basic and Secondary Education" (Bloom and Cohen 2002). So even secondary education, until the last few years a program for a minority of the world's children, is now to be universalized. And again the right and responsibility to carry out this mission is explicitly global in character – all of us, apparently, are to have the responsibility to require all others, no matter what state they are located in, to have access to education through the secondary cycle.

The organized career

Entry. Associated with the enormous global expansion of education, larger and larger fractions of the occupational system are linked to educational attainment. The relative decline in strictly vocational education does not imply that education is less relevant to occupational attainment. The regularization of the education–occupation link, always under the purview of organizational rules, and often under the rules of the state, directly implies an increase in the social management or structuration of the life course. The individual, formally, chooses educational roles to an increased degree, and subsequently may have something like enhanced choice of occupational positions, but all this occurs under regulation. Certain jobs are inappropriate for persons with certain educational levels and lie outside the choice process. So more and more choice may be created, but more and more social regulation arises over the choices.

Organization of the Occupational Career. Globalization involves and produces a great expansion in the organizational structuring of society. Every sector, from education to health to production systems to government services, is more organized than in the past. And the organizations involved look less and less like traditional bureaucratic structures built around the authoritative control of collective goods. Bureaucracy declines and evolves into modern formal organizational systems (Brunsson and Sahlin-Andersson 2000; Drori et al. 2006). These modern organizations are rationalized structures built around the participatory roles of individuals, more than simple hierarchical forms carrying down what Weber called imperative authority. The modern form assumes an active participatory individual, not a passive member of an occupational community.

With these changes, more and more elaborate career choices and sequences can be identified and articulated. Individuals can formulate plans and prospects, and calculations become possible that once would not have been considered. They are, thus, individuals-as-projects, with active rights and obligations of participation. Similarly, organizations can produce articulate plans and programs (e.g., training, counseling) around individual career sequence prospects. And states can create rules defining appropriate processing rules (e.g., grievance procedures, rules for meritocratic decision-making): in some respects, these rules come under international human rights scrutiny too. Note that in all these matters, the individual's own choices and perspectives are to be taken into substantial account: the shift from bureaucracy to organization is a shift from decision-making about collective needs to decision-making about matters that involve personal development and choice considerations. The shift involved can be found, more or less globally, in every type of organization – schools, business firms, governmental agencies, health and welfare organizations, and so on. And criticisms of organizations of these sorts are more likely to involve complaints about the slowness with which the now-required changes have taken place, not the extreme character of the actual changes. Theoretically, here, we are discussing the shift from "manpower planning" perspectives toward occupational structuring and allocation to "human capital" perspectives. And within the human capital tradition, the further shift from objectified and technical notions of this capital (as social resource) to increasingly social and cultural and now psychological notions centered on the perspective of the individual person.

The effects on the individual person are to legitimate expanded self-oriented, articulated planning-like activities (Giddens 1991). Schneider and Stevenson (1999) provide useful statistical data, showing the extraordinary expansion in the articulateness and complexity of American teenagers' reflections of their futures from the middle of the twentieth century to its close. These authors emphasize the extraordinary optimism involved, and the likely anomie involved resulting from the inevitable failures (they are reporting on a world in which the typical young person articulates planful hopes far beyond any realistic possibility). In our discussion here, we emphasize a different aspect of the matter: the fact of the legitimated articulateness itself (not its realism). The lives of the young people are discussable in universalistic terms. They can be discussed by the young people themselves. And they can properly be discussed by these young people in terms of their own desires, plans, intentions, and choices.

Retirement. In the same way, obviously, modern occupational sequences more often end in formal retirement, and the organizational rationalization generated by globalization expands its scope. More traditional pension arrangements are often expanded but are modified to take into account the expanded and choice-laden empowerment of the modern individual. This is a public phenomenon, explicitly and articulately structured around the individual's life course, and commonly incorporating the perspective of the individual and some of their choices and needs. Riley and Riley (1994) discuss this as involving a shift from constraints on the life course to the integration of that life course (around, naturally, the perspective of the individual person).

Identity

A striking feature of the liberal system is the organization of the identity as a property of the individual person (rather than collectives like families, ethnic groups, or nations). The abstract principles of human rights involved are well developed at the global level (Ramirez and Meyer 2002) and spread rapidly to national levels (McNeely 1995; Frank and McEneaney 1999). Modern identities are, to a much greater extent than in the past, (*a*) properties of the individual, (*b*) chosen by the individual, and (*c*) freely alterable by the individual through the life course (Frank and Meyer 2002). So the modern individual chooses (and may at any time rethink) not only a religion, but also, surprisingly, an ethnicity (Lieberson and Waters 1988; Snipp 1992), and in good part a gender identity (chosen, in principle, from a list that is longer than two). And of course, familial membership is also, increasingly, an individual choice – divorce is commonly legitimated, and the separation of child from improper parents increasingly protected.

At the high point of the national state, of course, the identity of citizenship and national culture was managed quite intensely (Weber 1976). With globalization, this has come loose too. It is easier to change national citizenships and common to maintain at least two (Jacobson 1996). National cultural identities are more difficult to enforce, now, and cultural and linguistic identities are increasingly a matter of individual choice. And they can be changed by choice through the life course. Thus, a French state that devoted enormous time and energy to standardizing language and culture, and eliminating peripheral languages and cultures, now provides schooled instruction in a good number of them. It is a global principle that states should do this.

In the same way, nationalism and national foci decline worldwide in school instruction, which now celebrates both global solidarity and local diversity and choice (Frank et al. 2000).

Note that the identity choices celebrated in the global system are commonly defined as global human rights – that is as rights to be protected, no matter what local state is involved, by everyone in the world. These choices, thus, are universalized and standardized in the global system. One cannot now properly choose to live in a country which restricts one's religious choices or those of one's neighbors.

Health

Welfare states, traditionally, make arrangements to protect health (as defined by the welfare state). But also in leading liberal states, notably in the United States, citizens often utilize health services at high rates (e.g., through market-like arrangements) and appear to have even greater faith than traditional welfare state citizens in the powers of medicine and science generally.

Globalization has seen a considerable expansion in individual's legitimate claims to, and apparent faith in, modern health institutions. And indeed, health is commonly recognized as a general global human right (Inoue 2003): the recognition was symbolic with the foundation of the modern WHO; but in recent decades, the claims have become more and more real and urgent. The AIDS crisis has intensified all this.

Concomitantly, the nature of the health claims legitimated in the modern world has shifted considerably. Inoue (2003) discusses the shifts in detail. Essentially, they are shifts from the traditional welfare state model, in which the corporate community (or medical authorities) define what health is, toward a more liberal model in which the individual person (the emphasis is often on individual women) defines health needs. And associated with this change is a dramatically increased emphasis on individual health education and public communication associated with individual health decisions. Health is thus seen from the point of view of the individual life course rather than the corporate community. Health concerns, in the traditional welfare state, focused on individual health, too. What seems to have changed is the active conception of the participation of the individual and the expansion of the conception of that individual as a central choosing actor in the pursuit of and definition of health.

Thus, the health sector changes character as it moves from a more national and welfare state focus toward a global system. Health comes to be seen from an individual perspective, as linked to the individual's own choices and life-course trajectory.

THE LIFE COURSE IN THE WORLD SOCIETY

Standardization and universalization

In all the areas discussed above, globalization – by weakening the charisma of the national state and strengthening that of the individual person – generates universalizing and standardizing forces. For instance, education becomes a general human right everywhere and is seen in roughly the same terms everywhere. So also with health, or human rights, or political participation, or subjective self-expression. Statistics can now be kept, and reported worldwide, on every aspect of the individual development and life course. Lives and life courses can be compared and are to be seen in, ultimately, the same terms.

So the same social system that elaborates the perspective of the individual, and the life-course choices to be made by that individual, also standardizes and universalizes both the individual and the choices involved. We can now know in detail, from almost every point in the world, the educational, health, political, or attitudinal states of the individuals involved.

Globalization permits the formulation of sweeping human social goals, and indeed, the United Nations has generated a variety of such goals. Interestingly, most of them are formulated in terms of the individual human life course. This is certainly the case with the classic human rights declarations, of course – dramatic statements about the political and civil rights of persons and the economic and social rights, too. More recently, we have the Millennium Development Goals, most of which also celebrate progress formulated in terms of the life course of individual persons (see http://www.developmentgoals.org):

1. Eradicate extreme poverty and hunger
2. Improve maternal health
3. Achieve universal primary education
4. Combat HIV/AIDS, malaria, and other diseases
5. Promote gender equality and empower women
6. Ensure environmental sustainability
7. Reduce child mortality
8. Develop a global partnership for development

Global liberalism

A core theme of this essay concerns the cultural and political meaning of the expanded liberal individualism that is spread by the global order of the last half-century. In many analyses (particularly those focused on the extremes of a revanchist neo-liberalism), the liberal system is about markets, markets are about exploitation, and the subjective freedom of market participants is reactive false consciousness. In the view put forward here, global liberalism has spread as a political, cultural, legal, and quasi-religious model of collective action and organization. The explosion of subjectivity in the modern world is legitimated (and on a global scale) and constitutive (also on that scale), and by no means a sort of neurotic mass reaction of individuals themselves. It is important to spell out the point.

We have focused throughout this essay on the global expansion of all sorts of individual-centered institutions historically associated with many forms of the welfare state. All these expanded rules of individual life-course choice and free variability seem, in some analyses, to be prescriptions for massive anomie and social disintegration. And this is a common theoretical picture of the freedoms of individualism in the modern world, following old critiques of "mass society" (e.g., Putnam 2000). This imagery is fundamentally mistaken, as it omits the core social controls of this kind of society. Such controls, classically celebrated by Tocqueville (2000 [1835]) and the Scottish philosophers (Silver 1990) and elaborated by the American social control theorists (e.g., Mead 1956; Cooley 1964) discipline the life course by disciplining the individuals who nominally steer it and whose perspectives are celebrated. Thus the nominally free American individual is under continuous pressure from an extended set of also-free peers and associations. These pressures, celebrated by the social control theorists, were recognized and bitterly criticized by generations of American artists and intellectuals, who could find real freedom only on the streets of Paris.

The idea is that the extraordinarily expanded agency of the modern individual is acquired from collective cultural sources and legitimated by them (Meyer and Jepperson 2000). Thus long years of socialization and discipline go into their construction – the expanded educational systems of modern societies both indicate and result from this.

Thus the choices individuals make must, under modern conditions, be presented with elaborate justification. Individuals are to pretend to be responsibly choosing individual persons, and to respect the individuality of others: naturally, this greatly constrains choices. Life-course choices (and all sorts of opinions) are to be made and justified responsibly, with reasonable arguments respecting the individual's own personhood as well as that of others. The individual is to be a coherent person over time, with calculated relations to a past and a future: the life course and attention to it as a project are increasing requirements.

As a consequence, in the modern system opinions and choices are a good deal more disciplined than might be expected – organized around the standardized and legitimated self infused with culturally conferred agency as a project (Chapter 5). Any individual, at any stage of the life course, may have a broader range of possibilities than in the past. And these possibilities may be somewhat more disconnected from particular social roles. But the overall variance is substantially constrained – the range of plausible motives, perspectives, and considerations.

CONCLUSIONS

Modern globalization, overall, has produced an enhanced focus on the individual and the individual's life course. This individual is decreasingly linked to the nation-state as a corporate structure and is increasingly seen as a legitimate member of the global community – a member with standard rights and responsibilities.

Further, the individual life course is defined from the point of view of the individual person, rather than the local or national society as a whole. The life course is not to be externally planned so as to fit into an orderly local or national community, but is to reflect the evolving choices and participation of the individual person himself or herself.

Thus, life-course institutions associated with participation, choice, and individual empowerment expand – education, identity choice, occupational choice, political participation, health choice, and so on. And some institutions, once organized around corporate social authority (such as traditional vocational education or classic health arrangements and institutions of the welfare state) reorganize around the participatory and choosing individual life course. The individual as a project, reflecting the dominant liberal tradition, is central.

Obviously, it is difficult to make assessment of how all this works out, and for whose benefit (if any) it redounds. The ancient arguments over the virtues of modernization in general, and the celebration of the individual in particular, are now repeated on a global scale. Do people (and which people) gain by the rapid spread of norms valuing the individual life course and the individual's perspective on the life course, or lose by the economic and political exploitations legitimated by their nominal empowerment? The point of our discussion is not to celebrate the benefits of the brave new liberal world. It is to call attention to two related phenomena: the public social emphasis on life-course issues in structuring social organization; and the public social legitimation of the perspective (and choices) of the individual as centrally involved in the life course.

REFERENCES

Alber, Jens and Guy Standing. 2000. Social Dumping: Catch-up or Convergence? *Journal of European Social Policy* 10 (2):99–119.

Benavot, Aaron. 1983. The Rise and Decline of Vocational Education. *Sociology of Education* 56 (2):63–76.

Berkovitch, Nitza. 1999. *From Motherhood to Citizenship*. Baltimore, MD: Johns Hopkins Press.

Bloom, David and Joel Cohen. 2002. Education for All: An Unfinished Revolution. *Daedalus* 131 (3):84–95.

Boli, John and George Thomas (eds.) 1999. *Constructing World Culture*. Stanford, CA: Stanford University Press.

Brunsson, Nils and Kerstin Sahlin-Andersson. 2000. Constructing Organizations: The Example of Public Sector Reform. *Organizational Studies* 21 (4):721–46.

Cooley, Charles. 1964. *Human Nature and the Social Order*. New York: Schocken Books.

de Tocqueville, Alexis. 2000. [1835]. *Democracy in America*. New York: Bantam.

Deacon, Bob, with Michelle Hulse and Paul Stubbs. 1997. *Global Social Policy*. London: Sage.

Drori, Gili, John Meyer, Francisco Ramirez, and Evan Schofer. 2003. *Science in the Modern World Polity*. Stanford, CA: Stanford University Press.

—————— , and Hokyu Hwang (eds.) 2006. *Globalization and Organization*. Oxford: Oxford University Press.

Djelic, Marie-Laure. 1998. *Exporting the American Model*. Oxford: Oxford University Press.

Finnemore, Martha. 1996. Norms, Culture, and World Politics: Insights from Sociology's Institutionalism. *International Organization* 50 (2):325–47.

Flora, Peter and Arnold Heidenheimer (eds.) 1981. *The Development of Welfare States in Europe and America*. New Brunswick, NJ: Transaction.

Frank, David and Jay Gabler. 2006. *Reconstructing the University: Worldwide Shifts in Academia in the 20th Century*. Stanford, CA: Stanford University Press.

—————— and Elizabeth McEneaney. 1999. The Individualization of Society and the Liberalization of State Policies on Same-Sex Sexual Relations, 1984–1995. *Social Forces* 77 (3):911–44.

—————— and John Meyer. 2002. The Contemporary Identity Explosion. *Sociological Theory* 20 (1):86–105.

Giddens, Anthony. 1991. *Modernity and Self-Identity*. Cambridge: Polity Press.

Hasse, Raimund and Georg Kruecken. 1991. *Neo-Institutionalismus*. Bielefeld: Transcript Verlag.

Heidenheimer Arnold. 1981. Education and Social Security Entitlements in Europe and America, in P. Flora and A. Heidenheimer (eds.), *The Development of Welfare States in Europe and America*. New Brunswick, NJ: Transaction, pp. 269–305.

Inoue, Keiko. 2003. Vive La Patiente! Discourse Analysis of the Global Expansion of Health as a Human Right. Unpublished doctoral dissertation, Stanford University.

Jacobson, David. 1996. *Rights Across Borders: Immigration and the Decline of Citizenship*. Baltimore: Johns Hopkins Press.

Jakobi, Anja. 2006. The Worldwide Norm of Lifelong Learning: A Study of Global Policy Development. Unpublished doctoral dissertation, University of Bielefeld.

Jepperson, Ronald. 2002. Political Modernities. *Sociological Theory* 20 (1):61–85.

—————— 2002. The Development and Application of Sociological Neo-Institutionalism in J. Berger and M. Zelditch (eds.), *New Directions in Contemporary Social Theory*. Lanham, MD: Rowman and Littlefield, pp. 229–65.

Kaufmann, Franz-Xaver. 1986. The Blurring of the Distinction 'State versus Society' in the Idea and Practice of the Welfare State in F.-X. Kaufmann et al., (eds.), *Guidance, Control, and Evaluation in the Public Sector*. Berlin and New York: De Gruyter, pp. 127–38.

Lieberson, Stanley and Mary Waters. 1988. *From Many Strands*. New York: Russell Sage.

Luhmann, Niklas. 1997. Globalization or World Society: How to Conceive of Modern Society? *International Review of Sociology* 7 (1):67–79.

Luo, Xiaowei. 2006. The Spread of a 'Human Resources' Culture in G. Drori et al. (eds.), *Globalziation and Organziation*. Oxford: Oxford University Press, pp. 225–40.

McEneaney, Elizabeth. 2003. Elements of a Contemporary Primary School Science, in G. Drori et al. (eds.), *Science in the Modern World Polity*. Stanford, CA: Stanford University Press, pp. 136–54.

McNeely, Connie. 1995. *Constructing the Nation-State*. Westport, CT: Greenwood.

Mead, George Herbert. 1956. *The Social Psychology of George Herbert Mead*. Chicago: University of Chicago Press.

Meyer, John. 1986. The Self and the Life Course: Institutionalization and Its Effects, in A. Sorensen et al. (eds.), *Human Development and the Life Course*. Hillsdale, NJ: Erlbaum, pp. 199–216.

—— Francisco Ramirez, Richard Rubinson, and John Boli-Bennett. 1977. The World Educational Revolution, 1950–1970. *Sociology of Education* 50 (4):242–58.

—— —— Yasemin Soysal. 1992. World Expansion of Mass Education, 1870–1970. *Sociology of Education* 65 (2):128–49.

—— John Boli, George Thomas, and Francisco Ramirez. 1997. World Society and the Nation-State. *American Journal of Sociology* 103 (1):144–81. Reproduced in Chapter 8.

Mills, Melinda and Hans-Peter Blossfeld. 2003. Globalization, Uncertainty and Change in the Early Life Course. *Zeitschrift Fuer Erziehungswissenschaft* 6:188–218.

Monahan, Susanne, John Meyer, and W. R. Scott. 1994. Employee Training: The Expansion of Organizational Citizenship, in W. R. Scott and J. Meyer (eds.), *Institutional Environments and Organizations*. Thousand Oaks, CA: Sage, pp. 255–71.

Parsons, Talcott and Gerald Platt. 1973. *The American University*. Cambridge, MA: Harvard University Press.

Putnam, Robert. 2000. *Bowling Alone*. New York: Simon and Schuster.

Ramirez, Francisco and John Meyer. 2002. *Expansion and Impact of the World Human Rights Regime*. Stanford, CA: Institute for International Studies, Stanford University.

Riley, Matilda and John Riley. 1994. Structural Lag: Past and Future, in A. Foner, R. Kahn, and M. Riley (eds.), *Age and Structural Lag*. New York: Wiley.

Sahlin-Andersson, Kerstin and Lars Engwall (eds.) 2002. *The Expansion of Management Knowledge*. Stanford, CA: Stanford University Press.

Schneider, Barbara and David Stevenson. 1999. *The Ambitious Generation*. New Haven: Yale University Press, 1999.

Schofer, Evan and John Meyer. 2005. The World-Wide Expansion of Higher education in the Twentieth Century. *American Sociological Review* 70 (6):898–920.

Silver, Allan. 1990. Friendship in Commercial Society. *American Journal of Sociology* 95 (6):1474–504.

Snipp, Matthew. 1992. Sociological Perspectives on American Indians. *Annual Review of Sociology* 18:351–71.

Soysal, Yasemin. 1994. *The Limits of Citizenship*. Chicago, IL: University of Chicago Press.

Stichweh, Rudolf. 2000. *Die Weltgesellschaft: Soziologische Analysen*. Frankfurt: Suhrkamp.

Strang, David and Patricia Chang. 1993. The International Labor Organization and the Welfare State. *International Organization* 47 (2):235–62.

—— and John Meyer. 1993. Institutional Conditions for Diffusion. *Theory and Society* 22 (4):487–511. Reproduced in Chapter 6.

Thomas, George, John Meyer, Francisco Ramirez, and John Boli. 1987. *Institutional Structure: Constituting State, Society, and the Individual*. Beverly Hills, CA: Sage.

Weber, Eugen. 1976. *Peasants into Frenchmen*. Stanford, CA: Stanford University Press.

14

The Individual

The Profusion of Individual Roles and Identities in the Postwar Period

In recent decades, the individual has become more and more central in both national and world cultural accounts of the operation of society. This continues a long historical process, intensified by the consolidation of a more global polity and the weakening of the primordial sovereignty of the national state. Increasingly, society is culturally rooted in the natural, historical, and spiritual worlds through the individual, rather than through corporate entities or groups. The shift has produced a proliferation and specification of individual roles, accounting for what individuals do in society. It has also produced an expansion in recognized individual personhood, accounting for who individuals are in the extrasocial cosmos and fueling elaborated personal tastes and preferences. Where it has been contested, the shift to the individual has also produced a rise in specializing identities (e.g., in such domains as ethnicity or gender). These offer accounts of individuals' distinctive linkages to the cosmos, and they serve to bolster individual claims to standard roles and personhood. Over time, special-izing identities tend to get absorbed into roles and personhood. And in turn, expanded roles and personhood provide further bases for specializing identity claims. Because many theorists mischaracterize the relationship of specializing identities to roles and personhood, the literature often overemphasizes the anomic character of the identity explosion and the closeness of the coupling between social roles and identity claims. On the contrary, specializing identities tend to be edited to remain within general rules of individual personhood and to be disconnected front the obligations involved in institutionalized roles.

Originally published as:

David J. Frank and John W. Meyer. 1998. The Profusion of Individual Roles and Identities in the Post-War Period. *Sociological Theory* 20: 86–105.

For comments on earlier drafts, we thank the reviewers of *Sociological Theory,* as well as John Boli, Mark Brogger, Frank Dobbin, Robert Freeland, Ron Jepperson, Georg Kruecken, Ann Swidler, Mary Waters, and participants in Stanford's Comparative Workshop. Direct correspondence to David John Frank, Harvard University, Department of Sociology. William James Hall 504. 33 Kirkland Street. Cambridge. MA 02138. E-mail: frankdj@wjh.havard.edu.

	Problems of location in society	Problems of location in the extra-social cosmos
Problems for nation-states	loss of corporate role, bureaucratization (Putnam, 2000; Bellah et al., 1996)	decline of corporate identity, conflict
Problems of persons	proliferation and rigidification of individual roles, the iron cage (Weber, 1978; Foucault, 1973; Tocqueville [1836] 1966; Riesman, 1950)	bloating and fragmentation of individual identities, anomie (Gergen, 1991; Giddens, 1991)

Figure 14.1. The problems of individualization

The individualization of modern society has been a main topic of sociological theory and research from the beginning, with primary attention given to the problems associated with individualization. These problems are seen to be of two general types: on one side, the expansion of a stultifying individual role structure, increasingly encaging persons in bureaucratic society, and on the other side, rupture of the individual identity structure, leaving persons anomic and unmoored in the cosmos.[1] The two problems are seen to feed each other, and they take form both at the level of the person and at the level of the nation-state. We array the positions in Figure 14.1, which shows the problems of individualization for persons and nation-states as they are located in both society and the extrasocial cosmos. For the nation-state, according to the literature, contemporary individualization means a dangerous weakening of corporate role and identity, opening space for heightened social conflict. The nation-state maintains organizational centrality, but it does so as a soulless bureaucratic individual role structure. For persons, meanwhile, individualization is seen to result in an overwhelming proliferation of roles and identities, the former tending toward defacing rigidity and the latter toward unbalancing fluidity.

While this depiction of individualization is undoubtedly useful – we use it to launch our argument below – it is distorted in important ways. In taking up the problematic aspects of the process with so much fervor, sociologists have painted a picture of individualization with more tension and turbulence than seems empirically to be accurate. Ordinarily, the elaboration and transfer of roles and identities to individuals (sometimes from nation-states and other corporate bodies) occur quite

[1] Roles refer to what one does in society, identities refer to who one is in the cosmos. In some social settings, the two are collapsed in an identity-role matrix, where who one is necessarily determines what one does. With modernity, we argue, the two are increasingly differentiated. And a core theme of this chapter is that contemporary identities and organized roles are sharply decoupled.

routinely, with great legitimacy, bearing few obvious signs of destabilization and, on the contrary, striking evidence of global integration. It is this argument we develop below.

THE DECLINE OF THE NATION-STATE
AND THE RISE OF THE INDIVIDUAL

In several respects, World War II and its aftermath sharply shifted the balance of legitimated actorhood from nation-states to individuals in every type of polity, advancing the individual as the main element of reality and thus primary repository of legitimate roles and identities.[2] This happened first as the defeat and utter stigmatization of fascism undermined many remnants of corporate collective identity, most particularly the nation-state. And it happened second with decolonization and the expansion of the nation-state system to the whole world. Many earlier forms of nationalism rooted in racial (natural), spiritual (religious), or historical claims (e.g., to primordial dominance of territories and populations) lost legitimacy. The new forms of nationalism – however strong – arose on the identities and needs and choices of individual persons, not of corporate societies. Thus even as nation-states grew organizationally, and increasingly penetrated society (Thomas and Meyer 1984), their corporate actorhood declined, and they decreasingly put forward corporate (e.g., religious or military) purposes of their own (Fiala and Lanford 1987). New and reformed nation-states presented themselves as associations of individuals, serving the public goods of societies composed of individuals, and they increasingly came to define themselves around the goals of progress and justice for their people as individuals. Thus, for example, Ministries of War (operations of the state) were increasingly transformed into Ministries of Defense (operations for the people) (Eyre and Suchman 1996).

The very same changes reinforced the generalized actorhood of individual human persons. The defeat of fascism, the fall of colonialism, and the conflicts of the Cold War made for a dramatic rise in the cultural centrality of individual

---

[2] In Western history, the fundamental entitivities occur in several forms. A medieval system organized them around an opposition between celestial and fallen realms, at both individual and collective levels (Swanson 1971). Over time, the rise of democratic political, capitalist economic, and scientific cultural institutions reshaped this older system, promoting the legitimation of (a) the individual person, developing into a citizen, and (b) the corporate collective community, developing into a nation-state (Hall 1986; Mann 1986). Individuals acquired enhanced standing as citizens in increasing domains (Marshall 1948) and gained personhood on economic, political, and socio-religious dimensions (Meyer et al. 1987). At the same time, societies acquired standing around nation-states, with nationalist histories, ethnic identities, and spiritual ties. They became the central actors in history (Frank et al. 2000). Between individuals and states, each with identities legitimating action, other former or potential loci of human identity are weakened (Beck 1992). Occupations, organizations, and family systems all lost most of their direct ties to spiritual or natural forces (e.g., Ramirez and Meyer 1998; Ramirez and McEneaney 1997). The whole process leaves individuals and nation-states as the primordial entities.

rights, and for the formulation of these as "human" rights claimed in the world as a whole, rather than "citizenship" rights claimed against particular states (Brubaker 1996; Lauren 1999; Soysal 1994). It is now the sociocultural obligation of authorities great and small to protect an enlarged set of rights of individual human beings everywhere. Modern discussions of the matter call attention to the differentiated perceptions of the individual rights accorded, by dramatizing the number of failures in implementation. The heightened modern awareness of human-rights implementation failures, characteristic of social theory and research in their normative roles, probably lowers attention to the extraordinary expansions in the acknowledged rights themselves.

Economic and cultural changes under way in the postwar period have reemphasized the same shift. The continuing globalization of free-market capitalism chips away at the actorhood (and thus identity base) of the nation-state, even as it enhances the individual (Sassen 1998). Likewise, the globalization of culture and the world-wide expansion of mass education have spread knowledge across nation-state borders and into individual depositories (Giddens 1991; Meyer, Ramirez, and Soysal 1992).

In all of these ways, the individual became more central as the fundamental cultural locus of social membership and identity after World War II, and the primordiality (if not the organizational centrality) of the nation-state and other corporate entities declined. Out of these two shifts, a new model of society and identity has developed, mainly based on the individual. Consider the core institutions of any modern society, and the ways constitutional changes around the world have altered the depiction of them. What is the modern economy? It is by definition the product of the needs and choices (based on prior utilities and thus identities) of individuals as workers, investors, inventors, and consumers, and it is meant to benefit this society of individuals (rather than, e.g., the autonomous goals of the state). And the modern political system? It is tamed from primordial status (by which we mean rooted in religious or natural reality rather than seen as socially or culturally constructed), and is instead made to reflect the choices of the public of individuals, and to serve the needs of this republic. The modern cultural and religious system? It is meant to transform the collective rules and edicts of faith into sovereign individual choices and needs, based on personal understanding and experiential verification (Wuthnow 1988; McEneaney 1998).[3]

---

[3] It is probably not essential for a human community to account for itself – to elucidate its origins or explain its functions. The practical facts of interdependence and communication, without much theorizing, may be functionally sufficient. But many societies, perhaps especially more complex ones, do contain self-referential explanatory accounts, to be used in collective mobilization. Potentially, they come in many forms. Since Jaspers's "axial age," modern civilizations tend to explain themselves in terms of identities, which root society in a natural, spiritual, and historical cosmos (Eisenstadt 1986). According to many authors, Western culture draws especially sharp boundaries between society and this cosmos, stripping the gods, nature, and even history of virtually all capacity to "act." The division mobilizes society, while taming and demystifying the environment in which society finds its motives, identity, and power. This means that in the modern West, unlike in many settings, humans and human society are constituted as *actors* against a lawful natural, spiritual, and historical backdrop (Chapter 5).

Many observers have criticized these shifts as both reflecting and opening a Pandora's box of privatized, anomic, willful, and conflict-laden individual claims, and as destroying capacities for collective action through, for example, the culturally unified and sovereign nation-state (Bellah et al. 1996; Brown 1987; Putnam 2000; Schlesinger 1992). This view underemphasizes a third great change in the status of the individual. Even as the modern system undermines the primordial sovereignty of national (and other) collectives, it asserts global solidarities. Individual rights are human, not citizen rights, and they amount to claims on the whole world society. They are accompanied by individual responsibilities to respect the human rights of others on a now-globalized basis, and both governmental and non-governmental associations concerned with the issues have grown exponentially (Smith 1995; Boli and Thomas 1999; Lauren 1999).

The society to which the individual human belongs, with all its conflicts, has also importantly globalized – it has by no means contracted to the subnational level – and local claims (e.g., ethnic ones) are usually tightly linked to globalized models of entitlement and self-determination (e.g., Eade 1994: 388). Increasingly, the individual is seen as a member of a highly rationalized and scientized world: interconnected by the global ecosystem, overlaid by worldwide networks of production and exchange, permeated by international associations and organizations, and undergirded by universal (often scientific) understandings. The recent growth of "world society," the umbrella for all human beings, has been dramatic (Boli and Thomas 1999).

The statelessness of this world society adds fuel to the explosion of a globalized picture of both the individual and the individual's environment. Lacking the capacity to generate much positive world law, forces of social control push (often with ideologies that seem fairly extreme) for the recognition of "natural" laws – scientific, legal, and historical – that tend to reinforce the individual's unbreachable sovereignty. For instance, in the absence of much capacity for global lawmaking, those concerned with the human condition may try to develop a natural law about the developmental needs and essential rights of children in light of society's future: dependence on them (Chabbott 1999).

Overall, in an expanding and globalizing society of increasing complexity, corporate nation-state primordiality is weakened and the individual is strengthened as the central producing and benefiting entity at the beginning and end of all the elaborating steps of rationalization (Calhoun 1994). The redistribution of entitivity and actorhood to individuals in this way involves a tripartite expansion in the institutional structure. First, it gives rise to expanded and detailed individual roles in society, firmly linked to the rationalized collectivity (via, e.g., the gross national product).[4] The proliferating roles discipline individual choices, but they are justified in terms of broadened individual benefits and freedoms (and indeed they recast many

---

[4] Notice that, in contrast to some theorists (e.g., Appiah 1996: 79; Tilly 1996: 7), we sharply distinguish "identities" from "roles," and see the two as highly decoupled. The former describe the individual's place in the cosmos (nature, spirit, or tradition), while the latter describe the individual's place in society.

aspects of traditional control systems, such as religion, in terms of individual choices and needs). Second, in this way, rapid cultural, political, and economic rationalization also gives rise to the expanded authority of individual "personhood" – the master human identity generalized to a universal scale and imbued with elaborate rights – on which basis arises enormous cultural expansion in the legitimate range of free personal tastes and preferences.

These long-term processes – with individuation driving expansions in both the role structure and the structure of personhood – have heightened in recent decades, with globalization and the concomitant weakening of the primordiality (or distinctive identity and sovereignty) of more corporate units, such as the nation-state, the family, and traditional occupational and religious bodies. The individual person, bounded and authoritative, is increasingly culturally defined as the root element and primary actor in reality.

The third component of this wider cultural accounting system is the number of specializing identity claims that have received so much attention lately – of African Americans and women, Greek Cypriots and pagans – and that make the individual central in every sense (most recently transcending yet more completely the family and the primordial nation-state). Where cultural construction expands analyses of nature, history, or spiritual domains, or where the expanding general needs and rights of the individual confront a new or contested domain, identity claims arise – beyond universal personhood – to distinctive roots in nature or history or the spiritual world. These claims amount, for the most part, to dramatic assertions of the general needs and rights of individual personhood, and they are organized under individual (rather than corporate) rights. Specializing identity claims are not particularistic violations of expanded modern individualism, in other words, so much as new or contested fulfillments of it. As one Asian American wrote to Dear Abby: "What am I? Why I am a person like everyone else!" (quoted in Waters 1990: 159).

In the long run, successful identity claims tend to be absorbed into general personhood and routinized in roles in society (Gamson 1995). In this way, the more exotic specializing identities, legitimized, become choices available to persons in general, and ultimately part of the fabric of rationalized society. For instance, over time Irish American ethnicity loses some of its identity-ness – i.e., its tight linkages to particular blood or heritage – and becomes a choice or taste within the realm of generic personhood. Waters (1990: 158) reports the following exchange:

> Q: Would you say that being Irish is important to you now?
> A: Well, I don't know. I have fun being it. I would not know what to say. I have never been anything else. I am proud of it, but I am not really 100 per cent anyway. And my husband, he doesn't have a drop in him and you should see him on Saint Patrick's Day.

Irish becomes a role an individual can play, and part of the general structure of personhood. Thus, in contrast to most theorists, we see the rise of specializing identity claims – in such areas as gender, religion, and ethnicity – less as reactions to individual role problematics or personhood crises (Gergen 1991) than as special cases of common underlying institutional processes. Identities arise concomitant with roles and personhood linking these to the wider cosmos.[5] And all three faces of modern individualism are highly cultural in character, rather than idiosyncratic outcomes of particular local situations. They are formed in very general or universalistic terms, occur in forms that are scripted worldwide, and are addressed to the wider world at large. Thus, in explaining their recent expansions, we emphasize the broad cultural changes that increase the overall legitimacy and supply of individual accounts, not just shifts in the experiences, interests, or opportunities of particular groups.[6]

THE EXPANDED INDIVIDUAL

We have described processes that put the individual at the center of the world stage – the central actor within society and the dominant locus of identity linkages to the extrasocial cosmos. These processes unleash forces that on the one hand free the individual to claim a widened array of personal rights and specializing identities. On the other hand, however, the very same processes incorporate and tame the more-liberated individual into an expanding human society.

Expanding the rationalized role structure

Despite Durkheim's early lead ([1893] 1964), social scientists in recent decades have given much more attention to the dramatic identity movements associated with modern individualism than to the more routine expansion of the ordinary fabric of modern society. Nevertheless, change in the latter area has been intensive and worldwide. Many more, and more specified, roles are available to individuals now than in the past.[7] Just as medieval societies elaborated their structures upward to the kings and gods, and just as earlier modern societies developed into technological

---

[5] All these processes seem to some observers most striking in the core liberal countries – the United States especially – where the individual already stands as the central-most author of society (Frank, Meyer, and Miyahara 1995; Jepperson 2000). In these countries, individual *choices* and *tastes* are legitimated as the driving force behind every aspect of economy, polity, and society. So the elaboration of personhood and of specializing identities emphasizes natural, spiritual, and biographical forces behind drives and choices – sometimes in ways that seem exotic. Identity expansion may be less extreme in societies retaining more collective and communal elements (Brubaker and Cooper 2000: 3), but while varying cross-nationally, the identity explosion is clearly a general phenomenon, affecting persons and societies throughout the world (e.g., Altman 2001). In part, we argue, this is because global integration moves virtually all countries toward more individuated models of the person and more individual-centered models of society.

[6] In sociology, the groups are usually based on race and ethnicity (e.g., Waters 1990; Nagel 1995), or gender and sexuality (e.g., Schwalbe 1996; Weeks 1996). Religion is still relevant (e.g., Wuthnow 1988), but as we note below, class and occupational identities are the foci of fewer claims and less attention.

[7] To the extent to which most theorists have considered individual roles in relation to identities, they have envisioned a tightly coupled opposition – a dominating machine against which individuals struggle to maintain "identity" (see Gleason 1996). In contrast we see a complementarity – an elaboration of society around individuals in the form of roles, and an elaboration of the cosmos around individuals in the form of identities (Meyer et al. 1987).

detail, so modern societies reach down and elaborate around the individual. More occupational roles are created, as are more dimensions of education, training, and aspiration (Stevenson and Schneider 1999). Family roles are articulated, with detailed instruction and legal regulation (e.g., of spousal abuse) on how to manage newly liberated desires and choices (Frank and McEneaney 1999). Informal recreational activities are formalized, so that one can take detailed lessons in the right and wrong way to golf or sing, and so that direct or indirect state subsidies are available for such activities as they are now incorporated into the collective good. Traditional religious and ethnic cultures are rationalized in role performances (on holidays, in particular) that can be taught in school and specified for any outsider in the press. The rationalized role structure generally expands.

As the process goes on, the roles that emerge are differentiated from the traditional identity-role matrices in which they may once have been located. For example, in order to motivate recreational role activities, such as skiing, one no longer needs to evoke heroic nature, Nordic heritage, or any other identity. A bit of taste will do. Similarly, as many have noted, occupational roles have become mostly disconnected from the more diffuse identities involved in a class or estate structure, or even a national one – so that there are ways to be a good schoolteacher, but less and less a good German or Irish one.[8] Individual identities enter into the rationalized role structure as a matter of empirical practice, but their influence is very much muted in the cultural accounts given (Schleef 2000). Thus it is increasingly hard for a person with the identity of "woman" to say she plays the role of "housewife" because "that's what women do." The identity-role accounting, invoking the woman/mother identity-role matrix, is illegitimate. The preferred accounting depicts the woman as a sovereign individual person with a taste for domesticity: "That's what I choose to do."

As the role structure reaches down to, and elaborates at, the individual level, an opened menu of activities becomes available – to work, play, strategize, and express (Stevenson and Schneider 1999). Within this elaborated role structure, however, a good deal of scripting occurs, with detailed specification of how to fulfill the various roles – to be a good teacher, parent, skier, or whatever. Individuals have increased possibilities for choice and decision in other words, but the rationalized system exerts much social control too. The rationalized role structure disciplines choices within a frame, leaving open domains of uncertainty about which roles to choose but providing more and more structure about proper ways to behave given the chosen roles. One can elect rather freely to be a schoolteacher or husband, but proper conduct once in such a role – guided by calculation or consultation with skilled professionals (Giddens 1991) – is more tightly constrained than in the past.

While the rationalized role structure thus limits some individual behaviors in something like Weber's "iron cage," it also affords substantial advantages in the forms

[8] Only a few occupational roles – e.g., those that are stigmatized (drug dealer, prostitute) and those that claim special inheritance (princess, psychic) – still link individuals to the spiritual, natural, or traditional cosmos, and thus furnish much identity.

of clarity, legitimacy, and often considerable social resources. If the rationalization of material from an old identity-role matrix eliminates excitement (as it has for lesbians and gays: see Epstein 1999; Plummer 1999), the process provides greatly enhanced social standing, the benefits of which usually outweigh the benefits of distinction. Thus, much effort is devoted to routinizing matters originally rooted in identity, with social movements seeking to legitimize themselves with incorporation into established role structures (Gamson 1995).

Thus, we argue that:

1. The greater the expansion and rationalization of society around the individual, the greater is individual role differentiation.[9]

This process is intensified by the increasing cultural dependence on the individual person as the modern source of all meaning and action (in contrast, for instance, to the nation-state or the gods). As the individual becomes sacralized as the supra-societal wellspring – through ties to nature, spiritual forces, and history – individuals become the ultimate in almost every sense, and ultimately equal in their core personhood. In a complex and stratified modern system, this adds to the intensity of individual role differentiation. Because the modern system cannot justify variations in stratificational value in terms of "inherent" differences in personhood, stratification must be justified in terms of immediately rational functional and coordinative requirements. This takes place in much modern organizational structure, or in terms of rationalized principles of personnel allocation, as in the elaborated modern educational system (Meyer 1994).

2. The greater the emphasis on (equal) personhood as the identity root of society, the greater is role differentiation for individuals.

Thus we argue that the current period has seen a great expansion in the numbers and articulation of roles for individual persons, fueled not only by expanded social complexity but also by the increasing centrality of the equal individual as the foundation for all of society. We suggest that this expansion in the system of rationalized individual roles occurs in all institutional sectors (though more so in some than others): for instance, economic and occupational, religious and educational, familial and recreational. Vastly expanded models of society are in place, rooted in the roles of individuals.

Personhood and taste

In the course of expansion, the rationalized role structure tames many alternative courses of preference and action into decisions and choices with correct answers: There are quite explicit rules, for example, on how to play the role of "professor" (Shils 1982). But the proliferation of rationalized roles does something else too. It

---

[9] This proposition and those that follow describe properties of a main cultural system that characterizes core countries and, increasingly, world society. It is this system that is our unit of analysis.

reinforces the status of the individual human being, and authorizes persons to have and exercise individual tastes (neither correct nor incorrect). Globalization, which empowers individuals under natural law and weakens alternative sovereignties, does the same thing with great force. As the ultimate producer and consumer of all social goods, the individual person gains extraordinary ontological standing, with legitimate tastes, interests, and needs: Consultants (psychologists, spiritualists, and school counselors) abound to help individuals cultivate and develop them.

Individual personhood is the standardized master identity of the modern system, celebrated worldwide in documents such as the United Nations Declaration of Human Rights and in global institutions such as democracy, the free market, and the psychological sciences. Personhood as an identity can be claimed on a global basis (obviously with varying effectiveness, but with little dispute about the moral validity of the claim). It is also defended at national and local levels, in institutions such as education, citizenship, and welfare (Rauner 1998). Personhood involves, in principle, an enlarged set of needs and rights and capacities to choose lines of activity. But there are, even in principle, constraints that involve accepting the personhood claims of others. One cannot validly claim, on the basis of spiritual or natural or historical virtues, to be more of a person than others, and in this way, modern globally legitimated personhood is distinguished from many traditional forms of identity, and in some measure tamed.

Personhood accords broadened *and equal* rights to choice and taste. For example, moderns can claim exceptionally varied tastes in food, unconstrained by religion, nationality, or class. Of course the rationalized role system constrains on some food preferences in the name of health and safety, but the ability to build a secure food stratification, with high and low cuisines, is very limited (cf. Ferguson 1998). Tastes, like personhood, are equal. The same principles hold with marital and other personal relationships – one advertises unique tastes, not standardized role performances, and one seeks matching uniqueness in partners (Buchmann and Eisner 1997). So also with music, art, and other cultural matters, which increasingly flout distinctions of high and low taste, and float rather freely in personal option pools (Peterson and Simkus 1992). Likewise occupations, which become choices or tastes rather than inherited or semi-obligatory matters connected to family or traditional class categories. And so also with nationality: The modern person must be careful not to claim much distinction on a national basis. All persons have more or less equal rights, and the special status of citizenship is weakened (Soysal 1994; Jacobson 1996). Choice maps, and the tastes to navigate them, are open.

The opened ranges are all justified on the basis of personhood – the master identity in the modern system – offering individuals dense ties to realms prior and external to the functioning society. In nature, the individual is Homo sapiens, a member of a single species with a long natural evolution, united with all other persons by way of deep biological (and in this sense, psychological) similarities. The individual human also has the same ultimate spiritual certification, equal before the moral law (and many international legal principles rooted in the natural law). In increasing measure, the individual human is also part of a shared world history (and national or civilizational distinctions are now muted – Frank et al. 2000). The general movement is toward a common and equal human identity shared by all individuals. Conflicts about this occur only at extreme margins – regarding the identity status of the fetus, the dying, and sometimes the extremely defective. Overall, we argue that:

3. The more the individual stands as the ultimate source and beneficiary of modern society, the stronger is the master identity personhood, which legitimates a wide array of personal rights, capacities, preferences, interests, and tastes.

The foundation of universal personhood, with its authorized needs and tastes, is produced rather directly as part of the cultural theory on which modern societies are built. Personhood is also produced indirectly, through the expansion of the rationalized role structure confronting individuals. Many of the choices and decisions of individuals are highly structured in a system that specifies correct answers (one may choose whether or not to smoke, but there is no question of what is right). But rationalization generates more taste-based alternatives, too. Occupational role activities are specified in great detail, but moderns may reasonably choose an occupation based on their taste. There are correct ways to play the role of a mother, and these are promulgated by education, laws, and other controls, but modern women may choose – on "personal" grounds of taste – whether to bear children or not (Berkovitch 1999). Such choices involve the promulgation of individuated needs and tastes:

4. The greater the expansion and differentiation of the rationalized role structure, the greater the development of the master identity personhood, with associated legitimate individual rights, capacities, needs, preferences, interests, and tastes.

Thus, in balance with the elaborated individual role system, a contemporary society generates an elaborated theory of individual personhood that legitimates and justifies enlarged individual tastes. Causality is reciprocal here – more personhood generates more roles, and more roles generate more personhood (Meyer, Boli, and Thomas 1987). Both components follow from overall societal expansion, from the rise of the individual, and from the deconstruction around the individual of more corporate entities.

The rise of specializing identities

The changes discussed so far – the elaboration of individual roles in society and the rise of the master identity personhood – represent the primary pathways of contemporary expansion. They provide a cultural account for practically all of the institutions of global rational society. For instance, they stand at the heart of "education for all," which provides individual access to all sorts of knowledge (Chabbott 1999). Likewise, they center the universal declaration of human rights, the worldwide celebrations of democracy and the free economy, and so on. Virtually all of this now-rationalized material is justified and motivated in terms of individual role demands and human personhood. And this has been the main development of individuation in the contemporary period – in most cases proceeding routinely, barely noticed by social scientists.

To these general trends, however, there are exceptions. These occur at the frontiers of individualization, reflecting disputes, conflicts, and transitions in the whole process, and they receive much attention. Conflicts and boundary expansions generate waves of identity movements around the claims of individuals demanding recognition of the legitimacy of their distinct properties.

Some of these specializing identity claims locate the individual in nature, from which a person may derive a wide variety of particular abilities, disabilities, perceptions, or desires, such as sexual orientations. Others root the individual in a spiritual or transcendental environment, including one or another god or essence, with associated qualities, needs, or preferences. Still other identity claims embed the individual in a unique tradition or history – ethnic, familial, or personal – which may be used to explain diverse particular individual properties or actions (e.g., as a "survivor" of one or another abuse or as an inheritor of a particular ethnic background). In all of these cases, the idea is that the self is more than a current action system, and is a special case of the standard individual person. The self, it is asserted, reflects a pattern institutionalized in a distinctive and authoritative supra-societal environment (Jepperson 2000).

Specializing claims arise in two general areas. They arise where the expanding modern system is penetrating older corporate orders – many of them once regarded as "private" (Zaretsky 1994) or external – reorganizing and rationalizing them on a more individualistic basis. And they arise where expanded analyses of nature (e.g., sexual drives), history (e.g., ethnic traditions), and the spiritual world (the new religions) produce new opportunities for specializing claims. Some types of situations can be noted.

First, the mobilization of specializing identity claims is characteristic of the reconstitution of older corporate orders in rationalized and individualized terms. In particular: (*a*) There is an ongoing reformulation of the formerly elaborate family system into a network of individuals, freeing sexuality and gender from earlier social constraints. The process produces identity claims which abound in new groups of entitled individual persons – women, gays, lesbians, children, the aged, and so on. (Notice that some of the first specializing identities to arise from the breakdown of the family have almost disappeared with routinization: the "divorcee" is an example.) (*b*) Similarly, the further breakdown and rationalization in human-rights terms of the nation-state and nationalism generates waves of new ethnic identity claims worldwide: As nation-states lose corporate identity, individuals are increasingly free to adopt their own individual ethnic identities (e.g., Kunovich and Hodson 1999: 649; Tsutsui 2000). (*c*) Along similar lines, the continuing breakdown of religious controls and the globalization of religious systems produce waves of claims from new spiritual explorers (Wuthnow 1988).[10]

But note how little, by way of specializing identity claims, is produced from the modern occupational system, despite fairly rapid social change. The occupational

---

[10] In the famous battle cry of the character Stephen Dedalus, James Joyce perfectly forecasts these three dissolutions of the corporate order: "1 will not serve that in which I no longer believe whether it call itself my home, my fatherland or my church."

system has long been incorporated into rationalized society, with only remnants of its old corporate aspect – guilds (and their saints) – left to destroy. Thus the creation and destruction of occupations occur with few specializing identity repercussions. ("The last of the stenographers" rings none so resonantly as "the last of the Mohicans.") The general expansion of personhood, with its legitimated individual tastes and capacities, needs and preferences, sufficiently accounts for occupational matters. In a similar way, few identity claims are now generated from the destruction of estate society – the diffuse identity claims associated with peasants and aristocracies have long since been rationalized.

As a second main source of specializing identity claims, expansions of rationalized society and personhood involve the incorporation of all sorts of formerly stigmatized, demeaned, or excluded persons and activities. Expanded personhood offers room for the promotion of formerly hidden qualities and tastes as natural and human. The groups involved are likely to claim specializing identity status – with unique ties to history, nature, or the spiritual world – to bolster their entry into legitimate societal membership. And they are likely to claim distinctive status in terms of the individual human rights of their members, who are empowered in the contemporary system, not the corporate rights of groups, which are not. Examples include many individuals once categorized as handicapped, perverted, or antisocial.

In such cases of conflict and stigmatization, the paths to standard personhood and role performance are cleared by specializing accounts. The need is intensified because the groups involved commonly face quite real resistance. Thus, over and above the legitimated free tastes of personhood, the new sexual and gender identities are asserted with particular status vis-a-vis nature, spiritual ties, or history. The same claims are made about newly mobilizing formerly excluded ethnic and racial groups, disabled persons, and so on. The incorporation of formerly deviant or subordinated people and activities into the system of expanded individualism thus leads to the proliferation of specializing identity claims.[11]

Third, ongoing individuation produces some specializing identity claims in formerly dominant groups, as with the "reactive ethnicity" of white Americans faced with the civil rights movement, or the elaborate identity claims of the anti-abortion movements in their defense of more corporate family arrangements (Luker 1985). Similarly, men develop some identity accounts in the face of feminists (Schwalbe 1996), and heterosexuals discover identity in the face of lesbians and gays (Katz 1995). All claim new linkages to distinct natural, spiritual, or historical roots.

Fourth, extensions of personhood produce conflicts between competing identity claims, reinforcing the inclination to develop specializing identities over and above standard personhood. For instance, the individual identities linked to national citizenship conflict with the expanding individual rights associated with subnational ethnic groups, reinforcing the specializing mobilization of each conflicting party. Or

---

[11] Many theorists become mired in the "paradox" of identity – its simultaneous assertions of similarity and difference within society (Scott 1996; Brubaker and Cooper 2000). In our view, there is no paradox. Specializing identities displace difference to realms *outside* society (in natural, spiritual, and historical domains), in order to clear the way for equal access to roles and personhood.

expanding rights linked to general personhood conflict with the rights claimed by specific national or ethnic groups, as in the conflicts over female genital circumcision (Boyle and Preves 2000). These situations generally raise the supply of identity accounts.

Finally, the rationalization and globalization of the extrasocial cosmos tills new soil for the rooting of specializing identities. The realm of nature, for example, has expanded enormously in the hands of scientists over recent decades, producing many new identity bases, such as those derived from psychological and genetic characteristics (e.g., Kessler 1990; Fausto-Sterling 1993). Meanwhile, the spiritual realms expand with globalization, providing a more varied terrain in which to root specializing identity accounts. And analyses of the histories of all sorts of groups provide much material that can be used to ground new identity claims. In all of these cases, the cultural expansion of the cosmos is fueled by pressures for accountings of the individual in society. And in all these cases, the new cultural material is available not only to groups building broader agendas, but also to groups and individuals engaged in identity differentiation as essentially play activity (as with genealogical hobbies, Civil War reenactment games, and a variety of religious explorations).

Overall, thus:

5. The greater the expansion of individualism as a cultural account – of the rationalized roles held by individuals and of personhood as master identity – the greater the specializing identity claims. They occur especially with regard to new or contested ties to the cosmos.

Thus our arguments take issue with standard sociological narratives that see specializing identities as an escape from regimenting roles or as a salve for the alienation of mass society (functional arguments from the right: e.g., Gergen 1991; Gallagher 1997). They also depart from explanations that depict the rise of identity categories as extensions of elite political and economic controls (functionalism from the left: e.g., Foucault 1973; Miller and Rose 1994). In the extreme, both positions depict the proliferation of identities as anomic in character – as both cause and effect of societal breakdown and resurgent localism and particularism (Brown 1987; Schlesinger 1992; Putnam 2000). And both positions conceive of modern identity claims as closely tied to the social organizational role system: either reacting to its stresses or collapsing into it.

In contrast, we see identities as integral to the modern system – a general cultural property – rather than as responses to modernity's contradictions and stresses. Specializing identities are fundamentally linked to the modern expansion of the status of the individual, and are tied to expanded (and sometimes conflict-laden) claims to universal personhood in a rationalized and global world. At the microsocial level of individual experience, identity claims sometimes may be reactions to the stresses of modernity and the burdens of restrictive roles. But at the more macrosocial (e.g., national and supra-national) and cultural levels we address, identity claims fulfill expansions in modern rationalization. Very directly, the modern system provides opportunity for identity differentiation by culturally weakening the primordiality of corporate entities and locating the individual in an increasingly analyzed natural, spiritual, and historical frame: The individual is the core source and beneficiary of society. Less directly, the modern system provides opportunity for identity differentiation by elaborating a highly individuated role system, which provides an arena for ever-multiplying individual needs and tastes: Every new link in the causal chains constructing rationalized society supports a newly enlarged picture of the individual with new possibilities for identity. Conversely, amplifications in personhood and specializing identities expand and construct new roles in the rationalized society (Meyer et al. 1987).

In short, the same broad forces of individuation that produce expanded modern role differentiation and expansions in the tastes associated with personhood also work to facilitate specializing identity differentiation both as a general cultural process and as a set of political claims against older constraints. All the specializing identities that arise are not equal, of course. Those associated with the breakdown of older stratifying corporate orders tend to have more political significance, while those arising from the expanded cosmos tend to be more playful. The former characterize the old European core, while the latter are more common in the United States. In this sense, as is commonly recognized, the high level of identity work in the United States typically involves rather low levels of conflict.

THE EFFECTS OF IDENTITY CLAIMS

We have discussed the ways in which the general expansion of the individual is central to the modern cultural accounting system. The process drives elaboration of (*a*) the rationalized role structure, which links nominally autonomous individuals to society; (*b*) authoritative general personhood, with its enlarged capacity for taste; and (*c*) specializing individual identities, which tie the individual to the expanded cosmos, and which often attempt to unclog blockages in the first two, more routine, individual expansions. We turn now to effects running the other way: from expanded identity claims back into the structure of rationalized society.

The properties of specializing identity claims

The master individual identity of the modern system is personhood. Tastes and preferences simply based on this generalized structure legitimate much of modern society. In the nature of normal, non-specially-identified personhood, one claims the right to express this particular culture, that style of sexual behavior, or the other spiritual experience and belief. But when the reach of personhood to cover some taste or activity is contested or not yet established, specializing claims arise. Cultural tastes may be legitimated in the name of a formerly suppressed ethnic group, whose language (for instance) was excluded from the former nationalist educational system, giving rise to historical identity claims (Hobsbawm and Ranger 1983). Formerly prohibited sexual behaviors and stigmatized handicaps may be defended with claims to unique biological natures and thus identities (Hobbs 1975; Rosario 1997). Ridiculed beliefs may be defended with reference to particular religious experiences and connections (Wuthnow 1978).

The contemporary rise in all this specializing identity material has produced strong reactions among critics, who see the process as representing the fragmentation of the self and disintegration of society against a past of more standardized and presumably integrating homogeneity. And enough conflicts do arise to provide satisfying examples for these critics. But by and large, the criticisms are based on misunderstandings of the nature of modern identity movements, and of the properties of the claimed identities.

First, modern specializing identities are legitimately claimed by individuals as individual rights to the expression of needs and choices. They are rights *within human personhood,* not against it, and attempts to ground special claims in authoritative corporate groups (as with religious cults thought to transcend the individuals involved) are strongly resisted. Specializing identities amount to claims asserting that legitimate qualities have not been properly recognized as features of standard personhood and thus require special markers in order to be incorporated.[12]

Second, this means that modern specializing identity claims continue the long historic process of undercutting the power of corporate groups. Individuals may claim ethnic, gender, or spiritual identities rather freely; representatives of these identities, on the contrary, are restricted in their freedom to claim power over individuals. For instance, no new legitimated religious orders with binding power to monopolize the future decision rights of the individual arise, and old religious and ethnic corporate bodies are reduced to voluntary associations. Members of ethnic groups informally may try to discipline their compatriots into proper ethnic identification (encouraging, for example, within-group marriage), but the legal and cultural rights of the modern individual stand in the way of effective enforcement.

Third, thus neither society nor identity advocates can do much to properly enforce membership in an identity group. Individuals are increasingly free to claim, deny, or change their ties. In principle, one can claim to be dyslexic, Irish, and female one day, and the next day to be not specially abled, Scottish, and male (Lieberson and Waters 1988; Snipp 1989). Society – and the groups involved – can decreasingly impose these categories on an individual.

Fourth, this means that the meaning associated with specializing identity claims is restricted. They cannot really be claims to superior status in the allocation of power and resources, though some protections or recompenses may be involved. The specializing identities are put forward under broad norms of personhood that acknowledge the equal personhood of others. By and large, this means they are heavily expressive, and they tend to emphasize matters of aesthetic taste or lifestyle (food, dress, and language, not occupational rights, for instance) (Bellah et al. 1996), beyond the general assertion of personhood.[13]

---

[12] The preeminence of personhood over specializing identity appears in a commemorative plaque placed by the Black Veterans of Malcolm X College: "In Memoriam to the Black Veteran. One God... One Aim... One Destiny. From the Beginning Of Time to Eternity."

[13] Thus, even as the intermarriage rate of American Jews has dipped to around 50 per cent, there is a klezmer revival (Leiter 2000). It is the expressive identity, not the old identity-role matrix, that flourishes. Likewise, the hill tribes of Thailand are "identified" by variations in dress and housing much more than variations in economic or political rights.

Fifth, the links between identity claims and rights and obligations in the rationalized role structure of society are strikingly weak. Bluntly, specializing identities may be very poorly correlated with behavior. One may claim to be gay or straight or bisexual, without engaging in the associated behavior (as in the claim that all women who resist patriarchy exist somewhere in the lesbian continuum: see Rich 1983). And for that matter one may announce a clear gender identity without having the expected sexual organs (Green 1994). One may claim an ethnicity on the most tenuous grounds (Lieberson and Waters 1988; Waters 1990), knowing neither the language nor the customs of the claimed identity, and perhaps lacking even the appropriate ancestry in the main or entirely (note the novelist who claimed to be Irish his whole life [Priall 2000]). One may validly claim a spiritual or religious identity, say in accounting for an exotic taste in food, but then change it (and the associated taste) tomorrow, or simply claim the identity without engaging in the food choice at all.

6. The more specializing identity claims assume equal personhood, the more they take the form of individual rights rather than enforceable obligations, and the less they relate to role activity.[14]

Given these principles limiting special identity claims, what then is their point?

The impact of specializing identity claims

In the modern system, specializing identity claims are political and cultural assertions more than action ones (Bernstein 1997; Melucci 1989). They attempt to change the rules and boundaries of proper personhood and the rationalized role structure, not principally to behave within the extant system. The claim to an ethnic identity, over and above run-of-the-mill tastes legitimately derived from personal background, activates a driving spiritual, natural, or historical force that must be recognized in society. The specializing claim to a gender identity has a similar character – asserting something of the true nature of the individual that a just society must recognize as falling within the domain of personhood. Sometimes the assertion involved seeks to change the political structure of an immediate interaction situation – requiring the participants as proper persons to recognize a new dimension of personhood, as with an ethnic speech style or sexual preference. Sometimes it is a collective demand for massive political change – establishing rules to legitimate an ethnic culture in national politics or eliminating prohibitions on sexual conduct, or requiring that public spaces be accessible to special individuals – that extends the boundaries of normal and equal personhood to new groups, activities, or tastes.

In the current period of expanded legitimate individuality, many special identity claims have been put forward, and many have been quite successful. The right and

---

[14] This is clearly not true of ascribed identities, in which older identity-role matrices, marking inelastic "types" of persons, remain in force. Many such matrices, such as those around race, are disintegrating, but others, for instance, around the severely mentally retarded, persist. In these cases, identities severely constrain roles and personhood. For a vivid description of the matrix, see Barth (1996: 302).

capacity of national states to privilege particular ethnic cultures, for instance, has been greatly circumscribed, as has the right to legally constrain freer gender and sexual tastes (e.g., Frank and McEneaney 1999).

7. To the extent that specializing identity claims seek normalization in routine personhood, they tend to address the normative and political systems rather than role activities and relationships.

When a special identity claim is successful, the defended tastes and behaviors acquire cultural and political support as falling within the range of normal personhood. And thus the associated excitement and mobilization tend to be reduced, as the identity aspects of the claims – their dramatic rooting in nature or spiritual realms or history – devolve to the normal and mundane.

8. To the extent that specializing identity claims are successful, they are absorbed into normal personhood, as ordinary individual needs, tastes, preferences, and choices.

Thus, the specializing identity claims that remain alive and active in a modern system are those that face some continuing barriers or blockages. On the one hand, American society can absorb ethnics from central and eastern Europe as part of the standard range of normal persons, and the ethnic mobilizations and claims from such groups tend to be limited. On the other hand, African American and American Indian populations, facing continuing social and legal boundaries, remain more distinctive (e.g., Gonzales 2001). So also with contested gender identities of many sorts. And in American society, which has great absorbing capacity in many domains, religious identities retain some vitality because of the separation of religion and political life (cf. rational choice models of the same phenomenon [Finke and Stark 1992; Warner 1993]). These principles make the complete incorporation of religious identities in American national life difficult.

The absorbing of personal identity in rationalized society

We described above the ways that specializing identity claims tend to become absorbed in the routines of normal personhood. Vital histories and biological properties become normal tastes and styles, for which explanations are unnecessary, and exotic claims are moderated. The same society that generates special identity claims first constrains them (e.g., under the rules of equality) and then absorbs them in routine individuality (as it has, by and large, many once-strong identities: e.g., bastard, orphan, and widow).

In like manner, the tastes of normal personhood tend to be absorbed into the rationalized role structures of modern society (Thomas et al. 1987). Many have noted the absorbing power of the modern system (e.g., Marcuse 1992), though fewer have connected this absorbing power with the system's capacity to generate constantly new tastes and identity claims, and thus the equilibrium that tends to result.

Over time, legitimate tastes and preferences tend to be rationalized and disciplined in the modern system. They are schooled, organized, and linked to the overall economy. Thus, for example, the mother of an infant may now exercise a legitimate taste to return to work – a choice most difficult under the old identity-role matrix. And her choice will be facilitated by an elaborated role structure that will feed, clothe, bathe, and care for her child, even to the point of pumping, storing, and delivering the mother's own breast milk. And all such activities will contribute to society – enriching the GDP and enlarging the domains of freedom. With incorporation, much of the material once stored in the identity "mother" gets redistributed to standard personhood and the rationalized role structure.

DISCUSSION AND CONCLUSION

We have seen contemporary changes in modern society as greatly expanding the space for the individual as core to the modern cultural account. This continues a long process of rationalization in terms of the individual, accelerated in recent decades by globalization, development, and the further breakdown of corporate collective life (prominently, the national state as a strong collective actor).

The expansion of society around the individual in the form of roles drives expansion of the cosmos around the individual in the form of personhood, and vice versa. When older corporate or normative systems pose barriers to expansion and when rationalization opens new realms of the extrasocial cosmos, claims to specializing identities arise – to distinct personal rootings in unique natural, historical, or spiritual locations prior to society and interaction. Over time, specializing identities tend to be absorbed in normal personality and, in turn, to flow into the rationalized role structure, with its differentiated definitions and regulations. Thus the modern system produces some rough equilibrium between what is personal identity and what is social role performance.

The trends we analyze are clearly visible in most developed societies, and in developing ones, too. They are most obvious in, and indeed generally thought to be characteristic of, the liberalism and individualism of American society. The United States has, for almost two centuries, been a world leader in expanding those dimensions of individuation stressing individual choice. The United States has had expanded rationalized individual role systems, with early educational expansion, the elaboration of formal organizations and associations, the rapid differentiation of occupational systems, and highly organized religious and recreational systems. And on the personhood side of the equation, the United States is famous for producing and supporting the blossom of claims to religious, natural, and historical selfhood, with all the exotica of extreme self-expression finding a home.

But if the analysis focuses on the individuation of human needs and entitlements (rather than choices), assessments of where the identity explosion is most prominent will likely shift. The maintenance of special individuated entitlements based on gender, ethnicity, region, community, and so on, may be much more substantial in developed countries other than the United States (Heidenheimer 1981; Soysal 1994). This is notoriously true when assessments of individuated welfare arrangements are involved – a variety of northern European countries score very high

(Koopmans and Statham 1999). It is well to remember Tocqueville's analysis of ways in which American empowered choices produce narrowed zones for sharp identity differentiation ([1836] 1966).

On a more comparative scale, we may suppose developed societies have changed in the same individuating directions (see Inglehart and Baker (2000) for quantitative examples). Forces such as globalization and Europeanization and the ideologies associated with them tend to reinforce expanded individuation, and weakened corporate identities, everywhere. And with these forces one finds in accompaniment both expanded rationalized role systems (educational, occupational, and organizational structures of great articulation) and broadened subjective personhood (deeply rooted in world human rights doctrines).

While conflict and resistance most certainly continue, the legitimate alternatives to some form of the individuation we have discussed seem weak in contemporary world society. It is difficult to maintain strongly legitimated corporate identities with national or subnational monopolies, and thus to restrict the flowering of elaborate specializing identity claims and claims to expanded tastes rooted in general personhood. It is also difficult to maintain a more traditional model of rationalized society built around group structures rather than highly elaborated and expanded individual role systems. Intellectuals envision Shangri-Las with the capacity to resist the system: here a modernized Japan with traditional family and organizational systems, there an Iran or Afghanistan with vitalized enforcements of traditional religious scripts, over there a successful socialist order, and back somewhere tribes that retain their culture (e.g., Escobar 1995). But resistant alternatives, under conditions of expansion and globalization, seem very fragile. They violate, on the one side, the norms of organizational rationality set by the regime of liberal individualism. They violate, on the other, basic principles of human rights that certify as legitimate and routine forms of individual self-expression and identity that, a few decades ago, would have seemed very extreme indeed.

REFERENCES

Altman, Dennis. 2001. *Global Sex*. Chicago, IL: University of Chicago Press.

Appiah, K. Anthony. 1996. Race. Culture, Identity: Misunderstood Connections, in K. Anthony Appiah and Amy Gutmann (eds.), *Color Conscious: The Political Morality of Race*. Princeton, NJ: Princeton University Press, pp. 30–105.

Barth, Fredrik. 1996. Ethnic Groups and Boundaries, in Werner Sollors (ed.), *Theories of Ethnicity: A Classical Reader*. Basingstoke: Macmillan, pp. 294–324.

Beck, Ulrich. 1992. *Risk Society: Towards a New Modernity*. London: Sage.

Bellah, Robert N., Richard Madsen, William M. Sullivan, Ann Swidler, and Steven M. Tipton. 1996. *Habits of the Heart: Individualism and Commitment in American Life*. Updated edn. Berkeley, CA: University of California Press.

Berkovitch, Nitza. 1999. *From Motherhood to Citizenship: Women's Rights and International Organizations*. Baltimore, MD: Johns Hopkins University Press.

Bernstein, Mary. 1997. Celebration and Suppression: The Strategic Uses of Identity by the Lesbian and Gay Movement. *American Journal of Sociology* 103:531–65.

Boli, John and John W. Meyer. 1987. The Ideology of Childhood and the State: Rules Distinguishing Children in National Constitutions, 1870–1970, in G. M. Thomas, J. W. Meyer. F. O. Ramirez, and J. Boli (eds.), *Institutional Structure: Constituting State, Society, and the Individual*. Newbury Park, CA: Sage Publications, pp. 217–41.

—— and George M. Thomas. 1999. *Constructing World Culture: International Nongovernmental Organizations since 1875*. Stanford, CA: Stanford University Press.

Boyle, Elizabeth Heger and Sharon E. Preves. 2000. National Politics as International Process: The Case of Anti-Female-Genital-Cutting Laws. *Law and Society Review* 34:703–37.

—— and John W. Meyer. 1998. Modern Law as a Secularized and Global Model: Implications for the Sociology of Law. *Soziale Welt* 49:275–94. Reproduced in Chapter 15.

Brown, Richard Harvey. 1987. Personal Identity and Political Economy: Western Grammars of the Self in Historical Perspective. *Current Perspectives in Social Theory* 8:123–59.

Brubaker, Rogers. 1996. *Nationalism Refrained: Nationhood and the National Question in the New Europe*. Cambridge: Cambridge University Press.

—— and Frederick Cooper. 2000. Beyond Identity. *Theory and Society* 29:1–47.

Buchmann, Marlis and Manuel Eisner. 1997. The Transition from the Utilitarian to the Expressive Self: 1900–1992. *Poetics* 25:157–75.

Calhoun, Craig. 1994. Social Theory and the Politics of Identity, in Craig Calhoun (ed.), *Social Theory and the Politics of Identity*. Oxford: Basil Blackwell, pp. 9–36.

Chabbott, Colette. 1999. Development INGOs, in J. Boli and G. Thomas (eds.), *Constructing World Culture*. Stanford, CA: Stanford University Press, pp. 222–48.

de Tocqueville, Alexis. [1836] 1966. *Democracy in America*. New York: Doubleday.

Durkheim, Emile. [1893] 1964. *The Division of Labor in Society*. New York: Free Press.

Eade, John. 1994. Identity. Nation and Religion: Educated Young Bangladeshi Muslims in London's 'East End'. *International Sociology* 9:377–94.

Eisenstadt, Shmuel. 1986. *The Origins and Diversity of Axial Age Civilizations*. Albany, NY: State University of New York Press.

Epstein, Steven. 1999. Gay and Lesbian Movements in the United States: Dilemmas of Identity, Diversity, and Political Strategy, in Barry D. Adam, Jan Willem Duyvendak, and André Krouwel (eds.), *The Global Emergence of Gay and Lesbian Politics*. Philadelphia, PA: Temple University Press, pp. 30–90.

Escobar, Arturo. 1995. *Encountering Development: The Making and Unmaking of the Third World*. Princeton, NJ: Princeton University Press.

Eyre, Dana and Mark Suchman. 1996. Status, Norms, and the Proliferation of Conventional Weapons, in Peter Katzenstein (ed.), *The Culture of National Security*. New York: Columbia University Press, pp. 79–113.

Fausto-Sterling, Anne. 1993. The Five Sexes: Why Male and Female Are Not Enough. *The Sciences* (March/April):20–5.

Ferguson, Priscilla Parkhurst. 1998. A Cultural Field in the Making: Gastronomy in 19th-century France. *American Journal of Sociology* 104:597–641.

Fiala, Robert and Audri Gordon Lanford. 1987. Educational Ideology and the World Educational Revolution, 1950–70. *Comparative Education Review* 31:315–32.

Fillieulle, Olivier and Jan Willem Duyvendak. 1999. Gay and Lesbian Activism in France: Between Integration and Community-Oriented Movements, in Barry D. Adam, Jan Willem Duyvendak, and André Krouwel (eds.), *The Global Emergence of Gay and Lesbian Politics*. Philadelphia, PA: Temple University Press, pp. 184–213.

Finke, Roger and Rodney Stark. 1992. *The Churching of America, 1776–1990*. New Brunswick, NJ: Rutgers University Press.

Foucault, Michel. 1973. *Discipline and Punish*. New York: Random House.

Frank, David John and Elizabeth H. McEneaney. 1999. The Individualization of Society and the Liberalization of State Policies on Same-Sex Sexual Relations, 1984–1995. *Social Forces* 77:911–44.

—— John W. Meyer, and David Miyahara. 1995. The Individualist Polity and the Centrality of Professionalized Psychology. *American Sociological Review* 60:360–77.

—— Suk-Ying Wong, John W. Meyer, and Francisco O. Ramirez. 2000. What Counts as History: A Cross-National and Longitudinal Study of University Curricula. *Comparative Education Review* 44:29–53.

Gallagher, Catherine. 1997. The History of Literary Criticism, in Thomas Bender and Carl E. Schorske (eds.), *American Academic Culture in Transformation: Fifty Years, Four Disciplines.* Princeton, NJ: Princeton University Press.

Gamson, Joshua. 1995. Must Identity Movements Self-Destruct? A Queer Dilemma. *Social Problems* 42:390–407.

Gergen, Kenneth J. 1991. *The Saturated Self: Dilemmas of Identity in Contemporary Life.* New York: Basic Books.

Giddens, Anthony. 1991. *Modernity and Self-Identity: Self and Society in Late Modern Age.* Stanford, CA: Stanford University Press.

Gleason, Philip. 1996. Identifying Identity: A Semantic History, in Werner Sollors (ed.), *Theories of Ethnicity: A Classical Reader.* Basingstoke: Macmillan, pp. 460–87.

Gonzales, Angela. 2001. American Indian Identity Matters: The Political Economy of Ethnic Boundaries. PhD dissertation. Department of Sociology, Harvard University.

Green, Richard. 1994. Sexual Problems and Therapies: A Quarter Century of Developments and Changes, in Alice S. Rossi (ed.), *Sexuality across the Life Course.* Chicago, IL: University of Chicago Press, pp. 341–61.

Hall, John. 1986. *Powers and Liberties: The Causes and Consequences of the Rise of the West.* New York: Penguin.

Heidenheimer, Arnold J. 1981. Education and Social Security Entitlements in Europe and America, in Peter Flora and Arnold J. Heidenheimer (eds.), *The Development of Welfare States in Europe and Americaw.* New Brunswick, NJ: Transaction Books, pp. 269–304.

Hobbs, Nicholas. 1975. *The Futures of Children: Categories, Labels, and their Consequences.* San Francisco, CA: Jossey-Bass.

Hobsbawm, Eric and Terence Ranger (eds.) (1983). *The Invention of Tradition.* Cambridge: Cambridge University Press.

Inglehart, Ronald and Wayne Baker. 2000. Modernization, Cultural Change, and the Persistence of Traditional Values. *American Sociological Review* 65:19–51.

Jacobson, David. 1996. *Rights across Borders: Immigration and the Decline of Citizenship.* Baltimore, MD: Johns Hopkins University Press.

Jepperson, Ronald Lee. 2000. Institutional Logics: On the Constitutive Dimensions of the Modern Nation-State Polities. Unpublished manuscript. Department of Sociology, University of Tulsa.

Katz, Jonathan Ned. 1995. *The Invention of Heterosexuality.* New York: Dutton.

Kessler, Suzanne J. 1990. The Medical Construction of Gender: Case Management of Intersexed Infants. *Signs* 16:3–26.

Koopmans, Ruud and Paul Statham. 1999. Challenging the Liberal Nation-State? Postnationalism, Multiculturalism, and the Collective Claims Making of Migrants and Ethnic Minorities in Britain and Germany. *American Journal of Sociology* 165:652–96.

Kunovich, Robert M. and Randy Hodson. 1999. Conflict, Religious Identity, and Ethnic Intolerance in Croatia. *Social Forces* 78:643–74.

Leiter, Robert. 2000. A Little Bad News, a Little Good News. *New York Times,* September 23, p. A19.

Lieberson. Stanley and Mary C. Waters. 1988. *From Many Strands: Ethnic and Racial Groups in Contemporary America.* New York: Russell Sage Foundation.

Luker, Kirstin. 1985. *Abortion and the Politics of Motherhood.* Berkeley, CA: University of California Press.

Mann, Michael. 1986. *The Sources of Social Power.* Cambridge: Cambridge University Press.

Marcuse. Herbert. 1992. *One-Dimensional Man,* 2nd edn. Beacon.

Marshall, T. H. 1948. *Citizenship and Social Class.* New York: Doubleday.

McEneaney, Elizabeth H. 1998. The Transformation of Primary School Science and Mathematics: A Cross-National Analysis, 1900–1995. PhD dissertation. Department of Sociology, Stanford University.

Melucci. Alberto. 1989. *Nomads of the Present: Social Movements and Individual Needs in Contemporary Society.* Philadelphia, PA: Temple University Press.

Meyer, John W. 1994. The Evolution of Stratification Systems, in David Grusky (ed.), *Social Stratification.* Boulder, CO: Westview, pp. 730–7.

—— and Ronald L. Jepperson. 2000. The 'Actors' of Modern Society: The Cultural Construction of Social Agency. *Sociological Theory* 18:100–20. Reproduced in Chapter 5.

—— John Boli, and George M. Thomas. 1987. Ontology and Rationalization in the Western Cultural Account, in G. M. Thomas, J. W. Meyer. F. O. Ramirez, and J. Boli (eds.), *Institutional Structure: Constituting State, Society, and the Individual.* Newbury Park, CA: Sage Publications, pp. 12–37.

—— Francisco O. Ramirez, and Yasemin N. Soysal. 1992. World Expansion of Mass Education, 1870–1990. *Sociology of Education* 65:128–49.

—— —— —— and Francisco O. Ramirez. 1997. World Society and the Nation-State. *American Journal of Sociology* 103:144–81. Reproduced in Chapter 8.

Miller, Peter and Nicholas Rose. 1994. On Therapeutic Authority: Psychoanalytic Expertise under Advanced Liberalism. *History of the Human Sciences* 7:29–65.

Peterson, Richard A. and Albert Simkus. 1992. How Musical Tastes Mark Occupational Status Groups, in M. Lamont and M. Fournier (eds.), *Cultivating Differences.* Chicago: University of Chicago Press, pp. 152–86.

Plummer, Ken. 1999. The Lesbian and Gay Movement in Britain: Schisms, Solidarities, and Social Worlds, in Barry D. Adam. Jan Willem Duyvendak, and André Krouwel (eds.), *The Global Emergence of Gay and Lesbian Politics.* Philadelphia, PA: Temple University Press, pp. 133–57.

Prial, Frank J. 2000. Patrick O'Brian, Whose 20 Sea Stories Won Him International Fame, Dies at 85. *New York Times,* January 7.

Putnam, Robert D. 2000. *Bowling Alone: The Collapse and Revival of American Community.* New York: Simon and Schuster.

Ramirez, Francisco O. and John W. Meyer. 1998. Dynamics of Citizenship Development and the Political Incorporation of Women, in Connie McNeely (ed.), *Public Rights, Public Rules.* New York: Garland, pp. 59–80.

—— and Elizabeth H. McEneaney. 1997. From Women's Suffrage to Reproduction Rights? *International Journal of Comparative Sociology* 66:6–24.

Rauner. Mary. 1998. The Worldwide Globalization of Civics Education Topics, 1955–1995. PhD dissertation, Stanford University.

Rich, Adrienne. 1983. Compulsory Heterosexuality and Lesbian Existence, in Ann Snitow, Christine Stansell, and Sharon Thompson (eds.), *Powers of Desire: The Politics of Sexuality.* New York: Monthly Review.

Riesman, David. 1950. *The Lonely Crowd: A Study of the Changing American Character*. New Haven, CT: Yale University Press.

Rosario, Vernon A. 1997. *Science and Homosexualities*. New York: Routledge.

Sassen, Saskia. 1998. *Globalisation and its Discontents*. New York: The New Press.

Schiller, Nina Glick. 1994. Introducing Identities: Global Studies in Culture and Power. *Identities: Global Studies in Culture and Power* 1:1–6.

Schleef, Debra. 2000. 'That's a Good Question!' Exploring Motivations for Law and Business School Choice. *Sociology of Education* 73:155–74.

Schlesinger, Arthur D. 1992. *The Disuniting of America: Reflections on a Multicultural Society*. New York: Norton.

Schooler, Carmi. 1990. Individualism and the Historical and Social-Structural Determinants of People's Concerns over Self-Directedness and Efficacy, in Judith Rodin, Carmi Schooler, and K. Warner Schaie (eds.), *Self-Directedness: Cause and Effects Throughout the Life Course*. Hillsdale, NJ: Erlbaum, pp. 19–49.

Schwalbe, Michael. 1996. *Unlocking the Iron Cage: The Men's Movement, Gender Politics, and American Culture*. New York: Oxford University Press.

Scott, Joan Wallach. 1996. *Only Paradoxes to Offer: French Feminists and the Rights of Man*. Cambridge, MA: Harvard University Press.

Shils, Edward. 1982. The Academic Ethic. *Minerva* 20:107–208.

Smith, Anthony D. 1987. *The Ethnic Origins of Nations*. Oxford: Basil Blackwell.

Smith, Jackie. 1995. Transnational Political Processes and the Human Rights Movement, in Louis Kriesberg, Michael Dobkowski, and Isidor Walliman (eds.), *Research in Social Movements, Conflict and Change*, vol. 18. Greenwood, CT: JAI, pp. 185–220.

Snipp, C. Matthew. 1989. *American Indians*. New York: Russell Sage Foundation.

Soysal, Yasemin Nuhoglu. 1994. *Limits of Citiienship: Migrants and Postnational Membership in Europe*. Chicago, IL: University of Chicago Press.

Stevenson, David and Barbara Schneider. 1999. *The Ambitious Generation*. New Haven, CT: Yale University Press.

Swanson, Guy. 1971. An Organizational Analysis of Collectivities. *American Sociological Review* 36:607–23.

Thomas, George and John W. Meyer. 1984. The Expansion of the State. *Annual Review of Sociology* 10:461–82.

—— —— Francisco O. Ramirez, and John Boli. 1987. *Institutional Structure: Constituting State, Society, and the Individual*. Newbury Park, CA: Sage Publications.

Tilly, Charles. 1996. Citizenship, Identity, and Social History, in Charles Tilly (ed.), *Citizenship, Identity and Social History*. Cambridge: Cambridge University Press, pp. 1–17.

Tsutsui, Kiyoteru. 2000. World Human Rights Pressures and the Global Rise of Ethnic Social Movements. Unpublished manuscript, Stanford University.

Warner, R. Stephen. 1993. Work in Progress toward a New Paradigm for the Sociological Study of Religion in the United States. *American Journal of Sociology* 98:1044–93.

Waters, Mary C. 1990. *Ethnic Options: Choosing Identities in America*. Berkeley, CA: University of California Press.

Weber, Max. 1978. *Economy and Society*. Berkeley, CA: University of California Press.

Wuthnow, Robert. 1978. *Experimentation in American Religion*. Berkeley, CA: University of California Press.

—— 1988. *The Restructuring of American Religion*. Princeton, NJ: Princeton University Press.

Zaretsky, Eli. 1994. Identity Theory, Identity Politics: Psychoanalysis, Marxism, Post-Structuralism, in Craig Calhoun (ed.), *Social Theory and the Politics of Identity*. Oxford: Basil Blackwell, pp. 198–215.

15

Law

Modern Law as a Secularized and Global Model: Implications for the Sociology of Law

The Enlightenment view of humanity, adopted by social scientists, places the rational, opportunistic individual at the center of the universe. The unique personality of this individual (charismatic, ambitious, and passive) and his or her local milieu (resources, class standing, networks, and ethnicity) creates his or her unique identity and interests. Under the functional or consensus perspective, individuals trade in some of their "uniqueness" and "interests" to form institutions which benefit the collective. The legal system is one such institution. Individuals agree to abide by its laws and decisions to increase certainty in their lives and to protect themselves from the selfish interests of others. The legal system is used instrumentally to solve collective problems. Standing in opposition to the functional perspective, but sharing many of the same Enlightenment assumptions, is the conflict perspective. According to this perspective, because of the uniqueness of each individual, pursuits of interests and expressions of identity do not converge, but rather clash in a cacophony of conflict. Law is a coercive, repressive system linked to the winners of the conflict.

These perspectives often treat legal systems as irrelevant in the modern process of globalization (see, e.g., Sklair 1995). According to one popular perspective, "international law" develops simply to coordinate the global economy. After all, it is frequently pointed out, there really is no international legal system – national legal systems lack jurisdiction over the international realm (Franck 1990). Others see law

Originally published as:

Elizabeth Heger Boyle and John W. Meyer. 1998. Modern Law as a Secularized and Global Model: Implications for the Sociology of Law. *Soziale Welt* 49:275–294.

This chapter is reprinted from *New Challenges for the Rule of Law: Lawyers, Internationalization, and the Social Construction of Legal Rules* (Yves Dezalay and Bryant Garth, editors). It was first presented at a conference co-sponsored by the American Bar Foundation, the John D. and Catherine T. MacArthur Foundation, and the University of California, Santa Barbara. We extend our appreciation to Bryant Garth and Yves Dezalay for organizing that conference. Special thanks to Gary Hamilton and Susan Silbey for their thoughtful critiques. We are also indebted to the following colleagues who provided feedback on earlier drafts of the work: Jeffrey Broadbent, Dan Cooperman, Frank Dobbin, David Frank, Mayra Gómez, Jennifer Pierce, Sharon Preves, Francisco Ramirez, Joachim Savelsberg, Perry Seymour, the members of the University of Minnesota international relations colloquium, and the members of the Stanford University comparative sociology workshop.

as more opaque and imagine the law and its authority to be the products of social functioning and the interests and powers involved (e.g., Black 1982).

Our perspective is different from these "realist" accounts. We propose that individuals do not construct legal systems (or other systems) to reflect inherent interests or identities. We propose that individuals *derive* their identities and interest from some perceived natural order and create legal systems to reflect these higher "platonic ideals." We do not, here, advocate or subscribe to such ideals. But we see the modern state and legal system as in good part organized around them. Like God in an earlier era, they become the center of action and interests in the modern world. From this perspective, finding the proper function for an international rule of law is problematic. Law is neither inherently functional nor repressive. Law is important for its linkage to perceived universal principles and as a source of identity for individuals and, importantly, nation-states.

For example, consider that legal rules, principles, standards, and ideas now flow very rapidly around world society. Similar legal themes appear, in waves, on a very wide-spread basis. This is difficult to understand if we take only a realist and "bottom-up" view of the law as the product of local conflicts, powers, and interests: such processes would engender internationalization rather slowly out of evolving interaction and interdependence. But it is very easy to understand if we add a more institutionalist view of the law – and the sovereignty of the modern state, with which it is now linked – as constructed out of a common and universalistic world cultural frame. In this chapter, we develop such a view, and show its implications.

The arguments of contemporary sociological institutionalism are useful here. Institutionalists stress (*a*) the dependence of contemporary rationalized organization on wider cultural environments and (*b*) the rationalism and universalism, and now globalization, of those environments (e.g., Thomas 1987; DiMaggio and Powell 1991; Meyer 1994). In these views, the modern nation-state system is governed by cultural assumptions derived from earlier religious principles. These cultural assumptions provide nation-states with clearly specifiable goals such as obtaining "justice" through a "rule of law."

The purpose of this chapter is not to criticize other explanations of law and the consequences which follow from their assumptions. Rather, the focus of this chapter is to note some of the distinctive consequences for legal systems which follow from a more institutional and cultural perspective. Further, we do not intend to imply that laws and actions are always in conformity. On the contrary, because law reflects spiritual ideals, we do *not* expect a high degree of correspondence between law and action. We take up this issue again later in the chapter.

BACKGROUND

It is generally understood that the historical sources of modern rationalized law and legal systems are ideas and assumptions about a religious or transcendental cosmos. Modern legal systems, now more or less worldwide, stem historically from the law and culture of the Catholic Church, which itself carried on re-codified traditions from the Roman Empire (Anderson 1976; Berman 1993: 35–54). Other universalistic religious traditions could, under favorable circumstances, have generated worldwide legal arrangements of some sort, but in historical reality, the Western traditions, diffused through colonialism and military, political, and cultural hegemony, played this role.[1]

In the feudal world, no general sovereign existed who could or wanted to create general law. God's will, carried in the Church, governed, and the suggestion that humans as secular individuals could refine and generalize law was blasphemy. Jurists were bad Christians (David and Brierly 1984; 1 Corinthians 6; cf. Greenhouse 1986). In the thirteenth century, law began to develop outside the Church, though carried by its culture, Latin language, organization, and professionals (Berman 1993). With the legitimized development of the state (Strayer 1970) and its universities, and of urban life and commerce, civil and common law as well as a Thomistic celebration of Reason acquired some authority. Reason, reflecting the myth of Rome, was universalistic, like divine law. Regional customary law, including "national" law, was scorned, as giving no expression to universalistic justice (David and Brierly 1984: 2).

In the modern period, with the slow destruction of the authority of the Church and the triumph of the State, rulers – whether kings or legislators – became the creators and carriers of law. The assumptions of universalism and rationality embedded in modern Western thought prompted the increasing globalization of the world system (see generally Weber 1958; Habermas 1984), including the globalization of the nation-state form and the related universalistic legal system. Thus, legal systems are a constitutive element of that form of society known as the modern nation-state. The two arose concomitantly each lending legitimacy to the other. National legal systems emerged more through the global system rather than through local organization.

Although law and legal systems are produced and changed by particular "societies," they carry socio-cultural meanings and values about a larger natural and spiritual environment. Many modern lines of thought about the law also see it as rooted in notions of justice which transcend individual interests, as with traditions emphasizing "legal science," "natural law," and so on (Black 1821; Nonet and Selznick 1978). We take seriously the idea that modern legal systems historically and currently rest on exogenous cultural assumptions. These assumptions shape both the content of laws and the particular organization and meaning of legal systems.

The modern system's pretenses, and much social scientific theory about the law, take the triumph of the State and its claims at face value. The source of law's legitimacy has become so embedded, so taken for granted, that the supranational character of law is given little attention (see David and Brierly 1984; Blankenburg

[1] Many former colonies now maintain dual court systems, one system which applies "state law" and one system which applies "customary law." Even in these systems with their emphasis on autonomy, there is little doubt that "customary law" is influenced over time by "state law" (see, e.g., Sierra 1995).

1994; see also Gaete 1991).[2] In its place arise pictures of the contemporary world as "secularized," and the legal decisions of nation-states are seen as those of autonomous "actors" in history (cf. Carter 1993). This is an important mistake. The rise of the State indeed essentially destroyed the organizational authority of the Church, but it did so, in our view, by absorbing, and thus becoming dependent on, a secularized version of the wider culture carried by the Church. The processes are dialectic and continue throughout modern history. In claiming autonomy and sovereignty under various secularized principles of rationality and universality, both the nation-state and the law that is partially its creation intensify their dependence on these secularized principles.

LAW AND THE NATION-STATE SYSTEM

First, the expanded autonomy and sovereignty of the modern state was legitimated and supported by secularized (often scientized) versions of universal principles. So not only scholars (David and Brierly 1984: 17), but also legislators and kings justified their nominally autonomous authority in terms of principles of law that were universal in spirit and scope. One cannot read the great claims of the French or American (or later national, and still later socialist) revolutionaries, without seeing these highly dramatic justifications in terms of putatively universal principles. In recent years, the state becomes central in universal declarations of human rights (Shue 1980; Donnelly 1989). The modern state and its purposes move center stage under the claimed cultural umbrella of (formerly divine) law, now turned into science and "natural" law (even now, direct reference to spiritual forces often remain). Sovereignty is a peculiar claim: it is a claim to autonomous decision power, but under exogenous universal principles and addressed to an exogenous and often universal audience. The idea of sovereignty itself emanates not from each nation independently but from the *global* recognition of the nation-state form.

Second, law, with remarkable uniformity (see Boli 1987), creates states which are "defined" by and constituted from legally assumed "societies" (Bendix 1964; Marshall 1964). As the legitimate basis of their authority, modern states claim to be made up of constitutive elements beyond the legislator: "society" is discovered, and individuals appear as "citizens." Here again is a wholesale absorption of earlier religious principles of equality in the eyes of God, now secularized and defined in terms of principles of scientific and natural law. Not only the great mobilizing power of the modern nation-state (Tilly 1975, 1990), but also a form of cultural dependence, is its claim and capacity to incorporate society and individuals in its structure. Society and citizenship are defined in terms of universalistic cultural rules such as

---

[2] Despite the "separate" national tracks along which legal systems developed over the last 200 years, the basic spirit and purpose of law continued to be tied to the "secular religious" principles of justice, sovereignty, and science. As law became increasingly central to the modern nationalist project, these exogenous forces extended first to the legal profession and currently to specific legal procedures (see, e.g., Frase 1990; Black and Coffee 1994).

the scientific principles of social development, natural or scientific principles of individual rights, and later scientific or natural laws concerning the environment. Justice, defined in terms of universal principles, comes to be a constitutive function in this system.

These processes of building nations and societies continue, expand, and intensify in our own period. The long-term expansion of the nation-state model around the world (Strang 1990; Anderson 1991) and penetration of the model into more and more domains of social life (Chapter 8; Thomas 1987; Meyer 1994) create a world in which standardized models of the nation-state are organized at the world level, understood to apply universally, and at least in form enacted by practically every nation-state. The expansion of the nation-state system extends and elaborates the rationalistic and universalistic culture on which it depends. In the postWorld War II period, global structuration occurs exponentially (Magnarella 1995): with explosions in central intergovernmental organizing (e.g., not only the UN system, but also many other organizations) and even greater expansions in world non-governmental organizing (Otto 1996; Boli and Thomas 1997).

Global society has developed extremely elaborate conceptions of the collective purposes of the state in managing society (see the general reviews in Chapter 8 or Finnemore 1996). It contains comprehensive doctrines of economic and social and political development, often with standardized measures of "success" (e.g., the GDP per capita, now gone worldwide). And it contains very elaborate visions of social and individual rights and justice (Ramirez and Meyer 1992), now including justice and equality across age, gender, sexual preference, and ethnic and racial lines (Berkovitch 1994; McNeely 1995; Dryzek 1996: 476–8). It also now includes elaborate and standardized conceptions of the proper relationship of societies to their natural ecosystemic environment (Frank 1998).

It is all phrased quite universally[3] and is justified in terms of the scientific and natural law understanding of a universalized and rationalized cosmos. The result is the modern picture of the environment (Frank et al., forthcoming), society, and the individual person (Frank, Meyer, and Miyahara 1995). The impact on typical nation-states is enormous. First, all this universalism aids in legitimating the global spread and stability of these entities (Strang 1990; McNeely 1995). But it also impacts formal structure – and often practice – in the widest variety of areas (Chapter 8; Meyer 1994; see also Donnelly 1989). Formal isomorphism, around universalized principles, is a dominant trend, despite the enormous practical variation among countries in resources or cultural traditions.

Thus, the modern nation-state is very much a creature of a theoretically imagined community (Anderson 1991), and the theoretical imagination is prominently a worldwide rationalistic and universalistic model of state, society, and the individual (Thomas 1987).

---

[3] Naturally, some countries resist pressure to conform to a notion of natural law, particularly outside the West, but even these countries engage in rationalizations based on Western ideas in the international realm (e.g., Crystal 1994).

IMPACT ON THE LAW AND THE LEGAL SYSTEM

In two ways, as discussed above, the wider universalistic culture of modernity impacts the law. First, modern legal systems are rooted in the nominal sovereignty of the national state. But as we discuss above, this sovereignty principle comes with dependence on the wider legitimating rationalistic culture. Thus the legislators and lawyers and judges are creatures of the nation-state organization (variably across national distinctions such as the civil/common law [Jepperson and Meyer 1991; or Boyle 1996]). Even the most despotic dictator now claims to represent the interests of a nation's citizens. But in playing these roles, they are also creatures of the wider culture in which the state is embedded and dependent on its definitions and conceptions: the servants of the state are involved in the business of applying putatively universal and rational principles of science and natural law, and of the rational pursuit of progress and justice, to their local polities.[4]

Second, wider universalistic and rational principles apply not only to the state, but also to every aspect of the status of society, its functional groups and interests, and the individuals in it. The law and lawyers play an independent role. Professionalized, the lawyers and law have direct responsibilities to reflect the overall rationalized and universalized principles to a myriad of particular situations, not all of which may be covered by the interests of a particular state. The law is above the particularities of the state and is to speak a wider universalistic truth. Liberal and/or common law contexts emphasize this independence and all democratic countries in the modern world, almost by definition, claim independent judiciaries. The law is thus dependent on wider truths, organized by scientists, social scientists, and professionalized knowledge of all sorts about nature, society and its interests, and individuals (Chapter 8; Meyer 1994). We note once again that these "truths" may or may not actually exist – the important point for this chapter is that actors in the modern world operate *as if* they exist.

IMPLICATIONS OF THE DEPENDENCE OF THE MODERN LAW ON GLOBALIZED, RATIONALIZED, AND UNIVERSAL CULTURAL PRINCIPLES

An understanding of the "secularized religious" dependence of the law aids in understanding modern legal systems. Law is at once derived from, and ostensible evidence of, general but powerful rules of nature. The connection to religion also illuminates the organization of the modern world system around a central principle –

---

[4] The states which fail to follow these roles are the exceptions which prove the rule. For example, when Iraq challenged notions of sovereignty by occupying Kuwait, it was labeled a rule-breaker and soundly condemned by the international community (see, e.g., Kahn 1992).

not God's will, but similar universal ideas carried through sovereignty. Agency rather than predestination determines the future, "social" change exists and can be systematically analyzed, and "neutrality" replaces doctrine. The modern system of sovereign nation-states, like God's will at an earlier time, encompasses reality and becomes the foundation which explains the world.[5] Bringing attention to the – necessarily imperfect – correspondence between modern legal systems and taken-for-granted beliefs in universal ideals helps make sense of issues raised in the sociology of law.

The closer a rule system is tied to ideas of universalism, the more, we argue, it will manifest the characteristics described below. Resource capacity is a competing explanation for conformity, but the effects of that variable are less clear. If a new human rights doctrine arises, a core country like Sweden is likely to learn of it early on and have many professionals who can translate the new doctrine into policy. On the other hand, these same resources could allow Sweden to resist or modify the new doctrine, an option unavailable to resource poor countries. Although having more resources enables core organizations to conform, having less resources simultaneously limits peripheral organizations' ability to resist or modify the operating frame. While resources undoubtedly play a role, links to the universal ideal frame seem more consistently and predictably important.

While the assumption and integration of universal principles is most profound at the international and nation-state levels, over time these ideals penetrate many other spheres. Business organizations adopt elaborate due process procedures (Edelman 1990), schools forbid corporal punishment, and even families come under increasing pressure to conform to universal standards. These latter spheres come under the influence of universal principles later and more indirectly than nation-states. They maintain more discretion and more idiosyncrasies. Consequently, they make useful points of comparison with the exogenous focus of national legal systems. We refer generally to entities in these spheres loosely as "organizations."

The contrast with mundane rule-making in the non-sovereign sphere, or in countries with competing religious universals (e.g., some Islamic countries), illustrates what law looks like within organizations which are less linked to exogenous universal principles or assumptions about sovereignty. To operationalize the continuum of linkage to putative universal principles, one could consider the extent to which an organization's identity was linked to the sovereignty of the nation-state and to the international community. One could also consider organizational, associational, and professional ties. In the case of typical nation-states themselves, these cultural and associational linkages would, of course, be extremely high. Among non-sovereign organizations, state monopolies (e.g., schools) or organizations with major state oversight should be more linked to universal ideals than more local and economically competitive organizations.

The global diffusion of the nation-state form (including the modern legal system) was facilitated by its universalism and the rationalism. To summarize the implications

---

[5] *Quod semper, quod ubique, quod ab omnibus creditum est* [The thing which has been believed always, everywhere, and by all] (Saint Vincent of Lirens ca. 450).

of rule system dependence on universal cultural principles, we propose the following three general themes:

1. The closer an organization is tied to the global and putatively universalistic system, the more its rule system will participate in the diffusion and expansion of universal principles through (*a*) the adoption of laws and legal discourse consistent with international cultural accounts, (*b*) isomorphism, and (*c*) the extension of its jurisdiction into more areas of the organization.

2. The closer an organization is tied to the global and putatively universalistic system, the more its rule system will engage in the ritualized enactment of law through greater (*a*) ceremony surrounding law, (*b*) decoupling between law and social reality, (*c*) elaborate restrictions on how to find the truth.

3. The closer an organization is tied to the global and putatively universalistic system, the more its rule system will assume the existence of an integrated and rationalized cosmos by (*a*) adopting scientific methods of inquiry, (*b*) relying explicitly on the idea of rationality, and (*c*) decoupling abstract justice rules of the system from concrete assessments of the justice of particular outcomes, (*d*) efforts to find and maintain consistency, and (*e*) the drive to expansion.

This section of the chapter is organized around these three general themes. We discuss each in turn.

Diffusion and expansion

The assumption, built into all modern legal systems, that the law reflects universal principles, produces a consequence that realist theories cannot well explain. The organization of legal systems and laws themselves are remarkably similar around the world despite much local cultural and material variation. This suggests that over-arching principles are prompting conformity, while local differences are creating small variations.

1. *Exchange of laws, rules, and legal discourse.* Across nation-states, laws diffuse much more rapidly than theories emphasizing local interests and culture would predict. And they diffuse in ways not predicted by theories seeing them as dependent on local or national sovereignty boundaries. This can easily be explained in terms of our arguments. States maintain their legitimacy through their responsiveness to perceived universal principles. National laws become an important symbol of the acceptance of these perceived principles. So laws readily diffuse across state boundaries in the United States (Walker 1969). And, now, they rapidly diffuse, around the world, from national constitutions (Boli 1987) to legal policy (Chapter 6; McNeely 1995) down into particular domains.

The content of the international ideals that diffuse has been discussed at length elsewhere (e.g., Meyer, Boli, and Thomas 1987). In general, the ideals are consistent with Western notions of individual rights and progress. The more a nation-state is linked into the international system, the more its rules will follow these basic ideas.

Rape laws provide an example of this. Highly universalistic legal systems make no distinctions between categories of persons. All types of women and men can perpetrate and be the victims of rape. Weakly universalized systems have entirely different legal rules for different types of people. In some Islamic countries, Hudood [religious] laws apply to Muslim rapists, and civil laws apply to other rapists. Some legal systems lie between these two extremes, as when countries have only one legal system which applies to all persons, but which differentiates between different kinds of persons, that is, the rape of a prostitute versus the rape of other types of women (Frank 1998). The greater the linkage to the international system, the more laws' application and content will conform to platonic ideals.

It is routine for legislators, law professors, and even courts to cite principles established in courts operating under an entirely different sovereign: the cross-national citing of cases and decisions has increased dramatically in the current period (see, e.g., Robinson 1996; Strauss 1995; Rosenberg 1997). It is also true that the principles of international law (including international governmental and even non-governmental organizations) routinely appear in legal decisions in particular countries, despite the extreme ambiguity in sovereignty involved. And international courts begin to take conformity across nation-states as evidence of universal principles. The European Court of Human Rights is a case in point (Harris, O'Boyle, and Warbrick 1995: 8–11, 580). Since its inception in 1955, over 25,000 claims have been filed with the Court. Consensus among European nations has a considerable impact on the decisions of the court. A state with a unique policy within the European community is particularly at risk of an adverse judgment (see *Tyrer v. UK,* A 26 para 31 [1978]). This result occurs because European consensus is deemed inspired by a common, universal law.

In all these cases, underlying assumptions of universalism make for the easy flow of legal rules across the boundaries of nominal sovereignty. The flows of legal rules seem most extreme when high and general principles, for example, of human rights, about the scientized environment or about national socioeconomic progress are involved (see, e.g., Dezalay and Garth 1995). Fundamental principles, contrary to much theory, may flow more easily than less fundamental adaptations. This characterizes a world in which local structures are envisioned in terms of universal rules. It probably describes much better the world of the high culture of the law (see Risse and Sikkink, forthcoming) than that of practical or mundane organizations dealing with local issues on local principles.

In the same way, the organizational system of the law permits the flow of participants and communication across sovereignty boundaries more readily than conventional theories might suppose. Legal cultures and discourse flow readily across state and national boundaries. United States legal research resources such as Lexis and Westlaw routinely include the codes and legal decisions of non-US sovereigns. Law firms specializing in international law now flourish and hold prestigious positions within the legal community. Hiring lawyers from other countries becomes routine for law firms as well as corporations, and transnational legal practice guides appear with increasing frequency (e.g., Campbell 1982; Pritchard 1991). Legal culture and discourse assemble themselves easily in international governmental and non-governmental organizational arenas (Boli and Thomas 1997). General legal expertise, it is assumed, carries across particular systems of law and training. This depends on the assumption that common underlying principles are involved.

On the other hand, at the localistic extreme, practical organizational rules, set out in non-legal situations, flow slowly across organizational boundaries. These rules are geared to satisfying local clientele. Even within the same multinational corporation, corporate rules tend to vary from country to country (see Hofstede 1980, for attitudinal data). The allocation of responsibilities to particular departments or occupations, the exact definitions of employee rights: rules such as these are expected to differ significantly from organization to organization. It is routine to assume that organizational cultures might naturally differ in different contexts: this becomes a problem only when the high legal culture intervenes.

2. *Isomorphism among legal systems.* The ideas given above suggest an implication that is often observed in specific cases, but less often noted in general. Legal systems – supposedly linked to particular societies, but in our view reflective of much common cultural material – are often much more similar than might be expected. Nation-states differ by ratios of 100 to 1 in resources per capita. They differ enormously in local cultural traditions. It is therefore surprising how similar their legal arrangements tend to be. The literature naturally emphasizes differences in property rules, family law, and the like, playing up what are often quite modest differences. It is more realistic to note how similar these systems are and how much they change in parallel. For instance, formal legal rules about human rights show a great deal of isomorphism and isomorphic change, despite enormous differences in practice and practical circumstances (Chapter 8; McNeely 1995; Risse and Sikkink forthcoming).

The intensification and expansion of world society and culture in the postWorld War II framework, and the creation of many new nation-states highly dependent on this framework, has greatly increased world pressures for legal isomorphism. We could therefore expect to find increases on this dimension in the current period, and more rapid rates of change toward isomorphism. We would also expect to find expansions in the number of domains (e.g., the environment, family law, etc.) in which rapid isomorphism occurs.

Prevailing theories of a more realist vein would suggest that legal isomorphism among countries obtains particularly in social areas (e.g., the economy) with relatively high international interdependence. Our argument is that it obtains when there is great perceived similarity of identity (Chapter 6) and can explain rapid legal diffusion in areas with quite low interdependence: rationalized family law, human rights principles, many environmental domains, education, medicine, and the like. In fact, an extreme version of our argument would treat much intersocietal interdependence as slowing down – not speeding up – diffusion and isomorphism, since it tends to create networks of differentiated and opposing interests and mobilization.

A striking feature of modern world legal development is its isomorphism precisely in domains with relatively low levels of exchange and interdependence. Family arrangements are viewed as a core cultural difference from place to place. One might expect that law and the state would allow wide latitude for variation in a sphere so central to the transmission of local culture. But when these systems are legalized, for example in terms of human rights, pressures for coherence and consistency rise, and consultants and advisors and legal principles flow readily across national boundaries. Recent expansions of law to encompass issues formerly left to a parent's discretion (spanking, female circumcision, etc.) raise the issue of cultural autonomy, but come down strongly on the side of universal principles (see, e.g., Boyle and Preves 1998; Frank 1998). A proper family does not beat its children, and the state has an obligation to insure that this is so, a proper family is the union of two individuals with equal rights to marital dissolution, and so on. From family planning to childrearing to divorce, the legally established meaning and "purpose" of the family has been surprisingly standardized around the world.

Other domains outside of international interdependence have also become the focus of laws consistent with the universalized ideas. Despite obvious geographic differences, the proper relationship of individuals to the environment has an assumed uniformity, and regulation looks very similar from one nation-state to the next. The role of women in society is another example. Recent articles have suggested that the state has not only negative obligations to refrain from abusing its citizens, but also a positive obligation to insure a more even distribution of power between men and women (Etienne 1995; Stetson 1995; Schuler 1992). Another example is military strategy, a key element of sovereign autonomy. Legal restraints on particular types of warfare, such as the use of chemical weapons or landmines, are often readily accepted throughout the international system (Price 1997). Theories of globalization based on local movements or interdependencies have a hard time explaining the pressure for uniformity in areas such as these. Nations, like Toqueville's Americans, may be most similar at the points at which they most stress their uniqueness and autonomy.

3. *Expanding jurisdiction of legalized rule systems.* Legal decision-making not based on the system of universal principles is the target of much suspicion. So myths about the importance of the universal ideals are maintained, despite the diversity of local social organizations and cultures. The modern expansion of the nation-state into many more domains – family life, the environment, economic regulation, and so on – is accomplished through the extension of standardized legal rules. Alternatives such as arrangements of hierarchical domination over, rather than penetration of, local segments are undercut. This explains, in modern times, the increasing reach of the law into areas which were previously unregulated, including rule-making in non-sovereign organizations. Belief in the correctness of universal principles mandates a concern that segmentation or indirect control will undermine sovereignty. Modern sovereignty seems to call, not so much for organizational domination, as for the legalized penetration of standardized rules. So relations between spouses, parents and children, employers and employees, buyers and sellers, or teachers and students are managed by ever-expanding direct legal application of general principles rather than simply by organizational domination.

Organizations which are linked to exogenous universal principles pick up this idea (or are required to), and, at least in appearance, subordinate themselves to such principles, acknowledging their lack of complete sovereignty. They often voluntarily attempt to link into the universal principles themselves and accept legalized controls. They also expand their subordinated rule-making authority into more areas of the organization and into more areas of employee lives. They formalize maternity leave and set up on-site daycare, create proper grievance procedures and systems of employee rights, and incorporate the appropriate professionals (Meyer and Rowan 1977; DiMaggio and Powell 1983). The correctness of all this is taken for granted.

The dependence of modern states and legal systems on wider models and the elaborated and universalistic character of these models create a situation in which the widest variety of social interests and social problems lead to expansions of legalization both in national societies and in the world as a whole. This is most striking in the peripheries of the world, where the availability of expanded general models leads both states and local interests to build elaborated rules and claims. Injustices and inefficiencies are seen that would otherwise be taken for granted. But the effects occur in core countries, too, and in the world as a whole: all sorts of interests, grievances, and problems lead both states and local actors to participate in the expansion of the system to cover, for instance, newly perceived environmental problems.

Thus, the widest variety of local interests and problems, in the modern context, can feed into the overall expansion of globalized legal arrangements as well as their penetration of local life.

Ritualized enactment

As in all situations in which transcendent principles are at issue, the law is enacted and enforced in highly ceremonial ways (Chapter 4). While general ideas are broadly understood, the ability to translate reality into a legal framework is limited to specialists – lawyers and judges. We discuss three dimensions on which the legal system tends to be distinctive. It is difficult to explain these properties without resort to our arguments about the extent to which the law carries and depends on assumptions of higher values.

1. *Ceremony.* Rule systems which are more closely tied to exogenous universal principles enact law in highly ceremonially constituted contexts. This maintains the special status of the law and suggests its separateness from, and superiority to, ordinary individual decision-making. Legislators, judges, and even lawyers take special oaths and occupy special positions with distinctive rights and responsibilities. Courts are highly ceremonial places. Witnesses swear before God to tell the whole truth, and perjury is the most serious of transgressions. Just as sinners were central to, but disassociated from, Church rituals, so too the public is distanced from court-room rituals. Legal proceedings are conducted on behalf of the public; the public is expected to contribute in certain limited respects (e.g., as jurors in common law countries), but the heart of the courtroom is the area from which the ordinary public

is barred. In this way courts are easily distinguished from the mundane society around them.

Further, within nation-states, lawyers generally make up a bounded and nominally unified profession, despite the diversity of their activities. Analogous to a priesthood, there are elaborate rituals of socialization, principles of professional unity, and extremely sharp designations of who is, and who is not, a lawyer. Learning the arcane rhetoric of law (*habeus corpus, replevin, appellee,* etc.) is an important aspect of becoming a lawyer (Sarat and Kearns 1994). Stringent controls characterize entry into the legal profession – in the common law world, through lawyers' voluntary associations; in the civil law world, through controls exercised by the state (Abel 1988). Within the legal profession, those lawyers with the closest ties to universal principles of justice (e.g., constitutional law professors) or science (e.g., patent lawyers) are those with the highest prestige (see Heinz and Laumann 1982; see also Abbott 1988). In modern nation-states, those who find or interpret the law have special insight into the universal principles, and are clearly distinguishable from those who merely try to live according to the law.

Note how distinctive national legal systems are from proto-legal rule-making and enforcement in contexts in which the high culture of modernity is less invoked. Typical organizations make mundane rules routinely. Examples might include: decisions about subunit responsibilities and resources, detailed rules about travel allowances or office supplies, rearrangements of roles and their authority, the specification of particular office hours, or systems for handling complaints. Organizations can often create such rules rather casually through payroll employees, minor administrators, or committees, enact them without much ceremony (Zhou 1993), and enforce them in organizationally routine ways. Until recently, organizations did these things without much blessing from a symbolically unified and bounded legal profession (Dobbin et al. 1994), though legalization has now increased.[6] Rather, it was assumed that responsible people could interpret the rules without any special knowledge. Creating and changing routine rules did not legitimate or delegitimate management in a typical organization because management was not understood as trying to implement higher universal principles. As organizations become more dependent on exogenous ideals to maintain their legitimacy, they may begin to develop special pre-designated spaces and procedures to deal with problems and "independent" departments (i.e., human resources departments) to deal with employees.

2. *Decoupling between law on the books and reality.* Nation-states, because of their ostensible link to universal principles, also produce extreme decoupling of the law from practical social life (Chapter 4; Weick 1976; March and Olsen 1976). Law expresses and defines society in terms of the general principles on which it depends, and doing so makes it important to bound the law from mundane social reality. We

---

[6] Rules which have been considered mundane historically are coming under increasing pressure to conform to external legal guidelines, e.g., firing employees (Edelman, Abraham, and Erlanger 1992).

are not suggesting that there is no relationship between law and action – both are influenced by the putatively universal principles. Because law is more a reflection than an instrument of these principles, however, it is unlikely to have great, direct influence on much social action above and beyond the general effects of globalization.

Reality, practicality, and ease of use are emphatically not what the law is about. The law is about principle and the belief in some greater good, at least in part transcending any specific society or situation. Laws are as much invocations of perceived universal ideals and symbols of state legitimacy as they are routine concessions to various special interest groups. This explains why national laws emerge for which practical society shows more ambivalence than enthusiastic support (e.g., right to strike laws or laws giving rights to unpopular minorities). It also explains why legal systems have a profusion of symbolic, impractical rules (Gusfield 1986; Duster 1970), unenforced rules (Black 1982), and legal fictions (Fuller 1967; Olivier 1975).

The actual invocation of law is a dramatic step, infrequently taken, although the threat to invoke the law is omnipresent. Contracts are written but not used (Macaulay 1969); elaborate criminal court procedures are created but not employed in dealing with the vast majority of discovered deviations (Kaplan and Skolnick 1981). Judges create legal fictions to maintain the immutability of the law long after social change has reduced the actual terms of the law to nonsense. This is difficult to explain from most theoretical points of view. Why would impracticable, unenforced rules and principles be so common and so important? But the law survives and expands, in our view reflecting substantially different considerations than the practicability or wisdom of implementation.

From our point of view this decoupling is central to the national project. While decoupling characterizes all sorts of rationalized organization (Meyer and Scott 1991), decoupling occurs particularly in areas where corporate self-interest and extra-organizational legal requirements conflict (see, e.g., Chapter 4; Edelman 1990). In other words, decoupling occurs at precisely the point where the law intrudes.

The less a rule is linked explicitly or implicitly to ideals outside the organization, the less separation of "spirit" and "practice" is possible. If an office closes at 5 p.m. for no particular reason – just because – it is quite different from an office that closes at 5 p.m. as a requirement of state law. In the latter case, closing the office at 5.15 p.m. has numerous interpretations. Are the office employees being exploited? Are office clients at this particular location receiving an unfair advantage over clients who live across town? In our view, decoupling reflects not the extreme practical difficulties faced by the law, but rather the extraordinarily important and universalized culture on which it depends and which it must reflect. We propose that organizations, such as the nation-state and its legal system, which are more tied in to universalistic cultural accounts will have less specific enforcement provisions and more unused, unenforced rules and procedures than more localized, mundane organizations.

The decoupled character of legal systems is sometimes (and rather reasonably) taken to be an indicator of their ineffectiveness and functional unimportance. This may be realistic in dealing with some traditional legal systems, but misses important points in approaching the modern one. The modern system is decoupled precisely because it is so linked to universal models and standards, despite the limited and variable character of local social life. These universal ideas are available, not only to states and some lawyers, but to a wide variety of local interests and potential grievants as well. Despite the practical constraints and limitations of local circumstances, some wider perspectives are empowered by the expanded and universal character of the models. Local actors can look at their limited situations in terms of great rules about socioeconomic progress and social justice: mobilizing resources and sometimes concrete resource networks can be envisioned and are sometimes available. Thus, social interests and forces feed into the expansion and penetration of the wider models and lead to the creation of new variations in these models.

3. *Restrictions on determining truth.* Ritualization also appears in the legal obsession with "proper" evidence. Rule systems which imagine more links to universal principles tend to have elaborate restrictions on proof. In modern courts, "tainted" evidence, regardless of its probity, is strictly limited. In general, individuals may only speak for themselves: if others try to speak for them this is deemed "hearsay." The introduction of evidence into the courtroom is surrounded by elaborate ceremony. Evidence is formally introduced. The chain of possession is carefully reconstructed. The judge determines admissibility, and only then is the evidence considered. Who can bring a claim is also circumscribed. In general, individuals and organizations cannot bring claims for the common good, as that would belie the special access of courts and the state to the universal principles.

Organizations outside the system of universal principles are more likely to consider any pieces of information which come to their attention in trying to resolve issues. Any person presenting information may well be listened to. "Relevance" has a broader scope. Evidence flows informally, perhaps through gossip. The ritualized enactment of universal principles occurs in organizations with more links to global cultural accounts through formal rule systems which limit evidence, claims, and the standing to bring claims.

The assumption of an integrated and rational cosmos

Modern legal systems rest on the ideas that natural and social worlds occur in a unified and lawful context, and that this context can be understood in an integrated way. The core of this integrated system is a belief in rationality. Many features of modern law can be understood in these terms.

1. *The scientific progress of the law.* Modern national legal systems are more dependent on expanding scientific or scientized knowledge, including scientific methods, than the rule systems of non-sovereign organizations. Expert witnesses are commonly used in both legislation and court activity (Stryker 1994). And increasingly expert witnesses include social scientists, as in the gender discrimination lawsuit brought by Ann Hopkins against the Price Waterhouse accounting firm in

the 1980s. Susan Fiske, a well-known American social psychologist, figured prominently in the trial court's judgment (Hopkins 1997). Economics becomes the basis for numerous legal doctrines. Lawyers routinely hire jury experts and survey potential juries to predict outcomes. Criminal cases rest on the ability of the FBI crime laboratory to stick meticulously to its scientific mandate. Scientized knowledge about nature and the rational causal principles derived from its laws have extraordinarily high standing. Legal systems which are tied into universal principles also tend to follow a scientific model. For example, Harvard Law School in 1870 adopted a "scientific" method for learning and understanding law which quickly spread to, and still exists in, most US law schools (Friedman 1985:321–2).

In more recent times, the world is frequently considered a "laboratory" wherein national laws become natural "experiments" (see Black and Coffee 1994; cf. Zimring and Hawkins 1973). And legal cases mimic the aura of scientific experiments, for example, when jurors undertake the rigorous testing of the null hypothesis of the defendant's innocence. Legal systems exalt science and rationality.

Scientific methods are less likely to be employed in the day-to-day operations of a typical organization. Organizations often make policy decisions on the basis of hunches and interests. Typical organizations are less likely to systematize the actions of employees and more willing to let things drift. As universal and legalized principles in the current period penetrate nonsovereign organizations, the organizations are more likely to depend on the knowledge of professional and scientific consultants. They might employ scientists as in-house psychologists, economists, and the like. They might also enthusiastically recruit experts to systematize how employees approach their work.

2. *Rationality is expanded and invented.* In the modern period, rational motivation replaces religious explanations for individual action. Typically, the existence and importance of this rationality is taken for granted. National legal systems constantly search for rational, or rational choice, explanations to underlie legal rules and decisions. Elaborate scientific and rationalistic analyses are sought to adjudicate issues around the "battered wife syndrome," "repressed memory syndrome," or issues of effective legal deterrence. Numerous legal scholars suggest or assume that crime occurs after individuals rationally weigh the costs and benefits of committing crimes. Crimes and criminals who do not fit the model well are minimized as unimportant in understanding crime generally or brought imaginatively into a rational frame. Elaborate literatures arise, and their conclusions are routinely cited in the courts and legislative hearings. Courts also routinely measure individuals according to "reasonable person" standards. Would a reasonable person rationally believe that his or her conduct could lead to great bodily harm or death? Could a reasonable person be misled by the conduct of the defendant? Just as all individuals at one time had access to God through penance and prayer, now all individuals are assumed to have access to "universal truth" through rational thought.

Note how much more casual all this is in non-legal organizational rule-making. Mundane organizational rules depend on such analyses, to be true, but the urgency involved seems dramatically lower. In business, personal preferences may figure prominently in the allocation of work, and personal contacts may form the basis of continued business with particular suppliers or clients. In families, expressiveness is the key, and rationality still seems out of place. Weighing the costs and benefits of each potential spouse when deciding who to marry seems inappropriate (and callous), for example.

3. *Decoupling between the justice of the system and the justice of particular outcomes.* Unfortunate outcomes are more easily explained as resorts to higher principles in rule systems linked to universal ideals. When a system is linked to justice as a universal principle, then the system does not need to justify every outcome it produces. Rather, these rule systems are legitimated by their linkage to universal justice. Thus, in the 1200s, death could be an unfortunate side effect of determining whether a person was a witch, such as when suspected witches were tossed into water with stones tied to their feet. Those who sunk (and perhaps drowned) were deemed innocent; those who floated were deemed true witches and were burned at the stake. The witch trials emphasized "truth" over "justice": it was more important to know whether a person was a witch than to have a just outcome for the accused. Similarly, modern national legal systems are often unconcerned with particular outcomes, although the universal principle of sovereignty inverts the religious universals, emphasizing "justice" over "truth." Under the modern universal law, a dead body and a smoking gun may not be enough to convict a guilty person if the state did not follow the proper procedure in accusing him. In both the religious and the sovereignty systems, problematic outcomes are sometimes celebrated in the name of higher universal principles.

At the other end of the continuum, the practical effects of decisions are central to mundane organizational decision-making, even though ordinary organizations are increasingly subjected to institutional pressures for legalization (Chapter 4). Justice and truth are considered after assessing the impact of any outcome on the future of the organization. Complaints by disgruntled employees against the owner's son might be ignored or minimized regardless of their merit. Complaints by an important client are likely to be acted upon even if unfounded. Such inconsistency is rarely noted, but if it does come to the attention of management, organizational authorities "not wanting to stand on principle" might justify it as good business. Depending on the strength of an organization's ties to exogenous universal principles, its rule system may focus more on fair process than specific outcomes, and it may emphasize merit over lockstep or familial justifications for promotion and pay.

4. *The search for consistency.* National legal systems assume the importance of ultimate consistency, while more mundane organizational rule-making authorities may not. Inconsistency is seen as irrational, and extreme efforts are made to rule it out in civil law systems with detailed codes and internal coordinating committees (Blankenburg 1994: 264) and in common law systems with elaborate structures of hierarchical courts (Damaska 1986). Inconsistent rules provide counter-evidence to the idea that legal systems are based on universal principles and thus represent a serious threat to legitimacy. The emphasis on consistency by nation-states occurs

both within and increasingly across jurisdictions. Legal doctrines of one country (e.g., inheritance, rules of evidence) are assumed to exist in all others (see, e.g., Malinowski 1934). Much argumentation and citation is devoted to finding and rooting out inconsistency: if different courts, states, or now even countries have different conclusions on fundamental matters, something is wrong.

There are at least two strategies for dealing with perceived inconsistencies. The first response is to change inconsistent laws or overturn inconsistent cases on appeal. The second, and probably more prevalent response, is to "explain" the inconsistency. To a scientist, this is the imposition of scope conditions; to a lawyer, this is distinguishing cases or laws. Scholars seek to derive universal principles from diverse national laws (see, e.g., Frase 1990 [sentencing]; Black and Coffee 1994 [securities]; LoPucki and Triantis 1994 [bankruptcy]). The ideal of consistency is one source of the extreme decoupling discussed earlier. Unenforced rules allow the legal system to avoid the head-on conflicts which might threaten secular religious assumptions about universality. Legal fictions are devised so that "the internal coherence of the new with the old is ensured, and thus the systematic unity of the whole law" (Savigny 1840).

This is all quite different in mundane organizational rule-making and enforcement. It is not surprising or troubling to discover that Corporation A gives ten weeks of unpaid maternity leave while Corporation B gives six weeks of paid maternity leave. It is easy to understand, and not an urgent problem, if one organization has different rules than another and if the two rule systems are inconsistent. As putative universal principles increasingly penetrate organizations and become a source of legitimacy for corporate actions, consistency becomes more important to organizations. They develop elaborate job descriptions which insure that any individual can take on a job without changing the fundamental character of the organization. They get external validation of their conformity to universal standards such as ISO-9000 procedures (Mendel 1996). Formal advancement mechanisms insure the consistent treatment of all employees (Sutton et al. 1994). And management techniques, such as Taylorism or more recently McDonaldization (Ritzer 1993), maintain consistent decision-making in numerous contexts.

5. *The Drive to Expansion.* The dependence of modern legal systems on universal models and standards linked to scientific and rationalistic analysis of a broader nature produces much pressure and opportunity for expansion and globalization. Legitimated social interests have many incentives to support their claims with expanded scientific and rationalistic analysis. They find new efficiency claims (e.g., with economic analysis) to support and stabilize themselves; new medical, social and psychological analyses to empower justice claims; and new environmental analyses to support both individual and collective interests. On the other side, the elites of national states search for similar grounds with which to legitimate and stabilize their authority. The activities of all these parties operate to expand and further globalize the legal arrangements produced, providing an expansive dynamic for the whole system. We can imagine that a more closed world state system would find devices to block the processes of discovery and analysis involved: in the modern world, no

central authority exists to block the expansions in cultural knowledge and authority which expand and globalize legal arrangements.

CONCLUSION

One useful conception of modern legal systems is that they emerge to serve coordinative functions in increasingly complex and interdependent economies and polities. This is undoubtedly true. But focusing solely on this explanation misses important features of these systems that can better be explained in terms of their common historical and contemporary dependence on an evolving world cultural frame – originally religious, and now secularized in terms of very general lawful principles about the physical world, the proper goals of state society, and the natural status of individuals and interests within society. Taken-for-granted principles define and regulate sovereignty, rationality, collective goals, individual rights and interests and justice: these lead to the alignment of interests and actions under common legal principles.

This view can help explain many features of modern legal systems: their surprising isomorphism, even in domains with little interdependence; their ritualization and decoupling from practical reality; and their rationalism, and chronic search for consistency. A legal world is produced with much more commonality – diffusion, isomorphism, and shared rationalism – than would result from more realist models of power and interest in growing interdependence.

This is a world which attempts to control dissension and resistance through the dynamic expansion of integrated and universalistic models justified by analyses of nature and rationality. Dissension and resistance, then, feed into expansion and globalization by locating new claims – for instance, for new rights, for socioeconomic development, or for environmental protection – within the models and the analyses of nature on which they are based. Both the forces of control and the forces of resistance lead to the expansion of generalized and universalistic legalized frames. The system may be hegemonic – and certainly is Western in its notions of justice and progress – but it also empowers an extraordinary range of both powerful and relatively powerless interests to take mobilized action that has the effect of both expansion and globalization.

REFERENCES

Abbott, Andrew. 1988. *The System of Professions: An Essay on the Division of Expert Labor.* Chicago, IL: University of Chicago Press.

Abel, Richard. 1988. Lawyers in the Civil Law World, in Richard Abel (ed.), *Lawyers in Society. Volume Two. The Civil Law World.* Berkeley, CA: University of California Press, pp. 1–53.

Anderson, Benedict. 1991. *Imagined Communities. Reflections on the Origins and Spread of Nationalism.* London: Verso.

Anderson, Benedict. 1972. *Java in a Time of Revolution: Occupation and Resistance, 1944 to 1946.* Ithaca, NY: Cornell University Press.

Bendix, Reinhard. 1964. *Nation-Building and Citizenship: Studies of Our Changing Social Order.* New York: Wiley.

Berkovitch, Nitza. 1994. From Motherhood To Citizenship. The Worldwide Incorporation of women into the Public Sphere in The Twentieth Century, PhD dissertation. Stanford University, Stanford, California.

Berman, Harold. 1993. *Faith and Order: The Reconciliation of Law and Religion.* Atlanta, GA: Scholars Press.

Black, Donald. 1982. The Boundaries of Legal Sociology. *Yale Law Journal* 81:1086–100.

Black, Bernard and John Coffee, Jr. 1994. Hail Britannia? Institutional Investor Behavior Under Limited Regulation. *Michigan Law Review* 92 1:1997–2087.

Blackstone, Sir William. 1821. *Analysis of the Laws of England.* London: J. Sharpe.

Blankenburg, Erhard. 1994. The Infrastructure for Avoiding Civil Litigation: Comparing Cultures of Legal Behavior in the Netherlands and West Germany. *Law & Society Review* 28: 789–808.

Boli, John. 1987. Human Rights or State Expansion? Cross-National Definitions of Constitutional Rights, 1870–1970, in George Thomas, John W. Meyer, Francisco Ramirez, and John Boli (eds.), *Institutional Structure. Constituting State, Society, and the Individual,* Newbury Park, CA: Sage, pp. 133–49.

—— and George Thomas. 1997. World Culture in the World Polity: A Century of International Non-Governmental Organization. *American Sociological Review* 62:171–90.

Boyle, Elizabeth Heger. 1996. Litigants, Lawbreakers, Legislators. Using Political Frames to Explain Cross-National Variation in Legal Activity. PhD dissertation. Stanford University, Stanford, California.

—— and Sharon Preves. 1998. Sovereign Autonomy Versus Universal Human Rights: The Bases for National Anti-Female-Genital-Excision Laws. Unpublished manuscript. University of Minnesota, Minneapolis, Minnesota.

Campbell, Dennis (ed.) 1982. *Transnational Legal Practice: A Survey of Selected Countries.* Deventer: Kluwer Law and Taxation Publishers.

Carter, Stephen. 1993. *The Culture of Disbelief: How Americans Trivialize Religious Devotion.* New York: Basic Books.

Corillon, Carol. 1989. The Role of Science and Scientists in Human Rights. *Annals of the Academy of the American Political Science Association* 506:129–40.

Crystal, Jill. 1994. The Human Rights Movement in the Arab World. *Human Rights Quarterly* 16:435–54.

Damaska, Mirjan. 1986. *The Faces of Justice and State Authority: A Comparative Approach to the Legal Process.* New Haven: Yale.

David, René and John Brierly. 1984. *Major Legal Systems in the World Today: An Introduction to the Comparative Study of Law.* London: Stevens & Sons.

Dezalay, Yves and Bryant Garth. 1995. Merchants of Law as Moral Entrepreneurs: Constructing International Justice from the Competition for Transnational Business Disputes. *Law & Society Review* 29:27–64.

DiChiara, Albert and John Galligher. 1994. Dissonance and Contradictions in the Origins of Marihuana Decriminalization. *Law & Society Review* 28:41–78.

DiMaggio, Paul and Walter Powell. 1991. Introduction, in Walter Powell and Paul DiMaggio (eds.), *The New Institutionalism in Organizational Analysis.* Chicago, IL: University of Chicago Press, pp. 1–40.

Dobbin, Frank, John Sutton, W. Richard Scott, and John Meyer. 1994. Equal Employment Opportunity and the Law: The Construction of Internal Labor Markets. *American Journal of Sociology* 99:396–427.

Donnelly, Jack. 1989. *Universal Human Rights in Theory and Practice*. Ithaca, NY: Cornell University Press.

Dryzek, John. 1996. *Democracy in Capitalist Times. Ideals, Limits, and Struggles*. New York: Oxford.

Duster, Troy. 1970. *The Legislation of Morality. Law, Drugs, and Moral Judgment*. New York: Free Press.

Edelman, Lauren. 1990. Legal Environments and Organizational Governance: The Expansion of Due Process in the American Workplace. *American Journal of Sociology* 95: 1401–40.

—— Steven Abraham, and Howard Erlanger. 1992. Professional Construction of Law: The Inflated Threat of Wrongful Discharge. *Law & Society Review* 26:47–84.

—— Howard Erlanger, and Christopher Uggen. 1997. The Endogeneity of Law. Unpublished manuscript, University of California at Berkeley.

Etienne, Margareth. 1995. Addressing Gender-Based Violence in an International Context. *Harvard Women's Law Journal* 18:139–70.

Finnemore, Martha. 1996. *National Interests in International Society*. Ithaca, NY: Cornell University Press.

Fuller, Lon. 1967. *Legal Fiction*. Stanford, CA: Stanford University Press.

Frank, David. 1998. Sex and the State. Individualization, Globalization, and the Reconstitution of National Policies, 1945–1995. Grant proposal to the United States National Science Foundation, Harvard University.

—— John Meyer, and David Miyahara. 1995. The Individualist Polity and the Presence of Professionalized Psychology: A Cross-National Study. *American Sociological Review* 60: 360.

—— Ann Hironaka, John Meyer, Evan Schofer, and Nancy Tuma. Forthcoming. The Rationalization and Organization of Nature in World Culture, in John Boli and George Thomas (eds.), *World Polity Formation since 1875: World Culture and International Non-Governmental Organizations*. Stanford, CA: Stanford University Press.

Frase, Richard. 1990. Comparative Criminal Justice as a Guide to American Law Reform: How Do the French Do It, How Can We Find Out, and Why Should We Care? *California Law Review* 78:539.

Friedman, Lawrence. 1985. *History of American Law*, 2nd edn. New York: Simon and Schuster.

Gaete, Rolando. 1991. Postmodernism and Human Rights: Some Insidious Questions. *Law and Critique* 2:149–70.

Galanter, Marc. 1989. *Law and Society in Modern India*. Oxford: Oxford University Press.

Giddens, Anthony. 1990. *Consequences of Modernity*. Stanford, CA: Stanford University Press.

Greenhouse, Carol. 1986. *Praying for Justice: Faith, Order and Community in an American Town*. Ithaca, NY: Cornell University Press.

Gusfield, Joseph. 1986. *Symbolic Crusade: Status Politics and the American Temperance Movement*, 2nd edn. Urbana, IL: University of Illinois Press.

Habermas, Jürgen. 1984. *The Theory of Communicative Action, Volume 1: Reason and the Rationalization of Society*, translated by Thomas McCarthy. Boston, MA: Beacon Press.

Hamilton, Gary and John Sutton. 1989. The Problem of Control in a Weak State: Domination in the US, 1880–1920. *Theory and Society* 18:1–46.

Heinz, John and Edward Laumann. 1982. *Chicago Lawyers: The Social Structure of the Bar*. New York and Chicago, IL: Russell Sage Foundation and American Bar Foundation.

Hopkins, Ann Branigar. 1997. *So Ordered: Making Partner the Hard Way*. Amherst, MA: University of Massachusetts Press.

Jepperson, Ronald and John Meyer. 1991. The Public Order and the Construction of Formal Organizations, in Walter Powell and Paul DiMaggio (eds.), *The New Institutionalism in Organizational Analysis*, Chicago, IL: University of Chicago Press, pp. 204–31.

Kahn, Paul. 1992. Lessons for International Law from the Gulf War. *Stanford Journal of International Law* 28.

Kaplan, John and Jerome Skolnick. 1981. *Criminal Justice. Introductory Cases and Materials*. Mineola, NY: Foundation Press.

Kidder, Robert. 1984. *Connecting Law and Society. An Introduction to Research and Theory*. Englewood Cliffs, NJ: Prentice Hall.

LoPucki, Lynn and George Triantis. 1994. A Systems Approach to Comparing US and Canadian Reorganization of Financially Distressed Companies. *Harvard International Law Journal* 35:267–343.

Macaulay, Stewart. 1969. Noncontractual Relations in Business: A Preliminary Study. *American Sociological Review* 28:55–67.

Magnarella, Paul. 1995. Universal Jurisdiction and Universal Human Rights: A Global Progression. *Journal of Third World Studies* 12:159–71.

Malinowski, Bronislaw. 1934. *Law and Order in Polynesia: A Study of Primitive Legal Institutions*. New York: Harcourt, Brace.

March, James and Johan Olsen. 1976. *Ambiguity and Choice in Organizations*. Bergen: Universitetsforlaget.

Marshall, T. H. 1964. *Class, Citizenship, and Social Development*. New York: Doubleday.

McNeely, Constance. 1995. *Constructing the Nation-State: International Organization and Prescriptive Action*. Westport, CN: Greenwood Press.

Mendel, Peter J. 1996. The Institutional Development of Global Production: The Case of the ISO 9000 International Management Standards. Paper presented at the Conference on Standards & Society, Third Annual Meeting of the European Academy for Standardization, Stockholm, Sweden, May.

Meyer, John. 1994. Rationalized Environments, in W. Richard Scott and John W. Meyer (eds.), *Institutional Environments and Organizations*. Newbury Park, CA: Sage, pp. 28–54.

—— and W. Richard Scott. 1991. The Organization of Societal Sectors. Propositions and Early Evidence, in Walter Powell and Paul DiMaggio (eds.), *The New Institutionalism in Organizational Analysis*. Chicago, IL: University of Chicago Press, pp. 108–42.

—— and Brian Rowan. 1977. Institutionalized Organizations: Formal Structure as Myth and Ceremony. *American Sociological Review* 83: 340–63. Reproduced in Chapter 4.

—— John Boli, and George Thomas 1987. Ontology and Rationalization in the Western Cultural Account, in George Thomas, John W. Meyer, Francisco Ramirez, and John Boli (eds), *Institutional Structure: Constituting State, Society, and the Individual*. Newbury Park, CA: Sage, pp. 12–38.

—— —— —— and Francisco Ramirez. 1997. World Society and the Nation-State. *American Journal of Sociology* 103: 144–81. Reproduced in Chapter 8.

Nadelmann, Ethan. 1990. Global Prohibition Regimes: The Evolution of Norms in International Society. *International Organization* 44: 479–526.

Nonet, Philippe and Philip Selznick. 1978. *Law and Society in Transition: Toward Responsive Law*. New York: Octagon Books.

Olivier, Pierre. 1975. *Legal Fictions in Practice and Legal Science*. Rotterdam: Rotterdam University Press.

Otto, Dianne. 1996. Nongovernmental Organizations in the United Nations System: The Emerging Role of International Civil Society. *Human Rights Quarterly* 18:107–41.

Price, Richard. 1997. *The Chemical Weapons Taboo*. Ithaca, NY: Cornell University Press.

Pritchard, John. 1991. *Law Firms in Europe: The Guide to Europe's Commercial Law Firms*. London: Legalease Europe.

Ramirez, Francisco and John Meyer. 1992. The Institutionalization of Citizenship Principles and the National Incorporation of Women and Children, 1870–1990. Unpublished manuscript. Stanford University, Stanford, California.

Robinson, Mary. 1996. Constitutional Shifts in Europe and the US: Learning From Each Other. *Stanford Journal of International Law* 32:1.

Rosenberg, Gerald. 1997. Do Not Go Gently into that Good Right: The Pernicious Effects of First Amendment Jurisprudence on the High Court of Australia. Paper presented at the Law & Society Association Meetings, St. Louis, Missouri, May.

Risse, Thomas and Kathryn Sikkink. Forthcoming. The Socialization of International Human Rights Norms into Domestic Practices: Introduction, in Thomas Risse, Stephen Ropp, and Kathryn Sikkink (eds.), *The Power of Human Rights: International Norms and Domestic Change*. Cambridge, MA: Cambridge University Press.

Ritzer, George. 1993. *The McDonaldization of Society*. Thousand Oaks, CA: Pine Forge Press.

Savigny, F. C. 1979 [1840]: *System of the Modern Roman Law*, translated by William Holloway. Westport, CN: Hyperion Press.

Schuler, Margaret. 1992. *Freedom from Violence: Women's Strategies from Around the World*. New York: United Nations Development Fund for Women (UNIFEM).

Shue, Henry. 1980. *Basic Rights. Subsistence, Affluence, and US Foreign Policy*. Princeton, NJ: Princeton University Press.

Sklair, Leslie. 1995. *Sociology of the Global System*, 2nd edn. London: Prentice Hall.

Stetson, Dorothy McBride. 1995. Human Rights for Women: International Compliance with a Feminist Standard. *Women & Politics* 15:71–95.

Strang, David. 1990. From Dependency to Sovereignty: An Event History Analysis of Decolonization, 1870–1987. *American Sociological Review* 55:846–60.

—— and John Meyer. 1993. Institutional Conditions for Diffusion. *Theory and Society* 22:487–511. Reproduced in Chapter 6.

Strauss, Paul. 1995. Beyond National Law. *Stanford Journal of International Law* 36:373.

Strayer, Joseph. 1970. *On the Medieval Origins of the Modern State*. Princeton, NJ: Princeton University Press.

Stryker, Robin. 1994. Rules, Resources, and Legitimacy Processes: Some Implications for Social Conflict, Order, and Change. *American Journal of Sociology* 99:847–910.

Sutton, John, Frank Dobbin, W. Richard Scott, and John W. Meyer. 1994. The Legalization of the Workplace. *American Journal of Sociology* 99:944–71.

Thomas, George. 1987. Revivalism, Nation-Building, and Institutional Change, in George Thomas, John W. Meyer, Francisco Ramirez, and John Boli (eds.), *Institutional Structure. Constituting State, Society, and the Individual*. Newbury Park, CA: Sage, pp. 297–314.

Tilly, Charles. 1990. *Coercion, Capital, and European States, A.D. 990 to 1990*. Oxford: B. Blackwell.

—— 1975. *Formation of National States in Western Europe*. Reading, MA: Addison-Wesley.

Trevino, A. Javier. 1996. *The Sociology of Law: Classical and Contemporary Perspectives*. New York: St. Martin's Press.

Walker, Jack. 1969. The Diffusion of Innovation Among the American States. *American Political Science Review* 63:880–9.

Waters, Malcolm. 1996. Human Rights and the Universalisation of Interests: Towards a Social Constructionist Approach. *Sociology* 30:593–600.

Weber, Max. 1958. *The Protestant Ethic and the Spirit of Capitalism*, translated by Talcott Parsons. New York: Scribner.

Weick, Karl. 1976. Educational Organizations as Loosely Coupled Systems. *Administrative Science Quarterly* 21:1–19.

Zhou, Xueguang. 1993. The Dynamics of Organizational Rules. *American Journal of Sociology* 98:1134–66.

Zimring, Franklin and Gordon Hawkins. 1973. *Deterrence: The Legal Threat in Crime Control.* Chicago, IL: University of Chicago Press.

16

The European Union

The European Union and the Globalization of Culture

INTRODUCTION

The European Union is clearly a rather stateless, or centerless, polity. It is made up of many different nation-states and other actions. These, though highly and increasingly interdependent, are nevertheless sovereign and autonomous. Their polity, thus, appears organizationally to be an elaborate, expanding, and intensifying network of relationships among the component nations and states – a "network polity" (Kohler-Koch 1999). In this, Europe is very much like the global society, and it is difficult to make sharp distinctions between Europe as a political form and the world: perhaps for this reason, it is also difficult to draw definite boundaries between Europe and a physical, social, and moral space and the wider world society. The world polity is also, organizationally, a stateless "network polity," an expansive system of associations and linkages (Boli and Thomas 1999).

How are such systems held together, in the absence of authoritative centers and sharply maintained boundaries? The answer is that a political-organizational picture of Europe, or the world, is very incomplete. The polity of strongly legitimated actors in networks presumes some basic common cultural principles (Andersen 2000). And the operation of such a polity generates and expands such principles (Tocqueville 1836). In other words, the organizational picture of the European (or the world) polity is very incomplete if one does not take into account the cultural material that is intrinsic to it.

Understanding Europe, thus, requires comprehending not only its organizational structure, but also the institutionalized base on which this structure rests (and which it operates! to further institutionalize). Social arrangement can, of course, be built on or institutionalized in many different ways (see Jepperson 1991 for a rather definitive discussion). Theories, and social realities, differ in where institutionalization is located. The concept of institution simply refers to a location of meaning and identity outside the social system under examination.

Originally published as:

John W. Meyer. 2001. The European Union and the Globalization of Culture', in Svein S. Andersen (ed.), Institutional Approaches to the European Union (Arena Workshop 3). *Oslo: Arena, pp. 227–45.*

For example, one can imagine a Europe whose basic structure was institutionalized in the rules and powers of a world state, or a European constitution and state. In such cases, the institutional base for social action is to be found in the real organizational controls provided by the wider or historical context. Alternatively, one can imagine a Europe whose basic structure was found to have a strong, expressive, distinct, and primordial identity. In this case, institutionalization refers to the power of traditional expressive culture.

Neither of these forms is obtained in Europe, which is stateless and which also lacks strong primordial collective identity and boundaries – indeed the exact definition of Europe and its people is uncertain, variable, and for most participants, unknown. The institutional base on which Europe is built is cultural, but not primordial and expressive. It lies in a set of rationalistic cultural models.

By culture, here, we thus do not mean the marginal or expressive values, perceptions, and tastes that realist theories leave just room enough for. Nor do we mean demonic primordial forces. We mean basic cognitive and rationalistic models of identity and action that are obtained as a matter of social reality, and define logics of appropriateness for the constituted "actor" of the system (Olsen 2000). We mean, thus, such core, and expanding, rules of the game as the principles that the world is made up of nation-state actors with universalized rights and powers, that these are made up of universalistically entitled and empowered individual persons (Soysal 1994), that the nation-states have wide and common responsibilities and capacities to rationally pursue progress and justice, that they act in a common physical and social environment, and that they should be universalistically analyzed rationally and scientifically. Given such common assumptions, it is understandable that complex networks arise and that these networks operate to intensify the common assumptions.

Core to European, and global, political society are cultural notions of a "natural law" kind about human rights and capacities (Soysal 1994), the scientific and rational properties of (and analysis of) the environment (Frank et al. 2000a), and the responsibilities of nation-state actors to pursue standard goals of progress and justice in a rational way (Chapter 8). We discuss here the logic of this system, and the directions in which it is developing.

BACKGROUND

Both modern social theory and ideologies in political reality define the world as made up of strong sovereign nation-state actors. Interaction and interdependence in the wider world produce, not a super-state United Nations or European Union, but continuously expanded and expanding doctrines about the rights and responsibilities of the nation-state components. The nation-state is thus seen as an expanded purposive agentic actor. In the extreme, nation-states stand alone, operating in an institution-less anarchic context.

Some institutional theories, in reaction, postulate partly hidden controls at a more global level, rooted in economic or military dominance (e.g., Wallerstein 1974 and elsewhere, Tilly 1992). Such arrangements are real enough, but lack the legitimacy to be really constitutive of the larger standardizing systems we see empirically in place in Europe and the world. Other reactive theories see societies as rooted in primordial cultural institutions, though these theories suggest extreme diversity, and have difficulty accounting for the obvious standardized actorhood of national-states as well as for the rise of so much European and global institutional structure.

A more fruitful version of a cultural story derives from the "bounded rationality" tradition. A version of this line of thought, emphasized by March and Olsen (1989), understands that nation-states are supposed and licensed to be actors. But real hard-wired actorhood is generally impossible (it requires goals, means-ends competence, clear resource models, extraordinary knowledge of a predictable world outside the boundaries, control capability, and extreme levels of decision capability). Institutions, including cultural ones (e.g., habits), fill in the gaps so created. The key insight for our purposes is that the system of rational actors produces and depends on a lot of common cultural material.

In most versions of this line of thought, the actors (in this case, national states or polities) produce the needed cultures and habits on their own. In other words, the same units both act and interpret what they are doing.

This special case is interesting. But it seems clear that most of the time, the culture used by actors to achieve the pretense of hard-wired rational purposive actorhood is taken from the wider environment. And changes in this culture are stored there. Nation-state actors help do this. So do all sorts of other groups, as we discuss below.

THE SCRIPTED NATION-STATE ACTOR

Much research has demonstrated that nation-states tend to be isomorphic with scripts in their environments, and they tend to change with these scripts (Meyer et al. 1997).

Thus, core matters of identity and purpose are highly scripted. Boli shows that national constitutions are quite similar, and change in similar ways in adaptation to current fashion. McNeely (1995) and Ventresca (1995), both show similar effects in national data systems. Fiala and Lanford (1987) show the scripted character and change in national educational goals. Asserted national goals cluster around the purposes of national development or progress, and justice or rights for individuals.

Similarly, models of development are quite similar, and flow downward from the system. This was true of Keynesian models (Hall 1989), and is also true now of hyperliberal ones. Finnemore (1996) shows that in the early post-War period expanded national science efforts entered the equation, and Jang (2000) shows the consolidation of national ministries in the area. Barrett and Frank (1999) show the entry of population control doctrine into the system and its extraordinary effects in promulgating national policy.

Doctrines of individual rights flow in similar ways. Berkovitch (1999) and Bradley and Ramirez (1996) both show this for the status of women, and Frank and McEneaney (1999) for the status of gays and lesbians. Boli and Meyer (1978) show the effect for children's rights, and a number of researchers have tracked the similar world diffusion of programs protecting the elderly. But the rights associated in world ideology with individual personhood have greatly expanded as a general matter, as in the United Nations Declaration.

Education, combining both individual rights and societal development, has been a focus of research (Meyer et al. 1992a, b). Educational expansion patterns, curricular structures, and equalization efforts, all flow through a professionalized international world, producing pronounced world isomorphism.

Decoupling: The effects noted above are especially striking because changed environmental institutions are incorporated in very unlikely parts of the world. Policies change independent of practices, which also change in similar directions. Thus, worldwide educational reform generates expansion essentially everywhere (Meyer et al. 1992a). It also generates waves of national policy encouraging expansion (Ramirez and Ventresca 1992). The two phenomena are dramatically correlated across time. But they are uncorrelated (or even a bit negatively correlated) across individual countries, because disimplementation is as common as implementation, and because policies and plans are often formed in reaction to failed practice (which continues to fail).

The dramatic parallel changes in decoupled policy and practice often go unnoticed because the wider cultural system works through the creation of perceived crises and social problems: it would be very bad form, for instance, for a serious intellectual to call attention to worldwide improvements in the status of women or children. It is necessary to imagine that despite all the policy changes, not enough has really happened. Or, phrased differently, the onrush of policy conceptions of needed changes so greatly outruns the changes in practice as to create an appearance of regress. The perceived worldwide crises in the abusive conditions of life of children are an obvious example. Another notable example is the continuing perception of the crisis or failure or potential failure of Europe to meet the requirements for its survival.

Europe: The effects promoting long-run organizational isomorphism, as discussed here, are dramatic in Europe, and the effect of the European Union intensifies them. Studying this, however, requires recognizing an opposing effect. Strong and developed countries are more able to sustain alternative models of nation-statehood than are depressed peripheries (e.g., Germany, but not Namibia, can sustain an officially stratified secondary educational system against the general liberal and comprehensive models). In any analysis of the effect of the European Union on isomorphism, this effect must be controlled.

MECHANISMS

The core mechanism for isomorphism proposed here works through the cultural character of nation-state identity. Aspiring to join the world, or Europe, as a nation-state, much local cultural material is forgotten, and the legitimated wider purposes and techniques are adopted. A striking feature of isomorphism is how eagerly it is pursued, and how voluntary the organizational form.

This means that interested or committed outsiders can be most "helpful," rather than controlling or coercive. If a nation-state is already committed to world-standard schooling, for instance, the outsider is helping it achieve its own ends. The wider world is filled with this kind of consultant individual or organization.

Similarly, internal groups pursuing their own goals can use the culture of the wider system to "help" their nation-state achieve its true mission of justice. Modern gays and lesbians, for instance, are protagonists not only for their particular interests, but also for human rights in general (Frank and McEneaney 1999). They – and essentially all other groups – come equipped with lawyers more than guns. And their lawyers talk about universal human rights. It is thus a legitimated collective contribution, in the modern system, to pursue specific interests under valuable general contributions.

Note that all the parties in this system seem to gain, not by being actors, but by telling the nation-state actors what they ought to do. The system of rationalized actors, in other words, generates massive amounts of cultural otherhood (Chapter 5). This is the posture of the disinterested consultant, more in touch with the truth than his own interests; or of the scientist, disinterestedly analyzing the problems of economic development or global warming; or of the nongovernmental association, advocating the general universal good or truth rather than specific interests of its own members.

Many of the "interest groups" perceived by political scientists as making up the modern system are principally not interest groups at all. Their posture, rather, is what we call otherhood here. This characterizes, for instance, a high proportion of the international nongovernmental associations examined by Boli and Thomas and their colleagues (1999): they speak, not for grubby interests, but for the world collective good.

The general point here is that a system of legitimated rational actors, given the utter implausibility of actorhood, creates massive amounts of otherhood – an explosion of controlling cultural material. Tocqueville (1836), analyzing the cultural homogeneity and intensity of stateless America, made the argument long ago.

Otherhood – the constant elaboration of expectations for actors – is a driving force behind the often-surprising expansion of the European system. Realist social theories that do not recognize its power (or even existence) have had the greatest difficulty accounting for Europe. Europe is all otherhood, not action. It is the observation of the competitive threat from America and the political/military one from the USSR, and the resultant expectation that something must be done. It is the shocked observation of two massive wars (three, if one counts the Cold one) and a holocaust, and the expectation that something must be done. It is the constant discovery of large and small crises. All this work is done by people in their capacity of observers, not principally by interested actors.

Thus, the space for the political entrepreneurship that has characterized European development is essentially cultural in character. This is why there are so few heroes and so little drama to the process: it is made up, not of actors, but of observers and commentators, associations and professions, and scientific analyses.

EUROPE AND THE WORLD AS CULTURAL

Increased interdependence and perceptions of it, together with statelessness, generate an enormous explosion in rationalized culture (and others to promulgate it). It is in many interests for this to happen.

Nation-states, operating under expanding pressures, want consultants to legitimate and stabilize themselves – to impress their people, fight off competing elites, and to deal with their neighbors. Regimes that violate conventions face survival problems in such competitions (Thomas and Meyer 1980), and if conformity is difficult in practice, planning and consultance can at least display respect for the verities.

Nation-states, further, often have few good and legitimate mechanisms with which to pursue their interests and needs in the neighborhood: funding a culture of cooperation and some organizations to match makes sense. Strategic friendliness, at the level of the American individual, was well understood by Tocqueville (1836). In Europe, which lacks individual citizenship, the emergent principle of Euro friendliness applies more to organizations and states.

Other groups in the world, pursuing broad agendas like the environment, human rights and social justice, or social progress, are similarly well-advised to create cultural controls over nation-states. And groups internal to particular societies are probably better advised to develop external cultural material, and to link up to it, than to pursue more narrowly political action. A Batswana who loves a particular species of animal, for instance, will make little headway with the Botswana state. If, on the other hand, he/she can interest the World Wildlife Fund, and various cultural systems for objectively classifying his preferred animal as endangered, he is in an excellent position. Otherhood rather than interested actorhood, here as elsewhere, is the right solution.

Thus, many state, societal, and supra-societal forces work to create culture. The result is an explosion of intergovernmental organizations, but a much greater explosion of international nongovernmental ones. Boli and Thomas and their colleagues (1999) have documented this explosion, which occurs in every dimension of rationalized social life. The organizations involved carry scripts which will permit even a very weak nation-state to be a real proper actor (Finnemore 1996). Of course, as always, autonomous actorhood in human systems requires one to be practically identical with the other autonomous actors: this was Tocqueville's point (1836).

Beyond organizations, much of the material involved is coded in sciences and professions, which themselves have expanded enormously. Every aspect of European and international society tends to support this professional and scientific principles (natural law, as we will note below) become the way in which supranational rules are grounded in the absence of a positive state (and the presence of hyper-actor states).

Scientization and the expansion of nongovernmental organizations, has been especially striking in Europe, as Boli and Thomas (1997) note. The European non-state, as many have noted, is quite a modest formal organization (Kohler-Koch 1999).

Europe is to be found in networks of association, and in the professional and scientized cultures that are linked with these. The world, as a system, has something of the same character.

RESULTS: THE EUROPEAN SYSTEM

Organizationally, Europe is not much of an actor, as many have noted. It is mainly filled with otherhood – rules and associations advising actors and regulating what national and organizational actors do and are responsible for. It develops in this way so as not to compete much with the pretenses of national political actorhood. Its strength lies in a network structure (Kohler-Koch 1999, and others), but even more in the cultural materials institutionalized in this network (Andersen 2000).

The culture involved is the culture of rationalization, which pretends to be no culture at all, but natural law. At the bottom are putatively natural human rights, with something parallel to scientific justification. In the middle, there is the natural law of socio-economic development and the market. On top is the scientized environment. Each of these structures provides a cultural ontological base on which Europe can exist without a state. Interestingly, the modern world polity has exactly the same character, with exactly the same bases. Thus, the boundaries between the European Union and Europe in general are obscure (and most participants do not know them), as are the exact boundaries between Europe in any form and the wider world. For many purposes, Europe can be seen as an especially intense form of an elaborating global system.

European states now derive their justifications from these rules, and have interests in expanding them (and stabilizing their structures as well as influencing their neighbors). So do all sorts of groups internal to the European states, as well as supra-state associations. As a result, the cultural material involved expands very rapidly: human rights, environmental concerns, and rules of social development. The same things, exactly, are true of the world as a whole.

Lacking actorhood, Europe (and the world) lacks identity too. Some of this results from the lack of much distinction between Europe and the wider world – there appears to be no distinctive European values. The environment, human rights, and the laws of socio-economic development seem to be about the same everywhere.

But some of the indistinct character of Europe derives from its character as cultural rather than positive actor. There is little European purpose, independent of its subcomponents. In one natural law tradition, meaning is located in the wider natural and moral environment, and the political function is simply to come to terms with this, not to engage in dramatic action.

As a result, Europe lacks clear boundaries, and clear citizenship. Relatively few people can accurately report what countries are part of which European associations and what countries are not. And the boundaries can change rather easily. Similarly, it is hard to say who is and who is not a European, and people themselves seem quite unclear about it. There is much discussion of the (more or less hypothetical) problem of a European identity, collectively or individually, but it seems a quite deliberate and natural product. Many forces actively sustain it, and bury Europeanness in natural law and natural rationality.

As one consequence, Europe differs from classic national states in being massively and deliberately boring. National states make up positive histories and dramas of action and action heroes, and the like. And this is certainly true of European nation-states, which are renowned for their colorfully murderous histories. But Europe itself is all gray men in gray Mercedes, discussing issues designed to be technical and mindbogglingly uninteresting. Europe is about warding off any really interesting action (which would, presumably, be dangerous, nationalistic, racist, and so on) with reasonable rules making it unnecessary.

Constructing Europe, thus, means getting rid of a lot of history and primordiality. And indeed, educationally, European national histories recede in importance without a corresponding rise in the construction of a European history (Frank et al. 2000b). Europe is about natural humans acting reasonably in a scientized environment. It is not about the expression of a primordial or historical trajectory.

This does not mean that European history disappears entirely. Rather, it remains as expressive material on the local and national levels, suitable for museums, television shows, and colorful local celebrations and tourist attractions. What is conspicuously missing, and deliberately so, is the construction of a distinct European history as a central cultural project. Also missing are the older nationalistic and oppositional depictions of national histories, which must be severely edited in the modern European context. It will not do now to emphasize the neighbors as enemies.

RESULTS: NATIONAL AND SUBNATIONAL

With expanded externally-defined responsibilities, nation-states continue their organizational expansion. Thus, the fashionable imagery of the New Public Management movement stresses decentralization, agency autonomy, accountability, independent assessment, and so on – all forms that amount to the fragmentation of state (Olson et al. 1998).

The new fragmented state is filled with more autonomous units. People are professionalized, not in Weber's sense, but as competent scientists in touch with specialized environments. Every part of such a state needs to be filled with professionals who are linked to Europe and the world, not loyal servants of the local King or Minister. States, and other organizations, develop as networks of professionalized "receptor sites" (Frank et al. 2000a) that tie local structures to a complex rationalized environment, and that can work to elaborate this environment and its fragmentation.

Beneath the level of rationalized large-scale state and other organizations lie the loci of identity – some national, others subnational. The system rests on elaborated pictures of human rights, including the right to a good deal of what is called "culture." Everyone, in a sense, becomes a member of a group of legitimized "indigenous people." Everyone is entitled to his own culture, so long as it doesn't really count (e.g., violate principles of the environment, of expanding rationalized market society, or of human rights). If something really counts in the European or world stratification system, subsidiarity disappears.

"Culture" in this sense is expressive material suited for museums. And empirical studies of the school curriculum suggest this view is correct. Dramas of unique national histories and projects drop out, and are replaced by a "social studies" view of a world in which everyone is a person like everyone else, and all cultures are ultimately similar and equal (Wong 1991; Frank et al. 2000b). There are some evil forces, but all types of persons and all cultures depicted are basically good. Languages and literatures become "media of communication" rather than repositories of unique and powerful cultures.

Persons, in this world, are pretty much all potential scientists, and science/social science are big winners (McEneaney 1998). Rational analysis and action is the correct approach. Culture, in this sense, is a collection of cute costumes, holidays, and stories.

Obviously, we argue that the whole frame here makes up a rationalistic culture: one whose institutionalization involves the assertion that everyone involved is more or less a rational actor.

CONCLUSIONS

The European system is, organizationally, a rapidly expanding system of lateral associations. It is, organizationally, almost centerless, though some legal and policy institutions make up a weak center. It depends on common rationalistic cultural assumptions about the nature of legitimate nation-state identities, the rights of humans, the rational properties of the environment (both physical and social), and so on. And European integration, as it proceeds, adds massively to the details of such cultural assumptions. Analogous to Skowronek's (1982) American state of courts and parties, the European state is a state of endless committees and definitions. In this, Europe is rather similar to the modern world political society.

Lacking clear collective or individual identities of cultural kinds, the culture of Europe is rooted in natural law – sciences of nature and human development, natural and scientific laws about human needs and rights, and strong notions of the responsibility and capacity of action (e.g., national states) to be rational and reasonable. Here again, Europe is similar to the wider world society, and the evolving national states in that society. The game is not to be interesting and dramatic and in tune with unique and particularistic historic identities. It is to be reasonable, and to keep everything in line. A good deal of history, indeed, must be suppressed in maintaining this posture.

REFERENCES

Andersen, S. S. 2000. How is the EU Possible? Workshop on Institutional Approaches to the European Union, Oslo.

Barrett, D. and D. Frank. 1999. Population Control for National Development, in J. Boli and G. Thomas (eds.), *Constructing World Culture*. Stanford: Stanford University Press.

Berkovitch, N. 1999. *From Motherhood to Citizenship*. Baltimore: Johns Hopkins University Press.

Boli, J. and G. Thomas. 1997. World Culture in the World Polity: A Century of International Non-Governmental Organization. *American Sociological Review* 62:71–90.

—— —— (eds.) 1999. *Constructing World Culture*. Stanford: Stanford University Press.

Boli-Bennett, J. and J. Meyer. 1978. The Ideology of Childhood and the State. *American Sociological Review* 43:797–812.

Bradley, K. and F. Ramirez. 1996. World Polity and Gender Parity. *Research in Sociology of Education and Socialization* 11:63–91.

de Tocqueville, A. (1836) 1966. *Democracy in America*. New York: Doubleday.

Fiala, R. and A. G. Lanford. 1987. Educational Ideology and the World Educational Revolution, 1950–1970. *Comparative Education Review* 31:315–32.

Finnemore, M. 1996. *National Interests in International Society*. Ithaca: Cornell University Press.

Frank, P. and E. McEneaney. 1999. The Individualization of Society and the Liberalization of State Policies on Same-Sex Sexual Relations, 1984–1995. *Social Forces* 77:11–44.

—— S. Wong, F. Ramirez, and J. Meyer. 2000. Embedding National Societies: Worldwide Changes in University History Curricula, 1895–1994. *Comparative Education Review* 44:29–53.

Frank, D., A. Hironaka, and E. Schofer. 2000. The Nation-State and the Natural Environment over the Twentieth Century. *American Sociological Review* 65:96–116.

Hall, P. (ed.) 1989. *The Political Power of Economic Ideas*. Princeton: Princeton University Press.

Jang, Y. S. 2000. The Worldwide Founding of Ministries of Science and Technology. *Sociological Perspectives* 43 (2):247–70.

Jepperson, R. 1991. Institutions, Institutional Effects, and Institutionalism, in W. Powell and P. DiMaggio (eds.), *The New Institutionalism in Organizational Analysis*. Chicago: University of Chicago Press.

Kohler-Koch, B. 1999. The Evolution and Transformation of European Governance, in B. Kohler-Koch and R. Eising (eds.), *The Transformation of Governance in the European Union*. London: Routledge.

McEneaney, E. 1998. The Transformation of Primary School Science and Mathematics: A Cross-National Analysis, 1900–1995. PhD dissertation, Stanford University.

McNeely, C. 1995. *Constructing the Nation-State*. Westport: Greenwood.

Meyer, J. 1994. Rationalized Environments, in W. R. Scott and J. Meyer (eds.), *Institutional Environments and Organizations*. Thousand Oaks: Sage.

—— and R. Jepperson. 2000. The 'Actors' of Modem Society: The Cultural Construction of Social Agency. *Sociological Theory* 18:100–120. Reproduced in Chapter 5.

—— F. Ramirez, and Y. Soysal. 1992. World Expansion of Mass Education, 1870–1970. *Sociology of Education* 65:128–49.

—— D. Kamens, A. Benavot, Y. Cha, and S. Wong. 1992. *School Knowledge for the Masses*. London: Falmer.

—— J. Boli, G. Thomas, and F. Ramirez. 1997. World Society and the Nation-State. *American Journal of Sociology* 1103:144–81. Reproduced in Chapter 8.

Olsen, J. P. 2000. Organising European Institutions of Governance, in H. Wallace (ed.), *Whose Europe? Interlocking Dimensions of Integration*. London: Macmillan.

Olson, O., J. Guthrie, and C. Humphrey (eds.) 1998. *Global Warning: Debating International Developments in New Public Financial Management*. Oslo: Cappelen Akademisk Forlag.

Ramirez, F. and M. Ventresca. 1992. Building the Institutions of Mass Schooling, in B. Fuller and R. Rubinson (eds.), *The Political Construction of Education*. New York: Praeger.

Skowronek, S. 1982. *Building a New American State*. Cambridge: Cambridge University Press.

Soysal, Y. 1994. *Limits of Citizenship: Migrants and Postnational Membership in Europe*. Chicago: University of Chicago Press.

Thomas, G. and J. Meyer. 1980. Regime Change and State Power in an Intensifying World State System, in A. Bergesen (ed.), *Studies of the Modern World-System*. New York: Academic Press.

Tilly, C. 1992. *Coercion, Capital, and European States*. Cambridge: Blackwell.

Ventresca, M. 1995. Counting People When People Count. PhD dissertation, Stanford University.

Wallerstein, I. 1974. *The Modern World-System*. New York: Academic.

Wong, S. 1991. The Evolution of Social Science Instruction, 1900–1986. *Sociology of Education* 64:33–47.

17

Universities

The University in Europe and the World: Twentieth Century Expansion

In this chapter, we review empirical data on the twentieth century growth of higher education around the world. Several observations are striking and clear. First, there was extraordinary expansion. Higher education became organized on a much larger scale. Second, this expansion was concentrated in the period after about 1960. Third, the expansion was worldwide, characterizing every sort of country. Growth rates in all types of countries tended to be rather similar. The expansion in Europe, characterized by long traditions of controlled and constrained growth, has been especially noteworthy. The European expansion is striking because it is associated with a dramatic supra-national "Bologna Process" forcefully driving organizational change that in other world regions occurs with less disciplined planning, pressure, and purpose.

The overall pattern of observations poses an explanatory puzzle. Most explanations of higher educational expansion, such as those emphasizing socio-economic demands or needs, focus on national-level factors. They will obviously not serve well to account for endemic worldwide growth. This chapter, which reflects sociological institutionalist theories, focuses on global changes and shifting cultural models to provide an account of the dramatic worldwide expansion of higher education (Chapter 8; Drori et al. 2003).

BACKGROUND

Higher education is a worldwide phenomenon. But research on higher education tends to focus on case studies of particular institutions or national systems. When it

Originally published as:

John W. Meyer and Evan Schofer. 2006. The University in Europe and the World: Twentieth Century Expansion, in G. Krücken, A. Kosmützky, and M. Torka, (eds.), Towards a Multiversity? Universities between Global Trends and National Traditions. *Bielefeld, Germany: Transcript-Verlag, pp. 43–60.*

This is a revised version of a paper published in *Die Hockschule* in 2005. The paper reflects analyses in Schofer and Meyer (2005). The research was funded by the Spencer Foundation. Many helpful comments were received from colleagues at Stanford, Halle-Wittenberg, Minnesota, and Bielefeld.

moves in a more comparative direction, as in the well-known work of Burton Clark (e.g., 1983), it tends to focus on arrangements in a fairly circumscribed world – mainly the wealthy, industrialized nations. These qualities are also characteristic of research on the specialized topic of higher educational expansion. Country case studies are the focus of attention. The impressive effort of Paul Windolf goes beyond that (1997), but the cases he compares – Germany, France, the United States, Italy, and Japan – are among the most developed countries.

Case study research is known for its ability to trace causal effects and their pathways in considerable detail. But it suffers from its virtues in that this literature has a pronounced tendency to attribute causal significance to particular and distinctive features of the case under examination. After all, a student who spent two years on a case and reported that there is little significant about it, and that its history parallels that of all the other cases, would be unlikely to receive a degree, let alone substantial academic attention. Thus the research literature on higher educational expansion tends to emphasize characteristics of particular countries or types of countries as lying behind rapid growth in the contemporary period. In the United States, for instance, it is common to discuss post-War expansion as resulting from political changes embedded in the "G.I. Bill" – legislation that facilitated higher educational access for returning veterans after World War II. In Britain, and Continental countries, interpretations can stress the post-War breakdown of the constraints supported by the old class systems, the demands of a "new economy," or the weakening of the capacity of the state to maintain controls (Ben-David and Zloczower 1962). In some such interpretations, especially in the early post-War decades, the breakdown involved was thought to support potentially destructive over-education, credential inflation, and rampant status competition (e.g., Dore 1975; Collins 1979; Fuller and Rubinson 1992 for a late reflection).

That sort of unease about higher educational expansion has greatly receded both in the policy world and in academic theory. One can now observe little concern about the dangers and costs of over-education (but see Lenhardt (2002) for examples of older and more conservative German reactions). This change in interpretation is a worldwide and global cultural phenomenon, and in this chapter we see it as playing a direct causal role in higher educational expansion everywhere. In recent years, it is especially highly organized in Europe, with the "Bologna Process," but it is really a global process, and the results are global in scope.

THE WORLDWIDE CHARACTER OF HIGHER EDUCATIONAL EXPANSION

Banks (2001) assembled data on higher educational enrollments for countries around the world from the late nineteenth century to the early 1980s. UNESCO provides similar data in recent years (e.g., UNESCO 2004). The definitions employed are fairly conventional, covering post-secondary education with enough of an academic character to be seen as comparable to traditional university-level work: the great majority of the enrollments are in fact in institutions called

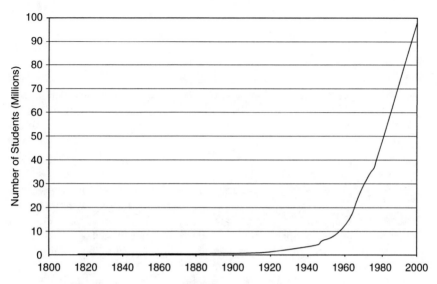

Figure 17.1. World tertiary students, 1815–2000

universities, or explicitly treated as university equivalent. We combined these two sources to construct a dataset that covers the whole world for the entire twentieth century (Schofer and Meyer 2005). There are undoubtedly missing data, but they are not likely to contribute much error, since the missing cases are typically colonies or poor countries early in the century, and these cases account for little or no enroll-ment. The overall global trend is depicted in Figure 17.1, which shows the extraor-dinary growth of higher education enrollments in a specific time period following World War II.

In 1900, only about half a million students were enrolled in the world, making up a small fraction of a single percent of the relevant age cohort. By 2000, about a hundred million students are involved, representing something like twenty percent of the relevant age cohort worldwide (UNESCO 2004; Schofer and Meyer 2005). And the great bulk of the growth occurred in the last four decades of the twentieth century. One can imagine an expansion of this magnitude as part of a world system of Western domination, like high-technology development or oil consumption (Wallerstein 1974). The idea is that the world tends to be a single economy organized around a sharply-defined and often exploitive class system. In this case, the expansion would occur principally in the developed world, with low rates of growth in developing countries. The world is an extraordinarily unequal social system, and it would certainly make sense to observe the fruits of extreme inequality in differential rates of educational expansion. Many interpretations of modern social change have this character, and there are interpretive efforts along this line in the case of higher education (e.g., Clark 1992). But this line of thought has some difficulty coming to terms with worldwide expansion, in all sorts of countries both central and peripheral. So there are reasons to be skeptical:

1. As an empirical matter, research on the expansion of mass education has shown that in the last half of the twentieth century high and comparable rates of expansion occurred in all sorts of countries, relatively independent of developmental levels.

2. As a theoretical matter, neoinstitutional theory in sociology emphasizes dramatically how much the institutions of modernity (as opposed to the actual income and resource levels nominally associated with these modern institutions) diffuse around the world independent of socioeconomic developments (see the summaries in Meyer et al. (Chapter 8) or Meyer and Ramirez (2000) for education). Mass education is clearly one of these institutions. Higher education seems to be another.

3. As a practical matter, higher education is one of those institutions whose costs may be scaled to the economic level of the country in which it occurred. As with other educational institutions, costs are mainly in salaries, and salaries can be low in poor countries. Further, there is no standard worldwide definition of educational standards (e.g., libraries, faculty competence, and research facilities), so an organization can be considered a university in a poor country that would be far beneath the scale of acceptability in a rich one.

The data on the issue are definitive. In Figure 17.2, we classify countries by world region as a simple way to show the results. The West (including the Anglo-American democracies) and Eastern Europe are set against the less developed regions of the world. We show the mean ratios of educational enrollment to overall population for

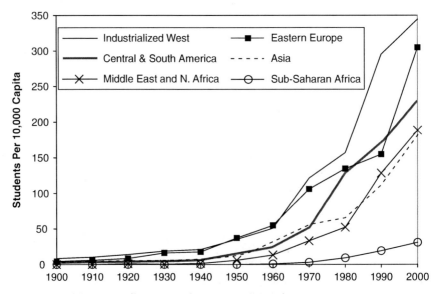

Figure 17.2. Tertiary enrollment per 10,000 capita, regional averages, 1900–2000

each region through as much of the twentieth century as we can. Two methodo-logical issues may be noted:

1. The ratios are calculated with the whole national population as denominator because in early decades of the century, precise age-group estimates are often missing. This turns out to create little error: analyses for the last half of the century using UNESCO data permit the employment of the appropriate denom-inator (customarily, the population aged 20–24) and show exactly the same patterns we report here.

2. Data availability changes mean that increasing numbers of countries are included in the analyses as time goes on. Schofer and Meyer (2005) show, by using constant sets of countries, that such more precise analyses show the same patterns as those reported here.

We can summarize the results simply. Roughly similar rates of growth are to be found in every group of countries that we can distinguish. Everywhere there is expansion. And everywhere this expansion is concentrated in the period since 1960. Even in Sub-Saharan Africa, which enters post-colonial society with almost no tertiary education, we find the same growth pattern that we note elsewhere. The African curve is far below the others (which are surprisingly similar), and that may lead a reader to misinterpret the data. In fact, the growth rate in Africa is quite high in this period and is very similar to that found in every other region. Some African countries now easily have enrollment ratios that exceed European countries' of a few decades ago. The data show a few interesting subtleties such as a slower rate of growth we note in Eastern Europe in the 1970s and 1980s. This interesting observation is analyzed in detail by several scholars with much better data than we present here. Their interpretations, consistent with our own, are noted below. For now, we need to call attention to the main observation. For every type of country, relatively independent of national resources, let alone national "needs," high growth in higher educational enrollments can be found in the period since the 1950s. Detailed analyses show that this pattern characterizes not just types of countries but almost all individual countries. As a result, gross tertiary enrollment ratios in European countries can exceed eighty percent.

Thus, higher education expansion in the modern period is principally a global pattern rather than a distinctive set of national patterns. However, some national variation is evident despite the massive global trend. Quantitative analyses presented in Schofer and Meyer (2005) explore the issue using pooled panel regression analyses over the period from 1900 to 2000 for a sample of roughly 100 countries. Statistical analyses show that higher educational expansion is a bit more rapid in richer countries, which could reflect both greater demand and more ready supply in such countries. And expansion is greater in countries with more expanded mass educa-tional systems, which could reflect the greater supply of candidates or more likely the processes of status competition celebrated in a long and distinguished literature (Boudon 1973; Dore 1975; Bourdieu and Passeron 1977; Collins 1979, 2000). On the other hand, perhaps this effect too indicates the same global process of educational expansion that the expansion of higher education does. Earlier research, indeed, shows that the worldwide takeoff of mass education took shape in precisely the same post-1950 time period that triggered the expansion of higher education (Meyer et al. 1992).

EXPLAINING THE GLOBAL PATTERN
OF EXPANSION

The global character of higher educational expansion contradicts some of the most traditional or conventional explanations of variations in educational systems. A pervasive functionalism runs through most of the literature, in particular stressing the impact of economic change in creating needs for expanded education to meet present or future labor force requirements. Present requirements can obviously show up in labor force demand, with scarcities, production bottlenecks, and the like. Future labor force requirements can show up through formal and informal processes of manpower planning.

Functionalist ideas are rooted in two main empirical claims, both of which are potentially problematic. First is the idea that economic change creates real labor market demands for highly educated individuals. The research literature has not observed much of a relationship between economic factors and educational change (Windolf 1997; Meyer and Ramirez 2000). For instance, Windolf (1997) did not find that patterns of industrialization could account for trends in higher education expansion while Schofer and Meyer (1995) find only a small (and somewhat unstable) effect. The sheer levels of enrollments – exceeding eighty percent in some European countries and well into double-digits within some agricultural Sub-Saharan nations – hint that educational expansion may be sharply decoupled from real economic demand. A second idea, which has received somewhat greater support in the literature, is that higher education produces functional benefits for the economy, and thus it is reasonable for states to pursue aggressive expansion. For instance, economists have repeatedly shown that mass education expansion has a large positive effect on national economic growth (Barro and Sala-i-Martin 1995). Also, Schofer et al. (2000) find that higher education enrollments in math and science have positive effects on economic growth. Finally, classic economic studies of "rates of return" show substantial public and private benefits of higher education (Psacharopolous 1982). While the latter "rate of return" studies involve dubious assumptions (for instance, that higher wages for degree holders reflect increased skills and efficiency rather than screening or credentialing effects), the literature hints that higher education may be a source of economic benefit. But research findings are mixed even on this issue. While enrollments in math and science may yield benefits, studies of overall tertiary enrollment fail to observe such an effect. In fact, in a number of studies, tertiary educational expansion shows statistically insignificant *negative* effects on subsequent national economic growth (Benavot 1992; Chabbott and Ramirez 2000).

For the Third World, functionalist ideas fail on the face of it. The occupational structures and economies of such countries by no means went through the kinds of growth that might have generated large-scale educational expansion. Typical Third World countries now have higher educational enrollment rates far above those of Germany, France, or Great Britain three or four decades ago – clearly exceeding any plausible labor market demand. For example, Kazakhstan now has as many higher education students as the whole world had in 1900 (Banks 2001; UNESCO 2004). The rapid expansion of tertiary education in modern African countries, despite consistent records of economic failure, makes it clear that economic development – and its functional requirements – is not a sufficient explanatory variable in accounting for educational expansion. Sociological institutionalist ideas are of much greater utility here (see, e.g., Meyer et al. 1997; Meyer and Ramirez 2000). These lines of thought decompose the problem into two components. First, they offer explanations of the *worldwide* character of the global expansion. Second, they offer explanations of the *expansionist* character of the global change.

1. *Explaining the global character of change*: Institutional theory emphasizes the worldwide commitment of countries to aggressive doctrines of both socio-economic progress and individual human development, and to the expanding ideologies that education is a key to this progress. A rapidly expanding world society built up the powers and responsibilities of a great many nation-states throughout the Third World. The idea that all countries, including the Third World ones, could develop (and develop rapidly) took firm hold. Thus, while countries differed enormously in economic development, their highly legitimated long-term goals came to be extremely similar. Copying expanded educational models made sense in terms of their common developmental goals, even if not in terms of their actual socio-economic realities. In other words, while functional theory cannot plausibly explain worldwide expansion, functional theory seen as a common world developmental ideology does the explanatory task rather well. Common goals and common models of how to pursue those goals create worldwide isomorphic educational change.

In explaining common worldwide change patterns in the field of education, institutional theory has a special advantage. Even to the most sophisticated empirical and theoretical analysts, the causal linkage between educational change and socio-economic progress is quite opaque (see Chabbott and Ramirez 2000 for a review). There is a worldwide ideological agreement that education is indeed a main source of social progress, but the character of the link is very unclear. This is a situation that generates the rapid diffusion of fashionable models of what an educational system should look like. Models can change rapidly, sometimes emphasizing the creation of technical skills and innovations through science and engineering, and at other times stressing the creation of socio-cultural integration through common cultural and social scientific understandings. American education has, thus, often been a kind of model for the world – but in the 1980s, a substantial literature emphasized the virtues of Japanese education (e.g., Rohlen 1983), and German education was something of an ideal before World War I. Overall, we can conclude that national systems of higher education are subject to global models and tend to change in line with changes in these models. The effect obviously intensifies after World War II. Principles of nationalism and celebrations of unique national trajectories did not look attractive after two World Wars and a Great Depression that were widely attributed to precisely such models. The delegitimation of nationalism and nationalist educational systems was, of course, especially striking in the European case. Post-War developmental efforts in Europe stressed the need to open up closed national systems of all sorts. This tendency is built into the European Union and dramatically celebrated in the recent Bologna Process efforts to explicitly internationalize higher education (Teichler 2002).

   2. *Explaining the expansionist character of global models*: We arrive at an understanding of the diffusion of global educational models in the modern period. We now need to address why the dominant and fashionable models of education tended so dramatically to emphasize expansions that would have seemed unreasonable and even dangerous in any earlier period. Obviously, the model of the properly developing society went through sharp changes. We can understand what happened if we consider the forces that limited higher educational expansion, in most countries and notably in European ones, in earlier historical periods. This is not difficult to do since the literature on higher educational systems historically stressed the "natural" character of constraints on expansion. By and large, this literature treats educational systems as generating personnel (and knowledge) for a real and rather closed national social system which itself changes rather slowly over time. A slowly changing distribution of occupations (and some other roles) is imagined. Each position in this distribution is thought to have knowledge and training requirements so that an educational system should ideally generate a distribution of persons matching the distribution of occupations (as well as mechanisms for placing the trained persons into the correct positions). An educational system that produces too few trained people will limit social development and even the effective maintenance of a fixed social order (Lenhardt 2002; Ramirez 2002). On the other hand, an educational system that produces more training than is needed can create severe problems: over-education is the core idea. Over-education can simply be inefficient as time and money are spent on unneeded years of training – this would be a concern from a classical liberal posture (Teichler 2002, for examples of concerns along these lines). But worse, over-education can be destructive. Unemployed schooled people are thought to be anomic and to experience dissatisfying unfulfillable yearnings. Masses of them may, it is thought, create much social trouble – revolutions of rising expectations that cannot be fulfilled by the existing social order (Huntington 1968). Ideas of this sort remain in the background during the modern period (see Lenhardt 2002, for examples), though without much effectiveness. Notions of "over-education" may maintain special sentimental value in Europe, in reaction to the sweeping changes produced by rapid educational change, and in particular by the dramatic legitimation of this supra-national change symbolized in the Bologna Process of recent years.

The old European state system thickly institutionalized more traditional educational models in both discourse and organizational practice. So the destruction of these models in the current period could confront a more aggressive conservatism in Europe than anything possible in weaker and newer national political systems in the rest of the world (Ramirez and Meyer 2002 for a discussion of the forces supporting exceptionalist ideas). This makes the dramatic success of the Bologna Process, which began with the most limited controversy and took on an impressive life of its own with the most astonishingly limited resistance, especially interesting. In any case, in an older (and especially European) model of education as necessarily adapted to a closed and slowly changing national society, constraints on educational expansion seemed very reasonable. And indeed, the traditional literature in the field treated constraints as normal. In particular, the state should play this role (especially in Europe – Ramirez 2002), and it was commonly understood that strong state systems control the sorts of unregulated and inflationary competition that might generate runaway educational expansion (Ben-David and Zloczower 1962; Collins 1979; and many others). In these lines of argument, educational expansion was likely to characterize modern societies in which state controls were insufficient, and broke down. This was the common interpretation of the early and unruly expansion of higher education in the United States.

An interesting specialized literature shows empirical results along this line even in the most recent period. Communist systems quite deliberately faced the issues noted above in the 1970s and 1980s, and across the communist world were able to stop the worldwide runaway higher educational expansion of the period (Lenhardt and Stock 2000). The idea was to keep educational expansion under control for several reasons: first, to keep political control in the hands of the party of the working class and out of the hands of an expanding population of experts (Konrad and Szelenyi 1979); and second, to keep training closely linked to real manpower requirements. Thus, in the modern period, strong central authority can keep higher education under control, and in the case of the Communist countries, did so. But we observe a good many strong national states in the world, with ample controls over their higher educational systems that are no longer able or willing to constrain educational expansion (e.g., France or Sweden). This suggests that Communist success in maintaining constraint reflected not only the centralized controls but also the older model of the closed society characteristic of Communist's (and especially in Europe, many other) more traditional ideologies (Ramirez 2002).

In the non-Communist world, a fundamentally changed model of society came into place in the post-War period. It was a model of a more liberal, participatory, and developing society in which much future progress could be built on educational expansion. And especially in Europe, with the rise of the European Union, it was a model of society as an open system in a much more globalized Europe and world: expanded education made sense as a broad strategy for national activity in this world (Ramirez 2002; Teichler 2002). And it was a broadly liberal model of society in much more than simply economic terms (Djelic 1998). Expansive individual capacity for action was seen as far more important than organizing schooling to fit people into a collective social organism. Human capital thinking in economics, political development theory in political science, post-structuralist theory in anthropology, and all sorts of interactionist theories in sociology, all reflected this picture of a national society resting on expanding individual capabilities. In this new picture, celebrated for example by the modern World Bank (2000), there could be no such thing as over-education. More educated people would create economic (and polit-ical, and social) progress. In this brave new world, expanded individual aspirations for more education were not indicative of social disorder and a "diploma disease" but were valid and highly legitimate sources of the collective good. Limited educational aspirations (and excessive controls over aspirations) came under ugly terms like "dropout." Similarly, collective processes generating expanded places in higher edu-cation were reconceptualized as, almost by definition, social and economic progress.

In short, the new model education became a core source for social and economic progress rather than a functionally necessary outcome of the demands created by such progress. Thus, it follows that expanded education resulted from the expanded and changed ideas about progress – found everywhere in the non-Communist world – rather than from the actual and highly variable course of real socio-economic development in the world. Expanded education reflected the universalized new goals and models, not the variable mundane realities of the world's economic and social systems.

SOURCES OF THE NEW MODEL

We can briefly reflect on the wider global social changes that undercut the older closed model of education and society, with its fears of over-education and anomie, and sustained the new vision of continuous development produced by individuals with greatly expanded schooled potential.

1. Undercutting the old model: World War II and the defeat of fascism, strikingly delegitimated nationalist corporatism (see Djelic 1998, for a discussion of the Marshall Plan response). So did the Great Depression, whose trajectory was under-stood to result from political failure. The primordial sovereignty of the closed national state and society, with ideas of the necessary sacrifice of individual attain-ments for the collective good, was deeply stigmatized, along with a variety of institutionalized European models. The failures of individual rights involved in the closed system were overwhelmingly obvious. Even the racist United States and colonialist Britain symbolically supported principles of global human rights in the Atlantic Charter. Thus, education increasingly came to be seen as properly organized for individual development (and collective progress resulting from this development) rather than for slots in the machinery of an organic national society.

2. Supporting the new model: Liberal national societies – particularly the United States – with their ideologies of the centrality of the expanded individual, dominated the post-War world. More than a military victory, their triumph had a cultural and ideological character. Liberal dominance created a whole new world political order (Chapter 8), filled with governmental and nongovernmental associations and infused with all sorts of doctrines about the virtues of indefinitely expanded education (Boli and Thomas 1999; Schofer 1999; Chabbott 2002). In recent years, this expanded world polity has generated pressures for "education for all," including ideas about the need for globally expanded secondary and higher education (World Bank 2000).

Further advantages lay in the confrontation with decolonization. A disorderly Third World, threatened by Communist ideas, could find a true and peaceful way to progress through expanded education. The actual Cold War competition made the discovery of pathways to national development an urgent matter, and education provided an obvious means. Universities were set up, and rapidly expanded, in the furthest Third World countries eager to achieve national integration and progress and to replace imperial elites with home-grown ones. Finally, the need for societies to function in an open global world rather than a closed national one was obvious. The atomic age made international military conflict unattractive as a means to progress, economic globalization and expansion offered obvious advantages to the skilled and competent, and political integration made expanded education a reasonable strategy.

All these changes hit on the European education and society with special force. The delegitimation of the older world was especially extreme. And the expansive supra-nationalization of the new world in discourse, organization, and very tangible reality was an overwhelming presence with the rise of the whole panoply of European institutions. In fact, forceful Europeanization and globalization often merge in modern European thinking about educational expansion. National policy-makers imagine their people and their countries have to compete on a vastly broader scale, with technical developments and human capacities requiring enormous educational expansion, standardization, and improvement. The new and emergent world polity is expansive and rationalized. And, even in Europe, it is stateless. As Tocqueville long ago noted in discussing American society, such social systems rely on forms of social control outside the state. A core mechanism of this sort, of course, is education, and theories of American educational expansion call attention to the roots of this expansion in American ideologies of social control. So the institutions of the new globalized world are all built on models of a more schooled population (Meyer 1977) as a core component of a world polity. Expanded and empowered individuals are central: expanded individual rights certainly include education and other rights (e.g., to health, to population control) rest on education.

Another mechanism of social control, also built into the higher education system, is science. In the modern rationalized but stateless world polity, science functions as a kind of common cultural frame and source of control (Drori et al. 2003). And the modern social order is highly rationalized, providing a fertile field for education: the modern business firm is a rationalized organization, as is the modern state, and the modern medical care system, the modern religious body, and so on. The models of rational organization that spread are essentially all rooted in the university and other institutions of higher education: it makes a certain sense in a stateless expansive Europe, or world polity, that managerialism and the business school would be the most rapidly expanding forms of education (the papers in Sahlin-Andersson and Engwall 2002).

All this scientization and rationalization, of course, transform higher education organizationally, beyond simply massive expansion. A striking feature of higher educational change around the world – and most dramatically in Europe – is its managerialist organizational reconstruction. In Europe, this is embodied in the

"Bologna Process" (Ramirez 2002; Teichler 2002). The old corporatist boundaries around the academic profession and its traditional university arrangements are undercut at every turn. Old exclusionary arrangement limiting the access of both types of students and types of knowledge to higher education tend to disappear. Students have choices and so do the old academic underclasses laboring under the old professors. And so do all sorts of formerly excluded interests in state and society who demand entry for their young as well as their substantive agendas. The "knowledge society" is linked to the university, and the linkage is a two-way street. The university is more dominant in society than ever before. But society is more dominant over the university than ever before, too (Schofer 1999). Thus, especially in Europe, the whole change gets organized, and its formal organization greatly expands. There is talk about accountability and measurement (of teaching and research, for instance). The old universities are forced to become something called "decisionmakers" (Krücken and Meier 2006). Resources are to be rationed and accounted. Categories from an older world of tradition and opacity are defined and standardized (unique degrees turn into BAs and MAs; specialized institutions are re-legitimated in terms of standard academic credits). Autonomous professors are assembled into rationalized organized units, and old privileges redefined in standardized accountings. One can describe it all as progress and/or as the destruction of tradition. Statistical evidence from pooled panel regression analyses of higher education enrollments provides strong support for these arguments. Quantitative measures of the rise of a liberal, democratized, and rationalized global culture have massive positive effects on national enrollments (Schofer and Meyer 2005). And, nations with strong ties to the world polity (e.g., measured by country memberships in international nongovernmental organizations) expand education more rapidly than do nations with fewer international ties. Results suggest that the world polity played a major role in encouraging the global expansion of higher education.

CONCLUSION

A wave of higher educational expansion, starting around 1960 and running into the present, characterizes the entire world. Its universality convincingly demonstrates that it is not driven by particular national characteristics like economic requirements or resources. Higher educational expansion is clearly part of a global model of society and of education. It gains power on a worldwide scale not because the world's societies are so similar but because their goals similarly focus on socio-economic progress and because education is seen in all dominant world ideologies as the main means to achieve progress.

Older notions of education as properly organized to fit people into positions in an established social order were undercut in the post-War period, most dramatically in Europe. The new model stressed education as a cause, rather than a necessary functional consequence, of economic growth and change. In economic thinking, human capital ideologies replaced the older model. In political and social life, models of expanded individual capability as creating progressive change replaced more static models, with their stress on orderly conformity to the social order. It is now difficult to conceptualize conventional older ideas like "over-education" as a real social problem. Expanded human potential, presumably to be carried along on a life-time learning basis, is seen as a source of social progress rather than of disorganization and anomie. It is linked to conceptions of an expansive global society built on greatly expanded conceptions of human rights and human potentials.

It is beyond our purposes here to discuss at length the effects of this revolutionary change. Obviously, a world in which masses of people have higher education even in the furthest periphery – and education in a common world culture – is transformed. Potentials for organized collective action are enormously enhanced. A sweeping world movement for the environment can be built on university science. A similar movement for organizational reform, standardization, and transparency can be built on rationalistic university social science. And a global human rights movement can celebrate the rights and capacities of highly schooled populations. Expanded collect-ive action possibilities produced by expanded education also increase potentials for conflict. A common universalistic world culture makes the extreme inequalities in resources characteristic of world society even more problematic. And it makes remaining cultural and religious differences the sources of conflict on a global scale. Under conditions of integration under common elites, inequalities can readily come to be seen as injustices and cultural differences as violations of supposedly common norms.

REFERENCES

Banks, A. S. 2001. *Cross-national Time-series Data Archive* [dataset]. Binghamton, NY: Computer Systems Unlimited.

Barro, R. J. and X. Sala-i-Martin. 1995. *Economic Growth*. New York: McGraw-Hill.

Benavot, A. 1992. Educational Expansion and Economic Growth in the Modern World, 1913–1985, in B. Fuller and R. Rubinson (eds.), *The Political Construction of Education*. New York: Praeger.

Ben-David, J. and A. Zloczower. 1962. Universities and Academic Systems in Modern Societies. *European Journal of Sociology* 3: 45–85.

Boli, J. and G. M. Thomas. 1999. *Constructing World Culture: International Nongovernmental Organizations since 1875*. Stanford: Stanford University Press.

Boudon, R. 1973. *Education, Opportunity and Social Inequality*. New York: John Wiley.

Bourdieu, P. and J. C. Passeron. 1977. *Reproduction in Education, Society, and Culture*. London: Sage Publications.

Chabbott, C. 2002. *Constructing Education for Development: International Organizations and Education For All*. London: Taylor & Francis.

—— and F. O. Ramirez. 2000. Development and Education, in M. T. Hallinan (ed.), *Handbook of the Sociology of Education*. New York: Kluwer Academic/Plenum Publishers, pp. 163–87.

Clark, B. 1983. *The Higher Education System: Academic Organization in Cross-National Perspective*. Berkeley: University of California Press.

Clark, R. 1992. Multinational Corporate Investment and Women's Participation in Higher Education in Noncore Nations. *Sociology of Education* 65 (1): 37–47.

Collins, R. 1979. *The Credential Society: An Historical Sociology of Education and Stratification.* New York: Academic Press.

—— 2000. Comparative and Historical Patterns of Education, in M. T. Hallinan (ed.), *Handbook of the Sociology of Education.* New York: Kluwer Academic/Plenum Publishers, pp. 213–39.

Djelic, M. L. 1998. *Exporting the American Model: The Postwar Transformation of European Business.* Oxford: Oxford University Press.

Dore, R. 1975. *The Diploma Disease: Education, Qualification and Development.* Berkeley: University of California Press.

Drori, G., J. W. Meyer, F. O. Ramirez, and E. Schofer. 2003. *Science in the Modern World Polity: Institutionalization and Globalization.* Stanford: Stanford University Press.

Huntington, S. 1968. *Political Order in Changing Societies.* New Haven: Yale University Press.

Konrád, G. and I. Szelenyi. 1979. *The Intellectuals on the Road to Class Power.* New York: Harcourt Brace Jovanovich.

Krücken, G. and F. Meier. 2006. Turning the University into an Organizational Actor, in J. W. Meyer, H. Hwang, and G. Drori (eds.), *Globalization and Organization: World Society and Organizational Change.* Oxford: Oxford University Press, pp. 241–57.

Lenhardt, G. 2002. Europe and Higher Education between Universalisation and Materialist Particularism. *European Educational Research Journal* 1 (2):274–88.

Lenhardt, G. and M. Stock. 2000. Hochschulentwicklung und Bürgerrechte in der BRD und der DDR. *Kölner Zeitschrift für Soziologie und Sozialpsychologie* 52: 520–40.

Meyer, J. W. 1977. The Effects of Education as an Institution. *American Journal of Sociology* 83 (1):55–77.

—— and F. O. Ramirez, 2000. The World Institutionalization of Education, in J. Schriewer (ed.), *Discourse Formation in Comparative Education.* Frankfurt: Peter Lang Publishers, pp. 111–32.

—— and E. Schofer. 2005. The University in Global Society: Twentieth Century Expansion. *Die Hochschule* 14 (2):81–98.

—— —— and Y. Soysal. 1992. World Expansion of Mass Education, 1870–1980. *Sociology of Education* 65:128–49.

—— J. Boli, G. Thomas, and F. O. Ramirez. 1997. World Society and the Nation-State. *American Journal of Sociology* 103 (1):144–81. Reproduced in Chapter 8.

Psacharopoulos, G. 1982. The Economics of Higher Education in Developing Countries. *Comparative Education Review* 26 (2):139–59.

Ramirez, F. O. 2002. Eyes Wide Shut: University, State and Society. *European Educational Research Journal* 1 (2):256–72.

—— and J. W. Meyer. 2002. National Curricula: World Models and National Historical Legacies, in M. Caruso and H. Tenorth (eds.), *Internationalisation.* Frankfurt: Peter Lang Publishers, pp. 91–107.

Rohlen, T. 1983. *Japan's High Schools.* Berkeley: University of California Press.

Rubinson, R. and B. Fuller. 1992. Specifying the Effects of Education on National Economic Growth, in B. Fuller and R. Rubinson (eds.), *The Political Construction of Education.* New York: Praeger, pp. 101–15.

Sahlin-Andersson, K. and L. Engwall. (eds.). 2002. *The Expansion of Management Knowledge.* Stanford: Stanford University.

Schofer, E. 1999. The Rationalization of Science and the Scientization of Society: International Science Organizations, 1870–1995, in J. Boli and G. Thomas (eds.), *World Polity in*

Formation A Century of International Non-Governmental Organization. Stanford: Stanford University Press, pp. 96–116.

—— and Meyer, J. W. 2005. The World-Wide Expansion of Higher Education in the Twentieth Century. *American Sociological Review* 70:898–920.

—— —— and F. O. Ramirez. 2000. The Effects of Science on National Economic Development, 1970–1990. *American Sociological Review* 65:877–98.

Teichler, U. 2002. *Towards a 'European Higher Education Area': Visions and Realities.* Kassel: Centre for Research on Higher Education and Work, University of Kassel.

UNESCO. 2004. *UNESCO Online Database.* New York: UNESCO Institute for Statistics, Online Publication.

Wallerstein, I. M. 1974. *The Modern World-System.* New York: Academic Press.

Windolf, P. 1997. *Expansion and Structural Change: Higher Education in Germany, the United States and Japan.* Boulder, CO: Westview Press.

World Bank. 2000. *Higher Education in Developing Countries: Peril and Promise.* Published for the Task Force on Higher Education and Society. New York: World Bank Publication.

PART IV

Bibliography of John W. Meyer's Writings

1. Stanley Budner and ——— . Women Professors. Bureau of Applied Social Research, Columbia University, 1961. Originally prepared for *The Academic Mind*, Vol. 2.
2. ——— . A Reformulation of the 'Coattails' Problem. In W. McPhee and W. Glaser (eds.), *Public Opinion and Congressional Elections*. Glencoe, Illinois, Free Press, 1962: 52–64.
3. ——— . Working Paper on Some Non-Value Effects of Colleges. Bureau of Applied Social Research, Columbia University, January 1965.
4. ——— . Collective Disturbances and Staff Organization on Psychiatric Wards: A Formalization. *Sociometry*, 31, 2, June 1968: 180–99.
5. Phillip E. Hammond, ——— , and David Miller. Profess, Publish, or Perish: Sources of Misperception. *Journal of Higher Education*, XL, 9, Winter 1969: 682–90.
6. ——— . The Charter: Conditions of Diffuse Socialization in Schools. In W. R. Scott (ed.), *Social Processes and Social Structures*. New York, Holt, 1970: 564–78. Reprinted elsewhere.
7. ——— . Effects of College Quality and Size on Student Occupational Choice. Technical Report 36, Laboratory for Social Research, Stanford University, 1970.
8. ——— . High School Effects on College Intentions. *American Journal of Sociology*, 76, 1, July 1970: 59–70.
9. ——— and James Roth. A Reinterpretation of American Status Politics. *Pacific Sociological Review*, 13, 2, Spring 1970: 95–102.
10. ——— , Elizabeth Cohen, Frank Brunetti, Sheila Molnar, and Erika Leuders-Salmon. The Impact of the Open-Space School Upon Teacher Influence and Autonomy. Technical Report, Stanford Center for Research and Development in Teaching, 1970.
11. ——— and Phillip E. Hammond. Forms of Status Inconsistency. *Social Forces*, 50, 1, September 1971: 91–101.
12. ——— . Comparative Research on the Relationships Between Political and Educational Institutions. In M. Kirst and F. Wirt (eds.), *Politics and Education*. Boston, D. C. Heath, 1971.
13. ——— . Economic and Political Effects on National Educational Enrollment Patterns. *Comparative Education Review*, 15, 1, February 1971: 28–43.
14. ——— , Christopher Chase-Dunn, and James Inverarity. The Expansion of the Autonomy of Youth: Response of the Secondary School to Problems of Order in the 1960s. Technical Report, Laboratory for Social Research, Stanford University, August 1971.
15. ——— and Barbara Sobieszek. The Effect of a Child's Sex on Adult Interpretations of Its Behavior. *Developmental Psychology*, 6, 1, 1972: 42–8.
16. ——— . The Effects of the Institutionalization of Colleges in Society. In K. Feldman (ed.), *College and Student*. New York, Pergamon, 1972: 109–26.
17. ——— and Richard Rubinson. Structural Determinants of Students' Political Activity: A Comparative Interpretation. *Sociology of Education*, 45, 1, Winter 1972: 23–46.
18. Frank Brunetti, Elizabeth Cohen, ——— , and Sheila Molnar. Studies of Team Teaching in the Open-Space School. *Interchange*, 3, 1972: 85–101.
19. ——— . Theories of the Effects of Education on Civic Participation in Developing Societies, SEADAG Paper Series, Southeast Asia Development Advisory Group: Asia Society, New York, 1972.
20. ——— and Richard Rubinson. Education and Political Development. *Review of Research in Education*, 3, 1975: 134–62.

21. —— , John Boli-Bennett, and Christopher Chase-Dunn. Convergence and Divergence in Development. *Annual Review of Sociology*, 1, 1975: 223–45.

22. Terrence Deal, —— , and W. Richard Scott. Organizational Influences on Educational Innovation. In J. Baldridge and T. Deal (eds.), *Managing Change in Educational Organizations*. Berkeley, McCutchan, 1975: 109–27.

23. Michael Hannan, John Freeman, and —— . Specification of Models for Organizational Effectiveness. *American Sociological Review*, 41, 1, February 1976: 36–43.

24. Elizabeth Cohen, Terrence Deal, —— , and W. Richard Scott. Organization and Instruction in Elementary Schools. Technical Report, Stanford: Stanford Center for Research and Development in Teaching, 1976; includes papers 25–6 below, 22 above.

25. —— , Susan Robbins, and Carl Simpson. Student Job Satisfaction: Who Likes School? In E. Cohen et al., *Organization and Instruction in Elementary Schools*. Technical Report, Stanford Center for Research and Development in Teaching, 1976.

26. W. Richard Scott, —— , Jo-Ann Intili, and Sally Main. The Staffing Structure of Districts and Schools. In E. Cohen et al. (eds.), *Organization and Instruction in Elementary Schools*. Technical Report, Stanford Center for Research and Development in Teaching, 1976.

27. —— . The Effects of Education as an Institution. *American Journal of Sociology*, 83, 1, July 1977: 55–77. Reprinted elsewhere.

28. —— and Brian Rowan. Institutionalized Organizations: Formal Structure as Myth and Ceremony. *American Journal of Sociology*, 83, 2, September 1977: 340–63. Also in J. Meyer and W. R. Scott, *Organizational Environments*. Beverly Hills, Sage, 1983: 21–44. Reprinted elsewhere, including W. Powell and P. DiMaggio (eds.), *The New Institutionalism in Organizational Analysis*. Chicago: University of Chicago Press, 1991: 41–62.

29. —— , Francisco Ramirez, Richard Rubinson, and John Boli-Bennett. The World Educational Revolution, 1950–1970. *Sociology of Education*, 50, 4, October 1977: 242–58.

30. Margaret Davis, Terrence Deal, —— , Brian Rowan, W. Richard Scott, and Anne Stackhouse. *The Structure of Educational Systems: Explorations in the Theory of Loosely-Coupled Organizations*. Stanford, Stanford Center for Research and Development in Teaching, 1977; includes papers 28 above and 33 and 52 below.

31. Marshall Meyer, John Freeman, Michael Hannan, —— , William Ouchi, Jeffrey Pfeffer, and W. Richard Scott. *Environments and Organizations*. San Francisco, Jossey-Bass, 1978; includes papers 32–34 below.

32. —— , W. Richard Scott, Sally Cole, and Jo-Ann Intili. Instructional Dissensus and Institutional Consensus in Schools. In M. Meyer et al., *Environments and Organizations*. San Francisco, Jossey-Bass, 1978: 233–63.

33. —— and Brian Rowan. The Structure of Educational Organizations. In M. Meyer et al., *Environments and Organizations*, San Francisco, Jossey-Bass, 1978: 78–109. Also in J. Meyer and W. R. Scott, *Organizational Environments*. Beverly Hills, Sage, 1983: 71–97.

34. —— . Strategies for Further Research: Varieties of Environmental Variation. In M. Meyer et al., *Environments and Organizations*. San Francisco, Jossey-Bass, 1978: 352–68.

35. John Boli-Bennett and —— . The Ideology of Childhood and the State: Rules Distinguishing Children in National Constitutions, 1870–1970. *American Sociological Review*, 43, 6, December 1978:797–812.

36. —— , Nancy Tuma, and Krzysztof Zagórski. Education and Occupational Mobility: A Comparison of Data on Polish and American Men. *American Journal of Sociology*, 84, 4, January 1979: 978–86.

37. —— , David Tyack, Joane Nagel, and Audri Gordon. Public Education as Nation-Building in America: Enrollments and Bureaucratization in the American States, 1870–1930. *American Journal of Sociology*, 85, 3, November 1979: 591–613.

38. —— and Michael Hannan. *National Development and the World System: Educational, Economic, and Political Change, 1950–1970*. Chicago, University of Chicago Press, 1979; includes papers 39–42 below, and 29 above.

39. —— , Michael Hannan, Richard Rubinson, and George Thomas. National Economic Development in the Contemporary World System, 1950–1970: Social and Political Factors. In J. Meyer and M. Hannan, *National Development and the World System*. Chicago, University of Chicago Press, 1979: 85–116.

40. —— , George Thomas, Francisco Ramirez, and Jeanne Gobalet. Maintaining National Boundaries in the World System: The Rise of Centralist Regimes. In J. Meyer and M. Hannan, *National Development and the World System*. Chicago, University of Chicago Press, 1979: 187–206.

41. —— and Michael Hannan. National Development in a Changing World System: An Overview. In J. Meyer and M. Hannan, *National Development and the World System*. Chicago, University of Chicago Press, 1979: 3–16.

42. —— and Michael Hannan. Issues for Further Comparative Research. In J. Meyer and M. Hannan, *National Development and the World System*. Chicago, University of Chicago Press, 1979: 297–308.

43. Elizabeth Cohen, —— , W. Richard Scott, and Terrence Deal. Technology and Structure in the Classroom. *Sociology of Education*, 52, 1, January 1979: 20–33.

44. —— . The World Polity and the Authority of the Nation-State. In A. Bergesen (ed.), *Studies of the Modern World-System*. New York, Academic Press, 1980: 109–37.

45. George Thomas and —— . Regime Change and State Power in an Intensifying World State System. In A. Bergesen (ed.), *Studies of the Modern World-System*. New York, Academic Press, 1980: 139–58.

46. —— . Levels of the Educational System and Schooling Effects. In C. Bidwell and D. Windham (eds.), *The Analysis of Educational Productivity II*. Cambridge, Ballinger, 1980: 15–63.

47. —— . Institutional Controls over Education. In H. Blalock (ed.), *Sociological Theory and Research*. New York, Free Press, 1980: 67–82.

48. John Boli-Bennett and —— . Constitutions as Ideology. *American Sociological Review*, 45, 3, June 1980: 525–7.

49. Francisco Ramirez and —— . Comparative Education: The Social Construction of the Modern World System. *Annual Review of Sociology*, 6, 1980: 369–99.

50. Francisco Ramirez and —— . Comparative Education: Synthesis and Agenda. In J. Short (ed.), *The State of Sociology*. Beverly Hills, Sage, 1981: 215–38.

51. —— . Review Essay: Kings or People. *American Journal of Sociology*, 86, 4, 1981: 895–9.

52. —— , W. R. Scott, and Terrence Deal. Institutional and Technical Sources of Organizational Structure. In H. Stein (ed.), *Organization and the Human Services*, Philadelphia, Temple University Press, 1981: 151–78.

53. Glenn Carroll and —— . Capital Cities in the American Urban System. *American Journal of Sociology*, 88, 3, November 1982: 565–78.

54. —— . Political Structure and the World Economy (Review Essay on Wallerstein), *Contemporary Sociology*, 11, 3, May 1982.

55. —— and W. Richard Scott. *Organizational Environments: Ritual and Rationality*. Beverly Hills, Sage, 1983 (rev. ed., 1992); includes papers 28, 33, 52, 56, 57, 58, 59, 60, and 61.

56. W. Richard Scott and —— . The Organization of Societal Sectors. In J. Meyer and W. R. Scott, *Organizational Environments*. Beverly Hills, Sage, 1983: 129–53. Revised version in W. Powell and P. DiMaggio (eds.), *The New Institutionalism in Organizational Analysis*. Chicago; University of Chicago Press, 1991: 108–40.

57. W. Richard Scott and ——. Centralization of Funding and Control in Educational Governance. In J. Meyer and W. R. Scott, *Organizational Environments*. Beverly Hills, Sage, 1983: 179–97.

58. ——. Organizational Factors Affecting Legalization in Education. In D. Kirp and D. Jensen (eds.), *School Days, Rule Days*. Philadelphia, Falmer, 1986: 256–75. Also in J. Meyer and W. R. Scott, *Organizational Environments*. Beverly Hills, Sage, 1983: 217–32.

59. ——. Innovation and Knowledge Use in American Public Education. In J. Meyer and W. R. Scott, *Organizational Environments*. Beverly Hills, Sage, 1983: 233–60.

60. —— and W. Richard Scott. Centralization and the Legitimacy Problems of Local Government. In J. Meyer and W. R. Scott, *Organizational Environments*. Beverly Hills, Sage, 1983: 199–215.

61. ——. Institutionalization and the Rationality of Formal Organizational Structure. In J. Meyer and W. R. Scott, *Organizational Environments*. Beverly Hills, Sage, 1983: 261–82.

62. ——. On the Celebration of Rationality: Some Comments on Boland and Pondy. *Accounting, Organizations and Society*, 8, 2/3, 1983: 235–40.

63. George Thomas and ——. The Expansion of the State. *Annual Review of Sociology*, 10, 1984: 461–82.

64. Martin Kohli and —— (eds.). Social Structure and the Social Construction of Life Stages. *Human Development*, Special Issue, 1984.

65. Krzysztof Zagorski, Rudolf Andorka, Nancy Tuma, and ——. Soziale Mobilität in Unterschiedlichen Sozio-Oekonomischen Systemen. In M. Niessen et al. (eds.), *International Vergleichende Sozialforschung*. Frankfurt, Campus, 1984: 25–61.

66. ——. Organizations as Ideological Systems. In T. Sergiovanni and J. Corbally (eds.), *Leadership and Organizational Culture*. Urbana, University of Illinois Press, 1984: 186–205.

67. David Baker, Yilmaz Esmer, Gero Lenhardt, and ——. Effects of Immigrant Workers on Educational Stratification in Germany. *Sociology of Education*, 58, 4, October 1985: 213–27.

68. John Boli, Francisco Ramirez, and ——. Explaining the Origins and Expansion of Mass Education. *Comparative Education Review*, 29, 2, May 1985: 145–68.

69. ——. The Self and the Life Course: Institutionalization and Its Effects. In A. Sorensen, F. Weinert, and L. Sherrod (eds.), *Human Development and the Life Course*. Hillsdale, New Jersey, Erlbaum: 1986: 199–216.

70. ——. Institutional and Organizational Rationalization in the Mental Health System. *American Behavioral Scientist*, 28, 1985: 587–600. Also in W. R. Scott and B. Black (eds.), *The Organization of Mental Health Services*. Beverly Hills, Sage, 1986: 15–29.

71. ——. Types of Explanation in the Sociology of Education. In J. Richardson (ed.), *Handbook of Theory and Research for the Sociology of Education*. Westport, Greenwood, 1986: 341–59.

72. ——. Myths of Socialization and Personality. In T. Heller, M. Sosna, and D. Wellbery (eds.), *Reconstructing Individualism*. Stanford, Stanford University Press, 1986: 212–25.

73. ——. Social Environments and Organizational Accounting. *Accounting, Organizations and Society*, 11, 4/5, 1986: 345–56.

74. ——. The Politics of Educational Crises in the United States. In W. Cummings et al. (eds.), *Educational Policies in Crisis*. New York, Praeger, 1986: 44–58.

75. ——, Klaus Hüfner, and Jens Naumann. Comparative Education Policy Research: A World Society Perspective. In M. Dierkes, H. Weiler, and A. Antal (eds.), *Comparative Policy Research*. Gower, Aldershot, 1987: 188–243.

76. ——— . Implications of an Institutional View of Education for the Study of Educational Effects. In M. Hallinan (ed.), *The Social Organization of Schools*. New York, Plenum, 1987: 157–75.

77. ——— , W. Richard Scott, and David Strang. Centralization, Fragmentation, and School District Complexity. *Administrative Science Quarterly*, 32, 1987: 186–201.

78. George Thomas, ——— , Francisco Ramirez, and John Boli. *Institutional Structure: Constituting State, Society, and the Individual*. Beverly Hills. Sage, 1987; includes 35, 44, 45, 69 above, and 102 below.

79. ——— , John Boli, and George Thomas. Ontology and Rationalization in the Western Cultural Account. In G. Thomas, J. Meyer, F. Ramirez, and J. Boli (eds.), *Institutional Structure*. Beverly Hills, Sage, 1987: 2–37. Reprinted elsewhere, including J. Meyer and W. R. Scott. *Institutional Environments and Organizations*. Thousand Oaks, Sage, 1994: 9–27.

80. Frank Dobbin, Lauren Edelman, ——— , W. Richard Scott, and Ann Swidler. The Expansion of Due Process in Organizations. In L. Zucker (ed.), *Institutional Patterns and Organizations*. Cambridge, Massachusetts, Ballinger, 1988: 71–98.

81. W. Richard Scott and ——— . Environmental Linkages and Organizational Complexity: Public and Private Schools. In H. Levin and T. James (eds.), *Comparing Public and Private Schools*. London, Falmer, 1988: 128–60. Also in W. R. Scott and J. Meyer, *Institutional Environments and Organizations*. Thousand Oaks, CA: Sage, 1994: 137–59.

82. ——— , Francisco Ramirez, Henry Walker, Nancy Langton, and Sorca O'Connor. The State and the Institutionalization of the Relations Between Women and Children. In S. Dornbusch and M. Strober (eds.), *Feminism, Children, and the New Families*. New York, Guilford, 1988: 137–58.

83. ——— , W. Richard Scott, David Strang, and Andrew Creighton. Bureaucratization without Centralization: Changes in the Organizational System of U.S. Public Education, 1940–80. In L. Zucker (ed.), *Institutional Patterns and Organizations*. Cambridge, Massachusetts, Ballinger, 1988: 139–67. Also in W. R. Scott and J. Meyer, *Institutional Environments and Organizations*. Thousand Oaks, CA: Sage, 1994: 179–205.

84. Yun-Kyung Cha, Suk-Ying Wong, and ——— . Values Education in the Curriculum: Some Comparative Empirical Data. In W. Cummings et al. (eds.), *The Revival of Values Education in Asia and the West*. Oxford, Pergamon, 1988: 11–28. Also in J. Meyer, D. Kamens, A. Benavot, Y-K. Cha, and S-Y. Wong, *School Knowledge for the Masses*. London: Falmer, 1992: 139–51.

85. ——— . The Social Construction of the Psychology of Childhood. In M. Hetherington, R. Lerner, and M. Perlmutter (eds.), *Child Development in Life-Span Perspective*. Hillsdale, New Jersey, Erlbaum, 1988: 47–65.

86. ——— . Levels of Analysis: The Life Course as a Cultural Construction. In M. Riley et al. (eds.), *Social Structures and Human Lives*. Newbury Park, Sage, 1988: 49–62.

87. ——— . Society Without Culture: A Nineteenth Century Legacy. In F. Ramirez (ed.), *Rethinking the Nineteenth Century*. New York, Greenwood, 1988: 193–201.

88. ——— . Conceptions of Christendom: Notes on the Distinctiveness of the West. In M. Kohn (ed.), *Cross-National Research in Sociology*. Newbury Park, Sage, 1989: 395–413.

89. ——— . Foreword. In J. Boli, *New Citizens for a New Society*. Oxford, Pergamon, 1989: xv–xviii.

90. ——— . Sources and Effects of Decisions. *Accounting, Organizations, and Society*, 15, 1/2, 1990: 61–5.

91. ——— . Individualism: Social Experience and Cultural Formulation. In J. Rodin, C. Schooler, and K. Schaie (eds.), *Self-Directness: Causes and Effects Throughout the Life Course*. Hillsdale, New Jersey, Erlbaum, 1990: 51–8.

92. Ronald Jepperson and ——— . The Public Order and the Construction of Formal Organizations. In W. Powell and P. DiMaggio (eds.), *The New Institutionalism in Organizational Analysis*. Chicago: University of Chicago Press, 1991: 204–31.

93. W. Richard Scott and ——— . The Rise of Training Programs in Firms and Agencies: An Institutional Perspective. In B. Staw and L. Cummings (eds.), *Research in Organizational Behavior*, 13, 1991: 287–326.

94. Aaron Benavot, Yun-Kyung Cha, David Kamens, ——— , and Suk-Ying Wong. Knowledge for the Masses: World Models and National Curricula, 1920–1986. *American Sociological Review*, 56, 1, February 1991: 85–100. Also in J. Meyer, D. Kamens, A. Benavot, Y-K. Cha, and S-Y. Wong, *School Knowledge for the Masses*. London: Falmer, 1992: 40–62.

95. ——— and Joane Nagel. Policy and Organization in Curriculum Development. In P. Ramatsui and C. W. Snyder (eds.), *Improving Instructional Quality*. Gaborone, Botswana, Macmillan, 1991.

96. ——— , Francisco Ramirez, and Yasemin Soysal. World Expansion of Mass Education, 1870–1970. *Sociology of Education*, 65, 2, April 1992: 128–49.

97. ——— , David Kamens, and Aaron Benavot, with Yun-Kyung Cha and Suk-Ying Wong. *School Knowledge for the Masses: World Models and National Curricula in the Twentieth Century*. London, Falmer, 1992. (Includes 84 and 94 above.)

98. ——— . The Life Course as a Professionalized Cultural Construction. In W. Heinz (ed.), *Institutions and Gatekeeping in the Life Course*. Weinheim, Deutscher Studien Verlag, 1992: 83–95.

99. ——— . The Social Construction of Motives for Educational Expansion. In B. Fuller and R. Rubinson (eds.), *The Political Construction of Education*. New York, Praeger, 1992: 225–38.

100. Suzanne Shanahan and ——— . Meanings and Effects of 'Income Inequality' in the Third World. Annual Meetings of the American Sociological Association, August 1992.

101. David Strang and ——— . Institutional Conditions for Diffusion. *Theory and Society*, 22, 4, August 1993: 487–511.

102. Frank Dobbin, John Sutton, ——— , and W. Richard Scott. Equal Opportunity Law and the Construction of Internal Labor Markets. *American Journal of Sociology*, 99, 2, September 1993: 396–427.

103. ——— , Joane Nagel, and C. Wesley Snyder, Jr. Interpreting the Expansion of Mass Education in Botswana: Local and World Society Perspectives. *Comparative Education Review*, 37, 4, November 1993: 454–75.

104. ——— . The Global Standardization of National Educational Systems. Research Bulletin of Studies on Secondary Education, 4, School of Education, Nagoya University, March 1993.

105. John Sutton, Frank Dobbin, ——— , and W. Richard Scott. Legalization of the Workplace. *American Journal of Sociology*, 99, 4, January 1994: 944–71.

106. ——— . The Evolution of Stratification Systems. In D. Grusky (ed.), *Social Stratification*. Boulder, Westview, 1994: 730–37, (2nd ed., 2001: 881–90).

107. W. Richard Scott and ——— . *Institutional Environments and Organizations: Structural Complexity and Individualism*. Thousand Oaks, California, Sage, 1994. Includes 73, 77, 79, 81, 83, 93, 101, 102 above, and 108, 109 below.

108. ——— . Rationalized Environments. In W. R. Scott and J. Meyer (eds.), *Institutional Environments and Organizations*. Thousand Oaks, Sage, 1994: 28–54.

109. Susanne Monahan, ——— , and W. Richard Scott. "Employee Training: The Expansion of Organizational Citizenship. In W. R. Scott and J. Meyer (eds.), *Institutional Environments and Organizations*. Thousand Oaks, Sage, 1994: 255–71.

110. ———. Foreword. In C. McNeely (ed.), *Constructing the Nation-State*. Westport, Connecticut, Greenwood Press, 1995: ix–xiv.

111. ———, John Boli, Francisco Ramirez, and George Thomas. Theories of Culture: Institutional vs. Actor-Centered Approaches. Annual Meetings of the American Sociological Association. Washington, D. C., August, 1995.

112. David Frank, ———, and David Miyahara. The Individualist Polity and the Centrality of Professionalized Psychology. *American Sociological Review*, 60, 3, June 1995: 360–77.

113. ——— and David Baker. Forming American Educational Policy with International Data. *Sociology of Education*, 69, Extra Issue, 1996:123–30.

114. ———. Otherhood: The Promulgation and Transmission of Ideas in the Modern Organizational Environment. In B. Czarniawska and G. Sevón (eds.), *Translating Organizational Change*. Berlin, de Gruyter, 1996: 241–52.

115. David Kamens, ———, and Aaron Benavot. Worldwide Patterns in Academic Secondary Education Curricula, 1920–1990. *Comparative Education Review*, 40, 2, May 1996: 116–38.

116. ———. Die Culturellen Inhalte des Bildungswesens (The Cultural Content of the Vessel of Education). In A. Leschinsky (ed.), *Die Institutionalisierung von Lehren und Lernen. Zeitschrift für Paedagogik*, 34, Weinheim, Beltz Verlag, 1996: 23–34.

117. ———, David Frank, Ann Hironaka, Evan Schofer, and Nancy Tuma. The Structuring of a World Environmental Regime, 1870–1990. *International Organization*, 51, 4, Autumn 1997: 623–51.

118. ———, John Boli, George Thomas, and Francisco Ramirez. World Society and the Nation-State. *American Journal of Sociology*, 103, 1, July 1997: 144–81.

119. Francisco Ramirez and ———. Dynamics of Citizenship Development and the Political Incorporation of Women. In C. McNeely (ed.), *Public Rights, Public Rules*. New York, Garland, 1998: 59–80.

120. Elizabeth Boyle and ———. Modern Law as a Secularized and Global Model: Implications for the Sociology of Law. *Soziale Welt*, 49, 3, 1998: 213–32. Also in Y. Dezalay and B. Garth (eds.), *Global Prescriptions*. Ann Arbor, University of Michigan Press, 2002: 65–95.

121. ———. Training and Certifying 'Unqualified' Teachers in Namibia. In C. W. Snyder, Jr., and F. Voights (eds.), *Inside Reform*. Windhoek, Gamsberg Macmillan, 1998: 103–54.

122. ———. Foreword. In O. Olson, J. Guthrie, and C. Humphrey (eds.), *Global Warning: Debating International Developments in New Public Financial Management*. Oslo, Cappelen, 1998: 7–13.

123. David Frank, Ann Hironaka, ———, Evan Schofer, and Nancy Tuma. The Rationalization and Organization of Nature in the World Culture. In J. Boli and G. Thomas (eds.), *Constructing World Culture*. Stanford, Stanford University Press, 1999: 81–99.

124. ——— and Elizabeth McEneaney. Comparative and Historical Reflections on the Curriculum: The Changing Meaning of Science. In I. Goodson, S. Hopmann, and K. Riquarts (eds.), *Das Schulfach als Handlungsrahmen*. Cologne, Böhlau Verlag, 1999: 177–90.

125. ———. Organizational Integration in Lesotho Primary Education: Loose Coupling as Problem and Solution. In C. W. Snyder, Jr. (ed.), *Exploring the Complexities of Education*. Gamsberg Macmillan: Windhoek, 1999.

126. ———. The Changing Cultural Content of the Nation-State: A World Society Perspective. In G. Steinmetz (ed.), *State/Culture: State Formation after the Cultural Turn*. Ithaca, Cornell University Press, 1999: 123–43.

127. ——— and Ronald Jepperson. The 'Actors' of Modern Society: The Cultural Construction of Social Agency. *Sociological Theory*, 18, 1, May 2000: 100–20.

128. David Frank, Suk-Ying Wong, —— , and Francisco Ramirez. What Counts as History: A Cross-National and Longitudinal Study of University Curricula. *Comparative Education Review*, 44, 1, February 2000: 29–53.

129. Evan Schofer, Francisco Ramirez, and —— . The Effects of Science on National Economic Development, 1970–1990. *American Sociological Review*, 65, 6, December 2000: 877–98. Revised version in G. Drori, J. Meyer, F. Ramirez, and E. Schofer, *Science in the Modern World Polity*. Stanford: Stanford University Press, 2003: 221–48.

130. Elizabeth McEneaney and —— . The Content of the Curriculum: An Institutionalist Perspective. In M. Hallinan (ed.), *Handbook of the Sociology of Education*. New York, Plenum, 2000: 189–211.

131. —— . Reflections on Education as Transcendence. In L. Cuban and D. Shipps (eds.), *Reconstructing the Common Good in Education*. Stanford, Stanford University Press, 2000: 206–22.

132. —— and Francisco Ramirez. The World Institutionalization of Education. In J. Schriewer (ed.), Discourse Formation in Comparative Education. Frankfurt, Peter Lang, 2000: 111–32.

133. —— . Globalization: Sources, and Effects on National States and Societies. *International Sociology*, 15, 2, June 2000: 235–50.

134. —— . Globalization and the Curriculum: Problems for Theory in the Sociology of Education. *The Journal of Educational Sociology*, (Japan), 66, May 2000. Also in H. Fujita (ed.), *Education, Knowledge, Power*. Tokyo: Shinyosha, 2000: 48–67. Portuguese edition in A. Nóvoa and J. Schriewer (eds.), *A Difusão Mundial Da Escola*. Lisbon: EDUCA, 2000: 15–32.

135. —— . Organizational Costs and Implications of Monitoring and Evaluation. In C. W. Snyder and T. Welsh (eds.), *Program Evaluation*, Vol. 2. USAID and Government of Ghana, Accra, Ghana, 2000: 139–75.

136. —— . The European Union and the Globalization of Culture. In S. S. Andersen (ed.), *Institutional Approaches to the European Union*. Arena, Oslo, 2001: 227–45.

137. —— . Reflections: The Worldwide Commitment to Educational Equality. *Sociology of Education*, 74, Special Issue, 2001: 154–8.

138. —— . Foreword. In A. Hoffman and M. Ventresca (eds.), *Organizations, Policy, and the Natural Environment*. Stanford, Stanford University Press, 2002: xiii–xvii.

139. Francisco Ramirez and —— . National Curricula: World Models and National Historical Legacies. In M. Caruso and H. Tenorth (eds.), *Internationalisation*. Frankfurt, Peter Lang, 2002: 91–107.

140. —— . Globalization, National Culture, and the Future of the World Polity. *Hong Kong Journal of Sociology*, 3, November 2002: 1–18.

141. —— . Globalization and the Expansion and Standardization of Management. In K. Sahlin-Andersson and L. Engwall (eds.), *The Expansion of Management Knowledge*. Stanford, Stanford University Press: 2002: 33–44.

142. David Frank and —— . The Contemporary Identity Explosion: Individualizing Society in the Post-War Period. *Sociological Theory*, 20, 1, March 2002: 86–105.

143. —— . Reflections on a Half Century of Mennonite Change. *Mennonite Quarterly Review*, 77, 22, April 2003: 257–76.

144. —— . Preface. In M. Hallinan et al. (eds.), *Stability and Change in American Education*. New York, Eliot Werner, 2003: vii–x.

145. Gili Drori, —— , Francisco Ramirez, and Evan Schofer. *Science in the Modern World Polity: Institutionalization and Globalization*. Stanford, Stanford University Press, 2003.

146. ——. Standardizing and Globalizing the Nation-State. *Sophia Aglos News*, 5, Sophia University, Tokyo, November 2004: 4–11.

147. ——. The Nation-State as Babbitt: Global Models and National Conformity. *Contexts*, 3, 3, Summer 2004: 42–7.

148. ——. World Society, the Welfare State, and the Life Course: An Institutionalist Perspective. *Conference on the Globalization of the Welfare State*, Hanse Institute for Advanced Study, Delmenhorst, Germany, February 2004.

149. Evan Schofer and ——. The World-Wide Expansion of Higher Education in the Twentieth Century. *American Sociological Review*, 70, 6, December 2005: 898–920.

150. ——. Management Models as Popular Discourse. In J. Alvarez, C. Mazza, and J. Pederson (eds.), *The Role of the Mass Media in the Consumption of Management. Scandinavian Journal of Management*, 21, 2, 2005: 133–6.

151. —— and Evan Scofer. Universität in der globalen Gesellschaft: Die Expansion des 20. Jahrhunderts (The University in Global Society: Twentieth Century Expansion). Die Hochschule, 2, 2, 2005: 81–98. Spanish revision, as "La Universidad en Europa y en el mundo: expansión el siglo xxi," in Volume 13 of the Revista Española de Educación Comparada, Universidad Nacional de Educación Distancia, Madrid, 2006: 15–36. English revision, The University in Europe and the World: Twentieth Century Expansion. In G. Krücken, A. Kosmützky, and M. Torka (eds.), *Towards a Multiversity? Universities Between Global Trends and National Traditions*. Bielefeld, Transcript Verlag, 2006: 45–62.

152. ——. John W. Meyer: *Weldkultur: Wie die westlichen Prinzipien die Welt durchdringen* (ed. by G. Krücken, trans. by B. Kuchler). Frankfurt, Suhrkamp, 2005. Includes 79, 117, 118, 120, 126, 127, 132, and 136 above.

153. Francisco Ramirez, Xiaowei Luo, Evan Schofer, and ——. Does Academic Achievement Lead to Economic Development? *American Journal of Education*, 113, 1, November 2006: 1–29.

154. Gili Drori and ——. Scientization: Making a World Safe for Organizing. In M. Djelic and K. Sahlin-Andersson (eds.), *Transnational Governance: Institutional Dynamics of Regulation*. Cambridge, Cambridge University. Press, 2006: 31–52.

155. Gili Drori, Yong-Suk Jang, and ——. Sources of Rationalized Governance: Cross-National Longitudinal Analyses, 1985–2002. *Administrative Science Quarterly*, 51, 2, June 2006: 205–29.

156. Gili Drori, ——, and Hokyu Hwang (eds.). *Globalization and Organization: World Society and Organizational Change*. Oxford, Oxford University Press, 2006. *Contains 157–60. below.*

157. Gili Drori, ——, and Hokyu Hwang. Introduction. In Drori et al. (eds.), *Globalization and Organization*. Oxford, Oxford University Press, 2006: 1–22.

158. ——, Gili Drori, and Hokyu Hwang. World Society and the Proliferation of Formal Organization. In G. Drori et al. (eds.), *Globalization and Organization*, Oxford, Oxford University Press, 2006: 25–49.

159. Gili Drori and ——. Global Scientization: An Environment for Expanded Organization. In G. Drori et al. (eds.), *Globalization and Organization*. Oxford, Oxford University Press, 2006: 50–68.

160. ——, Gili Drori, and Hokyu Hwang. Conclusion. In G. Drori et al. (eds.), *Globalization and Organization*. Oxford, Oxford University Press, 2006: 258–74.

161. David Frank and ——. Worldwide Expansion and Change in the University. In G. Krücken, A. Kosmützky and M. Torka (eds.), *Towards a Multiversity? Universities*

between Global Trends and National Traditions. Bielefeld, Transcript Verlag, 2006: 19–44.

162. David Frank and ——— . Foreword. In D. Baker and A. Wiseman (eds.), *The Impact of Comparative Education Research on Institutional Theory.* Oxford, JAI Press/Elsevier, 2006: xi–xvi.

163. Francisco Ramirez, David Suarez, and ——— . The Worldwide Rise of Human Rights Education. In A. Benavot and C. Braslavsky (eds.), *School Curricula for Global Citizenship*, Hong Kong, University of Hong Kong/Springer, 2006: 35–52.

164. ——— . World Models, National Curricula, and the Centrality of Individual. In A. Benavot and C. Braslavsky (eds.), *School Curricula for Global Citizenship.* Hong Kong, University of Hong Kong/ Springer, 2006: 259–71.

165. ——— . Foreword. In D. Frank and J. Gabler, *Reconstructing the University.* Stanford, Stanford University Press, 2006: ix–xvii.

166. Ronald Jepperson and ——— . Analytical Individualism and the Explanation of Macro-social Change. In V. Nee and R. Swedberg (eds.), *On Capitalism.* Stanford, Stanford University Press, 2007: 273–304.

167. Ronald Jepperson and ——— . *Doctrinal Individualism in Sociological Theory: The "Protestant Ethic Thesis" as Intellectual Ideology.* Department of Sociology, University of Tulsa, 2007.

168. David Frank and ——— . University Expansion and the Knowledge Society. *Theory and Society*, 36, 2007: 287–311.

169. ——— . Globalization: Theory and Trends. *International Journal of Comparative Sociology*, 48, 4–5, 2007: 261–73.

170. ——— , Francisco Ramirez, David Frank, and Evan Schofer. Higher Education as an Institution. In P. Gumport (ed.), *Sociology of Higher Education.* Baltimore, Johns Hopkins University Press, 2007: 187–221.

171. Emilie Hafner-Burton, Kiyoteru Tsutsui, and ——— . International Human Rights Law and the Politics of Legitimation: Repressive States and Human Rights Treaties. *International Sociology*, 23, 1, 2008: 115–41.

172. ——— . Reflections on Institutional Theories of Organizations. In R. Greenwood, C. Oliver, R. Suddaby and K. Sahlin (eds.), *Handbook of Organizational Institutionalism.* Thousand Oaks, Sage, 2008: 790–811.

173. ——— . Building Education for a World Society. In M. Pereyra (ed.), *Changing Knowledge and Education.* Frankfurt, Peter Lang, 2008: 31–49.

174. ——— . Afterword. In M. Boström and C. Garsten (eds.), *Organizing Transnational Accountability.* London, Elgar, 2008: 250–4.

175. ——— , Patricia Bromley-Martin, and Francisco O. Ramirez. Human Rights in Social Science Textbooks: Cross-National Analyses, 1975–2006. Annual Meetings of the American Sociological Association, Boston, 2008.

176. Gili Drori, ——— , and Hokyu Hwang. Global Rationalization and 'Organization' as Scripted Actorhood. In R. Meyer, K. Sahlin, M. Ventresca, and P. Walgenbach (eds.), *Ideology and Institutions.* 2009.

177. ——— . Reflections: Institutional Theory and World Society. In G. Kruecken and G. Drori (eds.), *World Society: The Writings of John W. Meyer.* Oxford, Oxford University Press, 2009.

178. ——— . World Society, the Welfare State, and the Life Course: An Institutionalist Perspective. In G. Kruecken and G. Drori (eds.), *World Society: The Writings of John W. Meyer.* Oxford, Oxford University Press, 2009. Adapted from 148 above.

Index

individuals 52, 53, 54, 119, 280–1,
  287–306
  roles 293–5
  specializing 297–304
individuals
  and actorhood
  decoupling process 120–1
  globalization 152, 155, 246
  and identity 52, 53, 54, 119, 280–1,
    287–306
  rights 44, 54, 276
  rationalization of 72
innovation 142, 145, 185
institutionalism, new/neo 10, 38–41
institutionalization
  defined 62, 80–1
  organizations 85
institutional theory 34–58
  core arguments 46–50
  globalization 41–6
  global models 47–50
  law 312
  social change 50–4
  world models 46–7
institutions 19
  as cultural accounts 75–7
  defined 62–3, 80
  and globalization 273–4
  and rationalization 87–9
  and rules 73–5
intellectuals 185
international relations 11–14
Islam: rape law 319
isomorphism
  educational systems 207–8
  European Union 338–9
  and globalization 158–60
  legal systems 320–1
  mimetic 2, 7, 39
  nation-states 170–1, 315
  organizations 90, 92, 120

justice 15, 24, 56, 59, 67, 74, 76, 77, 78, 80,
  81, 82, 114, 117, 144, 147, 157,
  160, 166, 176, 179, 181, 188, 189,
  191, 197, 199, 207, 211, 212, 215,
  218, 298, 312–2, 323, 324, 325,
  327, 331, 332, 334, 336–8, 345,
  346, 348, 349, 367

Keynesian policies: diffusion 140–1

labor
  child 50
  market 55;
  and higher education expansion 351
law 311–29

and ceremony 322–3
and consistency 327–8
and decoupling process 327
diffusion and expansion of 318–22
expansion of 328–9
institutionalist view of 312
international 319
natural law 290–1
  and modernity 316
  and nation-state system 290–1, 314–16,
    318, 321
  and organizations 317–18, 320, 322,
    323, 324, 327, 328
  and rationality 326–7
  and religion 316–17
  and ritual 322–5
  scientific progress of 325–6
League of Nations 180, 221
lesbians: rights 178, 260, 339
liberalism 116–18, 274, 282–3
life course 271, 276–82, 284
loose coupling 10, 12, 20, 24, 72, 115n6, 217

macrostructuralism: Meyer and 19–20
management
  education 248
  globalization 242–50
  organization studies 5–11
markets 86, 244–5
Marxism 136
modernity 17
  and culture 178–9
  defined 142
  and diffusion 142–5
  and law 316
  and nation-states 177
  and religion 55–6
  social institutions of 273
money: and economics 56
moral authority 75, 76
motherhood, 304, see also women
myths
  formal structures 6, 87–9
  organizations 99, 101
  rational institutional 90–2, 93

nationalism 144 n19, 289 *see also* cultural
  identity
national societies *see* societies: national
nation-states 164–90
  as actors 38, 114, 171–2, 259
  as collectivities 67
  and culture 166–7, 176, 340
  decline of 288–92
  decoupling process 172–4
  and diffusion 134–5, 141, 180–1
  and education 173, 176, 199–200, 207

United States (*Cont.*)
   liberalism 274
   polity 133–4
universalism 275–6, 319
universities 40
   expansion 121, 203, 346–58
   history teaching 205
   interests 118
   science 257, 267
   structuration 160, 174

war 123; World War II 37, 190
Weber, Max 15
   and organizations 6, 8, 10
   and society, rationalization of 22, 72
welfare states 13, 272–3, 274, 275
women
   and education 50, 160, 171, 201–2, 203–4
   and rape laws 319

   and social change 52
   social role of 13
   see also motherhood
work
   culture of 70
   retirement from 280
   see also careers; child labor; labor market
World Bank 206, 354–5
world society
   actors 185–7
   collective 179–83
   culture 18, 168, 183–5, 187–8
   globalization 153
   heterogeneity 18–19
   nation-states 175–9, 180–1
   polity 221, 230
   sciences and professions 182–3
   statelessness 164–5, 185
   theory 1–2, 3
World War II 37, 190